CHAPTER ONE

The Ancient Religion of the Sun

WHAT IS THE ANCIENT RELIGION OF THE SUN?

Most people are somewhat familiar with the notion that people in the past worshiped the sun. And, many believe they did this because their understanding of the universe was much more simplistic than our own. But actually, it's quite the reverse. It's our understanding of them and of the spiritual nature of the universe that is so materialistic as to have overlooked the depth and meaning behind the ancient veneration of the sun. In the eighth chapter of this book, I give a summary as to the origins of why the sun held such a central place in the spiritual traditions of so many ancient cultures.

Although I use the phrase "sun worship," the veneration of the sun in more spiritually-advanced cultures was not a dumb devotion to the physical element. Instead, the sun was seen as and used to symbolize the supreme manifestation of the divine, as the greatest source of light and life. It was used not only as a symbol of the divine existing in the world around us, but also within us, as our own eternal Being.[1] The ancient Religion of the Sun was a great body of knowledge and metaphysical practice that taught someone how to realize this divinity within themselves and reunite with their higher Being, symbolized by the sun. This process was referred to as a path or way, and the journey of the sun throughout the year, through the two solstices and two equinoxes, symbolized its major stages, which is why so many deities experienced major life events at these times, why they were held sacred and celebrated by many ancient peoples, and why so many sacred sites were aligned to them.[2]

The ancient Egyptians are the most well-known practitioners of the ancient Religion of the Sun. This painting is from 1,300 BC, and shows the Egyptian ankh, symbol of eternal life, holding the sun.

A solar religion existing from ancient times is well-known in academia. For example, the Encyclopaedia Britannica entry on "sun worship" says:

> "Although sun worship has been used frequently as a term for "pagan" religion, it is, in fact, relatively rare. Though almost every culture uses solar motifs, only a relatively few cultures (Egyptian, Indo-European, and Meso-American) developed solar religions. All of these groups had in common a well-developed urban civilization with a strong ideology of sacred kingship. [...]
>
> The sun is the bestower of light and life to the totality of the cosmos; with his [...] all-seeing eye, he is the stern guarantor of justice; with the almost universal connection of light with enlightenment or illumination, the sun is the source of wisdom."[3]

Essentially, three major branches of ancient civilization are well-known to have practiced solar religions—namely those of the ancient Egyptians, Indo-Europeans, and Mesoamericans—although it also influenced and was practiced by numerous other cultures too, as I explain further on.

Indo-European is a broad term that includes a vast set of religious traditions that branched off over time. They include the Armenians in the Caucasus

THE ANCIENT RELIGION OF THE SUN

The Wisdom Bringers and
The Lost Civilization of the Sun

LARA ATWOOD

SŪRA ONDRÚNAR

PUBLISHING

Second Edition, published January 2021. Last updated November 2021.

ISBN 978-0-6487565-1-4

Requests for permission to reproduce copyrighted material may be emailed to the publisher Sura Ondrunar Publishing, visit suraondrunar.org.

Every reasonable effort has been made by the publisher to locate and acknowledge copyright owners, and obtain any necessary clearances. Please refer to the Copyright Acknowledgments section at the end of this book for the full list of works. If any works requiring clearance have unwittingly been included, or any corrections need to be made, the publisher will be pleased to do so at the earliest opportunity.

NON-PROFIT PRINCIPLES

The author does not receive any money for the writing or sale of this book, as she follows the ancient principle that spiritual knowledge should not be profited from. This book is sold by a not-for-profit publisher with the same principles who set its price to cover the cost of production, with any surplus going back into their operating expenses.

DISCLAIMER

This book contains general information on the topic of religion for educational use only. Neither the author nor the publisher are providing any service or advice to the individual reader.

While we endeavor to keep the information in this book up-to-date and correct, we make no representations or warranties of any kind, express or implied, about the completeness, accuracy, reliability, or suitability for any purpose. Any reliance you place on such information is therefore strictly at your own risk. You need to make your own enquiries to determine if the information is appropriate for your intended use.

This book is dedicated to all those brave men and women who made immense personal sacrifices to teach and preserve the knowledge of the Religion of the Sun through the ages.

··· CONTENTS ···

CHAPTER FOUR

The Lost Civilization of the Sun

Preface

Here is a short summary of how the information in this book came about (parts of this preface also appear in the book I co-authored with my husband, *Ancient Solstice*).

The ancient Religion of the Sun is not something my husband and I set out to find, or heard about from somewhere else. It's something we discovered unexpectedly.

In June of 2011, two weeks before the summer solstice, my husband Mark suggested we do something to celebrate it. I'd never celebrated a solstice or equinox before, at least not knowingly. I loved Christmas as a child, when the air seemed thick with magic, but only decades later did I find out it's a winter solstice festival. I'd grown up in a completely nonreligious household. We celebrated Christmas with stockings, milk and cookies left out for Santa Claus, and a decorated, fresh cut pine tree; all these customs, which I'd never questioned the origin of, I now know to have more in common with ancient Germanic pagan celebrations of midwinter rather than anything Christian, and this was the closest I'd ever come to celebrating any kind of ancient tradition. Mark on the other hand was raised a Catholic, in which Christmas (winter solstice) and Easter (essentially the spring equinox) are celebrated as the major festivals of the religion using symbols subsumed from ancient pagan traditions fused with those of early Christianity. He'd had metaphysical experiences as a child, and searched for spiritual truths beyond the Church. In his twenties, he'd watched the sunrise on the summer solstice at the ancient site of Arthur's Stone in Wales with just a few people, playing drums and guitars, and singing peaceful songs. The experience of seeing the sun emerge in all its majesty, bringing the ocean and emerald green hills to life, and resonating with the ancient stones, was quite powerful and had always stayed with him.

With this, our experience of the solstice and equinox, we began researching ancient traditions connected to the celebration of midsummer from around the world. Incorporating what we found, such as ancient Vedic mantras and

Eastern European customs, and using Mark's spiritual experience of what the event means, Mark created a ceremony to celebrate the summer solstice and posted it online.

Some of those who used this ceremony for their solstice celebration were deeply moved by their experience of it, and felt they would never be the same again. We realized there was a lot more to these ancient traditions than first seemed, and continued our research, this time preparing for the following autumn equinox. Over the course of a year between 2011 and 2012, we released web articles explaining the spiritual meaning of the autumn equinox, winter solstice, and spring equinox. Later, in mid-2013 we released a web article on the meaning of the summer solstice. We did this by researching a broad range of ancient sites, texts, and traditions, and then used Mark's spiritual knowledge and experience to help decipher them. Based on the symbolic meaning of these times of year, Mark also created ceremonies for each of them.

Mark's spiritual experience was essential to reconstructing the ancient meaning of the solstices and equinoxes, as many traditions that had preserved remnants of their practice had lost the deeper meaning of the symbols in their traditions, if they were even still kept alive. Mark has been a dedicated spiritual practitioner since 1990. Since then he has practiced a broad range of spiritual techniques derived from a number of ancient traditions, which we now know to be remnants of the lost Religion of the Sun.

And so, we began reconstructing the actual meaning of the solstices and equinoxes, and came to realize that a number of ancient people in the distant past had to have understood their deeper meaning at one time, and had sometimes incorporated these meanings into the sacred sites they aligned to the solstices and equinoxes, and into their rituals and celebrations.

We also came to realize that the path of the sun throughout the year actually correlates with the path to self-realization/enlightenment, etc., alluded to in many ancient wisdom traditions. My husband began this path in 1991, which is how he was able to decipher the meaning of so many teachings and symbols of the ancient Religion of the Sun.

In September of 2013 we compiled our web articles on the solstices and equinoxes, and released them as a free eBook (now only available in paperback and titled *Ancient Solstice*), explaining within it that there had once been a solar religion practiced across many parts of the world in ancient times, which had given rise to the building of many of the world's most enigmatic sacred sites, like the Great Pyramids of Egypt, the statues of Easter Island, Stonehenge in England, and countless others, each of which aligned to the solstices and equinoxes.

We began referring to this religion as "the Religion of the Sun"—a term we coined ourselves, but later discovered had been used in a handful of instances over the last few centuries, most notably by Thomas Paine, who was one of the Founding Fathers of the United States and likely a Freemason. Thomas Paine was the only one to employ it as any kind of formal title—using it to describe the religion that had been practiced from the remotest antiquity before spreading over large parts of the ancient world, and later being preserved in Freemasonry. All other uses (of which I have only found a number that can be counted on one hand) were merely passing and one-off, using it as a descriptive phrase for ancient forms of solar religion—mostly in books dating from over seventy years ago.

By this time I had done a massive amount of research by reading scores of ancient texts from numerous traditions (at least over one hundred from cover to cover) and researching the alignments of large numbers of ancient sites from around the world. Out of this, we included hundreds of excerpts from ancient texts as well as images of ancient sites and symbols in our book as supporting evidence.

Our eBook had been downloaded over thirty thousand times as of January 2016, when it was taken offline, due to it being extensively plagiarized, and was instead first published as a paperback book in September 2016 and is still available in this format today. We had provided the eBook completely free of charge (as well as our articles on the solstices and equinoxes, which were still online at that point), and anyone was able to download it without subscribing or registering for anything. As a paperback book, its price was (and still is) set only to cover publishing costs. We receive no money from the sale of any of our books, as it's against our principles to profit from spiritual knowledge.

Initially I had thought that the many different cultures evidenced as practicing the Religion of the Sun in some form had done so independently of one another. In my research, I had come across many similarities between the symbols of ancient cultures (even though they were never meant to have had any contact with one another), and had put this down to people within these ancient cultures coming upon the same spiritual knowledge through mystical experience and encoding it using the same symbols.

The first time I began to doubt this, however, was when I saw a statue of the Aztec goddess Coatlicue and noticed that she shared a number of striking similarities with the Hindu goddess Kali. Nevertheless, I pressed on with holding an isolationist viewpoint, as Wikipedia and its repeaters, which had saturated the top layers of internet search results for just about every term on ancient history, were adamant that everything in prehistory was definitely not connected, in any way, at all, period.

Looking back, I can't believe I didn't realize so much earlier how different ancient cultures must have had contact in prehistory. It was staring me in the face, with the exact same pyramid designs, symbols, etc., found from one continent to another. But I had been so indoctrinated to believe that they didn't, that all the glaring similarities were simply hiding in front of me in plain sight.

Left: The goddess Kali, a major deity in Hinduism in India. Right: The goddess Coatlicue, a major deity worshiped by the Aztecs in Mexico. The similarities between these images sowed the first seeds of doubt in my mind about my isolationist viewpoint.

The penny dropped only later, in March 2016, when researching ancient sites on the Internet (as part of preparing the first print edition of our book *Ancient Solstice*), I stumbled across the website of Martin Doutré, http://celt-icnz.co.nz. In his work, Doutré painstakingly analyzes the measurements used in the building and layout of many ancient sites in different parts of the world, and demonstrates that their builders used the same standard measurement system, and thus were part of or influenced by the same global civilization. Although Doutré does not discuss the Religion of the Sun, he does recognize that the builders of these sites venerated the sun. After reading some of his articles, Mark and I realized that the traces of the ancient Religion of the Sun that we had been researching and studying had originated from the same source in remote times, and had once been the religion of a post Ice Age global culture and civilization now lost. Mark and I named this civilization "the Lost Civilization of the Sun."

Months later, in September of 2016, Mark and I released an updated edition of *Ancient Solstice* to include a chapter titled "The Lost Civilization of the Sun," in which we shared our findings on this lost civilization. At the time, we traced it as much as we could throughout the world, and sourced its origin in a group of wisdom bringers who are likely to have been survivors of Atlantis. Since then, I've read some of the works of authors such as Thor Heyerdahl, Graham Hancock, and David Frawley, whose research has confirmed and added detail to what we had first realized in 2016 about the existence of such a lost civilization.

Throughout this time, our original articles on the spiritual meaning of the solstices and equinoxes, which we had first written between 2011 and 2013, still remained freely available online. They were shared a total of over twenty-three thousand times and viewed about half a million times as of March 2018, which is when we took them offline. We withdrew them because they were being plagiarized so much—excerpts from them had been copied and pasted into other people's websites without attribution over one thousand times. Our articles had become a world reference for the meaning of the solstices and equinoxes and ranked among the top results in search engines for terms like "winter solstice meaning," often above reference sites like Wikipedia.

Before releasing our articles, the actual deeper spiritual meanings of the solstices and equinoxes, as far as I'm aware, were not understood. We had searched through much of the material available in English at the time on their meaning when writing our articles, and found no single source that described what they meant. We were only able to do this ourselves after months of painstaking research into barely preserved ancient traditions, by deciphering the spiritual symbolism encoded into the ancient sites that were built to align to these times of year, and combining this with Mark's knowledge and experience of the path to self-realization/enlightenment.

After our articles were released, as a result, the spiritual meanings of the solstices and equinoxes became much more widely understood. Before this they had been fairly mundane seasonal celebrations, interpreted, usually from a modern Wiccan perspective, as to do with letting go of attachments, tuning into the rhythm of the seasons, giving birth to new personal projects, setting goals, etc.

In 2017, instead of writing articles, I switched to making videos. What I present in my videos is based on our findings and supported by my ongoing research. I also draw upon the research of other authors who have presented their own findings on lost civilizations, and whose work I admire and acknowledge. I have done so under the title "Sakro Sawel." This is another term Mark and I put together, this time by looking through online dictionaries of reconstructed Proto-Indo-European words. "Sakro" means sacred, and "Sawel" means sun in the ancient Proto-Indo-European language—we joined these words together to create Sakro Sawel (meaning "sacred sun"), the name for the YouTube Channel and website I use.

It's important to mention that our research was a journey—we in no way set out with a destination in mind when we first began writing about the solstice back in June of 2011. We had absolutely no idea what we were in for—we instead simply followed the evidence as it led us from one thing to another. We had no idea that a Religion of the Sun, wisdom bringers, or a Lost Civilization of the Sun had ever existed.

Both of us had been schooled in the mainstream, isolationist view of ancient history, and had never had any reason to question it. That's why our own discoveries each came as major shocks to us. For me, finding out about the Lost Civilization of the Sun particularly was what I call "a Truman Show moment"—as like in the film, when the character that Jim Carrey plays steps out of the false life he had been born into, I felt everything I had ever been taught and believed about ancient history was essentially a façade that had been constructed over reality, much like a Hollywood movie set. I felt betrayed, lied to, and awe-inspired all at the same time!, and incredibly grateful to have been given the opportunity to step out into a new world that made so much more sense, and which revealed the greatest religion in the world, and one of the most courageous and inspiring spiritual missions of all time.

As far as I'm aware, no one else has come to the same conclusions we have, in the way that we have. Although some researchers whom I greatly admire have pieced together the traces of a lost Ice Age civilization, and brought together a lot of information on the wisdom bringers and the influence they had on various cultures, as well as recognized the solar nature of Indo-European religions, and some of the similarities between sun worship in different cultures, I haven't seen anyone bring it all together to construct a coherent narrative that traces the origin of this religion as far back as possible, tying it in with the wisdom bringers, the legends of Atlantis, and numerous megalithic sites worldwide, as well as revealing the deeper meaning of its symbols and how to practice it. Essentially, we've tried to put together the whole package and tell the whole story of the Religion of the Sun, often spending seven days a week writing and researching for many months at a time, without charging anything, as we deeply care about this message and realize how important it is for people to know.

However, there is a difference between our methods of study and those of purely academic researchers. We not only write about the Religion of the Sun and research its evidence throughout history, but first and foremost, we practice it. Many people think you find out about things just by reading, but there is a limit to how much you can find out by reading alone. Ancient mystics discovered their knowledge through experience—one which is inner/metaphysical. The Religion of the Sun is a body of knowledge and a metaphysical practice that is directed toward the transformation of the individual, and thus someone can only truly uncover and understand its practice through practicing it and transforming themselves.

My husband was able to recreate its practice, not just from studying and researching its ancient remnants, but from his actual practice of it—including having out-of-body experiences using the same techniques practitioners of the ancient Religion of the Sun did. Likewise, someone can essentially have the same metaphysical experiences these ancient peoples did, and can thus penetrate into the true meaning of the symbols and writings they left behind, even when they are currently obscured or misunderstood.

Modern practitioners of the Religion of the Sun can and have seen many things, while out of the body, that were taught as part of the religion. This includes experiences of being shown and visiting such places as hell, called Xibalba, Narakam, Helheim/Niflheim, etc. in different ancient traditions, meeting the beings now called gods who founded the Religion of the Sun in ancient times, and, like my husband, seeing some of these beings in higher dimensions still using the ancient sites they built while alive on earth to initiate those worthy into deeper knowledge, such as the Great Pyramid of Egypt.

Since releasing the Sakro Sawel videos, a number of people have come to my YouTube channel after having an experience with the Being who in Nordic/ Germanic tradition became known as Odin and Wotan—to some he appeared in a dream; another he led out of a coma. I have also had the great fortune of meeting this Being in an out-of-body experience. This is the Religion of the Sun at work—it's a living practice, where the traditions of old are not locked in the past, but are alive as they once were, when the wisest of our ancestors were in touch with the other worlds, and through its practice, we are too.

CHAPTER ONE

The Ancient Religion of the Sun

WHAT IS THE ANCIENT RELIGION OF THE SUN?

Most people are somewhat familiar with the notion that people in the past worshiped the sun. And, many believe they did this because their understanding of the universe was much more simplistic than our own. But actually, it's quite the reverse. It's our understanding of them and of the spiritual nature of the universe that is so materialistic as to have overlooked the depth and meaning behind the ancient veneration of the sun. In the eighth chapter of this book, I give a summary as to the origins of why the sun held such a central place in the spiritual traditions of so many ancient cultures.

Although I use the phrase "sun worship," the veneration of the sun in more spiritually-advanced cultures was not a dumb devotion to the physical element. Instead, the sun was seen as and used to symbolize the supreme manifestation of the divine, as the greatest source of light and life. It was used not only as a symbol of the divine existing in the world around us, but also within us, as our own eternal Being.[1] The ancient Religion of the Sun was a great body of knowledge and metaphysical practice that taught someone how to realize this divinity within themselves and reunite with their higher Being, symbolized by the sun. This process was referred to as a path or way, and the journey of the sun throughout the year, through the two solstices and two equinoxes, symbolized its major stages, which is why so many deities experienced major life events at these times, why they were held sacred and celebrated by many ancient peoples, and why so many sacred sites were aligned to them.[2]

The ancient Egyptians are the most well-known practitioners of the ancient Religion of the Sun. This painting is from 1,300 BC, and shows the Egyptian ankh, symbol of eternal life, holding the sun.

A solar religion existing from ancient times is well-known in academia. For example, the Encyclopaedia Britannica entry on "sun worship" says:

> "Although sun worship has been used frequently as a term for "pagan" religion, it is, in fact, relatively rare. Though almost every culture uses solar motifs, only a relatively few cultures (Egyptian, Indo-European, and Meso-American) developed solar religions. All of these groups had in common a well-developed urban civilization with a strong ideology of sacred kingship. [...]
>
> The sun is the bestower of light and life to the totality of the cosmos; with his [...] all-seeing eye, he is the stern guarantor of justice; with the almost universal connection of light with enlightenment or illumination, the sun is the source of wisdom."[3]

Essentially, three major branches of ancient civilization are well-known to have practiced solar religions—namely those of the ancient Egyptians, Indo-Europeans, and Mesoamericans—although it also influenced and was practiced by numerous other cultures too, as I explain further on.

Indo-European is a broad term that includes a vast set of religious traditions that branched off over time. They include the Armenians in the Caucasus region where some theorize the Indo-Europeans originally migrated from; those in the Steppe regions to the north of the Caucasus like the Yamnaya and Scythian; those of the east, which are the Vedic/Hindu traditions found today in India and extending into Indonesia, Thailand, Cambodia, and China; those in the south, which includes Zoroastrianism in Persia (what is now Iran); the Hittites and Luwians of Anatolia; the Euphratic speakers of Mesopotamia who influenced the religions of the region, such as that of the Sumerians and surviving among the Yazidi; and those that spread westward into Europe, such as the Thracian, Slavic, Baltic, Germanic, Celtic, Scandinavian, Minoan, Mycenaean/Greek/Hellene, and later Roman pre-Christian religions. At one time, Indo-European traditions stretched all the way from Ireland in the west to Western China (from at least as early as 2,400 BC).

Solar religions in the Americas stretched over an equally vast area, and include those in Central America, like the Olmec, Aztec, and Maya—but also those in North America, among pre-Columbian peoples such as the Hopi and Zuni of the southwest and the stone and mound builders of the east, as well as in South America, among peoples such as the Inca, Chimú, Chachapoya, Moche, Tiwanaku, Muisca (and possibly Chinchorro), and others. Following the ocean currents, this solar religion also spread west to Easter Island, New Zealand, and the Pacific Islands.

The Egyptian branch of the Religion of the Sun extended much farther than Egypt itself, across North Africa, south into other parts of Africa, across to the Canary Islands, and following the ocean currents west of Egypt, connecting into the traditions of the Americas. Furthermore, I believe all three traditions of solar religion enumerated by Encyclopaedia Britannica—the Egyptian, Indo-European, and Mesoamerican—are each connected to one another, and I explore many of these connections in this book.

Although these solar religious traditions, and many others, are seen as disconnected and as having arisen organically out of the same instinctual impulse to deify those important natural elements necessary to survival, I have found much evidence to show that they are in fact very much connected and derive from the same body of profound knowledge in the very ancient past, and even from the same great spiritual teachers who traveled the world with the mission to spread it. This body of knowledge, my husband and I call the ancient Religion of the Sun.

As far as I am aware, this is the first comprehensive history of the ancient Religion of the Sun ever written, which also attempts to identify those who originated and spread it. After years of research, it is the first time the history of this religion has been told in such detail.

Following is a short summary of the origins and history of the Religion of the Sun, which I explain in more detail with references to evidence in the sections of this chapter that follow.

UNDERSTANDING THE PAST BY UNDERSTANDING THE PRESENT

Before we delve headlong into the past though, I think it's important to consider how we look at it. So often I find that people speculate about the past as though it bears no relationship to how things operate in the present. I've found that even scientists and respected researchers—seemingly otherwise rational people—come to conclusions about the past that don't correlate with any situations that we know about or have lived through ourselves.

Yet I think the soundest way to understand how things may have been in the past is to look for similar situations in the present.

For example, we only need to look at the spread of Western civilization to understand the spread of civilization in the past. Yet many believe this was impossible, seeing the oceans as some kind of impassable barrier essentially until the voyage of Columbus in 1492 across the Atlantic from Europe to America. But crossing the oceans is certainly achievable; people have even done it on their own in rowboats.[4] As I explain in chapter 4, the Norwegian adventurer Thor Heyerdahl crossed the Atlantic and Pacific Oceans in boats made according to ancient designs to prove ancient civilizations could do it.

Often people think of human movement in terms of invasions and exploitation, and yet there can be benevolent motivations too, and there are examples of this in the world today. People within organizations like the Red Cross, which were founded on Christian principles, have traveled the globe to peoples of all races, providing charity and helping to reestablish civilization after natural and man-made disasters.[5] Those teachers who spread the Religion of the Sun were likewise motivated by compassion and high religious ideals, often braving danger and hardship in order to care for the well-being of others.

If people think that shamans are responsible for advanced civilizations now lost, then take a look at the level of civilization achieved by surviving shamanic traditions today. The founders and great teachers of the Religion of the Sun were highly skilled, civilized, and educated people who built the greatest megalithic monuments on Earth using sciences still not understood by our own; these are not the traits of shamans like those alive today in Mongolia, Siberia, or the Amazon, and who were spread over much of Europe and Asia during the Ice Age.

If people think that civilization is only a few thousand years old, and yet anatomically modern humans have been around for at least 200,000 years, then you have to ask yourself, what were people, who were just like you and I, doing for 190,000 years or more. Just look at the pace of invention and innovation today. Such ingenious people have always been among us, and I'm sure they were just as restless to explore, understand, and traverse the unknown as such people are today. We've found only some of their inventions buried in the ground, just as ours will be one day.

THE TRACES WE'D LEAVE IF WE BECAME A LOST CIVILIZATION

Now that we're about to embark on the search for lost civilizations, I think it's also important to understand what kind of evidence we could expect to find. Again, understanding the present can give us an insight into the past.

Imagine if our civilization collapsed tomorrow. It can be from any cause—a killer virus, natural disaster, climate change, nuclear war, or meteor impact—after which the world enters a dark age where its technology and literacy are extinguished. Yet humans survive, and slowly rebuild their communities and lives. Now imagine yourself thousands of years later among the people of the future who were archaeologically investigating it. They are uncovering identical symbols, building styles, legends, remnants of similar sacred texts, etc., all over the world, and some of them are wondering why. In the case of Christianity for example, either identical or near identical churches, crucifixes, and statues of Jesus, are being unearthed in almost every continent and region. The people of the future would rightly conclude that there had once existed a lost global civilization that had, for the most part, shared a common religion.

When looking back at ancient history we see exactly the same thing. We find the same pyramid and megalithic designs oriented to the sun, using the same geometric principles and standard measurements, as well as building styles and techniques. Stepped pyramids, for example, can be found in a huge number of locations—in ancient Egypt, the Canary Islands, Mauritius, the Azores, the Maldives, Sicily, Sardinia, Russia, Central America, South America, Cambodia, and some of the Pacific Islands. In Sumer they were built as ziggurats, and in India and other parts of Asia they are known as stupas.[6]

We also find identical symbols in use throughout the ancient world. One of the most prolific of these is the swastika, an ancient solar symbol, which before it was adopted by the Nazi Party in 1920, was in use for at least twelve thousand years, and has been found in such widespread places as the Americas (North, Central, and South), the whole of Europe, Russia, the Middle East, and large parts of Asia (including India and China).

Not only that, but legends of the same great teachers and preachers of an ancient solar religion, who were associated with these symbols and the building of many of these sacred sites, like stepped pyramids, can be found in disparate parts of the world. Dressed in robes, and with supernatural abilities, they were the equivalent of Jesus in their day, and as with the image of Jesus, similar images and descriptions of them are found across continents.

Some of the great religious teachers of the ancient world (excluding Cernunnos, who is now remembered only as a god) depicted as seated in a cross-legged pose, which was associated with the sun god as discussed in chapter 4.

When looking at ancient history, it starts to become obvious that there was once a global civilization in ancient times that shared a common religion.

But where did it go?

Civilization has not always progressed in an upward trajectory. It has been punctuated and hurled backward by numerous cataclysms and societal collapses, followed by major population loss and movements, sometimes leaving little trace behind.

In his book *The World Without Us*, journalist Alan Weisman studied what would happen if one day every human being suddenly disappeared from the face of the earth. What he describes is how quickly and almost completely nature would reclaim what we've made. At what pace and to what degree largely depends on the location and materials used.[7] What's left exposed is mostly broken down, and what survives, sometimes indefinitely because it's buried, is swallowed out of sight. Ceramics and bronze items would await archaeologists—both common finds in digs today.

In terms of buildings, what lasts above ground are megalithic stone monuments, which would outlive all else. For example, according to Weisman, "Mount Rushmore's granite erodes at one inch every 10,000 years. At that rate, barring asteroid collision or a particularly violent earthquake in this seismically stable center of the continent [Mount Rushmore] will be around for the next 7.2 million years."[8]

The most enduring vestige of our civilization
will be Mount Rushmore in the United States.

That's why we so often find megalithic monuments of similar design throughout the world with successive layers of civilization buried around them. Yet even they don't last forever—of the seven wonders of the ancient world, only one remains, that being the Great Pyramid of Egypt, and even it is deteriorating since its casing was removed in the Middle Ages. Its exposed limestone blocks will dissolve so that in a million years from now it will look just like a hill.[9]

"The other six [wonders of the ancient world] were of even more mortal stuff: a huge wooden idol of Zeus plated in ivory and gold, which fell apart during an attempt to move it; a hanging garden, of which no trace remains among the ruins of its Babylonian palace 30 miles south of Baghdad; a colossal bronze statue on Rhodes that collapsed under its own weight in an earthquake and was later sold for scrap; and three marble structures—a Greek temple that crumbled in a fire, a Persian mausoleum razed by Crusaders, and a lighthouse marking Alexandria's harbor, which was felled by earthquake as well."[10]

~ ALAN WEISMAN, THE WORLD WITHOUT US

The seven wonders of the ancient world—only one of which remains today.

As great as they were, these ancient wonders were brought down by mere puffs of wind compared to the scale of disasters Earth has seen. In this book I discuss the massive global catastrophes that occurred at the ending of the last ice age, which resulted in the extinctions of megafauna, gigantic floods, global sea level rise, torrential rains, earthquake and volcanic activity, sudden extreme plunges and rises in global temperature, disruption of the circulation of the world's oceans, continent wide wildfires that burned up around

9 percent of the total biomass of the planet, thick clouds of smoke and dust that would have obscured the sun's light causing something like a nuclear winter for centuries, etc. These events would have buried, submerged, or destroyed most traces of any prior human occupation.[11]

> "There is a glaring lack of knowledge about our own past in the two million years between the oldest hominid bones found under the silt in Africa and the evidence of seafaring inside and outside the Straits of Gibraltar some six or seven thousand years ago. [...] Most of the human past is totally lost. Buried or effaced. In the course of two million years of human activity, ice has come and gone. Land has emerged and submerged. Forest humus, desert sand, river silt and volcanic eruptions have hidden from our view large portions of the former surface of the earth. The sea level has altered, seventy percent of our planet is below water and underwater archaeology has barely begun in coastal areas.
>
> We are accustomed to finding sunken ships with old amphora and other cargo beneath the sea, but speculation as to the discovery of other human vestiges on the bottom of the ocean remains a subject for science fiction writers."[12]
>
> ~ THOR HEYERDAHL, THE TIGRIS EXPEDITION

> "It's easy to make the assumption that nothing much was going on 15 or 20 or 30 thousand years ago because of the lack of records. Well, it's only when you begin to understand how extreme and how comprehensive some of these catastrophic remodelings of the earth have been that we can appreciate that really it would be surprising if much from these former ages even existed at all.
>
> [...] Once you begin to realize how extremely the environment has changed during the tenure of humanity of this planet, you can begin to realize that it's very possible we have built who knows how many levels of culture that have been basically erased and leave no trace other than through legends and folklore and tales and so on. And of course every ancient culture is consistent on that—of talking about a former order of things whether we call it the Garden of Eden, or Hyperborea, or Atlantis, or numerous other names. This is one consistent tradition we find from all over the world—this belief in a former order of things that basically succumbed to these great changes."[13]
>
> ~ RANDALL CARLSON

Remarkably, it's that which is committed to memory and passed on verbally in unbroken succession that outlasts most material structures. Is it so surprising then to find peoples with a rich culture and oral tradition telling of great past events, when little evidence of it except baffling megalithic structures now surrounds them? Parts of our story too would survive in places, preserved in local traditions, to the utter disbelief of people thousands of years later. Perhaps some would be preserved in books held within dedicated religious orders, written and rewritten, as the last paper or hide copies deteriorated. And of these, maybe a few would be committed to the walls of stone temples, where they become abridged and take on mythical form.

These are essentially the traces the lost religion and civilization of the sun have left behind. It's worth bearing this in mind, as we now turn our attention to the past.

SUMMARY OF THE HISTORY OF THE ANCIENT RELIGION OF THE SUN

The story of the Religion of the Sun, as far as I can ascertain, begins in a very distant past referred to in ancient Egyptian and Indo-European traditions as a golden age. This age was not golden in the sense of material gold, but in terms of expressing a time rich in spirituality, peace, and happiness. These golden ages are said to recur, just as the cycle of seasons do, but over very long periods of time—spanning at the very least, thousands of years. The last golden age is placed at least ten thousand years ago, and given different dates in different ancient texts and traditions. Based on ancient sources, I personally believe that a golden age likely occurred just over forty thousand years ago, and that the ancient Religion of the Sun derives from this time or earlier. In the records preserved in ancient Egypt, this age is when "the gods" are said to have lived, and established the first temple of the sun.

The ancient Egyptians had no word for "religion," as spirituality was seen simply as an expression of reality and not a separate discipline. In the Vedas (of the Indo-European tradition), the religion of this golden age is simply called "Sanatana Dharma," roughly translated to mean "the natural, ancient and eternal way."[14] The advanced peoples of the golden age were said in ancient texts to be able to perceive much more of reality than we can today, and thus were far more able to understand and explain it. Their most ancient knowledge, preserved in the oldest known sacred literature in the world, was a solar religion, and thus in this golden age, the Religion of the Sun was the understanding of reality. Only today is this perennial truth now seen, at best, as just one of the ways to interpret reality, as ancient texts of the Religion of the Sun state people's ability to perceive it has atrophied.

At that time, the world was in the last ice age, or more specifically, the last glacial period, which had begun about 110,000 years ago, and peaked around 20,000 years ago.[15] This ancient solar religion was said to have been practiced by a number of now lost civilizations, including a highly advanced civilization that existed during the last glacial period. This civilization is most popularly known as Atlantis, but references to it exist in a number of ancient sources where it is called by different names.

Over time, the spiritual level of humanity is said to decline, and the golden age comes to an end, giving way to increasingly lower ages of human spiritual development, just as in other cyclical phenomena in nature, such as the seasons in which the sun loses strength from summer through autumn to winter. The inhabitants of Atlantis are recorded as gradually losing their spiritual faculties and virtues, and becoming increasingly degenerate and aggressive, until finally, legends state that their island homeland (somewhere in the Atlantic Ocean) was destroyed by a great flood as a form of divine punishment.

This great flood is likely the same one found recorded in hundreds of native histories around the world, and most probably occurred around 9,700 BC, when an abrupt cataclysmic event ended the last ice age (which according to ancient texts, was most likely caused by an incoming celestial body[16]), and the period known as the Younger Dryas in the archaeological record, causing a massive global rise in temperatures and sea levels. Incredibly, this date coincides with the one given by the famous Greek philosopher Plato for the destruction of the lost civilization of Atlantis, even though Plato was of course unaware of when the Ice Age ended and that it was accompanied by massive floods worldwide.[17]

Legends state that among the several islands of Atlantis, one was home to religious institutions of the Religion of the Sun and a number of its high priests and sages. While most of the inhabitants of Atlantis perished in the cataclysm, a king and a number of sages were said to have been forewarned and survived. These survivors, whom I call "wisdom bringers," then embarked on a mission to spread the Religion of the Sun and the knowledge of civilization needed to create stable societies to support its practice across the world. Numerous accounts of indigenous peoples record their arrival—the descriptions of their appearance and what they taught share incredible similarities. I explore a number of these accounts in the third chapter of this book.

The religion they established became the basis of a number of ancient religions in different parts of the world—in Egypt; Britain; Europe; Russia; Mesopotamia; large parts of Asia; North, Central, and South America; and across the Pacific Islands. Remnants of the Religion of the Sun survive in many ancient wisdom traditions still practiced today that share remarkable similarities with one another.

Following in the wake of the wisdom bringers, a global culture and civilization arose which had adopted the Religion of the Sun, and further established it across the earth—by both land and sea. As far as I can tell, sometime after 9,700 BC this culture appears to have largely migrated from around the region of the Black Sea (the Caucasus and Anatolian region), where the megaliths of Göbekli Tepe (described as the world's first and largest temple) have now been discovered. My husband and I named this civilization "The Lost Civilization of the Sun," and I explore the evidence I have found through my research for its existence in the fourth chapter of this book.

The inhabitants of Atlantis, and the surviving wisdom bringers, had seafaring capabilities, as clearly recorded in numerous ancient sources. The global culture they gave rise to (The Lost Civilization of the Sun) also had seafaring capabilities, and this is largely how the same spiritual knowledge, symbolism, building techniques, alignments, mathematical and astronomical knowledge, etc., were diffused throughout much of the world. Mainstream academia does not generally accept that ancient peoples had the ability to make long ocean voyages from one continent to another, however, I present references to some of the evidence that they did in the fourth chapter.

Many of the most famous sacred sites on the planet were built as part of the practice of the Religion of the Sun, including the Great Pyramids of Egypt, the moai of Easter Island, Stonehenge in England, Tiwanaku in Bolivia, Machu Picchu in Peru, Cahokia in the United States, Arkaim in Russia, Newgrange in Ireland, and numerous others. These sites all align to the solstices and equinoxes—the four major stages of the sun's journey through the year.

Quite a number of these sites were also built so that a line can be traced across the earth intersecting them, some at mathematically symbolic degrees from one another, indicating they were built to align with one other by a seafaring civilization at some time in prehistory. Note that many of these sites were progressively renovated by later peoples over pre-established and extremely ancient sacred places.

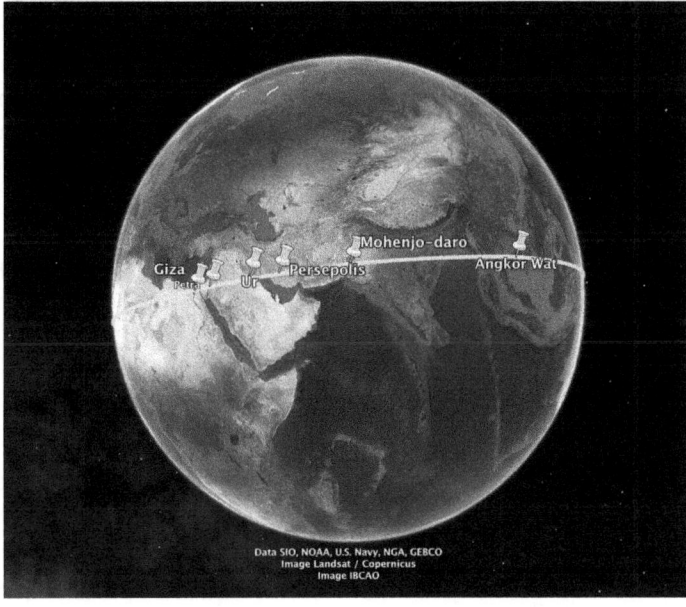

"The Great Pyramid is aligned with Machu Picchu, the Nazca Lines and Easter Island along a straight line around the center of the Earth, within a margin of error of less than one tenth

21

of one degree of latitude. Other sites of ancient construction that are also within one tenth of one degree of this line include: Persepolis, the capital city of ancient Persia; Mohenjo Daro, the ancient capital city of the Indus Valley; and the lost city of Petra. The Ancient Sumerian city of Ur and the temples at Angkor Wat are within one degree of latitude of this line. [...]

Many similarities between these sites have been well documented, including the use of perfectly cut and precisely placed monolithic stones, exact orientations to the cardinal points and astronomical orientations."[18]

~ JIM ALISON, EXPLORING GEOGRAPHIC AND GEOMETRIC RELATIONSHIPS ALONG A LINE OF ANCIENT SITES AROUND THE WORLD

The most ancient sites were aligned to the sun, so as to incorporate the sun itself into the place of worship as the focus of veneration. An old Hindu text (which as I discuss further on, also preserves a likely account of Atlantis) states that in ancient times, the sun itself was venerated, but that later, images of the sun were made and installed in places of worship instead. This would explain why ancient sites were so prominently aligned to the sun—and the more ancient, usually the more so. It also explains why the celebration of the solstices and equinoxes were so widespread and important.[19] It was so the sun could be worshiped directly.

"There was no image of the Sun-god in ancient times. His worship was performed only through his orb as this solar orb exists in the sky. Exactly like this the Sun-god was worshipped by his devotees in the form of the orb in ancient times but from the day Visvakarma [considered the teacher of ancient monument building in India] fashioned the sun-image in the anthromorphic form for the welfare of the whole world, his image was installed. His image form was definite according to the regulation from that time. The worship of the image (of the Sun-god) came to be initiated."[20]

~ SAMBA PURANA

I've found traces of the ancient Religion of the Sun almost everywhere in the world on every continent (except Antarctica), so great was its influence in the past. As part of its diffusion, many mystery/esoteric schools were established across the world—one ancient text states that these schools "spread to every corner of the Earth."[21]

Over time, however, many of the empires, cultures, and civilizations that had retained aspects of the Religion of the Sun collapsed or were destroyed. Its practice continued in some form in various outposts in some of the more remote regions of the world where it remained untouched for longer, including a number of isolated islands, such as Easter Island and the Canary

Islands—even up until a few hundred years ago. It also survived in some of the mystery schools that had been established across the earth, possibly in Egypt, Central Asia, India, Mesopotamia, and the Middle East. Some of these schools had to relocate to increasingly remote places in order to escape intensifying persecution, and hide within the guise of more recent religions, which had been forced on local populations upon pain of death. An example of this is the Knights Templar and the Freemasons, who preserved much of the knowledge of the Religion of the Sun from ancient times, but practiced it within the cloak of Christianity.

While the evidence for the existence of the Religion of the Sun has remained in scattered remnants left behind in various ancient texts, megalithic sites, and symbols, the actual information of how to practice the religion itself in any coherent and meaningful form was lost over thousands of years of suppression and persecution. Its practice had also degenerated terribly in many cultures, which either introduced horrific practices, such as human and animal sacrifice, that were never originally part of the Religion of the Sun, or retained them while also adopting some aspects of the Religion of the Sun that had been taught to them or their ancestors. My husband explains the practice of the Religion of the Sun in our book *Ancient Solstice*.

The ancient Religion of the Sun was a religion practiced across much of the ancient world in which the sun was seen as the supreme manifestation of the divine.

‹HAPTER TWO

Origins

To understand the origins of the Religion of the Sun, we'll start by looking at the oldest surviving references to it , which I have located through my research.

They are found in the oldest known sacred literature in the world, both in texts acknowledged by mainstream academia, and those that aren't, but that I nevertheless believe to be authentic, for reasons I'll explain.

As we would expect, it is in the cultures mentioned as practicing a solar religion—the Egyptian, Indo-European, and Central and South American—that we find them. And it is to these traditions that we now turn to find the earliest references to the Religion of the Sun.

THE EARLIEST REFERENCES TO THE RELIGION OF THE SUN

THE VEDAS OF INDIA

The Vedas are considered the oldest surviving sacred literature of Indo-European religion. They are the oldest scriptures of Hinduism, and are among the oldest known sacred texts in the world. They contain numerous clear references to the sun as the supreme godhead.

The Vedas were first written down about one thousand years ago in India, but were preserved prior to this through oral transmission—the general academic consensus is that they were first composed in India around 1,500 BC. However, there are scholars who believe they were composed thousands of years earlier than this. One such scholar is the Indian astronomer B. G. Sidharth who has analyzed the astronomical phenomena described in the Vedas and demonstrated that the earliest astronomical observations recorded in them must have been made prior to 10,000 BC.

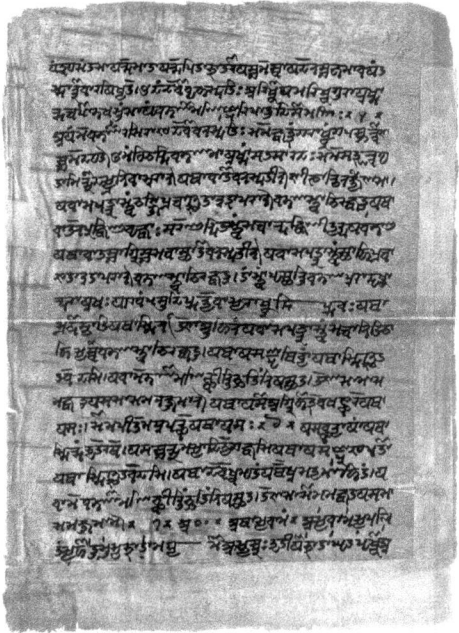

A page from the Atharva Veda, one of the four books that comprise the ancient literature referred to as "the Vedas."

"It is quite evident that the composers of Vedic literature were a highly intelligent, knowledgeable, and sophisticated lot with a long tradition of astronomy that itself implies observation and settlement. Apart from their incredible calendric accuracy, including knowledge of precession, such other advanced and modern concepts as the heliocentric theory are already expected of the semi nomadic, illiterate invaders that contemporary theory supposes. [...]

Once the astronomical and calendric character of Vedic literature is recognized, any number of astronomical dates tumble out. All of them show a continuous astronomical tradition beginning before 10,000 B.C. Many of these dates are couched in the typical allegorical style of Vedic and other ancient Indian literature. But there are a number of explicit dates also. A few are given below.

The Taittiriya Brahmana (3.1.2) refers to Ajaekapada, the nakshatra Purva Bhapada, rising exactly due east, a phenomenon that occurred around 10,000 B.C. when this asterism was at the autumnal equinox. [...]

Thus an amazing continuity of astronomy from about 10,000 B.C. to about 2500 B.C. can be seen in Vedic literature."[1]

~ B. G. SIDHARTH, PRECESSION OF THE EQUINOXES AND CALIBRATION OF ASTRONOMICAL EPOCHS

A similar position is held by Dr. David Frawley, an American Vedic teacher and author, and founder of the American Institute of Vedic Studies.

"The Vedic people had a calendar based upon astronomical sightings relative to the equinoctial positions going back from 2000 BC to at least 6000 BC, from the age of Taurus to that of Cancer. This Vedic calendar was modified periodically according to precessional changes which can be documented up to the positions found in Hindu calendars today."[2]

~ DAVID FRAWLEY, GODS, SAGES AND KINGS

The date of 10,000 BC, given by Sidharth, also correlates with a number of archaeological finds. The oldest known depiction of the symbol of the swastika—which is a solar symbol central to Vedic culture—was found carved onto the tusk of a woolly mammoth in Ukraine and is dated to at least 10,000 BC.[3] People from the Lepenski Vir site, in what is now Serbia, were found buried facing east (the direction of the rising sun) in the "butterfly pose"—a position in the practice of yoga, which traces its origins to the Vedas—and these burials date to between 9,500 to 7,200 BC.[4]

Example of someone from the Iron Gates Mesolithic culture found at Lepenski Vir buried in a yogic "butterfly pose."

The settlement of Lepenski Vir has been called "the first city in Europe," given its great age and high level of development.[5] The city was located so that a "double sunrise" on the summer solstice was viewable from it, and its religion centered around the sun.[6]

"The terrain was further surveyed with the theodolite and the astrogeodesy analysis was conducted in 2017. The results show that the "double sunrise" was visible from the northernmost part of the [Lepenski Vir] settlement. Viewed from the southernmost part, the summer solstice Sun rose on the southern part of the flattened top of Treskavac. So, the whole settlement was accurately measured according to the astronomical event."[7]

The first shrines of the Lepenski Vir city were eventually used as houses, but had originally been dedicated to the sun.[8] I suspect that the site was initially a place of religious pilgrimage because of its unique natural solstice alignment, but later became a permanent settlement.

"[Archaeologist Ljubinka Babović] asserted that every house was actually a small Sun shrine and that [the] plan of the settlement represents the astronomical movement of the Sun."[9]

These findings suggest that the culture of Lepenski Vir may provide the earliest known evidence of an Indo-European solar religion.

Other evidence connects Indo-European religion with what has been dubbed "the world's oldest temple."[10] The astronomer B. G. Sidharth has recognized astronomical myths found in Vedic literature as being depicted on columns at the ancient site of Göbekli Tepe in Turkey, dated to 9,600 BC.[11]

Pillars at the ancient site called Göbekli Tepe, located in modern day Turkey.

Additionally, there are geographical descriptions in the Vedas that also indicate their great age. In the following excerpt, David Frawley explains how the Saraswati river in India was referred to in Vedic literature as the largest in the country and one that flowed into the sea—using satellite imagery, scientists are now able to date when the now dried up Saraswati river matched the descriptions given for it in the Vedas, and thus, how long ago the parts of the Vedas that refer to it in this state are likely to have been composed.

"It is thus clear from the Rig Veda and the Vedic tradition that the homeland of its people is the Saraswati river. [...]

Was there ever a time in which this Saraswati river was a great river, perhaps the largest in India, as the Vedas say? [...]

Many sites of the Indus Valley culture, which flourished in the third and second millennia BC, have been found along its dried course showing that it was indeed an important site of ancient Indian civilization. Hence the Saraswati has been found to have been a great river, perhaps the greatest in India, as the Vedas say, but this takes us back to early ancient times, to the Indus Valley culture or before — much earlier than the time period given to the Vedas by modern scholars. [...]

The Vedic people could not have known that this river flowed of its own accord into the sea as the greatest river in India if they entered India in 1500 BC when the river had already dried up in the desert. It took many thousands of years for the Saraswati to change its course four times and then dry up by the time of the Mahabharata. That the Vedas knew of this river and its greatness certainly calls into question our entire view of human history. [...]

Modern scientific studies indicate that the Saraswati river dried up around 1800 BC, while its previous ocean-going flow ended perhaps as early as 8000 BC."[12]

~ DAVID FRAWLEY, GODS, SAGES AND KINGS

As further evidence for the antiquity of Vedic civilization, David Frawley notes that the ancient Hindu texts referred to as the Puranas contain long and detailed lists of kings, stretching back to the founder of civilization in India called Manu—who was a son and student of the sun god. These king lists cover a timespan possibly dating back to around 6,400 BC, although as Frawley says, the time allotted to each king's reign is currently speculative.

"The Puranas contain elaborate lists of kings, including many related seers, going all the way back to the legendary first king and first man, Manu. Many of these figures occur in the Vedas as well. [...]

Some scholars have tried to make a chronology out of the Puranic lists of kings. They show about one hundred and thirty-five kings starting with the first king, Ikshwaku [Ikshvaku], to the time of Mahapadma Nanda (c. 400 BC). The Greek historian Arrian's

Indicka (9.9), quoting Megasthenes, states that 'from Dionysos (Shiva) to Sandracottus (Chandragupta Maurya) the Indians counted a hundred and fifty-three kings over six thousand and forty-three years.' How many years we may give these kings is speculative. We may not want to afford them six thousand years, though this agrees quite well with the astronomical references in the Vedas [...].

Such an extensive list of kings counters the idea that the Hindus have no history and that their records do not go back very far. Their records in this regard are more extensive and no less legendary than those of other ancient cultures like Egypt and Babylonia."[13]

~ DAVID FRAWLEY, GODS, SAGES AND KINGS

I personally believe that much of the sacred literature of Hinduism, including the Puranas, contain stories that are far older than the texts themselves, and that some of the events they describe may even predate the destruction of Atlantis (for example, see references to Vimanas in a number of Hindu texts, literally translated as "aircraft"[14]).

David Frawley describes how the Vedas portray an ancient solar religion, and are likely only a remnant of this religion, which once spread throughout the globe.

"The *Vedas* contain spiritual, occult and cosmic secrets that we are just beginning to become aware of. The great India based religions of Hinduism, Buddhism, Jainism and Sikhism may represent only later aspects of ancient enlightenment traditions that were probably more common during the Vedic era. The *Vedas* represent the remains of these early traditions, of which there were no doubt many more.

Vedic literature portrays an ancient solar religion of Yoga and enlightenment, such as was once common throughout the entire world. The Sun is a symbol of the higher Self, the *Atman* or *Purusha* of yogic thought. This Vedic religion of light is a religion of consciousness, which is the supreme form of light."[15]

~ DAVID FRAWLEY

"This universal religion is the basis of the Vedic Aryan culture. It is the legacy of the great solar religion of enlightenment that prevailed throughout the ancient world, which set up ritualistic cultures ruled by priest and seer-kings. The Vedic peoples reflect this culture and its development."[16]

~ DAVID FRAWLEY, GODS, SAGES AND KINGS

References to the spiritual sun as the supreme godhead are found in the oldest sacred text of India, the Rig Veda:

"Arising from the surrounding darkness, seeing the higher light, we have reached the Godhead, the Divine Sun, the supreme light."[17]

~ RIGVEDA I.50.10

In summary, the astronomical and landscape descriptions in the Vedas, the corresponding archaeological finds of great age, and the lengthy king lists cited in later Vedic literature indicate that the Indo-European branch of the Religion of the Sun dates to 10,000 BC or earlier—at least a few hundred years before the end of the last ice age.

ANCIENT EGYPT

There are many references to civilization in ancient Egypt being extremely old—in some cases, even tens of thousands of years old. Alongside this, references state that the oldest religion of ancient Egypt was a solar religion—the first king and god as recorded in the annals and king lists of ancient Egypt was Ra, the sun god.[18] This is very similar to Vedic civilization, whose first king was said to be a son and student of the sun god Surya. However, as we will see, ancient Egyptian records stretch back much further than those found in the Vedas, to as far back as 39,500 BC.

Drawing of the sun god Ra-Horakhty. In Egyptian, as well as in Mesopotamian, Mesoamerican, and Indo-Iranian cultures, the sun was often associated with birds.

A number of famous Greek historians who wrote in the first few centuries BC had access to many more of the ancient Egyptian records than we do today, and even to the firsthand accounts of the Egyptian priests at the time. It was their opinion that the civilization of ancient Egypt was extremely old—in fact, the oldest.

"The Egyptians [...] were the most ancient of men."[19]

~ DIODORUS, LIBRARY OF HISTORY

Plato recounts how the Egyptian priest of the temple of Sais told his ancestor Solon, who lived in 600 BC, the following about the age of the records kept in Egypt:

"And whatever happened either in your country or in ours, or in any other region of which we are informed—if there were any actions noble or great or in any other way remarkable, they have all been written down by us of old, and are preserved in our temples. Whereas just when you and other nations are beginning to be provided with letters and the other requisites of civilized life, after the usual interval, the stream from heaven, like a pestilence, comes pouring down, and leaves only those of you who are destitute of letters and education; and so you have to begin all over again like children, and know nothing of what happened in ancient times, either among us or among yourselves. As for those genealogies of yours which you just now recounted to us, Solon, they are no better than the tales of children."[20]

~ PLATO, TIMAEUS

The very ancient age of Egypt is corroborated by a list of their high priests that stretches back over ten thousand years.

"They [the Egyptian priests] brought me into the great inner court of the temple [...] every high priest sets there in his lifetime a statue of himself [...] they traced descent through the whole line of three hundred and forty-five figures [...]. Before these men, they said, the rulers of Egypt were gods."[21]

~ HERODOTUS, BOOK OF HISTORY

Given that Herodotus was writing at around 440 BC, and using the Greek calculation of three generations per one hundred years, the lineage of high priests referred to would stretch back to around 11,940 BC.

Then there are a number of ancient Egyptian king lists that stretch back tens of thousands of years. Some of the references to such lists can be traced to an Egyptian priest of the sun at the temple of Heliopolis called Manetho who lived in the third century BC and wrote an extensive history of Egypt. His work did not survive, only references to it, which quote some of the dates he gave for the civilization of Egypt and its dynasties.

"What is curious but significant is that today's Egyptologists still use Manetho's dating, which is considered perfectly reliable for everything related to the 'officially' recognized dynasties; but they carefully avoid anything that relates to the prehistoric dynasties, while still regarding him as the 'Father' of Egyptology! Strange intellectual acrobatics in order to remain 'politically correct'! Mainstream Egyptology avoids talking much about Manetho, because they find some of the details he gives extremely disturbing. Manetho wrote for example that according to the stelae coming from the gods of the first (real) dynasty, more than 20,000 works were attributed to Thoth (Tehuti, Hermes). He also reported that these same gods reigned from 33,894 to

23,642 BC. It must be said that this is more than a little disturbing, coming from one whose work is the basis for the entire official chronology of the dynasties recognized as authentic. [...] Manetho gives us very interesting details on the dynasties called 'divine', which he divides into three categories: Gods, Heroes, and 'Manes'. He also explains that the category of the Gods was divided into seven sections, each having a god at its head, including Horus, Anubis, Thoth, Ptah, Osiris and Ra, and that 'these gods who originated from Earth then became celestial and associated with the stars as they reached heaven'."[22]

~ ANTOINE GIGAL, EGYPT BEFORE THE PHARAOHS

"These [i.e. Ptah, Ra, Thoth, Osiris, Set, Horus] were the first to hold sway in Egypt. Thereafter, the kingship passed from one to another in unbroken succession [...] through 13,900 years [...]. After the Gods, Demigods reigned for 1255 years; and again another line of kings held sway for 1817 years; then came thirty more kings, reigning for 1790 years; and then again ten kings ruling for 350 years. There followed the rule of the Spirits of the Dead [...] for 5813 years."[23]

~ EUSEBIUS CITING MANETHO, CHRONICLE OF EUSEBIUS

The total Manetho gives for the Egyptian kings following the first (real) dynasty is 24,925 years; he was writing around 300 BC, thus placing the beginning of Egyptian kingship earlier than 25,225 BC.

This figure is roughly comparable to the one given by the Greek historian Diodorus, who places their beginning in 23,100 BC.

"At first gods and heroes ruled Egypt for a little less than 18,000 years, the last of the gods to rule being Horus, the son of Isis. [...] Mortals have been kings of their country, they say, for a little less than 5000 years ..."[24]

~ DIODORUS SICULUS

An ancient text called the Turin Papyrus also records Egyptian kings stretching back tens of thousands of years.

"... Venerables Shemsu-Hor, 13,420 years; Reigns before the Shemsu-Hor, 23,200 years; Total 36,620 years."[25]

~ TURIN PAPYRUS

Essentially, what the Turin Papyrus states is that the first period of Egyptian kingship lasted for 23,300 years, and is when a lineage of gods was said to have ruled. This is followed by a second period of 13,420 years in which those called the "Shemsu Hor" reign. The term Shemsu Hor is loosely interpreted as "the followers of Horus." Horus was son of the wisdom bringer Osiris, and was later deified in ancient Egypt as a sun god. The name "followers of Horus" seems to have a double meaning. Firstly, it indicates that, in the succession of kings, the Shemsu Hor followed after Horus, who was the last of the "gods" to rule. A second meaning, based on a more precise and literal translation of their name is "'those who follow the path of Horus,' that is, the 'Horian way,' also called the solar way."[26] Meaning, they don't just follow Horus in succession, they follow the religion taught by him, which the path of the sun—the path to return to one's higher Being as the sun—lies at the heart of.[27] Their name has also been interpreted as the "divine pharaohs who came from elsewhere,"[28] indicating they did not originate in Egypt. The long reign of the Shemsu Hor is followed by the reign of the first dynastic kings of Egypt, starting at around 3,000 BC. This means the Turin Papyrus places the beginning of the Egyptian lineage somewhere around 39,500 BC!

This figure is corroborated in other historical accounts, which state:

> "Four times in this period [since the beginning of Egyptian civilization] (so they [the Egyptian priests] told me) the sun rose contrary to his wont; twice he rose where he now sets, and twice he set where now he rises."[29]
>
> ~ HERODOTUS, BOOK OF HISTORY

> "The Egyptians pride themselves on being the most ancient people in the world. In their authentic annals [...] one may read that since they have been in existence, the course of the stars has changed direction four times, and that the sun has set twice in that part of the sky where it rises today."[30]
>
> ~ POMPONIUS MELA (LATIN AUTHOR OF THE FIRST CENTURY)

As the author and researcher Graham Hancock has pointed out, based on the work of Schwaller de Lubicz, the reference to the sun changing where it sets and rises likely refers to the precession of the equinoxes, in which the sun on the equinoxes gradually rises and sets against different constellations. The time it would have taken to switch where it rises and sets to opposite positions, twice, would set the beginning of Egyptian civilization back to at least 39,440 BC.[31]

In addition, an Egyptian text in *The Kolbrin* states that during this time there have been numerous natural disasters that would have severely disrupted the seeming continuity of Egyptian civilization in the archaeological record, and perhaps buried or even swept away some of its older layers.

> "My land is old, a hundred and twenty generations have passed through it since Osireh [Osiris] brought light to men. Four times the

stars have moved to new positions and twice the sun has changed the direction of his journey. Twice the Destroyer has struck Earth and three times the Heavens have opened and shut. Twice the land has been swept clean by water."[32]

~ THE ANNEXED SCROLL 1, THE KOLBRIN

Although we have such clear references to the beginnings of Egyptian civilization stretching back tens of thousands of years, many simply shrug them off as fantasy, since there is no archaeological evidence to corroborate them...

Or is there?

Could it be hiding in plain sight—literally staring us in the face? An ancient version of Mount Rushmore that survived the destruction of virtually all else around it?

The age of the Great Sphinx is a hotly contested topic, as it is one of the few ancient sites in the world that clearly shows evidence of extreme antiquity.

Public debate about it got going in the early 1990s when the researcher John Anthony West and geologist Robert Schoch put forward the theory that the Sphinx and its surrounding enclosure show signs of heavy weathering from rainwater. They argue that deep fissures in the stone, which have almost entirely eroded away the original form of the Sphinx, were created by a long period of heavy rainfall. Today, Egypt is mostly desert—the last time the Giza Plateau experienced heavy rainfall was during the period called the Nabtian Pluvial, which lasted from 10,000-3,000 BC. This means the Sphinx must have existed during this time, but could also have been built earlier. Schoch places the age of the Sphinx at around 10,000 BC.[33]

The Great Sphinx. Notice the deep fissures in the stone wall surrounding
the sphinx and the scale of them in comparison to the people.

However, another prominent researcher in the field, Randall Carlson, believes the erosion is so great that the Sphinx could be at least 20,000-40,000 years old.[34] He came to this conclusion by looking at a number of studies that had measured the rate limestone erodes when subjected to weathering from water (including rainfall), as the Sphinx and surrounding enclosure is carved into the limestone bedrock of the Giza Plateau.[35] The results of his comparative analysis are stunning. One study showed that a coastal limestone cliff face subjected to the constant action of ocean waves had eroded at the rate of just 1 mm per year, which is approximately 0.039 inches.[36] Limestone tombstones in the south-eastern United States eroded at one inch in five hundred years.[37]

Additionally, he looked at the rate of weathering on a number of limestone quarries in Egypt, which have been definitively dated to the period between 1,200-2,000 BC, which is around 500-1,300 years after the Sphinx was apparently carved, and yet the pick marks on them are still clearly visible today, while the enclosure surrounding the Sphinx is weathered approximately seven feet in places.

This seems to be contradicted by dates obtained from the Sphinx Temple using a technique called "luminescence dating," which found that the limestone blockwork used to build the Sphinx Temple must have been laid between 2,850-2,500 BC.[38] However, Randall Carlson points to a study showing that at around 10,500 BC the Nile experienced massive flooding, which he proposes would have swept away all but the stone blocks heavier than one hundred tons[39]—and this is the estimated weight of the largest limestone blocks in the Sphinx and Valley Temples,[40] which would have definitely been in the path of a flooding Nile. Let's remember that the ancient Egyptian text from *The Kolbrin,* quoted earlier, said Egypt had been *swept clean* by water, twice.

I suspect the Sphinx Temple and Valley Temple were built by reusing the ancient blocks quarried from around the Sphinx that had been part of a much older structure ruined during these floods.

The Sphinx and its enclosure are not the only structures on the Giza Plateau that are extremely weathered—the little-known Tomb of Khentkawes and the wall surrounding the Khafre Pyramid are also carved from the limestone bedrock of the Giza Plateau, just as the Sphinx is, and both show the same signs of extreme weathering.[41]

To create a level foundation for the so-called Khafre Pyramid (the second largest of the three pyramids), the surrounding bedrock was dug out, forming an enclosure wall that runs parallel to the pyramid on two sides. The surface of this wall was first exposed when the foundation of the pyramid was built and therefore indicates its age.[42]

The so-called Tomb of Khentkawes is an ancient building located between the Great Sphinx and pyramids. At around 36,500 BC, when the major Giza monuments were most accurately astronomically aligned (as explained next), it corresponded to the position of the star Sirius, which is associated with the goddess Isis (the wife of Osiris) in ancient Egyptian religion.[43]

The astronomical alignments of the main structures on the Giza Plateau also indicate their great age. The author Robert Bauval discovered that at around 10,500 BC, the Great Pyramids aligned with the three stars of Orion's belt.[44] He and Graham Hancock argue that the monuments of the Giza Plateau all had their most dominant alignments at 10,500 BC, specifically at sunrise on the spring equinox—when the Sphinx aligned with the sun and the constellation Leo (which its form matches), and the Nile River with the Milky Way.[45]

However, although the date of 10,500 BC is one of the most popularly discussed, due to the precession of the equinoxes, it's possible that these alignments also occurred at an earlier time, around 36,500 BC. According to the researcher Armando Mei, the alignments were even more accurate at this date—and the most accurate they could be anywhere in the period between 100,000 BC to AD 2,000. The date of 36,500 BC also coincides more closely with the beginning of the king lists in Egypt, when it's said the gods ruled.

In summary, what we have that supports a date for the beginning of civilization in Egypt at around 39,500-36,500 BC is as follows:

1. The king list found in the Turin Papyrus.

2. The historical accounts of Herodotus, Pomponius Mela, and *The Kolbrin*.

3. The date of best match for the dominant astronomical alignments of the Great Pyramids and Sphinx.

4. The signs of extreme weathering on the Great Sphinx and its enclosure, as well as the Tomb of Khentkawes and the enclosure wall of the Khafre Pyramid.

As compelling as these things are, archaeologists often refute their validity by pointing to the fact that there is apparently no evidence for any kind of advanced civilization in ancient Egypt until the beginning of the dynastic age at around 3,100 BC. However, the Nile River—which the Great Pyramids and ancient Egyptian civilization were built along—creates one of the largest river deltas in the world, as it spreads out and drains into the Mediterranean Sea. Before the construction of a modern dam (the Aswan Dam), it flooded annually, spreading layers of silt out across the Nile Delta.[46]

> "We have here a clear reason why we do not and possibly can never know the details of the civilization which I believe really built the pyramids of Giza, because the home of their civilization and the original occupation levels of their capital at Sais are mostly buried at enormous depths below thousands of years' accumulation of mud and silt of the Delta."[47]
>
> ~ ROBERT TEMPLE, EGYPTIAN DAWN

This is one of the reasons why the Great Sphinx and Pyramids have outlasted any surrounding evidence for their builders.

And they will likely outlast modern civilization too. If today's inhabitants of Egypt were to suddenly disappear, their civilization along the Nile River would be swallowed up just as totally as the ancient one. The Aswan Dam would eventually be overwhelmed, unleashing the Nile, which would go:

> "[...] spreading out again across its former alluvial plains, and entombing whatever was built there in annual layers of silt. Within them, fire hydrants, truck tires, shattered plate glass, condominia, and office buildings may remain indefinitely, but as far from sight as the Carboniferous Formation once was."[48]
>
> ~ ALAN WEISMAN, THE WORLD WITHOUT US

So now that we have explored the possible age of civilization in Egypt, what do the most ancient records preserved in Egypt have to say about the religion practiced in these earliest times?

The walls at the Temple of Horus at Edfu in Egypt are carved with stone murals that preserve some of the most ancient accounts of the origins of Egyptian civilization, as well as its religion. These murals were considered the most important parts of much more ancient documents now lost. The following excerpts are from a book by the Egyptologist Eve A. E. Reymond who studied the murals and has provided the most authoritative interpretation of them.

> "We suspect that the texts which were used at Edfu to define the nature of the gods of historical times were originally parts of an extensive doctrinal document of an early date."[49]
>
> ~ EVE A. E. REYMOND, THE MYTHICAL ORIGIN OF THE EGYPTIAN TEMPLE

Entrance to the Edfu Temple in Egypt, the central door of which is engraved with a sun disk.

Just as in ancient Indo-European texts and traditions, like the Vedic, the ancient Egyptian texts describe a golden age of spirituality that once existed on Earth. In the Edfu murals, this time is called "Zep Tepi;" the exact sentence found on the walls of the temple of Edfu is "Ntr ntri hpr m sp tpy," which has been translated by Reymond as "when the gods manifested as humans at the first time."[50] These texts describe the creation of the world by the "Sun-God," and the establishment of the first temple by the gods as their home, which was the temple of the sun, in the most distant time described.

> "[...] the birth-place of the Sun-God, was regarded as the centre from which all the acts of creation were believed to have started. [...] When he (the Sun-God) opened his eyes, he had illumined the Two Lands, he divided the night from the day. The gods issued from his mouth and men from his eyes. Everything attains being in him.

> "[...] the Solar Temple was regarded as a real home of all the gods who took part in the origin of the temple and sacred lands. [...] The Early Primaeval Deities, being assembled in their train, praised the Sun-God who created the Ka on the First Occasion to the limits of Eternity."[51]
>
> ~ EVE A. E. REYMOND, THE MYTHICAL ORIGIN OF THE EGYPTIAN TEMPLE

These traditions clearly describe the establishment of the Religion of the Sun in the depths of prehistory by those referred to as gods (I explain who these gods were in chapter 5). Reymond also goes on to say that the homeland where this religion was first established may have existed as a real place.

> "The conception of the appearance of the primeval hin, homeland, might have had a realistic background. It seems to reflect the appearance of a very primitive sacred place as it might once have existed in the dim past of prehistoric Egypt."[52]
>
> ~ EVE A. E. REYMOND, THE MYTHICAL ORIGIN OF THE EGYPTIAN TEMPLE

But where was this real place?

The city of Heliopolis (meaning "city of the sun") in Egypt, where much of this knowledge had been preserved, was once said to contain the most magnificent temple of the sun, whose floor reflected the stars above, but which has, along with the entire city, been completely dismantled as its blocks were gradually taken away for building material, and is now little more than a litter of stones in the sand.

When Diodorus Siculus, the Greek historian, visited it in the first century BC, he was told by its inhabitants that Heliopolis was older than any other city in Egypt.[53] And, according to their traditions, theirs was the site of the first temple of the sun. As support for this, a line drawn intersecting each of the southeast corners of the three Great Pyramids points to Heliopolis, as they likewise do when drawn from other pyramid sites in Egypt.[54] Maybe the site of Heliopolis was first established when the Great Pyramids were.

There is something extraordinary about the Great Pyramids that provides another clue to the possible location of the primeval homeland mentioned in the Edfu texts, and its religion.

Researcher and author Robert Temple essentially reverse engineered (at least some of) the geometrical masterplan of the Great Pyramids and Sphinx. In short, what he discovered is that there were a number of overlapping plans that geometrically generated each other, incorporating numbers such as pi and the golden angle, both in two and three dimensions, interlocking in a cohesive whole, to create the entire ground plan of the Giza site, which must have been designed from its very inception. Temple concludes the designers must "have had a great deal of truly profound geometrical knowledge" to such a degree that he kept "getting the uncomfortable feeling that there are some deeper principles of geometry operating here than are apparent to us, or at least to me."[55] For a full explanation including diagrams, see Temple's book *Egyptian Dawn*.

What is of most interest to the discussion here, however, is perhaps the central aspect of this geometrical master plan—and that is how it creates a representation of the eye of the sun god Ra staring at the zenith of the sky.

> "The first thing one can do with the Perfect Square of Giza is to construct a giant Eye of Ra gazing upwards at the sky. It is a purely geometrical design, which is not physically represented on the ground. However, it is not just an arbitrary Eye of Ra, but is one which is constructed of two arcs and a circle, each of which intersects key points of the Giza monuments. [...] This giant Eye looks directly upwards at the meridian line which bisects the Perfect Square, and peers at the central point of both the day and night sky which we call the zenith. [...]
>
> This gigantic and invisible, but geometrically implied, Eye was only known to the designers and the priests, and of course, presumably to the gods. It lay there on the ground as an imagined construct in the minds of the priests, to pay invisible homage to the sun god. [...] To the minds of the Egyptian priests, sacred geometrical designs were thus similar to silent prayers: nothing can be seen, nothing can be heard, but they exist and are powerful because they have been fully and meticulously articulated within the mental secrecy of the most elaborate acts of worship by the high priests themselves. What could be more appropriate for a solar centre like Giza than that it should secretly represent a giant solar eye staring up at the sky."[56]
>
> ~ ROBERT TEMPLE, EGYPTIAN DAWN

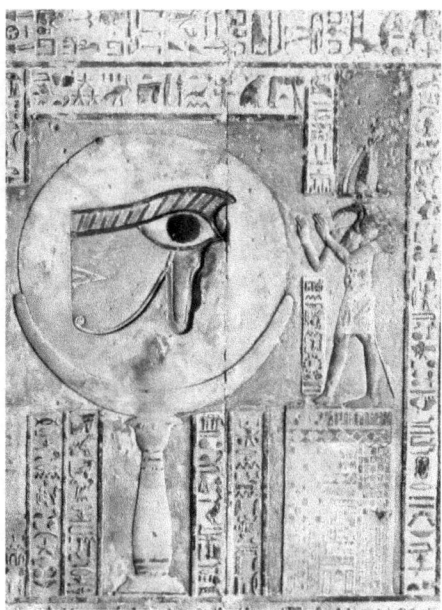

The eye of the sun god Ra being
worshiped by the wisdom bringer Thoth.

Looking again at Reymond's interpretation of the Edfu texts, could it be that the "birth-place of the Sun-God" where he "opened his eyes" and "divided the night from the day" and "created the Ka on the First Occasion" might be a reference to the opening of the solar eye in the ground plan of Giza, staring at the zenith of the sky, where his invisible Ka (or spiritual double) was first geometrically manifest? That "everything attains being in him" may describe the original purpose of the Giza site—as a place of the Religion of the Sun in which people reunited with their higher Being symbolized by the sun?

The religion described in the Edfu texts, which is that of the gods, is clearly a solar religion—the creator of the world is the sun god, and the first temple established in this primeval age is a temple of the sun.

Ancient Egypt had retained much of the knowledge about and from the golden age, and their religion and vast wealth of esoteric knowledge reflects this.

The sun became the most prolific symbol of divinity in ancient Egypt, and many references are found to the sun god across its most ancient texts, including the Pyramid Texts and the Book of Coming Forth by Day, commonly known as the Book of the Dead.

As research continues, it's looking possible that the Sphinx, and at least the bases of the Great Pyramids, were built tens of thousands of years ago by a people seen as "gods" by the surrounding population. This is when the ancient Religion of the Sun first identifiably appears in prehistory, being the religion of a distant golden age.

THE KOLBRIN

The Kolbrin is a little-known text, which unlike the Vedic and Egyptian texts mentioned earlier, is rejected by mainstream scholars. Instead, it is being studied by independent researchers such as Yvonne Whiteman. These researchers are gradually sifting through and finding evidence that corroborates *The Kolbrin's* texts with real historical and genetic finds. Many of the historical and genetic discoveries that correlate with *The Kolbrin* have only come to light after *The Kolbrin* was first published in 1994, lending credence to its authenticity.

Image of the book *The Kolbrin*, published by the Culdian Trust.

> "[...] it was only when I travelled to Egypt three years ago that gut instinct told me these incredible books had to be genuine and that I must try to authenticate them. Since then I have been researching here, there and everywhere to find links with other ancient works and locate archaeological and DNA evidence. One or two other enthusiasts have also been researching and having Eureka moments so that, bit by bit, the Kolbrin is emerging as a unique voice from the past."[57]
>
> ~ YVONNE WHITEMAN, GUIDE TO THE KOLBRIN

I've read *The Kolbrin* in its entirety and have come across numerous detailed and passing references that correlate with obscure archaeological finds that only someone who is broadly versed in ancient cultures from around the world would be able to pick up on. Given the volume of the text, and the extent of the events it describes, I believe it would have been a very complex and time-consuming undertaking to forge, and would have to have been written by a masterful expert in ancient history and archaeology, as well as ancient texts, religion, and philosophy.

It also contains esoteric knowledge that only someone with esoteric experience could know, which in my opinion, is almost nobody alive today.

The Kolbrin contains eleven books—six are Egyptian and five Celtic. However, these books contain accounts that cover a wider geographical area, including the Indus Valley, the Caucasus, Mesopotamia, Egypt, and Britain. They also contain an account of the first of Jesus' followers to arrive in Britain with Joseph of Arimathea.

This collection of texts was said to have been much larger, but was partially destroyed, and spent much time being safeguarded from persecution. After a long and perilous journey over thousands of years (even spending time buried beneath a cairn in Wales), the texts resurfaced in the private collection of an elderly sea merchant, who was a member of a hermetic organization and attended the councils of Welsh or other Celtic Bards and Druids. He brought them to New Zealand where they were made public for the first time.[58]

Given the events they describe, these books, or at least the accounts preserved in them, would be among the oldest in the world. Some of the accounts in *The Kolbrin* refer to events that may have happened thousands and even tens of thousands of years ago. They describe the possible interbreeding between humans and Neanderthals[59] (a species of humanoid that went extinct around thirty-seven to forty thousand years ago[60]), the destruction of a proto-Indus Valley civilization,[61] a number of great flood myths,[62] the bringing of civilization and religion to Egypt by Osiris, a more complete version of the epic of Gilgamesh, as well as accounts of the Religion of the Sun being taught far back in prehistory. I've found two such instances that stand out.

The first is the teaching a man named Habaris gives to the king of the Caucasus called Herthew, who was the son of a man called Dadam that was one of the Children of God (discussed in chapter 5) and known as "Firstfather." Dadam lived in the "gardenplace"[63] (also discussed in chapter 5), and an obvious parallel can be drawn to Adam of the Garden of Eden in Genesis. Interestingly, the name Abaris appears in the writings of the classical Greek historians, who state that he was a legendary sage of the Hyperboreans (whom the Greeks often identified as the Scythians, and Abaris was noted as wearing Scythian clothing), and priest of the sun god (whom they called Apollo).[64]

> "Thus far have I spoken of the Hyperboreans, and let it suffice; for I do not tell the story of that Abaris, alleged to be a Hyperborean, who carried the arrow [symbol of Apollo] over the whole world, fasting the while."[65]
>
> ~ HERODOTUS, BOOK OF HISTORY

The following excerpt from *The Kolbrin* records how Habaris taught the Religion of the Sun to the people of the Caucasus (Krowkasis) in ancient times.

> "He taught that men reach the true goal of life by transmuting lustlove into truelove. That true victory is gained only over the defeated bodies of their vanquished passions and baser selves. These and many other things were taught by Habaris, but many of his teachings displeased the people of Krowkasis [...]. So Habaris concealed many things from them and taught, by simple tales things within their understanding. He taught them the mysteries concerning the wheel of the year and divided the year into a Summer half and a Winter half [...] and established the folkfeasts of harvest-tide and seeding-tide.

[...] But Habaris instructed Herthew in the ways of the Otherworld. He taught him concerning the three rays from the central invisible sun, which manifest all things [...]."66

~ THE BOOK OF CREATION, FROM THE KOLBRIN

The Religion of the Sun spread with the migrations of Indo-Europeans from out of the Caucasus to places like Europe and Britain. Many elements of Arthurian mythology can be found in *The Kolbrin* which must have traveled to Europe with them, and I get the sense that King Herthew and Habaris are prototypes for King Arthur and Merlin.

The second clear instance of the Religion of the Sun being taught in the texts of *The Kolbrin* is in the accounts of Osiris, who became deified as the most central god in ancient Egypt. In *The Kolbrin*, he is a real person (called Yosira, Osireh, and Usira), who came to Egypt to teach the people the Religion of the Sun. He is what I call a wisdom bringer, and I discuss him in more detail in the following chapter.

> "In this fertile black land [Egypt] there are those who worship the sun and they call it the greatest and most bountiful among all gods, the Seer of Heaven, the Orb of Glory. They tell many tales about the coming of the Sun People and of the land from whence they came. They also tell of the squalid manner in which men dwelt before the Golden One [Osiris] led his people hence. [...]
>
> Then came the servant of the Sun [Osiris] and he it was who brought the people together and put rulers over them. [...] He showed them, man and woman, how to dwell together in contentment as husband and wife [...]. He instructed men in the sowing of corn and the growing of herbs. [...]
>
> Then when he departed he bade the people not to weep, for though he went to his father, the sun would adopt them as his children and all could become sons of the sun. Thus many became sons and servants of the sun and they believed what they had heard, that the sun was their father and the light of goodness overlooking the whole land. It is this light that sustains all living things but within it is the greater light which sustains the spirit. It is the light that enlightens the hearts of men. [...]
>
> When their guide and leader left, the people knew themselves as children of the sun."67
>
> ~ THE SCROLL OF KAMUSHAHRE, THE KOLBRIN

"[Osiris said] Behold the nature of man. Within him is a spark from the Divine Source and this is the Lord of the Body. This alone is everlasting, this alone of man is his true self. This spark is enwrapped within a heavy mantle of matter, it is enclosed in a covering of earthly clay. This spark alone is the seat of life, it alone has understanding and thought. Such things are not with the clay of the flesh, neither are they kin to the stones from which the bones come. The life within man radiates out from the enclosed spark, and through the blood endows the body with life and heat. Life gives forth heat and the greater the life the greater the heat. As the sun gives light and fire spreads heat, as the flower radiates perfume, so does the Central Light give forth a vaporous unseeable glow, and this our fathers called the Breath of God."[68]

~ YOSIRA [OSIRIS] IN THE TEACHINGS OF YOSIRA, THE KOLBRIN

THE STANZAS OF DZYAN

The Tashilhunpo Monastery in Tibet, where the Stanzas of Dzyan were said by Blavatsky to have been held.

The Stanzas of Dzyan is a text that was first brought to public attention by the author and founder of Theosophy, Helena Petrovna Blavatsky. What some believe is her masterwork—her book titled *The Secret Doctrine*, which was published in 1888—is based upon these Stanzas. *The Secret Doctrine* is structured so that Blavatsky analyzes and explains the meaning of each of these Stanzas verse by verse.

The Stanzas of Dzyan is a small text that Blavatsky says was held at the Tashilhunpo Monastery at Shigatse in Tibet where she read and translated it;[69] she said she spent several years studying in Tibet.[70] Blavatsky states that these Stanzas are extremely ancient and were originally written in a language called Senzar, which is a Tibetan word meaning "secret language" or "secret speech," and is said to be older than any known language in the world, used only by initiates.[71]

She states that a number of ancient texts have derived material from the Stanzas of Dzyan, including Genesis, and Vedic/Hindu, Egyptian, and Chinese texts.[72] For example, the famous Hymn of Creation in the Rig Veda is clearly an abridged version of the creation story found in the Stanzas of Dzyan. The Rig Veda was already published and well-known in Blavatsky's day, but there are other texts that share similarities with the Stanzas that were not. The Kalachakra texts of Tibetan Buddhism have only begun to be released to the public in the last couple of decades. The researcher David Reigle has discovered phrases that are completely unique to the Stanzas in the Kalachakra texts, helping to vindicate the authenticity of the Stanzas.[73] One of these phrases is "the great breath," which refers to the force behind the eternal motion of creation.[74] Interestingly, in the previous section, Osiris refers to "the Breath of God," possibly indicating some connection with the Stanzas.

Blavatsky implied that the Stanzas of Dzyan are taken from the still secret portions of the ancient Kalachakra literature. These secret portions originated long before Buddhism, and have been preserved within Buddhism from the ancient Vedic tradition Buddhism derived from. Blavatsky says that the Stanzas were first written in Central Asia after the destruction of Atlantis, and were dictated by the survivors and divine instructors of Atlantis to the "sons of Light"—who were the progenitors of the Indo-European civilization of our current age.[75]

Thus, they may have been written down around 9,700 BC. They are said to be older than the Vedas,[76] which as we've seen, already contain material dating to 10,000 BC. Taking that date as the basis of dating the Stanzas, some of the material in them could well refer to events that happened long prior to that date—potentially making their accounts the oldest known in the world. As an indicator as to the date of some of the events that the Stanzas describe, although it sounds incredible, they contain descriptions of various species of dinosaurs. Yet is this as incredible as it first seems? Since if we know about dinosaurs, it is surely possible that an advanced civilization destroyed by a global cataclysm could have known about them too, and the memory of them preserved somewhat simplistically in a text like the Stanzas of Dzyan.

I've found the Stanzas also contain central themes from the Religion of the Sun—including a creative trinity of Father and Mother who give birth to a Son, referred to as the "radiant Child of the two." This Son is associated with the sun, as he is in the Religion of the Sun.[77]

> "Behold, oh Lanoo! The radiant Child of the two, the unparalleled refulgent Glory: Bright Space Son of Dark Space, which emerges from the depths of the great Dark Waters. It is Oeaohoo the younger, the * * *. He shines forth as the Sun; he is the blazing Divine Dragon of Wisdom; the Eka (*one*) is Chatur (*four*), and Chatur takes to itself three, and the union produces the Sapta (*seven*), in whom are the

seven which become the Tridaśa (*the thrice ten*) or the hosts and the multitudes. Behold him lifting the Veil and unfurling it from East to West. He shuts out the above, and leaves the below to be seen as the great Illusion. He marks the places for the shining ones (*stars*), and turns the upper (*space*) into a shoreless Sea of Fire, and the One manifested into the Great Waters."[78]

~ THE STANZAS OF DZYAN

The Stanzas of Dzyan also include the story of the destruction of Atlantis and the mission of the wisdom bringers, which I explain more about in the following chapter.

ORAL HISTORIES

There are also oral histories of native peoples in the Americas that recount how their ancestors, in a very distant time, were visited by wisdom bringers who taught a solar religion. Although no dates are given in these histories, certain events they mention can be correlated with dates.

For example, the native Hopi people of the Four Corners region of the southwest United States have preserved oral histories that state there have been a series of three world ages that were each destroyed by global cataclysms. They state the First World was destroyed by fire coming up from volcanoes and raining down from above until it consumed everything. The Second World

Portrait of a Hopi girl, taken in 1900.

ended after the ice caps shifted, causing the world to spin off balance, mountains to plunge into the sea, the sea to slosh over the land, and the earth to freeze into solid ice.[79] This may correspond to the onset of the period known as the Younger Dryas at around 10,800 BC—when a cataclysmic event, possibly meteor impacts, caused global temperatures to plummet for over a thousand years[80]—or even to the beginning of the last glacial period over one hundred thousand years ago.

To survive these cataclysms humans had to take shelter within the earth (in what they describe as "ant hills") to afterward reemerge once it was safe to repopulate the world. This was said to happen at the end of the First and Second Worlds.

The Third World was destroyed by a great flood in which rain fell for a long time, continents sank, and tidal waves as high as mountains washed over the land. It likely corresponds to the rise in sea levels that occurred at around 9,700 BC. The Hopi say they survived on rafts which they traveled on across the ocean, stopping at a series of now submerged islands (likely in the Pacific Ocean), until arriving on the western shore of Central America, called the Fourth World. From here different clans migrated out across the entire continent. Their account shares similarities with that of the Maya of Central America, who are said to have originated from this migratory group.[81] This account preserved by the Hopi, but not limited to them, may record one of the earliest migrations to America.

> "The Hopis believe that the early Mayas, Toltecs, and Aztecs were aberrant Hopi clans who failed to complete their fourfold migrations, remaining in Middle America to build mighty cities which perished because they failed to perpetuate their ordained religious pattern. This may well be a case of the tail wagging the dog. It is more likely that the people who later called themselves Hopis were a small minority, perhaps a religious cult, who migrated north to the Four Corners area of our own Southwest."[82]
>
> ~ FRANK WATERS, BOOK OF THE HOPI

On arrival to the Americas the Hopi say they were met by Maasaw, whom they described as the caretaker of the land. He gave them a set of clay tablets to guide them, which have the symbols of the swastika and sun on them.[83] The Hopi still venerate the sun as the highest form of divinity, as did the Maya, Toltecs, Aztecs, and many other ancient civilizations of the Americas. Some Hopi believe that the tablets are ten thousand years old or more, and state that scientific dating methods have confirmed this.

> "You know, one time the scientist came to the Hopis and they said, 'We want to take a piece of the stone tablets.' They said 'We want to take the stone tablets to a scientific laboratory to determine how old they are.' The Hopis said, 'We know how old they are.' Well, the scientists said, 'We want to confirm it.' Well, the Hopis let them take a little piece, and they did that by the carbon dating method. They found these tablets were at least 10,000 years old, maybe 50,000. So when I say, 'Thousands of years ago, there were Native people that spoke of these things,' that's exactly what I mean. They told their children and thousands of years ago, their children grew up and told their children, and then their children grew up and told their children."[84]
>
> ~ LEE BROWN, SPEAKING IN 1986 AT THE CONTINENTAL INDIGENOUS COUNCIL, TANANA VALLEY FAIRGROUNDS, FAIRBANKS, ALASKA

Oral histories of the native peoples of Central and South America also describe a great deluge that wiped out a former age of humanity, and tell how afterward a Caucasian wisdom bringer traveled through their lands, and taught them civilization and religion. The religion this wisdom bringer taught is the Religion of the Sun. I've brought together many of these accounts in the following chapter.

Although no dates have been preserved in these histories, those of the Inca in South America for example, state that the wisdom bringer called Viracocha, who founded the Religion of the Sun there, also caused the building of the ancient site of Tiwanaku after a great flood. The clearly bearded image of Viracocha is carved into a stone monolith at this site. Although inhabited and renovated by people at a later date, a number of features at Tiwanaku indicate it was first established a long time ago, including a depiction of an elephant that would have gone extinct—depending on what species it was—at either 4,000 BC or between 10,800 and 9,600 BC.[85]

A carved monolith in the image of the wisdom bringer Viracocha at the ancient site of Tiwanaku. He has a beard and large round eyes, which are not Amerindian features.

But it's not just the remains of ancient sites and stone tablets that support the antiquity given by Native Americans to their oral histories. Genetic testing has now revealed that a number of Native American peoples have occupied the same land as their ancestors for thousands of years. This was discovered by comparing the DNA of ancient remains to modern indigenous people in the same region. The Quechua speakers who once peopled the Inca Empire, and those who speak Aymara and inhabit the region around Tiwanaku—both of whom preserve legends of Viracocha—are now known to have lived in the same area since at least 7,000 BC.[86] What this indicates is that their histories, particularly those of their beginnings, may also be at least that old.

These are just a few examples of oral histories containing accounts of the founding of the Religion of the Sun possibly over eleven thousand years ago.

REFERENCES TO HUGE SPANS OF TIME

Further evidence that lends credence to the Religion of the Sun dating from immense antiquity are the references to huge spans of time in the cultures and civilizations that were influenced by or practiced it in some way.

The ancient Egyptian sun god Ra in his "Boat of Millions of Years"–a phrase used to indicate eternity.

The king lists of Egypt stretch back over a period of tens of thousands of years, but in the ancient Egyptian Book of Coming Forth by Day, there are even references to periods of millions (and even billions) of years, as the boat of the sun god Ra is called the "Boat of Millions of Years."

> "Sun, your number is one, multiplied by millions. I am but a man with my thousand longings for unity. May we never cease to be. May there be no time in which a man must count the days toward some end. O, that life could be more than its garments. No before and no after, no exaltation but in the timeless one. The sun is striding over heaven, crossing distances of millions of years, and the hundreds of thousands of millions... one day of the sun. He set-rises, set-rises, set-rises over thousands of cities, trees and mountains and men. The distance of the instant. He has made an end to hours, and likewise counted them. In the morning, earth fills with light. Law and baptism. The one of us all, endures. It is our work under the sun."[87]
>
> ~ FROM THE ADORATION OF RA IN THE EGYPTIAN BOOK OF THE DEAD, TRANSLATED BY NORMANDI ELLIS

Vedic/Hindu literature also refers to numbers like this. It describes cycles of human civilization called Yugas that span millions and even billions of years.[88]

Like Vedic and Egyptian king lists, there are also Sumerian king lists that stretch back into the distant past and that likewise include names of seemingly mythical kings that precede those known to history. In the Sumerian records, however, these kings are said to stretch back not only tens of thousands, but hundreds of thousands of years—although some have noted that these seemingly impossibly long figures are likely to be symbolic of astronomical dates and cycles.[89]

In addition to this, as has been discussed by the author Graham Hancock in his book *Fingerprints of the Gods,* based upon the work of Professor Giorgio de Santillana and Hertha von Dechend in their book *Hamlet's Mill,* these civilizations also encoded the knowledge of the precession of the equinoxes into their literature and monuments.[90] The precession of the equinoxes is an astronomical phenomenon that takes place over an approximately twenty-six-thousand-year time frame.

Such concepts and observations of time indicate that these civilizations possessed knowledge that was very old and sophisticated. Both the ancient Egyptian and Vedic literatures claim there was once a golden age of spirituality on Earth, and that they preserved the religion from this age—and by referencing such long periods of time, it's at least possible they were aware of such a history existing, just as our civilization is aware of certain events taking place even millions of years ago too.

ATLANTIS

As we've seen, the accounts preserved in Vedic and Egyptian texts, in *The Kolbrin* and Stanzas of Dzyan, and in the histories of people such as the Hopi, are among some of the oldest in the world, and each is connected to a solar religion.

In the remainder of this chapter I trace the origins of these traditions ever further back in time, to a previous era of human civilization now lost, popularly referred to as Atlantis. Each of the sources that preserve some of the oldest references to a religion of the sun describe such a lost civilization, and their descriptions also share many similarities with one another.

In short, together these accounts, with much overlap, state that the Religion of the Sun was practiced on an island to the west of Egypt, by a people called a prior race or world (specifically the fourth; we today being the fifth), who had a moon-colored complexion, and were of a taller stature. They had developed a civilization more advanced than any other, and were considered a divine race, but had become proud and materialistic, had interbred with other humanoids, and as a result had lost their spiritual sense—which had been given by their inner/third eye. Their civilization, which had been built across a chain of islands, was destroyed suddenly in a terrible cataclysm, which included a great flood. All the islands are said to have sunk beneath the ocean overnight. This was considered a form of divine retribution for their mistakes. In this same disaster the world's megafauna became extinct (an event well-known to have occurred before the end of the last ice age).

There were great sages from this civilization, who themselves occupied a sacred island, likely one in this chain of islands. The accounts state that only those who were worthy/holy were saved, while those who weren't perished. The holy ones—these sages, who had survived the flood—became the progenitors and teachers of the fifth race, which I believe formed the basis of the Lost Civilization of the Sun, which it is said was ruled by the first divine kings. These sages and divine kings taught and instructed the people of our current age, and are what I call the "wisdom bringers."

These divine kings, sages, and wisdom bringers are recorded as the progenitors of humankind after a great disaster in many traditions still preserved today—for example, Ziusudra was a divine king and progenitor of Mesopotamian civilization, along with seven sages. Manu was a divine king and progenitor of Indian civilization, along with seven sages. Thoth was a divine king and progenitor of Egyptian civilization, along with seven sages and a number of other helpers, as was Osiris. Odin/Wotan was remembered as a divine king and progenitor of Germanic/Nordic civilization. Hotu Matu'a was a divine king and founder of the civilization of Easter Island along with seven explorers/priests.

Thus, the megalith and temple building, the civilization, and religion of each of these cultures are all likely to trace back to the survivors of Atlantis who instructed them in the Religion of the Sun. The Vedic/Hindu, Egyptian, Mesopotamian, and Persian religions have their root in this same religion, as do the pagan religions of Europe that have an Indo-European or Egyptian connection, as well as those of many of the people of North, Central, and South America, where similar wisdom bringers are also recorded as visiting and teaching religion, and no doubt many others.

Manly P. Hall was an author and thirty-third degree Freemason who famously wrote *The Secret Teachings of All Ages*, considered "a classic work of esoteric literature, divided into hundreds of entries examining aspects of myth, religion, and philosophy from around the world and throughout history."[91] In this work, he identified Atlantis as the origin of "sun worship" and the solar religion that formed an important part of the esoteric side of pagan religions.

> "Sun worship played an important part in nearly all the early pagan Mysteries. This indicates the probability of their Atlantean origin, for the people of Atlantis were sun worshipers. The Solar Deity was usually personified as a beautiful youth, with long golden hair to symbolize the rays of the sun. This golden Sun God was slain by wicked ruffians, who personified the evil principle of the universe. By means of certain rituals and ceremonies, symbolic of purification and regeneration, this wonderful God of Good was brought back to life and became the Savior of His people. The secret processes whereby He was resurrected symbolized those cultures by means of which man is able to overcome his lower nature, master his appetites, and give expression to the higher side of himself. The Mysteries were organized for the purpose of assisting the struggling human creature to reawaken the spiritual powers which, surrounded by the flaming ring of lust and degeneracy, lay asleep within his soul. In other words, man was offered a way by which he could regain his lost estate."[92]
> ~ MANLY P. HALL, THE SECRET TEACHINGS OF ALL AGES

Following are excerpts taken from a number of accounts that refer to Atlantis, including Plato's famous account, an ancient account told by Gurdjieff's father, oral histories from Native Americans, and various accounts found in Egyptian and Hindu sacred texts.

GREEK ACCOUNTS

Portrait of Plato, 350 BC.

The most famous account of Atlantis was told by Plato, who was a Greek philosopher that lived from around 425 BC to 347 BC, and who "is widely considered the most pivotal figure in the development of philosophy, especially the Western tradition."[93]

Here are a few extracts from Plato's famous retelling of the account of Atlantis that was told to his ancestor—the famous Greek lawgiver Solon—by a priest at the temple of Sais in Egypt in around 590 BC.

> "For many generations, as long as the divine nature lasted in them, they [the Atlanteans] were obedient to the laws, and well-affectioned towards the god, whose seed they were; for they possessed true and in every way great spirits, uniting gentleness with wisdom in the various chances of life, and in their intercourse with one another. They despised everything but virtue, caring little for their present state of life, and thinking lightly of the possession of gold and other property, which seemed only a burden to them; neither were they intoxicated by luxury; nor did wealth deprive them of their self-control [...]. By such reflections and by the continuance in them of a divine nature, the qualities which we have described grew and increased among them; but when the divine portion began to fade away, and became

diluted too often and too much with the mortal admixture, and the human nature got the upper hand, they then, being unable to bear their fortune, behaved unseemly, and to him who had an eye to see grew visibly debased, for they were losing the fairest of their precious gifts; but to those who had no eye to see the true happiness, they appeared glorious and blessed at the very time when they were full of avarice and unrighteous power. Zeus, the god of gods, who rules according to law, and is able to see into such things, perceiving that an honourable race was in a woeful plight, and wanting to inflict punishment on them, that they might be chastened and improve, collected all the gods into their most holy habitation, which, being placed in the centre of the world, beholds all created things. And when he had called them together, he spake as follows ... [the rest of the dialogue of Critias has been lost]."[94]

~ PLATO, CRITIAS

"[...] in those days the Atlantic was navigable; and there was an island situated in front of the straits which are by you called the Pillars of Heracles; the island was larger than Libya and Asia put together, and was the way to other islands, and from these you might pass to the whole of the opposite continent which surrounded the true ocean; for this sea which is within the Straits of Heracles is only a harbour, having a narrow entrance, but that other is a real sea, and the surrounding land may be most truly called a boundless continent. Now in this island of Atlantis there was a great and wonderful empire which had rule over the whole island and several others, and over parts of the continent, and, furthermore, the men of Atlantis had subjected the parts of Libya within the columns of Heracles as far as Egypt, and of Europe as far as Tyrrhenia. [...] But afterwards there occurred violent earthquakes and floods; and in a single day and night of misfortune all your warlike men [the Hellenes] in a body sank into the earth, and the island of Atlantis in like manner disappeared in the depths of the sea. For which reason the sea in those parts is impassable and impenetrable, because there is a shoal of mud in the way; and this was caused by the subsidence of the island."[95]

~ PLATO, TIMAEUS

The date given for the submergence of Atlantis by Plato is nine thousand years before the account of it was told to Solon, making it approximately 9,600 BC. Based on Greenland ice cores, the end of the last ice age is dated to around 9,700 BC, which is when there was an abrupt rise in global temperature, with "a speed in the natural climate change process never before seen in ice cores," said Jim White, who studied Greenland ice cores as part of a team of scientists. Another member of the team, Dahl-Jenson, said the change was so sudden it was "as if someone had pushed a button."[96] This was followed by a large rise in sea levels called "meltwater pulse 1B."[97] In other words, there was a large-scale and extremely sudden change in Earth's climate accompanied by an inundation of massive areas of land right around the time Plato gives for the submergence of Atlantis.

A number of arguments have been made against Plato's narrative, most commonly that Plato created the story in order to make a political point. Yet Plato begins his account by stating, "Then listen, Socrates, to a tale which, though strange, is **certainly true** [emphasis added], having been attested by Solon, who was the wisest of the seven sages,"[98] and continues to narrate it as nothing less than a real story, citing some of the most esteemed and respected men of his time as passing on the account from one to another until reaching him. Thus, this argument essentially rests on the claim that Plato was lying.

Other arguments contest the dating of Atlantis, for example claiming that the reference to nine thousand years ago was referring to lunar "years" (which are actually months) rather than solar years as is literally implied. Still others claim it must have been a scribal error, which added an extra zero—turning nine hundred to nine thousand. Yet this supposed error is made every time the figure of nine thousand is mentioned, and also when the figure of eight thousand years ago is mentioned, and the passing of one thousand years between them. These arguments, and others like it, rely on mistakes having been made in the text, or on interpreting things that are not literally stated.[99]

The fact that the date given by Plato so closely matches the timing of the end of the last ice age, and the huge earth changes that accompanied it, when Plato could not possibly have known about them, is beyond coincidence, and I think, proves that there is at least some truth to the story.

THE STANZAS OF DZYAN

The Stanzas of Dzyan include a story about the destruction of a prior civilization that shares many similarities with Atlantis. The entire narrative of the Stanzas explains creation and the history of the various ages of human life on earth over huge spans of time. Right at the very end it describes the fall of the fourth race, which is the race that preceded our own (ours is referred to as the fifth). The people of the fourth race are said to have achieved a high level of civilization, but had degenerated, and their islands were swallowed by water. Only those who were holy were saved—they became the progenitors of the fifth race. Then divine kings, whom I call the wisdom bringers, taught and instructed this fifth and current race—which is where the entire narrative of the Stanzas mysteriously ends.

"The Fourth Race developed speech. [...]

Thus two by two on the seven zones, the Third Race gave birth to the Fourth-Race men; the gods became no-gods; the sura became a-sura. [...]

Then the Fourth became tall with pride. We are the kings, it was said; we are the gods.

They took wives fair to look upon. Wives from the mindless, the narrow-headed. They bred monsters. Wicked demons, male and female, also Khado (dakini), with little minds.

They built temples for the human body. Male and female they worshipped. Then the Third Eye acted no longer.

They built huge cities. Of rare earths and metals they built, and out of the fires vomited, out of the white stone of the mountains and of the black stone, they cut their own images in their size and likeness, and worshipped them.

They built great images nine yatis high, the size of their bodies. Inner fires had destroyed the land of their fathers. The water threatened the fourth.

The first great waters came. They swallowed the seven great islands.

All Holy saved, the Unholy destroyed. With them most of the huge animals, produced from the sweat of the earth.

Few men remained: some yellow, some brown and black, and some red remained. The moon-coloured were gone forever.

The fifth produced from the Holy stock remained; it was ruled over by the first divine Kings.

. . . . Who re-descended, who made peace with the fifth, who taught and instructed it. . ."[100]

~ THE STANZAS OF DZYAN

To those who knew of these events, the story of the fourth race must have seemed utterly tragic—once they were a noble and wise people who had lived virtuously and venerated the sacred sun, but at some point, their civilization had turned to vanity. Thus, the divine kings had to "re-descend"—perhaps meaning that a number of great Beings had to take rebirth in a lineage of kings, which as we'll get to in chapter 3, is what some of the wisdom bringers were said to have done.

HINDU ACCOUNTS

References to Atlantis also appear in Hindu texts, where it is called "White Island," and a solar religion is said to have been practiced there. Remarkably, the inhabitants are described as they are in the Stanzas of Dzyan, as being moon-colored in complexion.

"Atala and Sveta Dwipa ('White Island') are not the only names for Atlantis in Sanskrit lore. Another name, Saka Dwipa, is used just as often in the Puranas; and according to the Sanskrit Dictionary (1974), Saka Dwipa means 'island of fair skinned people.'... The terms 'Atala' and 'White Island' are used also by the Bhavishya Purana (4th cent. B.C.). Here it is stated that Samba, having built a temple dedicated to Surya (the Sun), made a journey to Saka Dwipa, located 'beyond the salt water' looking for the Magas (magicians), worshippers of the Sun. He is directed in his journey by Surya himself (i.e., journeys west following the Sun), riding upon Garuda (the flying vehicle of Krishna and Vishnu) he lands at last among the Magas.

The Mahabharata (circa 600 B.C.) also refers to 'Atala, the White Island', which is described as an 'island of great splendour.' It continues: 'The men that inhabit that island have complexions as white as the rays of the Moon and they are devoted to Narayana... Indeed, the denizens of White Island believe and worship only one God.'"[101]

~ R. CEDRIC LEONARD, PRE-PLATONIC WRITINGS PERTINENT TO ATLANTIS

Blavatsky states that the Hindu texts called the Puranas, referred to in the excerpt above, drew some of their material from the Stanzas of Dzyan,[102] and this is why they likely contain similarities with it.

Following are some of the descriptions of Atala and its inhabitants taken directly from the Hindu text the Mahabharata, the oldest written parts of which date to around 400 BC.[103] They are so remarkable and detailed that I have reproduced them almost in full. Atala (referred to as White Island) is clearly described as an island located in the ocean where a sole god who is described as the sun is worshiped only.

This first account is narrated by Bhishma, a great warrior who was son of a king in Northern India.[104] Comments in square brackets are mine.

Bhishma narrating to an audience.

57

"On the northern shores of the Ocean of Milk there is an island of great splendour called by the name of White Island. The men that inhabit that island have complexions as white as the rays of the Moon and that are devoted to Narayana. Worshippers of that foremost of all Beings, they are devoted to Him with their whole souls. They all enter that eternal and illustrious deity of a thousand rays. They are divested of senses. They do not subsist on any kind of food. Their eyes are winkless. Their bodies always emit a fragrance. Indeed, the denizens of White Island believe and worship only one God. Go thither, ye ascetics, for there I have revealed myself! All of us, hearing these incorporeal words, proceeded by the way indicated to the country described. Eagerly desirous of beholding Him and our hearts full of Him, we arrived at last at that large island called White Island. Arrived there, we could see nothing. Indeed, our vision was blinded by the energy of the great deity and accordingly we could not see Him. At this, the idea, due to the grace of the great God Himself, arose in our minds that one that had not undergone sufficient penances could not speedily behold Narayana. Under the influence of this idea we once more set ourselves to the practice of some severe austerities, suited to the time and place, for a hundred years [many ancient texts state that some people had longer lifespans in the past]. Upon the completion of our vows, we beheld a number of men of auspicious features. All of them were white and looked like the Moon (in colour) and possessed of every mark of blessedness. Their hands were always joined in prayer. The faces of some were turned towards the North and of some towards the East [the direction of sunrise]. They were engaged in silently thinking on Brahma. The Yapa performed by those high-souled persons was a mental yapa (and did not consist of the actual recitation of any mantras in words). In consequence of their hearts having been entirely set upon Him, Hari became highly pleased with them. The effulgence that was emitted by each of those men resembled, O foremost of ascetics, the splendours which Surya [the sun god] assumes when the time comes for the dissolution of the universe. Indeed, we thought that Island was the home of all Energy. All the inhabitants were perfectly equal in energy. There was no superiority or inferiority there among them. We then suddenly beheld once more a light arise, that seemed to be the concentrated effulgence of a thousand Suns, O Vrihaspati. The inhabitants, assembling together, ran towards that light, with hands joined in reverential attitude, full of joy, and uttering the one word Namas (we bow thee!) We then heard a very loud noise uttered by all of them together. It seemed that those men were employed in offering a sacrifice to the great God. As regards ourselves, we were suddenly deprived of our senses by his Energy. Deprived of vision and strength and all the senses, we could not see or feel anything. We only heard a loud volume of sound uttered by the assembled inhabitants. It said, 'Victory to thee, O thou of eyes like lotus-petals! Salutations to thee, O Creator of the universe! Salutations to thee, O Hrishikesa, O foremost of Beings, O thou that art the First-born!' Even this was the sound we heard, uttered distinctly and agreeably to the rules of orthoepy [how language should be spoken]. Meanwhile, a breeze, fragrant and pure, blew, bearing perfumes of celestial flowers, and of certain herbs and plants that were of use on the occasion [only flowers and other plants were used for the sacrifice]. Those men, endued with great devotion, possessed of hearts full of reverence, conversant with the ordinances laid down in the Pancharatra, were then worshipping the great deity with mind, word, and deed. Without doubt, Hari appeared in that place whence the sound we heard arose. As regards ourselves, stupefied by His illusion, we could not see him [they did not have their third/inner eye open, like those of White Island did]. After the breeze had ceased and the sacrifice had been over, our hearts became agitated with anxiety, O foremost one of Angira's race. As we stood among those thousands of men all of whom were of pure descent, no one honoured us with a glance or nod. Those ascetics, all of whom were cheerful and filled with devotion and who were all practising the Brahma-frame of mind, did not show any kind of feeling for us. We had been exceedingly tired. Our penances had emaciated us. At that time, an incorporeal Being addressed us from the sky and said unto us these words, 'These white men, who are divested of all outer senses, are competent to behold (Narayana). Only those foremost of regenerate persons whom these white men honoured with their glances, become competent to behold the great God. Go hence, ye Munis, to the place whence ye have come. That great Deity is incapable of being ever seen by one that is destitute of devotion. Incapable of being seen in consequence of his dazzling effulgence, that illustrious Deity can be beheld by only those persons that in course of long ages succeed in devoting themselves wholly and solely to Him. Ye foremost of regenerate one, ye have a great duty to per-form. After the expiration of this the Krita age, when the Treta age comes in course of the Vivaswat [sun god's] cycle, a great calamity will overtake the worlds [the cataclysm that destroyed Atala/Atlantis?]. Ye Munis, ye shall then have to become the allies of the deities (for dispelling that calamity) [reference to the ancestors of the Indo-Europeans needing to help reinitiate civilization and religion following the destruction of Atala/Atlantis?].' Having heard these wonderful words that were sweet as nectar, we soon got back to the place we desired, through the grace of that great Deity.

When with the aid of even such austere penances and of offerings devoutly given in sacrifices, we failed to have a sight of the great Deity, how, indeed, can you expect to behold Him so easily? Narayana is a Great Being, He is the Creator of the universe. He is adorned in sacrifices with offerings of clarified butter and other food dedicated with the aid of Vedic mantras. He has no beginning and no end. He is Unmanifest."[105]

~ MAHABHARATA, BOOK 12, SANTI PARVA, PART 3, SECTION CCCXXXVII

Another similar account follows in which the Rishi Narada succeeds in getting to White Island.

Rishi Narada.

"Arrived at the spacious realm called White Island, the illustrious Rishi beheld those same white men possessed of lunar splendour (of whom I have already spoken to thee). Worshipped by them, the Rishi worshipped them in return by bending his head and reverencing them in his mind [using a more telepathic form of communication]. [...] and then sang the following hymn unto the Lord of the universe, '[...] Salutations to thee, O God of gods, [...] who is called Immortal, who is called Ananta (Sesha), who is Space, who is without beginning, who is both Manifest and Unmanifest as existent and not-existent things, [...] who is the four-headed Brahman, who is the Lord of all created Beings, [...] who is the Lord of the universe (or Indra), who is the all-pervading Soul, who is the Sun, who is the breath called Prana [...].'"[106]

~ MAHABHARATA, BOOK 12, SANTI PARVA, PART 3, SECTION CCCXXXIX

"[...] the great God addressed that ascetic and said, 'Go hence, O Narada, and do not delay! These worshippers of mine, possessed of lunar complexions, are divested of all senses and do not subsist upon any kind of food. They are, again, all Emancipate; with minds wholly concentrated upon Me, people should think of Me. Such worshippers will never meet with any impediments. These men are all crowned with ascetic success and are highly blessed. In ancient times they became entirely devoted to me. They have been freed from the attributes of Rajas [passion] and Tamas [destructive traits]. Without doubt, they are competent to enter me and become merged into my Self.'"[107]

~ MAHABHARATA, BOOK 12, SANTI PARVA, PART 3, SECTION CCCXL

The story of the origin of the accounts of White Island then follows. Those who narrated them record that they are incredibly ancient, having been passed down from guru to disciple over many generations.

"Bhishma continued, 'I have now repeated to thee the narrative that was recited by Narada (unto the conclave of Rishis assembled in the abode of Brahman). That narrative has descended from one person to another from very ancient times. I heard it from my sire who formerly repeated it to me.'"[108]

So how old is this account? The first to visit White Island are a group of ascetics. These ascetics are the brothers Ekata, Dwita, and Trita who are sons of Rishi Gautama[109]—considered one of the seven Vedic sages, called the Saptarishi[110] (I discuss these sages in chapter 3). Buddha is said to be a descendent of Gautama, which is why he is sometimes referred to as Gautama Buddha.[111]

Their visit is placed within what is called the Krita or Golden Age in the Hindu cycles of time. Interestingly, the account states that "a great calamity will overtake the worlds" during the following lower age, called the Treta, which is a possible reference to the global catastrophe that destroyed Atlantis/Atala.

The visit of these brothers to White Island is followed by another visit, this time by the sage Narada. He is a semi-mythical Vedic sage who is considered ancient, but has no verifiable biographical origin (said to be a son of the god Brahma). Both accounts of White Island are said to have first been told by Narada to a conclave of rishis. These rishis then passed it down within a secret order "from very ancient times." At some point Brahmanas (priests) united "in the days of yore," brought all the scriptures they possessed together, and extracted from them these important stories of White Island. The accounts of them continued to be passed down until being retold by Bhishma.[112]

Bhishma was said to have fought in the great Kurukshetra War which Krishna also participated in.[113] Based on textual, astronomical, and archaeological evidence, this war may have occurred as far back as 3,137 BC.[114] This means that Narada's account was already considered "very ancient" by this time.

Yet even Bhishma's account is not directly recited by him, instead being repeated by Suta (who is either a specific individual or someone from the class of Sutas who were tasked with narrating Hindu stories[115]).

> "Suta continued, I have now told you all that Vaisampayana recited
> to Janamejaya. [...] As regards myself, I heard this excellent narrative
> that has descended from generation to generation, from my sire who
> recited it to me in former times."[116]

The text in which these accounts of Atala appear (the Mahabharata) is entirely narrated by (a?) Suta, who was a pupil of Vyasa—considered the author of the Mahabharata.[117] Like Suta, Vaisampayana was also a pupil of Vyasa, and recited the story of Atala to King Janamejaya, who is thought to have lived some time between the twelfth and ninth centuries BC.

Clearly all these men were part of a very ancient oral tradition, which they carefully preserved. The Mahabharata is an amalgamation of material, which is believed to have taken the final form it has today around the fourth century AD.[118]

The Mahabharata being narrated to a crowd of gathered sages. This is how
extremely ancient stories were handed down and preserved in Vedic tradition.

This means that the account of Atala has been repeated and passed down over thousands of years.

There is another possible account of Atala/Atlantis from a different Hindu text. This text is called the Samba Purana, and was compiled in India from different sources. The oldest part of it is said to have been composed between AD 500-800. Other parts were added as late as AD 1500.[119] It's the oldest part that contains a likely reference to Atlantis, where it is called Saka Island.

The text is named after Samba, who is one of the sons of the well-known deity Krishna. It's presented as a dialogue between a king of the solar dynasty in India and Vasistha, who is one of the seven Vedic sages (I discuss these sages in chapter 3).[120] The sage espouses the benefits of sun worship, and in doing so narrates the story of Samba. In this story, Samba creates a temple dedicated to the sun god.

Nothing of Samba's sun temple remains. These are the ruins of a much later sun temple, also in India, called the Martand Sun Temple—destroyed by a Muslim ruler.

Some have identified Samba's temple with the Sun Temple of Multan (aka the Aditya Sun Temple) that was located on the banks of a major river in what was once Northern India (now Pakistan). For a time it was the most important sun temple in ancient India. It housed an image of the sun god made of pure gold, and was adorned with gold, silver, and gems (just like the most important sun temple of the Inca in Peru called Coricancha), but was later utterly destroyed by Muslims and had a mosque built over it.[121]

Because there is no one worthy to worship at this temple in Jambudvipa (identified as Asia[122]), the sun god orders Samba to go to Saka Island to find priests of the sun religion, and return to the temple with them. So Samba sets off on his flying vehicle Garuda for Saka Island.

> "Having been addressed by Samba [...] [the image of the sun god said]—O Pure Soul (Samba)! No person in the *Jambudvipa* is worthy for performing my worship. You may please bring Brahmanas devoted to my worship from the Saka island. This Saka island is beyond the salt ocean and is encircled by the milk ocean. It is heard that the Saka island is beyond the Jambu-island [Asia]. There are

sacred fellows who follow fourfold varna system. These are Magas, Mamagas, Manasas and Mandagas. Magas are mainly Brahmanas and Mamagas are Ksatriyas.

[...] These people are very happy because they follow their duty (Dharma) strictly. These people were made by myself through my splendor in ancient times. I myself instructed these people [in] the four Vedas with all secrets and these people are experts in various eulogies narrated in the greatly mystical Vedas composed by myself.

They meditate on me and constantly chant me and recite my name. They are engrossed in my thought, they are my devotees and they are my followers. They serve myself and they observe my vow. They wear a girdle round the waist and perform all rituals encoded in the code-books. They perform worship there in harmony with devotion always. In that island, the gods along with the Gandharvas, Siddhas and the Caranas roam about and entertain him along with them face to face.

[...] Therefore, you may please bring those Magas here from the Saka island for performance of my worship. O Samba! Go immediately mounting on the Garuda. Think about it.

Vasistha spoke—As is the order (of the lord), after soliciting the permission of the Sun-god, the son of Jambavati (Samba) being filled with great brilliance reached Dvaravati again and narrated the entire episode of the direct vision of the Sun-god to his father getting his vehicle Garuda and mounting on him, Samba started.

Thereafter, elated Samba arrived at Sakadvipa and saw there lustrous Magas as told by the Sun-god himself. They were worshipping the Sun-god with sacred incense and fragrant sticks etc. After saluting all of them and circumambulating, he asked about their welfare and appreciated them and said—'You people are very meritorious and are worthy to be seen by welfare-wishing people, as you people are busy continuously in the worship of the Sun-god and are capable of giving boon.' I am the son of Visnu (Krsna) and I am known by the name of Samba.

I have established the Sun-god on the bank of river Candrabhaga and I have been sent to you by him. Please get up and let us go there.

They said to Samba—'There is no doubt it will happen as you say'. The Sun-god has too told this to us earlier. There are eighteen families of Veda-expert Magas here who all will go with you there where is placed the Sun-god. Mounting these eighteen families on the Garuda, Samba restarted with great speed."[123]

~ SAMBA PURANA

The sun god states that he created the inhabitants of Saka Island in ancient times from his own splendor, making them "children of the sun."

The Magas (priest magicians) of Saka Island are called Sakaldwipiya Brahmins in Hindu lore, and came to be identified as a class of Brahmin priests in Northern India that were originally of Scythian descent[124]—specifically those referred to as the Saka in ancient times, who were descendants of Indo-Iranian/Aryan people and inhabited the Eurasian Steppe and Tarim Basin in China, and migrated into northwest India.[125] Thus Saka Island is usually postulated as being connected to the lands historically inhabited by Scythians, however, this is not conclusive.

In the Hindu literature called the Puranas, Earth is divided into seven islands (called the Saptadvipas) and seven oceans. These islands were said to have been part of one great landmass on Earth, but were broken apart (today there is clear scientific evidence that this is the case; the landmass is called Pangea, and is believed to have begun breaking apart 175 million years ago[126]). Based on their descriptions, Indologists have identified the location of six of these seven islands as Asia, Africa, Australia, North America, South America, and Oceania. Saka Island is the only one whose location remains unidentified.[127] Could this indicate it no longer exists, having sunk beneath the ocean (as Atlantis)? It seems more likely that the knowledge of Saka Island was preserved in Indo-Iranian/Aryan tradition and brought to India by Saka migrants. Thus, it's possible the story of Saka Island has far more ancient roots.

Sakas are likely to have also become known as the Shakyas in India, who worshiped the sun and who considered themselves kinsmen of the sun and as a solar race whose descent was traced back in one ancient genealogy to King Ikshvaku. In the next chapter, I explore the connections between this king and the wisdom bringers. Another text traces their lineage to one of the seven sages in Vedic tradition. Buddha, who was born a prince in India, was a Shakya.[128]

ANCIENT EGYPTIAN ACCOUNTS

In ancient Egyptian texts and histories there are a number of different references to Egyptian civilization having its origin in a prior civilization that had been destroyed.

The Greek historian Diodorus in his epic *Library of History* wrote of the origins of the Egyptians:

> "The Egyptians were strangers, who, in remote times, settled on the banks of the Nile, bringing with them the civilization of their mother country, the art of writing, and a polished language. They had come from the direction of the setting sun [the west] and were the most ancient of men."[129]

The direction of west possibly places their origin off the west coast of Africa, in the Atlantic Ocean, where the island of Atlantis is said to have sunk beneath the sea around 9,600 BC. This indicates that the Egyptian king lists stretching back tens of thousands of years may actually refer to kings of Atlantis, whose lineage continued in Egypt after Atlantis was destroyed.

The Egyptian wisdom bringer Thoth, who was later deified as a god. He was depicted as wearing a symbolic Ibis bird headdress.

Ancient Egyptian texts also contain accounts of a wisdom bringer called Thoth, who appears to have led the survivors of Atlantis to Egypt where he oversaw the establishment of civilization there.

> "Scattered though they may be, an interesting picture emerges from the numerous references to Thoth in the earliest writings of the ancient Egyptians—and that picture fits the theory of an Atlantean origin for this intriguing character. Although late writings depict him as a god, the earliest texts depict him as a king (The Palermo Stone versus The Coffin Texts; Faulkner, 1974).
>
> Thoth had just been described (Chapter LXXXV, Papyrus of Nu) as ruler of the "Western Domain"; but by the end of the New Kingdom he is called the "Lord of the West" (Seth, 1912). He is accredited with the invention of writing, mathematics, astronomy, and civilization in general (Budge, 1960). In addition to being the author of a large number of esoteric books, Thoth is also called the Scribe (Pyramid Texts; Book of the Dead, et al.); his Egyptian name, Tehuti, means "the measurer" (Budge, 1960).
>
> In summation, a catastrophe occurred which darkened the sun and disturbed the gods, but Thoth led them across the sea to an eastern country [Egypt]. Thoth is depicted as the "controller of the Flood," (Leyden Papyrus) and the Theban Recension includes the

Island of Fire in the Flood story. (Papyrus of Ani, Chap. CLXXV) Thus it appears that Thoth was once the ruler of an Island Kingdom beyond the western horizon before the Egyptian priests turned him into a god. The question therefore is: Was the Egyptian Tehuti-Thoth originally a migrant from Atlantis, and did he once rule as a king there?"[130]

~ R. CEDRIC LEONARD, WRITINGS OF THE EGYPTIANS

A similar story is told in the murals carved into the walls at the Temple of Horus at Edfu in Egypt, where Thoth is also mentioned as a survivor of a destroyed island. The researcher and author Graham Hancock has made correlations between the Edfu accounts and the description Plato gave of Atlantis.

"These inscriptions, the so-called Edfu Building Texts, take us back to a very remote period called the "Early Primeval Age of the Gods"— and these gods, it transpires, were not originally Egyptian, but lived on a sacred island, the "Homeland of the Primeval Ones," in the midst of a great ocean. Then, at some unspecified time in the past, a terrible disaster—a true cataclysm of flood and fire as we shall see— overtook this island, where "the earliest mansions of the gods" had been founded, destroying it utterly, inundating all its holy places and killing most of its divine inhabitants. Some survived, however, and we are told that this remnant set sail in their ships (for the texts leave us in no doubt these gods of the early primeval age were navigators) to "wander" the world. Their purpose in doing so was nothing less than to recreate and revivify the essence of their lost homeland, to bring about, in short: 'The resurrection of the former world of the gods ... The re-creation of a destroyed world.'

[...] At Edfu, [...] although the original sacred records are also gone, the extracts preserved in the Building Texts do seem to tell essentially the same story that Solon heard and passed on to Plato."[131]

~ GRAHAM HANCOCK, MAGICIANS OF THE GODS

The ancient Egyptian god Osiris was said to have been a divine king of Egypt, who like Thoth, also came from elsewhere, and is likewise credited with establishing civilization and religion in Egypt. And, like other wisdom bringers such as Viracocha of South America, Osiris was said to have traveled to the rest of the world establishing it in other places. And there is much evidence to suggest that Osiris, Viracocha, and Odin/Wotan (as well as other wisdom bringers) were either the same person, or people from the same group of people who shared this same mission.

The Egyptian wisdom bringer
Osiris, who was later deified as a god.

There are a number of accounts of Osiris in the Egyptian texts of *The Kolbrin*. In these accounts, it states that Osiris (referred to as Usira and Yosira) came to Egypt from a place called Ramakui. The descriptions of Ramakui share many similarities with the account of Atlantis given by Plato, the murals at the Temple of Edfu in Egypt, and the island of the fourth race described in the Stanzas of Dzyan.

Following is a description of Ramakui:

> "From Ramakui of the seven cities, Land of Copper, came the People of the Light and they brought with them, out of their transparent temples, the light that shines, when darkness falls, without being lit. Led by the Old Bald-Headed One, he whose name is not spoken, they came out of the West at the sunsetting. They came from the place where now the sun goes down; in the days when the Western wilderness was green and sand had not replaced the waters; when the outlands nourished cattle and sheep fed where now there is nought but rock and stone. The Tirdinians welcomed them not, but they passed safely through the westward places to the land of Ansibyah, and were succoured and fed. They brought to the people many things, for wise they were and learned. They were men of wisdom."[132]
>
> ~ THE SCROLL OF HERAKAT, THE KOLBRIN

The "light that shines without being lit" indicates some form of technology—possibly electricity, and thus provides a clue to the level of technology the Atlanteans had reached.

The "Western wilderness" is the outlying lands which lay to the west of Egypt—these are the now desert regions of North Africa known to have once been savannahs used for grazing livestock. Ansibyah sounds like a slightly scrambled version of Libya, which was once the name given to the land west of Egypt (the rest of North Africa), not just the country as it is now. Tirdinians sounds like Sardinians, the name of a people who inhabit the island of Sardinia in the Mediterranean.

Here's another excerpt from *The Kolbrin* about Ramakui.

"Men talk of the land of Oben, from whence they came. Not from Oben towards the South came men, for the great land of Ramakui first felt his step. Out by the encircling waters, over at the rim it lay. There were mighty men in those days, and of their land the First Book speaks thus: Their dwelling places were set in the swamplands from whence no mountains rose, in the land of many waters slow-flowing to the sea. In the shallow lakelands, among the mud, out beyond the Great Plain of Reeds. At the place of many flowers bedecking plant and tree. Where trees grew beards and had branches like ropes, which bound them together, for the ground would not support them. There were butterflies like birds and spiders as large as the outstretched arms of a man. The birds of the air and fishes of the waters had hues which dazzled the eyes, they lured men to destruction. Even insects fed on the flesh of men. There were elephants in great numbers, with mighty curved tusks. The pillars of the Netherworld were unstable. In a great night of destruction the land fell into an abyss and was lost forever. When the Earth became light, next day, man saw man driven to madness. All was gone. Men clothed themselves with the skins of beasts and were eaten by wild beasts, things with clashing teeth used them for food. A great horde of rats devoured everything, so that man died of hunger. The Braineaters hunted men down and slew them. Children wandered the plainland like wild beasts, for men and women became stricken with a sickness that passed over the children. An issue covered their bodies which swelled up and burst, while flame consumed their bellies. Every man who had an issue of seed within him and every woman who had a flow of blood died.

The children grew up without instruction, and having no knowledge turned to strange ways and beliefs. They became divided according to their tongues. This was the land from whence man came, the Great One came from Ramakui and wisdom came from Zaidor.

[...] Those who came with the Great One were cunning craftsmen in stone, they were carvers of wood and ivory. The High God was worshipped with strange light in places of great silences. [...] In

Ramakui there was a great city with roads and waterways, and the fields were bounded with walls of stone and channels. In the centre of the land was the great flat-topped Mountain of God.

The city had walls of stone and was decorated with stones of red and black, white shells and feathers. There were heavy green stones in the land and stones patterned in green, black and brown. There were stones of saka, which men cut for ornaments, stones which became molten for cunning work. They built walls of black glass and bound them with glass by fire. They used strange fire from the Netherworld which was but slightly separated from them, and foul air from the breath of the damned rose in their midst. They made eye reflectors of glass stone, which cured the ills of men. They purified men with strange metal and purged them of evil spirits in flowing fire.

We dwell in a land of three peoples, but those who came from Ramakui and Zaidor were fewer in numbers. It was the men of Zaidor who built the Great Guardian which ever watches, looking towards the awakening place of God. The day He comes not its voice will be heard."[133]

~ THE SCROLL OF EMOD, THE KOLBRIN

There are a number of things that are interesting to note in this description. The excerpt is taken from "the First Book" in ancient Egypt, which indicates the great age of the story, and that it was probably first told at the establishment of Egyptian civilization. It says Ramakui lay "at the rim," which may refer to the tectonic ridge that runs north-south through the Atlantic Ocean, and of which the islands called the Azores are the highest parts.

Satellite image of the Mid-Atlantic Ridge, running approximately north-south through the Atlantic Ocean, between the Americas on the left, and Europe and Africa on the right.

The flat-topped mountain of god in the center of Ramakui immediately brought to my mind the flat-topped stepped pyramids found in many parts of the world where the wisdom bringers are recorded as traveling. There are also flat-topped stepped pyramids on the Azores aligned to the summer solstice,[134] made from the naturally occurring red, black, and white stone found on the volcanic islands, just as these stones are said to naturally occur and were used for building in the accounts of Ramakui, Atlantis, and in the Stanzas.

Researcher Yvonne Whiteman suggests that both Ramakui and Zaidor may have been islands of Atlantis, and in *The Kolbrin*, the ancient Egyptians credit people from these places as the source of their spiritual knowledge.[135]

The texts of *The Kolbrin* indicate that the religion of the wise priests of Ramakui was sun worship. It was later referred to as "the firstfaith," indicating it was the first religion to be practiced, in which:

> "They hold one day in seven holy [what became our Sun-day] to The Creating God whom they worship in a transparent temple where the sun falls upon the heads of the worshippers."[136]
>
> ~ THE FIRSTFAITH BRINGERS, THE BOOK OF ORIGINS, THE KOLBRIN

> "They raised up temples to the sunlight and worshipped inside many pillars, but within the temples were inner temples where greater things were known."[137]
>
> ~ THE BOOK OF THE SONS OF FIRE, THE KOLBRIN

A text in *The Kolbrin* of Mesopotamian origin states that there was a great flood caused by an incoming celestial body, which Whiteman has calculated occurred at around 9,700 BC based on the details given in the text.[138] This is the same date of the abrupt ending of the last ice age with its massive global rise in sea levels as found in Greenland ice cores.

CENTRAL AMERICAN ACCOUNTS

There are possible accounts of Atlantis preserved in Central America among a number of its indigenous peoples.

The Aztecs stated that a race called the Quinametzin had populated the world in prior ages, including the very first, and were also the oldest known inhabitants of Central America. Their name means "giant people,"[139] and they were said to have been ten to twelve feet tall, the builders of pyramids, and once had a great civilization. However, at the height of their civilization, when they no longer venerated the gods, they and their civilization were destroyed by a great catastrophe as a form of divine punishment.[140]

The Otomi people, who are believed to have lived in the region before the Aztecs, called this race the Uema. They were described as giants also, who were god-like, built large cities and massive temples, were incredibly advanced, and were so strong they could lift huge stones without effort. They lived peacefully for countless generations in their thriving civilization until it was destroyed by a great flood.

There is a story passed down among the Chichimeca people (who descend from the same ancestors as the Aztecs), which says there was a very advanced and peaceful race of long-lived giants, who flourished during an era described as a paradise. However, their world was destroyed when the earth began shaking.

It's likely these histories were exchanged among the peoples of Central America as they came upon the great ancient cities and ruins in the region, and wondered who built them. The Aztecs learned and ultimately adopted their histories (and language) from the Toltecs who preceded them, and who became their ruling class. The Toltec royalty were seen as the descendants of Quetzalcoatl, and Quetzalcoatl was remembered as one of seven Quinametzin/giants who had survived the great flood. The Aztecs then traced their lineage to these seven giants.[141]

Thus the story of the origins of the Aztecs is really that of the Quinametzin, which they had adopted from the Toltecs. They traced their place of origin to an ancient lost land called Aztlán.

A drawing of the Mexica (ancestors of the Aztecs) departing Aztlán, from a sixteenth century codex.

In various accounts, Aztlán was an island that was home to a civilization of seven cities and great abundance. In the middle of the island was a great mountain, depicted as a flat-topped stepped pyramid (like the flat-topped mountain of god in the center of Ramakui mentioned in the previous section). There lived the great king and wisdom bringer Quetzalcoatl, whose servants were skilled in all the arts. They would fly forth at his command to any part of the world with infinite speed (could this be a reference to the Vimanas/aircraft of Hindu texts, and the flying vehicles recalled by the Hopi in the next section?). Also from Aztlán came seven brothers who went on to found nations and cities—likely the seven giants who survived the flood.

A geographical location for Aztlán has not been identified; even the Aztecs under King Montezuma had searched for it.[142]

The name Aztlán means White or Bright Land, or "the place of whiteness,"[143] and bears more than a passing resemblance to the name Atlantis. It seems clear to me that Aztlán was the center of the civilization of the Quinametzin/ Uema, and was another name for Atlantis.

NORTH AMERICAN ACCOUNTS

The indigenous Hopi people of the southwest of North America describe a series of world ages punctuated by great cataclysms (as do the Maya and Aztecs). The Third World, which is the world that preceded our own (the fourth), is described as having been occupied by a global seafaring civilization in possession of advanced technology that even included what sound like flying machines called "patuwvotas," described as shields that were made to fly by creative power. These craft were said by the Hopi to have been used by people of many countries and cities to attack one another. Corruption and war had come to the Third World as it had also come to the first two, and so the gods decided to destroy it with a great flood, which caused entire continents to sink beneath the ocean.

Afterward, the god responsible is recorded as saying:

> "Down on the bottom of the seas lie all the proud cities, the flying patuwvotas, and the worldly treasures corrupted with evil, and those people who found no time to sing praises to the Creator from the tops of their hills."[144]
>
> ~ FRANK WATERS, BOOK OF THE HOPI

Hopi elders have continued to recount these histories:

> "That world [the Third World] lasted a long time and as in previous worlds, the people spoke one language. The people invented many machines and conveniences of high technology, some of which have not yet been seen in this age. They even had spiritual powers that they used for good.
>
> They gradually turned away from natural laws and pursued only material things and finally only gambled while they ridiculed spiritual principles. No one stopped them from this course and the world was destroyed by the great flood that many nations still recall in their ancient history or in their religions.
>
> The Elders said again only small groups escaped and came to this fourth world where we now live."[145]
>
> ~ THOMAS BANYACYA (HOPI ELDER), SPEAKING AT THE UNITED NATIONS NATIONAL ASSEMBLY IN DECEMBER, 1992

GURDJIEFF'S FATHER

This is not Gurdjieff's father, but a painting of an
Armenian bard, which was a tradition he belonged to.

We move now to a final possible account of Atlantis. This one comes from
the author and teacher of mystical subjects, George Ivanovich Gurdjieff, who
was born in 1866 in Armenia, and became famous for his travels in search of
secret spiritual knowledge, and for the system of philosophy he taught that
derived from what he found.

His father lived in Armenia and was one of the last remaining bards/ashokhs
in an ancient tradition. Gurdjieff says that his father would often recite ancient
legends to him as a boy—one such legend referred to a brotherhood of wise
men who were the sole survivors of a great deluge that took place seven
thousand years before a later deluge (the date for which is not given). Like
Atlantis, this island was the center of a great civilization that existed on Earth.

> "There was another legend I had heard from my father, again about
> the 'Flood before the Flood' [...]. In this legend it was said, also in
> verse, that long, long ago, as far back as seventy generations before
> the last deluge (and a generation was counted as a hundred years),
> when there was dry land where now is water and water where now
> is dry land, there existed on earth a great civilization, the centre of
> which was the former island Haninn, which was also the centre of
> the earth itself. [...]
>
> The sole survivors of the earlier deluge were certain brethren of the
> former Imastun Brotherhood [meaning brotherhood of wise men],
> whose members had constituted a whole caste spread all over the
> earth, but whose centre had been on this island.
>
> These Imastun brethren were learned men and, among other things,
> they studied astrology. Just before the deluge, they were scattered
> all over the earth for the purpose of observing celestial phenomena
> from different places. But however great the distance between them,

they maintained constant communication with one another and
reported everything to the centre by means of telepathy."[146]

~ GURDJIEFF, MEETINGS WITH REMARKABLE MEN

Again we find similarities with other accounts–the essential elements being
that there was a great civilization that was destroyed, the main agency of
destruction was water, the center of this civilization had been an island, there
was a great priesthood of sages who had existed on this island, and these
sages were the only survivors.

If this legend proved to be true, and these sages had been spread across
the earth before the Deluge, it may explain how they gathered such advanced
astronomical and navigational knowledge, and how the knowledge of astronomical phenomena, such as the precession of the equinoxes, became
encoded into many ancient sites and sacred texts associated with the sages
who initiated our current era of human civilization.

One final parallel before we move on. When reading through the texts of *The
Kolbrin*, I was struck with how similar the name "Imastun"–the name given by
Gurdjieff's father to this brotherhood of sages–was to the term "Imain" found
in *The Kolbrin*. It was not just the similarity in name that struck me though, but
also its implied meaning. The term Imain is used in *The Kolbrin* where Habaris
instructs Herthew in the Religion of the Sun (as mentioned earlier), and implies
that Habaris was teaching Herthew knowledge from within an existing tradition, called Imain. Furthermore, this "Imain" knowledge was said to have been
given to Herthew in the Caucasus–the same region where Gurdjieff's father
lived (Georgia and Armenia), and recited the legend of "Imastun" to Gurdjieff.

> "Herthew grew to manhood there and always Habaris was at his side,
> instructing him in all the things he should know. He taught Herthew
> the Nine essential disciplines of Imain [...]."[147]
>
> ~ THE BOOK OF CREATION, THE KOLBRIN

Could such legends have survived in the same region over thousands of
years, almost right up until today? Gurdjieff himself remarked on the ability of
the bard/ashokh tradition to preserve information with incredible accuracy
over such long periods of time, saying:

> "One day I read in a certain magazine an article in which it was said
> that there had been found among the ruins of Babylon some tablets
> with inscriptions which scholars were certain were no less than four
> thousand years old. This magazine also printed the inscriptions and
> deciphered text—it was the legend of the hero Gilgamesh.
>
> When I realized that here was the same legend which I had so often
> heard as a child from my father, and particularly when I read in this

text the twenty-first song of the legend in almost the same form of exposition as in the songs and tales of my father, I experienced such an inner excitement that it was as if my whole future destiny depended on this. And I was struck by the fact, at first inexplicable to me, that this legend had been handed down by *ashokhs* from generation to generation for thousands of years, and yet had reached our day almost unchanged. [...]

I often regretted having begun too late to give the legends of antiquity the immense significance that I now understand they really have."[148]

~ GURDJIEFF, MEETINGS WITH REMARKABLE MEN

Tragically, Gurdjieff's father died defending his home in what some have called "the Armenian Genocide," and the priceless prehistoric tradition he preserved, bar a few remnants retold by Gurdjieff, died with him.[149]

A LIST OF SIMILARITIES

As we've now seen, Atlantis is just one name given to this advanced lost civilization—it was also likely called Atala ("White Island") and Saka Island in Vedic/Hindu texts; the home of the fourth race in the Stanzas of Dzyan; the Homeland of the Primeval Ones in Egyptian texts; Ramakui in *The Kolbrin*; Aztlán in Aztec tradition; the civilization of the Third World in Hopi tradition; and Haninn in the ashokh tradition of Armenia.

Following are similarities between them.

SEVERAL ISLANDS: Ramakui is described as an island, and as having seven cities; Aztlán is an island with seven cities; the lands of the fourth race are said to have comprised seven islands; Atlantis is described as an island empire that ruled over several others. The Homeland of the Primeval Ones, Atala and Haninn, are all islands.

OCEAN LOCATION: Atala and Saka Island are both located in the "ocean of milk." Atlantis is located in the Atlantic Ocean.

WEST OF EGYPT: Both Ramakui and Atlantis are said to have been located to the west of Egypt.

IMPRESSIVE CIVILIZATION: Atlantis is a great and wonderful empire; Haninn is a great civilization; Atala is of great splendor; the cities of the fourth race are huge; Ramakui is home to a great city.

CITIES, FIELDS, CHANNELS: Ramakui had a great city with fields and channels; Atlantis had a great city, a plain, and canals; the islands of the fourth race had huge cities; the Third World had "proud cities."

GIANT ANIMALS AND ELEPHANTS: Ramakui is described as being home to megafauna, and so are the islands described in the Stanzas of Dzyan. Ramakui, Atlantis, and the islands of the fourth race were said to have had elephants.

STONES OF RED, BLACK, AND WHITE: In Ramakui, stones of red and black (along with white shells) were used for building (of note is that a type of stone used in Ramakui was called saka, which may be connected to the name Saka Island in Hindu lore); in Atlantis stones of red, black, and white; on the islands of the fourth race stones of black and white.

MOON-COLORED COMPLEXION: The Stanzas of Dzyan state that the inhabitants of the islands of the fourth race had a moon-colored complexion. Hindu accounts state that the island of Atala was inhabited by those with complexions as "white as the rays of the moon," the name Sveta Dwipa means "white island," and Saka Dwipa means "island of fair-skinned people." The name Aztlán means "white land" and "place of whiteness."

SUBMERGED UNDER WATER: Ramakui is submerged overnight; Atlantis sinks overnight; the islands of the fourth race are swallowed by water; the Homeland of the Primeval Ones is submerged in a flood; the civilization of the Third World is destroyed by a great flood.

DESTROYED BY THE GODS: Atlantis and the Third World were both said to have been inhabited by a once spiritual people who degenerated; their civilization was then destroyed by the gods as punishment.

VOLCANOES: Both Ramakui and the islands of the fourth race are described as having volcanoes, and the inhabitants as using volcanic obsidian. As we shall see further on, a number of myths associated with wisdom bringers that recall a great cataclysm seem to describe a huge volcanic eruption, which appears to have played a key part in the destruction of Atlantis. The Mid-Atlantic Ridge, which the islands of Atlantis may have been located on or near, has numerous volcanoes along it.

Photo of some of the islands in the Azores, which lie along the
Mid-Atlantic Ridge, showing one of its volcanic peaks in the distance.

GREAT SAGES: The Holy who are saved from the islands of the fourth race are associated with the first divine kings and instructors of the fifth race. The Homeland of the Primeval Ones had been home to a number of great figures who became deified in Egypt as gods. From Ramakui came the People of the Light and the Great One who were clearly great spiritual figures led by a kind of priest. Saka Island was inhabited by Magas/priests. Haninn was the center of the Imastun Brotherhood.

RELIGION: The inhabitants of Atala worshiped the one god Narayana, who is compared to the sun. The priests of Saka Island worshiped the sun. The religion of Ramakui and the Homeland of the Primeval Ones was centered on the sun, as was the religion the Aztecs inherited from Aztlán.

As you can see, there are striking parallels between these accounts.

GEOLOGICAL EVIDENCE FOR ATLANTIS

The whole idea of Atlantis ever existing is largely derided based on the apparent fact that there is no geological evidence for a chain of islands, like those described by Plato, having ever existed in the Atlantic Ocean. However, this is based on an ignorance of numerous geological studies and processes, some of which are outlined here.

Firstly, let's look at where Atlantis was most likely located. It's the Egyptian priest at the temple of Sais, quoted by Plato, who gives the most detailed location:

> "This power [Atlantis] came forth out of the Atlantic Ocean, for in those days the Atlantic was navigable; and there was an island situated in front of the straits which are by you called the Pillars of Heracles [now known as the Straits of Gibraltar]; the island was larger than Libya and Asia put together [this is based on an ancient, not modern understanding of these locations], and was the way to other islands [there are numerous islands in the Atlantic that would have been exposed before the sea level rose], and from these you might pass to the whole of the opposite continent [the Americas] which surrounded the true ocean [the Atlantic]; for this sea which is within the Straits of Heracles is only a harbour [the Mediterranean], having a narrow entrance [the Straits of Gibraltar], but that other is a real sea [the Atlantic], and the surrounding land [the Americas] may be most truly called a boundless continent."[150]
>
> ~ PLATO, TIMAEUS

Taking this description, and looking at a map of the Atlantic during the Ice Age, before sea levels rose 400 feet (at around 9,700 BC), the most likely candidate for the location of Atlantis is the Azores Plateau, which is situated directly in front of the Straits of Gibraltar.

Despite the very exact directions given (they couldn't be more precise), many people have proposed numerous other locations for Atlantis, and all of them deviate from Plato's account in one way or another,[151] as most don't think there is any evidence for Atlantis in the location pinpointed by Plato.

As it turns out, however, there is clear evidence for sunken lands along the Mid-Atlantic Ridge in the region of the Azores. This has been collated and brought to the fore by the researcher Randall Carlson, based on numerous scientific studies.

Carlson offers a very simple and plausible explanation for the mechanism which caused the Azores Plateau to sink suddenly beneath the ocean at the end of the Ice Age—around 9,700 BC, which is just one hundred years off the date given by Plato for the submersion of Atlantis.

"If you understand geophysics at all or geology, you understand the concept of isostasy, which is basically a vertical redistribution of mass throughout the earth's crust. And so when you pile up say a two mile thick ice sheet over the North American continent [during the Ice Age], which was its thickest over Hudson Bay, what happens is the weight of that ice compresses the crust of the earth. In the case of North America there are regions that were compressed through what we call isostatic depression by as much as 2,000 feet. Now when you remove that weight [suddenly at the end of the Ice Age], the land begins to rebound, and if you look at aerial photographs of the shorelines around Hudson Bay you see that there are multiple shorelines elevated many hundreds of feet above modern sea level, and that's due to the rebounding, the isostatic rebound of the North American crust after the release of this tremendous load of ice."[152]

~ RANDALL CARLSON

Multiple shorelines at a bay on the Arctic coastline. The land is gradually rising/rebounding due to the reduction in glaciation after the Ice Age, creating a new shoreline each time.

The geological phenomenon Carlson is referring to is called "glacial iso-static adjustment"—a well-known process that is monitored globally by the U.S. National Oceanic and Atmospheric Administration (NOAA), specifically its National Geodetic Survey.[153] NOAA describes this phenomenon by saying:

> "Imagine lying down on a soft mattress and then getting up from the same spot. You see an indentation in the mattress where your body had been, and a puffed-up area around the indentation where the mattress rose. Once you get up, the mattress takes a little time before it relaxes back to its original shape.
>
> Even the strongest materials (including the Earth's crust) move, or deform, when enough pressure is applied. So when ice by the megaton settled on parts of the Earth for several thousand years, the ice bore down on the land beneath it, and the land rose up beyond the ice's perimeter—just like the mattress did when you lay down on and then got up off of it.
>
> That's what happened over large portions of the Northern Hemisphere during the last ice age, when ice covered the Midwest and Northeast United Sates as well as much of Canada. Even though the ice retreated long ago, North America is still rising where the massive layers of ice pushed it down."[154]
>
> ~ U.S. NATIONAL OCEANIC AND ATMOSPHERIC ADMINISTRATION (NOAA)

Carlson continues:

> "Well, when the ice melted that load was released from the land and was essentially dumped back in the ocean basins. Now you look at the Azores—essentially what you have in the form of the Azores is they're the peak of mountains that are part of what's called the Azores Plateau, and the Azores Plateau [...] is essentially cut almost right through the middle by the Mid-Atlantic Ridge, which is where the European Plate, the African Plate, and the North American tectonic plates come together, right. And the Azores Plateau itself is actually rocks made up of bedrock that was once part of the African Plate but in the process of sea-floor spreading it got left behind.
>
> Well, what you have now again with the Azores is a series of islands that are basically the peaks of mountains, right. Well if you drop sea level 400 feet you're basically doubling the size of all those islands.
>
> Now, if you take into account isostatic compensation, and you realize that the Mid-Atlantic Ridge—that suture that runs right down the middle of the Atlantic Ocean—is one of the most weakest and susceptible places for crustal repositioning on the planet [Carlson likens it to a hinge in another presentation[155]], you realize that

along there, there would probably be a concentration of isostatic effects. And the geology supports the fact that there was a massive subsidence along the Mid-Atlantic Ridge as a consequence of the rapidly rising sea level. And that subsidence may have been as much as one thousand to two thousand feet and maybe even more in places, and it's clear from the studies around the Azores that there was a focus of subsidence right along the Azores Plateau.

Well, when you combine the [...] sea floor dropping by several thousand feet and sea level rising by 400 feet, what you have there is during the Ice Age large portions of the Azores Plateau would have been above sea level. And then when you go into the studies of the Gulf Stream you realize that during the Ice Age the Gulf Stream shifted south about 500 miles further south that it now does, and it basically would have circumambulated right around the Azores Plateau—the emerged [above water] not submerged [below water], but emerged Azores Plateau.

Taking this in context, and of course I'm abbreviating this discussion immensely—if you were living on planet Earth during the Ice Age, probably one of the most benign places to have lived would have been on those Mid-Atlantic islands, and if there was a place where an advanced maritime culture—and I'm not talking now about [...] anti-gravity or [...] flying machines, or any of that stuff [...]. Who knows what they were up to, but Plato doesn't describe anything like that. If you look at what Plato describes, he describes an advanced maritime culture, and there's really nothing pseudo-scientific about theorizing the existence of an advanced maritime culture on the Mid-Atlantic islands during the Ice Age."[156]

~ RANDALL CARLSON

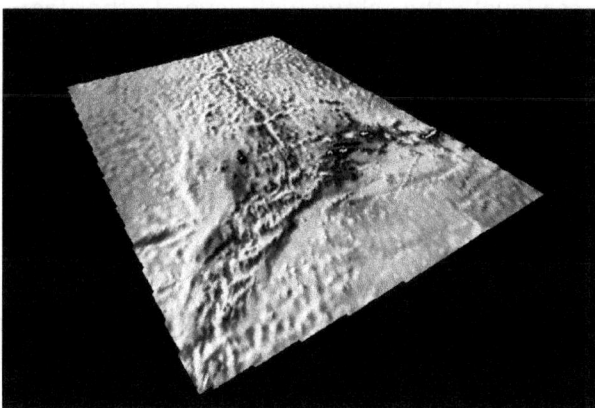

Image of the Azores Plateau, which is mostly underwater, but would have been a sizeable island. You can see the Mid-Atlantic Ridge running down the middle of it.

Given that North America is still isostatically adjusting, it's likely the Azores Plateau continued to also, which is why in Plato's account there was still a shoal of mud remaining after it submerged, which of course is no longer there, as it continued to sink further over time.

Carlson bases his conclusions about the Azores Plateau on the thousands of scientific papers he has read, which include studies that have found the following:

✦ Significant deformation of the earth's surface due to rise in sea levels from glacial melting at the end of the Ice Age. This deformation being caused by the increased amount of water and thus weight in the ocean basins, leading to lateral transfers of mass within the plastic zone of the earth's mantle (as it moves to fill areas that were formerly depressed by ice from surrounding areas—like a "memory foam" mattress). Those areas closest to the formerly glaciated areas, such as the Atlantic Ocean, are predicted to have experienced the largest and most significant displacement. This shifting would have caused seismic events like earthquakes and volcanic eruptions.[157]

✦ Dredging along the Mid-Atlantic Ridge (from beneath the ocean) has pulled up granitic material capped by shallow water limestone; this is a remnant of Africa's continental crust left behind when the continents separated. High amounts of magnesium calcite were found in the limestone, which only forms in the atmosphere—revealing the crust was above water at some time. This crustal block must have undergone large vertical movements, where for episodes it was above water.[158]

✦ Limestones recovered from the Mid-Atlantic Ridge at a depth of 950-1300 meters below sea level were a type formed in very shallow water (close to sea level). This, along with several other features of the limestone, indicates it spent time above the surface of the ocean.[159]

✦ Ridges running east-west along the length of the Mid-Atlantic Ridge indicate large-scale vertical movements along the ridge, as they cannot be explained by the normal process of lateral spreading caused by the separation of continents.[160]

✦ Massive amounts of earth from the west coast of Africa and the Canary Islands are spread over large distances into the Atlantic Ocean, likely caused by tsunamis arriving from the direction of the Mid-Atlantic Ridge loosening material from the land and then dragging it back into the ocean as they receded.[161]

✦ Dredging from level terraces beneath the sea on the Mid-Atlantic Ridge, of sediments ranging up to 3,000 feet in depth, showed evidence the land there must have at one time been above water but had become submerged or the sea had risen by two miles.[162]

✦ Dredging from the Mid-Atlantic Ridge pulled up beach sand deposited during the Ice Age, 300 miles away from any shallow water. It contained the remains of shallow water dwelling marine life.[163]

✦ Prehistoric beach sand was discovered in core samples brought up from the Mid-Atlantic Ridge from a depth of two and also three and a half miles, far from anywhere beaches now exist. The study concluded the sand must have existed on a beach at or near the surface of the ocean, and that the land had sunk or the ocean had risen two to three miles.[164]

✦ Core samples taken from a depth of 4,400 meters (more than 2.5 miles) below the ocean in the Atlantic found layers of continental sand—derived from the coastal shelf of a continent or large island. In the lowest level of the sand there were vegetable remains, such as twigs, nuts, and fragments of bark, again indicating a continental or island origin. In the uppermost levels of the sand, there were shells of shallow water creatures that had at one time lived at a depth of 100 to 200 meters below sea level.[165]

✦ The summit of a submerged seamount south of the Azores was sampled; one of its limestone cobbles was found to have a radiocarbon age of twelve thousand years. This suggests the seamount may have been an island, i.e. above water, within the last twelve thousand years, but had afterward been submerged by the ocean.[166] This aligns with the date for the submergence of Atlantis given by Plato.

There is also archaeological evidence for ancient, submerged human occupation in the Azores. In 2013, private yacht owner Diocleciano Silva discovered an 8000 square meter pyramidal structure at a depth of forty meters (131 feet) off the coast of Terceira Island in the Azores using his GPS. Images collected by Silva using GPS technology revealed the pyramid to be perfectly shaped, and "precisely oriented north-south, just like the pyramids of Giza, in Egypt" he said.[167] Perhaps the most remarkable thing about this discovery is that this pyramid was most likely submerged at the end of the last ice age, given the depth it is now located beneath the ocean. Silva found this pyramid purely by chance, meaning that there could be others like it awaiting discovery beneath the ocean.

GOLDEN AGE

Ultimately, the Religion of the Sun is said to trace to a time possibly even further back than the Ice Age civilization of Atlantis, to a far distant era often called "the golden age." References to a golden age are found, as we would expect, in some of the oldest sacred literature in the world in precisely those texts that contain the most ancient accounts of the Religion of the Sun, as well as of Atlantis.

In Egypt, this golden age is mentioned in the Edfu building texts, and is called "Zep Tepi," which translates as "when the gods manifested as humans at the first time."[168] It is a time when the sun god is praised, and the gods in human form raise the first temple to it.

Many Indo-European ancient texts also speak of a golden age. The Indo-Iranian/Zoroastrian, Vedic/Hindu, and Norse ancient texts all describe a series of cyclical ages of human civilization, starting with a golden age, in which people are virtuous, have greater spiritual faculties, and when the original Indo-European religion (the solar religion) they preserved remnants of is practiced by all. In Norse texts this golden age is called Gullaldr.[169] In Hindu texts, it is called the Krita/Satya Yuga. It is followed by three other successive ages that progressively decline in spirituality, making a total of four.[170] According to Hindu calendars we are living in the fourth and darkest age called the Kali Yuga.[171]

According to Hopi tradition we are also living in the fourth and most material age. Hopi oral history says that life began in a golden age, called Tokpela or the First World, which is associated with gold. The people of this world "knew no sickness," "understood themselves," and were "pure and happy"; they lived at one with each other and with all animals, and communication between them was telepathic. However, over time they began fighting and the animals fled from them in fear. Then the creator, the sun god, decided to destroy the First World, so that a few chosen survivors could start over. This First World is followed by a Second and Third that were also destroyed when their inhabitants became corrupt. With each world, the purity of consciousness successively decreased, so that the Fourth is now the most materialistic.[172]

At the end of the lowest age, those who have become immoral are finally purged from the earth in a great cataclysm so that a new golden age can begin, and as the Hopi say, people can be given a fresh start.[173] The Hopi, Hindu, and Norse traditions essentially indicate that a golden age occurred in the distant past, and describe the signs that will occur during the coming dark age, many of which correlate with events today.

It could be inferred from Egyptian texts that the golden age was when the Egyptian king lists state that the gods ruled as pharaohs, which could be as far back as around 39,500 BC. In Hindu texts, the golden age, or Krita Yuga, is estimated as occurring as far back as 11,500 BC in some interpretations, or millions of years ago in others. In a Zoroastrian text there are four ages, lasting three thousand years each, with the first being a purely spiritual one—and by this account, the golden age could have started anywhere from 10,000 BC.[174]

The Wisdom Bringers

After having explored some of the earliest references to the Religion of the Sun and its origins in a prior advanced civilization (popularly referred to as Atlantis) that was destroyed in a great cataclysm around 9,700 BC, and its even earlier origin in a "golden age" that may have existed tens of thousands of years before this, we now turn to what happened after Atlantis was destroyed. That is, we are now looking at what happened at the end of the last ice age, just under twelve thousand years ago or at approximately 9,700 BC.

The accounts we've already explored state that the survivors of Atlantis were a number of great sages and priests. I call these sages "the wisdom bringers," and it is these great figures I'll examine now.

WHO ARE THE WISDOM BRINGERS?

In numerous accounts, these wisdom bringers were said to have embarked on a mission to teach people all over the world the religion and arts of civilization that had existed from before a great flood. It's not surprising then, to find similar accounts of culture heroes and wisdom bringers turning up after a flood to teach religion and civilization in the oral histories of disparate indigenous people in continents and cultures across the world. As we shall see, each of these wisdom bringers are described as having a very similar appearance, of teaching the same things, and even in some cases, having exactly the same names. They are generally described as being bearded and Caucasian in appearance, wearing long robes, teaching the Religion of the Sun, and things such as agriculture, building, ethics, and monogamous marriage.

The Edfu building texts of ancient Egypt describe how their civilization was founded by a number of gods, including Thoth and Horus, who were accompanied by seven sages; in another it is Osiris who brings civilization to Egypt accompanied by seven strangers. This is paralleled by the story of the Sumerian civilization being founded by Ziusudra and seven sages called Apkallu, and in Vedic accounts by Manu and the seven sages. Easter Island was said to have been founded by King Hotu Matu'a and seven explorers. The peoples of Central and South America consistently describe a culture bringer who was accompanied by a number of helpers, and who came to reinitiate civilization after a great flood. He, or people like him who shared the same mission, were variously called Viracocha, Kukulkan, Quetzalcoatl, Bochica, Votan, etc. The name Wotan (pronounced Votan) also appears in Germany as the name of the wisdom bringer of the Germanic peoples, who corresponds to the wisdom bringer of the Nordic people called Odin. There are also similar legends in North America, where the wisdom bringer Maasaw appeared to the pre-Columbian Hopi people. The Slavic peoples also had a wisdom bringer, called Svarog.

The same bucket-like object held in an identical way by the wisdom bringers in Mesopotamia and Mexico, and carved onto one of the megaliths at Göbekli Tepe in Turkey.

A number of them are depicted as carrying a unique looking bag or bucket-like object, and as the researcher Graham Hancock realized, this object is carved onto one of the megaliths at the ancient site of Göbekli Tepe in Turkey, which incredibly, is dated to around 9,600 BC—the same date as given by Plato for the destruction of Atlantis. This date also coincides with a dramatic rise in world temperature and sea levels, and the end of the last ice age.[1] It is also the site where agriculture is said to have first developed (or was redeveloped) before spreading to other parts of the world—and agriculture is one of the main things these wisdom bringers were remembered as teaching.[2]

The spiritual teachings these wisdom bringers gave also share similarities: wherever they went the chief deity was associated with the sun, monuments of similar design were aligned to the sun at the solstices and equinoxes and festivals were held on these dates, solar theocracies were established, and the people they taught came to call themselves "the children of the sun."

Although these wisdom bringers became deified as gods, I believe they were at one time very real people who conducted one of the greatest missions in history.

Following are more detailed explanations of these wisdom bringers as they appeared to people across various cultures.

ACCOUNTS OF WISDOM BRINGERS

EGYPTIAN

A relief from the Temple of Edfu in Egypt, showing the wisdom bringers
Thoth and Horus on the right. The murals were badly defaced by Christians.

At the ancient Temple of Edfu in Egypt, its walls are inscribed with some of Egypt's most ancient records, including those of its beginnings. It describes how Thoth and Horus, who became known as gods, along with seven sages, and a company of builders and creators, set out in ships after their sacred island homeland sank beneath the ocean in a great disaster, to recreate new sacred lands elsewhere.[3] As explained in the previous chapter, this sacred homeland is likely one of the several islands of Atlantis, said by Plato to have been destroyed around 9,600 BC.

The ancient writings carved on the temple walls at Edfu in Egypt state that the mission of these survivors was to continue their creative work in other lands, recreating sacred places and restoring the primeval religion from the golden age and first time—the Religion of the Sun. As the researcher Graham Hancock states:

> "Their mission, in short, was to repromulgate the lost civilization and the lost religion of the days before the flood."[4]
>
> ~ GRAHAM HANCOCK, MAGICIANS OF THE GODS

In the texts of Edfu, their memory, and what they established, is said to have survived into known history, forming the basis of the historically recorded civilizations from which our own modern civilization is derived.[5]

In other ancient texts of Egypt, Osiris, who became the most well-known god of Egypt, is also credited with founding its civilization and religion. As outlined in the previous chapter, both he and Thoth are said to have come from an island lying in the ocean to the west of Egypt that had been destroyed.

In another account, Osiris is also said to have come from a land far to the east of Egypt, and is accompanied by seven strangers in his civilizing mission.

Drawing of Osiris.

> "Osireh came not into a land of powerful kings and great cities, but into a land of ignorant, unenlightened men. He came with seven strangers from a land far East of the Sea of Death, a land not as old as Egypt but long since dead and forgotten. [...]
>
> "Out of the Land of God, to the East, came Osireh who was one filled with the Spirit of God, the first Viceregent of God on Earth. Truly a god who walked among men, a true Son of God. He learned, by communicating with the heart of God, what lesser beings can hope to learn only by long contemplation of the Sacred Writings."[6]
>
> ~ THE ANNEXED SCROLL 1, THE KOLBRIN

The famous Egyptologist E. A. Wallis Budge (knighted in 1920 for his service to Egyptology and the British Museum) recounted many of the ancient beliefs and histories of Osiris. These clearly illustrate that Osiris was a real person who entered Egypt at some time in prehistory to teach the local people religion and civilization, later being deified as Egypt's most prominent god.

> "The general evidence derived from the Religion of Ancient Egypt showed that all the great fundamental beliefs centred in Osiris and his cult [...]. With the cult of Osiris was bound up all that was best in the civilization of Egypt during the Dynastic Period. It weaned the

primitive Egyptians from cannibalism and from cruel and barbarous customs, it taught them to respect human life and to regard man as the image of God, and his dead body as a sacred thing, it induced them to devote themselves to agricultural labours, and it improved their morality. Above all, it transformed them from nomad hunters and thieves into settled people with a god, a priesthood, and a worship, and taught them to believe in divine incarnation, and gave them a hope of resurrection and immortality, and of an existence in heaven, which, they were taught, could only be attained by those who had lived righteous lives upon earth, and through the mercy of Osiris.

The Egyptian texts now available enable us to trace the history of the cult of Osiris from the Archaic to the Roman Period with tolerable completeness, but its beginning is hopelessly lost in obscurity. [...]

No funerary inscription exists, however early, in which evidence cannot be found proving that the deceased had set his hope of immortality in Osiris, and at no time in Egypt's long history do we find that the position of Osiris was usurped by any other god. On the contrary, it is Osiris who is made to usurp the attributes and powers of other gods [...]."[7]

~ E. A. WALLIS BUDGE, OSIRIS AND THE EGYPTIAN RESURRECTION

Not only does Budge relate how Osiris was the founder of civilization and religion in Egypt, but that he also traveled the world to do likewise; and as we'll see further on in this chapter, there exist a number of accounts of other wisdom bringers arriving from the east (the direction of Egypt) by boat to Central and South America, who share remarkable similarities with Osiris.

"Having become king, he [Osiris] devoted himself to improving the condition of his subjects. He weaned them from their miserable and barbarous manners, he taught them how to till the earth and how to sow and reap crops, he formulated a code of laws for them, and made them to worship the gods and perform service to them. He then left Egypt and travelled over the rest of the world teaching the various nations to do what his own subjects were doing. He forced no man to carry out his instructions, but by means of gentle persuasion and an appeal to their reason, he succeeded in inducing them to practise what he preached. Many of his wise counsels were imparted to his listeners in hymns and songs, which were sung to the accompaniment of instruments of music."[8]

~ E. A. WALLIS BUDGE, OSIRIS AND THE EGYPTIAN RESURRECTION

"Osiris raised a large army, and he determined to go about the world teaching mankind to plant vines and to sow wheat and barley. [...]

Osiris became a benefactor of the whole world by finding out food which was suitable for mankind, and after his death he gained the reward of immortality, and was honoured as a god."[9]

~ DIODORUS, QUOTED BY E. A. WALLIS BUDGE, OSIRIS AND THE EGYPTIAN RESURRECTION

The Kolbrin also contains many texts that describe Osiris, his mission, and the spiritual teachings he gave. It too describes him as having been a real person, though having the divine within, who later became deified as a god.

"Now this Osireh, of whom I speak, is even he whom the people of this land have made a god, for the Twice Born who have wisdom have let it be thus. Call him man or call him god, it is a matter of small importance, for the boundary between them in not impassable."[10]

~ THE ANNEXED SCROLL 1, THE KOLBRIN

In *The Kolbrin*, Osiris is credited with a long list of things that he taught and established in Egypt, including religion, peace, prosperity, monogamous marriage, agriculture, irrigation, animal husbandry, the working of metals, pottery, and the building of temples and cities:

"Then there were no cattle or sheep and the land knew not the hand of man, it lay untilled and unwatered. No land was sown, for they who dwelt in it knew not the making of waterways, nor did they know how to command the water and make it flow at their behest. There were no cities and men dwelt in holes in the ground or in places where the rock was cleft. They walked in their nakedness or clothed themselves with leaves or bark, while at night they covered themselves with the skin of wild beasts. They fought with the jackal for food and snatched dead things from the lion. They pulled roots from out of the ground and sought for sustenance among things that grew in the mud. They had none to rule over them, nor had they leaders to guide. They knew not obligation or duty. None spoke to them about their manner of life and none knew the way of Truth. They were truly unenlightened in those days.

Then came the servant of the Sun [Osiris] and he it was who brought the people together and put rulers over them. He set Ramur up as king over the whole land. He showed them, man and woman, how to dwell together in contentment as husband and wife, and he divided their tasks between them. He instructed men in the sowing of corn and the growing of herbs. He instructed them in the tilling of the ground and the manner of cutting the waterways and channels. He it was who showed men the ways of the beasts of the field. He instructed men in the working of gold and silver and the making of vessels from clay. He instructed men in the hewing and cutting of stone and the building of temples and cities."[11]

~ THE ANNEXED SCROLL 1, THE KOLBRIN

Osiris established a solar theocracy, a rulership of divine kings as referred to in the Stanzas of Dzyan—which was likewise established in India, and in South America, where wisdom bringers also traveled.

"[...] Osireh was sad, his heart was heavy for the people, he knew their nature and the ignorance of their ways. Therefore, he assigned a protector to be the guardian of the people, one who knew Truth, who was an Enlightened One, who was greatest among the Twice Born. One to be an ever open channel to God, so that a flood of spiritual power should inundate the land, spreading bounty and peace over its expanse. [...]

The Appointed One was the King, the Pharaoh, the Light of God on Earth, the Vice-regent of God over Men. [...] He was the link, the bridge between God and man. His was the task to bring men the knowledge and awareness of divinity, and to preserve the special spirituality with which he was endowed in a select portion of one race. [...]

They were taught to regard the people as their own children, to be guarded, guided and inspired by the finest examples possible. The family of Pharaoh was to reach out to the very summit of aspiration, to aim for the pinnacle of goodness and spirituality. While the common people laboured under them, the whole life of the royal families was to be devoted to service and goodness, to the elevation of mankind, to the preservation and administration of justice."[12]

~ THE ANNEXED SCROLL 1, THE KOLBRIN

These pharaohs saw themselves as "sons of the sun" and as part of a solar dynasty.

"It is well known that the cult of Ra [the sun god], under one phase or another, was the form of Religion accepted by the Pharaohs, and the priesthood, and a limited aristocracy, from the middle of the Vth dynasty onwards. And as each king, beginning with Assa, delighted to call himself 'son of Ra,' and regarded himself as an incarnation of Ra, this is not to be wondered at."[13]

~ E. A. WALLIS BUDGE, OSIRIS AND THE EGYPTIAN RESURRECTION

Over time, however, *The Kolbrin* records how the pharaohs, who were originally enlightened men, became ordinary and the religion in Egypt eventually degenerated. However, the secret mysteries that had been taught by Osiris were said to have been safeguarded in temples and were symbolically preserved in allegorical tales down through the passage of thousands of years.

The sun was the highest symbol of divinity in ancient Egypt, and adorned the entrances of their temples. Egypt's greatest temples and monuments, such as the Sphinx, the Great Pyramids, the Temple Complex of Karnak, and the Osireion, all have solstice and equinox alignments.[14]

VEDIC

Manu and the seven sages being saved from the great flood by Vishnu as a giant fish.

Like in Egypt, the civilization and religion of India was said to have been founded, following a great flood, by a king of the sun dynasty, along with seven rishis/sages. This king is referred to by the name Manu—a name meaning "the first man," which has the same Proto-Indo-European language root as the English word "man." Manu was the title given to the man chosen by the god Vishnu (a deity encompassing all the Vedic sun gods[15]) to survive a catastrophic flood in a boat and then reinitiate civilization and religion. Manu was recorded as being a son of the sun god Surya as well as his student.

This story is told by Krishna, who is said to be an incarnation of Vishnu, in the most famous text of Hinduism, called the Bhagavad Gita.

> "The imperishable philosophy I taught to Viwaswana [also known as the sun god Surya], the founder of the Sun dynasty, Viwaswana gave it to Manu the Lawgiver, and Manu to King Ikshwaku! The Divine Kings knew it, for it was their tradition. Then, after a long time, at last it was forgotten. It is the same ancient Path that I have now revealed to thee, since thou art My devotee and My friend. It is the supreme Secret."[16]
>
> ~ KRISHNA IN THE BHAGAVAD GITA

As in Egypt, a solar theocracy of divine kings was established in India to preserve and teach the Religion of the Sun—passing it from before to after a great flood, which likely refers to the same flood that destroyed Atlantis. The "ancient Path" Krishna refers to is the path of the spiritual sun (the path to self-realization/enlightenment), which is central to the Religion of the Sun, and which my husband Mark explains in our book *Ancient Solstice*.

The wisdom bringer Manu is said to have gone on to reestablish the solar dynasty that had existed before the flood at the ancient city of Ayodhya, at the foot of the Himalayas.

> "Manu was said to have founded the solar dynasty at the great city of Ayodhya [...] just south of the Himalayan foothills that lead to Kailas. [...] This region marked by the Himalayan rivers is the land of Manu and Vivaswan [the sun god], the land of the Aryans and land of Soma. [...]
>
> This is not to say that Kailas was the center of Vedic Civilization. It is a remote mountain region at the roof of the world. It is more likely the home of the Vedic sages, the great yogis and seers who guided the culture, which grew up along the Saraswati river in the plains of north India."[17]
>
> ~ DAVID FRAWLEY, GODS, SAGES AND KINGS

As in ancient Egypt, these Vedic wisdom bringers and kings are identified with the sun, as Frawley states.

> "The Vedic seers and kings are identified with the Sun. The Vedic families descend from the Sun and the Moon."[18]
>
> ~ DAVID FRAWLEY, GODS, SAGES AND KINGS

Manu and the seven rishis were considered to have great spiritual knowledge and wisdom. In Hinduism, they're positions held by those deemed spiritually suitable. Different people are chosen to hold the position of Manu (or "first man") and the seven rishis in each age of human civilization, so that every age (or cycle of creation and destruction of human civilization) is founded by its own Manu and rishis.[19] This indicates that these positions were likely held across many different ages, and kept as a religious tradition, as they also were in Mesopotamia (explored further on).

As happened with the pharaohs of ancient Egypt, Krishna states that the divine kings of India also lost touch with the divine wisdom they were originally tasked with keeping, and that it was even forgotten altogether.

Remnants of the original solar religion have survived, however, in the Vedic/Hindu religion. Even today, many Hindus still chant the Gayatri mantra at sunrise, which is regarded as one of the greatest and most important mantras, and is dedicated to the spiritual sun.

"Let us adore the supremacy of that divine sun, the god-head who illuminates all, who recreates all, from whom all proceed, to whom all must return, whom we invoke to direct our understandings aright in our progress toward his holy seat."[20]

There exist many references to the path of the sun, and to the sun having a spiritual side as the highest visible manifestation of the supreme creator (known as Brahma, Narayana, etc.), in Vedic/Hindu texts.

The Sandhyavandanam is a Vedic ritual conducted at the transitions of the sun at sunrise, noon, and dusk. It is considered the oldest existing religious liturgy in the world, and is still used by Hindus today.[21]

There are Vedic/Hindu temples aligned to the sun that are based upon the same design as those found where the Religion of the Sun was also practiced, which is a flat-topped stepped pyramid, with a temple on top, approached by a staircase, and aligned to the sun at either the solstices or equinoxes, or both.

"[...] I had seen the variety of the most ancient Hindu shrines in Nepal. The oldest were best defined as ziggurats: a sun-orientated, terraced, and truncated pyramid with a long flight of ceremonial stairs up to a small temple on top."[22]

~ THOR HEYERDAHL, THE MALDIVE MYSTERY

This design became the basis of the later Buddhist stupa, and is found in a more ancient form in Mesopotamia as the ziggurat.

MESOPOTAMIAN

Sketch of one of the Apkallu made from a relief
at the ancient city of Nimrud in Mesopotamia.

The ancient civilization and religion of Mesopotamia (which includes the traditions of Sumer, Akkad, Assyria, and Babylon) was said to have been founded by the sage Adapa (later known as Oannes), who was one of seven sages, or seven enlightened ones, called the Apkallu.

As the author Graham Hancock has noted, there are many similarities between the descriptions of the seven Apkallu of Mesopotamia, and the seven sages described at Edfu in Egypt.[23]

> "The Apkallus mingled their magic with practical skills—such as laying the foundations of cities and temples. Similarly, the Seven Sages of the Edfu texts also had their practical, architectural side and many passages testify to their involvement in the setting out and construction of buildings and in the laying of foundations. Moreover, the Egyptians believed that "the ground plans of the historical temples were established according to what the Sages of the primeval age revealed to Thoth." This hint of a special connection between the Sages and Thoth is, of course, a further parallel for, as we've seen, the Apkallus were linked to Enki, the Mesopotamian god of wisdom. [...] The texts further disclose that the Sages of the mythical age were believed to be "the only divine beings who knew how the temples and sacred places were created" and were themselves the very creators of knowledge, which thereafter could only be passed on but not invented anew. This finds parallels in the Mesopotamian notion that since the time of the antediluvian Apkallus nothing new had been invented—with the original revelation simply being retransmitted and unfolded in later epochs. Without laboring the point further, therefore, it seems to me that the idea conveyed so strongly in the cuneiform inscriptions of ancient Mesopotamia of a project to recover and repromulgate antediluvian knowledge after a global cataclysm is, rather exactly, the same project that is set out in the Edfu Building Texts, which in turn bear uncanny and troubling resemblances to Plato's report of the destroyed Ice Age civilization of Atlantis."[24]
>
> ~ GRAHAM HANCOCK, MAGICIANS OF THE GODS

Two of them even share exactly the same name, as in the Edfu texts of ancient Egypt one of the wisdom bringers is known as Aa, and in the Hurrian tradition of Mesopotamia, one of the wisdom bringers was also known as A'a. Both are phonetically the same and are pronounced "ah-ah."[25] The Hurrian name A'a is another name for the sage Adapa, also known as Oannes, Enki, and Ea.[26]

In Mesopotamian tradition, as in Egypt, there are two separate accounts of the arrival of a wisdom bringer accompanied by seven sages. Yet although separate, both accounts are clearly connected. In the other account, civilization and religion was said to have been preserved and reinitiated after a great flood by a king and priest called Ziusudra, who was accompanied by seven sages[27] in a reed boat.[28]

Ziusudra is warned by the Sumerian god Enki in a dream that a great flood is coming, just as in Vedic accounts Manu is warned by Vishnu of an impending flood and is chosen to survive it and afterward reinitiate civilization. It's interesting to note that both Enki and Vishnu were considered as being either part fish or as having the ability to take the form of a fish. The Apkallu were sometimes depicted and described as wearing fish costumes, and as being able to live at sea.[29] The association between some of the wisdom bringers and fish may have arisen because they wore scale armor for protection (the use of which dates to at least 1,400 BC), and were seafarers. People with no knowledge of this technology may have interpreted them as being part fish.

Left: Drawing of an ancient relief depicting an Apkallu wearing a fish. Right: Reconstruction of medieval scale armor.

Like Manu, Ziusudra is not only a king but also a person learned in the religion that existed before the flood. There are so many similarities between these accounts that it appears Manu is the direct equivalent of Ziusudra simply preserved in a different but related tradition in India.

Enki orders Ziusudra to bury all the tablets of knowledge at the city of the sun called Sippar—this city is said to be in Armenia, and is the place where Ziusudra returns after the flood to unearth the buried tablets.[30]

As the author Graham Hancock notes, Sippar:

"[...] was one of the five antediluvian [pre-flood] cities remembered in Sumerian traditions [...]. What is envisaged here, therefore, is nothing less than a renewal of civilization after a global cataclysm—a renewal in which antediluvian knowledge was to be recovered and repromulgated."[31]

The city of Sippar is associated with the veneration of the sun god Shamash, earlier known as Utu.

The ancient Sumerians built structures called ziggurats that are essentially stepped pyramids topped with temples, like those found in the Americas. The Great Ziggurat of Ur, located in modern day Iraq, dates to at least 2,000 BC,[32] but was successively built over,[33] just as stepped pyramids in Central and South America were, and could therefore possibly be much older. It aligns to the summer solstice sunrise,[34] just as similar structures found worldwide also align to the solstices and equinoxes.

Like the civilizations of ancient Egypt and India, Sumerian civilization was also founded by divine kings who were said to have been descendants of the sun.[35]

PERSIAN

In the ancient Zoroastrian religion of Persia (roughly what is now Iran), the first man, and progenitor of the human race, is Yima, just as Manu is known as the first man, and progenitor of the human race, in India (although Yima's direct counterpart in Vedic religion is Yama, who was also a wisdom bringer and brother of Manu[36]). Like Manu of India, Yima is a king who is initiated into religion in a previous human age of civilization, and is forewarned of an impending disaster. In the following extract taken from the sacred texts of the Zoroastrian tradition called the Avesta—believed to have been written around 800 BC, although containing much older material—Yima is told to build a "Vara," which is a sort of bunker

Illustration of the Vedic Yama, who is the equivalent of the Zoroastrian Yima.

and underground city, in order to survive a catastrophe that will wipe out much of life on earth. He is also directed to store the best seeds of living things in order to repopulate the world afterward.

This story is told through a dialogue between Zarathushtra, who is also known as Zoroaster (the founder of Zoroastrianism, and reformer of the earlier Indo-Iranian religion of Persia), and the supreme god Ahura Mazda.

"Zarathushtra asked Ahura Mazda: O Ahura Mazda, most beneficent Spirit, Maker of the material world, thou Holy One! Who was the first mortal, before myself, Zarathushtra, with whom thou, Ahura Mazda, didst converse, whom thou didst teach the Religion of Ahura, the Religion of Zarathushtra?

Ahura Mazda answered: The fair Yima, the good shepherd, O holy Zarathushtra! he was the first mortal, before thee, Zarathushtra, with whom I, Ahura Mazda, did converse, whom I taught the Religion of Ahura, the Religion of Zarathushtra. [...]

And Ahura Mazda spake unto Yima, saying: 'O fair Yima, son of Vivanghat! Upon the material world the evil winters are about to fall, that shall bring the fierce, deadly frost; upon the material world the evil winters are about to fall, that shall make snow-flakes fall thick, even an aredvi deep on the highest tops of mountains. [...]

Before that winter, the country would bear plenty of grass for cattle, before the waters had flooded it. Now after the melting of the snow, O Yima, a place wherein the footprint of a sheep may be seen will be a wonder in the world.

Therefore make thee a Vara, long as a riding-ground on every side of the square, and thither bring the seeds of sheep and oxen, of men, of dogs, of birds, and of red blazing fires."[37]

~ YIMA AND THE DELUGE, AVESTA: VENDIDAD

Like many wisdom bringers, Yima is called a "son of the sun" (being the son of Vivaŋhat who is the same as the Vedic sun god Vivasvat/Vivasvan/Surya[38]) and is considered a divine king. He uses a gold poniard (which is a kind of slender dagger) to bore the earth. In the Avesta, this gold poniard is considered a symbol of royalty. The wisdom bringer called Viracocha in Peru is also remembered in the oral histories of the Inca as piercing the ground with a gold poniard[39]—another striking parallel between the memories of wisdom bringers recorded in different continents.

"Then I, Ahura Mazda, brought two implements unto him: a golden seal and a poniard inlaid with gold. Behold, here Yima bears the royal sway! [...] Then Yima stepped forward, in light, southwards, on the way of the sun, and (afterwards) he pressed the earth with the golden seal, and bored it with the poniard, speaking thus: 'O Spenta Armaiti, kindly open asunder and stretch thyself afar, to bear flocks and herds and men.'"[40]

~ YIMA AND THE DELUGE, AVESTA: VENDIDAD

The Zoroastrian religion shares many similarities with the Vedic, as both are derived from the same Indo-European source; this is the reason why the accounts of Yima and Manu are so similar. They are likely describing the same events, just remembered in two related traditions.

The builders of the ancient city of Arkaim and its surrounding settlements, located in the steppe of Russia, and currently dated to between 2,000-1,700 BC, were Proto-Indo-Iranian people who later migrated to Iran, bringing with them their language and religion.[41] They built Arkaim in an approximate swastika shape, and aligned it to the solstices and equinoxes.[42]

> "Scholars have identified the structure of Arkaim as the cities built 'reproducing the model of the universe' described in ancient Aryan/Iranian spiritual literature, the Vedas and the Avesta. The structure consists of three concentric rings of walls and three radial streets, reflecting the city of King Yima described in the Rigveda. The foundation walls and the dwellings of the second ring are built according to swastika-like patterns; the same symbol is found on various artefacts."[43]

Reconstruction of the ancient city of Arkaim.

The main city of Atlantis was also described in Plato's account as having being been laid out in a three ringed concentric pattern—perhaps indicating a connection between Yima and Atlantis.

The solstices and equinoxes have been celebrated for thousands of years in Iran. In an old Persian poem, the celebration of the spring equinox is attributed to Jamshid/Yima. Zarathustra was said to have highly emphasized the celebration of both the autumn and spring equinoxes.[44] Even today, the symbol of the winged sun disk, called the Faravahar and found engraved at Persepolis, is a national symbol, and the imperial throne of Iran is called The Sun Throne.[45]

This religion existed in Iran until Islam eventually took over, with sun festivals still held in medieval times as a vestige of it.[46] In the sacred texts of Zoroastrianism the sun is described as "the highest of the high" and is worshiped.[47]

The supreme deity Ahura Mazda is depicted identically to the Sumerian sun god Shamash as standing within a winged sun disk, which is very similar to the winged sun disk of the supreme god Ra, who was the sun god in ancient Egypt.

The sun god depicted almost identically across
three of the major civilizations of the ancient world.

NORTH AMERICAN

Hopi snake priests performing a ceremony in 1896.

When the Hopi people first arrived on the shores of America fleeing a great flood, they were met by a handsome man called Maasaw. He had been the head caretaker of the Third World, and had been reappointed by the Creator, the sun, as caretaker of the Fourth. Before the Hopi could settle in one place permanently, Maasaw said they were to migrate across the entire North and South American continents, so that their routes formed the symbol of the swastika; this was called "the pattern of the Creator's universal plan." He gave them a set of clay tablets to guide them, which have the symbols of the swastika and sun on them, and a magical water jar, which would allow them to settle in areas without water. He also directed them on how they would live once they arrived at their permanent home.[48]

Maasaw also told the Hopi to await the return of Pahana, their "Lost White Brother," who left for the east when they arrived. It is said that on his return the wicked will be destroyed and he will usher in the Fifth World, which will be a new age of peace. Pahana shares many similarities with the wisdom bringer of Aztec tradition, called Quetzalcoatl. There are Hopis today who still await Pahana's return, and are traditionally buried facing east to greet him.[49]

Hopi oral histories also describe how they were guided by "kachinas," who accompanied some of the clans on their emergence into the Fourth World, and originated so far back in the past that a song still sung about them is in a language the Hopi no longer understand.[50] These kachinas didn't enter the Fourth World as others did, and were not really people in the normal sense—but spirits who were sent to help and guide the Hopi clans by taking the form of ordinary people.

After completing the long migration, a number of Hopi clans were directed by the kachinas to settle. Under the instruction of the kachinas, these clans then built a religious center of four levels, resembling a pyramid, with its main door facing east (toward sunrise).[51] Its essential structure is the same as that of ancient esoteric schools in Tibet and India.[52] The first level was where initiates were taught the history of the three previous worlds. On the second, they were taught about the human body and "that the highest function of the mind was to understand how the one great spirit worked within man."[53] This was to prevent people from becoming evil again, and this world from being destroyed as the three previous ones had been. On the third level, they were taught about the workings of nature, and the use of plants as healing remedies. The fourth level was smaller, and only those who had a high level of conscience, and knowledge of the laws of nature, were admitted. Here initiates were taught about the stars, and how they affect nature and humans, as well as how to keep "the door on top of their heads" open to be able to converse with the Creator.

The Hopi were represented by the color red which was assigned to the west, the direction they had come from. But the kachinas said that one day there would come people of three other races—black, yellow, and white—and that they had to ensure that all these races lived together in brotherhood in this new world.

Tragically, the Hopi recount how this religious center was destroyed by a rival clan, and its whereabouts lost, though its description shares similarities with the ancient city of Casas Grandes in Mexico,[54] which was burned around AD 1340. Casas Grandes is aligned on the same longitudinal axis (with an error of only a few miles) as the ancient city of Chaco Canyon (discussed in the next chapter), which is located in the region where the Hopi permanently settled, and it's speculated the builders of both sites are connected.[55] This was the last time the Hopi saw the kachinas, who they believe returned to the spirit worlds of stars and far-off planets. However, the Hopi believe it's possible to become a kachina at death if one "obeys the law of laws and conforms to the pure and perfect pattern laid down by the Creator."[56]

Given the similarities between the Hopi, Aztecs, and Maya, and their common origin (discussed further on), I think the kachinas are likely the same as the followers of the wisdom bringers Quetzalcoatl/Kukulkan of Aztec and Maya traditions.

As in the ancient Egyptian, Inca, and Vedic religions, the Hopi see the divine sun as their creator and natural father, whom they call Taiowa/Tawa, the great sun spirit. Their veneration of Taiowa is expressed in a beautiful Hopi song, which the following lines are taken from:

The creator in Hopi mythology called Taiowa, who is depicted with feathers, just as the sun gods of ancient Iranian, Mesopotamian, and Egyptian traditions are.

> "Both male and female make their prayers to the east,
>
> Make the respectful sign to the Sun our Creator."[57]
>
> ~ SONG OF CREATION, FROM THE BOOK OF THE HOPI BY FRANK WATERS

EASTER ISLAND

The megalithic civilization on Easter Island was said to have been founded by a king called Hotu Matu'a who sent out seven explorers to the island after being warned in a dream that his own island homeland would sink. These explorers were considered sages, being known as "king's sons, all initiated men."[58] Note how similar this account is to that of Manu, Yima, and Ziusudra—all who are kings, who travel with seven sages, and who were supernaturally forewarned of an impending flood.

The moai facing the equinox sunset at Ahu Akivi.

Easter Island is famous for its giant standing stone statues called moai. Some of them are aligned to the sun at either the solstices or equinoxes. In local legends, it says that the seven explorers are represented by the seven moai at Ahu Akivi on Easter Island that face the equinox sunset.[59] They also faced the heliacal setting of the constellation of Orion at the autumn equinox (heliacal describes the conjunction of a star or constellation with the sun as it rises or sets). Conversely, shortly before dawn on the spring equinox, the constellation of Orion rises behind the central moai.[60] The constellation Orion was associated with the Egyptian wisdom bringer Osiris, and sites these wisdom bringers are associated with often incorporate alignments both to the sun and the constellation of Orion.

Other legends state that King Hotu Matu'a came with hundreds of settlers much later from a desert land to the east—specifically Tiwanaku in Bolivia—after navigating his way to the island to find refuge, as its existence was already known. It was said to have been settled before him by his "brother" who had come from the same land. When Hotu Matu'a arrived, the island seems to have been uninhabited, as structures like the precision-fitted polygonal stone wall at Vinapu (that faces winter solstice sunrise[61]) were already there but showed signs of being long abandoned. He seems to have recognized their builders essentially shared the same religion and origins as he did (both venerated the sun, and the same kind of ancient polygonal stonework is found in Peru, Egypt, and Anatolia, which are all places the earlier inhabitants of Easter Island have connections to), and the building of stone moai was resumed. One basalt moai was held to be particularly important, and it's thought it was the original prototype from which the others were carved.[62] Perhaps the two accounts of Hotu Matu'a's settling of the island became conflated—one being more ancient than the other.

There is archaeological evidence that seems to support the existence of a megalithic civilization on Easter Island earlier than currently thought. Although the moai are conventionally dated to between AD 1250-1500, there are indications that the building of the first moai dates to a far earlier time. Excavations led by Thor Heyerdahl found that the island was inhabited before AD 386.[63] And the geologist Robert Schoch, famous for his re-dating of the Great Sphinx of Egypt, has noted varying degrees of weathering and erosion on different moai as possibly indicating major differences in their age.[64]

The religion and culture of Easter Island has connections to the ancient civilizations in South America, Egypt, and India, and I think reveals more about how these civilizations and their religions were all connected in the past.

The name for the sun god both on Easter Island and in Egypt was Ra. This is likely why so many of the names on Easter Island include "Ra."[65]

Also, the Easter Island word Aku and the ancient Egyptian word Akhu are almost identical. On Easter Island, the Aku-Aku were supernatural spirits who were believed in local legends to have helped raise the giant statues,[66] and the stone platforms which some of the statues stand on are called Ahu. In ancient Egypt, the word Akhu means "beings of light" and "divine spirits."[67] Someone became spiritually transformed into an Akhu (also referred to as an Akh) if they successfully passed through the Judgement after death. From there they ascended to the heavenly region of the stars to live eternally among the gods,[68] and were able to influence events in the world. The Akh was often portrayed as a mummy.[69] Akhu was also the title given to the Shemsu Hor, "the followers of Horus," whose full title was Akhu Shemsu Hor, and corresponds to the predynastic kings of ancient Egypt.[70]

> "We also came across a curious passage in the ancient Egyptian *Book of What is in the Duat* which tells the initiate that he must 'stand up with the Gods Who Stand Up ('Ahau')'. These were supernatural beings said to have been 9 cubits or approximately 6 meters in height."[71]
>
> ~ GRAHAM HANCOCK AND SANTHA FAIIA, HEAVEN'S MIRROR

If we turn back to the description of the fourth race in the Stanzas of Dzyan in chapter 2, we see that they were said to be nine yatis high. Perhaps a yati was another name for a cubit? These supernatural beings, the Akhu, seem to be the race of the Atlanteans, descendants of the so-called Children of God (discussed in chapter 5), who were the builders of the great monuments in Egypt, and were likely of a much taller stature, which the builders on Easter Island venerated. Interestingly, the word Aku also forms part of the name of the ancient site Tiwanaku in Bolivia, where giant stone statues are also found, and from where people migrated to Easter Island.

To most the moai are utterly baffling—why on earth would anyone erect so many huge, identical statues? I remember reading that they were built in honor of the deceased chiefs of the island and were worshiped as ancestors, but I wondered why they all look the same. Surely, I thought, they would have been carved in the likeness of each chief. Then that night I had a dream. I was on Easter Island, and busy at work erecting statues all over it were Buddhist monks. They were all dressed

There are large stone statues at Tiwanaku, similar to those on Easter Island, which are thought to either represent the wisdom bringer Viracocha, or giants, some of whom in Aztec tradition were said to have survived the great flood as fish,[72] as some of the statues are depicted wearing fish scales like the wisdom bringers of Mesopotamia.[73]

the same, with the same saffron robes tied over their shoulder, and all with shaved heads—they looked identical. When I woke up, it dawned on me—of course the statues of Easter Island look the same! Where else do we see such identical statues? At Buddhist sites it's common to find countless statues of Buddha, who always looks the same. Buddhists imitate his appearance, and in doing so, also look the same. We all understand the reason for this today. Think about a Christian graveyard—there may be scores of gravestones in the image of Jesus, with the dead buried beneath him in the hope of salvation in the afterlife.

Christian gravestones, which repeat the
same images of crosses, Jesus, and angels.

A row of identical statues of Buddha.

I believe the moai are all built to resemble a great teacher and wisdom bringer of the Religion of the Sun—one who shares characteristics with Viracocha of South America, Shiva of India, and Osiris of Egypt, and may have been based on a belief that these wisdom bringers were the same person.

Viracocha was described as having elongated ear lobes, red hair, and a beard, and these statues have elongated ear lobes, possible beards (indicated by the prominent sharpened edge around the jawline),[74] and some have red lava stone for hair (a stylized form of hairstyle in which it's worn in a top knot).[75] They may have fulfilled a similar purpose to the sarcophagi of ancient Egypt in which the deceased pharaoh was depicted as Osiris in the hope of becoming resurrected like him[76][77]—being created for living and/or deceased chiefs/priests of Easter Island who hoped to become like Viracocha, whom they considered their ancestor (as we'll see next, the builders of Tiwanaku were known as the "Viracochas").

The moai of Easter Island may have been the symbolic Aku/Akhu of the deceased, and this may be the reason they had inlaid eyes that looked upward towards heaven (and thus why one of the indigenous names for the island is Mata ki te rangi meaning "eyes looking to the sky"[78]) as this is where the deceased hoped to ascend to—to the eternal realm of the stars.

As I discuss in chapter 4, they also have connections to the wisdom bringer Shiva in India, who is connected to the Germanic/Nordic wisdom bringer Wotan/Odin.

Left: Statues built by the Chachapoya culture in Peru, which look very similar to the statues of Easter Island. These were used as sarcophagi for the deceased, and give me reason to suspect they were based on the same burial practice found in Egypt in which the departed would be depicted as a mummy like Osiris (in this case possibly as Viracocha, who I believe may have been the same person as Osiris) in the hope of resurrecting to immortal life as he did. Right: Sarcophagi from ancient Egypt in which the deceased would be depicted as a mummy like Osiris. Thus, the Egyptian sarcophagi all essentially look the same, as do those of the Chachapoya, and the moai on Easter Island.

The hands of the moai statues point inward toward the sacrum area beneath the navel. Statues with the same hand position are found at the ancient site of Tiwanaku in Bolivia that Viracocha was said to have been involved in building, and at the ancient site of Göbekli Tepe in Anatolia dated to around 9,600 BC. In his book *Easter Island: The Mystery Solved*, Thor Heyerdahl outlines the many similarities between the artifacts and cultures of Tiwanaku and Easter Island (as well as the absence of Polynesian ones), including strikingly similar depictions of the sun god Viracocha in both places.[79] These connections have now been confirmed by genetic evidence (as discussed in the next chapter).

Almost the same design of statue found on Easter Island, at the site of Göbekli Tepe (dating back to 9,600 BC), in the remote Hindu Kush mountains among the surviving Indo-European Kalash people (which notably are erected for the deceased[80]), in Indonesia, and on Tahiti.

There is further evidence that connects the builders of the moai and the ancient peoples of Anatolia, as the moai were made with deep eye sockets in order to hold lifelike inlaid eyes. Stone statues with similar inlaid eyes were made by the ancient Hittites of Anatolia, the ancient cultures in Mexico, in Egypt with metal statues, and in Peru with wooden statues, revealing a path along which the practice was transmitted. Like the inhabitants of Easter Island, the Hittites worshiped the sun, and used seafaring reed ships.[81]

Graham Hancock, commenting on the similarities between Easter Island, Tiwanaku, and Göbekli Tepe stated:

"If all these are coincidences then their profusion is rather extraordinary—unless, of course, the same Magicians of the Gods who created and then buried the Göbekli Tepe time capsule at the end of the Younger Dryas some 11,600 years ago were also at work in Easter Island."[82]

~ GRAHAM HANCOCK, MAGICIANS OF THE GODS

These magicians Hancock refers to are the wisdom bringers, and I believe after teaching the Religion of the Sun in Egypt, they followed the ocean currents to Central and South America, where they taught it there too, and that either they or their followers then spread it to islands throughout the Pacific, including Easter Island. It's likely that there were multiple migrations to Easter Island from South America by people who shared the same religion and basic founding story.

The very first European explorers that came to Easter Island witnessed the natives worshiping the sun. The following describes what the Dutch explorer Roggeveen and his crew saw when they landed on the island in 1722.

"On shore the Dutchmen saw gigantic figures thirty feet high, with great cylinders on the tops of their heads, like a kind of crown. Roggeveen himself tells that the islanders lighted fires before these giant gods and then squatted down before them with the soles of their feet flat against the ground and their heads bent reverently. They began to raise and lower their arms with the palms of their hands pressed together. Behrens, who was on board the other ship, tells us that when the sun rose next morning they could see the natives on shore lying prostrate and worshiping the sunrise, and they had lighted hundreds of fires which the Dutchmen thought were in honour of the gods. This is the only time that anyone has described active sun worship on Easter Island."[83]

~ THOR HEYERDAHL, AKU-AKU: THE SECRET OF EASTER ISLAND

Most of the clan names on Easter Island were solar in nature, such as: "Sun," "Sun-rise," "Red of Sun-down," "Rainbow," and "Light."[84]

Evidence for the spread of sun worship can be found on islands across the Pacific. For example, just as in Egypt and on Easter Island, the sun was called by the name Ra on all the hundreds of Polynesian Islands in the Pacific Ocean.[85] In New Zealand the sun was also called Ra and was believed to represent higher kinds of knowledge,[86] as it does in Vedic religion. The schools of the Maori were called Whare-Kura meaning "House of Light," and were built to face the sun, with studies commencing at sunrise and finishing at the sun's zenith.[87] The Maori god Tane was said to have created the first man, and was symbolized by the sun.[88] The Moriori, who lived on the Chatham Islands nearby New Zealand, had as their primary gods Wai-o-rangi, who was considered the father of the universe, and Tami-te-ra, who was the sun god.[89]

When a Moriori man was dying, the person attending him was said to have pointed to the sun, saying "Ascend direct above to the beams of the sun, to the rays of the morning, ... to the source, to the sun."[90]

CENTRAL AND SOUTH AMERICAN

The wisdom bringer, who in Central America, was called Quetzalcoatl.

In Central and South America there are numerous oral histories among the various indigenous people that state their civilization and religion was brought to their lands, following a great flood, by a wisdom bringer who was accompanied by a group of disciples. These oral histories were recorded by the early Spanish chroniclers in the first couple of centuries after the conquest and even by some of the conquistadors themselves. Although there were lots of different tribes and civilizations throughout Central and South America, the oral histories of many of them describe these events with almost identical detail, even though some of them are not known to have had any contact with one another. Additionally, there are numerous ancient artifacts that have been discovered in Central and South America that depict these wisdom bringers clearly as Caucasian bearded men in foreign style dress, and the Inca even referred to them expressly as *mitimas*, meaning colonists or settlers.[91]

In Andean traditions (of Peru and Bolivia), this wisdom bringer is called Viracocha.

"There is some evidence to support the extreme antiquity of Andean civilisation in the legends of the indigenous peoples. Many of them mention a time in the distant past, when there was a great civilisation of demi-gods, called the Ñapac Machula (The Wise Old Ones), elsewhere called the Viracochas. Other legends speak of the destruction of the ancient civilisation by a great flood called the *Uñu Pachakuti*, which swept down the altiplano from the north, obliterating everything in its path. In some legends, Viracocha himself is portrayed as the one who restored the gifts of civilisation to humanity after he had destroyed his first creation in the *Uñu Pachakuti*."[92]

~ DAVE TRUMAN, ANCIENT ALIGNMENT IN THE ANDES HINTS AT A LOST GLOBAL HIGH CULTURE

Similarly, the legends of the Guna people of Panama and Colombia state that a great teacher appeared after a devastating flood.[93] Like so many other peoples of Central and South America, the Guna say that the world was created by a god who later destroyed it with fire, darkness, and flood because people had sinned. Again, as in other accounts, after this catastrophe a great teacher appeared; in the Guna account, he arrives on a plate of gold (symbol of the sun[94]). He shows people how to behave, what to name things, and how to use them, and is followed by a number of disciples who help him in his task.[95]

In a number of the oral histories, these wisdom bringers are said to have arrived in boats from the ocean to the east, the direction of Egypt. I believe some of the wisdom bringers remembered in the various Central and South American legends were possibly the same person as Osiris in Egypt, or people who traveled with him, as Osiris was said to have traveled the world teaching, and shares many similarities with the wisdom bringers of the Americas.

The wisdom bringers of Central and South America were described as tall, fair-skinned men with beards, blue eyes, blonde or red hair, and as wearing long flowing robes. The various peoples and cultures stretching from Mexico to Bolivia gave these wisdom bringers various names, and some even stated that they were visited by them more than once. The Inca called the wisdom bringer that visited them Viracocha (who was also known in pre-Inca Peru by different peoples as Con and Tici, later amalgamated to Con-Tici-Viracocha when the Inca realized they were all names of the same person[96]); the Maya called the wisdom bringers that visited them Kukulkan, Votan, and Itzamna; to the Aztecs he was called Quetzalcoatl; to the Muisca he was Bochica; etc. It's important to note that the peoples of the later civilizations of Central and South America, like the Aztecs, Maya, and Inca, were the descendants of much earlier peoples whose stories they preserved, and therefore their stories date from a time well before these civilizations rose to prominence.

In all of the histories, these wisdom bringers were credited with teaching things such as the knowledge of religion (specifically sun worship), hieroglyphic writing, agriculture, megalith and pyramid building, monogamous marriage, law and order, communal living, the building of houses, art, medicine, cotton clothing, peace, and the calendar systems known famously as the Aztec and Maya calendars.

Local legends state that these wisdom bringers, and those with them, traveled throughout large areas of Central and South America, building numerous ancient sites and teaching the local peoples, before departing by boat from the west coast of Ecuador[97] from where the ocean current flows toward the Pacific Islands and Asia, where mysterious ancient sites and legends of similar wisdom bringers are also found, in some cases bearing exactly the same name (being known for example as Tici in Peru and Tiki in Polynesia). Often the legends of one people have these wisdom bringers departing from them at the exact point a neighboring people describe them as arriving, and a number of the pre-Columbian cultures had already realized upon contact with one another that the wisdom bringers they each remembered must have been the same person, and had amalgamated them long before the arrival of the Spanish.

These wisdom bringers and their followers were credited with building and establishing the most ancient megalithic sites of Central and South America, which were later renovated and reused by later cultures over thousands of years. These sites include stepped pyramids and precision-fitted polygonal stone blocks aligned to the sun at the solstices and equinoxes, which are also found in other parts of the world these wisdom bringers are associated with.

Oral histories of the Inca describe how Viracocha oversaw the building of the ancient megalithic site of Tiwanaku/Tiahuanaco on the shore of Lake Titicaca in present day Bolivia. A stone monolith at Tiwanaku is carved in the image of Viracocha, who is portrayed as bearded with large round eyes, and wearing a risen serpent and sun. This site includes a stepped pyramid, a giant calendrical "sun gate," standing stones, and an ancient solar observatory. Local legends state that Viracocha established his first residence on the "Island of the Sun" on Lake Titicaca where a number of ancient ruins have been found.[98] Ancient ruins have also been found submerged beneath the lake, as the water level of the lake has risen over thousands of years.[99]

Illustration of sun worship at an ancient megalithic sun temple (called Coricancha) in Peru.

Viracocha is recorded as teaching the Religion of the Sun, as well as the arts of civilization needed to support its practice.

"We learn from various narratives that the 'preaching', 'teaching', and 'instructions' of Viracocha were of a religious as well as of a practical nature. He was anxious that the Indians should consider him the representative of the sun, a divine being in spite of his human appearance, which only differed from theirs in a lighter skin and a beard, and in his attire, consisting of a long robe secured with a girdle, and the habit of carrying a staff and a book-like object in his hands.

It is interesting to note from various accounts how anxious this legendary preacher was to teach the tribes that he and his followers were god-men, connected with the sun, and that they should be worshipped and obeyed accordingly as creators, lords and protectors, instead of the idols of the former age of darkness. We are told how they taught the natives agriculture and showed them which were edible plants; how they introduced irrigation of waste land; how they built stone statues either in memory of their own ancestry who survived the flood [at Pukara], or thus to 'create ancestors' for the already existing tribes [at Tiahuanaco]; how they instructed their subordinates in megalithic work and other stone sculpturing [...]."[100]

~ THOR HEYERDAHL, AMERICAN INDIANS IN THE PACIFIC

"Cieza de Leon, writing of the period 'before the rule of the Incas in these realms, and even before they were known', says the period of barbarism ended with the appearance of the personification of the sun on the Island of Titicaca: And immediately after this event, they tell that from the south [of Cuzco] there came and stayed a white man of tall stature, who, in his appearance and person, showed great authority and veneration... In many places they tell how he gave rules to men how they should live, and that he spoke lovingly to them with much kindness, admonishing them that they should be good with each other and not do any harm or injury, but that instead they should love each other and show charity. In most places they generally call him Ticciviracocha... In many parts, temples were built to him, in which they placed stone statues in his likeness [...]."[101]

~ THOR HEYERDAHL, THE BEARDED GODS SPEAK

Oral histories of the Maya of Central America describe the arrival of two similar wisdom bringers, one they called Itzamna and the other Kukulkan. Both were described as real historical people, who were bearded, and were credited with founding the civilization of the two branches of the Maya's ancestors.[102] Itzamna was said to have arrived from the east, from across the ocean, in the largest and most ancient migration called the Great Arrival,[103] while Kukulkan was said to have arrived from the west, later in time and with smaller numbers of people, being called the Lesser Arrival.[104]

Itzamna was said to have been the first priest of the religion of the Maya, to have invented their hieroglyphic writing, to have been the source of the Maya calendar[105] (which is incredibly advanced and able to calculate astronomical phenomena with precision over thousands of years[106]), and to have won people over not through his physical strength, but the greatness of his esoteric knowledge.[107]

Kukulkan was said to have arrived with twenty men, of whom he was their chief, and that these had bare heads and long beards, and wore long flowing robes and sandals.[108] They were remembered as ordering the local people to confess and fast, and to cease using weapons completely, even for hunting.[109] He was also said to have been a great architect and a builder of pyramids, and is credited with the building of a number of ancient sacred sites—specifically the ancient city of Mayapan, as well as structures at Chichen Itza, which are both located on the Yucatan Peninsula in Mexico.[110] Under his rule, the people were said to have flourished, experiencing abundant harvests, prosperity, and peace.[111]

Mural of the wisdom bringer Quetzalcoatl teaching the indigenous people of ancient Mexico. The mural is within the National Palace in Mexico City (center of the rulers of Mexico since the Aztecs) and is by Diego Rivera.

In the histories preserved by the Aztecs of Central America, their wisdom bringer was known as Quetzalcoatl, whose name has the exact same meaning as Kukulkan, which is "feathered serpent."[112] Both were remembered in such similar ways that the Aztecs and Maya came to realize they must have been the same person. It was said that the fame of the wisdom bringer Quetzalcoatl was so great, that pilgrims from distant nations even came to visit him in Mexico.[113]

There is evidence that Quetzalcoatl may have originally come from North India, as the Aztecs recounted that Quetzalcoatl said he had come from the cities of Huapalcalli and Tlapallan, which Gene D. Matlock has interpreted as the cities Bopal-Kala and Dhara-Palan respectively in Northern India.[114] There is an ancient depiction of Quetzalcoatl seated in a yogic pose (reproduced in this book), and as I discuss in the next chapter, languages of the Maya and Aztecs have been described by some linguists as Indo-European (bearing most similarities to Old High German and/or Sanskrit). The Maya and Aztec calendars began their last Great Cycle in 3,114 BC,[115] while the current and lowest age/Yuga in Hinduism began just twelve years later in 3,102 BC.[116] These are just a handful of similarities between Central American and Indo-European culture and religion.

"The mere idea of the cruel and bellicose Mayas having invented such a peace-loving doctrine as that of Kukulcan, the immigrant priest-king, is as surprising as the insistence on the part of these beardless natives on the flowing beards, fair skin, and long robes of this cultured wanderer and his followers. Nevertheless, his humanitarian teachings and cultural activities coincide completely with those of Quetzalcoatl. Moreover, while Aztec tradition has Quetzalcoatl disappearing eastward in the direction of Yucatan, Maya tradition has Kukulcan coming from the west, from the direction of Mexico. Brinton points out that one of the Maya chronicles opens with a distinct reference to Tula and Nonoal—names inseparable from Quetzalcoatl tradition—and he concludes: The probability seems to be that Kukulcan was an original Maya divinity, one of their hero-gods, whose myth had in it so many similarities of Quetzalcoatl that the priests of the two nations came to regard the one as the same as the other."[117]

~ THOR HEYERDAHL, THE BEARDED GODS SPEAK

The Pyramid of Kukulkan (the feathered serpent) at Chichen Itza in Mexico. This pyramid is built over a much older site.

Both Itzamna and Kukulkan were associated with the sun (and with serpents). Itzamna was associated with the Maya sun god called Kinich Ahau[118] (Ahau is a word also found in ancient Egypt), and was called *Lakin Chan* meaning "the Serpent of the East."[119] Kukulkan caused the building of structures at Chichen Itza in Mexico, where there is a stepped pyramid aligned to the sun at the winter solstice and the equinoxes—the light of the equinox sun creating a serpent on its staircase representing Kukulkan (the feathered serpent). Even though they were remembered as arriving at different times, their appearance and mission is described as incredibly similar—were they the same person returning at different intervals, or different people from the same group, or people who practiced the same religion and who had sought to teach it at different times?

The Tzeltal speaking people, who are a branch of the Maya of Mexico, record the arrival of a wisdom bringer called Votan, whose name is pronounced Uotan. This name shares remarkable similarities with the name of the Germanic wisdom bringer Wotan (Odin). In modern German, Wotan is pronounced "Votan" as the letter "w" is pronounced "v," but the earlier form of his name in Old High German was Wuotan[120] (where "w" in Old High German is pronounced as "w"), which is almost identical to the Tzeltal pronunciation Uotan. There are many more remarkable similarities between the Votan of Mexico and the Wotan of Europe, which I explore in the next section.

A depiction of the wisdom bringer Quetzalcoatl with a beard, taken from an ancient manuscript.

The name Votan/Uotan means "the heart," which is based on the Maya root-word tan, meaning "the breast."[121]

> "At some definitely remote epoch, Votan came from the far East. He was sent by God to divide out and assign to the different races of men the earth on which they dwell, and to give to each its own language. The land whence he came was vaguely called *ualum uotan*, the land of Votan. His message was especially to the Tzendals. Previous to his arrival they were ignorant, barbarous, and without fixed habitations. He collected them into villages, taught them how to cultivate the maize and cotton, and invented the hieroglyphic signs, which they learned to carve on the walls of their temples. It is even said that he wrote his own history in them. He instructed civil laws for their government and imparted to them the proper ceremonials of religious worship. [...] They especially remembered him as the inventor of their calendar. His name stood third in the week of twenty days [...]. As a city-builder, he was spoken of as the founder of Palenque, Nachan, Huehuetlan—

in fact, of any ancient place the origin of which had been forgotten ...
Votan brought with him, according to one statement, or, according
to another, was followed from his native land by, certain attendants
or subordinates, called in the myth tzequil, petticoated, from the
long and flowing robes they wore. These aided him in the work
of civilization. On four occasions he returned to his former home,
dividing the country, when he was about to leave, into four districts,
over which he placed these attendants."[122]

~ DANIEL G. BRINTON, AMERICAN HERO-MYTHS

The physical descriptions of these wisdom bringers share some remarkable
similarities with depictions of the ancient Druids of Europe.

"The chronicler Betanzos, who took part in the discovery of Peru,
recorded: ... When I asked the Indians what shape this Viracocha
had when their ancestors had thus seen him, they said that according
to the information they possessed, he was a tall man with a white
vestment that reached to his feet, and that this vestment had a girdle;
and that he carried his hair short with a tonsure on the head in the
manner of a priest; and that he walked solemnly, and that he carried
in his hands a certain thing which today seems to remind them of
the breviary that the priests carry in their hands.'"[123]

~ THOR HEYERDAHL, THE BEARDED GODS SPEAK

Left: This illustration of a Druid priest shows him with giant ear plugs, which Viracocha is also
represented as having. Painting is "An Arch Druid in His Judicial Habit" from *The Costume of the Original
Inhabitants of the British Islands* by S. R. Meyrick and C. H. Smith, 1815. Right: This depiction of a Druid
also mirrors the legendary descriptions of Viracocha and Votan as having fair skin, a long beard, and
carrying a staff in one hand and book in the other. Illustration from *Britannia Antiqua Illustrata*, 1676.

The wisdom bringer Quetzalcoatl was described as wearing the symbol of the red cross on his long white robe,[124] and Viracocha was depicted with the sun, serpent, and spirals on his robe[125]—all symbols found associated with the Religion of the Sun in many ancient cultures and sacred sites.

The wisdom bringers of Central and South America were also often described as carrying a staff,[126] which Odin (as a spear) and Osiris are also described as carrying. In an excerpt further on, Osiris uses a "staff of power" to perform a ritual. Legend has it that Viracocha used his staff to put out a large fire.[127] And so these wisdom bringers may not have carried a staff as a walking aid, but to serve some ritual/magical function.

Ceramic figurines from the pre-Columbian Chimú culture of northern Peru depicting Viracocha just like a Druid priest with long robe, beard, and large ear plugs. A cloth is wrapped around his head and fanned out in wing-like fashion, likely to portray him as either a feathered or horned serpent, which were symbols of the heavens.[128] Where else do we find winged and horned headwear? Among ancient Germanic and Celtic people.

> "That the conception of men with Caucasian-like characteristics might have been due to the sight of the first Spaniards is out of the question, since the traditions are supported by bearded prehistoric portraits carved in Tiahuanaco, Mocachi, and Cacha stone statues, and modelled in Chimbote-, Huamachuco-, Moche-, and Chicama anthropomorphic pottery, all properly ascribed to pre-Spanish — and most of them even to pre-Inca — time."[129]
>
> ~ THOR HEYERDAHL, AMERICAN INDIANS IN THE PACIFIC

There is vast amounts of evidence for the veneration of the sun being the most important religion of Central and South America—numerous ancient sites, including megaliths, temples, and pyramids, align to the solstices and equinoxes, and the sun was revered as the manifestation of the divine by the Aztecs, Inca, the Muisca, etc., stretching back into the oldest cultures and civilizations that existed there.

GERMANIC/NORDIC

The Eddas are texts that were written in the thirteenth century in Iceland based on earlier sources, and contain the most complete writings on Germanic and

Nordic religion known to exist. In them, the most revered figure is Odin—also known by the name Wotan in Germany. Odin/Wotan is most renowned for his seeking after and bringing people knowledge and wisdom, and teaching people the form of writing called runes—an alphabet in which each letter is considered symbolic of a natural force or principle. He is essentially the culture hero or "wisdom bringer" of the Germanic peoples.

Drawing of Odin.

There has been much speculation as to whether he was based on a real person. I believe there is evidence to show that he was, and that this person may have lived many thousands of years ago. I've discovered that Odin shares similarities with wisdom bringers in other parts of the world, and these similarities, I think, reveal more about who he may have been.

Odin the Wisdom Bringer

In reading texts of Norse mythology, I was surprised to find that there are actually clear allusions to Odin/Wotan being a wisdom bringer who traveled the world.

> "Odin is called Allfather because he is father of all the gods. [...] He is also called God of the Hanged, God of Gods, God of Cargoes; and he has also been named in many more ways, after he had come to King Geirrödr:

Then said Gangleri: 'Exceeding many names have ye given him; and, by my faith, it must indeed be a goodly wit that knows all the lore and the examples of what chances have brought about each of these names.'

Then Hárr made answer: 'It is truly a vast sum of knowledge to gather together and set forth fittingly. But it is briefest to tell thee that most of his names have been given him by reason of this chance: there being so many branches of tongues in the world, all peoples believed that it was needful for them to turn his name into their own tongue, by which they might the better invoke him and entreat him on their own behalf. But some occasions for these names arose in his wanderings; and that matter is recorded in tales. Nor canst thou ever be called a wise man if thou shalt not be able to tell of those great events.'"[130]

~ THE PROSE EDDA

Clearly Odin was considered human enough to "wander." However, most of what is written about Odin in Old Norse texts is mythological or supernatural. This is because Odin/Wotan was used as a storytelling and allegorical device by the skalds/poets who composed the Eddas, just as the gods of Hinduism were—a position held by Maria Kvilhaug who has a master's degree in Old Norse mythology, and has spent over a decade studying and interpreting its symbolism. In particular, Kvilhaug suggests that Odin was used by the skalds to symbolize the spirit.[131] In this way, a mass of events and characteristics were assigned to Odin.

Additionally, rulers and "magicians" in Germanic societies often took his name, and the accounts of these people associated even more events and traits with Odin. In the accounts of Saxo Grammaticus (a Danish historian who lived in the twelfth to thirteenth centuries), Odin is forced to leave his position to be replaced by another who assumes his name.[132] This indicates that by the time of the event referred to, the name Odin was already a title.

There is even evidence that a king from Scandinavia called Woden-Lithi, meaning the "servant of Odin," traveled by ship to Ontario, Canada in 1,700 BC where he established a trading post with the native Algonquian peoples and left a detailed series of petroglyphs (stone carvings), which depict, among other things, the sun god aligned to the winter solstice and equinox sunrises, and a sun ship.[133] These petroglyphs are a protected historic site located within the Petroglyphs Provincial Park

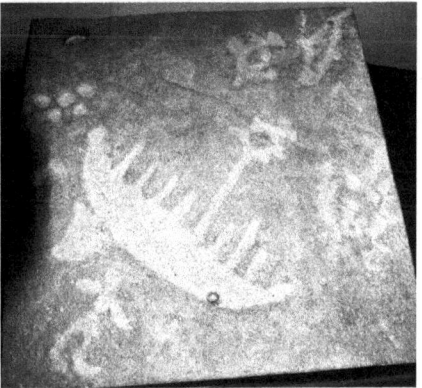

Cast of the sun ship petroglyph at Peterborough, Ontario, Canada.

in Peterborough, Ontario.[134] The name of the king further indicates that Odin was taken as a title by kings, but may hark back to an era of greater humility.

Kvilhaug believes that some of the events Odin was said to have gone through formed the basis of initiation rituals that kings undertook before they could rule.[135] Having completed the initiations of Odin, these kings were likely to have been viewed in some way as the embodiment of Odin. Viking Age warbands were also held together under the rule of a chieftain who embodied Odin.

> "Bonds of 'fictive kinship' were formed through feasting and drinking rituals, establishing a social hierarchy with religious connotations that maintained the rulers' position at the head of his war-band retainers as a 'father' figure, who almost certainly represented Óðinn. [...] Prominent aristocratic Iron-Age rulers clearly emulated the mythic qualities associated with Óðinn seeking direct access to his prowess as a warrior and magician."[136]
>
> ~ SHANTI OATES, THE HANGED GOD: ÓÐINN GRIMNIR

> "Wearing a one-eyed helm like that from Sutton Hoo, adorned in the imagery of his godhead, and possibly uttering words said to originate from the god himself, the ruler could literally transform himself into an image or manifestation of the god [Odin]."[137]
>
> ~ JOSHUA ROOD QUOTED IN THE HANGED GOD

> "That Kings were seen as bodily incarnations of gods in some way or other is common in many ancient societies [...]."[138]
>
> ~ MARIA KVILHAUG, THE SEED OF YGGDRASIL

In ancient Egypt, it was common practice for the pharaoh to emulate and aim to become Osiris by resurrecting like him. A similar practice was also adopted in Central and South America, where a long succession of kings took the name of their local wisdom bringer in claiming their descent from him, and thus their authority to rule.

> "If we turn to Mexico for a brief comparison, we find that the Aztecs speak of *Quetzalcoatl* as the Incas spoke of *Viracocha*. [...] Originally, Quetzalcoatl as well as Viracocha seems to have been the hereditary name of a hierarchical sequence, worshipping and claiming descent from a supreme god of the same name. Only with time have all the Quetzalcoatls, like all Viracochas, been amalgamated into one single deity-god and creator as well as human culture-hero and mortal benefactor."[139]
>
> ~ THOR HEYERDAHL, AMERICAN INDIANS IN THE PACIFIC

Thor Heyerdahl, just quoted, not only studied the accounts of the wisdom bringers of Central and South America, but he also spent the final years of his life searching for where Odin and the Æsir of Norse religion had originated from. I discuss Heyerdahl in detail in the next chapter. He used the descriptions given in the Old Norse texts, which state that Odin was a real person who wasn't born in Scandinavia, but migrated there, and had many sons who founded the Norse and Germanic royal families. All pre-Christian Norse and Germanic kings were expected to be a descendant of Odin.[140] Clearly they had believed Odin had been real enough to father human children.

> "Odin is not a god, he is a cultural hero and, consequently, can have a heroic prototype."[141]
> ~ THOR HEYERDAHL

The real person or prototype Odin may have been based on seems to trace back very far in time. The Roman historian Tacitus, who wrote about the beliefs of the Germanic people in the first century, stated that they believed they were descended from the three sons of Mannus, each of whom founded a tribe.[142] Scholars have identified at least one of these sons (arguments have been made for each) as Odin.[143] Interestingly, the son named Ing (Ingwaz in Proto-Germanic) founded the Germanic tribe called the Ingaevones, whose territory bordered the ocean—note the similarity with the name of the ancient royal family called the Inca in Peru, which was originally written "Inga" by some of the Spanish chroniclers;[144] this name lives on among the people called the Inga who are the descendants of an Inca colony that migrated from Peru to Colombia.[145] As has been pointed out by a number of scholars, this Germanic Mannus almost certainly corresponds to the Vedic "first man" and wisdom bringer called Manu who is said to have founded the first royal dynasty in northern India.[146] I explain more about these connections further on.

Similarities with Väinämöinen of Finland

But before seeking information about Odin from further afield, there is another figure in Europe who shares so many similarities with Odin it seems obvious the two are connected. That figure is Väinämöinen—a wise old sage who is the central character of Finnish folklore.

A number of scholars have noted the many similarities between Odin and Väinämöinen, such as the late Professor Emeritus of folklore at Helsinki University, Anna-Leena Siikala, who said, "Väinämöinen has an astonishing amount of characteristics that resemble [Odin]."[147]

One such obvious similarity is that both Odin and Väinämöinen were described as being masters of the runes or rune songs[148] and the first to have taught them to others. Matthias Castrén, the eminent nineteenth century Finnish ethnologist, philologist, and professor of linguistics at the University of Helsinki highlighted that their common characteristics include wisdom, knowledge, and experience. He states, "One of Väinämöinen's enduring epithets is eternal *tietäjä* [meaning wise man, knower] [...], and it is said Odin is 'wisest of all always'." They were both revered for "secret knowledge"–Odin describes the miraculous deeds he can perform by using secret, magical "songs," and Väinämöinen performs similar deeds, also by magic songs.[149] Like Odin, Väinämöinen was said to journey to the underworld, changing shape and encountering dangers, in search of knowledge or on a spiritual mission.[150] Both were able to use rune songs to control the forces of nature.[151] Interestingly, in *The Kolbrin* Osiris is also described as being able to draw upon the elements of nature through song.[152]

Like Odin, Väinämöinen was a culture hero and wisdom teacher—seen as both a high god and historical person.[153] He was the first man saved from the Great Flood, the renewer, and immortal ancestor.[154] Like Odin, he was a descendant of an ancient race of giants,[155] and was sometimes described as a giant.[156] His giant brothers were said to have built forts in Finland.[157] This likely refers to the ancient Neolithic megaliths called Giant's Forts or Churches in Finland that have solar alignments, particularly to the solstices,[158] which are said to have been built by giants who lived there or used them for religious purposes such as religious services.[159] [160]

Like other wisdom bringers, he was remembered as a seafarer—he taught the Finnish people seafaring skills,[161] and was the creator of the first boat.[162] He also taught agriculture,[163] how to make iron,[164] and fire.[165] He gave people a moral code to live by,[166] and was a teacher of both practical skills and spirituality.[167] "Väinämöinen knew the course of the stars, the moon, and the sun, which is why he was thought of as half man, half god."[168]

The institution whose spiritual leader was the tietäjä, which Väinämöinen is thought to have founded, is believed to have entered Finland during the Iron Age from contacts with Germanic-speaking cultures.[169] Germanic culture had a huge influence on Finnish culture and language.[170] Agriculture also became established in Finland in the same era as the tietäjä institution, replacing and transforming Finnic hunter-gatherer society and its shamans, who were its former ritual specialists,[171] [172] creating a unique Finnish culture. It was based on, or at least heavily influenced by, Germanic models, and Väinämöinen was its central figure, who is comparable to Odin, the central figure of the corresponding Germanic tradition in the same era.[173]

Therefore, it's possible that Väinämöinen may have been a Finnish deity who was merged with Odin, or was instead a local name for Odin. In either case, the information about Väinämöinen in Finland may preserve details about Odin that did not make it into the Norse Eddas, and thus provide a fuller picture of who Odin may have been.

Further details may also be found among the Sami, who are partly descended from some of the oldest inhabitants of Fennoscandia,[174][175] which includes the northernmost regions of Scandinavia, including northern Finland. Their oral traditions preserve the memory of the entrance of new peoples and practices to the region, associated with those called "sons of the sun."

The Sami believe that the sun is the father and the earth the mother of all life, and that they are children of the sun.[176]

In traditional poems, they trace their genealogy back to the sun. They describe a golden age that came to an end, after which two culture heroes restored world order and introduced marriage. One of them married the Daughter of the Sun[177] and she gave birth to the Son of the Sun.[178] This son took a giant as a wife, and gave birth to the ancestors of the Sami.[179] This belief has remained with them to the present day, as the Sami national anthem celebrates how they are "kin of the sun's sons,"[180] and they still identify as "Children of the Sun."[181]

The Sami celebrated the solstices and equinoxes,[182] and the Daughter of the Sun is one of their most celebrated deities—venerated as their protector and caretaker.[183] She and the sons of the sun may have been based on real people, as they were remembered as introducing new practices to the region,[184] and may be linked to a culture that entered Finland possibly between 2,000-500 BC,[185][186] associated with Väinämöinen, Indo-European people, and settled agriculture. What we possibly have here is a distant record of the followers of Väinämöinen, and thus possibly Odin, calling themselves "sons of the sun."

Indo-European Connections

Germanic religion derives from an older Proto-Indo-European religion, which broke off into different but related Indo-European traditions. Therefore, one of the first places to look for a possible source of who Odin may have been based on is in other Indo-European religions.

The Ossetians, who are modern descendants of the Scythians (a group within the Indo-European tradition who populated the Eurasian Steppe during the first millennium BC all the way from Eastern Europe to Western China) living in the Caucasus Mountains, have an indigenous religion called Uatsdin, also spelt Watsdin, Assdin, or Æss Din.[187] This is similar to the word Æsir, which is the name of a class of gods in Norse religion that Odin belongs to. Both Assdin and Æsir are derivatives of the word "as." In Assdin it refers to a tribe of Scythians called Alans.[188] In Old Norse ás is the singular term for a god; Æsir is the plural, meaning gods.[189] This same term is related to the class of gods called asuras in the Vedas.[190] In the Avestan language of Zoroastrianism (which is within the Indo-Iranian branch of languages) "Din" means divine "understanding" and "conscience"[191]—which are some of the same associations the name Odin has. "Ud" is the name for the universal self in Assdin religion,[192] and as mentioned earlier, Odin was used in the Eddas to symbolize the spirit. "Udi" is the name of another native people of the Caucasus.[193] These linguistic connections show that terms likely related to Odin and Æsir already had a history outside of Europe.

In one of the Old Norse sagas, Odin is described as a king from Asia who had many possessions in what has been identified as the Caucasus Mountains—the same place where the Ossetians now live. He was said to have fled Roman conquest by migrating to Northern Europe with "all the gods and many others." There he established kingdoms and temples, and taught the arts and runes.[194] It's therefore possible that "Odin" was already a title by this time held by a king of the Caucasus who migrated to Northern Europe and that he and his company were seen as godlike by the native Europeans. Thus, perhaps the Alans were identified as the Æsir gods.

The Alans are likely related to the Kalash people who have survived in a remote region of Northern Pakistan and maintained their ancient Vedic religion.[195 196] The connection between them provides another clue as to how a figure like Odin could share similarities with Vedic deities, as I discuss further on. Also of note is that one of the gods of the Assdin religion, called Æfsati, was most often portrayed as old, bearded, and one-eyed (like Odin) or blind (like Väinämöinen) and was a god of the hunt,[197] which Odin and Väinämöinen were strongly associated with.

That Odin was likely already a title by the time "Odin" is said to have migrated to Northern Europe in the sagas is evidenced even further afield. Chinese emperors and kings took the title Wu-Di or Wu-Ding, starting as early as 1,200-1,100 BC during the Shang Dynasty[198] (the second dynasty of China), and as I mention in the next chapter, there is evidence that Indo-European peoples migrated to China to form their first historical dynasties (and that people from the Shang Dynasty then migrated to Mexico where they influenced the Olmecs, which were the predecessors of the Maya). In Chinese, "Wu" means "warlike" and "Di" means "emperor."[199] In Scandinavia, Odin was seen as a god of warriors and kings, and so perhaps this was another meaning the title Odin held, and another reason why it was adopted by rulers in Scandinavia.

These kinds of connections indicate that much of the basis for Norse religion was brought to Europe by Indo-European peoples. There were numerous migrations of Indo-European peoples into Europe over thousands of years, and so it's possible that a deity connected to Odin may have been brought into Europe numerous times, as Kvilhaug has noted that figures in rock carvings dating back to the Bronze Age in Scandinavia (1,700-500 BC) may represent Odin.[200]

Similarities with Adinatha, Ikshvaku, and Shiva of India

Another Indo-European culture which the Germanic tradition shares many similarities with is the Vedic tradition preserved in India. This is because both derive from the same source. Over thousands of years, the different Indo-European traditions developed unique characteristics, with their earliest material sharing most in common.

> "The solar religions of ancient Europe were related not only to the Vedic, but to others of the ancient world and had similar ideas of illumination and enlightenment. Much of the spiritual roots of these ancient European teachings may therefore have become hidden by a veil of misunderstanding that came through the Christian conversion. [...]
>
> The further we trace the European languages back, the more they resemble Sanskrit. In fact it appears that the further back we go in time, the more ancient European and Vedic culture coalesce. The Rig Veda in this way may also be the oldest scripture of the European peoples."[201]
>
> ~ DAVID FRAWLEY, GODS, SAGES AND KINGS

There are numerous similarities between the Nordic and Vedic languages and religions. For example, the name "Scandinavia" has no clear etymology in Northern Europe, however, in India Skanda is the name of a warrior god (who is a son of Shiva), which would be an appropriate name for a land peopled by the warrior caste of the Aryans.[202] The name Skanda has possibly been found in the ancient writing of the Indus Valley Civilization in India, in the phrase "Skanda's people,"[203] which I think likely refers to the people, or some of them, who gave Scandinavia its name, also bringing their religion with them.

Studying the similarities between the religions within the Indo-European religious family, like the Germanic and Vedic, reveals more about their common source. This can also be applied to the study of who Odin was.

Because of their shared Proto-Indo-European root, a number of the Germanic/Nordic deities have a direct counterpart within the pantheon of Vedic deities. The Germanic god Thor, for example, is the equivalent to the Vedic god Indra—both are variants of the Proto-Indo-European thunder god Perkwunos.[204]

I believe the evidence shows that Odin also has a counterpart. This is found by way of the Jain religion, which shares many similarities with Hinduism and identifiably emerged in India between the seventh and fifth centuries BC,[205] although is said to have been taught millions of years ago by a great spiritual teacher called a *Tirthankara*, which indicates someone who has conquered the cycle of death and rebirth and now teaches others how to follow the same path.[206] The first Tirthankara of their religion was called Adinatha (also Rishabhanatha), whose various names mean "first lord," "lord of an era," and "first king."[207] He was considered the first teacher from whom all civilization developed, and who taught people all the things the wisdom bringers are usually credited with, such as marriage, agriculture, and writing, and was said to have established the first religious order.[208] He shares numerous similarities with Odin that are beyond coincidence, including a list of sons with names so similar to those of Odin that it is very likely they are variations of each other.[209] Adinatha was said to have lived millions of years ago, as having lived for millions of years, and as being 1,200 feet tall, so these figures are clearly not to be taken literally.[210]

Adinatha corresponds to Ikshvaku in the Vedic religion, who was a son of the "first man" called Manu—the founder of the sun dynasty at the city of Ayodhya in India, which is where it is said Ikshvaku was born and became the first "sun king."[211] In Germanic religion, Odin is the son of Mannus, who corresponds to the Vedic Manu. This means Adinatha/Ikshvaku and Odin were both considered sons of Manu/Mannus.

Adinatha is also considered the same person as Shiva in Jain and Vedic religion.[212] In the Vedas, Shiva is synonymous with the deity Rudra, and both are used to symbolize the spirit that pervades all of creation and are described as being present before creation is formed, just as Odin is in the Eddas.

The name of Odin's wife Frigg (as well as the goddess Freya who likely derives from the same original goddess), means "love" or "beloved one," which is very similar to the Sanskrit word priyā meaning "dear woman."[213] Pria was a goddess of the Proto-Indo-Europeans—who became known as Freya in Germanic languages, and Parvati in India,[214] after Indo-European languages diverged. The goddess Parvati was the wife of the wisdom bringer Shiva. Thus Odin and Frigg may correspond to Shiva and Parvati (aka Shakti), and were used to symbolize the primordial duality of masculine and feminine, just as Osiris and Isis were in ancient Egypt.

Like Odin, Shiva was known by a large number of names, revealing this same practice was followed by the peoples who revered them. Odin was described as having both a benevolent and ferocious side: "When sitting among his friends his countenance was so beautiful and dignified, that the spirits of all were exhilarated by it, but when he was in war he appeared dreadful to his foes."[215] Shiva and Rudra are the same deity—in the Rig Veda, Shiva is described as the kind and tranquil side, and Rudra the wild and cruel one.[216]

Shiva is also described as a solar warrior,[217] and the first great spiritual teacher who is said to have instructed the seven sages after the flood, before they traveled the world teaching people spiritual knowledge.[218] This clearly links Shiva (and thus possibly Odin) to the mission of the wisdom bringers.

Top left: Adinatha in India. Top right: Seal from the Indus Valley dating to around 2,500 BC depicting what is interpreted as Shiva (in his incarnation as Pashupati) in a yogic pose (likely the "butterfly pose"). Bottom left: The Celtic god Cernunnos who is equivalent to Shiva/Pashupati, on the Gundestrup cauldron found in Denmark and dated to between 150 BC to 1 BC. Bottom right: Sketch of stone artifact of Quetzalcoatl found in Central America (possibly from the ancient pyramid of Cholula).[219]

Additionally, the names Shiva, Osiris, and Dionysus (who was known as Orpheus to the Thracians), were at times used interchangeably in the ancient world. Each of them was associated with the constellation Orion,[220] as was Väinämöinen.[221]

Similarities with the Wisdom Bringers of Central and South America

"Often he [Odin] went away so far that he passed many seasons on his journeys."[222]

~ YNGLINGA SAGA

Odin is said to be known by "exceeding many names" because he traveled so much, and because people in different parts of the world named him in their own language.[223] Perhaps there is more truth to this than first appears, as remarkably, there are many similarities between Odin/Wotan as remembered in Europe, and the wisdom bringers called Votan and Itzamna in Central America, as well as Viracocha in Peru.

For a start, the physical description of the wisdom bringers in Central and South America share many similarities with those of Wotan/Odin. In both places, he is described and depicted as an old Caucasian man with a long beard, blonde or red hair and blue eyes, and as wearing a long robe, and holding a staff. The Maya wisdom bringer Votan/Itzamna is sometimes depicted with wings on either side of his head, just as the Germanic Odin/Wotan is.

> "In modern archaeology, Votan has been associated with the Maya 'God D' also known as Itzamná – 'Reptile House' – among certain Maya groups. He looks like an old man with sunken cheeks and flowing robes as a scribe would wear. He is tall sometimes he is associated with wings on his head along with a flat obsidian disk in the middle of his forehead. The ancient Maya prayed to him as a granter of k'uhul, a sacred life force energy used for healing."[224]
>
> ~ ROBERT BITTO, VIKINGS IN ANCIENT MEXICO? THE STORY OF VOTAN

ODIN

ITZAMNA (AS THE SUN GOD KINICH AHAU)

The names of these wisdom bringers are also nearly identical—in an older form of the German language called Old High German (a language no longer spoken), Wotan's name is Wuotan, and the name of the Maya wisdom bringer Votan was pronounced Uotan. The W sound in Old High German could be written in different ways—one of them gives the sound "uu,"[225] which would make the two names identical.

If this isn't astonishing enough, there is far more behind this similarity than most could ever imagine. The scholar Erhard Landmann compared Old High German with one of the Mayan languages called K'iche' and found numerous nearly identical words and phrases between them, which he documented extensively in his book *Weltbilderschütterung*. I discuss these linguistic connections in more detail in chapter 4. I also discuss genetic evidence, and further cultural evidence, that connects Europe and the Americas before Columbus.

That such unmistakable connections have been made, makes those that follow less mysterious.

Both the Germanic Wotan and Maya Votan had the third day of the week named after them. The third day of the week in English (as in other Germanic languages) is named after a variation of the name Wotan—which in Old English is Wōden. Thus Wōdnesdæg in Old English later became Wednesday in modern English. Likewise, the third day of the week in the Maya calendar was also named after Votan, who it was said gave the Maya their calendar, according to one Maya tradition.

Odin was said to have discovered and imparted the writing called runes. Likewise, Votan in South America is credited with bringing the language of hieroglyphic signs. The runic alphabet is usually associated with the Vikings, however, it has far more ancient roots. Runes are derived from an ancient alphabet that appears among the earliest Neolithic cultures of Europe, the megalithic cultures of the Mediterranean, and prehistoric Egypt (discussed further in the next chapter).

ODIN THE WANDERER

The Central American tribe called the Zoque, whose territory adjoined the Tzeltal speaking tribe of Maya, were visited by a wisdom bringer who is described as appearing where Votan departed from the Maya,[226] indicating they were the same person. The Zoque say this wisdom bringer was "their first father," and also "their Supreme God,"[227] just as Odin is described as the "Allfather" and the first father of the Germanic/Nordic peoples in the Eddas.

The Maya wisdom bringer Itzamna was associated with the Ceiba, the world tree of Maya mythology, just as Odin is with Yggdrasil (and Irminsul), the world tree of Germanic mythology. The Maya and Germanic world trees are similar in appearance, and are both described or depicted with a bird perched atop them.

IRMINSUL   CEIBA

The Maya wisdom bringer Itzamna and Germanic wisdom bringer Odin are both said to have the power of healing and were invoked by people seeking it, both are associated with royalty, regarded as creators of the world and supreme fathers, with great esoteric knowledge, and had the faculty of foresight. Both were known as great seers.

Additionally, the Maya wisdom bringer Kukulkan, and his Aztec equivalent Quetzalcoatl, were depicted as feathered serpents, and in Germanic mythology Odin transforms himself into a serpent, and later an eagle. The symbol of the feathered serpent is also found in ancient Egypt.

The name Wotan derives from the Proto-Indo-European root "wed," meaning "seer, prophet, the one who knows," which is related to the Sanskrit and Slavic word "veda," meaning "knowledge"[228] (and to the Old Norse word Edda, which is the name given to the texts where we find Odin deified). The name is also connected to the division of "vates" that were held in high esteem by the Celts and Germanic people, alongside the bards and Druids.[229] The vates were considered prophets, seers, healers, and diviners.[230] It's remarkable, then, that the wisdom bringers in Central and South America are described as looking like Druids. Also remarkable is that the name Itzamna means "divination or witchcraft" in Colonial Yucatec (a Mayan language), and "foretell or contemplate" in Nahuatl (the Aztec language).[231] This means that both the Indo-European name Wotan and Maya name Itzamna have near identical meanings as indicating someone who is a seer and diviner.

The name Viracocha has been compared to the Old High German words *vera cota*, meaning "the true god," which may make more sense than the meaning currently given to it, which is "foam/fat of the sea."[232] A very similar name appears in the Vedic texts of India. Virochana was a great teacher of the asuras (a class of gods that may be related to the Norse Æsir) whose name in Sanskrit means "the bright/illuminating/shining one," which are terms also used to describe the sun god.[233] It's interesting then, that in the legends of South America, Viracocha was said to have traveled with "shining ones."

But if all this wasn't enough... a friend of mine was able to fly a drone (with permission) near the Carajía sarcophagi of the pre-Columbian Chachapoya civilization of Peru.[234] I discuss this civilization in chapter 4, and its Celtiberian origin. These sarcophagi are located in an inaccessible location, high above a river gorge in the Utcubamba Valley in Peru (which is why they have survived looters).[235] He obtained some of the clearest images of these statues that exist. I was surprised when I first saw them, as at least one of the statues is clearly depicted as having one eye. I immediately thought of Odin, who is famous in Nordic tradition for having one eye—having sacrificed the other in order to obtain knowledge.

There would have been seven statues in total (one of them toppled over in an earthquake). They look similar to the seven moai at Ahu Akivi on Easter Island, where people who are genetically related to the Chachapoya/Celtiberians traveled (as discussed in the following chapter). These moai statues are said in local legend to represent the seven explorers who founded the island's civilization, and likely correspond to the seven sages or seven wisdom bringers in so many of the accounts presented here. As my friend pointed out to me, one of the Chachapoya statues is painted with a similar bag/bucket-like object that the wisdom bringers were sometimes depicted with. Interestingly, the locals call these statues the "ancient wise men."[236]

They face the rising sun, and were used to bury the elites of the Chachapoya,[237] just as statues were raised for the deceased elite on Easter Island.

Six remaining of the original seven Chachapoya sarcophagi. The furthest on the left was clearly made to have one eye (the other is just a slit). The second from the left has one eye that is much smaller than the other. The third statue from the left is painted with what looks like a handbag on his chest. One appears to be wearing winged headgear, and another wears headgear with horns. Ancient Egyptian-looking adornments are painted around their necks.

Could these statues again be telling us that Odin/Wotan was considered a wisdom bringer, or is there some other reason one of them was portrayed with one eye?

I believe Odin/Wotan is likely to have been a real person who was later deified as a god, just as the wisdom bringers Votan, Itzamna, and Viracocha were in Central and South America.

Similarities with Osiris of Egypt

Like Itzamna and Odin/Wotan, the ancient Egyptian wisdom bringer Osiris was also associated with the world tree (called the Djed pillar). Additionally, the Germanic Irminsul[238] [239] and Egyptian Djed pillar both symbolize the body and more specifically, the spine.[240] The Egyptian wisdom bringer Osiris was said to have left his wife Isis in charge of Egypt while he traveled the world, just as Odin's wife was left behind when he went away on long journeys. Osiris' son Horus, and Odin's son Balder, were both sun gods.

The name Osiris is actually vocalized and written as "Asar" by many Egyptologists.[241] In Old Norse, "ásar" essentially means something like "belonging to the gods," which is related to the word "Æsir," the name of the most important group of Nordic gods that Odin belonged to, and which is related to the Sanskrit word "asura,"[242] used to describe the gods in the oldest Vedic texts. A symbol used in Asar's (Osiris') name in Egyptian hieroglyphs is the throne, meaning "to sit, to be, to have power," which has the same meaning as the Sanskrit root "as."[243] The word "Asura" is also related to the name of the sun god "Ashur" which the name Assyria derives from.[244]

The wisdom bringer Osiris, in his form as the Djed pillar, symbolizing the spine, world tree, and axis mundi.

Sun Worship in Germanic/Nordic Religion

There is evidence that the Germanic religion preserved aspects of the Religion of the Sun from its Indo-European root.

> "For the later Norse eras (Vendel and Viking), the Sun seems to also have taken a subordinate backseat to most of the Gods in cosmology as the feminine Sunna, held as more or less equal with the masculine moon or Mani. But for the earlier Continental Germanic tradition, this does not seem to have been the case. The Sun was front and center in their rituals as their solar henges or 'Halgadoms' indicate, and their early use of the Fylfot or Fire-disk as a burning symbol of the Winter Solstice reflects the essentially Solar nature of old Germanic spirituality. The Sun was not a lesser deity for the Ur-Germans, or even their Saxon descendants—it was in Primal Position, an elemental principle perhaps even higher than the Gods, hence why it is embodied as a Rune—the mighty Sig or Sol rune [...].
>
> Sometimes the Irminsul is reconstructed with a solar-cross, representing the 'fire-whisk' at top, instead of wing-like branches.
>
> It is then no surprise that the popular notion of Odin being connected with the Sun, and more recently with the revived Sonnenrad [sun wheel] symbol, was well-known folk knowledge, even among later

generations of post-conversion Saxons who may not have been totally sure how Odin could be both a Sun-God and also a Germanic 'Ares' at once."[245]

~ CYRUS GORGANI, THE IRMINSUL, REAL RUNE MAGICK

Expert in Norse mythology Maria Kvilhaug holds a similar opinion.

"During the Bronze Age, the Sun was in fact the most important, central deity of Scandinavia, represented by discs and various energy wheel symbols. From countless rock carvings, we see testimonies of her central importance, her dominance in fact, in the public cult. She was worshipped through ritual dances and acrobatics, and carried as an emblem on the shields of warriors, or depicted as the emblems of the inner power of priests. In the Viking Age, however, it would seem that the Sun goddess has withdrawn from the cult and from the mythical lore – but it would also seem that her withdrawal is only skin deep. If we look at countless standing stones, often memorial stones, dating back to the Viking Age and some centuries before, we see that the symbols of the Sun – the swirling discs – were extremely common, as they were in art and jewellery. If we look to the written lore, that which has been left to us, we might find that the ancient Sun goddess, once undoubtedly the Great Goddess of Scandinavia, shows up with different shapes and names."[246]

~ MARIA KVILHAUG, THE SEED OF YGGDRASIL

Ancient rock carving in Sweden of people worshiping the sun.

The sun was symbolized as a goddess in Nordic texts, but a historical account of sun worship in Germany suggests that Wotan may have also been associated with the sun. The Proto-Indo-European,[247] Scythian,[248] Luwian, Hittite,[249] and Vedic religions, which the Germanic religion is related to, included both a male sun god and female sun goddess, and so it seems that somewhere along the way, it was the goddess who came to the fore in Scandinavia.

The following account of sun worship in Germany was written down some-time between AD 967-973 by Widukind of Corvey, who was a Saxon that wrote an important chronicle about Germany at the time. He was proud of his people and their history,[250] unlike some of the other historical writers regarding Germanic religious customs.

> "When morning was come they set up an eagle at the eastern gate [east being the direction of the rising sun], and erecting an altar of victory they celebrated appropriate rites with all due solemnity, according to their ancestral superstition: to the one whom they venerate as their God of Victory they give the name of Mars, and the bodily characteristics of Hercules, imitating his physical proportion by means of wooden columns, and in the hierarchy of their gods he is the Sun, or as the Greeks call him, Apollo. From this fact the opinion of those men appears somewhat probable who hold that the Saxons were descended from the Greeks, because the Greeks call Mars Hirmin or Hermes, a word which we use even to this day, either for blame or praise, without knowing its meaning."[251]
>
> ~ WIDUKIND OF CORVEY, DEEDS OF THE SAXONS

This account clearly describes worship at the rising sun with an altar dedi-cated to the god of victory, who is the sun. The use of Greco-Roman gods is confusing at first, but blogger about the ancient religion of Northern Europe, Cyrus Gorgani of Real Rune Magick, unpacks the meaning of each to reveal the identity of the unnamed Germanic god as being Wotan. For example, he states that the "'God of Victory' in Germanic languages consistently is ren-dered as the Runic name *Sig-Tyr*, or *Sieg-Tiwar* in the continental forms. This title is consistently used only for Odin in the Eddas."[252]

Many solar symbols can still be found in the Eddas, although veiled at first glance. In the Eddas, Odin is said to have sacrificed his left eye in pursuit of knowledge, leaving it in the well of memory in the underworld. Both the right eye of Horus in ancient Egypt and Shiva in India, were said to be the sun, while their left eye was the moon (which Horus also loses at one point). Thus, the remaining sole eye of Odin is thought by some to represent the sun,[253] [254] which is possibly why it's described as flaming and flashing in some of his names. It's likely derived from the one eye of the god Dyeus Phter—the Proto-Indo-European father of the gods—which was the sun,[255] as Odin assumes the role and many characteristics of Dyeus Phter in the Eddas. This sole, solar eye likely represents the third eye, which gives mystical insight (as Odin gains when one-eyed), and which the Egyptians also symbolized as the sun.

The symbology of the sun as being a single eye is very ancient, stretching back thousands of years in ancient Egyptian and Proto-Indo-European religion—references to it are also found in the Stanzas of Dzyan.

ODIN SOLE EYE   SOLAR EYE EGYPT   THIRD EYE INDIA

The various ways the spiritual third eye has been
depicted in European, Egyptian, and Indian traditions.

In Scandinavia there are ancient petroglyphs that depict the sun being carried in a boat, and a "Ship-Sun" is mentioned in the Prose Edda.[256] In the ancient Egyptian and Vedic religions, the sun was described as crossing the sky in a ship.

There are references in Norse texts to the solstices and equinoxes being important days.[257] And Odin, in his self-sacrifice on the world tree, symbolizes a major stage on the path to enlightenment, portrayed in the lives of many other solar deities, which is associated with the autumn equinox.[258]

SUN WHEEL SWEDEN

SUN WHEEL ARMENIA

Ancient sacred sites of the Germanic/Nordic people, which are aligned to the solstices, such as Externsteine and Goseck Circle in Germany, and the Ales Stenar stone ship in Sweden, also indicate the importance of the sun in their ancient religion.

For example, on the island of Gotland in Sweden (said to be named after Odin[259]), there are numerous ancient standing stones covered in solar symbols, like the swastika, and sun wheel of eternity (identical to those found in Armenia in the Caucasus).

Perhaps the most sacred site of the Germanic pagans who worshiped Wotan

Sun wheel symbol found in Sweden (on Gotland Island) and Armenia. Another variation of this symbol is the Slavic sun symbol called the Kolovrat. They are all variations of the prolific ancient Indo-European symbol called the swastika. They symbolize the motion of the eternal divine sun.

was Externsteine, located at a formation of naturally occurring rocks. At the highest point on the rocks is a small shrine carved into the stone. There is a hole carved above the altar which aligns to sunrise on the summer solstice, as well as to the moon at its most northerly extreme.[260] These times of year are when the light of the sun (both direct and reflected) is at its greatest, and indicate the prominence of the sun in Germanic paganism. There are a number of features at the site which indicate Wotan was worshiped here. Also at this site was a representation of the sacred pillar called the Irminsul, representing the sacred world tree, which Odin was said to have sacrificed himself on.[261]

Taking all this into consideration, Odin shares similarities with many wisdom bringers that also share similarities with one another—including Osiris of Egypt (who was associated with Dionysus of the Greeks), Itzamna/Votan of Central America (who shares similarities with those in South America like Viracocha), and Adinatha in India (who is said to be the same as Ikshvaku and Shiva). Over thousands of years, with the divergence of many different peoples who all continued to revere him, a mass of characteristics, stories, and names were attributed to him.

I believe Odin may have originally been the first priest, king, and "first father" of many of the Indo-European peoples after the great flood.

Apart from sharing a number of similarities with the wisdom bringers of Central and South America, India, and even Egypt, Wotan/Odin also shares similarities with the wisdom bringer of the Slavic peoples called Svarog, as explored next. Odin was even worshiped by Slavs in Germany and was associated with Svetovid—considered either the same as or a manifestation of Svarog in Slavic traditions.[262]

SLAVIC

Like the Vedic and Germanic/Nordic religions, the Slavic religion is another branch of the greater Indo-European family, which is why these three religions share many similarities with one another.

In Slavic tradition their culture hero, or wisdom bringer, is called Svarog, who is said to have taught them religion and civilization at a temple in the Caucasus Mountains following a great catastrophe.[263] He was associated with the heavens, fire, and the sun—his name is cognate with the Sanskrit word "svarga" meaning "heaven." In surviving records of Slavic mythology, he was one of the most important deities, and Slavic pagans still venerate the sun and Svarog today.

Modern carving of a Slavic god.

Many of the records of Slavic mythology have been destroyed or lost, and so the mentions of Svarog are scant, with some being contested—though all accounts of him correlate with the accounts of similar wisdom bringers in other cultures.

One of these few accounts is from a text called the Hypatian Codex. It is said to have been compiled in the thirteenth century, though drawing on much older documents about Russian history that were held in the Ipatiev Monastery in Russia at the time. The mentions of Svarog in this text are as follows:

> "(Then) began his reign Feosta (Hephaestus), whom the Egyptians called Svarog ... during his rule, from the heavens fell the smith's prongs and weapons were forged for the first time; before that, (people) fought with clubs and stones. Feosta also commanded the women that they should have only a single husband... and that is why Egyptians called him Svarog... After him ruled his son, his name was the Sun, and they called him Dažbog... Sun tzar, son of Svarog, this is Dažbog."[264]
>
> ~ HYPATIAN CODEX

The Russian translator was retelling a story set in Egypt and used the names of Slavic deities to replace the Greek ones, which an earlier Greek translator had most likely already inserted to replace the original Egyptian ones.

The story sounds very similar to the accounts of the Egyptian wisdom bringer Osiris, who was credited with bringing civilization to Egypt, of teaching monogamous marriage, and was associated with the sun, as was his son Horus. It's assumed that in place of Svarog's name must have been the name Osiris, and instead of Dažbog, the name Horus. It's quite interesting that the name Dažbog is often qualified by Slavic peoples as Hors (meaning "radiant" like the light of the sun),[265] and the Slavs also consider Hors a sun god, which is almost identical to the name Horus anyway.

The name Feosta (Hephaestus), mentioned in the Hypatian Codex, is the name of a very ancient Greek deity who shares a number of similarities with Svarog, and who the Egyptian priest that recounted the story of Atlantis to Plato's relative Solon, said had been the progenitor of the ancient Greek people, providing "the seed" of their race following the destruction of Atlantis.[266]

Hephaestus and Svarog are both associated with blacksmithing and its tools, such as the hammer and anvil, indicating they taught people how to work metal. The Germanic/Nordic wisdom bringer Odin is also associated with working metal, as it is he who established the blacksmithing of metal in Ásgard.

> "Then said Gangleri: 'What did Allfather then do when Ásgard was made? 'Hárr answered: [...] Next they fashioned a house, wherein they placed a forge, and made besides a hammer, tongs, and anvil,

and by means of these, all other tools. After this they smithied metal and stone and wood, and wrought so abundantly that metal which is called gold, that they had all their household ware and all dishes of gold; and that time is called the Age of Gold [...]."[267]

~ PROSE EDDA

A number of references to Svarog can also be found in *The Book of Kolyada*, which is a recent compilation of Slavic folklore and myths.

These folktales say that Svarog caused a catastrophe to befall the earth with the purpose of cleansing it of wickedness. This catastrophe seems to involve a celestial object with a tail of fire and smoke, followed by a volcanic eruption that billowed out a plume of smoke (described allegorically as a serpent that had crawled out from within the earth).

> "At the beginning of time, when Svarog struck with a hammer the flammable white part of the Alatyr stone, the Fire God Semargl was born from a spark carved out of stone, as well as all the heavenly Ratichi—warriors of Svarog. The radiant Semargl appeared in a fiery whirlwind, cleansing from all wickedness. He, as though the Sun itself, lit up the whole Universe. Beneath Semargl was a golden-legged horse with a silver coat of hair. Smoke became His banner, and the fire—a horse. There, where He was riding on His horse, a black scorched trail remained. From the great fire of Svarog, a godly wind arose—that is how the wind god Stribog was born. He began to fan the great flames of Svarog and Svarozhich-Semargl. The Great Black Serpent, born of the World Duck, bethought to imitate Svarog. He crawled up to Alatyr and struck it with a hammer. From this blow black sparks scattered around the world—that is how all the dark forces, demons-dasuni, were born. And then Semargl entered into a battle with the Great Black Serpent and his army. But Svarozhich lacked in strength, and the Red Sun faded. The Black Serpent flooded the whole earth with darkness/a haze."[268]

~ THE BOOK OF KOLYADA

This account shares similarities with those that describe the destruction of Atlantis, as examined in the previous chapter. It describes the catastrophe as coming to rid the earth of evil, the involvement of volcanic activity, and the presence of a wisdom bringer. The creation of black sparks may refer to the comet breaking into pieces in the sky or to volcanic projectiles, and the references to the fading of the "red sun" and to the earth being flooded with haze are certainly descriptive of a natural catastrophe.

The account continues. Svarog, as the sun, first loses the battle with the serpent of black smoke, but then tames and makes it plow the earth. This sounds like the "snake," as a symbol of the natural disaster, changed the face of the earth—perhaps causing mountains, valleys, and oceans to shift.

> "And then Svarog and Semargl grasped the tongue of the Black Snake with red-hot tongs, tamed it and harnessed it into the plow. Then the gods divided the earth by this plow into the kingdom of Yavi and the kingdom of Navi. In Yavi began to rule Svarog and Semargl, and in Navi—the Black Snake."[269]
>
> ~ THE BOOK OF KOLYADA

Odin, Thor, and other gods of Nordic mythology doing battle with a giant wolf and serpent—both symbols of cataclysm.

In the mythology associated with Svarog and Odin, a great serpent is said to exist in the underworld, and when it shifts or surfaces above the earth, it causes great calamities. In the Eddas, Odin sends this serpent (called the Midgard serpent) beneath the earth after a great flood, but it's said it will return at the times of the end, called Ragnarok. In Slavic, Germanic/Nordic, and even in the ancient Edfu texts of Egypt, a great evil serpent was used to symbolize the cataclysm that destroyed a previous civilization—likely Atlantis.

The Book of Kolyada continues, stating that after this catastrophe, the whole Earth is covered with blood, which is an allusion to a great flood, the water of which later drains through a fissure in the earth.

> "After the battle of the gods with the Black Serpent, Svarog and Svarozhichi descended to earth. And they saw that the whole earth

was mixed with blood. And then they cut Mother Earth, and she swallowed the blood."[270]

~ THE BOOK OF KOLYADA

This draining of the flood waters through a hole that opens in the earth is a common motif found across many accounts of the great flood.[271] The use of blood to symbolize the flood waters also appears in Germanic mythology in the Eddas.

"The sons of Borr [one of these sons is Odin] slew Ymir the giant; lo, where he fell there gushed forth so much blood out of his wounds that with it they drowned all the race of the Rime-Giants, save that one, whom giants call Bergelmir, escaped with his household; he went upon his ship, and his wife with him, and they were safe there. And from them are come the races of the Rime-Giants [...]."[272]

~ PROSE EDDA

Following this great disaster, Svarog goes on to establish a kingdom, from which a sacred world tree sprouts. The world tree is a symbol often associated with these wisdom bringers, including Odin/Wotan in Germanic legends, and Itzamna/Votan in Maya legends. Svarog is also associated with a sacred world tree, which is described in a very similar way to the world tree of Germanic mythology.

"On the site of the battle with the Serpent appeared the Riphean mountains. In the Riphean mountains above the White Alatyr mountain, from which flows the White River, Svarga was established by Svarog—the heavenly kingdom of the gods. On this mountain arose a sprout, which grew into the sacred Elm, connecting the world. The World Elm stretched its branches to the very skies. On the eastern branches of the tree Alkonost built a nest, and on the western side the bird Sirin, in the roots the Serpent moves. At the trunk, the heavenly king walks—Svarog himself, and with him— Mother Lada."[273]

~ THE BOOK OF KOLYADA

Not only does a sacred world tree grow following the cataclysm, but a great temple is constructed in the Caucasus Mountains around a stone where Svarog first teaches people.

"Following this great victory, a half-horse by the name of Kitovras (Known to the Greeks as Chiron) constructed a temple around the stone with the most sacred area in the temple, an altar, being the place where Svarog spoke with man. The myth mentions it was here where Svarog taught man how to make food with milk and cheese curds, which is why the Slavs considered such a meal was a gift from the gods. Since then, this stone has been sometimes attributed to Svarog and in this way he is seen as the creator of the mortal world. Svarog, unlike Veles, does not create the material world with words or magic, but rather his hands. He cared about the Slavs, giving them fire for the cold and to cook food as well as the Sun-Ra (sun) which later became the word for joy (Radost). He also came to the earth to plow the fields and gave the Slavs several gifts. The first, an axe of which to defend their native lands from enemies and the second being a bowl to prepare sacred drinks and the third being tongs of which to create forged weaponry. Finally, his last and possibly most important contribution was the creation of the two circles of time, one of the ground and one of space."[274]

~ SLAVIC MYTHOLOGY: SVAROG | СВАРОГ, A JOURNEY THROUGH SLAVIC CULTURE

It is interesting to note that in the Book of Kolyada, Veles also has the characteristics of a wisdom bringer.

"Then Veles asked Svarog to forge a plow for him, as well as an iron horse to match. Svarog fulfilled his request. And Veles began to teach people how to plant, to sow and reap, how to make wheat beer. Then Veles taught people faith and wisdom (knowledge). He taught how to make sacrifices correctly, taught stellar wisdom, literacy, gave the first calendar. He divided people into classes, gave the first laws. [...] Veles could not sit at home, he wandered about the world with his friends, sailed on the blue seas. Trading in some places, fighting in others. He survived/experienced a lot."[275]

~ THE BOOK OF KOLYADA

There are also a few accounts that describe the ancient worship of the Slavs before they were Christianized.

The Christian bishop and chronicler Thietmar of Merseburg, writing in the eleventh century, described a holy city called "Radegast," located in northern Germany, which belonged to a Slavic tribe. He stated that among the gods worshiped there the most important was *Zuarasici*, which has been identified either as Svarog or Svarozic.[276]

Another account called the Chronicle of the Slavs, written by a German priest in the twelfth century, stated that the god Svantevit (Svantowit) was the most important of all the Slavic deities.[277]

Svarozic and Svantevit are considered the equivalents of Svarog, and so these accounts reveal that Svarog was one of the most important deities of the Slavs.

Today, the sun is still revered as a central theme in Slavic paganism. Solar symbols are the most widely used, like the swastika, and the solstices and equinoxes are celebrated as sacred days. Many pagan Slavs worship the sun every morning.

Slavs celebrating the summer solstice, called Ivan Kupala.

CHINESE

In Chinese tradition, Fuxi and Nüwa are considered the only human beings to have survived a catastrophic flood. They were divine twins born of the god Hua Hsu, and were married on Kunlun Mountain, the home of the gods, in a land far west of China, even though they were brother and sister. They are considered to have taught all the arts of civilization, and were the originators of the I Ching[278]—the oldest religious scripture of Taoism, which is perhaps the most ancient surviving religion of China, and which contains many principles of the Religion of the Sun.

The divine couple Fuxi and Nüwa with their son. They are credited with founding Chinese civilization and likely correspond to the ancient Egyptian trinity of Osiris, Isis, and Horus.

> "In the beginning there was as yet no moral or social order. Men knew their mothers only, not their fathers. When hungry, they searched for food; when satisfied, they threw away the remnants. They devoured their food hide and hair, drank the blood, and clad themselves in skins and rushes. Then came Fu Xi and looked upward and contemplated

the images in the heavens, and looked downward and contemplated the occurrences on earth. He united man and wife, regulated the five stages of change, and laid down the laws of humanity. He devised the eight trigrams, in order to gain mastery over the world."[279]

~ I CHING

Osiris and Isis in ancient Egypt were likewise considered brother and sister, and divine twins, born of a god. There are so many parallels between the founding of Chinese civilization and ancient Egypt (as discussed further on) that it seems very likely to me that Osiris and Isis are the basis for Fuxi and Nüwa. *The Kolbrin* states that Osiris and Isis were not really brother and sister, but had come to be known as though they were.

> "Osireh did not at once take Neth to wife and this is little understood, but it was a thing that could not be done in those days. At first she was adopted by him as his sister, according to the custom. Later, men called her Esita, she being the same whom men call Esitis [Isis] in these days. [...] Then it was ordained that Osireh should marry his sister [...]."[280]
>
> ~ THE ANNEXED SCROLL 1, THE KOLBRIN

There are also many similarities between the founding of Chinese civilization and the Inca Empire of South America. The Inca Empire was said to have been founded by a divine couple who were both brother and sister, and husband and wife. Like the wisdom bringer known as Viracocha to the Inca, Fuxi and Nüwa survived a flood where most perished, and then proceeded to make human beings from clay to repopulate the world, using divine power to make them come alive.[281] Like the Inca, the ancient Chinese also celebrated one of their most important annual festivals at the winter solstice.[282] [283]

The similarities between Fuxi and other wisdom bringers continue. Like Osiris, Fuxi instituted marriage and taught writing; like Manu of India, he was considered the first human; and like Viracocha, was credited with the creation of humankind.[284] I suspect those who established civilization in China brought with them the story of their origins—the same one used by the ancient Egyptians and Inca.

As in Egypt, the first dynasties of China were preceded by semi-divine rulers. The first of these were called the Three Sovereigns—Fuxi, Nüwa, and Shennong. They "were said to be god-kings [...] who used their abilities to improve the lives of their people and impart to them essential skills and knowledge."[285] Importantly, Shennong is credited with teaching agriculture and what became known as Chinese medicine.[286] The Three Sovereigns were followed by the Five Emperors, described as "exemplary sages who possessed great moral character and lived to a great age and ruled over a period of great peace. [...]

These kings are said to have helped introduce the use of fire, taught people how to build houses and invented farming. [...] the invention of the calendar and Chinese script are also credited to the kings."[287] They are said to have been the ancestors of the first dynasties of China—namely the Xia, Shang, and Zhou, which as discussed in chapter 4, evidence indicates were founded by Indo-Europeans.

Left: Pagoda that is reminiscent of a stepped pyramid in the Chinese city of Xi'an, which is its most ancient city. Right: Not far from Xi'an are a number of ancient pyramids (discussed in chapter 4).

MORE SIMILARITIES

And so we have now looked at some of the accounts of a number of wisdom bringers as remembered in different cultures—namely Osiris and Thoth in ancient Egypt, Manu in India, the Apkallu and Ziusudra in Mesopotamia, Yima in Iran, Maasaw in North America, Hotu Matu'a of Easter Island, those in Central and South America variously called Votan, Itzamna, Viracocha, etc., as well as Odin/Wotan in Germanic lands, Svarog in Russia and other Slavic countries, and Fuxi and Nüwa in China.

But there are even more accounts than these, which I haven't covered. The author Laird Scranton touches upon some of them in his studies of comparative ancient religion, stating:

> "In each of these cultures [the modern-day Dogon tribe of Mali, the ancient Egyptians, the ancient Buddhists, the Tibetan Na-Khi tribe, and the ancient Chinese] there is an abiding belief that civilizing skills relating to agriculture, weaving, pottery, metallurgy, stone masonry, the domestication of animals, and written language—among others—were intentionally given to humanity in some remote era by knowledgeable, quasi-mythical ancestor-teachers or ancestor-deities. Each culture we have studied closely associates these instructed civilizing skills with important concepts of their creation tradition

(or cosmology). The purpose of this instructed civilizing plan is understood by the most knowledgeable initiates of these cultures to have been to raise humanity upward from the status of hunter-gatherers to that of farmers. From a similar perspective, the Dogon priests assert that one of the foremost purposes of the cosmology was to help mankind understand our own place within the larger processes of creation."[288]

~ LAIRD SCRANTON, POINT OF ORIGIN

We've already seen that the accounts of wisdom bringers share a number of similarities—in some cases this includes a similar origin (a flooded/submerged island), having been given the same prophetic warning of an impending cataclysm, of being present at the time of this disaster, of having the same appearance, teaching the same things, being associated with solar symbols and the symbol of the world tree, of traveling with seven sages, of traveling the world, having the ability to cross oceans in ships, of causing the building of great sacred sites, and even in some cases as sharing an almost identical name though separated by an ocean.

Since these wisdom bringers were said to have traveled the world, visiting different places and peoples, it makes sense to bring these various accounts together to gain a more complete picture of who these wisdom bringers were and what their purpose was.

SONS AND CHILDREN OF THE SUN

The halo these divine figures are often portrayed with is a depiction of the sun crowning someone's head. It denotes someone who is a "son of the sun." Female deities were also depicted with this halo, as both men and women can be "sons of the sun."

Each of these wisdom bringers was associated with the sun and/or taught a religion in which the sun was seen as the manifestation of the divine as the greatest source of light and life. Specifically, some even shared the honorific title of being called a "son of the sun." Yima, Manu, and Osiris were known as "sons of the sun" and Viracocha as a representative and child of the sun. The disciples of Quetzalcoatl were called "Sons of the Sun."[289] The sons of Osiris, Svarog, and Wotan/Odin were seen as sun gods. The Stanzas of Dzyan also make reference to "Son-Suns." Altogether, the numerous references across many different cultures indicate that this was a special designation that was very anciently held. It survived over thousands of years, as pharaohs in Dynastic Egypt called themselves "sons of the sun."[290] The indigenous Uru people who live on Lake Titicaca in Peru (where the wisdom bringer Viracocha visited) historically called themselves "Sons of the Sun."[291] The native Natchez people who preserved the culture of the North American mound builders were taught their solar religion by "Sons of the Sun."[292] The Shakya, whose genealogy is traced back to Manu's son Ikshvaku, called themselves "kinsmen of the sun."[293] The Sami of northern Europe descended from the "Son of the Sun." The Chimú of Peru said the lands they occupied were formerly inhabited by "sons of the sun."[294] And one of the last kings of the Tuatha Dé Danann of Ireland was called MacGréine, meaning "Son of the Sun."[295]

Wherever these wisdom bringers, or those who venerated them, traveled, peoples often called or saw themselves as the children of the sun, including the Aryans, Sumerians, ancient Egyptians, Maya, Inca, Sami, and Hopi.

> "The Aryans are described as children of the light, children of the Sun, adorned with gold. Its people and its kings are said to be descended from the Sun God."[296]
> ~ DAVID FRAWLEY, GODS, SAGES AND KINGS

Some of the earliest migrants recorded as coming into Britain in the texts of *The Kolbrin* are called "Tothsolars" and "sunfolk"—in other words, "sun people." They're said to have come through "Airana," likely referring to lands of the Aryans,[297] so it's interesting to note that Indo-European peoples may have called and considered themselves "people of the sun" in their various migrations over potentially long periods of time.

The term "children of the sun" appears to have two meanings. One acknowledges that all beings ultimately come from the stars, both in a material and spiritual sense—everything we see, and all the elements we're composed of, are made of the stuff of stars. Not only this, but our inner spiritual part, our consciousness, also has its origin in the spiritual fire of the sun and stars.[298] The term was also particularly used to refer to the people (also known as the Children of God) who are first recorded as practicing the Religion of the Sun, and whose descendants spread it to many parts of the world. I discuss these people in chapter 5.

A "son of the sun" is a more serious title, and belongs to those who have incarnated the part of their higher Being known as the Spiritual Son/Sun.[299]

WOMEN WISDOM BRINGERS

I have been asked: were there any women wisdom bringers? In most accounts the wisdom bringers were men, but I have come across two accounts of women so far.

The first comes from the Guna people who are indigenous to Panama and Colombia.[300] The wisdom bringer in their account was assisted by a number of disciples who were in turn followed by ten great sages, one of whom was a woman.[301]

The second account comes from the Tukano/Tucano tribe indigenous to the Amazon rainforest in Brazil, who say they were gifted the knowledge of civilization by a Daughter of the Sun.

> "The origin myth of the Tukano speaks of the time, eons ago, when humans first settled the great rivers of the Amazon basin. It seems that 'supernatural beings' accompanied them on this journey and gifted them the fundamentals upon which to build a civilized life. From the 'Daughter of the Sun' they received the gift of fire and the knowledge of horticulture, pottery-making, and many other crafts. 'The serpent-shaped canoe of the first settlers' was steered by a superhuman 'Helmsman.' Meanwhile other supernaturals 'travelled by canoe over all the rivers and ... explored the remote hill ranges; they pointed out propitious sites for houses or fields, or for hunting and fishing, and they left their lasting imprint on many spots so that future generations would have ineffaceable proof of their earthly days and would forever remember them and their teachings.' [...] In this period 'the spirit-beings prepared the land so that mortal human creatures might live on it.' Once that task had been completed, however, the supernatural beings returned to their otherworldly abodes."[302]
>
> ~ GRAHAM HANCOCK, AMERICA BEFORE

Clearly these were not supernatural beings, but real people who came to the Amazon to create civilization, appearing to the locals as god-like.

WHERE AND HOW THEY TRAVELED

From analyzing similar accounts of the wisdom bringers, we can get some idea of where they traveled.

The Greek historian Diodorus stated that Osiris traveled from Egypt to Ethiopia, then through Arabia to India (where he founded the city of Nysa in the Indus Valley), through Hellespont (now in Turkey) to Europe, and into Thrace.[303] Based on similar artifacts and accounts of indigenous peoples, it seems likely he also traveled from the west coast of Africa to Central and South America, and then onto a number of the Pacific Islands, before possibly traveling to parts of Asia, such as Indonesia.

Not all the legends of the wisdom bringers may be independent accounts however, as similar legends of the wisdom bringers preserved by Indo-European cultures, or those influenced by them, may be derived from one source before it later fractured into separate cultures—as the branches of Indo-European languages attest.

Essentially, some of the legends of the wisdom bringers may be organic, in that the wisdom bringers traveled to those specific places, and the local people preserved the memory of the event, which has survived up until the present day. Others may have been transferred with the diffusion of people who had been taught by the wisdom bringers, and took the recollection of the event with them wherever they went. As this people splintered into different cultures, with various migrations over thousands of years, the story of the wisdom bringers appeared in different places and took on unique characteristics in each, though sharing underlying similarities.

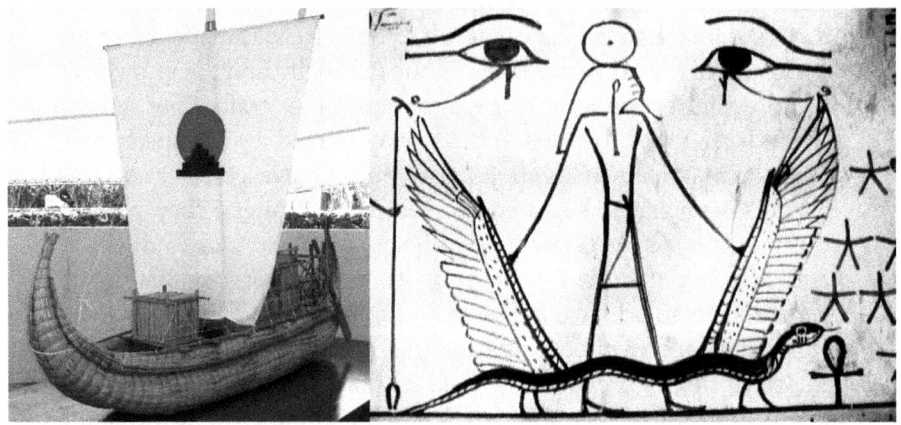

Left is a model of the reed boat Thor Heyerdahl used on his Tigris expedition, based on ancient designs, in which he sailed between the Indus Valley and Mesopotamia. To the right is the symbol of the feathered sun serpent from ancient Egypt. This is purely speculation on my part, but I believe the reed boats with sails and the sun symbol on them, which the wisdom bringers are likely to have traveled on, were also designed to be symbolic of the feathered sun serpent. This is a symbol with a special esoteric meaning, which is found depicted in Egypt, India, and the Americas. It depicts the trinity of creation as Heavenly Father (wings/eagle, which would correspond to the sail), Earthly Mother (serpent, corresponding to the boat), and Son (sun symbol, possibly painted on the sail).[304]

The wisdom bringers are recorded largely as traveling by boat, and as the great adventurer, ethnographer, and archaeologist Thor Heyerdahl discovered, the boats they are likely to have used were made of reeds, like those depicted in ancient Egypt, Mesopotamia, India, Easter Island, and the Caucasus, and are still made in South America (as explained in the next chapter). Heyerdahl tested this idea by actually crossing the Atlantic Ocean in a reed boat, and the Pacific Ocean in a balsa wood raft, which were both made according to ancient boat designs. He also traveled on a reed boat through the Persian Gulf and Red Sea (between what would have been the ancient civilizations of Mesopotamia and the Indus Valley).

"In the central position on the west wall [of the Sun Temple at Modhera in India] was a sculpture of Vishnu resting at sea on board his eternal serpent raft. It was a rather unlikely vessel. I could not avoid thinking of Con-Tic the pre-Incaic sun-god of Peru, and Quetzalcoatl, the Aztec sun-god of Mexico. They also travelled on this peculiar type of watercraft. In the legends of both areas they were bearded white foreigners who had come to bring to their forefathers sun-worship and the arts of civilization. [...] In Aztec tradition Quetzalcoatl travelled the ocean on a raft of snakes. In the iconographic art of the pre-Incas on the coast of North Peru Con-Tici is also shown traveling with his entourage on a serpent raft. A coincidence? Those of us who crossed the Atlantic on the bundles of the reed ship *Ra* had felt as if we were traveling on a bunch of undulating serpents.

Did these people share their legend because they had a common watercraft, or did they have a common watercraft because they shared their legend?"[305]

~ THOR HEYERDAHL, THE MALDIVE MYSTERY

Quetzalcoatl of Mexico and Vishnu of India, both considered sun gods, and both depicted as traveling the ocean on serpents.

SACRED SITES

Wherever these wisdom bringers traveled, or wherever their legends were diffused and preserved, sacred sites with the same or similar alignments and designs are found. Most commonly, this includes precision-fitted polygonal stone blocks, as well as stepped pyramids and standing stone megaliths.

The use of near identical ancient polygonal stone masonry can be found at ancient sites on Easter Island, in Peru, Turkey, Greece, Russia, the Maldives, Egypt, and a number of other places. Stepped pyramids can be found in a huge number of locations—in ancient Egypt, the Canary Islands, Mauritius, the Azores, the Maldives, Sicily, Sardinia, Russia (at the ancient site of Arkaim), Central America, South America, Cambodia, and some of the Polynesian islands. In Sumer they were built as ziggurats, and in India and other parts of Asia they are known as stupas. Standing stone megaliths can be found at Göbekli Tepe in Turkey, Armenia, Menorca, India, North Africa including Egypt, South Africa, Brazil, in the British Isles, and throughout Europe.

Ancient pyramids found across the world.

In South America, the sites the wisdom bringer Viracocha was said to have been involved in building lie along a straight line stretching over one thousand miles—called "The Way of Viracocha"—as it is said to correspond to the route he traveled through South America before departing across the Pacific Ocean. This "Way" also mirrors the alignment of the Milky Way on the summer solstice.[306]

"The alignment's association with Viracocha, the great Andean creator god, teacher and civiliser of humankind, is a highly significant one. Many legends concerning the feats of Viracocha speak of his undertaking a journey, from the city of Tiwanaku towards the

Northwest, eventually to leave the shores of South America's Pacific coast around the present day border between Peru and Ecuador. Viracocha's legendary journey, Sholten D'Ebneth revealed, corresponded with her own geometrical discovery of the alignment of many of the most ancient and sacred sites in the Andes, including the famous ones at Cusco (Cuzco), Ollantaytambo and, of course, the great and mysterious complex of Tiwanaku (Tiahuanaco). [...] it is perhaps worth pondering the sheer technical challenge of surveying this vast alignment across some of the most rugged, remote and mountainous terrain on earth. Indeed, my own research and that of others, indicate that the alignment could extend beyond Tiwanaku. [...] If my findings are correct, it implies that whoever surveyed the Way of Viracocha, not only had an understanding of the earth's curvature, but also understood the principles of spherical trigonometry. It is equally likely that those who undertook this work knew the dimensions of the Earth. The question then arose in my mind: could it be that Viracocha, the great teacher and restorer of civilisation in the Andes, in some way embodied the scientific knowledge of a sophisticated, but long forgotten high culture?"[307]

~ DAVE TRUMAN, ANCIENT ALIGNMENT IN THE ANDES HINTS AT A LOST GLOBAL HIGH CULTURE

The sites along The Way of Viracocha include massive polygonal stone block work and precision cut stones of enormous weight and proportions, and a number of them incorporate alignments to the sun at the solstices and/or equinoxes. Also found at these sites are people with naturally and artificially elongated skulls (which I discuss in the following chapter).[308]

The ancient sites connected to these wisdom bringers are all associated with the veneration of the sun, and are usually aligned to the solstices and equinoxes. I believe they were established as places where the Religion of the Sun could be practiced, and were encoded with its knowledge and sciences.

HOW AND WHAT THEY TAUGHT

There are further similarities between these wisdom bringers that shed light on the events of their mission.

Both Osiris and Viracocha were recorded as being surrounded by warriors, described as fighting men and faithful soldiers who were tasked with protecting them. Osiris is even said to have raised an army in order to travel the world teaching. They were also accompanied by those who preserved and handed down their more esoteric knowledge, kept only for initiates, given the identical name "shining ones" in the legends of both Peru and Egypt.[309] In Peru, it was said that the faithful soldiers and shining ones that accompanied Viracocha had the mission "to carry their lord's message 'to every part of the world.'"[310]

Osiris is recorded as having taught through the use of simple tales, and song and music, while imparting more advanced and esoteric knowledge only to those who were ready for it.

> "[Osiris said to his disciples] The light that is with me was kindled at The Supreme Source, which is the God of Gods. Therefore, my light shines with such brilliance that it must be veiled in part, lest it blind you. It is even as the sun be seen through a veil of cloud, it may be gazed upon for as long as desired. Seen thus it is a thing of beauty and mystery, not something which burns and consumes the eyes of the beholder. Therefore, even as I veil my light from you, so shall you veil your lights from the eyes of the uninstructed. Yet in all matters not pertaining to the light you shall instruct them in the fullness of Truth. In all matters concerning their bodies you shall instruct them in Truth. But in all matters concerning the Lord of the Body you shall instruct them with a light that is veiled."[311]
> ~ THE TEACHINGS OF YOSIRA [OSIRIS], THE KOLBRIN

> "Who taught men the nature and knowledge of God, but in the years left to him could not bring them to understanding? Who, then, veiled the great secrets in simple tales which they could remember and in signs which would not be lost to their children's children?"[312]
> ~ THE SCROLL OF EMOD, THE KOLBRIN

This is one of the reasons we find advanced knowledge (both of a spiritual and astronomical kind) encoded within simplistic tales in traditions connected to the wisdom bringers, alongside temples and mystery schools that preserved more profound and complex knowledge.

Viracocha, Itzamna, and Osiris were remembered as teaching using reason and through the greatness of their esoteric knowledge, rather than by force. In the books of *The Kolbrin*, Osiris was also said to have allowed the peoples he taught to keep their various gods and to fashion them in the likeness they wished, however, teaching them as many spiritual principles as they could understand. This could be one of the reasons why there are still local differences between those who were taught by the wisdom bringers, and why some of these places retained degenerate practices.

AGAINST HUMAN AND ANIMAL SACRIFICE

Although human sacrifice became associated with sun worship in some cultures such as the Aztec, both Quetzalcoatl and Osiris were recorded as forbidding it, along with violence and barbarity—stating that only flowers, incense, and fruits should be offered on altars.

"He [Quetzalcoatl] forbade the sacrifice of human beings and animals, teaching that bread, flowers, and incense were all that the gods demanded. And he prohibited wars, fighting, robbery, and other forms of violence to such an extent that he was held in affectionate veneration, not only by his own people but by distant nations as well, who made pilgrimages to his capital. The fact that the Aztecs, who excelled in human sacrifice at their pyramids and temples, still recollected a benevolent, pacifist culture-bringer whose teachings closely paralleled the Biblical Commandments so impressed the Spanish friars that they identified Quetzalcoatl with the Apostle Thomas—an exact analogy to the confusion of Viracocha with St Bartholomew in Peru."[313]

~ DANIEL BRINTON QUOTED BY THOR HEYERDAHL IN THE BEARDED GODS SPEAK

A Vedic ritual called a "yajna" being performed in India to Vishnu, who is a Vedic sun god. Only flowers, and foods such as butter, flour, seeds, and fruits are offered.

In the texts of *The Kolbrin*, Osiris goes so far as to risk his own life to save a man from being sacrificed. In this account, he draws fire from out of the air in order to protect himself from being attacked by those who were just about to perform a human sacrifice.

"When Yosira [Osiris] came to Kambusis he found there a man of the Hestabwis bound and prepared for sacrifice, and he cried out against the deed but none gave ear to his word. So, standing off, Yosira placed a staff of power upright into the ground and danced around it, singing the song for drawing forth the spirit. When they saw this, the people were wroth against him and called upon their charmers to curse him so he departed from the Earth. Their curses were ineffective and when one charmer approached the dance ring of Yosira, Yosira called forth a tongue of flame which consumed the charmer. Then the people became afraid and fled. So Yosira released the man who was bound upon the place of sacrifice, but he was not yet whole. Yosira also cursed all those who offered the Hestabwis as a sacrifice to their gods; since that day no man of the Hestabwis was ever slain upon the altars. [...]

Thus, when Yosira cried out against those who, while not permitting the slaying of men and women in their daily lives, nevertheless allowed a child to be slain as sacrifice, or buried beneath the pillars they raised up, he was condemned as an enemy of the gods."[314]

~ THE BOOK OF GLEANINGS, THE KOLBRIN

These excerpts reveal that the people Quetzalcoatl and Osiris tried to teach were already practicing human sacrifice and that Quetzalcoatl and Osiris tried to dissuade them from it. Unfortunately, they were ultimately unsuccessful, and these barbaric practices either persisted or were later revived.

"The Druids of Gaul and Britain offered human sacrifices, while it is claimed that the Irish Druids did not. This would appear to have been a corrupt after-growth imposed upon the earlier and purer sacrifice of fruits and flowers known in Atlantis, and due in part to the greater cruelty and barbarism in their descendants. Hence we find it practiced in degenerate ages on both sides of the Atlantic. [...]

The religion of the Atlanteans, as Plato tells us, was pure and simple; they made no regular sacrifices but fruits and flowers; they worshipped the sun.

[...] Quetzalcoatl, the founder of the Aztecs, condemned all sacrifice but that of fruits and flowers. The first religion of Egypt was pure and simple; its sacrifices were fruits and flowers; temples were erected to the sun, Ra, throughout Egypt."[315]

~ IGNATIUS DONNELLY, ATLANTIS: THE ANTEDILUVIAN WORLD

The accounts of Atlantis in Hindu texts also state that the only sacrifices made to the sun god were vegetarian foods and flowers. In the account where it is referred to as Atala (discussed in chapter 2), when a number of ascetics visit it they see its inhabitants worshiping one great god who appears as the sun, called Narayana. The sacrifices offered to this god are essentially the same as those offered in Vedic rituals today—only vegetarian foods.

"Narayana is a Great Being, He is the Creator of the universe. He is adorned in sacrifices with offerings of clarified butter and other food dedicated with the aid of Vedic mantras."[316]

~ MAHABHARATA, BOOK 12, SANTI PARVA, PART 3, SECTION CCCXXXVII

Following on the heels of this account, the narrator tells of an ancient dispute between "gods" and rishis over animal sacrifice. The Vedic rishis refuse to perform any kind of animal sacrifice, even at the behest of gods, saying that they are in the Krita/golden age, when such things are not done.

> "'Bhishma said, 'In this connection is cited an old narrative, O Bharata, of a discourse between the Rishis and the gods. The gods, once on a time, addressing many foremost of Brahmanas, said unto them that sacrifices should be performed by offering up *Ajas* as victims. By the word *Aja* should be understood the goat and no other animal.' The *Rishis* said, The Vedic Sruti declares that in sacrifices the offerings should consist of (vegetable) seeds. Seeds are called *Ajas*. It behoveth you not to slay goats. Ye deities, that cannot be the religion of good and righteous people in which slaughter of animals is laid down. This, again, is the Krita age. How can animals be slaughtered in this epoch of righteousness?'"[317]
>
> ~ MAHABHARATA, BOOK 12, SANTI PARVA, PART 3, SECTION CCCXXXVIII

In a Hindu account of Saka Island (likely Atlantis, and also discussed in chapter 2), the priests of its sun religion only offer flowers, fruits, and vegetarian foods in worship of the sun god.

> "They (*Maga* Brahmanas) are followers of the salvation and are dependent upon the philosophical action. They worship the lord Sun-god by offering pleasing flowers and fruits in the sacrifice. Like this, they drink the best oblations by performing sacrifices of cereals, plants and clarified butter, with chanting of the *mantras*.
>
> [...] In the performance of the sacrifice one form of the Sun-god is present in the fire and the second one which is giver of the light is present in the path of the wind in the sky [known as prana]. Above this the third form is that which is called solar orb. That orb is fitted with the hymns, shining eternal and without degeneration."[318]
>
> ~ SAMBA PURANA

Human and animal sacrifice is a sign of degeneration and of cruel people who do not have the sensitivity to perceive or connect with the spiritual forces in nature, or to feel the suffering of other forms of life and our common bond with them. This heightened perception and sensitivity is cultivated in the Religion of the Sun, and is even a prerequisite for it, as Osiris states:

> "I am the Dawnlighter and a torchbearer for the God of Gods. These are my words which you will do well to absorb, as the dry sands soaks up water. Though they are words of wisdom, they are useless

unless accepted by men who have control over themselves. They have no value to men who are unable to feel compassion for others or who close their ears to Truth."[319]

~ YOSIRA [OSIRIS], THE TEACHINGS OF YOSIRA, THE KOLBRIN

Ancient texts from Egypt and Britain, preserved in the *The Kolbrin*, explain some of the reasons why human and animal sacrifice is unnecessary and wrong, and what sacrifice in a spiritual sense really means.

"There is nothing on Earth that man can give God which could add to God's glory or increase what He has. The only acceptable sacrifice man can offer is service to the will of God, and God's will is that man should spiritualise himself and improve the Earth. To offer goods or money as a sacrifice is an insult to God, it is shirking the needful effort, evading the necessary duty and obligation; it is the easy way and not acceptable."[320]

~ ELOMA, THE KOLBRIN

"These are the only sacrifices to bring: Bodily lusts and passions, evil thoughts, lies, deceit, slander and all forms of wickedness. To offer the blood of harmless creatures is easy and cowardly, and an insult to He who created them. These are the offerings to dedicate to His service: Diligent study of the Good Books, wisdom, courage, moral purity and steadfastness, together with all things serving the purpose of good."[321]

~ THE LAST FOREST TEACHINGS (OF ELIDOR), THE KOLBRIN

"My desire is for love rather than futile sacrifices of burnt offerings, but it should not be a passive love but one expressing service in My Cause. A certain knowledge of right and wrong, with free choice of the former, is of greater value in My sight than pointless ritualistic worship. I derive no pleasure from the wasteful shedding of blood from bulls and lambs. I gain nothing from the fat of sheep and the flesh of goats. I am the Creator of All, so what can men give that would increase My greatness? Men are misled if they believe that their sins can be purged by vain rituals. Only active goodness can obliterate the stain of sin. [...] The ultimate in goodness is to actively combat all the root causes of evil. Those who are my true followers live a life of service and goodness. They live in harmony with their neighbours, harm none and do not shirk the burdens and obligations of earthly existence. [...] They who devote their lives to My service must do more than love and worship Me, for such service entails the elevation of mankind, the spreading of good and the combating of evil. They must not only fight against the ungodly, but also overcome the wickedness welling up in their own thoughts. They who love Me desire the wellbeing of all men, and their souls are filled with harmony and peace. Dearer to Me than their love for Me is the labour and tribulations of those who serve Me. I am their end. I am never the God of Inertia but the God of Effort; if you offer no more than deeds done in My service or in conformity with My design, then you serve Me adequately."[322]

~ THE BOOK OF GLEANINGS, THE VOICE OF GOD, THE KOLBRIN

SUPERNATURAL ABILITIES

Incredibly, like Osiris, Viracocha was also recorded as having the power to draw upon fire. And like Osiris, he uses it only when in dire need—in order to defend his own life.

The Spanish chroniclers Juan de Betanzos and Pedro Cieza de León both narrated the same account of Viracocha using fire to save his life, as told to them by the local indigenous people.

> "The natives had heard from their forefathers that Viracocha was much beloved, because he was humane and benevolent to all, and because he cured sick people, but that when he came to the neighbourhood of Cacha the Cana-people assembled to kill him. As they approached the place where he was, they saw him kneeling with his hands stretched out towards the mountains, as if praying for divine help.
>
> [...] he caused fire to fall from the skies and begin burning a hill near the place where the Indians were. And when the Indians saw the fire and were afraid to be burnt up, they dropped their weapons and ran forth to Viracocha, throwing themselves on the ground before him. When he saw this, he took a staff in his hands and went forth to the fire and gave it some blows with the staff until the fire was put out. When this was all over he spoke to the Indians and told them he was their creator."[323]

As a memorial, the Canas built a great stone statue of Viracocha around twelve feet tall. This statue was still standing when the Spanish arrived, who said it "represented a man of good stature, with a long beard measuring more than a palmo." However, it was later destroyed by the Spanish clergy.[324]

The ability to draw fire out of matter and the atmosphere is the control over a special type of energy that exists within everything. It is the same solar force many of these wisdom bringers were associated with; the fire that exists within all matter is ultimately the same as the fire of the sun.[325]

There are also many other supernatural abilities these wisdom bringers are recorded as having. Others include having the power to heal, bring people back to life, foresee the future, speak other languages, and surround entire lands with magical protective walls to keep out dark spirits. The priests of Ramakui (Atlantis) were said to be able to astral project (have out-of-body experiences), making "their soul depart from the body at their command and return as they willed."[326] Likewise, Odin was also said to be able to astral project, as his body would lie as if dead or asleep, but he would be "off in a twinkling to distant lands."[327] In *The Kolbrin* it says that the misinterpretation of this practice partly led to the development of mummification.[328]

FROM A GROUP

Given the scale of the undertaking they were tasked with, although some of the wisdom bringers may have been the same person, it's highly unlikely that all of them were. Instead, it's more likely they were people from the same group with the same mission, or lived at different times but practiced the same religion—perhaps even being from the same religious order that survived through time. Their memory may have also been transferred across different cultures, being passed on over time, preserved by some civilizations, and lost by others. It's also likely that the number of sages recorded as setting out on this mission was seven for a symbolic reason.

This number was important in the ancient Religion of the Sun, as evident in the Stanzas of Dzyan, and as later artwork in ancient Egypt and India shows, where deities associated with the wisdom bringers are depicted along with seven risen golden serpents.

Left: The Egyptian wisdom bringer Osiris (in his form as Sokar-Osiris), with seven risen sun serpents.
Right: The Hindu deity Vishnu (who saves Manu and the seven sages from the flood), with seven risen serpents.

In Central and South America, these wisdom bringers were also very much associated with serpents, for the same symbolic reason. A risen serpent is symbolic of the risen kundalini—the purified and transformed energy that is raised up the spine in the practice of alchemy, which curves like a serpent.[329]

On the path of the spiritual sun, the kundalini is raised seven times, in each of the seven bodies that exist across the various dimensions, and it is these bodies that are used as the vehicles of the aspect of the higher Being known as the Spiritual Son/Sun to manifest within.[330] The Spiritual Son/Sun and his seven bodies (with their seven risen serpents) is symbolized by the divine king traveling with the seven sages, and in Vedic literature as the sun god Surya driving a chariot pulled by seven horses.

These wisdom bringers were also associated with birds—sometimes being referred to as serpents, sometimes as feathered serpents, and in other cases as part bird. They are found depicted as part bird of prey in ancient

The Vedic sun god Surya being pulled in a chariot driven by seven horses.

Egypt, as the seven sages were said to resemble falcons; in Mesopotamia the seven sages were depicted as part bird of prey,[331] and on Easter Island the wisdom bringers were associated with bird men. Great religious significance was placed on mythical figures illustrated as human beings with bird heads in places where the memory of the wisdom bringers was preserved, and these were usually portrayed as sailing on reed boats.[332]

The bird and its feathers (particularly those of prey that fly the highest) are symbolic of the heavenly sky father. A feathered serpent is symbolic of the three forces of creation—Father/positive/masculine (bird), Mother/negative/feminine (serpent), and Son/neutral/neuter (sun). Someone who is referred to as a feathered serpent is one who has incarnated these three forces within themselves, and has thus attained an advanced spiritual level.[333] In the sun-worshiping civilizations on both sides of the Atlantic, the feathered serpent was used as a symbol of the supreme god and ancestor of the royal dynasty—it appears in religious art from Mesopotamia and Hittite Syria to Egypt, and from Mexico to Peru.[334]

In the Vedic texts of India, the first man Manu, and the seven sages, are appointed to watch over an entire age, and with the passing of each age, a new "Manu" and new sages replace them.[335] This indicates that the positions of the seven sages were likely held as an ancient tradition, and may have been maintained with new candidates from within an esoteric order, possibly with missions going out at different times, renewing the legends and legacy of the wisdom bringers. Certainly other practitioners of the Religion of the Sun renewed its practice down through the ages.

As in Vedic tradition, the lineage of the seven sages was also said to have been preserved in Mesopotamia and Egypt. Graham Hancock points out that the Mesopotamian wisdom bringers called the Apkallu were replaced by other sages described in one case as being "two thirds Apkallu,"[336] indicating that the Apkallu were either part of or had established some kind of esoteric order that was maintained through time. The Edfu texts of ancient Egypt state that the knowledge established by the first wisdom bringers in Egypt was preserved by initiates who came after them.

> "The Edfu texts do not claim that these beings [the wisdom bringers] were immortal. After their deaths, we are told, the next generation 'came to their graves to perform the funerary rights on their behalf' and then took their places. In this way, through an unbroken chain of initiation and transmission of knowledge, the 'Builder Gods,' the 'Sages,' the 'Ghosts,' the 'Lords of the Light,' the 'Shining Ones' described in the Edfu texts were able to renew themselves constantly, like the mythical phoenix—thus passing down to the future traditions and wisdoms stemming from a previous epoch of the earth."[337]
>
> ~ GRAHAM HANCOCK, MAGICIANS OF THE GODS

In an Egyptian text of *The Kolbrin*, it says that such schools of initiation spread "to every corner of the earth," but that over time, their knowledge was lost.

> "Having joined the Twice Born each man has a choice, he can go on to higher development within the Realms of Light, or he can remain to help others. [...] The wisdom of the Twice Born has spread to every corner of the Earth, and Caverns of Initiation are opened everywhere. But increasingly, through the years, men have declined to undergo the austerities and trials essential to bring them into the clear light of Truth. Therefore, the places of initiation decay and their secrets are lost, men grope in the dark and try to open a door to which they have no key."[338]
>
> ~ THE HIBSATHY, THE BOOK OF THE SONS OF FIRE, THE KOLBRIN

REAL PEOPLE DEIFIED AS GODS

The wisdom bringers appeared so utterly alien, with such a different demeanor and such a vastly higher level of civilization, technology, wisdom, and spiritual ability than the peoples they visited, that they were perceived as godlike beings. This is also true of some of the accounts of peoples of the Lost Civilization of the Sun, such as the Tuatha Dé Danann of Irish mythology who were remembered as a divine race. Similar impressions are found in Maori mythology in which they referred to a race of "gods" they called Pakepakeha who were remembered as having fair skin and as always living on the sea.[339]

In the various ancient writings and histories, the wisdom bringers became deified as gods, as if they were never men. In other cases viewed only as men, as if never divine. But I believe at least some of them could have been born with a special mission, to found the spiritual beginnings of our age, and after their physical deaths, have continued with roles in the higher dimensions of existence.

For example, my husband Mark saw the wisdom bringer Thoth in an out-of-body experience he had, where he saw Thoth carrying out the role he's depicted as having in ancient Egyptian texts. In other out-of-body experiences, he's been in a chamber of the Great Pyramid with a number of the deities depicted in ancient Egypt, including the Egyptian deities Anubis and Thoth, as they used it to conduct rituals and initiations.

Left: A Taoist depiction of an out-of-body experience, titled "The Separation of the Spirit Body." Right: A more modern illustration of the same thing, from 1929. Although the "cord" connecting the bodies is portrayed as stretching from the head in these illustrations, in the accounts I've come across, those who've seen it have described it as stretching from other parts of the body as well.

I believe the being Mark saw was likely to have been the same person who arrived to Egypt as the wisdom bringer called Thoth. At some time he would have walked the path of the spiritual sun, have incarnated his own Spiritual Son/Sun, and reintegrated with his higher Being, and now has a role in higher dimensions, which Mark saw him carrying out. Those who have experiences like this bring back the knowledge of who the different Beings are and what roles they have, and these often become depicted in sacred texts and temples that later become mythologized, etc., where people who have reintegrated with their higher Being become referred to as "gods" in many cases as though they had never been human.

Some of the divine kings of Egypt and Hinduism could have been people like this, who had reintegrated with aspects of their own Being in life or had even been born with a mission to spiritually guide society and civilization. The ages of these divine kings may have been times when people had enough understanding to choose their leaders based on their level of spiritual wisdom—meaning they were times when a profound spirituality was much more valued and understood.

As I mentioned in the Preface, the Being known in the world as Odin/ Wotan/Votan/Uotan has appeared to quite a number of people in dreams, particularly as a spiritual guide, and even led someone out of a coma. I have also met this Being in a conscious out-of-body experience.

Ancient texts that preserve aspects of the Religion of the Sun, such as those of Hinduism, state that those who achieve a high enough spiritual level in life move onto other realms of existence to fulfill roles there after death, and likewise that Beings who have roles in higher realms can be born on earth to perform missions and further their own spiritual development at advanced levels. These Beings can thus be met and interacted with when we're in these higher realms ourselves, such as when we're dreaming, or in an out-of-body or near-death experience. We may also be able to sense these Beings around us at times, as the different dimensions interact with and interpenetrate one another.[340]

Illustration of a Hindu king ascending to heaven (svarga) as a reward for his spiritual practices and achievements, based on a story from the text called the Bhagavata Purana.

A similar belief was held by the ancient Egyptians. For example, the Egyptian priest Manetho explains that the gods of ancient Egypt "originated from Earth [and] then became celestial."[341] The stars, heavens, and celestial regions were always associated with these higher realms and dimensions in the Religion of the Sun, and thus these "gods" had actually once been people who had entered these higher realms after death.

I believe the wisdom bringers were Beings who had achieved an advanced spiritual level and who were born on Earth to perform a mission, while using the events of life and the difficulties they faced here in order to further their own spiritual learning and development.

CONCLUSION

I believe that the mission of the wisdom bringers was one of the greatest and most significant events in human history. Although the Religion of the Sun had been preserved from a previous golden age, and likely kept as part of a long esoteric tradition, this mission was its founding in our age.

These wisdom bringers risked their lives, traveling over stormy and shark infested waters, through jungles, mountains, and hostile terrain, devoting everything they had to this singular task, without which, our civilization would not have had the magnificent spiritual foundation it has. What they set in motion has reverberated across the ages. The sacred sites and knowledge they established have continued to inspire and elevate our spirits, perpetually compelling us to contemplate the deeper mysteries of existence.

Although far back in time, we not only see, but still feel the effects of what they achieved even now. These men are not just figures of the past, nor old gods relegated to lost religions and crumbling temples—many of them, like Thoth, Anubis, and Odin/Wotan/Uotan, as people have seen, are still watching over us today.

Nor is the religion they taught an old relic, to be looked down upon as something primitive in the presence of our modern times, as their astronomical, architectural, and spiritual knowledge still bewilders and captivates us today.

Their spiritual message is alive, connecting us, across time and space, to its founding heroes and the great legacy they sacrificed so much to leave us—the Religion of the Sun.

As we shall see next, many people all over the world took up this great religion, and from it a global civilization arose that furthered its practice over the thousands of years that followed.

CHAPTER FOUR

The Lost Civilization of the Sun

WHAT IS THE LOST CIVILIZATION OF THE SUN?

Continuing our journey, from a distant golden age, through Atlantis and its destruction, to the mission of the wisdom bringers, we turn the pages of the past to see what happened next. Following in the footsteps of the wisdom bringers, a now lost global civilization arose in their wake, having been empowered with both the knowledge of religion and the arts of civilization.

This civilization was the inheritor of knowledge from lost civilizations like Atlantis, and also the predecessor to the civilizations known to history (spanning the last five thousand years). It essentially existed from the end of the last ice age, surviving up until the last few hundred years in scattered remnants in some of the most remote parts of the world, but had once spread across large parts of it.

The predominant characteristic of this civilization was its religion, which was the Religion of the Sun, as this is what it ultimately centered around. It was responsible for the building of many megaliths, temples, and pyramids of similar design, which align to the sun, all over the world.

I use the word civilization here in the same way it's used in "Western civilization," to refer to those tribes, kingdoms, and empires spanning thousands of years over a vast geographic area, which essentially shared the same religious beliefs, cultural foundation, political system, and customs.[1][2] Although Western civilization is comprised of many different kingdoms and nations over long periods of time, some who even fought devastating wars against one another, speak different (though related) languages, and have quite distinct cultures, they all derived from Europe and essentially adopted and spread the same ideas, institutions, and religion, which became part of a global network of trade and migration.

This is why my husband and I named this civilization "The Lost Civilization of the Sun," because it was primarily focused around a solar religion, and also because it is "lost," as its existence is unknown to most, even though the evidence for it is factual and based on the accounts of real people accepted to academia, such as some of the first Spanish explorers to the Americas.

This chapter explores some of the evidence for the existence of the Lost Civilization of the Sun, which gave rise to many of the world's spiritual traditions that over time became fractured and dissipated, to many sacred texts that though existing in different traditions share the same source, and ancient megalithic sites whose builders over time became forgotten.

SIMILARITIES BETWEEN THINGS IN ANCIENT TIMES

Anyone who looks into ancient history with an open mind will find similar megalithic structures, temples, religious symbols, languages, measurements, building techniques, and descriptions (depictions, and even skeletons) of similar looking people, across much of the world—dating from thousands of years before known history, which only begins around 2,500 BC.

There are so many similarities that it would take many volumes to cover them—to any objective observer however, it is patently obvious that these similarities are beyond coincidence, and that there had to have been a common source they derived from that had the ability to traverse the oceans. Some people have even drawn up long lists of these similarities, which number over sixty when comparing ancient Egyptian and Mesopotamian with Central and South American civilizations. Even if there was a 1 percent chance these civilizations independently developed the same practice, the chance they did it sixty times is 1 percent to the power of sixty, which makes it practically impossible.[3]

Most of these similarities are all connected to the same religion—the Religion of the Sun, in which hundreds, if not thousands, of similarly designed pyramids, standing stones, henges, and temples were built across the world to align to the sun on the solstices and equinoxes, and which incorporated the same solar symbols, such as the swastika, double spiral, and feathered serpent, and were built in places where the Religion of the Sun is recorded as being practiced.

Some of these similarities may be due to the influence and spread of the lost civilization popularly referred to as Atlantis, which Plato describes as stretching into Egypt and Europe.

"Now in this island of Atlantis there was a great and wonderful empire which had rule over the whole island and several others, and over parts of the continent, and, furthermore, the men of Atlantis had subjected the parts of Libya within the columns of Heracles as far as Egypt, and of Europe as far as Tyrrhenia [meaning possibly into the Mediterranean as far as Italy]."[4]

~ PLATO, TIMAEUS

The empire of Atlantis may have spread even further, particularly into regions the Egyptians and Greeks who were involved in telling this story would have had less knowledge of, such as into areas of Asia and the Americas.

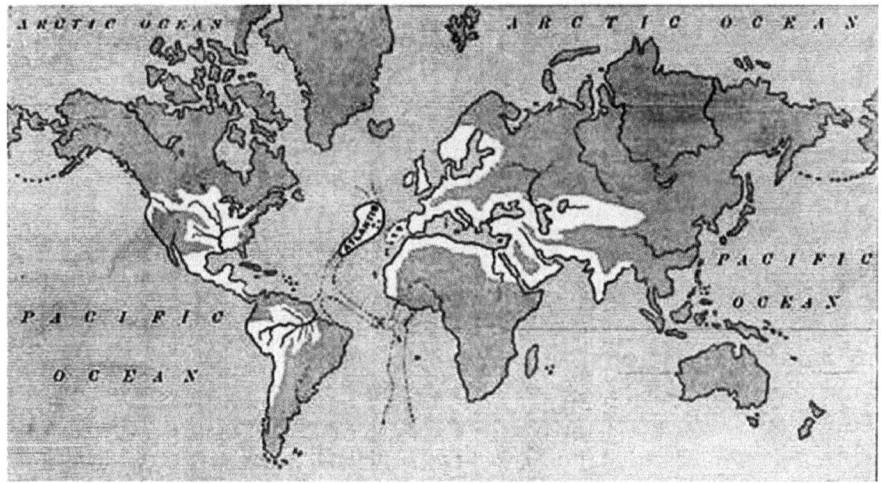

Speculative map of the Atlantean Empire from Ignatius Donnelly's book *Atlantis: The Antediluvian World*, 1882.

And so the very ancient sites that may predate 9,700 BC, and that share similarities, especially those that show evidence of advanced or unknown technology, could be remnants of the Atlantean empire, or even the work of the brotherhood of sages that existed in the times of Atlantis and which some of the wisdom bringers may have derived from.

Other similarities may be due to the wisdom bringers, who taught the same thing in the various places they traveled, with variances being due to existing local customs that were in some cases kept alongside the Religion of the Sun as it was introduced.

But the other reason, which I'll explore in this chapter, is that from out of what the wisdom bringers established, a global civilization and culture arose that followed the Religion of the Sun, and further spread it throughout the world.

SEARCHING FOR THE TRUTH OF THE PAST

I've used the available evidence to piece together what I can about the Lost Civilization of the Sun, but new pieces of evidence and breakthroughs in dating techniques and technologies, etc., can turn long-held assumptions on their head, and in the field of archaeology and genetics they tend to do so on an almost daily basis.

That's why from my personal perspective, my understanding of history is something fluid—and I feel that everyone should always be ready to reevaluate the accepted views of history. I've often had to completely change my own long-held views on history as I've come across new information, but I feel that's the only way to approach its study, as otherwise our views simply get in the way of truth. Ultimately, the only vested interest anyone should have in looking at history is in finding the truth, and the truth belongs to all of us to study, make sense of, and to use.

I think it's important to take into account that what we "know" about the past is entirely dependent on what has been unearthed so far. But we can't assume that what has been found is all that exists.

The discovery of the ancient temple complex of Göbekli Tepe in 1994 in Turkey has called into question the well-worn narrative that at the time of its building (and for thousands of years following it) humans had only existed as hunter-gatherers in very primitive style societies, incapable of megalithic building. It turns out now that this was wrong, and yet almost everyone was convinced it was true until the massive site of Göbekli Tepe emerged from underneath a completely unassuming hill. What else lies beneath the shuffling of our feet, where thousands of years of civilization bury the one before like layers of an onion?

It's turned out that we've forgotten and lost information about very recent civilizations, so is it that much of a stretch to think that we may have lost it about even older ones too?

Another example: laser technology is currently being used to reveal the massive, and I mean massive, extent of the ancient Maya civilization—much of which as it turns out, had been hidden by the dense jungle canopy of Guatemala. It is now believed that at its height, the population of the Maya could have reached between ten to fifteen million people!—far in excess of what was previously thought.[5]

Yet another example: the Osireion is a giant megalithic temple in Egypt that appears to have become buried under the shifting sands and later unearthed during the construction of the temple of the Pharaoh Seti I in around 1,280 BC, and later again along with the temple of Seti I in AD 1902, after both had become covered in sand! It turns out, huge things get forgotten, buried, and lost under the ground all the time. A similar thing even happened to the Great Sphinx, which too was either completely or almost completely buried in sand for millennia—something we might find hard to imagine today.

The Osireion temple in Egypt, which had, periodically, been
completely buried beneath the ground for thousands of years.

So when people say, "we know" there was no civilization back then, or "we know" these languages are not related to one another, etc., I always take it with a grain of salt.

I'm prepared to go wherever the evidence leads, and to look at as much of the available evidence as I can (within the limits of time, language, and availability). I've been doing this long enough to notice that many people come to conclusions without examining all the evidence available—usually ignoring the oral histories of people who have occupied lands for thousands of years, or inconvenient truths that conflict with their ideologies. Like this, their conclusions are based upon incomplete and skewed information, no matter how impressive they may sound.

I think it's important to be able to look at history from a neutral perspective, to be able to see and confront the ugliness of the past (even when it may pertain to our own ancestors), as well as to admire its great beauty (even if it pertains to the ancestors of others).

The people involved in the Lost Civilization of the Sun were not angels—they were ordinary people, and no doubt there were both good and bad among them. Think about the spread of Christianity with the expansion of Western civilization (although I believe the Religion of the Sun was more principled and contained a far greater depth of wisdom). Some Christian missionaries were extremely compassionate, while other Christians were fiendish con-quistadors and inquisitors, yet all of them essentially spread the teachings, symbols, and building styles of the same religion (to greater or lesser degrees, as much of Christianity is a distortion of Jesus' teachings as explained further on), which as a result left its mark on almost every region on Earth.

When I started researching, I had the impression there wasn't much evidence for things like Atlantis and what I now call the Lost Civilization of the Sun. But the more I look, the more evidence seems to tumble out everywhere, even for questions that I thought would never have an answer. Much of this evidence is simply unknown because it is forgotten and buried in old books in libraries, archives, and museums, or is omitted from popular discourse because it has been attacked and ignored. The evidence for a lost civilization has become almost as lost as the civilization itself. There is so much evidence to recover and bring together, that it would take many lifetimes to go through it, so I am only presenting what I have come across so far (or have been sent), and what stands out as important to providing an overview.

So let's get started on exploring the evidence for the Lost Civilization of the Sun—the following is a summary of as much as I've been able to piece together so far. It is by no means complete, and my research is always ongoing.

EVIDENCE

Some of the oldest sacred texts in the world, as discussed in the second chapter, which preserved remnants of the Religion of the Sun, such as the Stanzas of Dzyan and *The Kolbrin*, tell us not only about Atlantis and how it ended in a great cataclysm, and how the wisdom bringers then traveled across the world to reinitiate civilization and religion, but also about how the Lost Civilization of the Sun began.

The Stanzas of Dzyan provide a few, information-packed lines:

> "All Holy saved, the Unholy destroyed. [...] The fifth produced from the Holy stock remained; it was ruled over by the first divine Kings. .... Who re-descended, who made peace with the fifth, who taught and instructed it......"[6]

That is, those who were considered "Holy" or "worthy" were saved from Atlantis, as other flood accounts corroborate, and were led to safety. They had been considered the fourth race; the fifth were their offspring. They were ruled by the first divine kings in the solar theocracies established by the wisdom bringers, and were instructed by them.

It's interesting that those who were saved from the fourth race "made peace with the fifth," indicating that perhaps there was enmity between them. In Plato's account, Atlantis is at war, just before its demise, with the forebears of the Greeks, called the "Hellenes." Today, this term is often used generally to describe Greeks, but originally referred to the descendants of Zeus or Deucalion (who in Greek legend was the man who survived the flood).[7]

ARCHAEOLOGICAL EVIDENCE

In ancient Mesopotamian accounts of the great flood, the survivors make landfall in Armenia.[8] Not far from there, in eastern Turkey, the ancient site Göbekli Tepe was unearthed—a site which dates to 9,600 BC (the date of the destruction of Atlantis), and contains references to Vedic astronomy on its pillars, as well as the bucket-like object some of the wisdom bringers are depicted as carrying.

Many lines of evidence converge at Göbekli Tepe, but also in the vicinity. From 9,500 BC, the first signs of agriculture appear close by in the Levant,[9] and agriculture is one of the main things taught by the wisdom bringers. Klaus Schmidt, who discovered Göbekli Tepe in 1994, was quoted as saying that he believed agriculture was first invented, and disseminated into the wider region, by the people who built Göbekli Tepe's monumental stone circles because of the division of labor required to construct the site. Its complexity and thus the level of organization required to build it indicates that the project wasn't overseen by shamans, but by some kind of institution, perhaps a kind of priesthood.[10] Such an institution may have been related to what became the Vedic priesthood, as further evidence reveals next.

The most ancient evidence for what has come to be known as Indo-European culture, as far as I am aware, has also been found in this wider region at a similar time. As mentioned in the second chapter, this includes the oldest known depiction of the symbol of the swastika, which was found in Ukraine (dating to 10,000 BC). It also includes the artifacts of the culture of Lepenski Vir in Serbia (dating to between 9,500 and 6,000 BC), such as their ancient burials in yoga positions and their sun shrines.

The oldest depiction of a swastika in the world, found carved into a bird effigy made of mammoth ivory, dating to 10,000 BC and discovered in Ukraine. This effigy bears a resemblance to the Slavic deity known as Mater Sva, who was the wife of the wisdom bringer Svarog, and was depicted as a bird with her symbol a variant of the swastika.[11]

In addition to this, around thirty kilometers from Göbekli Tepe is another ancient sacred site called Nevali Cori. It shares a number of design features with Göbekli Tepe, and its oldest layer is relatively contemporaneous with it.

Both sites are associated with some of the oldest statues in the world. The statue called Urfa Man was discovered ten kilometers from Göbekli Tepe—it is currently "the oldest naturalistic life-sized sculpture of a human," and is dated to 9,000 BC,[12] which is contemporaneous with both Göbekli Tepe and Nevali Cori. Urfa Man is similar in design to the statues found on Easter Island and at the ancient site of Tiwanaku in Bolivia—both places where the wisdom bringers are recorded as visiting.

The statue of a man's head found at Nevali Cori shares similarities with the Brahmins or priests of Vedic religion, and with the headdress of the Egyptian pharaohs. It is believed to have been that of a priest; apparently it was found within a temple area at Nevali Cori, but had been partially destroyed—the face having been broken off. The back of the head has remained intact, and shows a serpent as if it's climbing up the back of the head to the crown. As noted by

B. G. Sidharth, this "rising serpent" looks very similar to the religious ponytail worn by Vedic priests even still today, stating "Even a not-too-well informed Indian can make this out to be the sculpture of a Vedic priest, because such a hairstyle is a dying, but still alive tradition in India today.[13] [...] Egyptian and Sumerian priests also had tonsured heads, but without the typical Vedic sikha depicted in the Nevali Cori sculpture."[14] Egyptian pharaohs and deities were also depicted with a serpent risen over their forehead. The serpent is very likely to symbolize what is known as the risen kundalini.

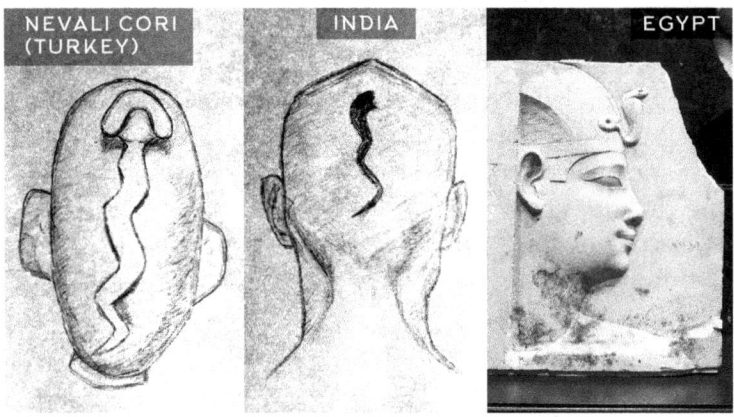

Left: A sketch of the back of the damaged head found at Nevali Cori. Middle: The "sikha" ponytail worn by some Vedic priests. Right: The serpent risen over the forehead of an Egyptian pharaoh.

This archaeological evidence indicates that the area of origin for Indo-European civilization and religion (which as explored earlier was a solar religion) after the end of the last ice age was in the regions around the Black Sea, including Anatolia. It also appears to be the cradle from where the Lost Civilization of the Sun first emerged. As we'll see next, what appears to have spread with it are the Indo-European languages.

LINGUISTIC EVIDENCE

Languages are a bit like sets of genes. Linguists can discover relationships between cultures based on commonalities in their languages. They can see whether cultures had contact with one another, and whether they derive from the same source.

Origins of Indo-European

Today, the language family spoken by most people in the world is Indo-European. Nearly half the world's population speaks a form of Indo-European as their first language[15]—including English, almost all European languages like Spanish and French, Slavic languages, Persian, and Hindi (a derivative of Sanskrit, the language of the Vedas).

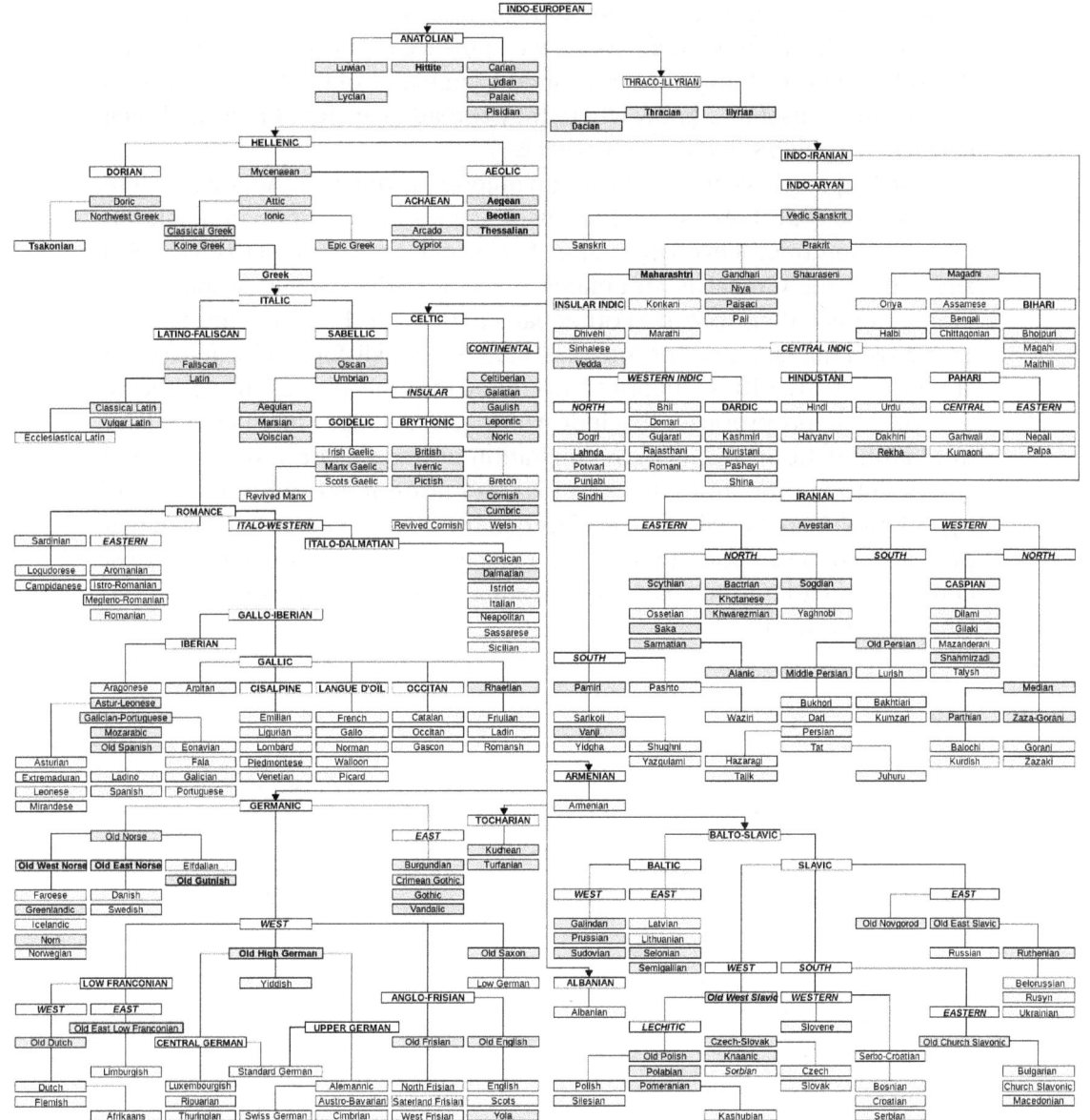

Partial diagram of the tree of Indo-European languages.

The Indo-European family of languages has a long history stretching back to at least 7,800-4,500 BC. Linguists believe that all Indo-European languages—whether Italian, Greek, Hindi, Persian, or Russian, etc.—all derive from an ancient mother tongue they call Proto-Indo-European.

During the last two hundred years, linguists have worked to reconstruct this original Indo-European protolanguage by comparing the numerous Indo-European child languages it broke off into, which they postulate happened over thousands of years with the migrations of its speakers. By doing this, they've also tried to locate where and when these protolanguage speakers are likely to have originated.[16] Since we know that Indo-Europeans carried the Religion of the Sun and they formed a large part of the Lost Civilization of the Sun, it's useful to know where they spread in ancient times, and their language can help show us where that is.

Some linguists have traced the origin of Indo-European to Anatolia, where some of the oldest archaeological evidence for Indo-European religion is found. Others trace it even more specifically to the coastline of the Black Sea and foot of the Caucasus Mountains. These theories usually propose that Indo-European then spread to other parts of the world with the first farmers who began migrating out of Anatolia (where Göbekli Tepe is located) from around 7,000 BC.[17] These theories are referred to as the "Anatolian hypothesis."

Another theory proposes that Indo-European languages spread much later, from around 4,000 BC, with the migration of peoples from the Ukrainian steppe into Europe and Asia, and for this reason it is called the "Steppe hypothesis." Genetic evidence analyzed in the last few years has proven that people from the steppe did migrate to places like Europe and India, almost certainly spreading Indo-European language as they did, supporting the Steppe hypothesis.[18]

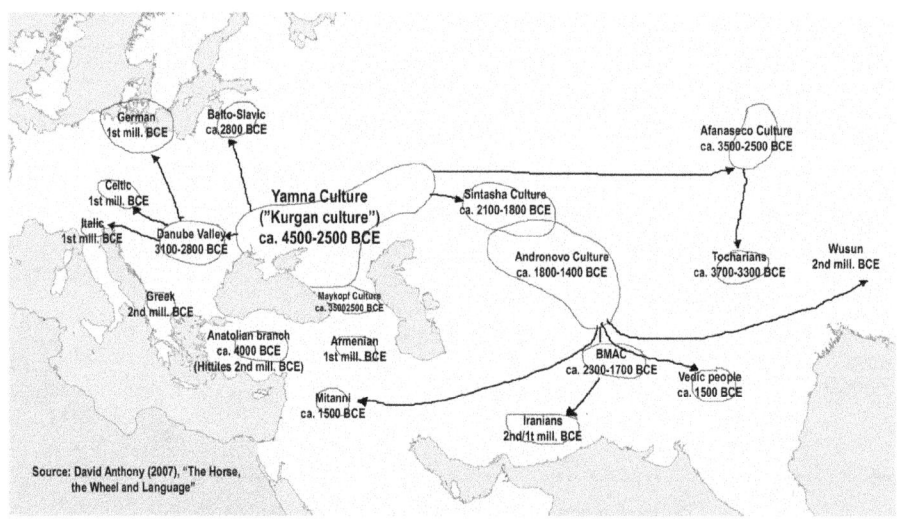

Map of a proposed spread of Indo-European language
and culture according to the Steppe hypothesis.

But the question remains whether the steppes were the first place where Indo-European was spoken, or whether it originated further back in time, elsewhere. It's possible that both the Anatolian and Steppe hypotheses are true, and that Indo-European language expanded out of Anatolia with the first farmers, experiencing a second major wave of expansion thousands of years later with migrants from the steppes.

However, the Anatolian and Steppe hypotheses are not the only theories out there; they are just the two most commonly considered. I personally suspect that Indo-European language, religion, and culture originates much further back in time (sometime prior to 9,700 BC) as indicated in Indo-European traditions. So to me, what the following studies indicate is where and when Indo-European language is evidenced as being spoken after 9,700 BC, providing valuable insights as to where the Religion and Lost Civilization of the Sun may have spread.

This first study supports the Anatolian hypothesis.

"There are two competing hypotheses for the origin of the Indo-European language family. The conventional view places the homeland in the Pontic steppes about 6000 years ago. An alternative hypothesis claims that the languages spread from Anatolia with the expansion of farming 8000 to 9500 years ago. We used Bayesian phylogeographic approaches, together with basic vocabulary data from 103 ancient and contemporary Indo-European languages, to explicitly model the expansion of the family and test these hypotheses. We found decisive support for an Anatolian origin over a steppe origin. Both the interred timing and root location of the Indo-European language trees fit with an agricultural expansion from Anatolia beginning 8000 to 9500 years ago. These results highlight the critical role that phylogeographic inference can play in resolving debates about human prehistory."[19]

~ MAPPING THE ORIGINS AND EXPANSION OF THE INDO-EUROPEAN LANGUAGE FAMILY BY REMCO BOUCKAERT ET AL. REPRINTED WITH PERMISSION FROM AAAS.

A similar study by two authors of the study above, Gray and Atkinson, supports both the Anatolian and Steppe hypotheses, as they found evidence that Indo-European languages originated in Anatolia, but experienced a major divergence coinciding with later migrations from the steppe. In their study they analyzed a matrix of eighty-seven languages using "computational methods derived from evolutionary biology." Essentially, they looked at languages and the way they mutate as though they were genes. They found the initial divergence of Indo-European languages must have occurred around 7,800-5,800 BC, and that the now dead Hittite language of Anatolia was the most senior of the Indo-European language family.[20] Their results showed the:

"[...] Hittite lineage diverging from Proto-Indo-European around 8,700 years BP [before present], perhaps reflecting the initial migration out of Anatolia. Tocharian, and the Greco-Armenian lineages are shown as distinct by 7,000 years BP, with all other major groups formed by 5,000 years BP. This scenario is consistent with recent genetic studies supporting a Neolithic, Near Eastern contribution to the European gene pool. The consensus tree also shows evidence of a period of rapid divergence giving rise to the Italic, Celtic, Balto-Slavic and perhaps Indo-Iranian families that is intriguingly close to the time suggested for a possible Kurgan expansion [from the steppe]. Thus, as observed by Cavalli-Sforza et al., these hypotheses need not be mutually exclusive."[21]

~ LANGUAGE-TREE DIVERGENCE TIMES SUPPORT THE ANATOLIAN THEORY OF INDO-EUROPEAN ORIGIN BY RUSSEL GRAY AND QUENTIN ATKINSON. REPRINTED WITH PERMISSION FROM SPRINGER NATURE.

A study by Gamkrelidze and Ivanov also supports an Anatolian origin, as they found a frequency of words in Proto-Indo-European that describe a mountainous landscape, which they say fits the location of eastern Anatolia and Transcaucasia, backed by the Caucasus Mountains, and not the flat and featureless landscape of the steppe. They also found that the consonants of Proto-Indo-European are closer to those of the Germanic, Armenian, and Hittite child languages than to Sanskrit, which is the reverse of what had been previously thought.[22] They concluded that the landscape described by the Indo-European protolanguage lies somewhere around the southern shores of the Black Sea curving east across Anatolia, and north to the Caucasus Mountains.[23]

Armenian scholars are also contributing research to the field in support of the theory that the origin of the ancient homeland of Indo-European civilization and language was the Armenian/Caucasus region.

"According to studies in the Armenian Highlands and in surrounding territories Armenian used to be a spoken language more than 9000 years ago. New studies have come to testify that these surrounding territories were also the ancestral Homeland of Arian tribes, the ancestors of Indo-Europeans. From then on, these tribes started moving from their Homeland, the Armenian Highlands, and its surrounding territories, to countries where they live at present on territories between Europe and India. The ancient maps of the world, also testify that Armenians (hay-armens) are the ancient inhabitants of South Western Asia, and that Armenia is one of the ancient countries of the world."[24]

~ ANCIENT WRITTEN SOURCES OF EUROPEAN NATIONS ABOUT THEIR ANCESTRAL HOMELAND—ARMENIA AND ARMENIANS BY ANGELA TERYAN

The supreme symbol of divinity in Armenia was the sun, and a profusion of solar symbols have been found in Armenia, including petroglyphs of the swastika and solar cross dating from the seventh to the fifth millennium BC.[25]

"According to studies a great many words in Armenian as well as in other Indo-European languages, have the root ar, which is the name of the God, in them. Other ancient Armenian words like arev (sun), arpi (dawn), arshaluys (dawning), arusyak (dawn), artsat (silver), aragil (stork), etc., that have the meaning of light, sparkle and white, allow us to say that primarily Ar meant light. Ar is always present (whether overtly or covertly) in the Armenian language and in the consciousness of each Armenian as well as in Arian tribes. Ar is the Creator, Space, Light, Heaven and Earth, God, bright mind, culture, art, flora and fauna, some personal and geographical names, and a mythological hero...

It should also be mentioned that for Armenians Ar, the god, was identical with the Sun-god. Without the existence of this god there would be no people, no nature, no flora and fauna on Earth."[26]

~ ANCIENT WRITTEN SOURCES OF EUROPEAN NATIONS ABOUT THEIR ANCESTRAL HOMELAND—ARMENIA AND ARMENIANS BY ANGELA TERYAN

Interestingly, one of the leading geneticists in the groundbreaking 2015 study that almost certainly confirmed that people from the steppes spread Indo-European languages,[27] wrote in 2018 that the available genetic and linguistic evidence so far indicated to him that Indo-European languages likely originated among a population living in Iran or Armenia.

"This suggests to me that the most likely location of the population that first spoke an Indo-European language was south of the Caucasus Mountains, perhaps in present-day Iran or Armenia, because ancient DNA from people who lived there matches what we would expect for a source population both for the Yamnaya and for ancient Anatolians. If this scenario is right the population sent one branch up into the steppe-mixing with steppe hunter-gatherers in a one-to-one ratio to become the Yamnaya as described earlier - and another to Anatolia to found the ancestors of people there who spoke languages such as Hittite."[28]

~ DAVID REICH, WHO WE ARE AND HOW WE GOT HERE

Further evidence of interest has come to light, which could possibly lend support to the Anatolian hypothesis, though it is not conclusive. Symbols from Göbekli Tepe have been identified in the script of an ancient Indo-European speaking people who lived in Anatolia between approximately 2,000 BC and 900 BC in a study by Robert Schoch and Manu Seyfzadeh. They identified "at least four symbols directly related to iconography found at Göbekli Tepe" in the hieroglyphic script of the extinct Luwian people, who spoke Luwian—an Indo-European language within the Anatolian branch of languages, closely related to Hittite. Among the matching symbols, Schoch and Seyfzadeh found that one carved on a pillar at Göbekli Tepe was "almost identical" to the Luwian icon for "god." The authors argue therefore, that the T-shaped pillars of Göbekli Tepe were meant to symbolize a god or gods.[29] These similarities indicate some kind of religious and linguistic continuity in the region possibly stretching back to 9,600 BC, which is remarkable, given that Göbekli Tepe was intentionally buried at around 8,000 BC and not unearthed again until 1994. However, there are other sites that clearly resemble Göbekli Tepe, and were built sometime during the first millennium BC. They are called Taulas, and are located on the island of Menorca,[30] which today is part of Spain (the more ancient megalithic temples of Malta also share similarities, though less obviously); this shows that some continuity in the tradition of Göbekli Tepe was maintained. It's unknown how and why these similarities exist, but it's certainly interesting that an Indo-European speaking people in Anatolia would use such a symbol for one of their most important words.

Indo-European in Eastern Europe

Currently, the earliest known forms of writing in the world (though contested) are found among the Iron Gates Mesolithic (which includes the site of Lepenski Vir) and Vinča cultures.[31] The artifacts that bear writing date back to 5,500 BC in both these cultures.[32] [33] The researcher Michel Gérald Boutet has claimed to have deciphered them using Proto-Indo-European,[34] revealing the peoples of these cultures may have spoken an Indo-European language.

> "In my opinion, as I have demonstrated, the Inscriptions of the Danube civilization can be successfully translated when using a reconstructed proto-alphabet obtained from a comparative study of the oldest known models and applying it to the Proto-Indo-European lexicon. Therefore, no need for a Rosetta Stone in order to find the underlying language. And, if you honestly look at it, you can't discount it. It was long believed that the Old Europeans of the Lower Danube River Basin had little to do with the Indo-European peoples who, according to the Kurgan theory of Gimbutas (1956), resided much further east in the Steppes region above the Black Sea. It now seems that they developed a sophisticated literate society which they diffused around the Black Sea territories. At least, this is what can be concluded."[35]
>
> ~ MICHEL GÉRALD BOUTET

Boutet's research, if correct, suggests that Indo-European language existed and spread earlier than the Steppe hypothesis allows. Found among the oldest Vinča inscriptions is the symbol of the swastika,[36] which was one of the most prominent symbols of Indo-European religion.

A Vinča bowl engraved with what Boutet has interpreted as the Indo-European word for sun, "Suelua."[37]

Indo-European in Ancient Greece

The Linear B script used by the Mycenaeans of Greece.

The script of the Vinča culture is possibly related to the scripts of both the Mycenaeans of ancient Greece and the Minoans of Crete. The Mycenaeans were the first distinctively Greek civilization; they were preceded by the Minoans who inhabited Crete and other nearby islands, although the two civilizations existed together for a time, before Minoan civilization collapsed. The script used by the Mycenaeans is called Linear B, while that used by the Minoans is called Linear A. Linear B has been deciphered, and is considered the first written record of the Hellenic branch of Indo-European languages (which includes Greek), while Linear A is considered undeciphered. However, Dr. Gareth Alun Owens, a British-Greek academic who is well-known for his studies of Linear A and B, "postulates that the phonetic values of ninety-percent of Linear A characters correspond to those of Linear B figures of similar appearance."[38] Owens believes the language of the Minoans, expressed using Linear A, was also Indo-European, stating "we recognise a clear relationship between Linear A and Sanskrit, the ancient language of India. There is also a connection to Hittite and Armenian. This relationship allows us to place the Minoan language among the so-called Indo-European languages."[39] Genetically, the Mycenaeans are largely similar to the Minoans (with an added steppe component).[40] And both Linear A and B share similarities with the script of the much earlier Vinča culture,[41] which as mentioned in the previous section, may have expressed Proto-Indo-European.

The Minoans also have numerous cultural and religious similarities with the ancient Indus Valley Civilization in India,[42] where Sanskrit, an Indo-European language, was also possibly spoken, and the kinship of Minoan language to Indo-European languages, particularly to Sanskrit, lends further support to this. According to the blogger Bibhu Dev Misra, some of the Linear A signs look exactly like those of the Indus script. Additionally, Astrid van den Kerkhof and Peter Rem, of the Delft University of Technology in the Netherlands, have translated a number of Minoan names using Sanskrit, such as the name of the legendary judge King Minos using the Sanskrit stem "mino/minu" which means "to judge."[43]

It's very likely, then, that the language of the Minoans and Mycenaeans, the earliest known literate civilizations of Greece, was Indo-European.

Indo-European in Central and South America

Maya script.

Scholars have identified similarities between Indo-European languages and ancient languages in Central and South America, so much so, that some have claimed they must belong to the Indo-European branch of languages, having diverged at some distant time in the past.

The German scholar Erhard Landmann has found numerous similarities between one of the languages of the Maya called K'iche', and that of the Aztecs called Nahuatl, with Old High German, and provides extensive comparisons as evidence in his book *Weltbilderschütterung*, first published in 1993.[44] Landmann states that even the word K'iche' is related to the Old High German word Duiche/Duisce, which became the German word Deutsch, meaning German.[45] The Maya terms used to refer to their hieroglyphic signs are "vuoh, tap" and "buoh, tap," which possibly correlates to the Old High German word "buohstap" that became the German word "buchstabe" meaning "letter."[46]

Landmann is not the first or only person to find such similarities. A well-known Maya researcher, called Charles Étienne Brasseur de Bourbourg, found similarities between K'iche' and his native Flemish language, which is a Germanic language related to Old High German. In his book *Grammaire de la Langue Quichée* (Grammar of the K'iche' Language) published in 1862, he listed dozens of similarities between German and K'iche' words, both in phonetics and meaning.[47]

On the surface, this seems untenable, as the first inscriptions in Maya script are dated to 300-200 BC,[48] but Old High German isn't attested until AD 750 in Europe (and even then was a term that encompassed a number of Germanic dialects[49]). However, all Germanic languages, including Old High German, are thought to derive from Proto-Germanic, which in turn derived from Proto-Indo-European. Both Proto-Germanic and Proto-Indo-European are reconstructed languages. That is, there are no surviving speakers of these languages, nor any known inscriptions or texts written in them. They have been put together by linguists by comparing related Indo-European languages to one another. Old High German is one of the first attested Germanic languages, but Germanic language itself is much older. Scholars may have found similarities between languages using Old High German or Flemish, because they are the languages they are most familiar with, and are attested.

A number of languages of the Americas have also been compared to other Indo-European languages, namely Sanskrit and Old Norse.

The Guna/Kuna people are native to the jungles of Panama, and are discussed further on. A study conducted in 1924-1925 found that their language had a structure like Sanskrit and shared over sixty words with Old Norse.[50]

Thomas Stewart Denison (1848-1911), who was a highly respected nineteenth century American publisher, philologist, educator, and writer, authored a number of books comparing the language of the Aztecs (and Toltecs), called Nahuatl, to Indo-European languages. He published an extensive vocabulary of Nahuatl, and examined around thirty languages in order to understand it, which became his life's quest. In doing so, he found Nahuatl was closest to Sanskrit, although he claimed it must have been older than Sanskrit and originated from a time before Indo-European languages diverged.[51] Earlier, in 1861, Professor Sir E. B. Tylor of Oxford University, writing in his book *Anahuac*, had found sixty-four Mexican words that were comparable to Sanskrit.[52]

The Hopi people of the North American southwest speak a language that belongs to the same family of languages as Nahuatl, called Uto-Aztecan.[53] This may be why the researcher Gene Matlock has found many similarities between Hopi words and Sanskrit, and identifies the Hopi as migrants from Central Asia.[54] Frank Waters, who spent much of three years living in a Hopi house and recording their traditions from thirty of their elders, found numerous similarities between their religion and that of Hinduism, as well as to customs of the Aztecs and Maya.[55]

Vicente Fidel López was an Argentinian historian, lawyer, and prominent politician (serving as national deputy and Minister of Finance). Writing in 1871, after ten years of research, he determined that Quechua, the language of the Inca, was an Indo-European language, which showed closest affinity to Sanskrit.[56] As the blogger Neeta Raina has pointed out, even the name Peru means "sun" or "golden mountain" in Sanskrit. The name of the greatest sun temple of the Inca, called Coricancha/Korikancha, can also be translated using Sanskrit. Kancha means "gold" or "golden" or "that which pertains to the Sun," and to "all that glitters," likely describing the temple, which was famously decorated with large amounts of gold and jewels. Korit, as Raina says, means "'scraped out' or 'budded from' or 'sprouted from' and may refer to the sculpted life size statues of animals and plants of pure gold that decorated the temple complex."[57] As mentioned earlier, Coricancha was decorated similarly to the Sun Temple of Multan in India, and this no longer seems such a strange connection. Likewise, many other important religious terms in Quechua can be translated using Sanskrit,[58] and today there are Vedic practitioners who claim to have identified over one thousand Sanskrit roots in Quechua, as well as numerous similarities between the ancient religions of the speakers of these two languages.[59]

The Peruvian doctor Pablo Patrón Faustos, writing in 1907, instead found that Quechua and Aymara (the language of the indigenous peoples of the Andean Altiplano around Lake Titicaca), as well as many Native North American languages, shared similarities with Sumerian and Akkadian (a Semitic language that partly converged with Sumerian).[60]

There are a number of possible scenarios which could explain why Sanskrit and Sumerian words may be found in Quechua, as speakers of Sumerian may have also influenced it, and as it turns out, Sumerian, and to a lesser extent Akkadian, both contain Indo-European words as explained next.

The similarities between these languages don't exist in isolation, as these cultures share many other things in common, some of which are covered in this book.

Indo-European in Mesopotamia

The Sumerian civilization that flourished in Mesopotamia (now southern Iraq) between 4,500-1,900 BC is considered one of the oldest in the world, and according to academic consensus, was the birthplace of writing (using a script called cuneiform). The language they spoke, called Sumerian, is considered a language isolate, meaning it is not known to be related to any other language.[61]

However, evidence is emerging that Sumerian speakers may have been preceded by Indo-European speakers in the region. The language they spoke has been termed Euphratic.[62]

> "For many decades now, leading Assyriologists have speculated on the existence of an early population in the 4th millennium B.C. that preceded the Sumerians, hitherto generally regarded as the first settlers of the region. Evidence for such a population comes from place names, the names of deities, technical vocabulary and even from environmental terms. Such speculation has proven fruitless, since no linguistic group or archaeologically attested society could be shown to be related. However, in a number of recent publications

data have been presented that suggest that one such linguistic group is indeed comparable -- the Indo-European family of languages. Polysyllabic terms lacking a Sumerian etymology can be demonstrated to resemble segmentable Indo-European words with comparable meanings. Furthermore, the cuneiform writing system can be shown to preserve traces of Indo-European influence in its sign values and in its sign composition.

If the alleged pre-Sumerian population in Mesopotamia was indeed Indo-European, then it stands to revolutionize our perception of very early Indo-European society [...]. All evidence suggests that they settled in the region as 'peaceful agriculturalists' no different in character from other societies of the Ancient Near East. Although it would be the earliest known Indo-European society by well over a thousand years [...]."[63]

~ UNIVERSITY OF COPENHAGEN

"In a series of recent articles (Whittaker 1998, 2001, 2004, 2004/2005, 2005), evidence based on both lexical and epigraphic data has been put forward suggesting that one major ethnic group contributing to the culture of the Uruk period was Indo-European in speech. This language, which manifests itself in all the areas suspected to have been influenced by a 'foreign' element, has been dubbed Euphratic [...]. Traces of this language can be found preserved primarily in the technical and elite vocabulary of Sumerian and, to a lesser extent, Akkadian, and attest to a prolonged period of intensive contact. It is worth noting that two of the three leading theories on the location of the Indo-European 'homeland,' those of Gamkrelidze and Ivanov (1995 [1984]) and of Renfrew (1987), envision Indo-Europeans in a zone flanking the northern and western reaches of Northern Mesopotamia, namely Transcaucasia and Eastern Anatolia respectively."[64]

~ PROFESSOR GORDON WHITTAKER, UNIVERSITY OF GÖTTINGEN, GERMANY, THE CASE FOR EUPHRATIC

As implied in the excerpts above, these findings have implications for the debate over the origin of Indo-European languages, and support the Anatolian hypothesis.

Indo-European in China

Chinese scholars have also found similarities between Indo-European and the Old Chinese language. A paper by Tsung-tung Chang is devoted to demonstrating the similarities between these languages and how they relate to the founding of civilization in China, saying:

"Considering all these linguistic facts, the thesis presents itself that Old Chinese emerged as a mixed language, though spoken with Proto-Chinese native tongue, using mainly the Proto-Indo-European idiom which seems to have stretched from Mongolia to Europe during the third millennium B.C. in the northern part of the temperate zone.

Historically the emergence of Old Chinese should be connected with the founding of the Chinese Empire by Huang-ti, the Yellow Emperor, with whom the Chinese still identify themselves today. According to Chinese historiography, he was the founder of the first state of China as well as its high civilization. [...] This emperor must have had an appearance of northern white people, as the epithet "Huang-ti" can etymologically be interpreted as "blond heavenly god" [...].

Huang-ti is mentioned also as the founder of Chinese language [...]."[65]

~ TSUNG-TUNG CHANG

Just as Landmann has identified Mayan and Aztec languages as sharing most similarities with Germanic Indo-European language, Chang likewise finds Old Chinese to be most similar to Germanic.[66]

Chang places the founding of the Chinese Empire between 2,700-2,400 BC,[67] which is when a large wave of Indo-European people traveled west to enter Europe. Traveling east to enter China, the Indo-Europeans could account for Chinese civilization being said to have originated from a mountain far in the west—specifically Kunlun Mountain, which likely corresponds to the Kunlun Mountains range that borders the Tarim Basin in China, where Indo-European speakers lived thousands of years ago.

Map showing the Tarim Basin with the Kunlun Mountains (shan) forming its southern border.

He also concludes that the Tibetan language shares commonalities with Indo-European, saying, "I would surmise that Tibetan may have emerged as a mixed language with an aboriginal and Proto-Indo-European substratum and an Altaic superstratum." The Indo-European contribution, he suggests, was likely to have come from the Tocharians[68] (the ancient Indo-European inhabitants of the Tarim Basin in China discussed further on).

Another Chinese scholar, Zhou Jixu, comes to the same conclusion, stating:

> "By combining their own imported cultural factors with those of the native culture, the Huang Di people gradually developed a splendid new civilization in the Xia, Shang, and Zhou dynasties. They superseded the original native people to take the leading role on the stage of Chinese history. That the Huang Di nation was a branch of the archaic Indo-European people is one of the most remarkable facts thus far known to human history. But a large number of Indo-European words in Old Chinese language clearly attest to this fact.
>
> [...] The European people from the west of the central Asian steppe brought new cultural components to the Yellow River valley in about 2300 BC. They combined their advanced techniques, such as bronze metallurgy, metal tools and arms, and chariot and tamed horses, with the native developed agricultural culture in the area of the Yellow River and the Yangtze River. This combination grew into the splendid civilizations of the Xia, Shang, and Zhou dynasties."[69]
>
> ~ ZHOU JIXU

Zhou Jixu has written a number of papers demonstrating the similarities between the Old Chinese and Proto-Indo-European languages.[70] This includes the correspondence between the highest god in Proto-Indo-European, called Dyeus, to the great god Tees in China. Interestingly, Tees was worshiped in China every midwinter with a sacred fire ritual, as the smoke was thought to reach up into his heavenly abode.[71] This reveals that the winter solstice was perhaps the most important sacred day of the year, celebrated with fire, which is considered divine and related to the sun in Indo-European religion (and the Religion of the Sun), with the smoke used to carry prayers and wishes to heaven, as is the ancient Vedic/Indo-European religion in India. Today, the winter solstice is still celebrated as one of the most important festivals of the year in China, where it is called Dongzhi.

The earliest Chinese dynasties conquered and absorbed the earlier agricultural Yangshao culture of the Yellow River valley in China, which existed from around 5,000-4,000 BC.[72] The Yangshao culture shares a number of similarities with the Cucuteni-Trypillia culture of Eastern Europe,[73] which as we've seen earlier, may have spoken an Indo-European language. The Cucuteni-Trypillia are the first culture known to use the yin yang symbol,[74] [75] now famous in China, and this is more evidence for the presence of related people in both places. It appears that both phases of Chinese civilization may be connected to Indo-European language speakers.

Similarities between the Scripts of Ancient India and Easter Island

The Indus script is the name given to the writing system used by the Indus Valley Civilization between 3,500-1,900 BC—now mostly located in Pakistan though considered part of India's ancient religious and cultural heritage.

Current academic consensus maintains that the Indus script remains undeciphered as there is no way to verify any proposed translation.[76] However, a decipherment was proposed by independent researcher Suzanne Redalia Sullivan in 2011 using Sanskrit, which is an Indo-European language,[77] [78] and which I personally find compelling.

The builders of the megalithic statues on Easter Island used a hieroglyphic script called Rongorongo, which to date, also remains untranslated. However, it shares numerous similarities with the Indus script.[79] To be clear, the Rongorongo and Indus scripts contain over fifty glyphs that are not just similar, they are *essentially identical*, and were discovered to have used identical phrases to one another.[80] Additionally, both the Indus script and Rongorongo have been found to be written boustrophedonically (using a form of bidirectional writing).[81] One of the first European expeditions to Easter Island found that the language spoken there was not Polynesian and was unidentifiable.[82]

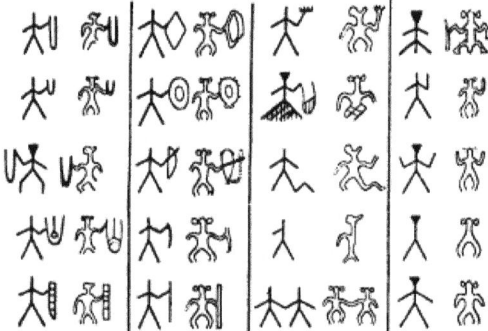

Just one small comparison of Indus script on the left of each column, to Rongorongo on the right.

Similarities have also been found between Indus script and ancient petroglyphs in Brazil,[83] which feature Celtiberian characters[84] (related to runes), as well as to runes themselves.[85] As to the origin of the Indus script, Sullivan believes it derives from even earlier writing systems, saying "it is evident that Indus Script [...] has borrowed signs from other, older writing systems, such as Proto-Canaanite Script, Sumerian pre-cuniform, and an Indus script-like writing system used by Dravidian speakers."[86]

Runes and the Earliest Forms of Writing

Runes are the letters of an alphabet that was used to write the Germanic branch of Indo-European languages; the earliest runic inscriptions date to

AD 150. They are generally believed to derive from the alphabet used by the ancient Phoenicians. However, there is evidence that both the runic and Phoenician alphabets derive from a far more ancient source.

> "It seems now fairly clear that there were three systems of writing in Egypt, and each of these is first known with a different race. The geometrical marks of the alphabetic system appear with the first prehistoric people, who seem to have been Libyans. They belonged to the west, and were the source of all the Mediterranean alphabets... the long priority of alphabetic signs in Egypt leaves the tradition of Phoenician origin [of the alphabet] out of the case... Even Diodorus [Siculus] did not believe in it... When we see how widespread was the full alphabet, it is plain that the Phoenician hold only a small part of the whole. There are 23 letters that were used in Egypt, Karia, and Spain, all unknown in Phoenicia. There were 10 other letters which the South Arabian had in common with the Mediterranean and the Runes of Northern Europe, yet all unknown in Phoenicia. It seems obvious that there was a very widespread alphabet, from which at a much later time the Phoenician selection was formed."[87]

~ SIR FLINDERS PETRIE (ONE OF THE MOST FAMOUS AND RESPECTED EGYPTOLOGISTS)

The prehistoric Libyans that Petrie identifies as the origin of the first alphabetical signs are discussed further on.

The earliest alphabetic writing in the world is considered to be Proto-Sinaitic script found in Egypt, which was based on ancient Egyptian hieroglyphs, and is dated to between 1,850-1,550 BC. It's said to have given rise to the Phoenician alphabet, which in turn gave rise to many others, including the Greek alphabet, followed by the Etruscan, which gave rise to the Latin (the alphabet we use today).[88] Similarities have also been found between Phoenician and the Indus script.[89]

However, artifacts of the Vinča culture dated to around 5,000 BC include signs that are identical to the form of runes.[90] There are also Vinča symbols that are the same or similar to those of Ogham and Linear B. Thus, these

Euboenisk-Griska	Hefðbundin Etrúiska	Forn Etrúiska	Siðari Etrúiska	Latina	Hljóð-gildi
A A	A	A	A	A	[a]
B	ﻮ			B	[b]
< C	↑	)	)	C G	[k]
D	◁			D	[d]
ᖴE	Ǝ	Ǝ	Ǝ	E	[e]
F	↑	↑	↑	F	[w]
I	I	I	⍗	(Z)	[z]
⊟H	⊟	⊟	⊟⊘	H	[h]
⊕⊗O	⊗	⊗O	⊙O		[tʰ]
I	I	I	I	I	[i]
K	⅄	⅄		K	[k]
L	↲	↲	↲	L	[l]
ᛙM	ᛞ	ᛞ	ᛙ	M	[m]
ᛘN	ᛘ	ᛘ	ᛘ	N	[n]
⌶	⊞				[s]
O	O	O		O	[o]
Γ	↑	↑	↑	P	[p]
M	M	M	M		[ʃ]
ᛩ	ᛩ	ᛩ		Q	[q]
P	◁	q	◁	R	[r]
ᛋ	ᛋ	ᛇ	ᛇ	S	[s]
T	T	T	ᛏᚱ	T	[t]
ᚢVY	Y	Y	V	V	[u]
X	X	X			[ks]
Φ⏀	φ	Φ	⏀		[pʰ]
ᚤᚢ	Y	Y	ᚤ		[kʰ]
		(88)	8		[f]

Characters of the Etruscan language, which was the basis for Latin. Anyone familiar with runes will recognize some among the Etruscan letters.

ancient alphabets may derive from a single ancient source, which would be the most ancient known form of writing in the world. Tellingly, the derivatives of this writing system were used by the Lost Civilization of the Sun which preserved the memory, and thus possibly the system of writing, originally taught by the wisdom bringers.

Language Similarities across the World

While some may brush off the linguistic similarities presented here as mere coincidence, the Swiss linguist Dr. Arnold Wadler stated that the probability of having the same root word with the same meaning in unrelated languages is 1 in 4.9-11.025 billion.[91] He devoted decades of his life to the study of the similarities between world languages, and found many between those that are considered unrelated, often in terms to do with the Religion of the Sun.[92]

The presence of related scripts and languages across these sun-worshiping cultures suggests that they were part of the same global culture and civilization that had been founded or influenced by people carrying the same religion.

EVIDENCE OF SEAFARING CAPABILITY

Many people don't think that the sun-worshiping civilizations of the ancient world, separated by oceans, were connected, because they believe that ancient people didn't have the ability to make transoceanic journeys. However, there is plenty of evidence to show that they did.

Apart from the cultural, religious, linguistic, and genetic evidence for transoceanic contact, there are also ancient depictions of seafaring ships, descriptions of ocean travel, and evidence for maritime trade. The evidence could fill a book in itself, so here are just some examples which relate to the spread of the Religion of the Sun.

In many places the wisdom bringers were said to have traveled, and the Lost Civilization of the Sun spread, there are depictions of ships, usually made of reeds, carrying the sun. Sometimes these ships are the purely mythological vehicle of the sun which it uses to cross the sky, but sometimes they are large, realistic reed boats, with wisdom bringers, cargo, and sometimes numerous people on board, along with the sun or sun god.

In ancient Egypt, a boat is used to sail the sun god Ra through the hours of the day and night, and descriptions of the sun traveling across water by boat is found in Egypt's earliest known texts, the Pyramid Texts.

In the Vedas, ships (and horses) are used as metaphorical and symbolic vehicles of the sun.[93]

> "The Sun mounted the luminous ocean, having yoked his straight-backed horses. The wise have led him like a ship through the water. [...] By this vessel may we gain the protection of the Gods, by this vessel may we cross over all narrowness (V.45.10-11)."[94]

However, even in this excerpt, the ship of the sun is also a vessel by which people can travel.

The Prose Edda of Germanic/Nordic tradition refers to a sun ship, and sun ships are carved into Bronze Age petroglyphs in Scandinavia. They were carved as petroglyphs on Easter Island,[95] and were also depicted in Sumer and in artifacts of the Phoenicians. Sun ships clearly had a religious significance, but were also used practically.

> "Reed ships with the sun god, bird-men, and other deities on board and sometimes with deck structures, horned cattle, and other evidence of major dimensions are extremely common on the oldest Sumerian seals and occasionally occur as far up the twin rivers as the Hittite territory of southern Turkey. [...]
>
> Recently a Phoenician jar, decorated with realistic reliefs of reed boats carrying a radiating sun on deck, was found by divers off the ancient Phoenician port of Cadiz on the Atlantic coast of Spain."[96]
>
> ~ THOR HEYERDAHL, EARLY MAN AND THE OCEAN

The depictions of sun ships made of reeds are very ancient. In Azerbaijan, a country in the Caucasus region, there are some of the oldest known petroglyphs in the world—in total there are more than six thousand, the oldest of which are believed to be forty thousand years old.[97] Among them are numerous depictions of boats of three types, including those made of reeds with the sun at their prow—the oldest of these dates to between 10,000 and 7,000 BC, making them the oldest known images of reed boats and sun ships in the world.[98]

Similar petroglyphs of reed boats have been found in Egypt and date to between 8,000 and 5,000 BC,[99] and were also found on Easter Island,[100] dating to unknown antiquity.

AZERBAIJAN   **EGYPT**   **SWEDEN**

Left: Boat petroglyph in Gobustan in Azerbaijan with the sun at the prow. Middle: Ancient Egyptian boat with the sun also at the prow. Right: Drawing of petroglyph found in Sweden depicting a boat carrying the sun.

> "Reed boats and reed boat illustrations have been found throughout the Mediterranean from Mesopotamia, Egypt, the coasts of present-day Syria, Lebanon, and Israel by way of Cyprus, Crete, Corfu, Malta,

Italy, Sardinia, Libya, Algeria, and out through the Straits of Gibraltar to the Atlantic coast of Morocco. [...]

Such reed boats have been in sporadic use from Mesopotamia to Atlantic Morocco until the present century, while rock carvings and cliff paintings from Egypt and the Algerian Sahara show that they were already in use five, six, or perhaps seven thousand years ago. [...]

One is struck by the fact that the majority of these sickle-shaped vessels have a numerous crew, sometimes fifty men or more. In addition to the double steering oar, some show forty or more rowing oars in the water, while a considerable number have mast and rigging and in many cases a large hoisted sail. The great dimensions of these vessels are indicated not only by the large number of men and oars, but also by the fact that horned cattle and other large animals are dwarfed on their decks."[101]

~ THOR HEYERDAHL, EARLY MAN AND THE OCEAN

Reed boats are evidenced as being the oldest form of sea-going vessel in the world, having many advantages over wooden planked ships that were invented and used much later.

"When the artist employed by the early pharaohs depicted legendary vessels assigned to the period of the early gods and first divine ancestors of man, these were invariably shown as sickle-shaped reed boats constructed of papyrus stems lashed together and commonly terminating with a symbolic papyrus flower at each gracefully up curved end. Here, too, the sun-god, bird-headed deities, and other ancestral culture heroes of all kinds were invariably shown performing all their water travel on papyrus vessels, never on wooden craft. The ancient artists show only the later historic pharaohs using wooden boats side by side with the older form of papyrus vessel and by the second millennium B.C. nearly all the larger ships appeared to be of sewn planks; only hunting vessels and poor men's craft continued to be of bundled papyrus. [...]

A review of the evidence gained from predynastic boat designs incised on cliffs from Egypt to Algeria, from subsequent Mesopotamian and Mediterranean art, from the sequence of ships as recorded by the artists of the pharaohs, from the oldest buried vessels like the papyri-form wooden ship of Cheops, and from discoveries made during experiments with papyrus boats in the open ocean, shows that the planked ship with hull was chronologically secondary to the reed boat in serving man in deep-sea navigation."[102]

~ THOR HEYERDAHL, EARLY MAN AND THE OCEAN

A reed boat on Lake Titicaca in Peru, where the wisdom bringer Viracocha is said to have traveled and established his capital. Reed boats are still made and used by the local people today.

Further evidence suggests that the inhabitants of ancient Egypt could make voyages across the ocean in remote prehistory, long before the first dynasties at around 3,000 BC. This includes a fleet of ships of "advanced design capable of riding out the most powerful waves and the worst weather of the open seas" dated to 3,000 BC found buried near the ancient site of Abydos,[103] the location of the Osireion temple (associated with the wisdom bringer Osiris).

> "Moreover I knew that the earliest wall paintings found in the Nile Valley, dating back perhaps as much as 1500 years before the burial of the Abydos fleet (to around 4500 BC) showed the same long, sleek, high-prowed vessels in action. [...]
>
> Could an experienced race of ancient seafarers have become involved with the indigenous inhabitants of the Nile Valley at some indeterminate period before the official beginning of history at around 3000 BC?"[104]
>
> ~ GRAHAM HANCOCK, FINGERPRINTS OF THE GODS

Other evidence includes the discovery in Egypt of an ancient seaside port (currently the most ancient known and accepted to mainstream academia) dated to 2,500 BC,[105] and references in the most ancient texts of Egypt—including the Pyramid Texts—to large and sophisticated ships.[106]

A port dated to the same time has been discovered at one of the major cities of the Indus Valley Civilization in Pakistan, which is known to have been used to conduct maritime trade with Mesopotamia.

> "A Mohenjo Daro seal depicted a reed ship with cabin, bipod mast, and twin rudder oars, just like those in ancient Sumer and Egypt

[...]. Sailing their reed ships between Mesopotamia, Bahrain, and the Indus Valley, the merchant mariners of old could have carried tons of cargo [...]."[107]

~ THOR HEYERDAHL, THE MALDIVE MYSTERY

Seal from Mohenjo Daro in the Indus Valley
depicting a reed boat with land-finding birds on board.

Writing in his book *Gods, Sages and Kings*, David Frawley demonstrates that the writers of the Vedas referenced oceans and ocean-going ships numerous times, stating that "the Vedas are a product of a maritime culture."[108]

"The modern, generally Western idea, is that the Rig Veda is the product of a nomadic people invading India from the northwest, who, therefore, could not have known anything of the sea. [...] However, this idea does not come from the Veda itself. [...] Even a modern scholar like Griffith, though he clearly does not allow that the early Vedic people had any contact with the ocean, is compelled to translate various Vedic terms as 'ocean' or 'sea' nearly a hundred times in his translation of the text. [...] The image of the ocean permeates the entire text of the Rig Veda. [...] The scope of Vedic geography is quite large [...]. Yet the oceanic symbolism appears to be the most common."[109]

~ DAVID FRAWLEY, GODS, SAGES AND KINGS

Frawley goes on to demonstrate that references in the Vedas indicate the Vedic people may have had colonies across the ocean, with which they traded,[110] and that "the Vedic people in part were refugees from some hostile land across the sea."[111]

"Like the story of Bhujyu, their story gives the image of Vedic ancestors as saved across the sea or flood by the grace of the Gods. In this regard the Vedic Manu is himself a flood figure and he may be related to such early Vedic ancestors."[112]

~ DAVID FRAWLEY, GODS, SAGES AND KINGS

Here is an excerpt from the Vedas describing long migrations across water, needing "constant oars and quarters":

"Agni, give us a ship for our vehicle and house, with constant oars and quarters, which can take across our heroes and benefactors and our people to safety (I.140.12)."[113]

Sanchoniatho, the Phoenician historian who lived around 1,200 BC, said that Byblos, Lebanon's first city, was founded by a divine race who had better ships than they (the Phoenicians are supposedly the first civilization in the world to have seafaring ships).[114] There is evidence that this pre-Phoenician culture navigated the Mediterranean and the shores of the Atlantic at least as early as 4,500 BC, perhaps being the source of or contributing to the megalithic cultures in Malta, Iberia, Ireland, and mainland Britain.[115]

> "From the Greek historians we learn that the Phoenicians were the first to build sailing vessels and navigate the open sea. Today, we know, thanks to archaeology, that this was only what the Greeks believed. Ships had sailed the seas off the shores of Lebanon and Egypt long before Phoenician times. Prepharonic petroglyphs and pottery decoration from Egypt illustrate large reed ships with double cabins, sail, and rigging. And when the first splendid Hittite sun-temples were recovered from under the sand in Asia Minor, tall ships with sails were found carved in relief on the stone walls. They had been carved centuries before Phoenician times and yet they had sails and rigging as complex as those used millennia later on the caravels of Christopher Columbus."[116]
>
> ~ THOR HEYERDAHL, THE MALDIVE MYSTERY

In short, ancient depictions and/or descriptions of sun ships can be found in the Caucasus, Egypt, Mesopotamia, Scandinavia, Easter Island, and India, and reed ships (often carrying the sun/sun god and wisdom bringers) in the Caucasus, Egypt, Mesopotamia, Anatolia, the Mediterranean, the Indus Valley, Libya, Morocco, Peru, Bolivia, and Easter Island, revealing a connection between the ancient sun-worshiping civilizations that existed in these places.

> "The ocean-going reed ship is not the only one of the specialized culture traits common to the pre-European civilizations on both sides of the Atlantic which is difficult to explain by theories of independent invention. It is the one culture element, however, that could explain how the other transatlantic parallels were born."[117]
>
> ~ THOR HEYERDAHL, EARLY MAN AND THE OCEAN

It's likely that when the wisdom bringers and those of the Lost Civilization of the Sun traveled or migrated anywhere, they raised the banner of the sun, in both seeking to spread the knowledge of the Religion of the Sun, and in securing the protection of divinity (as the sun) on their long and treacherous journeys across the ocean in reed ships.

Ships made of reeds disintegrate rapidly, and leave no archaeological trace behind. What would remain are ancient depictions of them, traditions of boat making using reeds, and evidence for cultural, religious, linguistic, and genetic exchange across continents—which is exactly what we find.

THOR HEYERDAHL

Thor Heyerdahl pictured with statues of the wisdom bringers from South America. This photo was taken in 1955 when he was forty years old.

In support of the extensive archaeological, textual, genetic, and historical evidence of a lost global civilization that had seafaring capabilities are the expeditions of Thor Heyerdahl.

Thor Heyerdahl (1914-2002) is described as "one of history's most famous explorers."[118] He conducted a number of archaeological excavations and expeditions in different parts of the world. Most famously, he crossed oceans using reed and balsa boats made according to ancient designs, in order to prove conclusively that ancient people could have crossed the oceans in ancient times, and thus diffused their culture and civilization throughout disparate parts of the world.

There is perhaps no single person who has done more to research the Lost Civilization of the Sun than Thor Heyerdahl, even though he never called it this nor stated his purpose as such. He hinted at something like it however, when he said:

"The sun was the father of all life, the ocean the womb where all life began. Today this is the accepted version of evolution, irrespective of the many varying hypotheses as to the driving force that produced it. Thus modern science has confirmed an old belief, for in the genealogies of the great ancient civilizations, the sun was honored as man's first ancestor. The sun is therefore an important part of the riddle we are going to tackle. [...] By accepting the sun as the father of all life, we give credit to the wisdom or intuition of the people we are about to follow across uncharted seas."[119]

~ THOR HEYERDAHL, EASTER ISLAND: THE MYSTERY SOLVED

"People think I'm just an adventurer. They don't realize that all my projects are related like pearls on a string — that they're part of a single pattern."[120]

~ THOR HEYERDAHL QUOTED BY BETTY BLAIR, THOR HEYERDAHL IN AZERBAIJAN

Thor Heyerdahl photographed during his Kon-Tiki expedition in 1947. The image of the sun god and wisdom bringer Kon-Tiki (Viracocha) is painted on the sail behind him.

His sea voyages included the two "Ra" crossings over the Atlantic Ocean, from the west coast of Africa to the Caribbean region of America. The boats and expeditions were named after the Egyptian sun god Ra, and prove that a wisdom bringer from Egypt like Osiris could have traveled using a reed boat from Egypt to Central and South America, where similar legends of wisdom bringers are found.

They also included the Kon-Tiki expedition, which was made using a balsa wood raft constructed according to ancient methods that crossed the Pacific

Ocean from South America to the Polynesian islands—the same route the sun god Kon/Tiki/Viracocha, the wisdom bringer of Peruvian tradition, is likely to have taken, according to Peruvian and Polynesian legends. The film made of the expedition won an Oscar.

> "This voyage on the 'Kon Tiki' in 1947 was my first experience with a small vessel on the open ocean. From then on, I began organizing archaeological excavations. My first was in 1952 to the Galapagos Islands. The next was to Easter Island in 1955-56. That was the first time I saw carvings of those large sickle-shaped ships. They were the same type as those in ancient Egypt and Mesopotamia."[121]
>
> ~ THOR HEYERDAHL, SCANDINAVIAN ANCESTRY

His Tigris expedition involved building "the largest reed ship to have been made in four thousand years."[122] The aim of this expedition was to "sail between the regions of the three ancient civilizations: Mesopotamia, the Indus Valley and Egypt." Heyerdahl's "objective was to show that they could have had contact via sea routes"[123] in ancient times.

> "I came to the conclusion that the Egyptians who built the pyramids left behind art and technology of an incredibly high level. They would not have continued to build boats made of reeds if they had considered such vessels to be primitive and ineffective. So, I decided that there must be something wrong with our scientific theories. All the literature that I had read at the university had said that boats made of balsam wood would absorb water and sink.
>
> So I went on to prove that these scientific theories were wrong. The Kon Tiki raft kept afloat for 101 days until we arrived in Polynesia. In Egypt it was said at the Papyrus Institute that papyrus reed would absorb water and sink after two weeks. Again, I decided to trust the ancient pharaohs more than modern scientists who have never even seen a papyrus ship. That's how I came to build my first reed boat. Together, with an international crew of seven people, we sailed for two months. The reed boat was still afloat."[124]
>
> ~ THOR HEYERDAHL, SCANDINAVIAN ANCESTRY

Every boat Heyerdahl used to cross the ocean was decorated with a symbol of the sun or sun god. Heyerdahl clearly understood that what connected many seemingly disparate and prehistoric civilizations was a common religion and culture that centered around solar symbols, solar theocracies, and "sun-worship," and that many of the depictions of their ancient vessels were shown "carrying" the sun.

A model of the boat that Thor
Heyerdahl used on his Ra II expedition.

"I believe I've opened the locked door to the hidden evidence that the vessels of antiquity permitted unrestricted voyages in pre-European times and that there is a complex global root relationship between all those rapidly growing civilizations that suddenly grew up with evidence of advanced boat building some 5,000 years ago."[125]

~ THOR HEYERDAHL QUOTED BY BETTY BLAIR, THOR HEYERDAHL IN AZERBAIJAN

"For a long time, I've been puzzled by the fact that three great civilizations surrounding the Arabian peninsula appeared in about 3,000 B.C. as ready-developed, organized dynasties at the same astonishingly high level and all three were remarkably alike. The definite impression is that related priest-kings at that time came from elsewhere with their respective entourages, and imposed their dynasties on areas formerly occupied by more primitive or, at least, culturally far less advanced, tribes. [...]

But where could they have come from? Is there a 'zero hour for civilized man'? I've been convinced for quite some time that the clues to this mystery, no doubt, lie in the prehistoric boat petroglyphs which are found on widely scattered continental shores and islands all over the world and even near dried-out waterways deep inside the Sahara Desert. Petroglyphs and rock paintings of watercraft represent the earliest known illustrations of human architecture and even predate pictures of dwellings or temples. I've seen such sketches from below the equator in Polynesia to above the Arctic Circle in Northern Norway. Everywhere they testify to the fact that boats were of extreme importance to early man as they provided security and transportation millennia before there were roads through the wilderness."[126]

~ THOR HEYERDAHL, THE AZERBAIJAN CONNECTION

Photograph of the reed boat Viracocha II that was built according to ancient designs and sailed between the coast of South America and Easter Island, proving the ancient civilizations in both places could have been founded by the same people and wisdom bringers. The expedition was led by Phil Buck who was inspired by Thor Heyerdahl.

Thor Heyerdahl continued working until his death at the age of eighty-seven in 2002. Interestingly, his very last project was entitled "the search for Odin," which was carried out in the Caucasus region—in the countries of Azerbaijan and Russia. It was an expedition, sadly, he was unable to complete. Heyerdahl's search was for more than Odin though—it was for the very beginnings of civilization. After traveling the world, from Egypt to India, and from Peru to Easter Island and across Polynesia, his search for the origins of the civilization had led him to the Caucasus.

> "To find images of boats that date back to the Mesolithic period (10th–8th millennium BC) in such a place as Gobustan was an important event for the much-travelled Thor Heyerdahl, who claimed that world civilization had existed long before the emergence of the Egyptian, Mesopotamian and Indian cultures and that it had spread via the sea before people started to use overland transport. [...] He said that the Gobustan images of boats were the oldest in the world and that Azerbaijan was the centre of supposed world civilization."[127]
>
> ~ MALAHAT FARAJOVA, BOATS IN ROCK ART OF GOBUSTAN

This appears to be the final conclusion Heyerdahl had reached. He organized excavations looking for this great mother civilization, but ran out of time. In some ways though, he hadn't, as the man who had insisted that civilization was spread and diffused around the world by ancient, "sun-worshiping" seafarers, and had risked his life crossing the ocean in reed boats multiple times to prove it, had found the oldest depiction of ships in the world—and reed sun ships at that.

"The uniqueness of the Gobustan boat drawings, the clean quality of the images and, mainly, their age amazed Thor Heyerdahl. They were more original than the numerous depictions of boats he had seen in South America, the Pacific islands, Asia and Africa. Moreover, the earliest depictions of boats in these regions dated to the middle of the 4th millennium BCE. All this indicated that the Caspian Sea and, specifically, the western Caspian-Caucasus zone was the oldest seat of boat-building. Thor Heyerdahl also drew attention to the fact that depictions of boats he had seen in Egypt featured the sun disc positioned in the middle of the boat. In Egypt the disc, as a symbol of all the living on earth, is an incarnation of the Egyptians' main god, Ra. This image, displayed to the boat and its crew, acted as an amulet to ensure a safe voyage. This was the first time Thor Heyerdahl had seen the image of the sun on the prow of a boat [...]."[128]

~ GOSHGAR GOSHGARLI, THOR HEYERDAHL AND AZERBAIJANI ARCHAEOLOGY

Heyerdahl had the ability to think in both linear and lateral ways, and had a strong sense of intuition when it came to his research, which I believe is incredibly important when looking to solve ancient mysteries of global proportions, and allowed him to fit many pieces of the puzzle of the Lost Civilization of the Sun together.

GENETIC EVIDENCE

Genetics is a new tool in the kit of researchers of history. Where cultural and linguistic similarities have been taken as merely suggestive of contact between ancient peoples, genes are now providing incontrovertible proof. The following genetic studies, which I've brought together, are revealing the identity of the people who spread the Lost Civilization of the Sun, and where they traveled.

Paracas Culture, Peru

Only recently (February 2018) has genetic evidence revealed beyond any doubt that a type of Caucasian/European people migrated across the ocean via boat thousands of years ago to Peru.[129] The skeletons of these people were first discovered in the 1920s on the coast of Peru, at Paracas (the location of the largest natural bay on the Peruvian coastline), and many more have been discovered since.[130] The people whose remains were genetically tested are believed to have died in the range of 850 to 2,000 years ago.[131] Many of them still had red or red-blonde hair intact, and appear to have been the noble or royal class of the Paracas culture.[132] They were found to have some of the largest elongated skulls in the world,[133] and the adults were also tall, being approximately six feet to six feet and two inches tall.

In 2013, a team of researchers headed by biologist Brien Foerster and researcher L. A. Marzulli began scientific work on the Paracas skulls. Their initial analysis revealed that the elongation was not caused by cranial deformation alone, as they found the skulls had a volume up to 25 percent larger and 60 percent heavier than normal, which cannot be caused by head binding or flattening, which only changes skull shape.[134]

Elongated skulls from Paracas on display in a museum in Peru.

Over five years, Brien Foerster and a team of researchers worked with the permission of the Peruvian government to genetically test the Paracas skeletal remains.[135] Genetic samples were sent to three separate labs. Eighteen skulls were originally tested, but only twelve yielded results, as in six the DNA was too badly degraded.[136] The genetic results came back from labs in Canada and the USA in 2018.[137]

Only their maternal DNA was tested (at the time of writing this, their paternal DNA is in the process of being tested[138]). The results indicate that they had red hair, fair skin, and blue or green eyes. A summary of the results finds that one had haplogroup U2e1;[139] another was T2b;[140] another H1;[141] and another H2a.[142]

Haplogroup U2e1: According to Eupedia is "found in Mesolithic Sweden, Estonia and Latvia, in Neolithic Ukraine, in Bell Beaker Czechia, in the Corded Ware and Unetice cultures, and in EBA Alsace."[143] According to blogger Genetiker, specifically in "Copper Age Corded Ware and Bell Beaker cultures in Germany, [and] the Early Bronze Age Unetice culture in Germany."[144]

T2b: According to Eupedia is "found at high frequencies throughout Europe (especially around the Alps) and at lower frequencies in North Asia, Central Asia and the Middle East."[145] According to Genetiker, "It has been present all over Europe since the Early Neolithic, and it has been found in Late Neolithic samples from Morocco."[146]

H1: According to Eupedia is "by far the most common subclade in Europe, representing approximately [more] than half of the H lineages in Western Europe." Its "highest frequencies are observed in the Iberian peninsula, southwest France and Sardinia."[147] According to Genetiker, "it's been that way since the Neolithic. H1 has also been found in Guanche samples from the Canary Islands."[148]

H2 and its H2a subclade: According to Eupedia are "found throughout Europe and in the Caucasus."[149] According to Genetiker, H2a specifically "has been found in Early Copper Age samples from Eastern Europe, but it has also been found in samples from the Copper Age Remedello culture of Italy, the Copper Age Corded Ware and Bell Beaker cultures of Germany, the Early Bronze Age Unetice culture of Germany, and in a Bronze Age sample from Scotland. H2a has also been found in Guanche samples from the Canary Islands."[150]

Speaking in a video in February 2018, Foerster gave an overview of the genetic results, stating:

"The basic overview is this: there is a predominance of haplogroups U2e and also H, H1, H1a, and H2. Now if you study the source of these haplogroups, where do you wind up on the planet? In Peru? No. In South America? No. In the Americas? No. The Caspian and Black Sea area, what we call the Caucasus. Again look at the characteristics: light skin, red hair, in some cases blonde hair. The source of red hair is not Ireland or Scotland, or Scandinavia—it's the area of Iran, Iraq, and the Caucasus mountains."[151]

Blood results from an earlier study[152] also support the non-Native American origin of the Paracas nobility. Of the fourteen Paracas remains tested, Foerster stated that less than half were type O, there was a small percentage of type B, a high percentage of A, and very high percentage of AB.[153] If the Paracas were Native American, they should have yielded entirely type O results, which they did not.[154] Interestingly, the AB blood type they were highest in is very rare, occurring in only 3 percent of the world's population.[155]

Foerster has become an expert on elongated skulls, and has pointed out that the two places in the world where the largest elongated skulls have been found are Paracas in Peru, and the Caucasus region.[156]

Just south of the Caucasus region is also where the oldest known elongated skulls have been found, with the earliest examples dating to between 9,000 to 8,000 BC in *Homo sapiens*,[157] and at least 45,000 years ago in Neanderthal skulls[158] (both of these oldest examples were found in the same cave in northern Iraq).

"Originally, head flattening was instituted to 'distinguish certain groups of people from others and to indicate the social status of individuals.' In Europe the practice was most popular with tribes that emigrated from the Caucasus region of Central Asia [...]. Indeed, that region is where the remains of the earliest suspected practitioners of artificial cranial deformation were discovered."[159]

~ CHRIS WHITE, HEAD SPACE: BEHIND 10,000 YEARS OF ARTIFICIAL CRANIAL MODIFICATION

Apparently naturally elongated skulls have also been found in tombs in Egypt dated to before 4,000 BC, in the tombs of the ancient megalithic culture of Malta, and among the early cultures of Tiwanaku in Bolivia;[160] thus the Paracas DNA may provide genetic clues to the identity of the founders of all these ancient sun-worshiping civilizations.

The Paracas venerated the wisdom bringer Kon (which is another name for Viracocha), who was a son of the sun and depicted with red hair.[161] [162] The Viracochas—the followers of the wisdom bringer called Viracocha who arrived with him and were said by the Inca to be his descendants—were described as having red hair, just as some of the Paracas people had. Those who emigrated to Easter Island from the civilization Viracocha established in Peru and Bolivia (with its center at Tiwanaku) also had red hair; in old photos and sketches some of their descendants have the highest foreheads I've seen in living persons, and they carved wooden statues of themselves with elongated skulls.[163] One of the stone moai statues on the island was depicted as female, and as having an extremely elongated head.[164]

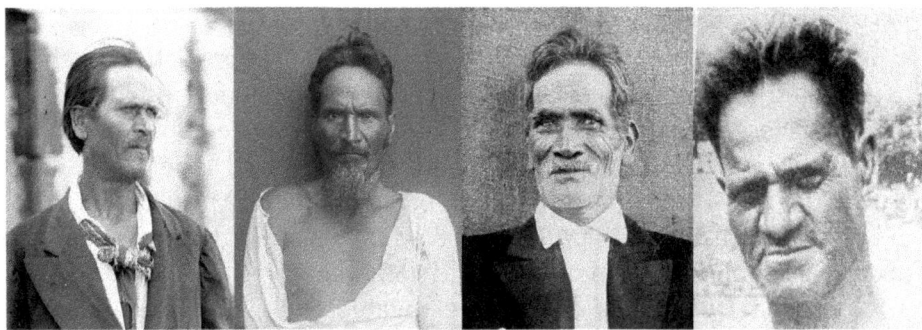

Native men from Easter Island with naturally high foreheads. Left: Photo of Kaitae taken in 1886—he was the closest descendant of the last king of Easter Island called Maurata.[165] Center left: Photo of Tepano taken in 1884.[166] Center right: Photo of Te Haha taken in 1914—he was a nobleman of the elite Miru clan, and was an attendant of the second last king of Easter Island called Nga-ara.[167] Right: Nicolas Pakomio, who was the son of a chief called Pakomio Maori. Pakomio lived from 1816 to 1909 and was one of 15 out of 1,500 natives who survived the Peruvian slave raid of 1862 and made it back to the island alive. He had lighter skin and hair than other natives on the island.[168]

Cranial deformation was practiced in many parts of the world—it was seen as a sign of nobility and of someone with a greater degree of spiritual perceptivity. This appears to be based on an attempt to imitate the race of people the Paracas nobility are descended from.

Additionally, *The Kolbrin* states that the Children of God interbred with other humanoids, giving birth to the first person they had ever seen with red hair, and who was said to have lived around the Caucasus region, where the most ancient and (apart from the Paracas) largest elongated skulls have ever been found. Today the incidence of red hair coincides most closely with the paternal haplogroup R1b (discussed further on).[169] Perhaps the Children of God had elongated skulls, and as the text indicates, were another as yet unclassified type of humanoid, as the Paracas genetic tests have revealed that among the known Caucasian haplogroups were five haplogroups unknown both among modern and extinct humanoids.[170] These unknown haplogroups may represent unknown races or species of humanoid that are now extinct. Three medical experts have emphatically stated that because of the abnormalities of the Paracas skulls they should be classified as a subspecies of human, which they would call *Homo sapiens sapiens paracas* (as opposed to just *Homo sapiens sapiens*).[171] As I discuss in the next chapter, the Children of God possibly had some kind of extraterrestrial genetic input.

Easter Island

In 1971, blood samples were collected from natives of Easter Island who were very carefully selected to exclude anyone who had possible European admixture from later settlers. In 2005-2006, DNA testing carried out on these samples revealed that most of the individuals sampled were descendants of a chief called Pakomio Maori (mentioned in the previous image caption). One of Pakomio's sons (possibly the one in the previous photograph on the right), and four of his male offspring were shown to have European DNA. The immunologist Dr. Erik Thorsby wrote in his 2012 paper that they "belonged to the R-M173 [R1] haplogroup typical of Europeans and had a Y-STR [paternal] haplotype found in middle and southern Europe. [...] The particular haplotypic combination has [...] the world highest frequency among Basques [...]."[172]

The Basques are a people who inhabit north-central Spain and south-western France. On their paternal side, they are 100 percent Western Europeans of "Steppe Ancestry" (on their maternal line European hunter-gatherer), but without the later population admixtures that affected Europeans in the region from the Iron Age onward.[173] This means that their paternal line is a kind of two-thousand-year-old time capsule. This is interesting, because as we'll see further on, there is clear evidence that the Chachapoya culture was founded by people of the Celtiberian, Castro, and Talayot cultures who left the region of Spain around two thousand years ago to settle in South America, and thus would have been genetically similar to the Basques.

Thorsby's study also found an Amerindian contribution to the genepool from prehistoric times, most closely related to the Aymara people who are indigenous to the Tiwanaku region in Bolivia, which is the capital established by Viracocha, and exactly where Easter Island oral histories stated that migrants to the island came from! Thorsby writes that the study was not able to ascertain when these Amerindian genes came to Easter Island, only that "it must have occurred early."

A later study on different native Easter Island individuals also found haplotypes only present in Aymara Amerindians living around Lake Titicaca where the megalithic city Tiwanaku is located.[174]

Chachapoya Culture, Peru

DNA testing has been carried out in the remote former territories of the Chachapoya culture on local people who display fairer skin, hair, and eye colors than Amerindians, or who had children with these features. All males tested yielded the presence of the male haplogroup R1b (most commonly found in Western Europeans), as well as other European haplogroups. A wider sample needs to be collected to ascertain the date of this admixture, but so far the permission to do this hasn't been granted.[175]

Locals are well aware that the Chachapoya had people among their civilization that were of a different genetic origin, and were there before the Spanish. Even the sign outside a Chachapoya museum plainly states that the Chachapoya were described as looking different to the other tribes in the area, saying, "Many of the questions [regarding the origins of the Chachapoya] come from the description of the chroniclers of the colonial era. They reported that the ancient Chachapoya settlers were different from those in the other regions of the Andes. They described them as taller, whiter and more beautiful. What does all this mean?" The sign features a photo of a little, fair-skinned blonde girl from the former region of the Chachapoya.[176]

These different looking descendants of the Chachapoya are known locally as "gringuitos," which essentially means "white foreigner" in Spanish, and also as "mushas," which is an indigenous Quechua term that means "colored hair," and is used to indicate their ancestors and heritage.[177]

An anonymous blogger called Genetiker has examined DNA results of select Chachapoya mummies (he argues that geneticists have purposely tested mummies without Caucasoid features to avoid the controversy surrounding them). Nevertheless, he identified one of the mummies (called NA50) as having 30 percent Caucasoid admixture, saying, "The calls for NA50 show that he was positive for L773, one of the SNPs that defines haplogroup R1b1a2-M269. [...] My K = 4 ADMIXTURE analysis of the Chachapoya samples identified NA50 as having 30 percent additional Caucasoid admixture, more than any of the other samples had. At the time I dismissed that finding, in the belief that all of the non-Amerindian admixture for the samples with fewer than one thousand SNPs was noise. But with the Y-SNP calls for NA50 showing that he was positive for an R1b-M269 mutation, I now suspect that the additional Caucasoid admixture detected in NA50 is real."[178]

Unfortunately, there appears to be a concerted effort to obscure the genetic origins of the Chachapoya. However, as we will see further on in this chapter, the cultural evidence overwhelmingly identifies them as descended from ancient Celts who lived in Iberia (mostly modern-day Spain).

Ancient Peruvian Blood Types

Testing has been done on the blood types of ancient mummies from a number of cultures in Peru—specifically the Paracas, Nazca, Huari, Ica, Inca, Tarapaca Colonial, and Murga Colonial (listed in date order from oldest culture to youngest). All of the cultures had individuals of blood type O, which is the typical Amerindian blood type. However, they also had at least one individual of type A and/or B and/or AB. Generally, the older the culture, the higher the proportion of individuals with A, B, and AB blood types.[179] The paper published in 1976 states, "The results indicate the presence of A, B, AB and O blood groups in America prior to known European contact. This suggests the need for a revision of concepts of blood groups in the American Indian."[180] The paper authors note that since 1933 a number of other studies had tested ancient American remains, and also found individuals with A, B, and AB blood types, further noting that only the findings of all group O types had gained general acceptance. A follow up paper in 1978 states, "In Peru all ABO blood groups were found in the period from 3000 B.C. to 1400 A.D.; from this period to 1650 only A and O were seen. In Chile no B or AB was noted either in pre-Columbian or Colonial mummies. This confirms the archaeological concept that the Chilean Indian was culturally as well as genetically different from the Peruvian Indian."[181] The paper authors called for a revision of concepts of blood groups in Native Americans, since they were believed to only have O type blood. The findings indicate that there were non-Amerindians who were more prevalent among the ancient cultures of Peru (where, not coincidentally, there are many megalithic ancient sites similar to those in Egypt and Europe), but who disappeared in the later phases of Peruvian culture before the Spanish arrived.

There have been a number of studies done on blood types of Amerindians over the past few decades. They reveal a number of different races may have come to the Americas in migrations both from the east and west.

> "It was once contended that all American Indians other than the Blackfoot (who were high in A) were of blood type O. Asian B was said to be absent. Now, however, we know that B occurs in over half the samples of American Indians, particularly among Nancy Yaw Davis's (2000) possibly Japanese influenced Zuni, and that all four ABO blood types were present in pre-Columbian Peru, especially in earlier times.

As early as the 1950s, it was noticed that the Diego blood factor, an East and Southeast Asian type, also occurred among American groups but was absent in the North. [...] I cannot cover the details here, but suffice it to say that a variety of "foreign" genes, especially from Afro-Asiatic and southern Asian parts of the world, occur again in the Western Hemisphere, not randomly, but with definite concentrations, especially in Mesoamerica and in the Central to Southern Andean region. This seems impossible to assign to mere happenstance, and Mediterranean/Middle Eastern and greater Southeast Asian/Oceanian inputs appear to be the only believable explanation.

I may mention, as well, Asian HLA links with Ecuador and Colombia, links also supported by presence there of an uncommon type of human Tlymphotropic virus also found among the Ainu of Japan, and the absence of the normal Asian and American mtDNA 9-by deletion. All this is congruent with Betty Meggers's Jomôn-in-Ecuador proposals (Meggers, Evans, and Estrada 1965)."[182]

~ STEPHEN C. JETT, PRE-COLUMBIAN TRANSOCEANIC CONTACTS

Chinchorro Culture, Peru

The Chinchorro are a very ancient culture that lived in Peru and Chile. They are the oldest known culture in the world to practice mummification, and the oldest in South America known to have practiced cranial deformation.[183] They naturally mummified their dead in the local desert conditions—the earliest examples of which date to around 7,000 BC. Later, they also very carefully artificially mummified their dead—the earliest examples of which date to around 5,000 BC.[184] As with many of the ancient mummies of Peru, there are mummies among the Chinchorro that have fine red, light brown, and auburn hair.[185]

The blogger Genetiker has examined the genetic results of one of the mummies of the ancient Chinchorro culture, saying "with a series of calculator and admixture analyses, I discovered that a Chinchorro DNA sample dated to 3972–3806 BC contained approximately 30 percent European admixture: This Chinchorro sample has been included in all of my admixture analyses since then, and all of those analyses have consistently shown it to be about 30 percent European."[186] Genetiker states that "pre-LGM [Last Glacial Maximum] Europeans remain one possible source of its European admixture" and that "European hunter-gatherers with some early European farmer admixture could be another."[187] This could indicate that a very ancient European migration reached South America, perhaps followed by a much later one of early farmers, and that one or both of these European migrant types contributed to DNA in South America.

Haplogroup X

X is a mysterious maternal haplogroup that is found on either side of the Atlantic Ocean, particularly its subclade X2. Wikipedia states, "Subclade X2 appears to have undergone extensive population expansion and dispersal around or soon after the Last Glacial Maximum, roughly 20,000 years ago. It is more strongly represented in the Near East, the Caucasus, and Southern Europe and somewhat less strongly present in the rest of Europe. The highest concentrations are found in Georgia (8%), Orkney (Scotland) (7%), and among the Druze community in Israel (27%). Subclades X2a and X2g are found in North America, but are not present in native South Americans."[188] It's not found in all Native North American tribes however; its highest occurrence is found in the Ojibwa of the Great Lakes region in the northeast of the continent.[189]

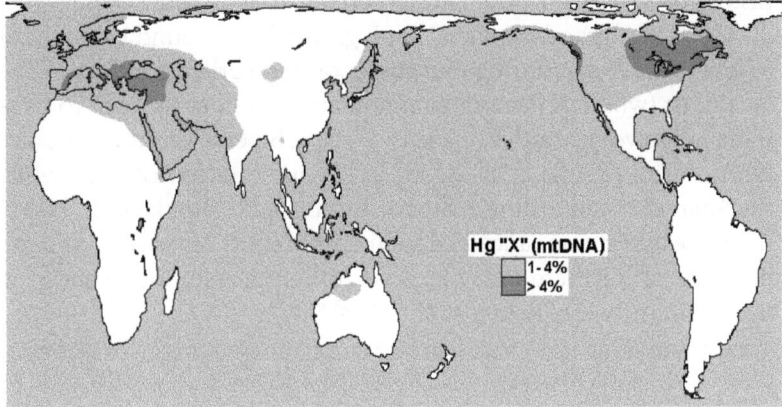

Map of frequency of haplogroup X among modern populations.

This haplogroup is considered one of the founding haplogroups of North America, but as yet, no one has been able to identify how it got there.

A 1998 paper seeking to identify the migratory route of those carrying haplogroup X into North America states that it may have arrived either 12,000-17,000 or 23,000-36,000 years ago.[190]

"Median network analysis indicated that European and Native American haplogroup X mtDNAs, although distinct, nevertheless are distantly related to each other. Time estimates for the arrival of X in North America are 12,000–36,000 years ago, depending on the number of assumed founders, thus supporting the conclusion that the peoples harboring haplogroup X were among the original founders of Native American populations. To date, haplogroup X has not been unambiguously identified in Asia, raising the possibility that some Native American founders were of Caucasian ancestry."[191]

~ MTDNA HAPLOGROUP X: AN ANCIENT LINK BETWEEN EUROPE/WESTERN ASIA AND NORTH AMERICA?

Kennewick Man is the name given to the remains of a man found in Washington State in the United States dated to approximately 7,000 BC. He belonged to the haplogroup X2a, currently only found in North America among particular Native American peoples. His features have been described as predominantly "Caucasian" looking.[192] A 2001 study was able to identify haplogroup X in people living in the Altai Mountains of Siberia (who exhibit both Mongoloid and Caucasian features) at a frequency of 3.5 percent.[193] However, writers of a 2015 paper on the origins of haplogroup X2a in North America, state:

> "[...] unlike the other American mitochondrial haplogroups (A–D), which have clear parental haplotypes persisting in contemporary Siberian populations, there is no clear record of the evolutionary history of X2a in any population (Fernandes et al. 2012; Reidla et al. 2003). X2a's "grand-parental" haplogroup, X2, is found throughout, at low levels today throughout much of the world, including in the Near East (where X is more common and therefore thought to have initially evolved), South Caucasus, Europe, Siberia, Central Asia, and North Africa (Reidla et al. 2003). It is important to note that while the Altai people in southern Siberia exhibit X2 (Derenko et al. 2001), their lineages are not ancestral to those of North Americans, and the presence of X2 there today appears to be the result of recent gene flow from the west (Reidla et al. 2003)."[194]
>
> ~ RAFF AND BOLNICK, DOES MITOCHONDRIAL HAPLOGROUP X INDICATE ANCIENT TRANS-ATLANTIC MIGRATION TO THE AMERICAS? A CRITICAL RE-EVALUATION

More findings, research, and genetic testing of modern populations are needed to find the missing ancestral link between X2 and its offshoot in North America X2a.[195]

Could haplogroup X be linked to the legends of a white race in the north-east of North America where ancient sites like those in Europe and the British Isles are found?

Ancient Egypt

Geneticists were surprised when they genetically tested ninety ancient Egyptian mummies from the archaeological site of Abusir el-Meleq, which was inhabited from at least 3,250 BC until about AD 700 (although the tested samples were from individuals who died between around 1,400 BC to AD 430). The site was held in high religious regard and used as a burial ground because of its connection to the worship of the wisdom bringer Osiris. The results released in 2017 are described as "the first reliable data set obtained from ancient Egyptians," and are summarized by the paper's authors as follows:

"We find that ancient Egyptians are most closely related to Neolithic and Bronze Age samples in the Levant, as well as to Neolithic Anatolian and European populations. When comparing this pattern with modern Egyptians, we find that the ancient Egyptians are more closely related to all modern and ancient European populations [...] the substantially lower African component in our ~2,000-year-old ancient samples suggests that African gene flow in modern Egyptians occurred indeed predominantly within the last 2,000 years."[196]

> ~ VERENA J. SCHUENEMANN ET AL., ANCIENT EGYPTIAN MUMMY GENOMES SUGGEST AN INCREASE OF SUB-SAHARAN AFRICAN ANCESTRY IN POST-ROMAN PERIODS

They go on to qualify this by stating:

"However, we note that all our genetic data were obtained from a single site in Middle Egypt and may not be representative for all of ancient Egypt. It is possible that populations in the south of Egypt were more closely related to those of Nubia and had a higher sub-Saharan genetic component, in which case the argument for an influx of sub-Saharan ancestries after the Roman Period might only be partially valid and have to be nuanced."[197]

In 2010, genetic testing was done on eleven ancient Egyptian mummies in an attempt to identify the family of the most famous pharaoh—the boy king Tutankhamun. Researchers stated that they were able to identify a number of his close relatives, including his parents, and to ascertain Tutankhamun's cause of death.[198] Their findings were aired on television, including in a Discovery Channel documentary. Incidentally, footage from this documentary showed some of the DNA data, which has still never officially been released to the public despite several requests.[199] Only part of the study results were published in the Journal of the American Medical Association, which were the snippets of Y-DNA used to identify Tutankhamun's relatives. But more of this Y-DNA data appeared in the footage, enough that the Swiss personal genomics company iGENEA was able to reconstruct the paternal genetic profile of Tutankhamun.

Managing director of iGENEA, Roman Scholz, said in an interview, "Maybe they didn't know what they showed, but we got sixteen markers from the Y chromosome from these pharaohs."[200]

iGENEA was able to ascertain that Tutankhamun, his father Akhenaten, and his grandfather Amenhotep III, belonged to the paternal haplogroup R1b1a2, which less than 1 percent of modern Egyptians belong to, but more than half of Western European men do.[201] Scholz said, "We think the common ancestor lived in the Caucasus about 9,500 years ago."[202]

Ancient Ethiopia

Another surprise was in store for the geneticists who sequenced the first ever ancient African human genome—belonging to a man who died around 2,500 BC in Ethiopia. While most closely related to modern Ethiopians, he was also found to share ancestry with the first farmers who migrated from southeastern Anatolia into Europe around 7,000 BC—this ancestry correlates most closely with modern day Sardinians and people of the ancient Linear Pottery culture (c. 5,500-4,500 BC[203]) in parts of Central and Eastern Europe. This allowed the geneticists to extrapolate that several thousand years ago there was a massive migration into Africa of farmers from West Eurasia.[204] [205] Dr. Andrea Manica, who conducted the research said, "We know now that they [the farmers from Eurasia] probably corresponded to a quarter of the people that already lived in East Africa (at that time)."[206] Their genes spread all the way down the coast of East Africa to South Africa,[207] where ancient standing stones are found. Their genes are also found in populations across North Africa to varying degrees.[208]

> "Using Mota [the ancient man tested] as an unadmixed African reference and the early farmer LBK [Linear Pottery culture] as the source of the West Eurasian component, it is possible to reassess the magnitude and geographic extent of historical migrations, avoiding the complications of using admixed contemporary populations. We estimated a substantially higher Eurasian backflow admixture than previously detected, with an additional 4 to 7% of the genome of most African populations tracing back to a Eurasian source. Moreover, we detected a much broader geographical impact of the backflow, going all the way to West and Southern Africa. Even though the West Eurasian component in these regions is smaller than in Eastern Africa, it is still sizable, with Yoruba and Mbuti, who are often used as African reference populations, showing 7% and 6%, respectively, of their genomes to be of Eurasian origin."[209]
>
> ~ GALLEGO LLORENTE ET AL., ANCIENT ETHIOPIAN GENOME REVEALS EXTENSIVE EURASIAN ADMIXTURE IN EASTERN AFRICA, REPRINTED WITH PERMISSION FROM AAAS.

The conclusion of these findings so far is that people with the same ancestry—the ancient first farmers of Europe—migrated into North Africa thousands of years ago, and they or their descendants migrated down the coast to South Africa. It seems probable they were the builders of the ancient standing stones of Northern Africa and South Africa, just as they are likely to have been in Europe.

Haplogroup R1

A haplogroup that is closely linked to the Lost Civilization of the Sun, and to Indo-European language and culture, is the paternal (Y chromosome) haplogroup R. This haplogroup is thought to have originated in North Asia just before the Last Glacial Maximum (26,500-19,000 years ago), and has been found in the remains of a twenty-four-thousand-year-old boy from the Altai region, in south-central Siberia. The boy was found to be most closely related "to the modern populations of Europe and South Asia [Afghanistan, Bangladesh, Bhutan, the Maldives, Nepal, India, Pakistan, and Sri Lanka], the two regions where haplogroup R also happens to be the most common nowadays (R1b in Western Europe, R1a in Eastern Europe and Central and South Asia, and R2 in South Asia)."[210] As noted further on in this chapter, in the ancient texts the Vedas and the Avesta (which are both written in Indo-European languages) there are indications that their oldest parts were authored by people who had once lived in the Arctic (in the northernmost regions of Siberia), and the R1 subclades of haplogroup R are one of the main paternal haplogroups of those who are believed to have spread Indo-European languages.

Haplogroup R split into R1 and R2, and R1 further diversified into R1a and R1b. "The oldest forms of R1b [...] are found dispersed at very low frequencies from Western Europe to India, a vast region where could have roamed the nomadic R1b hunter-gatherers during the Ice Age."[211]

At around 8,500 BC, R1b people are believed to have been in eastern Anatolia, where the genetic diversity of R1b is greatest (suggesting it was the post Ice Age homeland of this haplogroup), before they moved southwest into the Levant and Africa, and north into the Pontic-Caspian steppe where it later became one of the dominant haplogroups among Proto-Indo-European speakers.

They are believed to have been the first to domesticate cattle. Since all taurine cattle alive today have been found to descend from a population of just eighty aurochs, the expansion of R1b people can also be traced archaeologically through the movement of domesticated cattle. These cattle herders appeared in central Syria, then the Southern Levant, and then in Egypt—specifically at Nabta Playa at around 7,000-6,500 BC, where there are ancient standing stones. They then spread out across most of northern and eastern Africa, as at that time, the Sahara was a vast savannah with plenty of grass for cattle; later the climate changed and it became the desert it is today.[212] Again, ancient standing stones are found throughout the region these people inhabited. It may come as no surprise that the cow and/or bull became a central sacred symbol wherever they traveled (among the ancient Egyptians and Indo-Europeans).

An article on Eupedia, an online resource of European heritage, states "But the most compelling evidence that R1b people related to modern Europeans once roamed the Sahara is to be found at Tassili n'Ajjer in southern Algeria, a site famous for petroglyphs (rock art) dating from the Neolithic era. Some paintings dating from around 3000 BCE depict fair-skinned and blond or auburn-haired women riding on cows."[213]

Those of the haplogroups R1b and R1a carry genetic markers for fair skin and hair, including red and blond hair, which is found among some of the earliest descriptions of those who established the Lost Civilization of the Sun.[214]

R1b subclades have been found among the ancient people of the Iron Gates Mesolithic culture in Serbia and Romania,[215] the Guanches of the Canary Islands, natives of Easter Island, descendants of the Chachapoya in Peru, and the Egyptian Pharaoh Tutankhamun; while R1a is found among the Brahmin caste in India.

R1 has also been found to high degrees in certain tribes of North Amerindians—being the most common paternal haplogroup after Q-M242, which is the predominant paternal haplogroup of all North Amerindians.[216] I suspect it was largely brought to North America by Celts who likely built the ancient stoneworks in the northeast and were described in Amerindian legends as "a fierce race of white warriors" (as I explain further on), as the R1b haplotype occurs to the greatest degree in those tribes in the Great Lakes region of North America,[217] [218] [219] where copper was mined and likely taken back to Europe during the Bronze Age.

The Guanches, Canary Islands

The Guanches were the indigenous inhabitants of the Canary Islands when the Spanish arrived and conquered them in 1496. They worshiped the sun and built stepped pyramids (as described further on in this chapter). Although there is no record of where the Guanches originated from, four genetic studies (one published in 2009, two in 2017, and another in 2019) of Guanche remains pre-dating Spanish arrival have found that there were essentially two distinct populations on the islands that may have come in two large migrations, "with the second migration wave affecting only the islands closer to the African continent," said Dr. Fregel, geneticist of the most recent 2019 study.[220] This would account for the two physical types of people described by various explorers to the islands—those closer to Africa were described as having darker complexions, while those islands to the north were inhabited by people with fair skin, blonde hair, and blue/green eyes, being the earlier inhabitants of the islands.[221]

Painting from 1764 of captured Guanche men being presented to the King and Queen of Spain. Notice they are fair-skinned.

Two of the studies found that the majority of Guanche remains were "genetically most similar to modern Berber populations from northwest Africa."[222]

What came as a surprise to geneticists, however, was the large component of European farmer ancestry. The 2017 paper by Rodríguez-Varela et al. says, "the Guanches carried early European famer (EEF)-like ancestry [...]. The EEF component is strongly associated with early Neolithic famers from Anatolia and Europe (as well as present-day Sardinians)."[223] The 2017 study by Ordóñez et al. found three paternal haplogroups among the remains tested. Two of them are found most frequently today in west and northwest Africa; one highest among Amazigh/Berbers and the other among the Dogon people of Mali (mentioned further on). The third was R1b-M269, and was found in seven out of the sixteen ancient individuals.[224] The 2009 study also found the haplogroup R1b-M269 at a frequency of 10 percent among the remains they tested.[225] Note that this is exactly the same haplogroup the blogger Genetiker claimed to have found in one of the ancient Chachapoya of Peru. This particular type of R1b haplogroup is the most common paternal haplogroup in European men today.

The 2019 study, which only tested maternal DNA, states, "We obtained complete mtDNA genomes from 48 ancient human remains sampled in 25 different archaeological sites. Our sample set covers the entire archipelago and a time span of 1,200 years [...] the majority of haplogroups observed are of Eurasian origin, most with a Mediterranean distribution. This result is expected, as recent aDNA data from North Africa has indicated the presence of Neolithic European lineages as early as the Late Neolithic period (~5,000 BP). [...] Most lineages observed in the ancient samples have a Mediterranean distribution, and belong to lineages associated with the Neolithic expansion in the Near East and Europe [...]."[226]

The language spoken by the Guanches also provides clues as to whom they were related. Although linguists have attempted to classify it as Berber, it remains unidentified, and appears only to have adopted some Berber words but is otherwise unrelated to it.[227] It also contains words of Proto-Indo-European origin,[228] as well as words that share similarities with those spoken in other places where similar peoples with a religion of the sun existed—including Central America, ancient Egypt, and Iceland (where a language of the Germanic branch of Indo-European is spoken).[229] For example, the word "Hu" in Guanche is a "preformative indicating greatness or holiness."[230] This same word with the exact same meaning is said to have been used by the Druids and Welsh of the British Isles to refer to a great leader of theirs called Hu Gadarn, who led them from "where Constantinople is now" (Anatolia) to Britain.[231] Although mocked as a modern forgery, this tale, and many others like it, also appear in *The Kolbrin*, which contains lengthy accounts of the various migrations into Britain in prehistory.

ANCIENT MIGRATIONS

Wherever ancient sun-worshiping people tended to travel, standing stones, pyramids, henges, earthworks, temples, mounds, and settlements were built that aligned to the solstices and equinoxes.

> "In remote antiquity, there was a very mobilized group of cousin nations who traveled across the entire globe and wherever they settled long term they built code-bearing complexes to preserve and teach their sciences. To ensure that profound scientific knowledge would not be lost, they erected precisely positioned pyramid and hump mounds, concentric ring mounds, geometric earth embankments, henges complete with internal stone markers, standing stone circles, obelisk complexes, sighting pits, cairn markers, etc. In each case the selfsame measurement standard, as well as length and angle codes on one site will duplicate that found on another, even a continent or two removed."[232]
>
> ~ MARTIN DOUTRÉ, THE CHINESE PYRAMIDS AT XI'AN, SHAANXL

Using their great astronomical, navigational, and surveying knowledge, they were even able to align sacred sites to one another across vast distances. In Ireland for example, sacred sites were aligned from its east to west coast (also in alignment with the equinox sunrise), stretching a distance of 135 miles. This alignment is called the Millmount-Croagh Patrick Alignment.[233]

ARKAIM CIRCLE

STONEHENGE

GOSECK CIRCLE

Additionally, many sites in different countries were built using similar principles. For example, the ancient sacred sites of Goseck Circle in Germany (dated to 5,000 BC), Stonehenge in England (dated to 3,000 BC but being modified up until 1,520 BC), and Arkaim in Russia (dated to between 2,000 to 1,700 BC), were all built on the same latitude. This latitude is a very special one for a number of reasons. It is "the exact latitude at which the midsummer sunrise and sunsets are at 90 degrees to the Moon's northerly setting and southerly rising. This particular phenomena is only possible within a band of less than one degree of which Stonehenge and Goseck lies in the middle-third."[234] It is also "one of two unique latitudes in the world where the full Moon passes directly overhead on its maximum zeniths."[235] It can be no coincidence that each of these sites lie on this latitude, are laid out in concentric circles, and have multiple astronomical alignments, providing strong evidence that they are connected to each other.

This time of the Lost Civilization of the Sun was a time in which large numbers of people cooperated in the building of giant structures with incredible precision (sometimes using materials from vast distances away) and incorporating advanced alignments, which would have required times of relative peace and prosperity. It was also a time when many remote places of the world were explored and inhabited for this purpose.

Following are just a few examples of the spread of this civilization to different parts of the world.

EASTERN EUROPE

The earliest known cities in the whole of Eurasia, and the largest in Europe at the time (the fourth millennium BC) and possibly anywhere in the world, were those in Eastern Europe.[236] They belonged to the Cucuteni-Trypillia people. About 3,000 of their sites have been found spread over large parts of what is now Ukraine, Moldova, and Romania; including "mega-sites" containing as many as 3,000 structures inhabited by 20,000-46,000 people.[237]

Reconstruction of a Cucuteni-Trypillia mega-site.

They were also building some of the largest temples in Europe. One of their temples (called the Nebelivka temple), which is the largest ancient temple found in Europe so far, dated to 4,000 BC, had its main axis aligned to the equinox sunrise, so that "On the equinox day, the sunlight passed through the main gate, through the entrance to the temple and lit the central altar No. 7. In the dark temple, the altar, covered with red clay, shone in the rays of the sun."[238] Other altars within the temple aligned to sunrise on the winter and summer solstices.[239]

CT civilization, Nebelivka temple.
4000 BC.

A recreation of an ancient temple of the Cucuteni-Trypillia civilization in Ukraine. It's adorned with a host of solar symbols, including those detailed in this section: the yin yang, double spiral, and swastika. At the apex of the temple are the horns of the solstice, and the axis of the temple was aligned to equinox sunrise. These symbols would appear in later European cultures, such as the Minoan and Western European megalithic cultures.

Like the earlier culture of Lepenski Vir, the Cucuteni-Trypillia also centered their religion around the sun, and used symbols later central to the Religion of the Sun, such as the swastika, double spiral, analemma/infinity symbol,[240] and yin and yang. There is also evidence they may have migrated to distant parts of the world. A paper published in 2013 found remarkable similarities between the very distinct and beautiful style of ceramics used by the Cucuteni-Trypillia with that of cultures in China (Yangshao), Thailand (Ban-Chiang), and North America (Anasazi). The swastika was also used as a common symbol in each.

"A puzzling similarity has been observed in some of the ceramics and figurines in several cultures in Eastern Europe (the Trypillia-Cucuteni culture, 6500 - 5500 years before present [ybp]), Thailand (the Ban-Chiang culture, between 7400 and 3800 ybp), China (the Yangshao culture, between 8000 and 4000 ybp), North America (the Anasazi-Mogollon culture, between 7500 ybp and present time). It is remarkable that the ceramics of these four cultures match each other in 17 (45%) of the 38 indicators used to distinguish archeological ceramic piece in the comparative research. Remarkably, all four cultures with look-alike ceramics also use the swastika as a common symbol. We advance the hypothesis that all four cultures are connected by the Aryan (bearers of R1a) migrations between 5500 and 3000 ybp. While the Aryan migrations in Eurasia are well verified by DNA data, those in the Americas are not known as yet. Consideration of R1a haplotypes among Native Americans do not conflict with the hypothesis."[241]

~ A DNA GENEALOGY SOLUTION TO THE PUZZLE OF ANCIENT LOOK-ALIKE CERAMICS ACROSS THE WORLD BY ANATOLE A. KLYOSOV AND ELENA A. MIRONOVA

Left: Anasazi ceramic from North America. Center: Cucuteni-Trypillia ceramic from Eastern Europe. Right: Yangshao ceramic from China. Notice the same use of spirals and zig zags. This is just a quick comparison I made using freely available images—an internet search finds comparisons people have made of designs that share identical motifs.

The paper goes on to say that these ceramics share similarities with the even older Iron Gates Mesolithic culture of Lepenski Vir.

> "The dates given here are for the cultures, not for the ceramics, which—if dated at all—are often not reliably dated. All the cultures are ancient; the Trypillian culture, which belongs to the Proto-Slavic region of Vincha-Tordosh-Keresh-Cucuteni-Trypillia cultures of 8000 - 5000 ybp, reveals some similarity with ceramics and other artifacts of the Mesolithic Lepenski Vir culture in Serbia, dated at least 9400 - 8200 ybp using strontium isotope measurements (Boric & Price, 2013). It is remarkable that these cultures—separated by thousands of miles—designed ceramics and figurines that bear similarities that cannot be regarded as accidental."[242]

Another symbol shared between the Cucuteni-Trypillia culture and later Chinese culture, is the yin and yang symbol (which is a symbol related to the cycles of the sun), the earliest known example of which is found in the Cucuteni-Trypillia culture, again revealing a connection between these regions in ancient times.

NORTH AMERICA

There are numerous oral histories, artifacts, and ancient sites, which attest to the existence of a number of phases of lost civilization in North America connected to the ancient Religion of the Sun.

One of the clearest accounts comes from Lucy Thompson, who was one of the first Native American women to write down the oral histories of her people (which she did in 1916). She describes how there was a civilization that spread across North America when her people first arrived:

Photograph of Lucy Thompson taken in 1916.

"When the Indians first made their appearance on the Klamath river it was already inhabited by a white race of people known among us as the Wa-gas. These white people were found to inhabit the whole continent, and were a highly moral and civilized race. They heartily welcomed the Indians to their country and taught us all of their arts and sciences [...]. For a vast period of time the two races dwelt together in peace and honored homes, wars and quarrels were unknown in this golden age of happiness. No depredations were ever committed upon the property of their people, as the white people ruled with [a] beacon light of kindness, and our people still worship the hallowed places where once they trod. Their morals were far superior to the white people of today, their ideals were high and inspired our people with greatness. After we had lived with these ancient people so long, they suddenly called their hosts together and mysteriously disappeared for a distant land, we know not where [...]. It was a sad farewell when they departed from this land, for our people mourned their loss, as no more have we found such friends as they, so true and loyal. In their farewell journey across this land they left land-marks of stone monuments, on the tops of high mountains and places commanding a view of the surrounding country. These land-marks we have kept in repair, down through the ages in loving remembrance. I have seen many of these land-marks myself (and often repaired them) that they left as a symbol of the mystic ages and the grandeur of a mighty nation that passed in a single season [...]. This is said to be the reason why some of our people are very fair. Some of the Indians are still looking for their return to the earth, when they come back it is believed that peace and happiness will reign supreme again over this great land and all evil will be cast out."[243]

~ LUCY THOMPSON, TO THE AMERICAN INDIAN: REMINISCENCES OF A YUROK WOMAN

According to Thompson, this white race departed toward the north, returning in the direction they were believed to have first entered the Americas, and that "thousands of years had elapsed since then."

Ancient Cities of the Southwest

Another account was recorded in 1857 by Nelson Lee, a member of the Texas Navy who was held captive by a Comanche tribe for three years. During his captivity, he was told the following by the Comanche chief called Rolling Thunder:

"Innumerable moons ago, there was a race of white men, ten feet high, and far more rich and powerful than any white people now living, who inhabited a large range of country, extending from the rising to the setting sun. Their fortifications crowned the summits of the mountains, protecting their populous cities situated in the intervening valleys. They excelled every other nation which was flourished, either before or since, in all manner of cunning handicraft—were brave and warlike—ruling over the land they had wrested from its ancient possessors with a high and haughty hand. Compared with them the palefaces of the present day were pygmies, in both art and arms. They drove the Indians from their homes, putting them to the sword, and occupying the valleys in which their fathers had dwelt before them since the world began. At length, in the height of their power and glory, when they remembered justice and mercy no more and became proud and lifted up, the Great Spirit descended from above, sweeping them with fire and deluge from the face of the earth. The mounds we had seen on the tablelands were the remnants of their fortresses, and the crumbling ruins that surrounded us all that remained of a mighty city."[244]

Rolling Thunder had taken Lee on a long journey, into a wide desolate valley surrounded on all sides by high mountains. On their journey, Lee recalls they passed man-made mounds atop many mountains, resembling ancient fortresses. In the valley, Rolling Thunder led Lee to the ruins of an ancient city with a great number of buildings that had once lined spacious streets; amid them was what appeared to be a church-like building with walls of cut stone two feet thick and in some places fifteen feet high. It was at these ancient ruins Rolling Thunder related his account. Lee says that all the Comanche tribes believed the same about the origin of these ruins.

Of the account, Lee wrote:

> "It would, indeed, be difficult to adopt any other hypothesis than the one entertained by the chief. The evidence before me was too clear and palpable to be controverted, that at some period, more or less remote, this valley had been inhabited by a people skilled in architecture and evidently possessing, in a high degree, a knowledge of mechanism and the arts."[245]

In the region once roamed by the Comanche there are ancient ruins that match Lee's description. Today they are commonly attributed to a people known as the "Anasazi," which is a Navajo word meaning "ancestors of our enemies," who archaeologists currently believe inhabited the region from the twelfth century BC. Hundreds of their sites, including multistory stone cities (some six stories high), mountain top ruins/fortresses, and road systems (some with roads 30 feet/10 meters wide and stretching for a combined distance of 180 miles/300 km) are scattered across a vast area of the states of Colorado, New Mexico, and Arizona.[246] Note that both Thompson and Rolling Thunder attribute the ancient stone structures atop high mountains to the white races they described.

Ruined city of the Anasazi, with thick, high walls made of cut stone, just as Lee described.

A number of the Anasazi's ancient cities incorporated sun temples and complex solar and celestial alignments. Major sites include Mesa Verde in Colorado (which contains Cliff Palace) and Chaco Canyon in New Mexico. Advanced geometry was used in their design, such as the golden ratio, Pythagorean triangle, and Golden Rectangle, which were also used in ancient sites in Egypt and Europe.[247] They were built using a standard unit of measurement of 30.5 cm, which is a tiny fraction more than a standard foot today at 30.48 cm;[248] the foot has a long history, as it was used by a number of ancient civilizations, including the Egyptian, Greek, Harappan/Indus Valley of Pakistan/India, and Neolithic Britons who built Stonehenge, though its length varied.[249]

In Hopi oral histories, the Anasazi were described as a "peaceful and prosperous people" who had "worshiped the sun" and lived in the region since "time immemorial."[250] The Hopi call them the "Hisatsinom," meaning "ancient people,"[251] and are believed (among other Pueblo peoples) to be descended from them. DNA analysis of elite burials from Chaco Canyon, including the richest ancient burial in the Southwest United States, dated to between 800-1,130 AD, revealed that they were all part of a ruling family who were related to each other through matrilineal descent.[252] They practiced cranial deformation, and one had six fingers,[253] which is a physical characteristic associated with giants.[254][255] A number of Pueblo peoples, including the Hopi and Zuni, still maintain a system of matrilineal descent and share (to low degrees) the same haplogroup as the elite of Chaco, B2[256]—believed to have originated in East Asia. Interestingly, this haplogroup is not found in populations along the migratory path said to have been taken by all Native Americans through Siberia and Beringia.[257][258] As noted earlier, that ceramics of the Anasazi are remarkably similar to those found among certain cultures of East Asia.

Settlements of the Hopi were built to mirror the constellation of Orion and the star Sirius on the ground, and also align to the solstices;[259] the solstices and these stars still feature centrally in Hopi ceremonies.[260] This practice of aligning sites to these specific stars and to the sun is found at the Great Pyramids of Egypt, and many other sacred sites around the world associated with the Religion of the Sun.

An illustration showing what the huge ancient
settlement of Chaco Canyon would have looked like.

Remarkably, Rolling Thunder's account echoes the story of the rise and fall of the Atlanteans as told by Plato. The "Great Spirit" who descended from above, to sweep the giants away with flood and fire, sounds like a meteor.

But what are we to make of it, since the more advanced structures of the Anasazi are thought to have been built between 750-1300 AD?

A possible contributor to Anasazi culture, which may provide some answers, are the Amazigh people of North Africa (commonly referred to as Berbers).

Left: Photograph of the so-called "Cliff Palace"—an ancient site of the Anasazi, which was clearly built within a cliff face as a means of fortification and protection. Right: Dwellings in the Bandiagara Escarpment in Mali, which were used by the Dogon people as a means of fortification and protection, and look incredibly similar to those of the Anasazi.

The Anasazi site of Mesa Verde shares a number of similarities with the Bandiagara Escarpment dwellings of the Dogon people in Mali, West Africa. The Dogon recount how their ancestors took refuge in these dwellings in the fourteenth century to escape Islamization. They displaced their earlier inhabitants and builders called the Tellem, which in the Dogon language means "those who were before us."[261] There is a tribe of Berber speaking people still living to the north of these cliffs called the Tamaha, who refer to themselves as T'Iullem-meden, meaning "they, the Iullem tribe" and who may well be descendants of the Tellem.[262]

Evidence for the presence of the Amazigh has been found in the Southwestern United States. Rock inscriptions in languages from North Africa have been identified there,[263] and the Hohokam culture (specifically from AD 1,000-1,130), whose territory was adjacent to that of the Anasazi, shared some similar customs with the Amazigh.[264] As mentioned earlier, the Canary Islands were largely populated by those genetically similar to the Amazigh, who are likely to have used it as a stopping point on the way to the Americas. A haplogroup was found among the ancient inhabitants of the Canaries that today is found at the highest frequency in the Dogon, who possibly interbred with the Tellem.[265]

The Dogon provide further evidence for these connections as their religion has a number of similarities with that of the ancient Egyptians.

"[...] key aspects of Dogon cosmology lend themselves to consistent correlation with various enigmatic elements of ancient Egyptian cosmology [...] the pervasive cultural, civic, and religious parallels that can be drawn between the Dogon and the ancient Egyptians strongly suggest a long period of close contact between the two cultures at some early point in Egyptian history [...]."[266]

~ LAIRD SCRANTON, THE COSMOLOGICAL ORIGINS OF MYTH AND SYMBOL: FROM THE DOGON AND ANCIENT EGYPT TO INDIA, TIBET, AND CHINA

Might that point of contact have been via the Amazigh? The Dogon state that they received their knowledge from wisdom bringers called Nommo who were primarily symbolized by the sun, and were referred to as serpents.[267] Were these teachers from among the Tellem/Amazigh? The Amazigh essentially descend from Eurasian people from the Levant who migrated into North Africa around twelve thousand years ago, and later mixed with farmers from Europe (most likely from Iberia) who migrated to North Africa during the Neolithic.[268] [269] They were among the people called Libyans in ancient times, which was the name given to the inhabitants of the land west of Egypt extending to Morocco (rather than just the territory of modern Libya).[270] They are recorded primarily as worshiping the sun, as well as a number of the most ancient and well-known gods of Egypt, such as Osiris, Neith/Athena, and Ammon/Amun, who some even believe originated from among the ancestors of the ancient Libyans. The Libyans also influenced the Greek pantheon of gods during a period of peaceful relations between the two cultures,[271] and the same Greek symbol of the labyrinth found on ancient coins from Crete is held sacred by the Hopi,[272] possibly indicating that some mixture of Greeks and Libyans traveled to the American southwest. The influence of the ancient Libyans may provide an explanation for the use of ancient Egyptian and Pythagorean geometry, as well as the foot as a unit of measurement, in Anasazi sites.

Is it possible that some of these ancient sites were first established by a race of white giants (Atlanteans), and later occupied, renovated, and built over by some of their distant descendants—the "ancient enemies" of the Navajo, and perhaps also the Comanche? Evidence for human habitation in the area is currently dated to as far back as 10,000 BC.[273] Certainly the history of the American Southwest is very ancient and multifaceted, but always seems to have been connected to the veneration of the sun.

The Mound Builders

Large numbers of ancient earthen mounds were built across vast regions of eastern North America—in the areas of the Great Lakes, Ohio River Valley, and Mississippi River Valley. They were often built as flat-topped pyramids[274] similar in design to those found in Central America, but without the stone exterior. The earliest evidence for them has currently been dated to approximately 5,500 BC (however, as most have been destroyed, there were possibly older sites).[275] They are located beside rivers connected to the ocean that ancient seafarers could have navigated along, and there is evidence that many did.[276] Many of these earthworks also align to the solstices and equinoxes.[277]

Map of mound sites in North America.

A survey of Amerindian oral traditions concerning the earthworks of eastern North America found that many tribes did not know who built them or what their purpose was. Others said they were built by their ancestors, with some saying they had a military purpose. For example, legends of the Cherokee and Choctaw tribes say there was a race of white giants whom their ancestors vanquished when they arrived in Mississippi.[278] One account said the mounds were built by a "strange white race" and by "white men from a foreign country;" another said "foreign peoples from the south;" and another said "giants."[279] One Amerindian tradition stated that their ancestors came from the west, but that the earthworks of Ohio were "raised by white Indians" who came from the ocean to the east. Other tribes said they were occupied by a series of Amerindian people, but that the mounds were actually built in ancient times by a people of whom they knew nothing about, and had no name for.[280] Some earthworks were found to be in use by Amerindians, but they ascribed their construction to a prior race from a much more ancient time.[281] Also associated with the mounds are numerous discoveries of skeletons of giant stature.[282]

"When these early explorers and settlers came upon these things [the ancient mounds and earthworks of North America] they were wonderstruck. Well of course they begin to turn to the native inhabitants of the region to enquire as to what was the origin of these things. And consistently through every single report that was published from the 1700s to the end of the 1800s, was the same:

the current tribes that lived there could furnish no information about them other than to say these were built by the ancient ones who were here before us, the 'Nunnehi,' 'the people who could travel anywhere' to use the term of the Cherokee. [...] It's interesting that when the excavations were done they would frequently find skeletons within the mound, which led the earlier researchers to conclude that they were burial mounds [...]. Typically what they would do is they would find that there were two types of skeletons. One skeleton that was near the surface, they would excavate it, and this is the one that would get sent to the museum, that would go to the Smithsonian [...] and so forth. When they would excavate down further, they would discover at the base of some of these mounds there were skeletons who as soon as they were exposed to light and air crumbled to dust. Now there were clearly two ages of skeleton [...]. The assumption was that the skeletons removed were skeletons of the builders, however, ignored in that is the obvious fact that there were two very distinct ages of skeletons [...]. By finding skeletons which were almost certainly intrusive burials, it misled researchers into thinking that these were the skeletons of the builders. If these were the skeletons of modern tribes or the immediate ancestors of the modern tribes—that explains the phenomena, there's no mystery here at all [...]."[283]

~ RANDALL CARLSON, ARCHAIC AMERICA: THE EARTHWORKS MYSTERY

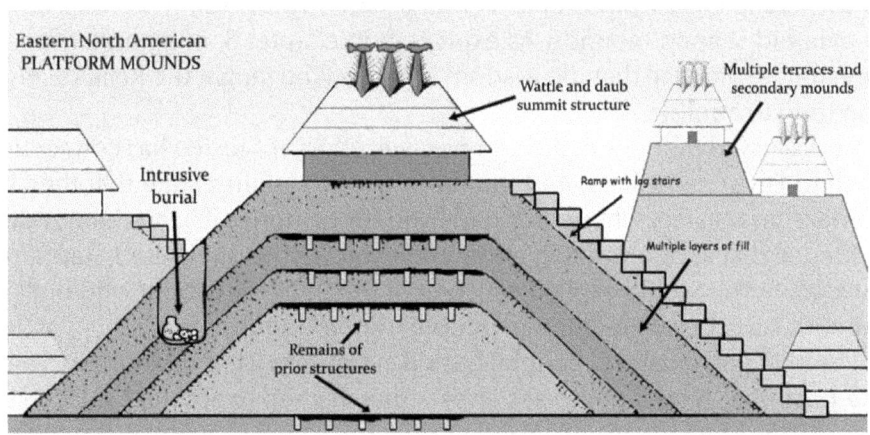

Cross-section of a typical pyramidal platform mound. Like the pyramids of Central America, they were often built over multiple times, and intrusive burials were added at a later date.

The Natchez are a Native American people who inhabited the Mississippi Valley, where they built mounds. They are the only Mississippian culture with a complex form of social organization to have survived long after European colonization,[284] and therefore information about their religion and origins may provide valuable insights into the mound builders of North America.

"Traditional Natchez religion venerated the Sun, which was represented by a perpetual fire kept burning in a temple. All fires in a village, including the sacred fire, were allowed to die once a year on the eve of the midsummer Green Corn ceremony, or Busk. The sacred fire was remade at dawn of the festival day, and all the village hearths were then lit anew from the sacred flames."[285]

~ ENCYCLOPEDIA BRITANNICA

Histories of the Natchez recall that their solar religion, and the sacred fire they kept perpetually burning, were first brought to them by "Sons of the Sun," who established themselves as their rulers.[286] These rulers were called "Suns" and the king the "Great Sun."[287] Just like the Inca royal family, the rulers of the Natchez claimed descent from the sun. And just like those of the Anasazi, inherited their status through the female line, with the Great Sun's mother called the "Female Sun." They also established a four-tiered caste system,[288] like that found in the Vedic religion of India.

Like some of the cultures of Central and South America, the Natchez practiced human sacrifice. When the king died, all the wives and servants of the king were expected to commit suicide, or were ritually sacrificed, in order to accompany him in the afterlife.[289] Evidence for this horrific practice has been found at one of the most famous mound sites in North America, called Cahokia.[290] Strikingly, it was also practiced by the pharaohs of ancient Egypt during the First Dynasty (3,100 BC-2,900 BC),[291] and by the emperors of the Shang Dynasty in China (as well as later dynasties), who were buried in pyramid shaped mounds. As explained in chapter 3, human sacrifice is a degenerate practice that the wisdom bringers who taught the Religion of the Sun tried to abolish.

As discussed further on, the Olmec civilization of Mexico has connections both to Egypt and China, and traditions of the Natchez state that they had come from Mexico, where they had lived for centuries,[292] and there is other evidence that supports a migration into what is now the United States from Mexico.[293] This would explain why one of the traditions about who built the mounds said they were "foreign people from the south."

The elite personages (a couple) buried at Cahokia were orientated towards the post of a "woodhenge" at Cahokia that aligned to summer solstice sunrise.[294] This again ties in with Natchez religion, which clearly saw the summer solstice sunrise as a time of spiritual rebirth. The burials date to between 1,000-1,100 AD when Cahokia was at its peak and its cultural influence extended along the length of the Mississippi from the Great Lakes in the north to where it terminates into the Gulf of Mexico in the south.[295]

The buried elite male was covered in beads laid out in the shape of a falcon, so that he resembled the "Birdman" who often appears on ancient artifacts at Cahokia. In some traditions, the Birdman is interpreted as a heroic figure whose sons fought off a race of giants.[296] Could these giants have been the first mound builders? There are two separate accounts from 1891 and 1906 of skeletons of larger than ordinary size being excavated from mounds at Cahokia, some of which crumbled to dust once exposed to the air,[297] likely due to their great age.

Ross Hamilton, who has conducted an extensive survey of the traditions related to the mounds and has compared them to archaeological discoveries, states that:

> "It seems that the tall people at least shared the status of being the first inhabitants of Indian memory, and that the smaller-in-stature folk lived among or in proximity to them from remotely ancient times. The Tall Ones tended to live together, consolidating their presence [...]."[298]
>
> ~ ROSS HAMILTON, A TRADITION OF GIANTS: THE ELITE SOCIAL HIERARCHY OF AMERICAN PREHISTORY

But after a time of living apart, the tribes who inhabited the west began expanding east, resulting in great wars:

> "Thousands of years ago in central North America, long before Cahokia and the Mississippian moundbuilding societies, there was a great and broad-ranging civil war. [...] The nomadic tribes of plains and prairies engaged for some time an eastern woodland adversary, and the battleground spanned a broad geography starting from the wide boundary of the ancient Mississippi eastward. It witnessed many battles and by its end sustained a radical loss of life bordering on mutual genocide. In sum, the great tribes of the west encountered the great nation of the east, and the resultant history—or rather prehistory—in due course shaped the pre-Columbian world far more than is presently understood."[299]
>
> ~ ROSS HAMILTON, A TRADITION OF GIANTS: THE ELITE SOCIAL HIERARCHY OF AMERICAN PREHISTORY

This explains why native traditions state that those who built the mounds were either unknown, were giants, or a white race. It also explains why the mounds were remembered as having a military purpose, as some were built solely for that reason. By 1,000 BC, Hamilton states that the nation of giants was eradicated, but that some survived as a special group who assumed, "a position at the apex of a hierarchical structure intimate with a population possessing average stature."[300] This would explain why mound building continued, and why in some traditions the mounds were remembered as being built by the ancestors of Native Americans.

The oldest evidence for mound building in North America currently dates back to around 6,500 years before the rise of Cahokia. Mound building in North America then followed a sequence, with various sites being built then abandoned (and sometimes later refurbished), and other mound sites afterward being built elsewhere and likewise abandoned, etc., down through thousands of years by different cultures, who, as Graham Hancock states:

> "[...] all shared the same mound-building obsession and continued to express it in the same ways. [...] Despite the fact that different cultures were involved at different periods, every resurgence of mound-building was linked to the reiteration and reimagination of the same geometrical and astronomical memes. This was not "chance" or "coincidence." [...] It's not unreasonable, therefore, to suppose that some kind of cosmic "sky-ground" religion lay behind the alignments to the solstices and the equinoxes at Watson Brake and at the other early sites—a religion sufficiently robust to ensure the continuous successful transmission of a system of geometry, astronomy, and architecture over thousands of years."[301]

It's likely that the tradition of mound building stretches back to the times of Atlantis, and was continued by its survivors (white giants), firstly as part of their own civilization, and then later by those whom they mixed with and taught.

DNA testing of ancient remains buried within mounds at the Hopewell Mound Group in Ohio showed that on their maternal line they were Amerindian and shared a unique genetic mutation with the elites buried at Cahokia.[302] This reveals there was a connection between the elites at two major mound sites, and therefore likely also between the knowledge behind their use and construction. Amerindian peoples have also preserved some of the astronomical knowledge encoded into the earthworks in their religious myths,[303] showing a continuity with the original builders.

A woodhenge (circle of wooden posts) at the site of the Cahokia Mounds in the U.S. state of Illinois, which like its British counterpart Woodhenge (near Stonehenge), also has alignments to the solstices. The combination of standing circle and mound is also a feature of ancient Neolithic sites in Europe.[304]

It's clear that from their inception, these sites were used for the ancient veneration of the sun, and that the practice of mound building, and the religion of the sun associated with it, was passed on, but that at some point later in its history became distorted with practices like human sacrifice.

Circular and Geometrical Earthworks

NEWARK, OHIO

AMAZON RAINFOREST

GOSECK CIRCLE, GERMANY

AVEBURY, ENGLAND

STONEHENGE, ENGLAND

Ancient circular earthen banks and ditches, which are called "henges," on opposite sides of the Atlantic.

Among the numerous mound and earthwork sites of the Americas are those that are circular and geometrical, often consisting of an earthen ditch and bank, which is astronomically aligned, particularly to the solstices and equinoxes. These sites are located in Ohio in North America, and the Amazon in South America. Researchers have noted many similarities, and sometimes identical features, between them and those at the ancient sites of Avebury and Stonehenge in England, which even date to the same time periods.[305] So far hundreds have been uncovered in the Amazon, where evidence for occupation dates back to approximately 2,500 BC. Although the alignments of the Amazonian earthworks have not yet been studied, three have already been identified as likely having alignments to solstices.[306]

Circular earthworks aligned to the solstices have a long history in Europe. Descendants of the Iron Gates Mesolithic culture are believed to have built the first ancient circular earthwork sites in Central and Eastern Europe between 4,800-4,600 BC,[307] [308] including Goseck Circle in Germany, which is aligned to winter solstice sunrise. Stonehenge in Britain also started out as a circular earthwork aligned to the solstices, believed to have been built by the so-called Windmill Hill people.[309] Those in Central and Eastern Europe were the first known farmers in the region, and likewise the Windmill Hill people were the first to bring farming to Britain. Striking similarities have also been found between their scripts,[310] further indicating some continuity between these European earthwork building cultures.

I think it's most likely that those who built these sites in Europe were involved in building them in the Americas, and that they were used as sacred places of the ancient Religion of the Sun.

The Stone Builders

Two dolmens on opposite sides of the Atlantic.
Left: Dolmen in New York state. Right: Dolmen in Wales.

Then there are the builders of the thousands of stoneworks, cairns, dolmens, and chambered passage mounds of the northeast. Three counties in the states of New York, Connecticut, and Vermont have the highest known density of them. In the region of New England alone, it was estimated in the 1930s to have 250,000 miles of stone walls. Chambered stone mounds in the area are built just like those found on the other side of the Atlantic along Europe's west coast, and like their European counterparts, have openings to allow beams of light to penetrate them at the solstices and equinoxes. Over two hundred of these ancient stone solar temples have been identified in New England.[311] For example, the so-called "calendar chamber" in Connecticut has an opening that allows a beam of light to enter on the equinoxes, while chambers in Maine and Massachusetts are similarly designed to allow the light of the sun in on the summer solstice.[312] In Europe, some of the most famous chambered passage mounds include Gavrinis, which is located on an island off the coast of France and is dated to around 3,500-3,000 BC, and is aligned to the winter solstice.[313] Newgrange in Ireland dates to around 3,200 BC, and also aligns to the winter solstice.[314] Likewise, Maeshowe in Scotland aligns to the winter solstice, and dates to between 3,000-2,500 BC.[315] Others align to the summer solstice and equinoxes.

Similar ancient stone chambers on opposite sides of the Atlantic. Left: Stone chamber in New York state. Right: Stone chamber in France dated to 4,700 BC, making it one of the oldest in Europe (it is aligned almost exactly to winter solstice sunrise).[316]

A number of the stone chambers in North America were found to have inscriptions in them, and artifacts with inscriptions were also discovered in association with them. Dr. Barry Fell, Professor Emeritus at Harvard University, identified the scripts they were written in as Ogham, Iberian, and Phoenician, and was able to translate them as dedications to the sun god of the Celts called Bel and that of the Phoenicians called Baal. Many also include solar symbols, like the eye of the sun god and solar cross, as also found in Europe.[317] A journalist and archaeologist independently claimed to have found hundreds of Ogham inscriptions across the Mississippi River Valley and the South West,[318] and another researcher has found Ogham at the Anasazi site Mesa Verde where it marks a solar alignment.[319]

Ogham is a form of writing first attested in Ireland, and inscriptions carved in stone are found in Ireland and west Britain (most numerously in Wales).[320] It was used to write the Old Irish language (an Indo-European language) and is dated to between the first century BC to fourth century AD. However, it may have much older roots, as a number of identical characters appear in the script of the Iron Gates Mesolithic and Vinča cultures.[321]

This account of one of the first colonial settlers in the Kanawha Valley in West Virginia provides further evidence for who their builders were:

> "Near the summit of the mountain dividing the waters of Loup and Armstrong creeks, in Fayette county, West Virginia, there is found the remains of a very remarkable stone wall, which was well known by the first white settlers in the Kanawha Valley, and to the Ohio Indians who passed along this route in hunting and other expeditions [...].
>
> The late Dr. Buster who was among the first white residents of the Kanawha valley, resided at the foot of this mountain [...]. No white man had ever occupied the ground upon which his father built his cabin, according to record; and the history of the pale face here, is absolutely complete within this family. [...] In my last interview,

about 1877, though a very old man, his mind and body were still active and vigorous. He remembered talking to the Indian 'medicine men' in his boyhood, as they frequently passed up the river, and discussed this wall and numerous relics of bones, stone implements and pottery found all over the surrounding bottom lands. According to his statements the Indians knew of these monuments, but claimed no part in them. One of their legends sets forth the fact that the Kanawha Valley had been occupied by a fierce race of white warriors, who successfully resisted the approach of the 'red man' from the west for a long time, but had finally succumbed, and passed away in death. The Indians claimed never to have occupied the valley, except for hunting expeditions; that they found these relics old when they first entered; and that their origin was beyond his records.

Though such legends are not always reliable, a careful study of the conditions, habits of the people, and the bones found at the foot of the mountain, inevitably leads to more than the suspicion of a prehistoric race, differing from the North American Indian in physiognomy, character and habits."[322]

~ HISTORY OF THE GREAT KANAWHA VALLEY: WITH FAMILY HISTORY AND BIOGRAPHICAL SKETCHES

The ancient copper mine in Michigan in the Great Lakes region (northeast) of the United States was said in local native legend to have been mined by "fair-haired marine men" who left behind petroglyphs of a sailing ship and solar cross—the copper they mined has been suggested to have fueled the Bronze Age in Europe,[323] where a solar religion dominated. Evidence for mining activity there dates as far back as 6,000 BC.[324] Many other artifacts, language similarities, oral traditions, and ancient sites, too countless to list here, link ancient North America to Britain.[325]

I believe, as a number of other researchers do, that the stoneworks, dolmens, and chambered mounds in the northeast of North America were built by the seafaring megalithic civilization that stretched from the Mediterranean (including the island of Malta where similarly designed solar temples were built), to along the Atlantic coast of Europe as far as Scotland.[326] And that the Celts and Phoenicians, who came to inhabit these European territories, continued to build upon the civilization these megalith builders established both in Europe and in the Americas. It's possible that what they established in the Americas was considered as much a part of their civilization as that in Europe. The Celts called their kingdom in the American northeast "Iargalon," meaning "the land beyond the sunset."[327]

This is certainly possible, as the Celts had a powerful navy—Julius Caesar stated that one of the Celtic tribes had 220 seaworthy ships, far stronger than those of the Romans, against which he fought his greatest naval battle, saying

232

"The ships were built wholly of oak, and designed to endure any force and violence whatever; the benches which were made of planks a foot in breadth, were fastened by iron spikes of the thickness of a man's thumb; the anchors were secured fast by iron chains instead of cables, and for sails they used skins and thin dressed leather [instead of canvas, which is weaker]."[328] The Romans won the battle, destroying the Celtic navy, and it's from about this time onward that further Celtic artifacts, inscriptions, and sites cease in North America.[329] Those Celts who must have remained in North America eventually succumbed to invasion.

Some cultures from the Old World made more of an impact on the New than others, but many left their mark. Reams of evidence, presented in the works of Fell, clearly indicate that for thousands of years peoples from the Old World traveled to North America and established networks of trade, colonies, schools of learning, and religious sites. These people included the Phoenicians, Celts, Celtiberians, Tartessians, Basques, Carthaginians, Libyans, Egyptians, Greeks, Arabs, Chinese, Japanese, Norse, and Hebrews. All of them left their imprint on North America either through artifacts, inscriptions, language, and/or sites. Relations were apparently peaceful with the indigenous people, who were eager to share, trade, and learn, and the Atlantic Ocean, and to a lesser extent the Pacific, were sailed frequently, as were the river systems of North America—connecting Asia and Europe with the Americas, until the Roman conquest of Europe, which led to the demise of this once busy ancient transoceanic network.[330]

> "The advanced mathematical principles, found encoded into precisely positioned, purpose-built surveying markers around Ring o' Brodgar and the greater Orkney Islands [in Scotland], tell us the following facts with indisputable clarity:
>
> By about 3000 BC the cousin Caucasoid nations living around the Mediterranean and throughout Continental Europe, were making ocean traversals to the Americas in their very seaworthy, large, planked sailing ships. For this otherwise dangerous undertaking they used Britain as a main staging area and had established several expansive open-air universities for teaching mathematical principles of navigation and cyclic astronomy. In the British Isles great sprawling schools, offering intensive-comprehensive courses, were laboriously built at Avebury Henge and Durrington Walls Henge in Wiltshire, England, as elsewhere.
>
> This European preoccupation with exploration would go a long way towards explaining why such a high percentage of the Algonquian Indian language of North America, extending to the Great Lakes region and almost across the entire continent, contains many clearly

identifiable ancient Basque words (the same word used for elbow, foot, head, breast, shoulder, guts, lake, river, louse, birch bark, ocean, boat, snow (falling), snow (on ground) etc.). Moreover, it's a very ancient form of the Basque tongue, uninfluenced by Indo-Aryan admixtures that crept into the Basque language at later epochs.

[...] Also, ancient European structures, cultural-symbolism and writing are found in profusion up and down the Eastern seaboard of the United States, with Hebrew, Phoenician, runic or ogham scripts, etc., seen as far inland as Minnesota, Oklahoma, Ohio, New Mexico, etc. Caucasoid remains are found in Nevada, extending to the Windover bog of Florida or from Mexico to Peru (the Cloud People) & Bolivia, etc. A very high percentage North American Indians carry the European 'Y' chromosome and many tribes in both North and South America have oral traditions of the white tribes that their ancestors vanquished. The same measurement & angle standards employed to build ancient Mediterranean-European structures were used to build the huge geometric earthmound complexes of Ohio and Pennsylvania, as well as the temple structures of South America."[331]

> ~ MARTIN DOUTRÉ, RING O' BRODGAR, ORKNEY ISLANDS: GATEWAY TO THE AMERICAS

The inscriptions at the ancient stone chamber sites in Northeast United States, along with their alignments, clearly indicate they were religious places used for sun worship.

CENTRAL AND SOUTH AMERICA

The Aztecs of Central America, and Inca of South America, did not claim to have built many of the ancient sacred sites they occupied.

Oral histories of the Inca say that the ancient megalithic sites in Peru and Bolivia were built by the bearded, fair-skinned men that had come to their lands with Viracocha.

> "When the Spaniards came to Lake Titicaca, up in the Andes, they found the mightiest ruins in South America—Tiahuanaco. They saw a hill reshaped by man into a stepped pyramid, classical masonry of enormous blocks beautifully dressed and fitted together, and numerous large stone statues in human form. They asked the Indians to tell them who had left these enormous ruins. The well-known chronicler Cieza de Leon was told in reply that these things had been made long before the Incas came to power. They were made by white and bearded men like the Spaniards themselves. The white men finally had abandoned their statues and gone with their leader,

Con-Ticci Viracocha, first up to Cusco, and then down to the Pacific. They were given the Inca name of viracocha, or 'sea foam' because they were white of skin and vanished like foam over the sea. [...] When the Spaniards reached the shores of Lake Titicaca, they heard from the Indians there too that Con-Ticci Viracocha had been chief of a long-eared people who sailed on Lake Titicaca in reed boats. [...] The Indians added that it was these long-ears who helped Con-Ticci Viracocha transport and raise the colossal stone blocks weighing over a hundred tons which lay abandoned at Tiahuanaco."[332]

~ THOR HEYERDAHL, AKU-AKU: THE SECRET OF EASTER ISLAND

There is much evidence that many of the "Viracochas" or "fair skinned bearded men" who had traveled to South America with the wisdom bringer Viracocha, remained and settled there in outposts that became part of a network of sites throughout the world on well-traveled sea routes. For example, at least hundreds of mummies with red, blonde, and light brown hair have been discovered in Lima, Paracas, and Nazca in Peru.[333] There are also numerous ancient artifacts that have been found throughout Central and South America that depict Caucasian, bearded men, including painted wall frescos, statues, and rock carvings. For a thoroughly comprehensive and detailed examination of these artifacts, as well as beautiful photographic reproductions of them, I recommend the book *American Indians in the Pacific* by Thor Heyerdahl.

A mummy found near the ancient Nazca Lines in Peru. This woman had very fine plaited, strawberry blonde hair, and is just one of hundreds of ancient mummies in Peru with fine blonde, red, or brown hair.

The Aztecs stated that their knowledge had come down to them from Quetzalcoatl and his followers,[334] who were described as "astrologers and necromancers, marvelous poets and philosophers, painters as were not to be found elsewhere in the world, and such builders that for a thousand leagues the remains of their cities, temples and fortresses strewed the land."[335] Diego Duran, a friar and author of one of the first Western books on the Aztecs, said that whenever he asked an indigenous person "who cut this pass through the mountains, or who opened that spring of water, or who built that old ruin," the answer was, "The Toltecs [the predecessors of the Aztecs[336]], the disciples of Papa [Quetzalcoatl]."[337] As discussed in chapter 2, the Aztecs stated that Quetzalcoatl and his followers were from a race of giants, and these giants were said to have built the ancient site Teotihuacan (which includes the Pyramid of the Sun and shares a number of similarities with the Great Pyramids of Egypt[338]) as well as the pyramid of Cholula,[339] which may be the most ancient pyramid in the Americas.

The Aztecs, the Maya, and the Inca all renovated existing ancient sites, in some cases multiple times (for example, a number of Maya and Aztec pyramids have been discovered to have been built over in at least five successive layers of restoration). Each of these civilizations also attempted to revive the religion of the original builders. While most are familiar with these cultures, few realize they were preceded by others who were far older, like the Olmec, Chimú, and Chinchorro, who were likely to have been preceded by even earlier cultures themselves. The author Richard Cassaro has also noted incredible similarities between later Maya and Balinese temple architecture, revealing there was contact between Indonesia and Central America.[340]

A model of the Cholula Pyramid in Mexico dedicated to the wisdom bringer Quetzalcoatl, showing multiple phases of its building, as the original sacred site was continually built over by different peoples—until finally being topped by a church. The original pyramid possibly dates to at least 6,500 BC, making it the oldest known in the Americas, and as having been built thousands of years before the Aztecs.[341] The Aztecs said it was first built by the giant Xelhua, surnamed "the Architect," who had survived the great flood.[342]

The Inca

The Inca Empire is the most famous ancient civilization in South America, and is generally thought to have been founded by local pastoralists sometime in the early thirteenth century.[343] However, a rare manuscript written in 1644 by a Spanish explorer and priest living in Peru, who claimed to have crossed the Andes no less than seventy times, states that the Inca Empire has much more ancient and foreign origins.

According to the accounts he transcribed, the first Inca king was preceded by ninety-three pre-Inca rulers! The manuscript starts by describing the settling of the Americas by peoples who arrived from across the ocean; the Spanish author speculates they came from Armenia and the Middle East.[344] Their foreign origin would explain why the Spanish invaders described the Inca rulers as fair-skinned and haired, and why some of the Inca mummies have fair, fine, and wavy hair.[345] They were said to have lived for a long time in peace, and gradually spread over all of South America.[346]

These first rulers were called Amautas, and did not live in Cuzco as the later Inca kings would, but at Ollantaytambo—whose original name meant "House of the Dawn"[347]—where there is an ancient pyramid aligned to the winter solstice sunrise, and many megalithic ancient sites.[348] Amauta is a Quechua word meaning "master of great wisdom." These Amautas were a special class of wise men who were the most highly educated and respected in the later Inca Empire.[349] They became advisers to the Inca nobility, and were known as interpreters of the sky and stars, and keepers of knowledge.[350] They maintained the knowledge of all sciences, history, morality, and religion through an oral tradition, which they were tasked with passing to all future generations throughout the Empire.[351]

As noted earlier, the Inca and pre-Inca civilizations (together with the ancient civilizations of Mexico) share over one hundred cultural similarities with the ancient civilizations of Egypt and Mesopotamia. Many of the Inca and pre-Inca cultural artifacts are essentially identical to those of Egypt, differing only in local style.[352] Also noted in different parts of this book are the similarities shared with the ancient civilization of India.

The Guna/Kuna

In 1924, Richard Oglesby Marsh led a scientific expedition into one of the most dangerous places in the world—the Darien jungle of Panama. There he discovered "white" indigenous people still living according to their ancient traditions among the tribe known as the Guna or Tule. After a harrowing journey, on which a number of the scientists lost their lives, Marsh was granted an audience with one of their chiefs, who was the latest in a long line of hereditary kings, and was allowed to spend time among the Guna and learn about their society.

"[...] I was astonished to learn of the high level of political organization they have achieved. Not only did they have an hereditary feudal government, but courts of law with a recognized code of precedents.[353] [...] Like all the Indians of the San Blas coast, brown as well as white, they proved far superior in intelligence and character to any other Indians I had even encountered, either in North or South America, and not excepting the Pueblos of our own Southwest. Their civilization was far more advanced, and their political practices, ethical standards, and practical arts more perfected. Their treatment of women and children alone would set them apart. I never saw a woman or child among them who did not look happy. They speak of their women as "flowers," and their manner toward them is as gentle and considerate as one would expect from that poetical idea."[354]

~ RICHARD O. MARSH, BLOND INDIANS OF THE DARIEN JUNGLE

The chief allowed Marsh to take three "white" Guna back with him to the United States; there they were studied by leading scientists, ethnologists, and linguists.[355] They made detailed recordings of their language, and came to the conclusion that it had a structure like Sanskrit and shared numerous similarities with Old Norse.[356] Tule, which is the name the Guna call themselves, is very similar to Thule, the name of an island or region in the most northerly part of the world in ancient Greek writings, which has been identified with places like Iceland and Norway[357] where Old Norse was spoken.

The "white Indians" that Marsh saw are known today to have a particular type of albinism (which affects the same gene that produces blue eyes[358]) at one of the highest rates in the world.[359] According to Guna traditions, the first of these "white" people was called Mago/Mako—the father of the sun who was sent to them by god. His albino descendants were venerated as "Grandchildren of the Sun" and "Children of the Moon."[360] The Guna recount how God regularly sends human emissaries to correct people on earth when they become corrupt, and that when this fails, God punishes them with catastrophes. Some people learn, but others become evil, and even degenerate into "animal people." After one of these catastrophes, in which the world was upturned, Mago arrived as a prophet, but was later called back to God. Four more cycles of corruption, emissaries, and catastrophe followed—the last a flood. The final emissary of this present age was Ipeorkun/Ibeorkun,[361] who arrived on the disk of the sun,[362] taught them various arts of civilization, gave them the text of God's Way,[363] and likely instructed them in their religious practices associated with the sun.[364]

On his expedition, Marsh encountered a number of ancient structures in the Panamanian jungle which he determined were abandoned pyramids:

"They were certainly not natural, but man-made—small primitive earth pyramids [...]. As soon as I reached the top of the hill, I saw that it was unquestionably artificial or artificially altered. The top was perfectly level. The edges were straight lines to uniform slopes. [...] The general effect of the hill was a truncated pyramid, a design common to most of the ancient cultures of Central and South America. The terraced amphitheatre was unusual, but its purpose was apparent."[365]

Marsh also found the Guna had a high degree of morality, stating:

"Except for the Chocois themselves, all the tribes of Darien are monogamous, and they have, besides, quite the highest standard of sexual morality I have encountered anywhere in the world. When I say this, I do not except the white men of the United States."[366]

Others who joined Marsh in his contact with the white Guna claimed to have been shown a book of their ancient writings by a head priest, and stated that it was hieroglyphic.[367] This led Marsh to conclude that the Guna had once been part of a great civilization, which had already collapsed before the arrival of the Spanish:

"I am more and more convinced [...] that Darien in very ancient times was the seat of a highly developed culture which was destroyed long before the coming of the Spaniards. Certain remnants of it are still preserved among the Tule tribes."[368]

In 1925, Marsh took part in the uprising of the Guna against the Panamanian government. He appealed to the United States, who helped broker a peace treaty between the Panamanians and the Guna, which ultimately resulted in the protection of the Guna lands and customs, as well as the granting of some autonomy.[369] As part of this, the Guna adopted their own flag. It features a swastika, which is their ancestral symbol called Naa Ukuryaa, said to symbolize "the four sides of the world" or the place from where the world's people emerged.[370]

The ethnic flag of the Guna, which is golden yellow like the sun.

The Chachapoya

The Chachapoya were a large pre-Inca civilization in the remote mountain ranges of Peru. At one time their population numbered half a million,[371] and their city called Kuélap high up in the mountains is one of the largest ancient ruins in the world (with a mass three times that of the Great Pyramid of Egypt[372]).

The absolutely massive fortified walls that were built around the entire Chachapoya settlement of Kuélap high up in the Andes Mountains of Peru.

They were described as fair skinned by the Spanish invader Pedro Pizarro, who stated, "The people of this kingdom of Peru were white but of a tawny hue, and among them the Lords and Ladies were whiter than Spaniards. I saw in this land an Indian woman and a child who did not differ from those who are white and blond. These people say that the latter were the children of the heathen gods [meaning they were descendants of those who came to Peru with the wisdom bringer Viracocha]."[373] The chronicler Pedro Cieza de León similarly described them as, "the whitest and most handsome of all the people that I have seen in the Indies."[374]

Today, there are still people living in the remote regions of the former Chachapoya civilization who are white and blond and whose DNA traces to Europe (as explained earlier in this chapter).[375] The building style and cultural artifacts of the Chachapoya also trace back to Europe—specifically to the Castro, Celtiberian, and Talayot cultures of Iberia (in regions of what is now mostly Spain). This has been thoroughly documented by Professor Hans Giffhorn, who proposes that the peoples from these cultures crossed the Atlantic, traveled up the Amazon River, and founded the Chachapoya civilization in the Amazonian Andean Mountains. These journeys would have been possible, as crossing the Atlantic using the ocean currents would have been easier/safer than the sea crossings known to have been made by the Celts of northwest Iberia to Brittany and Ireland.[376] The journey from the Atlantic up the Amazon River to the territory of the Chachapoya was also possible, as this same journey was made by Spanish explorers in 1538 and 1542.[377]

The unique building style of the Chachapoya is found nowhere else in Central or South America, and yet is identical to that of the Celts in Iberia. Celtiberian artifacts and practices have also been found among the Chachapoya. Evidence points to them arriving in South America around two thousand years ago,[378] at a time when they were being conquered by the Romans,[379] to a large island at the mouth of the Amazon River, called Marajo. The local people stated that their ancestors saw strange men with red beards make landfall there. Petroglyphs of ancient Celtiberian script have also been identified near the coast of Brazil.[380] The culture on Marajo suddenly began to make complex ceramics in styles similar to that of the Celtiberians and became what is now considered the highest developed ancient culture in Brazil.[381]

The settlement of Los Millares in Spain, in use approximately 4,000-2,000 BC (where depictions of sun ships have been found [382]). Artistic reconstructions of Kuélap show it would have looked very similar.

Left: Chachapoya hut in Kuélap in Peru (note the lozenge decoration, which is found in the megalithic artwork of Europe). Right: Celtiberian hut in Spain.

The Celtiberian connection to the Chachapoya is further proof that cultures of the Old World had contact with the New, and knew of the existence of the Americas. After their arrival, the Celtiberians may have recognized themselves as being related to earlier Old World migrants to the Americas, or perhaps knew of their existence already. There is much evidence that suggests there were already existing trade relations between the Old and New Worlds (for example the presence of tobacco was found in ancient Egyptian mummies dated to 1,070-395 BC—a plant only found in the Americas at the time[383]). And there were likely to have already been well-established colonies.

On Marajo Island, where the Celtiberians appear to have landed, there are ancient mounds and earthworks like those in the northeast of the United States and the British Isles, dating back to at least 1,000-300 BC, which is also when evidence for widescale plant cultivation appears there.[384] This suggests that earlier peoples, like the Celts of Britain, arrived before them, possibly to an established port, the knowledge of which may had been handed down to them by their ancestors. Earthworks with near-identical features in some cases to the henges of the British Isles are found farther up the Amazon River in the Rio Branco area of Brazil (as noted in the previous section).

This may explain why the Chachapoya told the Spanish they were descendants of the Viracochas. They would certainly have identified themselves as a later arrival of their ancestors, feeding into the already established Lost Civilization of the Sun in the Americas. The Celtiberians are known to have venerated the sun (and moon),[385] and what is believed to be a ceremonial area at Kuélap is aligned to the equinoxes.[386]

Left: Drawing of the physical type I think is closely represented by the Chachapoya statues (the man is Conor McGregor, a famous Irish boxer and MMA fighter). Center: Chachapoya statues, which appear to have stylized beards. Right: Statues on Easter Island.

The Celtiberians were a Celtic (Indo-European) speaking people who inhabited central-eastern Iberia along the coast (today mostly in Spain) in the last few centuries BC. They have been shown to have derived from the earlier Castro culture of Iberia,[387] and are most closely genetically related to Iberians who migrated to Britain between 5,000-4,000 BC. People in the region where the Castro culture existed are still known for their fair skin, and green and blue eyes.[388] The Celtiberians are likely descendants of a large maritime, megalith-building Celtic culture that stretched along the west coast of Europe from around 3,000 BC.[389]

They went on to build a large and peaceful civilization in South America. Archaeologist Alfredo Narváez believes that due to the enormous size of their Kuélap fortress it must have been built on a voluntary basis as a communal, ritual, and religious center.[390] This huge undertaking would not have been possible without the help, cooperation, and integration of the indigenous people.[391]

The Chachapoya fortress city at Kuélap has been compared to Machu Picchu, and resembles the ancient stone city in Zimbabwe (said in local legend to have been built by another fair-skinned people[392] and that also has solar and astronomical alignments[393]), as well as the cities of the Anasazi in North America. A stone head kept at a museum in the former territory of the Celtic Castro culture is identical in design to those created by the Chachapoya.[394] Additionally, these statues bear a resemblance to the iconic giant stone statues on Easter Island.

EASTER ISLAND

The presence of the "Viracochas" is also found on Easter Island, where the ancient stone statues were built in the image of Viracocha. Oral histories state that a king called Hotu Matu'a came to Easter Island from "a sun-dried land, in the same direction as Peru, with long-ears among his followers."[395] This land was the region around Tiwanaku, which Viracocha was said to have built, and which shares many similarities with the artwork, sculpture, and practices of Easter Island.[396] As explained earlier, genetic evidence has proven this to be true, with the presence of DNA specifically found in the indigenous Aymara of the region around Tiwanaku found in the natives of Easter Island.

The Dutch and Spanish explorers who first landed on Easter Island in 1722 and 1770 respectively, both stated that they saw people of Caucasian appearance amid a very ethnically mixed population. The Dutch also saw the island's inhabitants worshiping the sun. One of the first natives to board their ship seemed to be a priest; he wore a crown of feathers, had elongated earlobes, and was described as "a completely white man." According to the indigenous tradition, the Caucasians were descendants of the earliest people who had come to the island:

> "[...] according to the traditions of the natives themselves, many of their ancestors in olden times had white skin, red hair, and blue eyes."[397]
>
> ~ THOR HEYERDAHL, AKU-AKU: THE SECRET OF EASTER ISLAND

Left: Drawing of a man on Easter Island made during James Cook's expedition in 1777. Right: Another drawing of a chief on Easter Island made during Theodore de Flore Lappelin's expedition in 1872.

The Spanish noted that some of the fair inhabitants were very tall, bearded, and had shades of brown and reddish hair. The red lava stones placed on top of the statues on Easter Island were said to represent the red hair of the first divine founders of the island, and some of the fair-skinned men with reddish hair were said in local histories to be descended from them.[398]

> "The Spaniards met on the island tall, fair men. Two of the biggest were measured and were respectively 6 feet, 6 1/2 inches and 6 feet, 5 inches tall. Many had beards, and the Spaniards found that they were quite like Europeans and not ordinary natives. They noted in their diaries that not all of them had black hair: the hair of some was chestnut brown, and in other cases it was even reddish and cinnamon-colored."[399]
>
> ~ THOR HEYERDAHL, AKU-AKU: THE SECRET OF EASTER ISLAND

The author David Childress noticed that the red lava stones on the statues looked like the topknot the Hindu god Shiva is depicted with, leading him to conclude that the moai of Easter Island are statues of devotees to Shiva.[400] The red lava stones are called "pukao," meaning "topknot," because of the type of hairstyle they are said to represent. It was custom for high ranking men on Easter Island to wear their hair like this.[401] Shiva is also depicted with this hairstyle, and it's custom for ascetics in India (called sadhus), particularly those who venerate Shiva, to wear their hair in a topknot in imitation of him.[402]

Evidence indicates that Shiva was one of the primary gods worshiped in the Indus Valley Civilization in India.[403] This and further evidence connecting Easter Island to the Indus Valley (such as the similarities between Rongorongo and the Indus Valley Script, the practice of ear elongation, the use of reed ships, and the worship of the sun), indicate that the statues could well be connected to Shiva.

The hands of the moai point to their sacrum, the seat of creative energy, and in local tradition the moai were said to be phallic symbols;[404] Shiva is often symbolized by a lingam, considered a phallic symbol, which portrays him as the generative and creative power of all existence.[405] This means that the moai may be a kind of Shiva-linga, though symbolically connected to resurrection in the afterlife. The statues of the Chachapoya (discussed in this book), and the statue found at Urfa near Göbekli Tepe, which look similar to the moai, are portrayed with an erect phallus, as Osiris sometimes is. This symbol of generative power is likely to have been associated with resurrection, and thus the statues could have acted in the same or a similar way to the sarcophagi of ancient Egypt, in which the deceased would be portrayed as Osiris in order to resurrect like him.

Based on these connections, along with those already discussed in chapter 3, beliefs about the wisdom bringers Shiva (and also Odin, who is connected to Shiva), Viracocha, and possibly Osiris, may have been associated with one another by those who migrated to Easter Island and may have even originated from the same wisdom bringer.

Top Left: Sadhu in India with topknot hairstyle of the sect who worships Shiva. Top Right: Drawing of a native from Easter Island with topknot hairstyle. Bottom Left: Statue of Shiva with stylized topknot and elongated earlobes. Bottom Right: Moai on Easter Island with a stylized red stone topknot and elongated earlobes.

INDIA

Recent genetic studies have concluded that Indo-European-speaking people, who inhabited the Eurasian steppe, migrated into Northern India at around 2,000-1,500 BC[406]—their DNA (essentially the paternal haplogroup R1a) is found to a high degree particularly in the Brahmin or priestly caste of the Vedic/Hindu religion,[407] and contributed up to 30 percent of the genepool of people living in India today.[408] This supports the theory that these migrants brought the Vedic religion and Indo-European language to India.

However, what's still contested is whether there is evidence for Vedic religion (and Indo-European language) in India far earlier. Some scholars have interpreted the ancient Vedic texts as describing the landscape of Northern India as it existed thousands of years prior, as discussed in chapter 2. Others claim to have found archaeological evidence of Vedic religion in India dating to before the proposed steppe migration. For example, the ancient Indus Valley city of Dholavira, dated to around 3,000 BC,[409] has been identified as being laid out according to principles of architecture enumerated in the Vedas,[410] and contained a solar observatory.[411] Possible fire altars in Vedic style have been unearthed at the Indus Valley city of Kalibangan in which worshipers would have faced the rising sun.[412] And evidence for horses (integral to Vedic culture) have been found at Indus Valley sites dating back to 2,600 BC.[413]

While on an archaeological expedition in the region, Thor Heyerdahl visited sites in the Indus Valley and found the same building styles he had seen in other ancient sun-worshiping civilizations like in Peru and Egypt (such as the use of butterfly clamps in megalithic construction, polygonal masonry, and stepped pyramids), as well as the ancient practice of ear elongation and cotton cultivation. He noticed that the Sun Temple of Modhera in the Indus Valley region, which had been built in a stepped pyramid form, and was aligned so that on the equinoxes the sun would illuminate the temple, had been built over an older, demolished structure, which had used megalithic butterfly clamps.[414] Looking at images of the Sun Temple, I noticed that it shares unique motifs with the ancient site of Puma Punku, which is part of Tiwanaku in Bolivia.

There are also over one thousand rock-cut cave temples in India, some of which are aligned to the solstices and equinoxes. Those considered the oldest have doorways cut in a trapezoidal shape with machine-like precision into solid granite (an extremely hard stone) in a strangely beautiful, unadorned, monolithic style. This same monolithic style is found at ancient sites in Peru and Egypt, such as the Osireion and Great Pyramids, while megalithic trapezoidal doorways are found most frequently at ancient sites in Peru.

There is no evidence for their local development in India; instead, these and similar caves have been dated based on inscriptions and artwork carved into them. There are several Buddhist and Hindu rock-cut sculptures and inscriptions at what is believed to be the oldest cave site, which are known to have been added later,[415] and I think all of this kind of stonework was an embellishment made by later peoples.[416]

Top Left: Plan of the Modhera Sun Temple. Although the latest structures were built after AD 1026, the temple was built over an earlier structure and may have retained the same layout. Top Right: Pool at the Modhera Sun Temple with stepped pyramid motifs. Look closely at the reflection in the water, and see how it was used to create the same symbol at Puma Punku. Center Right: The same motif incorporated into the temple at Modhera, but using a much more elaborate style. Bottom Left and Right: Motifs, which look very similar to those at the Modhera Sun Temple, carved into Puma Punku, which is part of the ancient site of Tiwanaku in Bolivia. Both sites used megalithic blocks and butterfly clamps. Puma Punku displays a highly sophisticated knowledge of stonework, as the blocks are carved with machine-like precision. There are several features at Tiwanaku and Puma Punku which indicate they are likely to be much older than they're currently dated.[417] As discussed earlier, Tiwanaku was said in local histories to have been built by the followers of Viracocha.

Left: Entrance to one of the caves in India, with trapezoidal doorway. Center: Similar trapezoidal doorway at the ancient site of Ollantaytambo in Peru, center of the Amautas. Right: Trapezoidal doorway at the ancient city of Cuzco in Peru, later center of the Inca.

Considered together, Heyerdahl found the traits of the Indus Valley Civilization to be most comparable to the ancient civilization of Peru and Bolivia. This led him to conclude that mariners from the Indus Valley had traveled to South America via the Atlantic Ocean; those associated with the civilizations in both places (i.e. the seafaring, step pyramid and polygonal wall building, sun and Shiva worshiping Redin who were the first inhabitants of the Maldives off the coast of India and appear to have formerly inhabited the Indus Valley, and the Viracochas of Peru) were described as having fair skin, blue eyes, and red/brown hair, as well as elongated earlobes.[418]

> "The idea seemed at first too fantastic to consider seriously. I had long suspected that Middle East culture had reached tropical America by sea centuries before Columbus [...]. There were also those scholars who had speculated on prehistoric voyages from India, by way of the Pacific, to America. I myself, like almost everybody else, had rejected such conjectures as geographically without sense. By the time the prehistoric voyagers from India had reached the Asiatic shores of the Pacific, they would still have half the circumference of this planet left to cross before reaching America. [...] Nobody seemed to realize that America lay much closer to India westwards by way of the Atlantic Ocean; nor that this course would, furthermore, be favored by the elements."[419]
>
> ~ THOR HEYERDAHL, THE MALDIVE MYSTERY

These connections add further weight to the similarities between the ancient civilizations of India, South America, and Easter Island that have already been covered, such as those between the languages of Sanskrit and Quechua.

There are further indications of contact between India and other ancient cultures. For example, there are a number of ancient standing stones in India with solar alignments like those found in North Africa and the British Isles.[420] And as already discussed, there are also connections with the Minoans of Crete.

Ancient standing stones in India, like those found in many other parts of the world. In India there were also megalithic trilithons like Stonehenge.

A very unique and specific marking that was painted on the body of some Australian Aborigines has been found on one of the pillars of Göbekli Tepe.[421] Geneticists know that there was a migration from India to Australia at around 2,000 BC,[422] and this may be the source of the ancient marking. But how would Indians have known about it from Göbekli Tepe, which was buried in the eighth millennium BC, unless there was some kind of contact with the site's builders or their descendants? Interestingly, there are signs of Vedic religion in Anatolia around that time, as discussed in chapter 2.

The earliest known site of agriculture in the region of India is at Mehrgarh, now located in Pakistan, which is believed to have been the predecessor to agriculture in the Indus Valley Civilization. The use of agriculture at Mehrgarh dates back to 7,000 BC.[423] The researcher Yvonne Whiteman has located the "gardenplace" of the Children of God, as described in *The Kolbrin*, as having been at Mehrgarh sometime in the distant past.[424] Was some lineage of knowledge preserved there that left no genetic trace? And were there other migrations into India, prior to 2,000 BC, which geneticists are yet to discover?

NEW ZEALAND

The people of the Lost Civilization of the Sun also got as far as the island country of New Zealand, described by some as the "ends of the earth," as it is almost the farthest place they could have traveled by boat from Egypt and Eurasia. The evidence of their existence there also reveals a lot about whom they were and where they came from. Legends of the local Maori people, whose ancestors colonized New Zealand in around AD 1300, described the civilization of people they found when they arrived as being Caucasian in appearance.

> "In Maori oral traditions and history, these more ancient residents that the first Maori immigrants encountered were universally described as 'uru-kehu' and 'kiri-puwhero', which in physical terms means people with light, reddish-pinkish skin colouration and reddish hair."[425]
>
> ~ MARTIN DOUTRÉ, ARCHAEOASTRONOMER AND AUTHOR OF WWW.CELTICNZ.CO.NZ

Extensive research by the archaeoastronomer Martin Doutré has identified standing stones that align to the solstices and equinoxes in New Zealand, as well as "bullauns," which are small cup holes carefully carved into the rock. Bullauns are characteristic of ancient sites in the British Isles, and standing stones with solar alignments are found throughout the British Isles and Europe.

> "The use of bullauns, stemming from Neolithic Age ritual cleansing and 'holy wells' traditions still practised in Continental Europe and Britain, was equally prevalent in New Zealand. The Pagan European

bullaun ritual practices were adopted by the early Christian church and bullaun bowls became the 'baptismal fonts' or holy water vessels of the church for baptism, sprinkling or christening rituals."[426]

~ MARTIN DOUTRÉ, THE ANCIENT SURVEYING STRUCTURES ON THE BOMBAY HILLS

Cave burials that have been accidentally unearthed in New Zealand have been found to possibly contain the remains of ancient Caucasian skeletons.

"Burial caves all over New Zealand contain the remains of red, brown or blond haired Indo-European skeletons."[427]

~ MARTIN DOUTRÉ, MEGALITHIC NEW ZEALAND

This prior civilization in New Zealand was mostly wiped out by Polynesian tribes who eventually took over the islands. However, a very small number of these ancient inhabitants survived by hiding in remote places, or by being hidden by friendly Polynesian tribes. Some of the last remaining people in New Zealand that trace their lineage to these inhabitants are called the Ngati-Hotu, whose descendants today still retain their light hair, fair skin, and green eyes.

A lot of other evidence of the presence of these people in New Zealand still exists, too numerous to detail here. Much of their culture was absorbed by the Polynesians (who came to be known as a distinctive group called the Maori) who had been welcomed into their society and taught their practices. The spiraling patterns of the famous Maori facial tattoos for example, which the Maori record as having been taught to them by these fair-skinned people,[428] were similarly found on the faces of ancient Indo-European mummies discovered in the Tarim Basin in China.

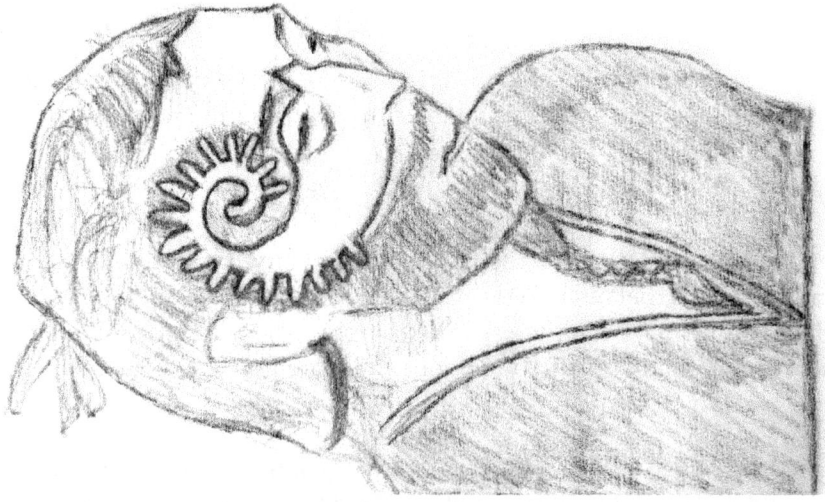

The mummy called "Cherchen Man" who has a double sun spiral painted in yellow ochre across his face, similarly to how yellow ochre is used by Vedic religious practitioners today.

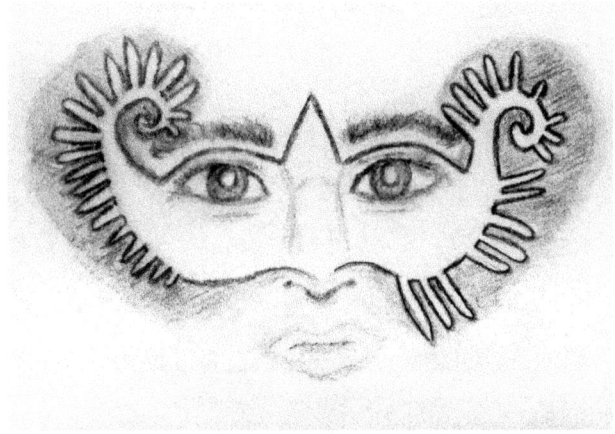

Artist's rendition of the entire double sun
spiral painted across Cherchen man's face.

Artist's rendition of the sun spirals painted in yellow ochre
on one of the female mummies found at the Tarim Basin.

The double spiral was one of the most prominent symbols of ancient Europe
as a symbol of the movements of the sun, and is found in the artwork of the
seafaring megalithic culture that stretched from the Mediterranean along
the Atlantic coast of Europe. It has been found etched into stone in Malta,
Scotland, and Ireland—where it adorned or was associated with ancient sites
aligned to the solstices and equinoxes.[429]

Spirals etched into the stone entrance to
Newgrange, which aligns to winter solstice sunrise.

Facial tattoo of a Maori chief. "Note the use of the double spirals,
in miniature, on each side of the nose and larger spirals on each
cheek. The cheek spirals are marked by double lines, which track
the Sun's movement inward to the centre of the spiral (Solstice)
where it turns and moves toward the Equinox (marked by the
bridge of the nose). The Sun then continues its journey to the
other Solstice position on the opposite side of the face."[430] ~ Martin
Doutré. The lines found on the face and forehead represent the
days between equinoxes—a similar concept, as Doutré has pointed
out, found in the nemes headdress worn by Egyptian pharaohs.

"[A] well-preserved Caucasian mummy from Ürumchi, China shows a 'double spiral' design painted on the face adjacent to the nose. The unravelling spiral straightens then crosses to the nose. An identical spiral, unravelling in the same clockwise direction, is fashioned on the opposite side of the face. Archaeologists assessing these 3000-4000 year-old mummies, recognise that the people were Sun worshippers and the designs painted onto the faces of the dead were in veneration of their Deity.

The double spiral design has been used by European peoples since before megalithic times, as one of the foremost symbols of antiquity. It was prominently displayed in Megalithic Great Britain until the Iron Age, when its usage began to diminish. [...]

Long after the Northern Europeans had their former Sun aligned religion supplanted through ruthless Christianisation, the selfsame pre-Christian beliefs, far beyond the reach of Rome, remained intact and unthreatened in New Zealand. Although enforced amnesia terminated age-old astronomical knowledge in the North, it persisted pure and undefiled at the base of the South Pacific...until the coming of the Pa or fortress Maori warrior/ cannibals.

Evidence would suggest that the 'double spiral' represented the Sun sitting at a Solstice position (the innermost part of the spiral), then winding out of that position to the Equinox and continuing yet further to the other Solstice position. [...] Inasmuch as early Europeans, either in the Mediterranean Basin or in the far-flung colonies, used the Sun as the vicarious representation of their spiritual God RA, the annual movements of the Sun were of tremendous religious significance.[431] [...]

Maori oral traditions clearly state that the art of moko facial tattooing was taught to Maori-Polynesians by the Turehu people who occupied New Zealand for thousands of years before the arrival of the Maori.[432] [...]

The Maori Moko [which is the spiral Maori facial tattoo] [...] is a sophisticated solar calendar. Virtually every part of the design celebrates the movements of the Sun God RA, who, in pre-colonial New Zealand was known by that exact name and vocal rendition. The endless journey of RA is shown again in the design around the mouth, with the Vernal and Autumn Equinoxes occurring at the position of each nostril and the Sun's Solstice change of direction occurring each side of the chin cleft. [...]

Many researchers can readily see the glaring similarity between Maori and pre-Celtic design, sufficient to show that both art forms stem from the same origins. These artistic expressions were used equally by the Pictish, Hebrew, Assyrian, Mayan, Mycenaean and Scythian civilisations."[433]

~ MARTIN DOUTRÉ, MEGALITHIC NEW ZEALAND

The sun god was most prolifically called Ra in ancient Egypt, which clearly connects this early civilization of people in New Zealand and their spiritual knowledge to Egypt, along with other evidence.

The Egyptian sun god Ra.

Left: A native man from Easter Island with a traditional facial tattoo that appears to show the journey of the sun. It looks similar to Maori facial tattoos and the nemes headdress worn by Egyptian pharaohs. Right: Nemes headdress on the death mask of the Pharaoh Tutankhamun.

However, Europe and Egypt are not the only places they have connections to. Family history, passed down by some of the surviving ancient fair-skinned people of New Zealand, recounts how their ancestors had traveled to New Zealand by boat from the regions of present-day India and Iran.

Monica Matamua of the Ngati-Hotu tribe in New Zealand, whose family has preserved the story of their origins in Persia, underwent a DNA test as part of the National Geographic DNA Ancestry Project in 2005. Her results revealed a strong link to the region of Iran. Monica believes that her ancestors did not find New Zealand by mistake, but mapped their way to the country and have been there for at least seventy-four generations (from sometime before 3,000 BC).

> "There are 800 in our whanau. When the seven warrior waka arrived in New Zealand, my people were here. Our history says that our people first came to Aotearoa a long time back from what is now called Iran. If you go there today, the women still have moko, the black lips. Our people came here through Borneo."[434]
>
> ~ MONICA MATAMUA, NGATI-HOTU AND DESCENDANT OF THE TUREHU PEOPLE

This connects the ancient inhabitants of New Zealand with the Indo-European cultures that once spread throughout parts of Eurasia.

Oral tradition in New Zealand records how the ancient people who preceded the later Polynesian immigrants were known as "The Surveyors."

> "[...] in a very stimulating conversation with a learned Maori kaumatua-historian, he recounted an oral tradition passed down within his family that spoke of his ancestors arriving in New Zealand from India in 700 AD. Upon making landfall, his ancestors encountered a well-established civilisation that they called 'The Surveyors' ... because of their preoccupation with marking the landscape for overland surveying purposes. Although I was aware of many other names or terms used to describe the earlier civilisation (such as 'The Stonebuilders') this was the first time I had heard of them being called, specifically, 'The Surveyors' in the Maori oral histories."[435]
>
> ~ MARTIN DOUTRÉ, ANCIENT NEW ZEALAND SURVEYORS AND ASTRONOMERS

Evidence for this skill in surveying the landscape is found at sacred sites throughout the British Isles, which align to one another across vast distances, as well as in many ancient sites that align to each other from across the globe. It was this knowledge they precisely encoded into monuments, megaliths, and ancient cities around the world, and which they used to navigate across the earth.

NORTH AFRICA AND EGYPT

Stonehenge is the most famous megalithic site in Britain. Although most see Stonehenge as a completely unique site in the world, there existed other ancient sites that looked near identical to it, having the same gigantic stone "trilithons." These were located in North Africa, in present-day Libya and Algeria, as well as in India.[436] Other ancient megalithic trilithon designs have been found in the temples of Malta, in predynastic Egypt, and as entrances to the chambered mounds of Ireland,[437] which are all places with megalithic sites aligned to the sun.[438]

Row of ancient megalithic trilithons in Libya.

The connection between the ancient sites in North Africa and Stonehenge is further reinforced by the presence in North Africa of cairns, barrows, dolmens, and standing stone circles, just like those found in Europe and particularly Britain.[439]

> "The whole of North Africa is littered with megalithic remains of all sorts. In Libya, there is a vast number of 'trilithons,' which resemble those of Stonehenge in England.[440] [...]
>
> The widespread prevalence of over a hundred trilithons throughout Libya, some in groups, but often standing on their own, and many more torn down and destroyed, indicates a 'trilithomania' in Libya at some unknown prehistoric period [...]."[441]
>
> ~ ROBERT TEMPLE, EGYPTIAN DAWN

Although now mostly a parched wasteland, thousands of years ago North Africa was a green wilderness, which had been covered in lakes and rivers, and had once supported huge herds of cattle along with a large megalithic civilization. The area became the desert it is today starting sometime between 4,000-3,000 BC,[442] likely forcing its ancient inhabitants to leave. All that remains of this once great civilization are mostly toppled stones—in some cases only photos and sketches attest to the now destroyed or lost sites.

Still partially standing though in Morocco is the largest stone ellipse in the world, called Mzora. It marks the sunsets and sunrises of each of the solstices and equinoxes,[443] and its name likely means "the place of sunrise."[444] It shares a relationship with a number of other ancient sites in Egypt, Britain, and Armenia. Both Mzora and the ancient standing stones of Nabta Playa in Egypt (which are dated to around 4,800 BC) were built using the same geometrical principles (by using a Pythagorean right-angled triangle) that were also used in the standing stone rings of Britain, as uncovered through the research of Alexander Thom.[445] Researcher Bob Quinn also found numerous similarities between Mzora and the ancient mound Newgrange in Ireland, which aligns to the winter solstice sunrise.[446]

Left: Sketch of the Mzora standing stones in Morocco made in 1830. Right: Ancient standing stones in Armenia. Both share a name related to the word "dawn."

The name Mzora is related to the name Zorats Karer given to a site of ancient standing stones in Armenia, dated to around 5,500 BC. Both contain the word "zora," which is the Arabic word for "dawn" or "sunrise," and probably a loan word from a more ancient language.[447] Zorats Karer is believed to have been dedicated to the primary god of the Armenians, which was the sun, called Ari,[448] possibly related to the word Arian/Aryan. Interestingly, the first ancient African genome sequenced (discussed earlier in this chapter) showed the man, who lived around 2,500 BC, to be most closely related to a tribe in Ethiopia called the Ari, but also revealed he shared ancestry with the first farmers who migrated out of Anatolia.[449] Anatolia is the region where the oldest dated standing stones are found.

As explained further earlier, DNA from the first farmers of Europe has been found in ancient Egyptians from the dynastic period. The beginning of the dynastic period and the so-called first kings of ancient Egypt is generally placed around 3,100 BC. However, the actual king lists of ancient Egypt stretch back tens of thousands of years as discussed in chapter 2.

The beginning of the dynastic period in Egypt was really just the end of the reign of the predynastic/prehistorical kings of Northern Egypt, who were conquered by the first dynastic pharaoh called Menes.[450] The predynastic kings were referred to as the "Shemsu Hor" or "followers of Horus" (as mentioned in chapter 2).

As it turns out, the evidence for the existence of these predynastic Egyptian kings is found inscribed on the ancient Palmero Stone, which is currently the oldest widely accepted surviving historical text from ancient Egypt.[451] It contains a list of the kings of ancient Egypt. The first register on the Palmero Stone shows the names of nine predynastic kings of Northern Egypt. However, this line is damaged—if it were preserved, it's possible that it would have listed as many as 120 predynastic kings![452] Despite accepting the list of dynastic kings on the Palmero Stone as authentic, the existence of these predynastic kings is mostly denied by historians.

These predynastic kings seem most likely to have been related to those people whom the ancient Egyptians called Libyans.[453] The ancient city of Sais, where Plato's ancestor Solon was told the story of Atlantis, was inhabited by Libyans.[454] Their territory was described as stretching all the way from the west coast of Africa in Morocco to the western border of ancient Egypt.[455] They were depicted as tattooed with similar markings as the Amazigh/Berber people of Morocco,[456] and with similar patterns used by the ancient megalithic culture in Spain.[457] This, among other evidence, has led Robert Temple to propose that the predynastic Egyptians were the same as the ancient megalith builders whose sites can be found across North Africa, around the Mediterranean, stretching from Iberia along the Atlantic coast of Europe as far as Britain.

Drawing of ancient Libyan men based on a mural found in the tomb of Pharaoh Seti I, dated to around 1,279 BC. They wear feathers in their hair, which can be seen depicted in some of the headdresses of Egyptian gods.

"There are many ancient Egyptian pictures of Libyans from wall paintings and other sources [...]. Many of these show very clearly certain recurring design patterns which appear either on the clothing of the Libyans or as tattoos on their skin. Similarities may be seen between these and the design patterns [...] of the Spanish/Iberian megalith builders. [...] The main feature in both cases is the lozenge, or the recurring lozenge as a series. These similarities further substantiate the idea that the Libyans and the Iberian megalith builders had common origins, and it should be borne in mind that the examples of the Libyan designs are mostly more than a thousand years later, so that certain cultural continuities were clearly strong over immense spans of time."[458]

~ ROBERT TEMPLE, EGYPTIAN DAWN

Archaeological and genetic evidence has confirmed that sometime before 3,000 BC, peoples from the Neolithic cultures of Iberia migrated into Northern Africa.[459] As Temple points out, these cultures certainly had the ability to lift massive megalithic blocks, as their Dolmen of Menga in Spain has a roof stone weighing 180 tonnes.[460] Possibly as far back as 5,000 BC, this megalithic civilization was building mounds that have been compared in function to the pyramids of Egypt, as places for burials of the elite.[461] However, I believe there is evidence that some of the mounds of Europe were used for initiations in the Religion of the Sun, in the same way some of the pyramids of Egypt were, and that both were based on the same basic design sharing the same symbolism.[462]

In the Egyptian texts of *The Kolbrin*, the ancient Egyptian scribes and priests writing at the time clearly locate the original homeland of their race as Krowkasis, which as Yvonne Whiteman has pointed out, is closer to how the word Caucasus was written in ancient times: "Pliny the Elder in his Naturalis Historia derives the name 'Caucasus' from the Scythian kroy-khasis – 'ice-shining, white with snow.'"[463]

Photo taken in Georgia of the Caucasus Mountains.

> "Over subsequent centuries, Egyptian scribes wonder where their Motherland could have been. They consider all the geographical options where strange races live, and speculate whether the Motherland might have been Ramakui, Zaidor or some earlier civilisation. The Book of Origins states unequivocally that their cradleland was Krowkasis."[464]
>
> ~ YVONNE WHITEMAN, GUIDE TO THE KOLBRIN

The accounts of the wisdom bringer Osiris state that he did not travel the world alone, but raised an army to accompany him, indicating he traveled with a sizeable number of people. In *The Kolbrin*, the people who arrived to Egypt with Osiris are described as "sun people" and "children of the sun":

> "They tell many tales about the coming of the Sun People and of the land from whence they came. [...]

When their guide and leader [Osiris] left the people knew themselves
as children of the sun. They were warlike and subdued other people
in its name, and brought them under its rule. Then great temples
were raised up to it [...]."[465]

~ THE SCROLL OF KAMUSHAHRE, THE KOLBRIN

But what were the origins of the people who came with Osiris to Egypt and
formed the army he traveled with? Could this be how the people of Krowkasis
(the Caucasus) first came to Egypt, and were they the predynastic pharaohs
known as the Shemsu-Hor?

THE CANARY ISLANDS

The Canary Islands, located off the northwest coast
of Africa, is another place that served as a remnant
time capsule of this civilization of the sun until relatively recently, just as Easter Island and New Zealand
did. For thousands of years, people described as
fair skinned, blonde and red haired, and blue eyed
lived with Stone Age technology (there is no metal
in the Canary Islands), in a tropical paradise, until
they were invaded and finally wiped out by Spanish
conquistadors in 1496. The Spanish recorded their
observations of these native people whom they
called the Guanches. They wrote how they practiced
a solar religion, had a solar theocracy, built stepped
pyramids aligned to the solstices, used to offer
prayers to the rising sun, and practiced mummification—all characteristics of those who formed part of
this once great Lost Civilization of the Sun.

Statue of a Guanche
king on Tenerife in
the Canary Islands.

"An ancient network of pyramids are scattered across the earth in
places like China, India, the Maldives, Mesopotamia, Bosnia, Egypt,
Sardinia, Canary Islands, Antigua, Polynesia, Mexico, Peru, and others.
These pyramid-building nations who also practiced mummification,
were outposts established by those culture bearers who came at the
dawn of history, to introduce civilization to native people all over
the earth [...]. The Guanches outlasted nearly all of the others due
to their island remoteness and homogeneous population that were
never conquered until the Middle-Ages."[466]

~ GORDON KENNEDY, THE WHITE INDIANS OF NIVARIA

There are also some interesting linguistic connections that have been preserved in the language of the Guanches. For example, the Guanche word for

"heaven," which is "Atuman,"[467] contains "Atum," which was the name of the first god and supreme creator in Egypt, associated with the sun—in Old High German "Atum" means "breath," related to first life; while on Easter Island the name for god was "atua."[468] The name "Atuma" is also found in *The Kolbrin* as the name of the supreme god of the Children of God, and "Gatuma" is used as the name for a great king of the Caucasus.[469] The word "Gautam" is a Sanskrit name meaning "the sun," believed to have been used in the Vedic period, and was later an epithet given to Buddha as "Gautama."[470] The Sanskrit word "Atman" is similar, and is used as a term to denote one's true self, which is part of the supreme cosmic spirit Brahman,[471] who is identified as the sun, and contains the name of the Egyptian sun god Ra. It's interesting to find such striking linguistic connections between the Guanches, Egyptians, and Indo-Europeans, especially as they are to do with their religions, which also share many similarities. The word "Amen" was used by the Guanches as their word for the "sun"[472]—the same word which is now used to finish Christian prayers, and is closely related to a variation of the name of the ancient Egyptian creator god "Amun" as "Amen," who fused with the sun god to become "Amun-Ra" and "Amen-Ra." If you reverse the order of these words, you get something like Ramen, which is similar to Brahman.

> "The Guanches recognized themselves as custodians of an ancient spiritual legacy, and they were very devoted to their religion and spiritual practices. Like their European cousins, the Celts and Teutons, they looked upon the sun as the mighty emblem and instrumentality of the Godhead. Menceys were priest-kings within tribal territories on the islands, and like in ancient Peru they built solar temples and step-pyramids and claimed their descent and divinity from the sun.
>
> Solar religion manifests itself not simply in acknowledgement of the overt functions of the sun as provider of light and heat, but also in recognition of influences that are more wide-ranging than the elemental force itself. The sun is the great source of energy in almost all terrestrial phenomena, from the meteorological to the geographical, from the geological to the biological. Solar energy equals life.
>
> [...] the Guanches were monotheistic, but had a complex form of expressing the divine principle. Concepts like *'Life of the sky,' 'Sun God,' 'Sun spirit of the mountains,' 'Indweller of the universe'* and dozens of other spiritual metaphors were all part of the daily language, with religion being the central theme of their existence."[473]
>
> ~ GORDON KENNEDY, THE WHITE INDIANS OF NIVARIA

The Guanches provide further evidence of the ancient Lost Civilization of the Sun, as one of its various outposts that survived right to the end of the Middle Ages.

The Canary Islands where the Guanches lived and practiced their solar religion lies along the ocean current that travels from Morocco in northwest Africa, where the Berbers (whom the Guanches were genetically related to) still live, and Central America, where the Olmecs (who were the predecessors to the Maya) practiced a solar religion.

It is precisely where this ocean current departs northwest Africa in Morocco that the ruins of the ancient city of Lixus still partially remain. The origins of this city are unknown. Although attributed to the Phoenicians, the Romans called it "The Eternal City," because they believed it was the early home of the gods. Its oldest name is actually "Sun City" as it was built by unknown sun worshipers who aligned its gigantic megalithic walls with the sun.[474] I suspect it was established as far back as the times of Atlantis.

Lixus was likely a port from which ancient peoples of the Lost Civilization of the Sun, coming from throughout the Mediterranean, departed by boat for Central America, following the current across the Atlantic Ocean, sometimes possibly stopping at the Canary Islands on the way, which may be why there is evidence of solar religions at all points—at origin, along the way, and at the destination. This path across the Atlantic is essentially the same one Christopher Columbus followed on his journey to the Americas.

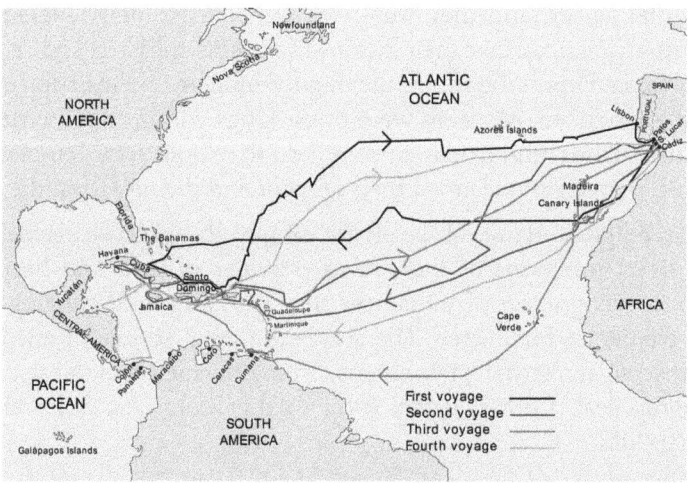

The four voyages Columbus made to the Americas. He followed a well-traveled ancient sea route from Spain (another ancient seaport was located in Morocco), sometimes stopping over at the Canary Islands, and landing in Central America (not far from where the Olmec established themselves).

CHINA (MEXICO AND EGYPT)

Where the ocean current from Africa terminates, on the coast of Mexico, there is an ancient site where a startling array of artifacts has been found. The site is called La Venta; it was inhabited by the sun-worshiping Olmec culture, and possibly dates back to 1,900 BC. Artifacts at the site clearly depict

African Negroid, Asian (likely Chinese), and Caucasian people. Some pieces bear astonishing similarities to Chinese and Hindu artwork, others depict Asians in numerous and difficult yoga postures, and still another depicts an East Asian-looking person in a yoga posture while wearing what looks like a pharaonic Egyptian headdress![475]

A giant 2.8m/9 ft high stone head with clearly Negroid facial features, found at an Olmec site in Mexico. Not one, but numerous heads like this were found at the site.

Left: A jade mask found at an Olmec site in Mexico, which looks incredibly similar to Chinese jade masks and guardian lions. Right: Chinese guardian lion.

The Olmecs are considered to be the predecessors of the Maya, and old records of the K'iche' speaking Maya people of Guatemala preserved in the Popol Vuh, which was written down in approximately AD 1550 based on oral tradition, confirm the presence of both black and white people in the tribes they were founded from, and say that they worshiped the sun:

"There they were then, in great number, the black men and the white men, men of many classes, men of many tongues, that it was wonderful to hear them. [...] They did not invoke wood nor stone, and they remembered the word of the Creator and the Maker, the Heart of Heaven, the Heart of Earth. [...] And they raised their prayers, those worshipers of the word (of God), loving, obedient, and fearful, raising their faces to the sky [...]. Thus they spoke while they saw and invoked the coming of the sun, the arrival of day [...]."[476]

~ POPOL VUH

Betty Meggers, who was an American archaeologist that worked for the Smithsonian and specialized in South American cultures, and Mike Xu, Professor of Chinese at Texas Christian University, put forward the theory that the Olmec civilization had been founded by migrants from China—specifically the Shang Dynasty (the second historical dynasty of China), which existed at the same time the Olmec culture first appeared. Xu found most similarities between Shang and Olmec artifacts and writing, so much so, that when he took Olmec motifs to China, experts asked him whereabouts in China he got them.[477]

One glaringly obvious thing that connects the ancient cultures of China, Mexico, and Egypt/Africa, are pyramids. At La Venta in Mexico there is a pyramid, considered one of the oldest in the Americas. Today, after more than 2,500 years of erosion, it looks just like a big canonical shaped mound of earth, but it was once a stepped pyramid like those found in ancient Egypt.[478] Stepped pyramids are found in both Mexico and Egypt, and are well-known; lesser known are the ancient pyramids of China (Central and Northern), of which there are at least thirty-eight. These ancient pyramids are mostly located at Xi'an,[479] which is one of the most ancient cities in China and one of the main places where Chinese civilization emerged.[480]

A model of one of the pyramids near Xi'an in China. Unlike many pyramids around the world, which are stepped, its sides are flat like those of the Great Pyramids of Egypt, and it is made of earth like the pyramidal mounds of North America.

Around 1912 a Western trader named Fred Meyer Schroder was told about the origins of the Chinese pyramids. He visited the Kumbum Lamasery, which contained the largest library of ancient records in all of Tibet, where he spoke to the Tashi Lama in charge. The lama stated that the oldest books of the monastery recorded that the pyramids were already considered old five thousand years ago. They didn't know who built them, only that they were men of ancient times. He also stated that their ancestors had dealings with people far more ancient than they who lived on a land beyond the great water (perhaps related to the builders of the Chinese pyramids, and from ancient Egypt or even Atlantis?). Another lama told Schroder that the Chinese emperors interred within the pyramids were buried in them long after the pyramids had actually been built.[481] This is yet another example of how ancient sacred places were reused, revered, and often renovated and altered by later cultures who were not the original builders.

There is more evidence that furthers the connection between ancient Egypt and the beginnings of civilization in China. The historical description of the topography of the Xia empire, considered China's first dynasty, matches that of ancient Egypt. Ancient bronze found in the city of Yin, the capital of China's second dynasty, was found to share the same characteristics as bronze in ancient Egypt, suggesting their ores came from the same African mines.[482] A number of the pharaohs and ancient Egyptian elite were Asian, as can be clearly seen from the facial features of their statues. In fact, there are so many similarities between the two places that a museum in Berlin, Germany, featured an exhibition in which it compared ancient Egyptian and Chinese civilization in five areas: writing, forms of government, religious beliefs, funerary cult, and daily life. The exhibition's webpage says, "Despite their enormous distance, both cultures developed similar structures, which are still recognizable today. [...] In some areas, Chinese and Egyptian art and culture reveal surprising correlations, in others interesting tensions emerge."[483]

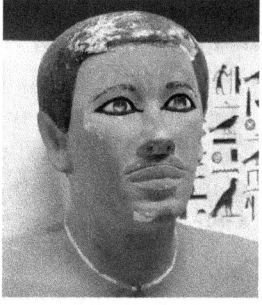

Top: Egyptian pharaoh with clearly Asian facial features—he was the Pharaoh Menmire-setpenre Amenmesse who ruled during the Nineteenth Dynasty (1,292-1,186 BC).[484] However, I have seen others with Asian features as far back as the Second Dynasty (2,890-2,686 BC).[485] Bottom: The Egyptian Prince Rahotep who was the half-brother of the Pharaoh Khufu (who is credited with commissioning the building of the Great Pyramid at around 2,560 BC, though, in my opinion, the evidence shows he only oversaw renovations and additions to the site[486]). He is depicted with life-like blue eyes made of glass and has Caucasian features (his skin is darkened from sun exposure—men were often portrayed with much darker skin than women in Egyptian artwork, as they spent most time outdoors). Both Caucasians and Asians appear to have been among the early Egyptian dynasties, as they likely also were in China.

As explained earlier, two scholars of Chinese studies have sourced the founding of Chinese civilization among Indo-Europeans, and there is archaeological evidence that appears to support this connection.

As touched on earlier, since the beginning of the 1900s, hundreds of Caucasian mummies, many with red and blonde hair, have been found in the northwest of China—the earliest dating to at least 1,800 BC.[487] These mummies have been called the Tarim mummies because they were discovered in what is today called the Tarim Basin.

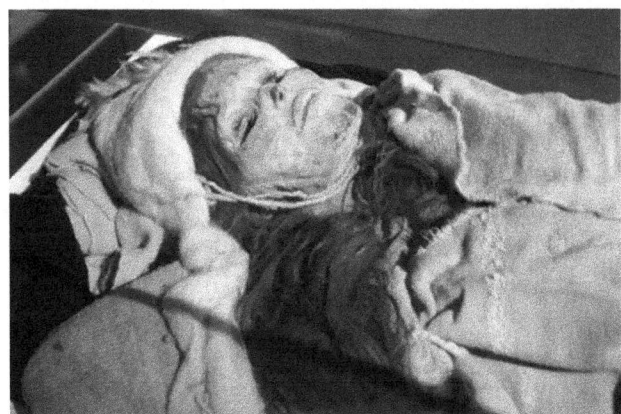

One of the Tarim mummies—a woman, with fine
features, fair skin, and fine chestnut colored hair.

They were found buried with tartan cloth, Celtic looking artifacts, what looks like a wizard hat[488] (which is similar in appearance to the ancient wizard hats made of gold and used as solar calendars in Western Europe[489]), and one with an artifact with a swastika on it. Their graves were marked with what look like dolmens from Britain, as well as standing stones.[490]

Textile expert Elizabeth Wayland Barber, who examined the tartan cloth, believes that its origins can be traced back to Anatolia, the Caucasus, and the steppe area north of the Black Sea. Her theory is that the people who wore this cloth migrated out from the Caucasus, dividing into two groups—one going east and another west.[491] A similar opinion is held by Professor Victor Mair of Pennsylvania University, who has studied the mummies and believes that the "early Europeans headed in different directions, some traveling west to become the Celts in Britain and Ireland, others taking a northern route to become the Germanic tribes, and then another offshoot heading east and ending up in Xinjiang"[492] in the Tarim Basin.

This is also supported by linguistic evidence. The Tarim people spoke an Indo-European language called Tocharian (which is now a dead language).[493] Tocharian is part of the centum branch of Indo-European languages (the other branch being satem), as are Western European languages like Celtic and Germanic,[494] and shares more affinity with Western European languages than with those Indo-European languages spoken in regions closer to it, like Persian and Sanskrit.[495] The split between the Indo-European speakers who ended up in Western Europe, and those who ended up in China, may have happened thousands of years ago. A study by linguists of the Max Planck Institute for the Science of Human History, and the University of Auckland, found that Tocharian is likely to have branched off from Proto-Indo-European and become isolated at around 5,900 BC,[496] which means Indo-European speakers may have been living in or near China from at least that time.

Genetic testing has also revealed their connection to early Indo-European migrations, as all paternal lineages of the tested mummies were R1a1a,[497] which is "thought to have been the dominant haplogroup among the northern and eastern Proto-Indo-European tribes, who evolved into the Indo-Iranian, Thracian, Baltic and Slavic people."[498] However, these people are associated with a different branch of Indo-European language (satem), and so the Tocharian language may instead have been brought to the region by an earlier people in the area whose paternal lineages were subclades of R1b. These R1b people in the region were possibly replaced by later R1a migrants,[499] and there are indications of this in their language as "the vocabulary [of Tocharian] shows the influence of Iranian and, later, Sanskrit" but retained "many of the most archaic elements of the Indo-European vocabulary."[500]

The ancient inhabitants of the Tarim Basin are further connected to the beginnings of civilization in China by a mountain range. The bearers of Chinese civilization, the founders of its first dynasties, and the religion of Taoism, which is a branch of the ancient Religion of the Sun, were said to have originated from a mountain far west of China, called Kunlun Mountain. Although this mountain became mythologized in China, it has a real location—the Tarim Basin is bordered to the south by the Kunlun Mountains. This is where the wisdom bringers of China, who correspond to Osiris and Isis in ancient Egypt, were said to have been married.

It's clear that ancient Indo-European, Chinese, Egyptian, Olmec, Maya, and even North American pyramid building civilizations are connected to one another. Most of the racial types involved—Caucasian, Chinese, and African Negroid—were among the people depicted in Egypt at different times, and are evidenced in the artifacts of the Olmecs in Mexico, and given the clear connections between these places, this no longer seems so surprising.

SOLAR THEOCRACIES

One of the main characteristics of the Lost Civilization of the Sun was its form of government, which was solar theocracy—meaning a government headed by someone who was both king and priest, who met the required spiritual level to rule, and who was a representative of the sun (seen as the supreme manifestation of divinity). These rulers were often called "sons of the sun" or "children of the sun." In China, the emperor was called "son of heaven." In Japan where there is still an emperor today, he is called "heavenly sovereign," and as in so many ancient solar dynasties, he and his family are seen as direct descendants of the sun (who in this case is personified as a goddess).[501]

These solar theocracies are recorded as being established by the wisdom bringers, and their first rulers selected by the wisdom bringers themselves, being those whom they considered most fit for the task. There is evidence for solar theocracies existing in India; Iran; Anatolia; Mesopotamia; Egypt; the Canary Islands; Ireland; among many tribes and civilizations of the Americas; on Easter Island, Hawaii and numerous other islands of the Pacific; in Indonesia; Japan; and in China. It is one of the main cultural similarities shared between many of the civilizations of the ancient world.[502]

This form of government as being practiced by the Guanches of the Canary Islands is described by Gordon Kennedy in his book *The White Indians of Nivaria* as:

> "Essentially, a theocracy, a form of government where the solar deity is recognised as the supreme ruler (heliotheism), which is administered on earth by priest-kings or Menceys [...]. Religion and patriotism were one and the same to the Guanches with no separation between church and state."[503]

Histories of the Native American Natchez people of the Mississippi Valley record how their solar theocracy was established.

> "In a time long past, people were living in ignorance and anarchy. The 'Sons of the Sun' pitied them and descended from heaven to the earth, bringing with them the sacred fire. The Sons of the Sun were a man and a woman, covered with the most beautiful ornaments ever seen. The people of the earth wanted to give them orders, but the Sons of the Sun did not accept this and demanded the people of the earth to unconditionally obey them and to follow them wherever they would lead them. The Sons of the Sun also required their leadership to be continued in perpetuity as a form of government through their family. The heavenly male divinity and Son of the Sun was called 'The', and he lived so long as to have known his great-grand-children and he created many institutions. It was him, who brought the sacred fire with him from the heavens, which burns continuously in their mysterious sacred temples. From The descended the kings of our present day and these kings bear the name 'Suns'."[504]

In Egyptian texts of *The Kolbrin*, this rulership, at some stage (as no dates are given), demanded extreme spiritual discipline and having passed the most difficult of spiritual tests.

Evidence reveals that the ruling class were often described or depicted as Caucasian in appearance, and had elongated earlobes as a sign of their nobility. For example, the rulers of Easter Island elongated their earlobes, as did the elite of the Inca, Aztecs, and Maya, and kings of India. The famous Egyptian royal family—Pharaoh Akhenaten, his wife Nefertiti, at least some of his daughters, and his son Pharaoh Tutankhamun—were depicted with elongated earlobes, and it's interesting that Akhenaten had tried to revive ancient sun worship. Other famous examples of this practice include the huge stone moai statues of Easter Island, and the depictions of Buddha, who was a blue-eyed prince of the solar dynasty in India.

> "The oldest known practice of ear extension was among the mariners in the prehistoric Indus-Valley harbor-city of Lothal where large numbers of big ear-plugs in the type used by the Long-ears in ancient Mexico, Peru and Easter Island have been found. In the subsequent epoch of India the Hindu rulers adopted the custom, but it was restricted to members of the royal families and images of the Hindu gods. Buddha had long ears because he was born and reared as a Hindu prince, and as Buddhism spread, the images of the long-eared Buddha spread wide and far over modern Asia."[505]
>
> ~ THOR HEYERDAHL, EASTER ISLAND: THE MYSTERY SOLVED

The first European explorers who landed on Easter Island in 1722, observed that ear elongation was still being practiced. Among what were described as the fair, dark, and red-skinned inhabitants of Easter Island, was a Caucasian-looking man who was clearly a ruler of some kind, and as their religion was not separate from their way of life, was also a priest.

> "Among the first who came on board the Dutch ships was a 'completely white man' who had a more ceremonious air than the others. He was ornamented with a crown of feathers on his head, which otherwise was close-shaven, and he had in his ears round white pegs as large as fists. This white man showed by his bearing that he was a prominent person in the community, and the Dutchmen thought that he might be a priest."[506]
>
> ~ THOR HEYERDAHL, AKU-AKU: THE SECRET OF EASTER ISLAND

Over the thousands of years that followed, those in places where these solar theocracies had been established would be eager to trace their lineage back to these original kings, in order to prove their divine authority to rule. Some of the royal families of Europe traced their lineage back to Odin/Wotan, kings in India traced it back to Manu,[507] whereas the Inca elite traced it to Viracocha. The golden crown worn by royals is likely a vestige of these solar theocracies, symbolizing the sun encircling the ruler's head with its projected rays.

Since the Atlanteans/Children of God had been considered a divine race, and had been the ancestors of the first royal rulers, the subsequent efforts royal families made in many parts of the world, including in native and tribal societies, to preserve their bloodline, was very likely an attempt to preserve these genetics.

> "[...] the natives still divided their ancestors in two categories according to the color of their skins, and [...] [said] that even the last king had been a quite white man. The white branch was looked up to with admiration and respect, and just as in the other South Sea Islands some leading personalities had to undergo special bleaching processes to be as much like their deified ancestors as possible."[508]
>
> ~ THOR HEYERDAHL, AKU-AKU: THE SECRET OF EASTER ISLAND

Likewise, the Inca of Peru followed the same custom:

> "When the Spaniards discovered the Inca Empire, Pedro Pizarro the chronicler wrote that, while the mass of Andes Indians were small and dark, the members of the Inca family ruling among them were tall and had whiter skins than the Spaniards themselves. He mentions in particular certain individuals in Peru who were white and had red hair. [...]
>
> Pizarro asked who the white-skinned redheads were. The Inca Indians replied that they were the last descendants of the viracochas. The viracochas, they said, were a divine race of white men with beards. They were so like the Europeans that the Europeans were called viracochas the moment they came to the Inca Empire. It is a historical fact that this was the reason why Francisco Pizarro, with a handful of Spaniards, was able to march straight into the heart of the Inca domain and capture the Sun-King and all his enormous empire, without the vast and valiant Inca armies daring to touch a hair of their heads. The Incas thought they were the viracochas who had come sailing back across the Pacific. [...]

> The Spaniards recorded that the ruling Inca families called themselves ore-jones, or long-ears, because they were allowed to have artificially lengthened ear lobes, in contrast to their subjects. [...] Pedro Pizarro pointed out that it was especially the long-ears who were white-skinned."[509]
>
> ~ THOR HEYERDAHL, AKU-AKU: THE SECRET OF EASTER ISLAND

Eighteenth century portrait of the eighth Inca king, who had taken the title of Viracocha, had elongated earlobes, and held a staff with a symbol of the sun.

This practice of the royalty in Peru elongating their ears can be traced to the direct orders of the wisdom bringer Viracocha himself:

> "It says that Con-Ticci Viracocha had long-ears with him when he sailed off westward across the sea. The last thing he did before he left Peru was to stop at Cusco in the north on his way from Lake Titicaca down to the Pacific coast. In Cusco he appointed a chief named Alcaviza and ordered that all his successors should lengthen their ears after he himself had left them."[510]
>
> ~ THOR HEYERDAHL, AKU-AKU: THE SECRET OF EASTER ISLAND

It appears that sacred kingship was not only indicated by having elongated earlobes, but also by sitting in a cross-legged pose (particularly the lotus or butterfly pose), which the Vedic/Hindu deities Shiva and Brahma, Jain deity Adinatha, Aztec deity Quetzalcoatl, Celtic deity Cernunnos, and Nordic deity Freyr (associated with the sun and sacred kingship) are all depicted in. Further evidence for this is found in the burials of ancient Indo-European peoples, in which individuals who may have been sacred kings were buried seated in what looks to be either the lotus or butterfly pose, as part of a tradition that spanned thousands of years.

The oldest known burials of people in the butterfly pose have been found at Lepenski Vir, which has been dated as far back as 9,500 BC, as mentioned in chapter 2. Burials of people that were likely to have been positioned in a lotus or butterfly pose have also been found in the later Bell Beaker, Corded Ware, and other Bronze Age Indo-European cultures of Europe that existed from around 2,500 BC. Those buried in this position were high-status males, and when taken together with the beliefs of other ancient Indo-Europeans, may have been considered sacred kings or god kings, called Devaraja in the Vedic tradition.[511] The continuity of this practice reveals that it was part of a very ancient tradition.

The lotus is an ancient solar symbol. In ancient Egypt it was a symbol of the sun and of resurrection, as a certain species (the blue water-lily, which was used most frequently in ancient Egyptian art) opens only during the day—closing, and sinking beneath the water at night, and reemerging in the morning—just like the sun. The yellow center of the flower, set against its blue petals, looks like the sun in the sky.

> "I am the holy lotus that comes forth from the light [...]. I have made my way, and I seek after him, that is to say, Horus [the resurrected Son/sun]. I am the pure lotus that comes forth from the field [of Ra, the sun god]."[512]
> ~ THE CHAPTER OF MAKING THE TRANSFORMATION INTO THE LOTUS, THE EGYPTIAN BOOK OF THE DEAD

In Maya culture, it likewise represented the resurrection of the sun from out of the underworld.[513] In Vedic religion, the god Brahma is said to have emerged from a lotus to create the world. He is depicted as seated in the lotus position upon a lotus, just as Buddha later was.

> "The Self is hidden in the lotus of the heart. Those who see themselves in all creatures go day by day into the world of Brahman [the sun] hidden in the heart. Established in peace, they rise above body-consciousness to the supreme light of the Self."[514]
> ~ THE CHANDOGYA UPANISHAD

In ancient Egypt, the lotus was also the birthplace and throne of the sun god Ra who created the world.

> "[...] the pool with the lotus, the very spot of [...] creation [...] was conceived as being the most sacred part of the primeval domain of the Sun-God since it is described as his [...] throne."[515]
> ~ EVE A. E. REYMOND, THE MYTHICAL ORIGIN OF THE EGYPTIAN TEMPLE

The lotus was clearly associated with the sun god and creator, and I believe the sacred kings, who were considered its emissary upon the earth, seated themselves like the sun god upon his lotus throne.

THE SAME SYMBOLS FOUND ACROSS THE WORLD

Symbols like the swastika, solar cross, double spiral, lotus, "Master of Animals," feathered serpent, and third eye, which are all symbols related to the sun, are found like footprints wherever the people of this civilization tread in their journeys. Many of the symbols they used had multiple layers of meaning, encoding both spiritual and astrological principles, as the same principles can be found operating both "above" and "below"—at a macrocosmic and microcosmic level, and also "within" and "without"—both within us, and in the world around us. My husband and I explore many of these symbols, what they mean, and how they can be found in the movements of the sun and the earth in our book *Ancient Solstice*.[516]

The swastika is one of the most prolific symbols of the ancient world, and appears in such widespread places as across the Americas (North, Central, and South), the whole of Europe (including Britain), Russia, the Middle East, and large parts of Asia (including India and China).

Another prolific symbol is that of the third eye—usually represented as a dot in the middle of the brow. The researcher and author Richard Cassaro has put together numerous images showing the third eye symbol used on ancient artifacts in Egypt, throughout Asia, and the Americas. The ancient Egyptians symbolized this third eye as the sun. At the same time, the sun was also seen as the eye of the supreme creator. In ancient Egypt, the sun was depicted symbolically as the eye of the sun god Ra, and to the Proto-Indo-Europeans it was the eye of the shining sky father Dyeus Phter.[517]

As discussed in the next chapter, the symbol of the third eye seems to originate from the inner sight that the Children of God were said to have possessed, and it spread to places where the Religion of the Sun was practiced. This third eye is atrophied within people today, and its remaining physical seat is the pineal gland within the brain.

LOST KINGDOMS

Both the mysterious lost civilizations of Hyperborea and Shambhala were recorded in legends as places where a solar religion was practiced.

Hyperboreans were described by the classical Greek historians as being a giant, divine race, who practiced sun worship, with a solar priesthood and theocracy, in a circular temple. The Greeks attempted to locate Hyperborea in a variety of places—in Europe, the Arctic Circle, the North Atlantic Ocean, the Urals in Russia, and Siberia, but came to no agreement. The location of Hyperborea has still not been conclusively identified.

"This island [Hyperborea] is situated in the north and is inhabited by the Hyperboreans, who are called by that name because their home is beyond the point whence the north wind (Boreas) blows; and the island is both fertile and productive of every crop, and since it has an unusually temperate climate it produces two harvests each year. Moreover, the following legend is told concerning it: Leto was born on this island, and for that reason Apollon [the sun god] is honoured among them above all other gods; and the inhabitants are looked upon as priests of Apollon, after a manner, since daily they praise this god continuously in song and honour him exceedingly. And there is also on the island both a magnificent sacred precinct of Apollon and a notable temple which is adorned with many votive offerings and is spherical in shape. Furthermore, a city is there which is sacred to this god, and the majority of its inhabitants are players on the cithara; and these continually play on this instrument in the temple and sing hymns of praise to the god, glorifying his deeds."[518]

~ DIODORUS SICULUS, LIBRARY OF HISTORY

"This god [Apollon] has as priests the sons of Boreas (the North Wind) and Khione (Chione, Snow), three in number, brothers by birth, and six cubits in height [which is about 9 feet or 2.7 meters]. So when at the customary time they perform the established ritual of the aforesaid god there swoop down from what are called the Rhipaion (Rhipaean) mountains swans in clouds, past numbering, and after they have circled round the temple as though they were purifying it by their flight, they descend into the precinct of the temple, an area of immense size and of surpassing beauty. Now whenever the singers sing their hymns to the god and the harpers accompany the chorus with their harmonious music, thereupon the swans also with one accord join in the chant and never once do they sing a discordant note or out of tune, but as though they had been given the key by the conductor they chant in unison with the natives who are skilled in the sacred melodies. Then when the hymn is finished the aforesaid winged choristers, so to call them, after their customary service in honour of the god and after singing and celebrating his praises all through the day, depart."[519]

~ AELIAN, ON ANIMALS

The ancient lost city of Shambhala was also said to have been inhabited by sages who practiced sun worship. References to Shambhala are found in the Kalachakra Tantra texts of Tibetan Buddhism, in which it is said that a king of Shambhala traveled to India and was there converted to Buddhism. He then brought the religion of Buddhism back with him to Shambhala, where it became the religion of the succession of kings who followed him, until the eighth decided to convert the entire population of Shambhala to Buddhism.[520] A sage of Shambhala called Suryaratha (whose name means "sun chariot") was expelled, along with twenty thousand of those who clung to "Surya Samadhi"[521] (meaning something like "union with the divine sun") and "the pure sun way," when they refused to convert.[522]

The Trundholm sun chariot found in Denmark and dated to around 1,400 BC. In Indo-European religion, the sun was seen as riding in a chariot, pulled by horses. Thus the name "sun chariot" connects the sage of Shambhala to Indo-European religion.

Shambhala may have been a real ancient city located in the Tarim Basin, now buried beneath the shifting desert sands, where the ancient Indo-European Tarim mummies who were painted with sun symbols were found.

"The text specifies that Shambhala was a kingdom 'north of the River Sita.' While no consensus exists among scholars regarding the historical reality of Shambhala, several scholars believe that Shambhala was an historical kingdom of a different name (circa 850-1250), located in present day Xinjiang province of northwestern China and in eastern Kyrgyzstan, and that the River Sita refers to the Tarim River. The Tarim River basin has been the home to several well-known Buddhist and Bon kingdoms, and there is climatological evidence that this area was once far less arid than it is now; the ruins of stupas are found throughout this vast region, now mostly buried under desert sands."[523]

~ NICK TRAUTZ, SHAMBHALA IN THE KALACHAKRA TANTRA

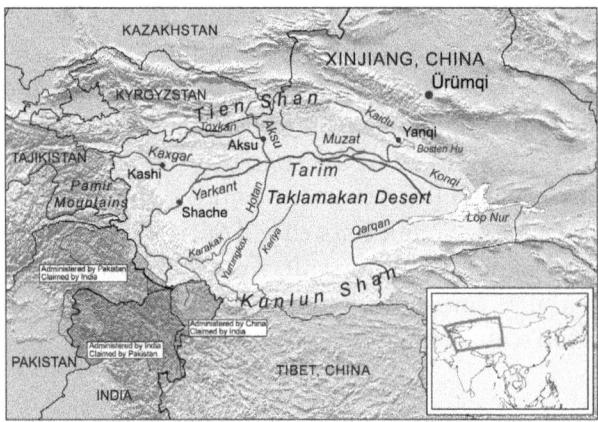

Map of the Tarim River Basin, possibly the location of the now lost kingdom of Shambhala.

Shambhala has become associated with Buddhism, but Buddhist texts state clearly that it was originally inhabited by people who practiced a religion of the sun.

ESOTERIC SCHOOLS

As part of the spread of the Lost Civilization of the Sun, esoteric schools were established in different parts of the world—all the way from Egypt, through Mesopotamia, India, Central Asia, Western China, Europe, and likely many other places.

The esoteric schools that Gurdjieff encountered in remote parts of Central Asia, around one hundred years ago, are very likely to have been remnants of them.

Gurdjieff writes about visiting two esoteric schools in particular, each of which he claims to have visited for some months.

The first was the Sarmoung Brotherhood, which had first been established in Mesopotamia (in the city of Mosul in present day Iraq) as early as 2,500 BC, but had relocated, according to Gurdjieff's account to somewhere in southern Uzbekistan or northern Tajikistan.[524] The knowledge of this school was said to be preserved by Aisors (who are of Assyrian descent).[525]

"What struck us most was the word Sarmoung, which we had come across several times in the book called Merkhavat. This word is the name of a famous esoteric school which, according to tradition, was founded in Babylon as far back as 2500 B.C., and which was known to have existed somewhere in Mesopotamia up to the sixth or seventh century A.D.; but about its further existence one could not obtain anywhere the least information. This school was said to have possessed great knowledge, containing the key to many secret mysteries."[526]

~ GURDJIEFF, MEETINGS WITH REMARKABLE MEN

As explored in chapter 3, the most ancient religion of Mesopotamia was said to have been founded by the seven wisdom bringers referred to as the Apkallu, who appear to be identical to the seven wisdom bringers of ancient Egypt who are likewise credited with founding the most ancient religion of Egypt. This religion was the Religion of the Sun, and was perhaps preserved in Mesopotamia within esoteric schools. Mesopotamia and Egypt shared many cross-cultural links over thousands of years, and their religions are widely recognized as influencing one another.

The Sarmoung Brotherhood was said to have relocated around the sixth or seventh century[527] to an area dominated by the Zoroastrian religion, also a branch of the ancient Religion of the Sun, which attributes its founding to similar wisdom bringers as explained in chapter 3. At a monastery here, Gurdjieff says he was reunited with a very close friend of his, who had been directed to the monastery by a Tamil Hindu.[528] Again, Hinduism derives from the Religion of the Sun, and attributes its founding to similar wisdom bringers as also explained in chapter 3.

Those within these traditions (Assyrian, Zoroastrian, and Hindu) clearly understood their common heritage enough to provide refuge to and recommend the same esoteric school, the Sarmoung Brotherhood.

The second esoteric school Gurdjieff says he visited was the World Brotherhood, which according to the descriptions he gave, was located in Kafiristan, somewhere between present day northeastern Afghanistan and northwestern Pakistan,[529] and which was likely established in the tradition of the ancient Vedic religion, which predominated and has even survived into the present day in the region,[530] and that again is a branch of the ancient Religion of the Sun. This monastery was said to be among three others belonging to the World Brotherhood, located in Tajikistan, Tibet, and India. A man from this brotherhood told Gurdjieff that centuries ago there had been numerous brotherhoods in Asia.[531]

Schools of knowledge were said to have been established in different places as part of a network, which sincere seekers of knowledge could have traveled between in ancient times when the peoples who carried the Religion of the Sun spread throughout Eurasia and different outposts around the world.

"In India there are only 'philosophical' schools. It was divided up in that way long ago; in India there was 'philosophy,' in Egypt 'theory,' and in present-day Persia, Mesopotamia, and Turkestan— 'practice.'"[532]

~ GURDJIEFF SPEAKING TO OUSPENSKY ON ESOTERIC SCHOOLS, IN SEARCH OF THE MIRACULOUS

Gurdjieff wrote about the "Most Holy Sun Absolute" as the source of all, and the need to create the sun within oneself,[533] among other principles of the Religion of the Sun. He derived much of his philosophy from the schools and mystics he encountered in Central Asia, revealing that some knowledge of the Religion of the Sun had survived among them.

These esoteric schools have not been located since, and are likely to have disappeared due to rampant violence and upheaval in the places they used to operate; their closure is a sign of the dark times in which we live.

The Religion of the Sun was also preserved within esoteric schools in Europe. It was kept within the religion of the Druids, Hermeticism, Gnosticism, mysteries pertaining to knights and Arthurian legend, the Knights Templar, and more recently Freemasonry.

Thomas Paine, one of the famous "Founding Fathers" of the United States, who was likely also a Freemason, wrote how the Religion of the Sun is the most ancient of religions and came from a time before recorded history. From these most ancient and unknown origins, he described how it spread throughout the ancient world and eventually emerged in Christianity and Freemasonry.

"Masonry (as I shall show from the customs, ceremonies, hieroglyphics, and chronology of Masonry) is derived and is the remains of the religion of the ancient Druids; who, like the Magi of Persia and the Priests of Heliopolis in Egypt, were Priests of the Sun. They paid worship to this great luminary, as the great visible agent of a great invisible first cause whom they styled 'Time without limits.' [...]

The Christian religion and Masonry have one and the same common origin: both are derived from the worship of the Sun [...].

At what period of antiquity, or in what nation, this religion was first established, is lost in

Portrait of Thomas Paine, 1792.

the labyrinth of unrecorded time. It is generally ascribed to the ancient Egyptians, the Babylonians and Chaldeans, and reduced afterwards to a system regulated by the apparent progress of the sun through the twelve signs of Zodiac by Zoroaster the law giver of Persia, from whence Pythagoras brought it into Greece [...].

The worship of the Sun as the great visible agent of a great invisible first cause, 'Time without limits,' spread itself over a considerable part of Asia and Africa, from thence to Greece and Rome, through all ancient Gaul, and into Britain and Ireland [...].

As the study and contemplation of the Creator [is] in the works of the creation, the Sun, as the great visible agent of that Being, was the visible object of the adoration of Druids; all their religious rites and ceremonies had reference to the apparent progress of the Sun through the twelve signs of the Zodiac, and his influence upon the earth."[534]

~ THOMAS PAINE, AN ESSAY ON THE ORIGIN OF FREE-MASONRY

Thomas Paine even wrote a poem titled "The Religion of the Sun" that was published in 1826, which I came across after having already begun using the term, and was searching for possible instances of where it had been used before.

Of the fifty-six Founding Fathers of the United States who signed the Declaration of Independence, at the very least nine were Freemasons (having verifiable records of association),[535] and so it can be said that the philosophy found in the Religion of the Sun had some influence in shaping the ideals and ideas of the men who gave the United States its great values, principles, and freedoms.

Tragically, Freemasonry was infiltrated over time by the sinister ideology of the Illuminati—something the first President of the United States, George Washington, who was a Freemason, cautioned against in a number of his letters.[536] Today, at its core, it is no longer a benevolent institution, as it has incorporated things that are not of the Religion of the Sun, but are instead diametrically opposed to it, though remaining cloaked by using many of the same symbols, but in some cases giving them other, sinister meanings.

WHAT HAPPENED TO THE LOST CIVILIZATION OF THE SUN?

So what happened to this once great civilization that spread across the globe in ancient times—why is it not common knowledge, and instead the period between 9,700 BC (the end of the last ice age), and 2,500 BC (the beginning of known history) a literal vacuum?

I personally believe it's because this great civilization, like many others, collapsed, and its fractured remnants eventually succumbed to invasions, persecution, and even genocide. This collapse appears to have taken place over a period of thousands of years, with scattered outposts surviving in some of the most remote places in the world—such as Easter Island, the Canary Islands, and New Zealand—right up until the last 250 to 500 years.

Civilization collapse is usually followed by a "dark age" of chaos and destruction, and often not much survives. It might be hard for us to imagine today, but in the ancient world, only a very small number of people could read and write. These people were usually among the elite and upper class. Therefore, when an ancient civilization collapsed, the knowledge of writing was easily lost. Those who survived were usually illiterate, and so the history of the civilization gone before was often not preserved in books, but in oral histories. Over time these tales are mythologized and simplified, as those who are told them have no experience or memory of the civilization themselves. Texts, artifacts, and entire cities can be destroyed either by natural disasters or by incoming peoples who care nothing about or are even hostile to those who preceded them, and take no care in preserving anything at all, and the few illiterate survivors with their sometimes simplistic tales are forced to flee and start again.

One devastating example of this is the total collapse of the great civilizations around the Eastern Mediterranean and Near East, which ended the Bronze Age, around 1,200 to 1,150 BC—described by one Professor of Classical Studies as "the worst disaster in ancient history."[537] It included the collapse of the Mycenaean kingdoms, Minoan civilization, Hittite Empire, Kassite dynasty, Egyptian Empire, and Assyrian Empire—whose territories stretched through Egypt, the Levant, Anatolia, Syria, Cyprus, Crete, Greece, and Mesopotamia.[538]

As great as these civilizations were, historians are still trying to work out why they collapsed, since the records of the events surrounding their destruction hardly exist. This is because the literacy of these civilizations was extinguished in the collapse, and was also severely reduced in much of the known world. It also led to a "Dark Age" that lasted hundreds of years. The Mycenaean civilization of Greece was one of the hardest hit, and the effects so severe it led to what are called the "Greek Dark Ages," which lasted four hundred years.[539] Not much survives such a meltdown, and so is it any wonder that the tales of Greek mythology became so simplistic? They are certainly no measure of the great civilizations they concern, but are merely the tattered remnants of their vague memory.

I suspect the collapse began with a fragmentation of peoples that had been taught the Religion of the Sun who formed their own tribes and kingdoms, and went their own separate ways. Hindu texts record some of these separations, as well as huge wars fought by these kingdoms against one another. I imagine they would have not only competed with one another locally, but also across continents.

The Bronze Age cultures in Europe, in which the sun had held much more importance, were replaced by those of the Iron Age, with horrifically violent and warlike Indo-European tribes, for whom gods of war became more prominent. It's possible that tribes of Scythians played a part in the Bronze Age collapse by laying waste to and plundering the already weakened civilizations of the Eastern Mediterranean and Near East.[540] Many of these tribes were seafaring raiders. The formidable Fomorians of Irish mythology, whom the Tuatha Dé Danann did battle with and defeated, were possibly a seafaring Slavic tribe.[541]

Those who preserved the deeper, more esoteric, and advanced knowledge of the Religion of the Sun were also persecuted, as so often happens when the spiritual level of any society declines and degenerates. An Egyptian text preserved in *The Kolbrin* tells of a fall into dark practices and the persecution, driving out, and murder of its keepers of wisdom. The keepers of this knowledge withdrew into esoteric schools hidden from the public, and to increasingly remote places.

> "The hosts of the Dark Ones were well skilled in battle and they drove out all those who stood against them. The forces of righteousness were scattered. The sacred shrines which stood before the veil of Truth were spoiled. The ornaments of beauty and the sacred vessels were taken away to be profaned by sin-soiled hands. The Enlightened Ones and the Twice Born were hunted down like beasts of the chase. They were slain and buried in the ground like dogs. Their resting places remained unmarked and unattended."[542]
>
> ~ THE BOOK OF THE SONS OF FIRE, THE KOLBRIN

Hopi oral history recounts that the Anasazi of North America were brutally tortured and massacred by an invading tribe from the north around the end of the 1300s. There is evidence that violent raids were led against the once peaceful Anasazi settlements, which increased in size and frequency between AD 900-1300. "That period displayed social and behavioural hallmarks of modern genocide [...] a concentration of previously dispersed groups in a relatively small area, mass graves, mutilation of bodies, killing of women, children and the elderly—and numerous large-scale attacks that eradicated villages."[543] At around 1270, people living in three large Pueblo villages were killed and possibly cannibalized. Within fifteen years of a particularly horrific and brutal massacre at Sacred Ridge in Colorado, it was abandoned and dwellings began being built along cliff walls in the region.[544] Anasazi sites were built in increasingly remote and hard-to-access locations in order to survive, to the point of being perched in seemingly impossible positions on cliff faces. There is evidence of both slow starving out as well as large scale and sudden violence.[545] Those who ruthlessly took over their beautiful cities abandoned them to ruin soon after, and the knowledge of the Anasazi almost faded completely from memory. The present-day Hopi and Zuni people are believed to be descendants of the survivors.

The following oral history about the Anasazi was told by Hopis to a U.S. government funded expedition that occurred between 1874 and 1875.

> "Formerly, the aborigines inhabited all this country we had been over as far west [sic] as the headwaters of the San Juan, as far north as the Rio Dolores, west some distance into Utah, and south and southwest throughout Arizona and on down into Mexico. They had lived there

from time immemorial—since the earth was a small island, which augmented as its inhabitants multiplied. They cultivated the valley, fashioned whatever utensils and tools they needed very neatly and handsomely out of clay and wood and stone, not knowing any of the useful metals; built their homes and kept their flocks and herds in the fertile river-bottoms, and worshiped the sun. They were an eminently peaceful and prosperous people, living by agriculture rather than by the chase. About a thousand years ago, however, they were visited by savage strangers from the North, whom they treated hospitably. Soon these visits became more frequent and annoying. Then their troublesome neighbors—ancestors of the present Utes— began to forage upon them, and, at last, to massacre them and devastate their farms; so, to save their lives at least, they built houses high upon the cliffs, where they could store food and hide away till the raiders left. But one summer the invaders did not go back to their mountains as the people expected, but brought their families with them and settled down. So, driven from their homes and lands, starving in their little niches on the high cliffs, they could only steal away during the night, and wander across the cheerless uplands. To one who has traveled these steppes, such a flight seems terrible, and the mind hesitates to picture the suffering of the sad fugitives. At the cristone [a volcanic dike, according to Ingersoll] they halted, and probably found friends, for the rocks and caves are full of the nests of these human wrens and swallows. Here they collected, erected stone fortifications and watch-towers, dug reservoirs in the rocks to hold a supply of water, which in all cases is precarious in this latitude, and once more stood at bay. Their foes came, and for one long month fought and were beaten back, and returned day after day to the attack as merciless and inevitable as the tide. Meanwhile, the families of the defenders were evacuating and moving south, and bravely did their protectors shield them till they were all safely a hundred miles away. The besiegers were beaten back and went away. But the narrative tells us that the hollows of the rocks were filled to the brim with the mingled blood of conquerors and conquered, and red veins of it ran down into the cañon. It was such a victory as they could not afford to gain again, and they were glad, when the long fight was over, to follow their wives and little ones to the south. There, in the deserts of Arizona, on well-nigh unapproachable isolated bluffs, they built new towns, and their few descendants, the Moquis [Hopi], live in them to this day, preserving more carefully and purely the history and veneration of their forefathers than their skill or wisdom. It was from one of their old men that this traditional sketch was obtained."[546]

~ ERNEST INGERSOLL, FROM ARTICLE PUBLISHED IN THE NEW YORK TRIBUNE ON THE 1874 HAYDEN SURVEY

Frescos at the Temple of the Warriors at Chichen Itza in Mexico show scenes of people with fair skin and blonde or dark hair being driven out and killed—with some depicted as scrambling to get into their ships to escape via sea, and others who were less fortunate being offered as human sacrifices.

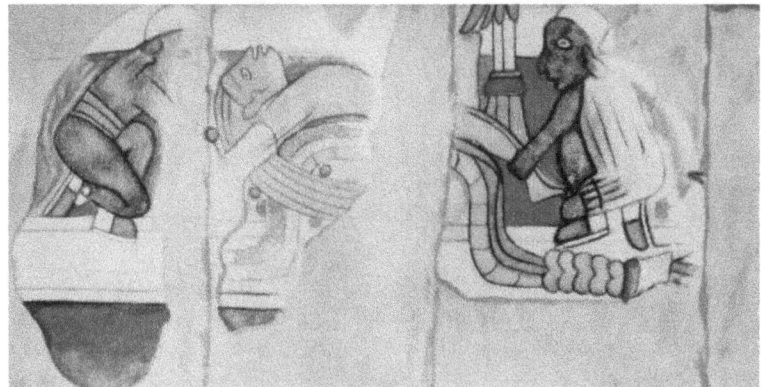

A mural from the Temple of the Warriors at the ancient site of Chichen Itza in Mexico. It depicts a man with fair skin and hair, being prepared as a human sacrifice.

Another mural from the same site showing a battle scene, with some of the site's inhabitants trying to pack their things and escape via the sea in what look like reed boats. They apparently lose, and are stripped naked and led away as captives.

Aztec codices show similar scenes, with warriors holding captured fair-skinned and sometimes bearded men by the hair, who would have surely been used as human sacrifices too.

By this time, the Aztecs were conducting military campaigns with the purpose of capturing as many people as possible to sacrifice them to the sun—it's estimated that between 20,000 to 250,000 people may have been sacrificed a year.[547] Numbers like this indicate how many peoples in the region may have been wiped out with mass executions like this. Human sacrifice is obviously a horrific practice that has nothing to do with the actual Religion of the Sun. The Aztec wisdom bringer Quetzalcoatl is recorded in oral histories as forbidding it, as explained in chapter 3.

Page of a mid-sixteenth century Aztec codex called the Codex Mendoza. It's interesting to note that the pose of holding captured prisoners by the hair in a sort of crouched, subordinate position, can be found prolifically in ancient Egypt.

Similar scenes were also carved at Nineveh in Mesopotamia, where people on reed boats are shown in battle at sea. Some of these boats are full of men and women who have their arms raised in prayer to the sun as they escape across the ocean.[548]

The Paracas people of Peru were invaded by a culture whom they taught their arts and sciences, but who later slaughtered and drove them out. This invading culture became known as the Nazca, though they were not the creators of the oldest Nazca Lines, but took over and continued to build upon them, and practiced human decapitation.[549]

Not long before the Spanish arrived, the Chachapoya were conquered by the Inca. The Inca sought to expand their empire, and in doing so, spread their solar religion, the arts of civilization, and infrastructure, and end the barbaric customs of those they conquered such as cannibalism, just as the wisdom bringers had done, and in many ways, it seems to have had mostly a positive effect. Ironically, the Spanish had sought to do the same (though in a far more brutal and destructive way), with their version of the Religion of the Sun in its new though distorted guise as mainstream Christianity.

> "[...] for the chief glory of the Incas and the veil with which they covered their ambition to expand the empire was to give out that they were moved by the desire to uplift the Indians from the inhuman barbarism of their present existence and to reduce them to a moral

and political way of life through the knowledge and worship of their father the Sun, whom they regarded as God."[550]

~ GARCILASO DE LA VEGA, ROYAL COMMENTARIES OF THE INCAS AND GENERAL HISTORY OF PERU

However, in the case of the Chachapoya, the Inca king desired to bring their civilization into his empire because of its great fame.[551] Those of the Chachapoya who survived the conquest were relocated by the Spanish (following their conquest) to Spanish style towns, where it's estimated that 90 percent of their population died over the next two-hundred years from poverty and disease.[552]

After the defeat of the Chachapoya, but just before the arrival of the Spanish, the Inca royal family met a horrific end at the hands of the last Inca king called Atahuallpa.

"[...] Atahuallpa destroyed the whole royal blood [of the Inca nobility], male and female, as we shall say, for he was a bastard, and feared lest the crown he had usurped should be taken away from him and given to a legitimate member of the royal family.

Not sated with [the blood] of two hundred of his brothers [...] he went on to drink that of his nephews, uncles, and other kinsmen up to and beyond the fourth degree, so that no member of the royal blood, legitimate or bastard, escaped. He had them all killed in different ways. [...]

When Atahuallpa had killed the males of the royal blood and the vassals and subjects of Huáscar [the legitimate king, whom he'd usurped through treachery], he went on to swallow the still unspilt blood of the women and children of the same stock [...]. He ordered all the women and children of the royal blood who could be found, of whatever age and condition [...] to be assembled and slaughtered in batches outside the city with various cruel tortures [...]. All the women who could be found throughout the kingdom were collected together, and intensive search was made lest any escape. A great many children were rounded up, both legitimate and otherwise, for the lineage of the Incas was the largest and most numerous in the empire [...]."[553]

~ GARCILASO DE LA VEGA, ROYAL COMMENTARIES OF THE INCAS AND GENERAL HISTORY OF PERU

All but one of the descendants of the original megalithic builders of Easter Island fell victim to genocide in around 1762 by later Polynesians who arrived to the island.[554] The megalithic builders were the fair-skinned "long ears" who were the earliest inhabitants of the island, while those who came later were called "short ears." The long ears were so called because they elongated their earlobes as mentioned earlier, and were described as "an energetic people, filled with plans for improving the island,"[555] the last of which was to clear the whole island of the lava stone littering the ground, in order to be able to use it for agriculture,[556] however, the short ears became tired of laboring at this task and decided to go to war against the long ears rather than continue. With the long ears gone, the island descended into a scene of hell, with rampant cannibalism and constant violence.[557] Prior to this, no weapons had been used on Easter Island, and the peoples there had coexisted peacefully.[558]

> "They have also persistent legends of a still earlier time of greatness when another people, the long-ears, had lived at peace with their ancestors, the short-ears. The long-ears had demanded too much labor of the short-ears, and in the end there had been a war in which nearly all the long-ears were burned in a ditch. From that day no more statues had been made, and many of those which were standing had been pulled down with ropes. Civil war, family feuds, and cannibalism marked the years that followed [...]."[559]
>
> ~ THOR HEYERDAHL, AKU-AKU

The earlier people of New Zealand who had venerated the sun god Ra were almost massacred and cannibalized to extinction by some of the Polynesian Maori tribes who had arrived later, and had been taught their arts and religion.[560] Following this, in 1835, invading Maoris from New Zealand massacred and cannibalized the indigenous Moriori people on the nearby Chatham Islands after seizing a European ship and learning that the Moriori were pacifists and were not likely to put up a fight.[561] The Moriori had lived there practicing a solar religion, completely peacefully. Their massacre was so severe it has been called a genocide.[562]

Photo of surviving Moriori people on Chatham
Island taken in the late nineteenth century.

In China, the military leader Ran Min, who reigned from AD 350-352, ordered the complete genocide of all non-Han Chinese peoples in the Chinese Empire. He decreed that any ethnic Chinese civil servant that killed and brought him the head of one "barbarian" (non-ethnic Chinese, indicated by their high big noses, deep set eyes, and thick full beards) would be greatly promoted in rank. He personally led a mass slaughter of "barbarians," killing over two hundred thousand men, women, and children in one day, mainly by decapitation. His military campaigns caused several million people of different races to flee.[563]

Remnants of the religion and civilization of the sun remained preserved in different traditions that had broken off into many branches, like that of the Druids, the pagans of Europe, the Slavs, Zoroastrians, and in secret mystery schools in places like Egypt, Greece, Rome, and the East. Unfortunately, much of the knowledge was lost, and the practice of these traditions degenerated terribly in many cases. These were then almost pulverized into oblivion by conquests and religious fanaticism over thousands of years. For example, the Roman conquest of Western Europe and its Celts and Druids, led by Caesar, was utterly horrific and devastating—as many as one million were killed, another million enslaved, and eight hundred of their cities destroyed.[564]

Many Roman emperors were initiated into mystery schools, which were very active in the region at the time. The last to be initiated was the Emperor Julian (into the Eleusinian Mysteries), who reigned from AD 361-363.[565]

What would go on to deliver a crushing blow was fermented in the Roman Empire, which had formerly been home to great religious diversity and a number of mystery schools—which even Roman emperors were initiated into.

Around AD 310, after the Roman state adopted Christianity, the persecution of pagans began in earnest within the empire—temples were vandalized, and access to them prohibited.[566] In AD 380, three Roman emperors issued a joint decree called the Edict of Thessalonica, stating:

"According to the apostolic teaching and the doctrine of the Gospel, let us believe in one deity of the Father, the Son and the Holy Spirit, in equal majesty and in a holy Trinity. We authorize the followers of this law to assume the title of Catholic Christians; but as for the others, since, in our judgement they are foolish madmen, we decree that they shall be branded with the ignominious name of heretics, and shall not presume to give their conventicles the name of churches. They will suffer in the first place the chastisement of the divine condemnation and in the second the punishment of our authority which in accordance with the will of Heaven we shall decide to inflict."[567]

This affected non-orthodox Christian sects and all non-Christians through-out the empire—a vast area that covered much of Europe, Egypt, the Levant, and Anatolia. Over 1,500 years later, in 1965, the Roman Catholic Church issued a decree recognizing the right of every person to religious freedom, and Pope John Paul II publicly prayed for forgiveness for what had been done.[568] But by this time, of course, so much had been destroyed.

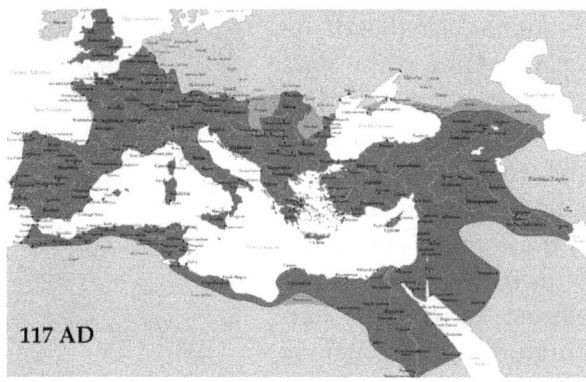

Extent of the Roman Empire in AD 117.

Over the next few hundred years, the old pagan religions in Europe, some of which had retained aspects of the Religion of the Sun, were often violently replaced with Judeo-Christianity, with many brutally executed for either refus-ing to convert or being suspected of heresy.

Toppling of a statue of the Slavic god Svantevit by
the Christian Bishop Absalon in Germany in 1169.

The Guanches survived for thousands of years in relative isolation on the Canary Islands off the west coast of Africa. They were so isolated that they remained in the Stone Age, and their islands were even said to have served as a place of spiritual refuge. That was until the Spanish conquistadors turned up in around 1402; they killed and enslaved so many of them as to have oblit-erated them and their culture entirely.[569]

The peoples of the Americas who preserved some memory of the Religion of the Sun were conquered by invading Europeans, and almost all their religion and history was destroyed. The tragic burning of Aztec and Maya codices by Catholic missionaries is well known; yet before they arrived, the first Aztec emperor had already burned all the historical codices in his possession, which contained information about those cultures that preceded the Aztec.[570] Many had awaited the promised return of the benevolent fair-skinned people their ancestors had treasured the memory of for thousands of years. Instead, those fair-skinned people who first arrived were no longer like the ones who had first arrived in ancient times.

Mongol and Muslim invasions changed the cultural landscape across Central Asia and the Middle East. With the advent of Islam (another religion largely influenced by Old Testament ideology), what had largely been safe in the East while the West was purged, now faced a scourging.

Unfortunately this still continues in parts of the Middle East today with the persecution of remaining spiritual minorities like the Yazidis by Islamic fanatics, and the deliberate destruction of ancient sites, which in some cases, are thousands of years old.

It's important to note though, that not every ancient culture, civilization, religion, or tradition is connected to this lost civilization, as many other practices and beliefs existed concurrently in many different parts of the world. The Lost Civilization of the Sun however, was a dominant influence.

Over the last few thousand years, many civilizations have periodically attempted to revive the ancient Religion of the Sun as it had been taught to their ancestors long ago, like the Inca, Aztecs, and Maya. One such famous attempt was made by the Pharaoh Akhenaten in Egypt at around 1,300 BC. It was even the state religion of the Roman Empire prior to Christianity. However, ultimately people were unable to understand and practice it sufficiently to be able to revive it.

A Roman coin from 313 AD depicting the sun god Sol Invictus behind the Roman Emperor Constantine. He would later make Christianity the state religion, following the sun god (Son of God) still, but in a new form.

With so many competing and invading peoples, all violently vying for power, a global civilization was no longer left—only tiny fragments surviving on the edges of society, and keepers of wisdom hanging on to ancient manuscripts in secret societies under threat of violence.

What happened to the Religion of the Sun, and the Lost Civilization of the Sun, is a true indictment against humanity, which according to ancient prophecies preserved in traditions of the Religion of the Sun, is now facing utter ruin and destruction in order to make way for a new golden age.

REMAINING QUESTIONS

While I have attempted to do my best to put together a narrative of the historical origins of the Religion of the Sun, by no means do I feel that I've found all the answers.

What I do feel I've been able to present is a coherent overview, which answers why many religions of the ancient world were centered around the sun, and where they came from.

However, the potential to continue researching and discovering connections is almost endless. I keep finding them on an almost daily basis, and sometimes it's not that there is too little evidence, but too much to get through.

Yet there are a number of hurdles. As could be expected, this includes trying to pin down definitive details of events and peoples in prehistory. Another is trying to put together a chronology without having dates for the events described in ancient texts and histories. There is always the risk of oversimplifying events because so much is unknown.

For example, there have been numerous cataclysms of great magnitude. Apart from the cataclysm that ended the period known as the Younger Dryas and the last ice age, there was also an earlier one at around 10,800 BC, which almost certainly involved a meteor impact that triggered the Younger Dryas plunge in global temperatures that lasted 1,200 years.[571] Since then, there have also been a number of largescale natural disasters, called bond/kiloyear events—just a few are estimated as having occurred at 6,200 BC, 3,900 BC, 2,200 BC, and 1,200 BC. Some of these events are known to have coincided with dramatic climate changes in parts of the world, which preceded the collapse of large ancient civilizations and the rise of others in their wake.[572] There is evidence that the kiloyear event at 3,900 BC was caused by meteor impact,[573] [574] though at a smaller scale than those that began and ended the Younger Dryas, and it's possible the others were too.

Matching these disasters to the various legends can become very difficult, as it seems to me that over thousands of years many of the legends of the various disasters among different cultures became abridged and perhaps even conflated with one another. Historians also existed in ancient times, and like us, they were often working with incomplete and sometimes confusing records, which they too were trying to make sense of.

Because my husband and I never set out with an idea we were trying to prove, because we simply allowed the evidence to take the lead, and because this concept of an ancient Religion of the Sun and Lost Civilization of the Sun is new, this book really reflects my ever-evolving understanding of the past. I have spent a lot of time going back and rewriting it as new information continually comes to light, and no doubt I will wish I could rewrite this edition you are reading now! It's not that the information is wrong, but that I find there is far more to something than was initially apparent, more people and cultures involved, more layers to the story, and a lot more evidence. Yet I have to stop somewhere as otherwise this book would never come out.

Therefore, I ask you to bear with me if I haven't acknowledged your culture or people where they should have been. I would never wish to ignore anyone who has played a part in this great story. I encourage you to add to the story, and fill in the missing gaps.

Given more time, there are many traditions I hope to research much further, such as those across Asia, in Africa, and the Pacific Islands, where I know legends of wisdom bringers also exist, as well as megalithic structures. I also hope to delve further into traditions I've already touched upon, bringing more to light about their connections to the ancient Religion of the Sun.

THE CENSORING OF HISTORY

So why is it that we hear so little about this once huge civilization of the Religion of the Sun—why don't we know of its story? It appears that there is a concerted effort to destroy all record of it, with evidence in many cases being bulldozed, reburied, or "disappeared."

Skeletons of giants, and of people and artifacts where they're "not supposed to be," are either destroyed, "lost," or ignored. And those who have the courage to investigate history with an open mind are usually attacked, ridiculed, and ostracized.

Mocking people like this is actually very common, not just in the field of history, but everywhere—as it's based on the "herd mentality" found existing in the animal (and thus human) psyche. It has taken different guises throughout history and always uses the terminology of its day, but the underlying mechanism is and will always be the same.

Those who deride what they don't know or understand form the lowest tier of those who suppress truth, as they are simply seeking to fulfill the basic instinct of gaining acceptance from their peers, which is determined by the majority/herd, not necessarily by what is right or true. Few people make the effort to research a given issue in any depth, usually just repeating what their figures of authority (leaders) tell them. When these figures have superficial knowledge themselves, or ideological agendas, then huge numbers of people can believe things that are completely false.

I believe, however, there is also a small number of people who both under-stand the truth of history and the psychology driving "the herd," and who have a malevolent self-interested agenda. I believe they encourage mocking and derision among "the herd" to keep people away from the truth of history, and that this small number of people form part of the highest tier of those who suppress truth.

Unfortunately, there are also many people in the middle, who wish to sup-press or distort truth for their own selfish and ideological interests—usually to serve political, religious, or cultural agendas of various kinds.

In many cases, the oldest surviving peoples of various regions across the globe have been credited with building ancient sites they never built, and even clearly state they never built (they often just renovated or made addi-tions to them). Despite this, there is a push in mainstream academia to ignore and belittle their oral traditions, and to credit them no matter what they say, thus replacing the histories they've preserved over thousands of years with a false and superficial story of their people. This may seem to serve the interests of native people in the short term, but I actually think it's ultimately working against them, as it's disassociating them from the great spiritual legacy they inherited and preserved, and preventing them from taking their place in its history.

It's my belief that we cannot live as though we were the people of the past and continue all the quarrels of our ancestors, but that we must be as we are now and work together to understand human history and uncover the spiri-tual legacy left to us all, respecting whatever part different races, peoples, and cultures played in it, even when they are not our own. The beauty of a flower is always beautiful wherever and whenever it grows, just as the flowering of knowledge and human potential is—can we as a humanity remove the envy and pride that is eating at our hearts and admire beauty simply for its own sake?

Whatever the cause of the suppression of history, ultimately, the effect is to rob humanity of the true understanding of its past. It's a kind of forced amnesia that completely reshapes our cultural narrative—serving to cut us off from the root. We're led to believe the past was only a primitive time, so that we reject the knowledge found within it, and instead turn to embrace a one-world, uniform monoculture of humanist materialism. When hard evidence is destroyed and ignored, and the oral histories of those who've occupied lands for thousands of years are sidelined, history becomes an incoherent mess of confusion and supposition—like a jigsaw puzzle whose pieces no longer fit. This serves to confound most people who look into ancient history, and leads them into a never-ending labyrinth of misinformation and conflicting so-called historical facts.

So often the questions of ancient history are presented as a mystery, as something we can never know the answers to. But I have come to realize that in many instances we *can* know, and that the evidence *is* out there. Ancient history is sometimes only a mystery because there are inconvenient truths people are choosing to ignore—truths that conflict with their ideologies, that they don't want to be ridiculed for stating, or want others to know. Don't be put off by them; be empowered to find the answers. There is a point where legend and history meet, where the figures of myth take human form. It's here we realize our connection to an immense and incredible past, and a legacy of sacred knowledge and places that still surround us, which we too can be part of.

Ultimately, the censoring and suppression of the traces of this civilization of the sun means the reburying of its spiritual knowledge. This knowledge is what the ancient wisdom bringers wished to give to humanity, and thus what humanity is ultimately being deprived of, which I hope in some way to help restore.

> "Oh, how little we know of the depths of the ages gone, how wide, how profound and deep is the knowledge we seek; a monument of stone, a stone bowl, a broken symbol, a hallowed unknown spot, a lodge of ruins, all this makes a golden page glittering with diamonds that trills the emotions with mysterious longings for truth and light in the depths unknown."[575]
>
> ~ LUCY THOMPSON, TO THE AMERICAN INDIAN: REMINISCENCES OF A YUROK WOMAN, 1916

Even though physical evidence can be decimated, the knowledge of the Religion of the Sun is really an inner knowledge and practice, and is taught by those who have the force known as the Spiritual Son within; this force is personified by the sun, which is why people who had this divine part within were associated with it. Wisdom bringers, such as Osiris, Viracocha, Odin/Wotan, Kukulkan/Quetzalcoatl, and much later Jesus, have all taught this knowledge anew and have worked to establish it in the world over different ages.

CHAPTER FIVE

The Children of the Sun

While the people of the Lost Civilization of the Sun spread the Religion of the Sun far and wide in their travels across the earth, I've found that the religion itself traces back to a far earlier people as revealed in many of the texts and traditions I've covered so far.

As far as I've been able to ascertain, the Religion of the Sun originated among a people considered divine in a number of ancient texts who lived during a golden age when this religion was considered Sanatana Dharma—the natural, ancient, and eternal way.

Piecing the various references together, they seem to have been much taller in stature, moon-colored in complexion, lived longer, had a larger brain capacity and possibly larger, elongated skulls, and had the ability to see clairvoyantly. They were more technologically advanced, and were the builders of some of the greatest megalithic monuments on Earth. They were also said to have possessed great spiritual knowledge.

> "[...] as far afield as Micronesia, South-east Asia, China, Peru, Greece and India there is a persistent tradition—as old as the hills—that a secret treasure was long ago stored away by a race of supermen who had been cruelly punished by the gods. Legends and scriptures hint that this treasure does not consist of gold or jewels but of occult knowledge [...]."[1]
>
> ~ GRAHAM HANCOCK AND SANTHA FAIIA, HEAVEN'S MIRROR

CREATED BY THE SUN GOD

They were considered so divine as to have been god's own children. For instance, in Plato's account, the Atlanteans are described as the seed of god, meaning, in other words, they were god's children.[2] In the Samba Purana, the sun god says that he created the inhabitants of Saka Island in ancient times from his own splendor, making them children of the sun/god. In the Stanzas of Dzyan, the fourth race were descendants of the gods called "suras." In *The Kolbrin* they are called "the children of god," while in some ancient texts and traditions they are referred to simply as "the gods."

William James Perry, who was a leader in cultural anthropology at University College London, spent more than seventeen years studying references to the "Children of the Sun" and "Sons of the Sun" in the most ancient traditions he could find, and located numerous accounts of them among peoples of the Americas, Africa, Europe, Mesopotamia, India, Japan, the Philippines, Indonesia, Australia, and Oceania. He discovered these traditions, though scattered across the world, shared fundamental similarities, one of the most common being that those considered the children of the sun had visited, or established themselves as the rulers of, various native peoples, and imparted their solar religion and the arts of civilization to them. Another similarity was that they were considered to have been born of god who was identified as the sun, and were considered gods themselves and immortal. Writing in the 1920s, Perry summarized his findings, saying:

> "[...] the Children of the Sun, who went all over the world and founded the states of the archaic civilization, were Sons of the Sun-God, born of theogamy and not of the union of mortals."[3]
>
> ~ WILLIAM JAMES PERRY, THE GROWTH OF CIVILIZATION

> "From one end of the region to the other, the Children of the Sun were looked upon as gods, that is, as beings far removed from the rest of mankind. They had great powers: they could control the weather, they could fly through the air, they could visit the world in the sky, and do all manner of things impossible to mortal men. In looking back to the days when the Children of the Sun ruled in Polynesia and elsewhere, a time is being considered when 'gods' walked the earth, divine beings incarnate as men, the like of which have not since been seen. The importance of this fact in the history of civilization, and especially in the study of mythology and tradition, cannot be exaggerated."[4]
>
> ~ WILLIAM JAMES PERRY, THE CHILDREN OF THE SUN: A STUDY IN THE EARLY HISTORY OF CIVILIZATION

It's possible that the various accounts of the Children of the Sun originate from the times of Atlantis and travels of the Atlanteans, from the mission of the wisdom bringers (who were descendants of the Children of God/the Sun), and from their descendants during the times of the Lost Civilization of the Sun, as these groups carried the title over the passage of thousands of years.

Their connection to the sky world was clearly a spiritual one, as in the Religion of the Sun, which they taught and followed, it is the place of heavenly and higher realms—being the source of the spiritual part that resides within every living thing and the return destination of those who attain spiritual immortality, which the Children of the Sun so determinedly sought. Yet when read alongside some of the ancient traditions covered in this book, I wonder whether their unearthly origins may have also indicated their distant extra-terrestrial heritage, and their travels to and from the sky their use of aircraft during the times of Atlantis.

ANCIENT WORLDWIDE CIVILIZATION

In a distant past, they were said to have lived over the entire face of the earth.

> "The forebears of all the nations of man were once one people, and they were the elect of God who delivered all the Earth over to them, all the people, the beast of the field, the creatures of the wasteland and the things that grow. They dwelt through long ages in the lands of peace and plenty. There were some who struggled harder, were more disciplined; because their forefathers had crossed the great dark void, their desires were turned Godward and they were called The Children of God."[5]
>
> ~ THE BOOK OF CREATION, THE KOLBRIN

Crossing "the great dark void" sounds like a description of crossing the darkness of space, and so this text seems to suggest that the ancestors of the Children of God could have had some kind of extraterrestrial genetic input.

This is corroborated by an ancient oral tradition preserved among Tibetan Buddhists, which I happened to stumble upon. Writing in 1977, the Russian-born author Andrew Tomas recounted a meeting he had with a lama from Tibet who was visiting a monastery at the foot of the Himalayas in India. The lama said that the tradition was from the Tashilhunpo Monastery in Tibet—the same monastery where Blavatsky stated the Stanzas of Dzyan were held—and that the legend was "as old as the Himalayas."

> "The lama began his story: 'Our oral teaching of the Tashi Lhunpo Monastery asserts that millions of years ago a number of superhuman beings, from another highly advanced world, came to earth for the acceleration of the evolution of this planet and its future mankind. [...] In appearance they were god-like giants. Among these angels was Mara, whom you call Lucifer or Satan. His important task was

to develop the concrete mind and individuality of man. In the course of ages he had accomplished his aim but when the Bodhisattvas and Tara appeared later in order to foster the heart of man, he refused to step aside. This was the revolt of Satan against the Rules or Cosmic Cycles. Since that time he does not bear the title of 'Light-bringer', or Lucifer, any longer. He is now the Prince of Darkness.

From then on the Bodhisattvas have had a double task: on the one hand of combating Mara's attempts to chain man to the earth and make him selfish, unscrupulous and warlike; and on the other, of working for the spiritual advancement of mankind, ordained by the law of cycles. This is what induces us to send Buddhas and Arhats to this world.

It is the lack of desire of the Terrestrial Ruler to cooperate with the Lord of the Sun and the Spirits of the Planets that has created a cosmic crisis. [...] The exalted beings of the sun and other worlds say to Satan—let your lamp shine but do not obstruct other and more glorious lights in starry space!'"[6]

This tradition states that superhuman, giant, god-like beings from a highly advanced civilization on another planet came to Earth to develop human life. Perhaps this is why in Genesis God is plural—and these gods create humans in their own image (emphasis added):

"And God said, Let **us** make man in **our** image, after **our** likeness [...]."[7]

Over the course of untold ages, possibly millions of years (as stated in ancient Hindu texts), these people witnessed and lived through a number of great cataclysms.

"Inner fires had destroyed the land of their fathers. The water threatened the fourth."[8]

~ THE STANZAS OF DZYAN

"Then came the day when all things became still and apprehensive, for God caused a sign to appear in the Heavens, so that men should know the Earth would be afflicted, and the sign was a strange star. [...] The mountains of the East and West were split apart and stood up in the midst of the waters which raged about. The Northland tilted and turned over on its side. [...] Some of the people were saved upon the mountainsides and upon the flotsam, but they were scattered far apart of the face of the Earth. They fought for survival in the lands of uncouth people. Amid coldness they survived in caves and sheltered places."[9]

~ THE BOOK OF CREATION, THE KOLBRIN

They were described as intermixing with other peoples, possibly other species of humanoids living on the earth at that time (such as Neanderthals, Denisovans, the ancestors of modern humans, etc.).

> "The first seven human shoots were all of one complexion. The next seven began mixing."[10]
>
> ~ THE STANZAS OF DZYAN

They were described as living in various places—notably "the cold northlands" (possibly the Arctic), Atlantis, the Indus Valley, and the Caucasus. For example, at some undetermined time, they are described as migrating southward from a northern land.

> "A race of men came out of the cold northlands. They were under a wise father and above them was The Grand Company which later withdrew in disgust. This race was The Children of God; they knew Truth and lived in the midst of peace and plenty. The Children of Men about them were wild and savage; clothed in the skins of beasts they lived like beasts. Even more wild were the Men of Zumat who lived beyond them."[11]
>
> ~ THE BOOK OF GLEANINGS, THE KOLBRIN

It's interesting that they are described as coming out of the "cold northlands," as the author, astronomer, and political leader of India, Lokmanya Bâl Gangâdhar Tilak, presented the theory in his book *The Arctic Home in the Vedas*, published in 1903, that the originators of the knowledge preserved in the Vedas and Zend Avesta must have once lived in the Arctic Circle. He came to this conclusion after a detailed analysis of the astronomical observations, myths, and references to migrations contained in these texts.

It's also interesting to note that part of Siberia within the Arctic Circle remained ice free during the last ice age,[12] and its climate was warmer during the Last Glacial Maximum than it is today. Randall Carlson suspects that this was because the location of the North Pole was positioned over Canada during the Ice Age, and shifted at the end of it closer toward Siberia (into the Arctic Ocean) due to the isostatic adjustment of the earth's surface, caused by the sudden melting of the northern ice sheets.[13]

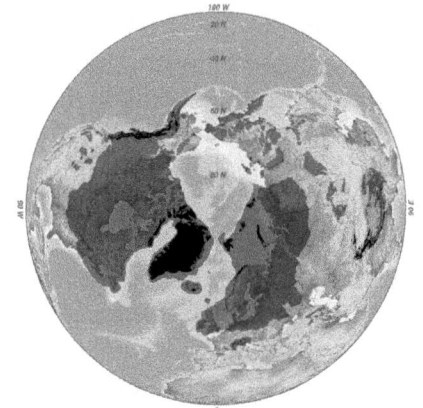

Map of the globe centered on the Arctic. Areas in black show the minimum extent of ice during the last ice age, and grey shows its maximum extent.

GIANT STATURE

The evidence indicates to me that the Children of God were so tall they would be considered giants in comparison to modern humans.

In oral histories, giants are often credited with building the ancient sites that are connected to the Religion of the Sun, and gigantic humanoid skeletons have actually been found buried within such sites, like the mounds of North America.[14]

There are thousands of scientific journals, old newspaper reports, photos, town histories, letters, diaries, ancient texts, and eyewitness accounts, which attest to the existence of humans who were much taller than we are today.[15] The heights of the discovered skeletons I've seen referenced range from about six feet five inches all the way up to twelve feet, and a vast number of them have reportedly been found— particularly on either side of the Atlantic in Europe and North America.

In Hindu accounts of the various epochs of human existence, called Yugas, giants were said to have lived during the earliest Yugas, being tallest and longest-lived during the golden age, but becoming shorter-lived and smaller in stature with the passing of each Yuga.[16] Likewise, the first age or "Sun" recorded in Aztec tradition was peopled by giants.[17]

In the Stanzas of Dzyan, the "fourth race/asuras" (who inhabited Atlantis) are described as nine yatis high. Although no one knows how long a yati is, the inference is that they were of great height. As discussed in chapter 3, one possibility is that a yati was the same as a cubit, which would mean they were thirteen and a half feet tall.

GIANT INDIAN SKELETONS

Roamed Indian Swamps 500 Years Ago Living on Shell Foods

Tampa, Fla. (AP).—Giant Indians who roamed Florida swamps 500 years or more, living on shell foods which they cracked with their teeth, is a picture unfolded by archeaologists who have delved into a burial ground on a gulf island near here.

The skeletons were discovered on a small section of land, where a lone fisherman has lived for years. Scientists estimated the bones are at least 500 years old and are remains of a tribe known as the Garibs, natives of the West Indies. They are believed to have inhabited the state and adjacent islands before the arrival of Spaniards in Florida.

The skulls, larger than those of current history, battered and crushed, indicated tribal battles. The jaw and teeth are unusually large. Likewise are the body bones, indicating the Indians of past ages were veritable giants in comparison with those of today.

Mounds similar to the one in which the bones were unearthed are common in the state.

The bones have been sent to the Smithsonian Institution for further examination.

A newspaper report published in 1922 in the United States about the discovery of giant-sized human skeletons. There are hundreds of such similar reports—and many end in the same way. The bones are sent to the Smithsonian, and are never seen again.

Some of these giants have been noted as having "the highest known skull vaults reported anywhere in the world" and "show the results of head shaping (deformation)."[18] These giants may have originally had naturally elongated skulls, and copying those with naturally high skull vaults is very likely to be the origin of the practice of skull deformation found in many parts of the world.

Ross Hamilton, who has studied the discoveries of giants in North America and written a number of books about them, says of the giants:

"According to the Native accounts [...] these people were, by-and-large, comely and attractive to the eye. Some of their ancient folk traditions held that they were [...] descended from a race of divinely endowed beings, but had through disgrace lost the mastery of earth-and-sky, devolving rapidly to plain mortals. At a time not as long ago as one might believe, a wiser humanity stewarded the earth to the condition of a true paradise. The people, fauna, and flora lived far longer than now, and as they became older, they continued to grow incrementally. The period of a person's youth took a very long time to fade."[19]

These accounts are corroborated by numerous archaeological finds, as giant skeletons have been unearthed in many parts of the world, perhaps most numerously in the United States. Skeletons uncovered there have also been found with grave goods that demonstrate they possessed a high degree of civilization.

"For sheer mind-blowing diversity, the discoveries across the state of Ohio may be the richest and most unusual in the country. Not only are there numerous finds of giants 8-10 feet tall, but there are also related finds that are equally astonishing. Among the most significant are the Cincinnati tablets inscribed with hieroglyphs, textiles that resemble those from Assyria and Babylon, a skull examined by a surgeon in Cincinnati that exhibits evidence of brain surgery that 'shows knowledge of practical surgery scarcely excelled at the present day,' as well as evidence of metallurgy, forges, slag, iron and even saws."[20]
~ RICHARD DEWHURST, THE ANCIENT GIANTS WHO RULED AMERICA

Other giants were found in copper armor, cloaks of pearls, iron helmets, and with shells from the Atlantic Ocean.[21] Navajo oral history states that there was a regal race of white giants they called the Starnake People, who ruled the West and enslaved lesser tribes, and had strongholds throughout the Americas. They were said to have operated mines, but met their end either because they were extinguished or "went back to the heavens,"[22] and these finds lend credence to the Navajo account.

In a number of oral histories, these giants were once a wise, peaceful, intelligent, and highly spiritual and advanced people who had created a paradise on earth. However, after countless ages of peace and prosperity, they are said to have become arrogant, having turned away from and transgressed divine laws, and were wiped out by a global calamity as a result.

The account of the Comanche chief Rolling Thunder, included earlier, stated that a race of white giants, ten feet high, had, at "the height of their power and glory, when they remembered justice and mercy no more" been swept "with fire and deluge from the face of the earth."

In the legends of the Inca, the wisdom bringer Viracocha, who was deified as a supreme creator, first created the world and then a race of giants to people it. Over time however, these giants became unruly, and so Viracocha being displeased with them, wiped them out with a great flood as punishment, which only two giants survived. Viracocha then created another, smaller people out of clay, whom he gifted with clothes, agriculture, language, and the arts,[23] and whom we are said to be descended from today. An almost identical story is found in the Germanic/Nordic texts the Eddas, in which Odin causes a flood that wipes out all but two of the "rime-giants,"[24] which are the race of giants that had existed in the first era since the creation of the world.[25]

The "War of the Titans" of Greek mythology is likely some echo of the battle between the giants of Atlantis and the Hellenes of Greece. The Titans were the first and oldest gods of the Greek pantheon; they were giants said to have ruled during a golden age. Their descendants were called the Olympians, who were known as the younger gods. They included Zeus, who is a derivative of the foremost god of the Proto-Indo-European pantheon, called Dyeus Phter, and from whom the Hellenes are believed to descend. This means, according to the genealogy of the Greek gods, the Hellenes were the descendants of Titans/giants. Zeus led the Olympians in a ten year rebellion against the Titans, eventually overthrowing them and banishing them to the underworld.[26]

Perhaps the Titans were Atlanteans, and the Olympians were Hellenes, who in Plato's account of Atlantis had gone to war with the Atlanteans when they sought to enslave them. The banishment of the Titans to the underworld may be some reference to their disappearance beneath the ocean at the sinking of Atlantis.

Depiction of Zeus throwing a thunderbolt at a kneeling giant, likely a Titan, carved at a temple in Greece dating to around 580 BC.

The War of the Titans is believed to have derived from legends of the Hittites, and dates back to the second millennium BC or earlier. In the Hittite version the Titans are instead called the Anunnaki, and were likewise depicted as giants. They were also the older class of gods, and were overthrown and banished to the underworld by the younger gods.[27] As discussed earlier, a number of the Children of God were said to have migrated to Mesopotamia, and became deified as members of the Anunnaki.

Ancient tablet showing the sun god Shamash as a giant and possibly with a larger skull, who was a member of the Anunnaki. It is dated to ca. 888-855 BC, and was found at the Babylonian city of Sippar (the city of the sun) in Iraq.

In Vedic/Hindu tradition, there were giants called Daityas, and it is said that at one time the whole earth had belonged to them. They were a clan of asuras who became power hungry, and fought against their half-brothers the devas.[28] Although originally one class of gods in Vedic texts, the asuras and devas divided and became pitted against one another in great wars,[29] which makes me wonder whether the Daityas/asuras were the equivalent of the Titans, while the devas were the equivalent of the Hellenes/Olympians. The Daityas are remembered as primarily worshiping Shiva and the sun god.[30]

Records of giants are also found in ancient Egypt, where they are the source of sun worship and the builders of pyramids and temples.

The Akhbār al-zamān (*The Digest of Wonders*) is a chronological account of the history of Egypt and its kings stretching from before the Deluge to relatively recent times. It was composed between AD 904-1140, but is based on much older sources. It states that Egyptian civilization was founded before the flood by a race of giants who had "sought a place to live apart from other men." They came to Egypt, walked along the Nile River and surveyed the country, which they saw was fertile and beautiful, and thus decided to make it their home. They went on to build the "tallest buildings and most magnificent monuments."[31]

The first king built a temple to the sun, as did many of his pre-flood succes-sors—who also built temples to light and fire. His son after him erected an idol of the sun, which was described as "the greatest of the Egyptian idols." These kings each reigned in the hundreds of years (just as in ancient Egyptian and Mesopotamian pre-flood king lists), as they were longer lived.

The last king before the Deluge had a number of dreams, warning of an imminent cataclysm. He consulted his chief priest, who in turn organized his priests to observe the stars to discern what this imminent cataclysm might be. They discovered that "a prodigy coming down from heaven and up from the earth would consume almost all men: this prodigy was to be a great flood, after which nothing would remain." After making further observations they concluded that despite the disaster, people would survive, and civilization would re-emerge. And so the king ordered the construction of great temples and monuments inscribed with all sciences and knowledge in the hope they would survive the cataclysm.[32]

After this flood, the first king was again a giant who was accompanied by thirty others. The chief priest from before the flood survived (likely a wisdom bringer), and instructed this new king in the knowledge from before the flood, teaching him to read the inscriptions left by the last pre-flood king—and so the legacy of the Religion of the Sun from before the Deluge was renewed.

As with the earlier kings, these also reigned for hundreds of years each. One of them "placed secrets in the pyramids [...] to imitate what had been done of old," and "uncovered the idols which the Flood had submerged," which they restored the worship of. Another built pyramids "as had been done in former times." Pyramid building after the flood was only in imitation of what had been done before it.

A number of following successors were giants, but eventually toward the end the kings are no longer described as giants.[33]

This historical account of giant men as the most ancient kings in Egypt is somewhat supported by archaeological evidence. In the early twentieth century, the famous Egyptologist Sir Flinders Petrie concluded, based on observations of predynastic skeletal remains, that there had been a race which was taller and had a larger cranial capacity than the surrounding pop-ulation, and was associated with the "Followers of Horus" (also known as the Shemsu Hor).[34]

The Basques, who are considered one of the oldest peoples of Europe, state in their legends that giants (called Mairuak) were the builders of the dolmens and stone circles found in the region. They say these giants were gradually displaced until they totally died out.[35] In Welsh legends, giants often held the position of king.[36]

This, and much other evidence, shows that there were giants who survived the flood. Some continued to practice their religion—building great temples and mounds aligned to the sun at the solstices and equinoxes, as well as to other complex astronomical phenomena. Others may have been installed as rulers because of the knowledge they possessed, and their stature. Among their dwindling numbers, they tried to maintain their genetics through intermarriage.

> "The very tall native people recorded early in American history were said to be of a time-honored tradition of selective mating or marriage both fragile and in a stage of imminent collapse. [...] Like European royalty, there apparently existed prescribed marital protocols among certain families. In the Eastern Woodland cultures of North America, there was an effort to preserve genetic lines sustaining, among other things, certain physical characteristics giving rise to a class of nobility over time."[37]
>
> ~ ROSS HAMILTON, A TRADITION OF GIANTS

Scene from an Aztec codex showing a group of natives killing a giant.

These giants appear not only to have intermixed among the natives of North America, but also in the Caucasus.

For example, old folk tales of the Caucasus, recorded in the Nart Sagas, speak of a tall, heroic, semi-divine, and long-lived race of warriors that had become prideful, and as a result, were eventually replaced by "people of small stature." This tall race was the Narts, and their sagas are believed to reflect Sarmatian, Scythian, and even Proto-Indo-European religion and culture.[38] Archaeological finds have corroborated these legends, as burials of Scythian warriors and nobles reveal they were tall and powerfully built, having longer arm and leg bones, and stronger bone formation, with some even exceeding six feet six inches / two meters in height. They dominated the people of smaller stature around them. In ancient historical accounts they were also described as unusually tall, and as having fair skin, red or blonde hair, and blue, green, or gray eyes.[39] As discussed earlier, those sharing the same physical characteristics were also tall. The Paracas nobility were up to six to six feet and two inches tall. The male fair-skinned inhabitants of Easter

Island were recorded as being up to six feet and six and a half inches tall. The Indo-European Tarim mummies in Western China include a woman nearly six feet tall,[40] and men who were up to six feet and seven inches tall.[41] By comparison, the average height of male hunter-gatherers in Europe was five feet and ten inches, while that of male European Neolithic farmers was five feet and five inches.[42]

There is evidence to suggest that some of the wisdom bringers were the result of this admixture, as there is reference to the wisdom bringer Odin/Wotan as being half jötunn—the term jötunn/jötnar being used to describe a race descended from the giant Ymir.[43] The wisdom bringers of Central and South America were also often described as tall. For example, the followers of Quetzalcoatl were described as "tall in stature, beyond the common race of men, and it was nothing uncommon for them to live hundreds of years. Such was their energy that they allowed no lazy person to live among them, and like their master they were skilled in every art of life and virtuous beyond the power of mortals. In complexion they are described as light in hue, as was their leader [...]."[44]

The evidence indicates that there was once a race of giants who had been known as the Children of God, although there may have been other races of giants too. To the shorter-lived and statured surrounding people they must have seemed so long-lived as to be immortal, and so advanced as to be god-like. They created the civilization of Atlantis, built many of the world's megalithic monuments, and were the source of the ancient Religion of the Sun. However, they interbred with other humanoids, and as they did, they progressively lost their stature and divine qualities, became shorter lived, smaller skulled and brained, and more animalistic and aggressive. This is how they are said to have degenerated into the warlike Atlanteans that the descendants of the surrounding peoples understood as having been punished by a great flood.

THE FALL

The demise of the Children of God is one of the most tragic and widely remembered events in ancient texts and oral histories. It seems to have been a pivotal turning point in the course of life on Earth.

In *The Kolbrin*, the Children of God are described as having a sacred "gardenplace" wherein there is a "tree of life" as well as a "moonchalice" and magical cauldron. Nearby the gardenplace is a stone circle containing a sacred grail.[45] These are all symbols that would later make their way into the mythology of Europe and Britain. There are also many references to what is obviously proto-Arthurian mythology in which a sacred grail would also later feature. *The Kolbrin* even states that some of these items were brought from Egypt to Britain, where they were kept by the Druids.[46]

Using references to place names and geographical features, Yvonne Whiteman has located the "gardenplace" in the Indus Valley region in what is now Pakistan (specifically Mehrgarh).[47] In the texts, the inhabitants of the gardenplace have connections to the peoples of the Caucasus, and at some point, the gardenplace is destroyed in a disaster (likely an earthquake), and most leave to dwell in the Caucasus region,[48] although some also go out among the surrounding tribes/peoples to teach them writing, laws, and building, and consequently become known as great, and even as gods, among them.

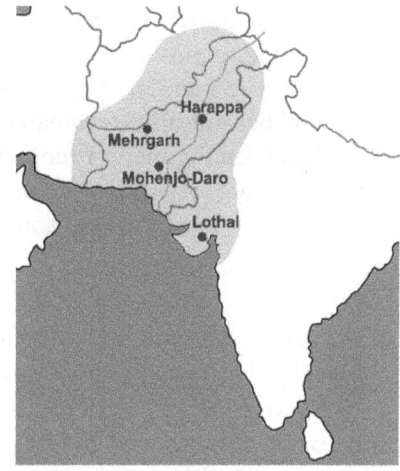

A basic map of the Indus Valley region, mostly located in what is now Pakistan.

The Children of God who inhabited the gardenplace had a sense of duty to help other people, as "teaching the wild men about them was a duty with which they had been charged,"[49] and they had initiated projects to do so, yet were never meant to mix with them. But eventually, the code was broken, and one of them mated with and had a child by a "Yosling," which Whiteman suggests could have been a Neanderthal.[50] I personally wonder whether Yoslings were modern humans who already had Neanderthal admixture. The mating with Yoslings was considered such a grievous sin that it was believed to have provoked the destruction of the gardenplace. It was remembered as the great "fall" of the Children of God. The description of the gardenplace and the events that occur there is clearly a much more detailed telling of the story of the Garden of Eden.

In addition to this, a number of different texts in *The Kolbrin* state that the Children of God mated with the Children of Men, and this too was considered such a grievous act that it was believed to have led to the great flood. Here is one example:

> "It came about that the sons of The Children of God mated with the daughters of The Children Men, who knew well the ways of men and were not reserved. The covenant had been broken and strange women were taken into the households, some even as wives, but though the daughters were lesser women, the sons were wonderfully big and mighty fighting men. [...] This was when the years of man's life were lessened because he became fully Earth-sustained [...]. In those days, there were many having the blood of The Children of God [...]. Therefore, the enlightening word of God came to Eloma [a great female teacher and visionary of the Children of God]. [...] Eloma had three sons and they all heard the voice of God and walked

with Him. Her firstborn son was Haryanah and he carried the word
of God to the Children of God who dwelt in the Northlands, for they
had forgotten His Ways. He married Didi, daughter of a great king
and became an even greater king; he had many sons who all became
kings among men of renown. Yahama, her secondborn son, carried
the word of God to those who dwelt towards the sunrising, and
Manum, her thirdborn son, carried it to those towards sunsetting."[51]

~ ELOMA, THE KOLBRIN

The above account is then followed by the devastating "Flood of Atuma."
It is clearly the same basic storyline found in Genesis, dating from a time
as the text says "when there were giants on the earth." It narrates how "the
Sons of God" mate with the "daughters of men," giving birth to "mighty men
who were of old, men of renown"—an event that is followed by the great
flood.[52] These Sons of God or their offspring by "the daughters of men" are
called Nephilim (the text is ambiguous as to whom the term applies to), which
has been translated most commonly to mean "giants," but also "the fallen
ones."[53] These Nephilim were known as great warriors, and were said to have
descended to the underworld, just as the Titans and Anunnaki were.

It's interesting to note that the offspring of the Children of God and Children
of Men are "wonderfully big," as in large or giant, and that they were "fighting
men," as the Atlanteans were giants who spent the final days of their civilization in wars of aggression. It's also interesting that the Children of God and
their descendants became great kings, and their names are very similar to
those found in the Vedas i.e. Yahama becomes Yama, Manum becomes Manu,
and Haryana is the name of a state in Northern India.

In ancient Egyptian religion, the west, specifically the place of the setting
sun, was called "The Land of Manu,"[54] which is the direction Manum travels (in
the above excerpt) to take "the word of God" to those who had forgotten his
ways, before the great flood. If they are referring to the same person, this may
mean that Manu traveled to Atlantis before it was destroyed. As described in
chapter 3, Manu is said to have survived this flood, and afterward established
a solar dynasty in Northern India. The region of Haryana in Northern India
(possibly named after his brother) is where some of the later books of the Rig
Veda are believed to have been composed,[55] indicating that they may contain
some of the knowledge carried by Haryanah.

Yima (the Iranian equivalent of Yama) and the Vedic first man Manu, were
both considered "sons of the sun" and kings of the sun dynasty who were taught
religion before the flood, and were tasked with surviving and reestablishing
it afterward. In the same text of *The Kolbrin* (called Eloma), a number of the
Children of God also migrate to Mesopotamia, where they raise cities, teach
writing and how to build with bricks, and become deified as members of the
gods called the Anunnaki,[56] which means something like "princely offspring."[57]

In Plato's account of Atlantis, the Atlanteans also succumb to "mortal admixture," and "their divine portion began to fade away, and became diluted too often and too much [...] and the human nature got the upper hand" and that like this they lost "the fairest of their precious gifts."[58] This mortal admixture suggests interbreeding between the inhabitants of Atlantis and ordinary humans. As with the Children of God, this was also said to have led to a great flood (which resulted in the destruction of Atlantis).

In the Stanzas of Dzyan the fourth race were the descendants of an earlier third race, who had sexually reproduced (two by two) across the earth, losing their "godliness" as they did. They then interbred with ordinary humans who had, what sounds like, a smaller cranial capacity:

> "[...] two by two on the seven zones [of the earth], the Third Race gave birth to the Fourth-Race men; the gods became no-gods; the sura became a-sura. [...] Then the Fourth became tall with pride. We are the kings, it was said; we are the gods. They took wives fair to look upon. Wives from the mindless, the narrow-headed. They bred monsters. Wicked demons, male and female, also Khado (dakini), with little minds."[59]
>
> ~ THE STANZAS OF DZYAN

This indicates that the Atlanteans (from the fourth race) were already the result of intermixing between the Children of God and other humanoids, and that this was the cause of their change of temperament and downfall. I suspect that Titans, Anunnaki, Nephilim, and asuras/Daityas were all names given to essentially the same people who were either the Atlanteans or related to them.

THIRD EYE

In *The Kolbrin*, the Children of God had their "Great Eye" opened and used this "inner eye" to see nonphysical things.[60] They are also described as having "twinsight," which is the ability to see "all the things of the Otherworld, not clearly but as through a veil."[61] In the Stanzas of Dzyan, the fourth race is described as having their third eye opened. The inhabitants of Atala (White Island) are described as being able to see the great god Narayana, whereas those who visited the island were not.

In the Maya account of creation, the gods attempt to create humans a number of times and fail, and each time have to destroy them in a cataclysm to start again—one of their failures devolved into monkeys.[62] At last they get it right. They create people who are described as not being born of any mother or father, but by a miracle of the Creator (being children of god). They are good and handsome, and have the figures of men. They are described as being able to see things instantly at a distance, which may indicate they were born with extrasensory perception:

"They were endowed with intelligence; they saw and instantly they could see far, they succeeded in seeing, they succeeded in knowing all that there is in the world. When they looked, instantly they saw all around them, and they contemplated in turn the arch of heaven and the round face of the earth. [...] The things hidden (in the distance) they saw all, without first having to move; at once they saw the world, and so, too, from where they were, they saw it. Great was their wisdom; their sight reached to the forests, the rocks, the lakes, the seas, the mountains, and the valleys. In truth, they were admirable men. [...] Then they gave thanks to the Creator and the Maker [...] 'we feel perfectly, and we know what is far and what is near. We also see the large and the small in the sky and on earth.' [...] They were able to know all, and they examined the four comers, the four points of the arch of the sky and the round face of the earth."[63]

~ POPOL VUH

But the text continues, saying this race had their clairvoyant vision taken from them, and the K'iche' believed they were descended from these blinded people:

"Then the Heart of Heaven blew mist into their eyes, which clouded their sight as when a mirror is breathed upon. Their eyes were covered and they could see only what was close, only that was clear to them. In this way the wisdom and all the knowledge of the four men, the origin and beginning [of the K'iche' race], were destroyed. In this way were created and formed our grandfathers, our fathers, by the Heart of Heaven, the Heart of Earth."[64]

~ POPOL VUH

In the Stanzas of Dzyan, after the fourth race "took wives from the mindless" and bred with those of "little minds," it was said "their third eye acted no longer" and because of their mistake, a great cataclysm utterly destroyed their island homeland.

Tibetan depiction of the third eye.

In *The Kolbrin*, the Children of God also lose their "twinsight" due to interbreeding with "Yoslings." A "Spiritbeing" casts them from the gardenplace, saying:

> "[...] you shall not again defile this place. Henceforth, the misty veil becomes an impenetrable barrier severing our two realms from each other, so they can no longer be easily spanned."[65]
>
> ~ THE BOOK OF CREATION, THE KOLBRIN

In yet another account, after "woman was tempted by the strength and wildness of the beast which dwelt in the forest, and the race of man was defiled again," the Great Eye closes.

> "The eye that sees earthly things is deceitful, but the eye that sees spiritual things is true. Then, because of the things that happened, the Great Eye that saw Truth was closed and henceforth man walked in falsity. Unable to perceive Truth he saw only that which deceived him, and so it shall be until his awakening."[66]
>
> ~ MAYA AND LILA, THE KOLBRIN

Note that one eye is described as seeing what is untrue, while the other sees what is true. This is likely the basis for Odin losing one of his eyes to gain sight of the truth. The inner eye which the Children of God once had is clearly the origin of the many depictions of the third eye in the ancient Religion of the Sun, and the religious preoccupation with attempting to reopen it.

Texts of *The Kolbrin* state that because of the interbreeding between the Children of God and other humanoids over a long period of time, the Children of God "passed into dust" and all that remained were ordinary humans.[67]

NOT AS FAR-FETCHED AS IT SEEMS

It may sound too extraordinary to be true that a race of giants who had extraterrestrial genetic input once lived on Earth. But it's not as far-fetched as it seems.

We now know, thanks to archaeology and the development of genetics, that very different races from our own lived hundreds of thousands of years ago, right up until the major expansion of modern humans around fifty thousand years ago. One of these humanoids had an average height between just three to four feet, making them "dwarves" compared to modern humans (though they are colloquially called "hobbits").[68] In fact, geneticists have now identified so many different ancient types of hominids that were so different to one another, a geneticist remarked, "we're looking at a *Lord of the Rings*-type world."[69] This kind of world is something we might find hard to imagine today, but is vividly preserved in many ancient traditions across the globe, which describe giants, dwarves, ogres, monkey people, etc.

Geneticists have so far identified five archaic humanoids who lived before seventy thousand years ago and who had diverged and remained unadmixed for hundreds of thousands of years. They are Neanderthals, two kinds of Denisovans, "hobbits," and modern humans. They have even identified a "superarchaic" population, which diverged between 1.4-0.9 million years ago and interbred with Denisovans. We've become accustomed to the human variation we see today, but as the American geneticist David Reich, who is known for his research into the genetics of ancient populations, points out, the humanoids that once lived tens of thousands of years ago were far more genetically varied than even the most genetically divergent races of modern humans are believed to be today.[70]

> "Seventy thousand years ago, the world was populated by very diverse human forms, and we have genomes from an increasing number of them, allowing us to peer back to a time when humanity was much more variable than it is today."[71]
>
> ~ DAVID REICH, WHO WE ARE AND HOW WE GOT HERE

The faces of archaic humanoids. Left: Homo floresiensis aka "hobbit." Center: Homo erectus. Right: Neanderthal.

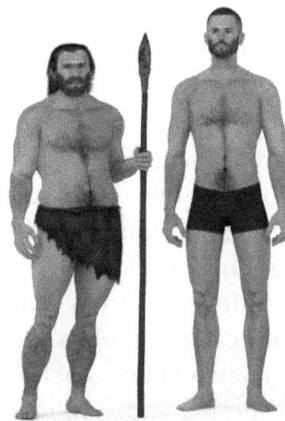

Digital illustration of a Neanderthal (left) compared to a modern West European (right).

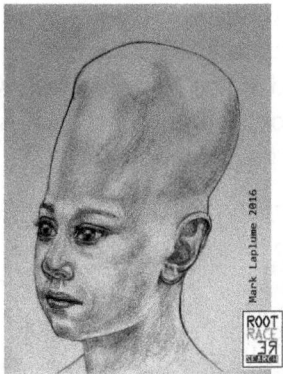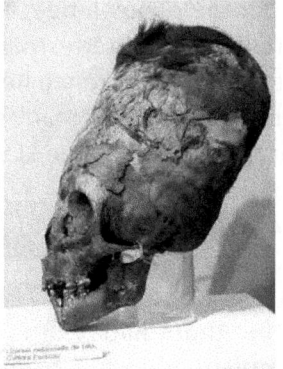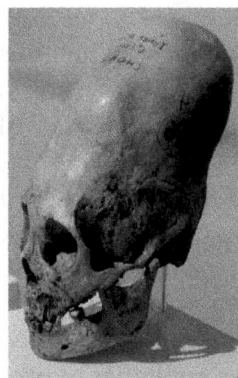

Left: Sketch by the artist Mark Laplume of a Paracas child estimated to be between five and ten years old, based on the skull in the central image, which used to be on display in the Regional Museum of Ica in Peru. Right: Paracas skull on display in the same museum. According to medical experts who studied their skull morphology, the Paracas should be considered another type of humanoid, potentially *Homo sapiens sapiens paracas*.

Reich is a professor in the department of genetics at the Harvard Medical School, and an associate of the Broad Institute. He believes there are probably more types of archaic humanoids yet to be discovered, and that the sequencing of some of their genomes has only been the beginning of "a torrent of findings that have disrupted many of the comfortable understandings we had before."[72]

Reich and colleges have also identified a number of "ghost" races that have long been extinct, but whose DNA geneticists have begun detecting in a number of different races today.[73] They have also identified mating or hybridyzation between some of these archaic humanoids and with certain races of modern humans, and have been able to calculate when this mating approximately occurred.

> "So far, DNA from two archaic human populations—Neanderthals and Denisovans—has been sequenced, and in both cases, the data made it possible to detect hybridization between modern and archaic humans that had been previously unknown. I would not be surprised if DNA sequenced from the next newly discovered archaic population will also point to a previously unknown hybridization event."[74]
>
> ~ DAVID REICH, WHO WE ARE AND HOW WE GOT HERE

So it's almost a scientific certainty that there are other archaic humanoids that geneticists are yet to discover. And it's possible that at least one of these may have had extraterrestrial genetic input.

The Disclosure Project, founded by Dr. Steven Greer in 1993, has coordinated over eight hundred U.S. government officials, including those working at high levels in military and intelligence agencies, and high-level defense contractors, to testify about their knowledge, and in some cases eyewitness accounts, of extraterrestrials and extraterrestrial craft. In 2001, over twenty of these witnesses spoke at a press conference held at the National Press Club in Washington, DC.[75] Although including many government officials, this was not a project involving or sanctioned by the U.S. government.

However, in 2017, the U.S. Department of Defense acknowledged that it has investigated UFOs as part of a secretive program. A Navy spokesperson also confirmed that there had been a number of unidentified and/or unauthorized aircraft that had entered military zones in recent years. Videos recorded by U.S. Navy pilots of three of these sightings were released to the public, and a Navy spokesperson stated that they represented just a fraction of the UFO incursions detected in Navy training ranges.[76] The footage of each of these sightings was taken aboard U.S. Navy Super Hornet jets using the

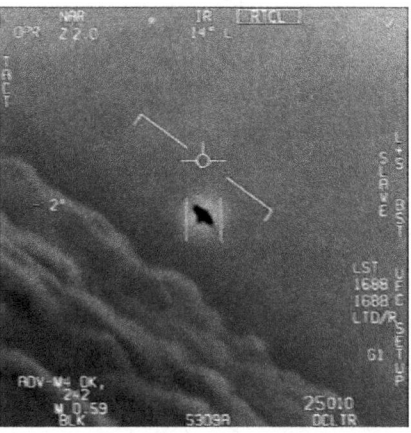

A UFO from the video "Gimbal" officially released by the U.S. Navy. Pilots exclaim they can see a whole fleet of these.

most advanced sensors and powerful tracking systems available.[77] One video showed an oval-shaped UFO that had no plumes, wings, or rotors, but had traveled at a mile per second, and easily outsped the jets.[78] A pilot exclaims that he can see a whole fleet of UFOs, although only one appears on camera.[79] One of the pilots said the object he saw moved in ways he couldn't explain—likening it to a ping pong ball bouncing off a wall. These videos were first released in 2017 and 2018 by a private company, but have since been officially released in 2020 by the Pentagon in order to confirm the footage is real.[80] That is, the most powerful and technologically advanced military in human history has admitted that there are craft, which do not belong to them, and are using technologies unknown to them, here, among us.

Between the confirmation of now extinct, archaic humanoids that lived tens to hundreds of thousands of years ago, and the acknowledgement by the U.S. Department of Defense of the existence of UFOs, the possibility that a race like the Children of God once lived on Earth becomes very real indeed.

The testimonies of the Disclosure Project witnesses, and the contact made by civilians using Dr. Greer's CE-5 protocols, reveal that extraterrestrials are not only highly technologically advanced, but also far more spiritually advanced than we are collectively. Interactions with them have shown they are concerned about the welfare of our planet and are working to ensure we don't destroy it (either through nuclear weapons or the irreparable destruction of the environment).[81][82] I believe our human race is so destructive they need to monitor us without getting involved directly, given our level of aggression and violence, to make sure we don't take our destruction to other planets and that this planet can support life into the future.

RELIGION OF A ONCE GREAT PEOPLE

While those among the Children of God may have been the source of the ancient Religion of the Sun, it's evident they were not the only ones able to practice it, nor attain its goal. In fact some are described as selflessly dedicating their time to teaching the peoples of other races around them. The wisdom bringers, some of whom may have been their descendants, also went to great lengths to teach peoples across the world the Religion of the Sun, even risking their lives to do so. They would not have bothered if the people they taught were unable to attain what they were teaching. Indeed what they taught, which has survived in a number of ancient texts and traditions, is that all people (and indeed all living creatures) have a spark of the divine within and that the ultimate purpose of life is for these sparks to reunite with their higher Being—so that "all [can] become sons of the sun."[83]

The ancient Religion of the Sun is the legacy of this once great people. I suspect they were the first to have called themselves "children of the sun," as they were considered to have been created by the sun god. Those who attempted to preserve their ancestry also called themselves children of the sun, and claimed direct descent from the sun, like the Inca, ancient Egyptian, and Vedic royal families, who established themselves as a ruling and priestly class in solar theocracies in the Lost Civilization of the Sun.

CHAPTER SIX

Jesus and the Religion of the Sun

JESUS THE GNOSTIC

Jesus taught the Religion of the Sun, but his true message and teachings have been greatly censored and distorted, and continue to be today. On one hand, Christians have rejected so much of his teaching (contained in numerous texts left out of the Bible) as to have a very incomplete and inaccurate view of him. On the other, many, particularly pagans, see Jesus as responsible for their historical persecution, and even as a complete forgery used for political control.

Virtually all modern scholars agree that Jesus was a real historical person due to the overwhelming evidence for his existence.[1] While it's true that many vested interests have used the figure of Jesus for political ends, this should not be confused with the actual person he was and what he taught, and there is much evidence for this, which many are unaware of.

Firstly, there is nothing in the words of Jesus that incites violence against any living thing. Scholars have noted that the explicit doctrinal source that the persecution of pagans by Judeo-Christians was based upon can be found in the texts of the Old Testament, and inferences in the works of Paul. Numerous such statements include:

> "You will not let a witch live."[2]
>
> ~ EXODUS 22:18

> "You must destroy all the places where the nations you are dispossessing served their gods, whether on high mountains, on hills, or under some leafy tree. Break down their altars, smash their

standing-stones to pieces, burn up their sacred poles completely and cut down the carved images of their gods. Exterminate their name from that place."[3]

~ DEUTERONOMY 12:2-3

As just one historical example of this, in 772 the Frankish King Charlemagne cut down the sacred Germanic Irminsul tree at the ancient site of Externsteine in Germany as part of his campaign to Christianize the Saxons. He returned ten years later to oversee the execution of 4,500 Saxons who had rebelled. The historian Alessandro Barbero says, "the most likely inspiration for the mass execution of Verden was the Bible," because Charlemagne wanted "to act like a true King of Israel." Barbero cites the biblical tale of the complete extermination of the Amalekites and the conquest of the Moabites by David as his likely inspiration.[4] These are stories from the Old Testament which were around before Jesus was born, and were later included in the Bible, which Jesus did not create.

Charlemagne overseeing the cutting down of the sacred Irminsul tree.

Texts in the Old Testament explicitly single out people who venerate the sun and stars as those who should be put to death, and this is likely why Jesus had to carefully veil his more esoteric message and instead use the events of his life as a symbolic teaching.

Jesus was considered a "sorcerer" and "Gnostic" (a pagan) by the supreme Judaic religious authority called the Sanhedrin as recorded in their text the Talmud.[5] [6] The ideology which led to Jesus' execution is the same ideology that led to the persecution of pagans by Judeo-Christians.

> "If a prophet, or one who foretells by dreams, appears among you and announces to you a sign or wonder, and if the sign or wonder spoken of takes place, and the prophet says, "Let us follow other gods" (gods you have not known) "and let us worship them," you must not listen to the words of that prophet or dreamer. [...] That prophet or dreamer must be put to death for inciting rebellion against the LORD your God [...]."[7]
>
> ~ DEUTERONOMY 13:1-3, 5

So what do texts attributed to Jesus say?

"If by gathering in a temple men feel they can better commune with God, then He will be there and that place will be holy. If within a circle of stones or before a symbolic image the soul of man may be stirred to attunement, then God will not absent Himself because of the Nature of the Place. He will meet man wherever man earnestly prepares for His coming. Though the temple may be holy to one man and the circle of stones to another, both places will be hallowed by God, if therein the souls of men are elevated to commune with Him."[8]

~ JESUS IN THE BRITAIN BOOK, THE KOLBRIN

Jesus portrayed as the sun.

Scores of texts containing the teachings of Jesus were excluded from the Judeo-Christian Bible, which was put together long after Jesus' death by people who were persecuting other Christians, including the followers of Jesus' esoteric teachings. Of the seventy-three books in the Catholic Bible, just four (five if you count Revelation) of them contain the direct teachings of Jesus, and even these were altered. Even some of the letters of Paul have been revealed by scholars to be forgeries.[9]

Instead, most of Jesus' teachings were banned and suppressed. The remnants of what survived can be found in the ancient texts of the Nag Hammadi Library, the Pistis Sophia, the Gospel of Judas, and the Gospel of

Pages from the ancient collection of texts called the Nag Hammadi Library that was discovered in 1945 buried in Egypt, containing never before seen teachings of Jesus.

Mary (Magdalene)—all of which have been rediscovered in the last 250 years, and are today called "Gnostic" to refer to the branch of people who followed Jesus' esoteric teachings. Other texts not accepted by mainstream academia, which I personally believe to be authentic, include *The Essene Gospel of Peace*, *The Gospel of the Kailedy*, and *The Kolbrin*.

THE FIRST TEMPLE OF SOLOMON DEDICATED TO SUN WORSHIP

Yet there is evidence that the earliest roots of Abrahamic religion (first attested in the Old Testament) may have been related to the Religion of the Sun. For example, the First Temple built by Solomon was oriented toward the rising sun, which people were described as worshiping.[10]

> "Then the Spirit lifted me up and brought me to the gate of the house of the LORD that faces east."[11]
>
> ~ EZEKIEL 11:1

> "He then brought me into the inner court of the house of the LORD [...]. With their backs toward the temple of the LORD and their faces toward the east, they were bowing down to the sun in the east."[12]
>
> ~ EZEKIEL 8:16

However, the sixteenth king of Judah, called Josiah, is recorded in the Old Testament as going on a campaign to eradicate sun worship from the temple. Josiah ordered the removal and burning of all the articles made for "the starry hosts." He then "did away with the idolatrous priests appointed by the kings of Judah to burn incense on the high places of the towns of Judah and on those around Jerusalem – those who burned incense to Baal, to the sun and moon, to the constellations and to all the starry hosts." He also "removed from the entrance to the temple of the LORD the horses that the kings of Judah had dedicated to the sun. [...] Josiah then burned the chariots dedicated to the sun."[13] The chariots and horses dedicated to the sun may have been the same as those that draw the sun in Indo-European religion.[14]

Scholars have noted numerous similarities between the solar monotheism of the Egyptian Pharaoh Akhenaten and the monotheism of Judaism.[15] Sigmund Freud explained this by saying that the god of Judaism was a fusion between the sun god of ancient Egypt and the Midianite god of the Old Testament.[16] The story of Noah is so similar to that of Manu and Ziusudra (as described in chapter 3) that I believe they are almost certainly describing the same event.

Further evidence for sun worship is found in the region of Qumran in the West Bank, where an ancient community called the Essenes once lived (one of the two groups Jesus is said to have spent time with, explained further on).

They are believed to have followed a form of Judaism. A room of one of their monasteries was aligned to the sun like the Temple of Solomon was.[17] They offered prayers to the sun, which they said was a practice passed down to them by their forefathers.[18] In nearby caves, the ancient texts called the Dead Sea Scrolls were discovered—which contain a solar calendar used to determine community feast days, which were celebrated on Wednesdays as the day the sun was created in Genesis[19]—along with a sundial.[20] The Essenes were likely survivors of the earlier solar religion of Judah before it became replaced with what's now known as Judaism.

> "And as for their [the Essenes] piety towards God, it is very extraordinary; for before sun-rising they speak not a word about profane matters, but put up certain prayers which they have received from their forefathers, as if they made a supplication for its rising."[21]
>
> ~ JOSEPHUS FLAVIUS, FIRST CENTURY HISTORIAN

What's clear is that sometime in its history, what became Judaism turned completely against the veneration of the sun, most likely during the reign of Josiah (c. 640-609 BC).[22] This may have led to some of the stories in the Old Testament being altered retrospectively.

JESUS' LOST YEARS

There is a marked gap in the recollection of Jesus' life as given in the Gospels—these are referred to as his "lost years" and occur from when he was twelve to thirty years old. The timing of these "lost years" is not random. During Jesus' time, it was Jewish custom that on turning thirteen, a boy was considered an adult, accountable for his own actions, and as having a number of responsibilities to fulfill in the religion.[23] Then, it wasn't until turning thirty that they were eligible to become a priest.[24] I believe it's no coincidence that Jesus disappeared precisely between these ages. By going away during this period, Jesus probably avoided entering mainstream Jewish religion, and was instead able to devote himself to study with at least two spiritual groups. He then returned at the accepted age of thirty to be a spiritual teacher.

The Gospels of Mark and Matthew indicate that during this time Jesus worked as a carpenter, but *The Kolbrin* gives more detail as to his whereabouts, saying that he traveled and spent time with two spiritual groups—namely the Nasarines and "the Society of Saints beside the Sea of Heavy Salt" (the Dead Sea),[25] and I've come across historical evidence to support this.

The Mandaeans are followers of an ancient Gnostic religion that survived in Iraq and Iran, who inhabited areas around Jerusalem and the River Jordan during the time of Jesus. Baptism is a central part of their ritual,[26] and Jesus was baptized in the River Jordan.

Ancient Mandaean texts state that Jesus, along with John the Baptist, became priests of the Mandaeans known as Naṣuraiia (Naṣoreans), which indicated someone who knew esoteric knowledge and white magic and observed the stars and omens.[27] This is very likely the basis of the references to Jesus being a Nazarene in the New Testament, as there are no references to a town called Nazareth existing until AD 200, and the New Testament references appear to be altered or misinterpreted, obscuring the real meaning of the phrase.[28] In the Jewish text the Talmud, written by Rabbis after Jesus' death, Jesus is referred to as "Jesus the notsri" (Yeshu ha-Notzri), which likely means Jesus the *Naṣuraiia* (Mandaean) / Gnostic.[29] The word Manda (from Mandaean) in Aramaic means "knowledge" just as the word gnostic means "knowledge" in Greek, and so Mandaeans were and are still considered Gnostic.[30]

The Mandaeans venerated the stars and sun as the home of light Beings and spiritual principles, and venerated the sun god Shamash who traveled across the sky in a boat, and who was depicted almost identically by the ancient Egyptians, Zoroastrians, and Mesopotamians. Texts and oral histories of the Mandaeans indicate they originated in ancient Egypt, but also possibly in the north, being connected to the Indo-Iranians.[31] They are also considered to be of the same religion as the Sabians, based in Harran in present-day Turkey (which at the time of Jesus was said to be a center of esoteric knowledge), who venerated the stars and made pilgrimages to ancient Egypt, and who had changed their name to escape persecution under Islam.[32] It appears Mandaean religion derived from the ancient Religion of the Sun, and Jesus became learned in it. Their sacred texts depict sun ships with the sun at the prow, just as is found in the ancient Caucasus and Egypt.[33]

Modern day Mandaeans in prayer.

The Mandaeans essentially believe that everyone contains a spark of light that originates from a great spiritual region of light, and has come into this dark world of matter. The mission of these sparks is to return to the light from where they came. Messengers are believed to be sent by the creator to rescue these light beings trapped in material bodies, by teaching them gnosis, or the knowledge of their true identity. The foremost among these is the "Son of Life."[34]

Anyone familiar with the ancient Gnostic text Pistis Sophia, in which Jesus teaches his disciples very high esoteric knowledge, will recognize he taught this same worldview.

Mandaean texts have been difficult to date, containing material from at least as early as the third century AD, but being edited until sometime after the advent of Islam.[35] They state that both John and Jesus had been Mandaean priests, and regard John as a great teacher, but later denounce Jesus as a rebel and heretic, who they say had betrayed secret doctrines and made religion easier.[36]

Jesus also appears to have spent time with the Essenes who lived by the Dead Sea (they are likely the Society of Saints beside the Sea of Heavy Salt referred to in *The Kolbrin*). The texts called the Essene Gospels of Peace possibly record teachings Jesus gave to this group on subjects not found in the Bible, such as on the spiritual in nature, and the divine feminine he calls the Earthly Mother—which he includes in the Trinity alongside the Heavenly Father and the Son of Man—as well as exercises for having out-of-body experiences and learning from dreams. The Hungarian philologist/linguist, philosopher, and psychologist, Edmond Bordeaux Szekely, claimed to have come across the Essene Gospel of Peace while studying at the Vatican in 1923, and published its translation, though the Vatican denies it ever existed.[37] Another collection of texts associated with the Essenes are the Dead Sea Scrolls, which have been authenticated. Certain parts of them contain similarities with Jesus' teachings, leading some scholars to feel that Jesus was at least influenced by the Essenes,[38] and this indicates he is likely to have had contact with them.

There are also claims that Jesus spent time in Britain, India, and Tibet, among other places. While it may be possible he did, the legends and texts used to support these claims are not considered historically reliable, and I personally don't find them reliable either.

JESUS AND THE RELIGION OF THE SUN

In ancient Gnostic texts Jesus taught about concepts many would consider Eastern, such as karma, reincarnation, and the cycles of lives. Many have noted the striking similarities between the teachings of Jesus and those of Hinduism, found both in the New Testament[39] and in texts that were omitted from the Bible.[40] Similarities have also been noted between Gnostic texts and the doctrine of Zoroastrianism.[41] One particular text shares the same central theme as the Eleusinian Mysteries of ancient Greece,[42] and the life of Jesus clearly shares many similarities with that of Osiris of ancient Egypt.[43] Jesus is also recorded as teaching both male and female disciples, and in one text, says Mary Magdalene is the most advanced among them. He also talks about the female aspects of divinity, such as the "Virgin of light" who judges people after death.[44]

In the ancient Gnostic texts and *The Gospel of the Kailedy*, in my view, a more accurate depiction of Jesus is given—as one who has the Spiritual Son/Sun within (being called a "son of the sun" in the terminology of the ancient Religion of the Sun), rather than being the literal only "Son of God"—whose purpose was to show people how to attain the Spiritual Son within themselves. Biblical scholar Bart Ehrman has demonstrated that Jesus never called himself God; instead, the view that he was literally God was adopted by his followers after his death.[45]

In *The Kolbrin*, Joseph of Arimathea is said to have gone to Britain just a couple of years after Jesus' crucifixion to establish a community near Glastonbury with a number of Jesus' followers; they eventually had an influence upon the beliefs of the people there, including on those of the Druids. A priestess of Glastonbury is described as having a recurring dream in which she sees the sun of the old religion of the Druids merge with the new sun of Jesus' teaching,[46] and so, as many people have recognized, the old solar religions became expressed through the life and teachings of Jesus.

In *Ancient Solstice*, my husband explains how Jesus carried out a spiritual mission, and that the people and events around him portrayed the stages someone goes through on the path of the spiritual sun (to enlightenment).[47]

My husband and I believe the whereabouts of Jesus between the ages of twelve and thirty may have been deliberately left vague in the accounts of his life. In my husband's view, the particular time and place Jesus was born into symbolizes how the Spiritual Son is born into the darkness of the world, and, on another level, into the darkness of someone's psyche on the path to source/enlightenment.[48] In the Gospels, Jesus knew he was going to be put to death, and it seems he tried to ensure this didn't happen before its appointed time, veiling much of his message to be able to stay alive long enough to complete the events he needed to go through and to gather a following. Had he taught openly in the society he was born into, he probably would have been killed even sooner than he was.

In the Gospel of Judas, Jesus is shown organizing his own betrayal with Judas as one of his closest disciples. It seems possible he also prearranged events with John the Baptist, whom he'd already spent time with as a Naṣuraiia, before they enacted his public baptism. Likewise, it's highly possible that Jesus gathered a close circle of followers in the time he spent with the Essenes, before he began his public teaching.

The story of Jesus' life would later become well-known, spreading the exoteric teachings he had given on how to lead a moral life, as well as those encoded into it about how to walk the path of the spiritual sun. Thus, it would fulfill two purposes: being an exoteric message the masses of people could take to literally, and an esoteric one people could read more deeply. Looking back into history, it seems those carrying Jesus' exoteric message, like Paul, were far more successful than those carrying his esoteric one. One by one, all the other groups who had practiced a more esoteric interpretation of Jesus' teachings were persecuted, either being exterminated or going underground, until they all eventually completely disappeared. Thus, a significant part of the story and message of Jesus was all but lost.

Cultures, civilizations, and peoples can carry the Religion of the Sun—and they once did over vast stretches of the earth—but it is those who had the Spiritual Son within, the "sons of the sun," that were the source of their spiritual knowledge and who ultimately came to create the conditions for all peoples to be able to learn the knowledge of the spiritual sun, and to fulfill life's spiritual purpose.

I believe Jesus was one such "Son of the Sun" and a teacher of the Religion of the Sun.

CHAPTER SEVEN

Summary of the Founding
of the Ancient Religion of the Sun

Based on what I've seen so far, here is a general outline of what I believe happened with the spread of the Religion and Lost Civilization of the Sun.

I believe that the Religion of the Sun dates back to a golden age, that these golden ages recur, and that it is the religion of every golden age, as it is an attempt to explain and systemize "the natural, ancient, and eternal way," which is better seen and understood the more spiritually perceptive people are.

It seems a golden age started around 40,000 BC, which is when some of the Egyptian king lists begin, and when some of the records of ancient Egypt appear to start. These records may not have been "Egyptian," but were later preserved by an esoteric order that survived in Egypt.

At this time, it appears there was a people remembered in ancient traditions variously called the "Children of God" and "children of the sun," who were very spiritually perceptive, and at least some of whom practiced the Religion of the Sun. They migrated out of a cold northern land at some indeterminate time when the climate became too cold. This may be the source of the legends of Hyperborea, where civilization began in a golden age, although the accounts of it appear to have become confused and conflated with other places over time.

As the ice sheets grew and increasingly trapped water, the amount of land on Earth increased, which the Children of God migrated into. They appear to have settled in different parts of the world—at least in the Indus Valley in South Asia, the Caucasus, Atlantis, Egypt, and the Americas.

The Children of God seem to have been much taller in stature, to have had a very pale (moon-colored) complexion, and a larger, elongated cranial capacity, which people all over the world later tried to mimic using techniques of cranial deformation. They were more spiritually perceptive (having their "inner eye" opened) and became the nobility among many ancient peoples, thus why cranial deformation came to denote these very things. The Children of God believed that it was important to preserve their genetics, which later resulted in intermarriage within royal dynasties even into relatively recent times, as with the Pharaoh Akhenaten in Egypt whose family were depicted with elongated skulls (though these clearly look to have been the result of artificial cranial deformation[1]) and who had tried to restore the practice of the Religion of the Sun (albeit in a very distorted way).

They are said to have been far more advanced than other humanoid species on the earth, and always cultivated the land around them, rather than being hunter-gatherers who lived by the chase. They are likely to have had some kind of extraterrestrial genetic input. Thus there was a huge gap between the level of civilization among the Children of God and other peoples; at some time in the past, descendants of the Children of God developed the highest known level of technology in prehistory, far surpassing that of any other people—as evidenced in megalithic monuments, ancient knowledge of mathematics and astronomy, etc. With their larger brain capacity together with their greater level of spiritual perceptivity, they are likely to have developed technologies that were in some ways more advanced than our own, which worked on different principles, and this may account for some of the ancient artifacts and descriptions of technology in ancient texts and oral histories that seem to have used techniques not currently known to our civilization.

There was an ancient priesthood of the Religion of the Sun who were from among the Children of God and their descendants, and were spread across parts of the earth. They were highly civilized and were great astronomers. The center of their religion was on an island in the Atlantic Ocean on the Azores Plateau, among a chain of seven, where a great and advanced civilization built by the Children of God developed, that later became known in legends as Atlantis (as well as Atala and Saka Island).

However, the descendants of the Children of God weren't limited to Atlantis, but lived and developed centers and cities in the Middle East, Asia, and the Americas. At first they lived alongside though apart from the "children of men." Ancient texts state they were not meant to mix with other types of ancient humanoids, but they eventually did over a long period of time. As a result, their descendants lost their divine qualities and ability to see into other dimensions, becoming more materialistic, aggressive, animalistic, and warlike.

Fractures developed between the descendants of the Children of God, and they fought wars against one another. Those of Atlantis degenerated and became materialistic, and sought to dominate through empire. As recounted by Plato, they were defeated by the "Hellenes," who must also have been a large and powerful civilization (likely also descendants of the Children of God). The wars between the Atlanteans and the Hellenes may have been some of the largest the ancient world has ever seen.

The ancestors of the Atlanteans had already lived through a terrible cataclysm in which the whole world seemed to have been destroyed and reborn through fire. Perhaps this occurred around 40,000 BC or earlier, or at 10,800 BC when a disastrous event caused global temperatures to plummet, initiating the period known as the Younger Dryas. It appears this did not destroy Atlantis or happened before Atlantis was built.

Then, at around 9,700 BC, a king of the solar dynasty who was also a priest of the Religion of the Sun was warned that another great catastrophe was imminent. This catastrophe was likely a meteor impact that ended the Ice Age and caused sea levels to rise rapidly, possibly overnight. It appears to have involved immense tectonic and volcanic activity along the Mid-Atlantic Ridge, and caused the islands of Atlantis to subside into the ocean amidst great shaking, leaving only the highest mountain tops above water (the Azores). It also seems to have triggered a massive flood, which swept over large areas of the earth, and is likely to be the origin of many of the myths of a great flood. The Indo-Europeans and ancient Egyptians used a serpent as a symbol of this disaster; it was said to cause the stirring of the earth (earthquakes), and was described as rising from within its bowels as a great plume of black smoke emitted from a volcano, just like a great black serpent.

This disaster was remembered as a symbolic fight between the gods and symbols of the disaster like the snake, which was defeated and sent back into its abode beneath the earth, and also the wolf (in Norse tradition), which may have symbolized the great clouds of smoke that appeared to stalk across the sky and "swallow" the sun.

Between the cataclysms of 10,800 BC and 9,700 BC, much of the evidence for prior civilization was destroyed or submerged beneath the ocean.

The king/priest and seven sages escaped the catastrophe on ships, along with a sizeable number of other people. Sages from within this religion may not only have escaped Atlantis, but may already have been stationed in different parts of the world.

They seem to have arrived firstly to Anatolia, where they gathered a large following and established an esoteric order. They taught the gathered survivors the Religion of the Sun and the arts of civilization, as well as megalith building, possibly resulting in the structures at Göbekli Tepe. Followers from among these people—perhaps being a mix of survivors from Atlantis and those descended from the Children of God in the Anatolian region—became the disciples of the wisdom bringers, and formed their army of "fighting men and faithful soldiers" as well as "the shining ones" who preserved their esoteric knowledge.

These followers were referred to as "sons" by the wisdom bringers. For example, in the books of *The Kolbrin*, Osiris refers to his followers as sons, and likewise Viracocha was said to have affectionately called all those he taught in South America his sons and daughters. Clearly these were not sons by birth, but I think gave rise to the concept that some of these wisdom bringers had large numbers of sons—Odin is said to have had up to seventeen, while Adinatha/Ikshvaku was said to have one hundred. Thus, these sons were also seen as having the same bloodline as the wisdom bringers, and as having the authority to establish royal houses and dynasties.

Most of the inhabitants of Atlantis perished, and the moon-colored race that had existed from the most ancient of times became almost entirely extinct, although some of their genetics appear to have been passed down and preserved in the area of the Caucasus, where it became the distinguishing feature of the earliest nobility of the solar dynasties that were established after the flood.

All the degeneration and wars that were said to have arisen from Atlantis were seen as being swept clean from the earth to provide an almost blank slate for the survivors to be able to begin again. However, with the descendants of the Children of God now mostly gone, the only hope for the survival of civilization and the Religion of the Sun into the future was to gather those who remained, and establish it among the surviving hunter-gatherers.

Together, the sages that preserved the Religion of the Sun then embarked upon the greatest mission in history—to teach the Religion of the Sun, and the arts of civilization, to peoples who were living primitively all over the world. They were so spiritually and technologically advanced that they appeared as gods walking the earth. What they taught became the basis of many ancient religions.

They caused the building of megalithic structures as sacred sites in many of the places they traveled, which also encoded the memory of what happened, as well as their spiritual knowledge and sciences, so that it could survive over thousands of years and perhaps even future cataclysms. The designs of some of these sites, such as the use of polygonal blocks, and of absolutely massive stones, indicate that they were built to survive severe disasters. This is likely because the memory of one was still fresh, and because those who built them knew that these disasters periodically recur. These sites were not only built to serve as sacred places for thousands of years, but they have also served to communicate the information encoded into them to people all over the world down through the ages. Countless people have been inspired by the very existence of these sites to search into the ancient spiritual knowledge of their builders, which may have even been part of their purpose.

Many of these sites were built in alignment with one another, and with the sun at the solstices and equinoxes. In some cases, they also seem to have been built on the sites of existing sacred places that the wisdom bringers already had knowledge of, and that had been destroyed or damaged in the cataclysms. The wisdom bringers used the same building techniques, designs, and measurements wherever they traveled, building pyramids, giant stone statues, and precisely fitted polygonal stone blocks of enormous size. Quality may have varied depending on the skill of the local people and the number of builders available. Surviving descendants of the Children of God or remnants of other giant races may have also gone their own ways, and continued to build megalithic structures using ancient techniques in different parts of the world.

Where accounts of their appearance exist, the wisdom bringers were often described as tall men, with fair skin, blue eyes, red and blonde hair, and as wearing long robes and symbols of the sun. They were known as "sons of the sun" and feathered serpents, who traveled on reed ships under the banner of the sun. They were renowned for their great esoteric knowledge and compassion, and were revered down through the passing of thousands of years as gods. From the perspective of the Religion of the Sun, at least some among them had reintegrated with their higher Being, symbolized by the sun.

They were remembered by different names among different peoples. Some of these names include Osiris/Asar, Thoth, Viracocha, Tici/Tiki, Itzamna, Quetzalcoatl, Kukulkan, Votan, Wuotan/Odin, Adinatha/Shiva/Ikshvaku, Manu, Yima, Ziusudra, Aa/Ea/Enki/Adapa/Oannes, Vishnu, Svarog, Hotu Matu'a, and Maasaw.

I believe some of the accounts of these wisdom bringers became conflated with later kings who wished to emulate and embody their power, and saw themselves as descended from their lineage and as preservers of their knowledge. Examples of this include the histories of Easter Island, the stories surrounding Odin, and the many Aztec and Inca kings who took the name of Quetzalcoatl and Viracocha respectively.

Clearly, a number of the wisdom bringers were also used as storytelling devices, as they take part in events over impossibly long periods of time and in supernatural feats such as the creation of the universe.

Many of the wisdom bringers went different ways to visit different people in order to cover large areas of land. Wherever they traveled, they established the Religion of the Sun and civilizations, as well as solar theocracies to preserve both. They installed leaders from among their followers, creating a nobility in many parts of the world.

The further back in time you go, the more similar the religions and traditions of ancient Egypt, Mesopotamia, and the Indo-Europeans become, which I believe is because they have the same source. The reason their king lists stretch back over thousands and even tens of thousands of years is because they are based on the existence of the same solar dynasty, which was seen as being ruled by "gods," but who I think were from among the Children of God. After the flood, there were then a number of solar dynasties established, which existed concurrently in different parts of the world.

Yet there was a common culture, civilization, and religion shared between them, as was taught to them by the wisdom bringers. They formed part of an overarching civilization that continued to travel and expand across the world, further spreading their knowledge and the arts of civilization. This Lost Civilization of the Sun also continued to build sacred sites, and periodically inhabited and renovated existing ones, many of which were left to them by the wisdom bringers. They also established cities along the same line around the earth, which in some cases, may have been on the site of cities that had existed before the flood.

While there were disputes, invasions, various migrations, etc., the people of this lost civilization largely retained their shared culture and religion, enough that the same temple building styles were maintained across the world over thousands of years—including standing stones, huge stone statues, stepped pyramids, and polygonal stone walls.

It's clear that the Religion of the Sun was also spread multiple times to the same places over thousands of years by various waves of migrating people who carried some form of it. Most often, later waves merged into older existing forms of it already present. This kind of layering and merging happened at least in Europe, Egypt, India, China, and the Americas.

Practitioners of the esoteric side of the Religion of the Sun continued to influence this civilization in different places and different times, and some of the esoteric orders established managed to survive over thousands of years at least in Egypt, Central Asia, and Mesopotamia.

This civilization existed for thousands of years at a time in Europe, Egypt, North Africa, Mesopotamia, Central Asia, Iran, India, Russia, and China, stretching all the way from Ireland to China, and connecting from Europe into the Americas to Easter Island and New Zealand. It may have also existed in other parts of the world too.

However, over time many of the cultures and peoples who had preserved the Religion of the Sun degenerated terribly, and more aggressive and brutal peoples continually overcame the more peaceful ones, replacing their cultures with increasingly barbaric and violent ones. Those who were more peaceful often fled to remote places of refuge where they preserved remnants of the Religion of the Sun, but after hundreds or even thousands of years, they too were eventually discovered and conquered by more militaristic and violent people. In places where people couldn't flee, knowledge was withdrawn into ever tighter secrecy within esoteric schools that moved when they could to increasingly remote locations.

Unfortunately, even these esoteric schools eventually lost track of the knowledge as their practitioners lost the ability to practice it in the ways ancient people did, particularly in relation to the more esoteric aspects of the path of the sun. When this happened, the knowledge was easily misinterpreted and distorted by those who did not have the spiritual experience needed to understand it, though it may have been repeated and partially preserved. Thus, it is something very fragile and easily lost even amidst an esoteric school, where knowledge was often communicated through symbols and metaphors, and privately between guru and disciple.

The headiest and most extravagant times of ancient civilization were not necessarily their finest, but may have been their most materialistic rather than their most spiritual, even though this is when they left the most evidence for their existence and are the times they are most remembered for.

Finally, after the Roman conquest of Europe, the Lost Civilization of the Sun completely collapsed, with only various remnants surviving in the Americas and remote places. The Iron Age saw the beginning of a horribly warlike time where much of the knowledge of the Religion of the Sun was lost and became supplanted with warlike gods and ideologies, or morphed into muddled and altered remnants. This was followed by a complete replacement in most parts of the world with Abrahamic religions. Although the teachings of Jesus carried the Religion of the Sun, they were mostly excluded from the Bible, which was instead mostly composed of the Old Testament and the letters of Paul. It was a darkening which the world has, for the most part, plunged further into.

There were times, however, when the Religion of the Sun partially bloomed again in various forms, as people who walked the path of the spiritual sun, and became "sons of the sun," taught it anew, or its influence was revived from ancient sources. For example, Hermetic texts (attributed to the Egyptian wisdom bringer Thoth) were largely the inspiration for the European Renaissance.[2] This would have happened many times over the last 11,600 years, just as it is today.

The Religion of the Sun and Lost Civilization of the Sun, as established by the wisdom bringers, had a profound impact upon world religions, culture, history, language, and civilization. Almost all religions today are either a result of or were influenced by them. Our civilization is a continuation of that founded by the wisdom bringers. And what these wisdom bringers taught gave rise to the greatest texts of ancient wisdom and most incredible ancient sites in the world. We are still largely living within their legacy today.

Why Did Ancient People Venerate the Sun?

It can be a bit hard for some people today to understand why ancient people would venerate the sun, or any natural phenomenon for that matter. In the ancient Religion of the Sun, what people were venerating however, was not the sun itself, but the divine manifesting through it, as the greatest visible source of light and life in creation.

The Abrahamic religious ideologies, which have permeated Western culture, have entrenched the worldview that the universe is merely the product of an almighty creator, perhaps devoid of any spiritual life or principles, which are portrayed as solely residing in a godhead that is separate from creation and unreachable until death.

This set up a divide between Abrahamic religions and all others, who were thus called "pagan." Pagans were essentially all the ancient forms of religion apart from the Abrahamic ones. Pagans were seen as those who worshiped the "powers of nature," and this was largely interpreted as primitive people simply trying to make sense of their world based upon what was important to their survival.

This may have been true in some cases. But in the Religion of the Sun it is instead based upon a profound understanding of creation. It is the result of perceiving the world in a very different way—being able to sense and see that creation is not only the product of the divine, but that the divine is also present within it, and that its attributes permeate it, forming the basis of its structure. It is a recognition that creation is an extension of the divine source, and is living and intelligent.

The K'iche' Maya people of Guatemala venerating the sun.

This is why the Eastern religions that derived from the ancient Religion of the Sun, like the Vedic and Taoist, describe the divine source as both permeating and transcending creation, and at the same time being both near and far away.

> "Whatever all this universe is, seen or heard of—pervading all this, from inside and outside alike, stands supreme the Eternal Divine Being."[1]
>
> ~ THE NARAYANA SUKTAM FROM THE YAJUR VEDA

> "The Self seems to move, but is ever still.
> He seems far away, but is ever near.
> He is within all, and he transcends all.
> [...] The Self is everywhere. Bright is the Self,
> Indivisible, untouched by sin, wise,
> Immanent and transcendent. He it is
> Who holds the cosmos together."[2]
>
> ~ THE ISHA UPANISHAD

> "The great Tao floods and flows in every direction. Everything in existence depends on it, and it doesn't deny them. It accomplishes its work without naming or making claims for itself. Everything in existence is clothed and nourished by it, but it doesn't lord over anything. Aimless, ambitionless, it might be called 'small.' Everything in existence returns to it, and still it doesn't lord over anything. Thus it might also be called 'great.'"[3]
>
> ~ LAO TZU IN TAO TE CHING

A number of ancient peoples clearly understood that divinity and its powers, forces, and principles manifest themselves through nature, which is why in the Religion of the Sun, natural objects, like the sun, stars, trees, fire, water, animals, etc., were used in spiritually symbolic ways. For example, the ancient Vedic fire ritual, called yajna, uses fire as a living expression of the divine fire and light of the sun. Those ancient Egyptians who had a greater understanding of spiritual knowledge, used various animals to symbolize the principles these animals express, rather than worshiping the animal itself.

The artwork of ancient Egypt is highly symbolic, using natural symbols
like the sun and animals to encode information about the nature of reality.

"The sages of old studied living things to a point of realization that God is most perfectly understood through a knowledge of His supreme handiwork—animate and inanimate Nature. Every existing creature manifests some aspect of the intelligence or power of the Eternal One, who can never be known save through a study and appreciation of His numbered but inconceivable parts. When a creature is chosen, therefore, to symbolize to the concrete human mind some concealed abstract principle it is because its characteristics demonstrate this invisible principle in visible action."[4]

~ MANLY P. HALL, THE SECRET TEACHINGS OF ALL AGES

In the ancient Religion of the Sun however, above animals, trees, and even fire, the sun was seen as the highest visible manifestation of the energy of the divine within creation. It is known to science that the stars created almost all the matter in the universe, and continue to create it even now, as they constantly produce and eject elements into space; this same view was held in sacred texts of the Religion of the Sun.[5]

> "Trees and animals, humans and insects, flowers and birds: These are active images of the subtle energies that flow from the stars throughout the universe. Meeting and combining with each other and the elements of the earth, they give rise to all living things."[6]
>
> ~ LAO TZU IN HUA HU CHING

But the sun was not only seen as having a material side; it also was understood to have an invisible spiritual side too.

> "In the majority of cases, the religions of antiquity agree that the material visible sun was a reflector rather than a source of power. The sun was sometimes represented as a shield carried on the arm of the Sun God, as for example, Frey, the Scandinavian Solar Deity. This sun reflected the light of the invisible spiritual sun, which was the true source of life, light, and truth. The physical nature of the universe is receptive; it is a realm of effects. The invisible causes of these effects belong to the spiritual world. Hence, the spiritual world is the sphere of causation; the material world is the sphere of effects [...]."[7]
>
> ~ MANLY P. HALL, THE SECRET TEACHINGS OF ALL AGES

These "invisible" realms are the otherworldly regions described in the ancient Religion of the Sun, where people go after death, and where "gods," etc., reside—today we call them other dimensions, where people have near-death and out-of-body experiences. Science now postulates that multiple parallel dimensions exist, which has been well-known to mystics for thousands of years. The sun, like everything, was also seen to exist in higher dimensions as not only the source of matter, but also of spirit—being the source of the eternal self of every living thing, arising from it like sparks of light.[8]

> "These two things, the spiritual and the material, though we call them by different names, in their origin are one and the same. This sameness is a mystery—the mystery of mysteries. It is the gate of all spirituality."[9]
>
> ~ TAO TE CHING

> "Imperishable is the Lord of Love.
> As from a blazing fire thousands of sparks
> Leap forth, so millions of beings arise
> From the Lord of Love [...]."[10]
>
> ~ MUNDAKA UPANISHAD

This is why followers of the Religion of the Sun called themselves "children of the sun," as they knew that ultimately, that is where our consciousness, our eternal self, has its origin.

The sun, fire, and electricity are all related, as all are ultimately forms of fire and light. This fire exists within all matter, and is what holds it together, giving it its color and form, as once the fire is released from any object, all that remains is grey ash/dust. Everything eats and absorbs forms of solar energy, either directly, as in when plants photosynthesize, or indirectly, when we eat plants or animals that have eaten plants themselves. This solar energy gives us vitality, powering our bodies, and is used to build all matter, which it is stored within. Thus, everything is a modification of fire and light, which has its origins in the sun and stars, with only time existing between us.[11]

This is why both fire and the sun held such a central place in the rituals, texts, temples, etc., of the ancient Religion of the Sun.

An ancient Vedic ritual called yajna being performed, in which fire is central, and symbolizes the sun. The element of fire is believed to be divine and thus able to convey messages between our physical world and the otherworldly, spiritual realms.

Additionally, consciousness was seen as just a spark of light—one part of a higher Self or Being that each person has, which the aim of the Religion of the Sun was to incarnate and return to. This higher Self/Being was associated with the sun, and the inward spiritual journey to reunite with it was referred to as a path to immortality, and is what my husband refers to as "the path of the spiritual sun."[12]

"The face of truth is hidden by your orb
Of gold, O sun. May you remove your orb
So that I, who adore the true, may see
The Glory of truth. O nourishing sun,
Solitary traveller, controller,
Source of life for all creatures, spread your light
And subdue your dazzling splendour
So that I may see your blessed Self.
Even that very Self am I!
May my life merge in the Immortal
When my body is reduced to ashes.
[...] O god of fire, lead us by the good path
To eternal joy."[13]

~ THE ISHA UPANISHAD

"That which is Brahman is light; that which is light is the Sun. [...] The king named after the wind, having made his obeisance to him and duly offered his homage, went, with his aim attained, to the northern path. There is here no going by any by-way. This is the path to Brahman. Bursting open the door of the sun, he departed by the upward path. On this point the sages declare;

Endless are the rays of that soul which abides like a lamp in the heart [...]. One of these rises upward which pierces the orb of the sun; by this, having passed beyond the world of Brahman, they attain to the supreme abode. [...]

Therefore yonder adorable Sun is the cause of creation, of heaven, and of emancipation."[14]

~ THE MAITRĀYAṆĪYA UPANISHAD

"The sun gives light and life to all who live,
East and west, north and south, above, below;
It is the prana of the universe.
The wise see the Lord of Love in the sun,
Rising in all its golden radiance
To give its warmth and light and life to all.
The wise see the Lord of Love in the year,
Which has two paths, the northern and the southern.
Those who observe outward forms of worship
And are content with personal pleasures
Travel after death by the southern path,
The path of the ancestors and of rayi,

340

To the lunar world, and are born again.
But those who seek the Self through meditation,
Self-discipline, wisdom, and faith in God
Travel after death by the northern path,
The path of prana, to the solar world,
Supreme refuge, beyond the reach of fear
And free from the cycle of birth and death."[15]
~ THE PRASHNA UPANISHAD

Most specifically, the sun was usually associated with a divine hero figure whose life corresponded to the path of the sun throughout the year—being born at the winter solstice, resurrecting at the spring equinox, and ascending at the summer solstice—with the time of the greatest light, the summer solstice, representing complete enlightenment. This is why many figures who either taught the Religion of the Sun, or who were used symbolically in it, experienced similar life events—like Osiris, Odin/Wotan, Mithras, and later Jesus.[16]

The birth of Jesus, traditionally celebrated around the winter solstice, symbolizing the birth of the spiritual sun/son at the darkest time of year, which on a deeper level, represents the birth of the spiritual sun/son within a person.[17]

Their lives were used as a symbolic spiritual teaching that allegorically revealed what someone goes through on the path to reunite with their higher Being. The correlation between their lives and the path of the sun occurs because spiritual principles are imbued in the natural world.[18]

Those who had journeyed on this path in life, later often became deified as "gods" in the Religion of the Sun. As these were people who had reunited with at least certain aspects of their higher Being, they became associated with the sun, becoming known as "sons of the sun."[19] This is why all Vedic deities were originally associated with the sun.

"The Vedic gods are all basically Sun Gods. The Vedic is a solar religion based upon a strong awareness of the Sun and its movement. All the Gods can be called Adityas or 'Sun Gods,' born from Aditi who may be identified with the heavens or the zodiac."[20]

~ DAVID FRAWLEY, GODS, SAGES AND KINGS

And in ancient Egypt, the realm of imperishability or immortality, was the stars—in fact, the aim was to become a star in a profound sense, which is a being of light.

"Thou shinest in the horizon, thou sendest forth thy light into the darkness, thou makest the darkness light with thy double plume, and thou floodest the world with light like the Disk at break of day. Thy diadem pierceth heaven and becometh a brother unto the stars, O thou form of every god."[21]

~ HYMN TO OSIRIS

The sun was also seen as a manifestation of a central, invisible sun—which was the central source of all light, and all creation. There is now possibly a scientific correlation with this in the "Electric Universe theory," which states that stars may be anodes of an electric current of energy flowing across the universe, and originating from the invisible plasma existing throughout it.[22] Thus, the source of energy/electricity powering the stars may be coming from some mysterious, invisible source—the central, invisible sun of the ancients.

For example, the sun is described by the Hopi as merely the face of the Creator, who otherwise remains unseen or invisible:

"[...] while the sun is himself a deity, the chief of our solar system, his is but the face through which looks the omnipotent Creator, Taiowa, who stands behind."[23]

~ FRANK WATERS, BOOK OF THE HOPI

Similarly, in Vedic/Hindu religion, Brahman is the invisible and formless source of all, while Brahma is a form of Brahman, born from the formless in order to create form. Both are identified with the sun—Brahman as its invisible/spiritual side, and Brahma as its tangible/physical one.[24]

Indeed, the Electric Universe theory postulates that the very basis of our universe is electrical energy, which manifests as fire, lightning, and the sun, which ancient practitioners of the Religion of the Sun have long seen as being connected and as expressions of one and the same divine energy. In Slavic religion for example, they were seen as the three faces of the one supreme god.[25]

"As the sun rises in the East, to give life to the day, so was the Devoted Priest placed in the East of the sanctuary, to open the services of worship and to instruct, like a father, those who came to him with understanding. In the ceiling above the candidates was the symbol of the sun and from it extended seven hands. This represented the sun of light dispending the vitalising forces of life from their fount within the circle of creative consciousness."[26]

~ THE HIBSATHY, THE BOOK OF THE SONS OF FIRE, THE KOLBRIN

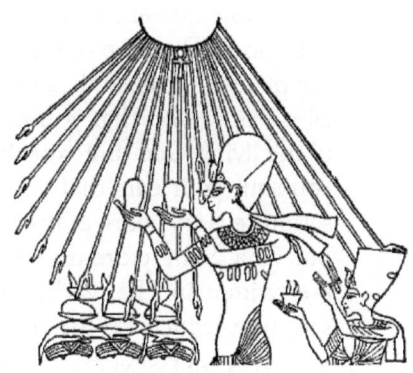

The sun portrayed in ancient Egypt with numerous extended hands.

A DIFFERENT WAY OF VIEWING THE WORLD

This understanding of creation is not something found solely with the rational mind—although it can be understood through reasoning to a point. It is something also intuitively felt and sensed. In particular, it is sensed by the conscious or divine part within us, recognizing and perceiving the divine in other living beings, and in the natural elements around us. The inner/third eye of the Children of God would have enhanced this ability greatly.

It is a way of perceiving creation that is innate and naturally observable, as I believe, creation wasn't made to be so complex or difficult to understand as to be out of reach to all except the greatest scientists and intellectuals—instead being designed so that its principles would be manifestly apparent to all those with the capacity to consciously observe them, allowing even simple, poor, and illiterate people the chance to fulfill the purpose of life. The sun and stars, therefore, are naturally observed and understood as light, and light as being transcendent and divine.

Jesus taught about this naturalistic way of perceiving, but these texts were excluded from the Bible, such as the one that follows:

"In everything that is life is the law written. You find it in the grass, in the tree, in the river, in the mountain, in the birds of heaven, in the fishes of the sea; but seek it chiefly in yourselves. For I tell you truly, all living things are nearer to God than the scripture which is without life. God so made life and all living things that they might by the everlasting word teach the laws of the true God to man. God wrote not the laws in the pages of books, but in your heart and in your spirit. They are in your breath, your blood, your bone; in your flesh, your bowels, your eyes, your ears, and in every little part of your body. They are present in the air, in the water, in the earth, in the plants, in the sunbeams, in the depths and in the heights. They all speak to you that you may understand the tongue and the will of the living God. But you shut your eyes that you may not see, and you shut your ears that you may not hear. I tell you truly, that the scripture is the work of man, but life and all its hosts are the work of our God. Wherefore do you not listen to the words of God which are written in His works? And wherefore do you study the dead scriptures which are the work of the hands of men?"[27]

~ JESUS IN THE ESSENE GOSPEL OF PEACE

The modern view is that understanding creation is reserved for those with great intellects, who can interpret the most difficult of equations. But objective human experience and observation is actually more real than any abstract theory or formula.

Scientific theories may advance our ability to observe creation at increasing levels of detail, which is of great use, but in terms of understanding the principles of creation, ultimately they reveal no more than what can be observed naturally (without the use of technology), as the same patterns and principles appear at all scales in nature, which is why creation is sometimes described as being both "fractal" and "holographic." This is why I think people would do best to understand the inherent and underlying principles of creation, rather than restricting themselves to dissecting specific and isolated phenomena.

The same fundamental mathematical patterns can be found in nature at all scales, indicating that all of nature is subject to the same inherent laws of creation.

This way of perceiving creation, I believe, was encoded in one of the most widespread symbols of the ancient Religion of the Sun, which Richard Cassaro has termed the "God Self Icon," but is known more commonly as the "Master of Animals." Cassaro has found evidence for this symbol being used across the ancient world—in Egypt, the Americas, Indonesia, India, Mesopotamia, Persia, England, Scandinavia, Italy, Greece, Nigeria, etc.[28]—existing as prolifically as the swastika. Understanding it is part of unlocking the secret to the worldview of those who practiced the Religion of the Sun.

The symbol referred to as the Master of Animals and the God Self Icon.

Left: Image from a Persian cylinder seal from the fifth century BC showing a Persian king in the God Self/ Master of Animals pose—note the winged sun disk above his head. This winged sun disk is also found above temple entrances in Egypt, symbolizing the same thing. Right: This God Self/Master of Animals icon is dated to 2,500 BC and is from Iran. Note that it has been carved onto a bucket-like object that looks similar to the one the wisdom bringers are often portrayed as carrying. Does this symbol have its origin in the knowledge that the wisdom bringers "carried" to different parts of the world? I think so.

The God Self/Master holds a staff or animal in each hand. The right hand represents use of and control over the rational, intellectual parts of our psyche (associated with masculinity), while the left over the intuitive and emotional (associated with femininity). Because our brains are "crosswired," the right side of our body is controlled by the left side of our brain, and vice versa (the left side of our brain processes the analytical and logical, while the right the emotional, sensory, and artistic).[29] I suspect they were portrayed as animals as the psyche belongs to our earthly, animal nature. The central figure represents what should use and exert control over our psyche, brain (both its right and left hemispheres), and body, which is consciousness—our eternal, spiritual part; our inner light.[30] This consciousness sits just behind and between our eyes (which if you notice, is where you "see" from), in the area of our pineal gland, which is the location of our atrophied third eye. The triptych temple entrance—which Cassaro has identified as being used at ancient sites in Egypt, Mexico, India, and Cambodia, as well as later Masonic buildings—essentially symbolizes the same thing, with a large central door, flanked by smaller doors to its left and right.

This was also symbolized in ancient Egypt in the design of their temples, in which the entrance was placed in between two higher walls (called pylons).

The entrance to the Temple of Edfu in Egypt (that records the history of the wisdom bringers). Above the central door is the image of a winged sun disk with two serpents.

Closeup showing the winged sun disk that so often adorns the entrances to temples in ancient Egypt.

This same symbolism is found at the Great Pyramids of Egypt. The sun on the summer solstice sets directly between the two largest of the Great Pyramids, crowning the sphinx with a halo of light.[31]

The "sun gate" at the ancient site of Tiwanaku in Bolivia, I believe, symbolizes the same thing as the ancient Egyptian temple entrances. This site is said to have been founded by the wisdom bringer Viracocha (who I believe could have been the same person as Osiris in Egypt). He was symbolized by the sun, and his image as the God Self Icon appears above the door, which aligns to the winter solstice sunrise.[32]

The stepped pyramid dedicated to the wisdom bringer Kukulkan in Mexico, who was also said to have founded the site. I believe this pyramid encodes the same symbolism as found in ancient Egypt and at Tiwanaku in Bolivia. Two serpents run down either side of the staircase—their heads can be seen at the base. These are the equivalent of the animals held in either hand by the God Self/Master. At the top of the pyramid is a triptych doorway, and above the central door is a now barely discernible face. I suspect it would have been the face of the sun god. The pyramid aligns to both the winter solstice sunrise and the equinoxes.[33] A similar temple design can be found across Asia too.

This light of consciousness was associated with the sun, which is why the central door of Egyptian temples was so often decorated with a sun above it, and the God Self was often a sun god. It is also why the third eye was often depicted as the sun.

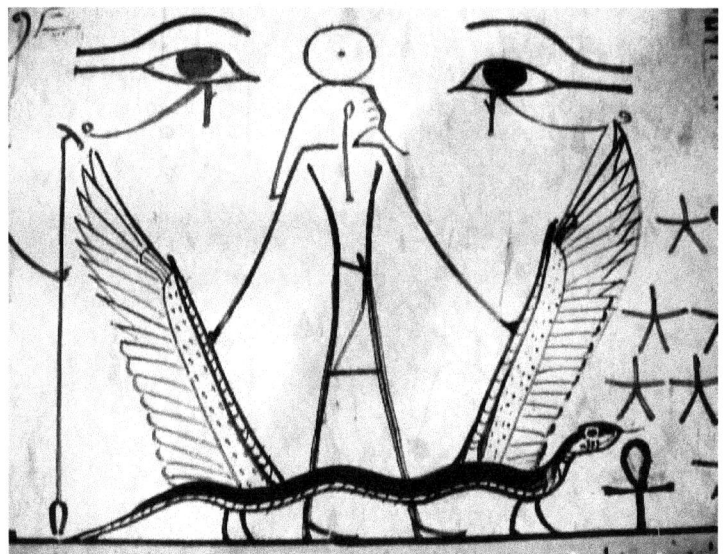

The third eye depicted in ancient Egypt with the symbol of the sun.

These symbols, among other things, illustrate a conscious perception that is both rational and intuitive. Too much intellectualism unbalances our perception, reducing creation to mechanical matter explained only through mathematical equations, ultimately leading to atheism, which we can see operating in the Western world. On the other hand, being led by feeling too much also creates imbalance, diverging into imagination and fantasy that doesn't correspond to reality, ultimately leading to religious superstition, dogmatism, and psychosis, which we can see occurring in religions (as well as other ideologies) today.

In the ancient Religion of the Sun, it was important to keep one's perceptions in balance, and in tune with reality. The most important thing, however, which was also key to achieving this balance, was to perceive from a point of conscious awareness, and to allow this consciousness to influence and control our brain (and body). This is done by perceiving, consciously and fully, in the present moment.[34]

It is through this conscious awareness that our own divine spark of light is manifestly conscious within us, allowing us to perceive the divine within creation,[35] and revealing among many things, the sun and stars as the outpouring of the great, creative divine light.

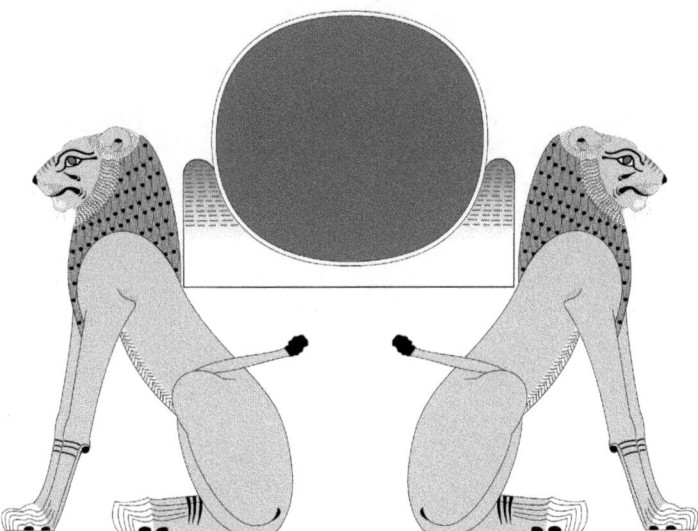

Perceiving consciously in the present moment was encoded in the symbol of the "horizon" and "Aker lions" of ancient Egypt. In this illustration, the sun rises between two mounds, and is the hieroglyph used for "horizon"—it is the basis of the pylon temple architecture discussed earlier. The horizon is held by two Aker lions, one facing west and the other east. They symbolize past (west) and future (east).[36] The sun symbolizes the present—that is consciousness, the divine Being, perceiving (seeing), like a spiritual eye (third eye) in the eternal moment.

Paracelsus, the great alchemist of the Renaissance, wrote in the 1500s:

"There is an earthly sun, which is the cause of all heat, and all who are able to see may see the sun; and those who are blind and cannot see him may feel his heat. There is an Eternal Sun, which is the source of all wisdom, and those whose spiritual senses have awakened to life will see that sun and be conscious of His existence; but those who have not attained spiritual consciousness may yet feel His power by an inner faculty which is called Intuition."[37]

Revival

Today, there are many people who are returning to and reviving the spiritual traditions of their cultures, countries, and ancestors. Because remnants of the Religion of the Sun survived in many of these traditions, what many people are reviving then, are aspects of it, which is why many of these revivals share common themes—particularly in relation to the sun and holding ceremonies on the solstices and equinoxes.

These revivals are sweeping across Europe and Russia, with Baltic, Hellenic, Slavic, Thracian, Scythian, Armenian, Germanic/Nordic, Celtic, and other pagan groups continuing to grow and multiply. But it's not just dedicated pagans who are feeling drawn back to their ancient roots. An eclectic ten thousand people gathered to watch the summer solstice alignment at Stonehenge in 2019,[1] which is opened to the public especially for the event, showing that there is a growing interest among people generally.

Many of these revivals are not only recognizing their common connections to one another and are sharing knowledge through such organizations as the European Congress of Ethnic Religions (ECER), but also within the greater Indo-European tradition. For example, the ECER has held a number of their annual conferences in India. A key organization in the ECER, the Lithuanian-based group Romuva, recognize that the Lithuanian language and religion is closely related to that of the Vedas, and have hosted joint ceremonies on the summer solstice with Hindu practitioners from India. Likewise, the largest druidic organization in the world, called the Order of Bards, Ovates & Druids, has jointly founded The One Tree Project to explore and celebrate "the idea that Indian and European culture share a common origin."[2]

A Hindu priest officiating a ceremony of the Romuva religion in Lithuania in 2009.

Revivals are also occurring in Central and South America. In 2009, the first indigenous president of Bolivia, Evo Morales (who is of Aymara descent), declared the winter solstice a national holiday,[3] and has taken part in traditional solstice ceremonies held at the ancient site of Tiwanaku, which are attended by thousands of Aymara people each year. He was even inaugurated for his third term in office dressed as an Inca emperor at Tiwanaku. Tens of thousands of people watch the winter solstice celebration of the Incas (called Inti Raymi) every year, enacted at the ancient site of Cuzco in Peru, while thousands gather to watch the equinox alignment at the ancient site of Chichen Itza and celebrate at the Pyramid of the Sun at Teotihuacan in Mexico.

Bolivian President Evo Morales (center) being inaugurated
in an indigenous ceremony at the ancient site of Tiwanaku.

Many tribes of North America have maintained their traditions, while others are being rekindled by a new generation. Such is the case with the Kitzit Laguna Youth Dance Group, which was founded based on Kyle Swimmer's wish, at the age of thirteen, to preserve the language and culture of his (the Pueblo) peoples.[4] The dancers of the group are between the ages of nine and twenty-two, and perform traditional dances at the ancient site of Chaco Canyon in New Mexico on the summer solstice.[5]

Some people, like the Yazidi in the Middle East, have suffered devastating genocide and sexual slavery at the hands of the Islamic terrorist organization ISIS, but have clung to their traditions over millennia despite unimaginable persecution, and whose story is now finally reaching a wider world.

In places like Iran, there is a growing interest in the country's ancient history[6] and the pre-Islamic religion of Zoroastrianism.[7]

And in India, where a branch of the Religion of the Sun has maintained its greatest continuity, it has layered and diverged in dizzying and countless ways over thousands of years.

However, it's important to realize that revival is a double-edged sword. Without discernment, what was both good and bad of the past can be resurrected. And like in the movie Jurassic Park, ancient monsters that had been laid to rest at great cost can stalk the earth again.

Over hundreds and even thousands of years many barbaric practices were incorporated into those cultures and traditions that preserved some remnant of the Religion of the Sun, and in some cases, there were cultures who already had barbaric practices, and were influenced by or adopted some aspects of the Religion of the Sun. That's why I believe it's important to be discerning when reviving ancient traditions—reviving only those things that are good, useful, and true. Blindly reviving everything makes no sense at all. This is to turn one's back on learning from the past, which is to regress, not progress.

To avoid this, I believe there needs to be a striving to find the pure, unadulterated root of the great truths taught by the wisdom bringers, and an understanding of the principles of the Religion of the Sun, which gave rise to times of great peace, high art and literature, a profound understanding of reality, perennial wisdom, advances in civilization, and most importantly of all, the spiritual transformation of the individual. It is when these principles are lost that civilization falls into decay, and it can't hope to regain any of its former glory without understanding and adhering to them.

Much of the knowledge taught and preserved within the Religion of the Sun, as well as its history, has been lost and destroyed, with even the record of its existence barely surviving. Often only scattered and fragmentary accounts of it remain, preserved across the various traditions it influenced or gave rise to, sometimes in folk songs, legends, ancient sites, symbolic artwork, and ceremonies. But the Religion of the Sun is much larger and broader than what has survived in any coherent form within many of these traditions—it was a body of knowledge that covered the entire spectrum of cosmology, and at its core the spiritual purpose of life. It provided the metaphysical practice and background philosophy of how to become a "son of the sun." Thus, a revival of the Religion of the Sun is more than outward ceremony and re-enactment—it is also the revival of its inner, spiritual practice. In our book *Ancient Solstice*, Mark decodes many of the obscured symbols, ancient sites, and texts of the Religion of the Sun, piecing together and reviving its practice and philosophy from the fragments preserved across various traditions.

Importantly, it was those who had made themselves "sons of the sun" that taught and revived the Religion of the Sun down through the ages, and who have likewise revived it today. On earth, they form the connection between heaven and earth necessary to do it, which is why sun gods and those with the Spiritual Son/sun within were sometimes referred to as mediators—communicating between the earthly and divine realms. In higher realms, these "sons of the sun" work to influence events here and communicate with people on earth through dreams and out-of-body experiences.

Whether lost in the fog of memory and long centuries of persecution, or trodden underfoot in so many layers of interpretation as to be barely discernible, the wisdom of the Religion of the Sun now runs like a hardly audible babbling stream throughout many traditional revivals. However, the interest is growing, as people continue to be magnetically and intuitively drawn to the understanding of life that feels so natural and just seems to "make sense." The earth, the stones, the sun, the stars, the light... are calling its children of the sun, and drawing them back into the grand, ancient prehistoric temples of those who felt the same indescribable pull thousands of years ago, and encoded the profound knowledge of life and the cosmos into the most grand edifices they could muster.

Although unknown to most, the Religion of the Sun, and the Lost Civilization of the Sun that carried it, is the richest source of ancient wisdom and mythology in the world. Its influence upon our own civilization cannot be understated. Even though its days of former glory have vanished—so far back in time as to have entered the realm of myth—its spiritual wisdom can still be read in ancient sites, sacred texts, and in living creation—and the actual practice of the Religion of the Sun has been made possible again today.

MORE INFORMATION

You can find more detailed and in-depth explanations of the path of the spiritual sun, why ancient people venerated the sun, and how to practice the Religion of the Sun, with hundreds of illustrations and examples from ancient sources in the book I co-authored with my husband, titled *Ancient Solstice*.

You can find my videos on the ancient Religion of the Sun through the website: sakrosawel.com

Appendix

THE PURPOSE AND MEANING OF THE EASTER ISLAND STATUES

While researching for this book, I think I may have worked out what the moai statues of Easter Island symbolized and what their purpose was. I decided to elaborate on this in an appendix so as not to interrupt the book.

Any theory about their purpose needs to answer a number of questions, and I present my theory and reasoning here in answer to them.

Why do they all look the same?

They are all carved in the image of the same deity, who shares characteristics with Shiva of India, Viracocha of Peru and Bolivia, and Osiris of Egypt. The statues have a red topknot of hair and elongated earlobes (and possibly beards). Viracocha was portrayed with or described as having red hair, a beard, and elongated earlobes, and was said to have instituted ear elongation among the ancient nobility of Peru and Bolivia. Shiva is portrayed with his hair in a topknot and with elongated earlobes.

Just as in ancient Egypt, where kings were buried in coffins depicting them as Osiris because they hoped to resurrect in the afterlife as Osiris did (becoming an Osiris), so too did the chiefs of Easter Island carve their statues in the image of their god in the hope of resurrecting in the afterlife as Osiris/Viracocha/Shiva.

The chiefs of Easter Island also imitated the appearance of the god that the statues represent, just as Buddhists dress in imitation of Buddha. The chiefs wore their hair in a top knot and elongated their earlobes (and grew beards).

Chiefs were also known to have worn headdresses of feathers, like those worn by the giant stone statues of the Toltecs at the ancient city of Tula in Mexico, which have been compared to the moai of Easter Island.[1] These statues are said to represent the warrior followers of Quetzalcoatl (the feathered headdress symbolizing Quetzalcoatl as the feathered serpent),[2] bringing another wisdom bringer into the mix of those already connected to Easter Island.

Why were they erected for deceased chiefs?

In ancient Egypt, the aim of the king was to become an akhu (also akh), which was a being of light that lived eternally among the gods. On Easter Island, the aku-aku were supernatural spirits believed to have helped raise the statues. Offerings of food were made to them, just as offerings of food were made to the deceased in Egypt. The aku of Easter Island could be petitioned for help, but could also inflict punishment if not appeased, just like the akhu of Egypt.[3]

In ancient Egypt, it was thought that only kings could become an akh after death—only later did this belief change to include the possibility that all people could become an akh. The chiefs of Easter Island are likely to have followed the earlier belief, which is one of the reasons why statues were not raised for everyone on the island.

In the Egyptian Book of What is in the Duat it says to stand up like the Ahau (the gods), and the platforms which some of the moai stand on are called Ahu. In Egypt there was a ceremony to raise the djed pillar (symbolic of Osiris)—making it stand up—which symbolized resurrection. The moai were likewise raised to stand up as an aku, like the gods, and represent the aku/akh of the deceased chiefs of Easter Island.

Why are they giant in size?

The Ahau of Egypt were considered to be giant in stature, which would explain why the moai are so large—they were in imitation of "the gods" (the earliest inhabitants of Egypt and the Children of God). However, oral histories of

Easter Island state that their size reflected the "mana" or mental power of the chief[4] (the near identical word "manas" has a similar meaning in Sanskrit[5]). This same mana was believed to have moved the statues to their places,[6] and so it seems to follow that the larger the statue, the greater the mana.

Why were they considered objects of ancestor worship?

The statues could have been worshiped as Viracocha, being built in his image, as the ancestor of the builders of the moai. The followers of Viracocha were considered his descendants, as they looked like him (having fair skin, red hair, and blue eyes) and were thus called the "Viracochas." The builders of the moai were also described as having fair skin and red hair, and had come from Tiwanaku which the Viracochas were said to have built, and are likely related to them. But I think there is more to it than that.

The chiefs on Easter Island who died were considered to have become immortal in the afterlife, living on as an "aku/akhu." The statue erected for them represented their aku/akhu. Chiefdom was hereditary, and so in worshiping the statues, the chiefs were venerating the representation (and possibly the physical dwelling) of the aku of past chiefs who were their ancestors.

In ancient Egypt, statues were seen as vessels for the life-force of the deceased[7] and so similarly on Easter Island, the moai statues are likely to have been vessels for the aku of the deceased chiefs. In fact, it was believed that the mana of the chief would flow into the moai at death,[8] which became its perpetual repository,[9] and this is why the moai were seen as the "living faces" of the chiefs.[10]

On Easter Island the aku were ancestor kings, just as the akh were in Egypt, and the statues that were believed to contain the akhs of these kings were venerated.

Why were they thought to be phallic symbols?

Oral tradition on Easter Island says that the moai are phallic. This seems to be because the statues were a kind of Shiva-linga, which is a symbol of the creative and generative force of the cosmos. And it seems that this generative power was associated with the ability to "regenerate" or resurrect in the afterlife, as Osiris was often depicted with an erect phallus while resurrecting. Perhaps these statues symbolized and/or sought to harness this force.

Why do their hands point to their sacral area?

They indicate the wish to harness the creative and regenerative powers for resurrection, which are found in the sexual energies that have their seat in the sexual organ. I suspect there was some knowledge of the use of sexual energies for spiritual transformation, as is found in some Hindu texts.

As my husband writes, these sexual energies, when harnessed spiritually, have the power of regeneration and confer immortality. The practice of harnessing them is essential to spiritual resurrection and the attainment of immortality.[11]

Since the chiefs of Easter Island sought to become immortal beings, the process of attaining immortality would have been very important to them (and their religion), and the symbolism of the statues indicates that the chiefs still retained some of the knowledge of that process, which once also existed in ancient Egypt.

Why do their eyes (when they had them intact) look up to the sky?

In ancient Egypt, the akh of the deceased was said to ascend to the heavenly realm of the imperishable stars to live among the gods. I think the same belief was held on Easter Island, and that the destination of the aku was the region of the stars, which is why the statues look toward the stars as their destination and home.

As a side note, the moai also had symbols carved onto their backs, the oldest of which have been identified as the sun, a rainbow, and rain.[12] The sun and rainbow were used in clan names on Easter Island. These symbols indicate that the statues were associated with the sun. In ancient Egypt, the akh not only ascended to the stars, but also joined the sun god Ra in his boat, which he used to cross the sky.[13] Viracocha was depicted as the sun, with rain coming from his eyes like tears, and the Inca considered rainbows as gifts from the sun god. Why these symbols would be carved on the backs of the moai like this, I do not know, though the statues at Tula also have sun disks carved onto their backs.[14]

Other Remarks

I believe Easter Island provides remarkable insight into the beliefs that were circulating and shared among peoples in the ancient civilizations of India, Egypt, and South America, as well as other places, as in some ways they are easier to see when removed from their source and isolated for a long time in such a sparse and remote place as Easter Island.

Credits

I would like to acknowledge Thor Heyerdahl for his work on uncovering the origins of the builders of the moai; Graham Hancock, Robert Bauval, and Santha Faiia for their discovery of some of the linguistic connections between the moai and ancient Egypt; and David Childress for his discovery of the connection between the moai and Shiva.

PUBLISHER'S NOTE

The author has worked very hard over nine years to put together this book, and the utmost has been done to ensure all sources are fully referenced and credited. It contains unique and original work, which is breaking new ground in its field, and the author should be properly credited if this work is used elsewhere.

In academia, there are rigorous standards and expectations requiring proper attribution when drawing upon the work of others. Outside this field, however, there often seems to be a "free for all" kind of attitude and plagiarism is rife.

Yet stealing is not ok, whether it is of physical items, a passage of writing, or something more intangible like an idea or a body of research—all of these things have cost their owner in time and effort. It's unethical and intellectually dishonest to present the ideas and research of another as if it were one's own.

If you have seen any work from this book that has been used without proper attribution, please let us know by contacting us, the publisher, through our website suraondrunar.org.

HOW TO CITE THIS WORK

If you would like to use this book as a source in your own work, at a minimum please include a reference to the author's name, the book title, and where applicable, the relevant page number(s) for any content or ideas referred to. In informal internet mediums like blog posts and online videos, a hyperlink back to the original source should also be provided where possible.

In formal publications, full citations should be used that follow any industry-recognized style guide. Here is an example of a formal citation of this book:

Atwood, Lara. *The Ancient Religion of the Sun: The Wisdom Bringers and Lost Civilization of the Sun*. 2nd ed. Sura Ondrunar Publishing, 2021, p. [Insert page number(s) where applicable].

References

TEXTUAL REFERENCES

For the sake of brevity, only the first instance of each source will include full publication details, with subsequent instances in the same chapter shortened, and the first instance in each subsequent chapter showing "see chap. X, n. X," meaning refer to chapter X, note X (the first instance of this source), for the full publication details.

CHAPTER ONE: THE ANCIENT RELIGION OF THE SUN

1. Atwood, Mark, with Lara Atwood. *Ancient Solstice: Uncovering the Spiritual Meaning of the Solstices and Equinoxes*. Updated 4th ed. Sura Ondrunar Publishing, 2021, p. 14-20.
2. Ibid., 26-30.
3. "Sun Worship." Britannica. https://www.britannica.com/topic/sun-worship.
4. "Ocean Rowing." Wikipedia. https://en.wikipedia.org/wiki/Ocean_rowing.
5. "International Red Cross and Red Crescent Movement." Wikipedia. https://en.wikipedia.org/wiki/International_Red_Cross_and_Red_Crescent_Movement.
6. Cassaro, Richard. "The Secrets of Asia's Pyramid Temples." RichardCassaro.com, February 16, 2017. https://www.richardcassaro.com/secrets-asias-pyramid-temples/.
7. Weisman, Alan. *The World Without Us*. St. Martin's Publishing Group, 2007, p. 17. Kindle edition.
8. Ibid., 181.
9. Ibid., 172.
10. Ibid., 173.
11. See the work of Randall Carlson, Graham Hancock's *Magicians of the Gods* Part II, and Graham Hancock's *America Before* Part VII.
12. Heyerdahl, Thor. *The Tigris Expedition*. London: Flamingo, 1993, p. 316-360.
13. Carlson, Randall. "Ice Ages, Atlantis, and the Azores Pyramid." YouTube, September 30, 2013, 27:50-28:20, 32:50. https://youtu.be/gQv8DPXwm8Q.
14. "Sanatana Dharma." Veda Wikidot. http://veda.wikidot.com/sanatana-dharma.
15. Briney, Amanda. "The Last Glaciation." ThoughtCo, March 14, 2018. https://www.thoughtco.com/the-last-glaciation-1434433.

16. Whiteman, Yvonne. "The Kolbrin | The Worldwide Flood: Who, Why, When, and Where." GrahamHancock.com, November 9, 2019. https://grahamhancock.com/whitemany11/.

17. Hancock, Graham. *Magicians of the Gods*. New York: Thomas Dunne Books, St. Martin's Press, 2015, p. 38. Kindle edition.

18. Alison, Jim. "Exploring Geographic and Geometric Relationships along a Line of Ancient Sites around the World." GrahamHancock.com, May 1, 2001. https://grahamhancock.com/geographic-geometric-relationships-alisonj/.

19. Atwood with Atwood, *Ancient Solstice*. Our book contains a detailed explanation of the religious importance of the solstices and equinoxes.

20. Srivastava, V. C., trans. *Samba-Purana*. Parimal Publication Pvt. Ltd., 2013, p. 87.

21. "The Hibsathy" in *The Kolbrin*. The Culdian Trust, 2014, p. 239. eBook.

CHAPTER TWO: ORIGINS

1. Sidharth, Burra G. "Precession of the Equinoxes and Calibration of Astronomical Epochs." Hyderabad: International Institute for Applicable Mathematics & Information Sciences, February 3, 2011. https://arxiv.org/pdf/1001.2393.pdf.

2. Frawley, David. *Gods, Sages and Kings*. Twin Lakes, WI: Lotus Press, 1991, p. 15.

3. "Mezine." Wikipedia. https://en.wikipedia.org/wiki/Mezine.

4. "On Slavic connections with... Buddha?" Cogniarchae, January 15, 2016. https://cogniarchae.com/2016/01/15/on-slavic-connections-with-buddha/; Boroneant, Adina, and Clive Bonsall. "Burial Practices in the Iron Gates Mesolithic." ResearchGate, January 2012. https://www.researchgate.net/publication/304826218_Burial_practices_in_the_Iron_Gates_Mesolithic.

5. "Lepenski Vir." Wikipedia. https://en.wikipedia.org/wiki/Lepenski_Vir.

6. Ibid.

7. Ibid.

8. Ibid.

9. Ibid.

10. Curry, Andrew. "Gobekli Tepe: The World's First Temple?" Smithsonian Magazine, November 2008. https://www.smithsonianmag.com/history/gobekli-tepe-the-worlds-first-temple-83613665.

11. Sidharth, "Precession of the Equinoxes and Calibration of Astronomical Epochs," 9.

12. Frawley, *Gods, Sages and Kings*, 72, 76.

13. Ibid., 133.

14. "Vimana." Wikipedia. https://en.wikipedia.org/wiki/Vimana.

15. Frawley, David. "December 2008 AOM: The Vedic Literature of Ancient India and Its Many Secrets." GrahamHancock.com, November 26, 2008. https://grahamhancock.com/frawleyd1/.

16. Frawley, *Gods, Sages and Kings*, 246.

17. *Rigveda*. Translation from the American Institute of Vedic Studies. https://www.vedanet.com/the-ancient-yoga-of-the-sun/.

18. Hancock, Graham. *Fingerprints of the Gods*. Crown/Archetype, 1995, location 6549. Kindle edition.

19. Diodorus Siculus. *Library of History*. Vol 1. Translated by C. H. Oldfather. Harvard University Press, 1989, p. 157.

20. Plato, *Timaeus*. Translated by Benjamin Jowett, 1817-1893. http://classics.mit.edu/Plato/timaeus.html.

21. Herodotus, *The Histories*. Book 2, Chapters 143-144. Translated by A. D. Godley. Harvard University Press, 1920-1925, http://penelope.uchicago.edu/Thayer/E/Roman/Texts/Herodotus/2B*.html.

22. Gigal, Antoine. "Egypt before the Pharaohs." Gigal Research, April 2010. http://www.gigalresearch.com/uk/publications-pharaohs.php.

23. Manetho. *History of Egypt*. Book 1. Translated by W. G. Waddell. Harvard University Press, 1940. http://penelope.uchicago.edu/Thayer/E/Roman/Texts/Manetho/History_of_Egypt/1*.html.
24. Diodorus, *Library of History*.
25. *Turin Papyrus*, quoted in Hancock, *Fingerprints of the Gods*.
26. Ibid., 213.
27. Atwood with Atwood, *Ancient Solstice*, 39 (see chap. 1, n. 1).
28. Gigal, "Egypt before the Pharaohs."
29. Herodotus, *The Histories*, Book 2.
30. Mela, Pomponius. *De Situ Orbis*, quoted in Hancock, *Fingerprints of the Gods*.
31. Hancock, *Fingerprints of the Gods*, 385-386.
32. *The Kolbrin*, 429 (see chap. 1, n. 21).
33. Schoch, Robert M. "Robert M. Schoch: Research Highlights. The Great Sphinx." The Official Website of Robert M. Schoch, May 29, 2018. https://www.robertschoch.com/sphinx.html.
34. Carlson, Randall. "Sphinx Quarry Erosion from Floods? / Durable Civilization? Cosmography 101, Class 32, Segment 3." YouTube, November 2008. https://youtu.be/IwVcNlykoVs.
35. Ibid.
36. Ibid.
37. Ibid.
38. Temple, Robert. *Egyptian Dawn*. London: Random House, 2010, p. 365.
39. Carlson, "Sphinx Quarry Erosion from Floods."
40. "Great Sphinx of Giza." Wikipedia. https://en.wikipedia.org/wiki/Great_Sphinx_of_Giza.
41. Sibson, Matthew. "Proof of an Ancient Origin: The Foundations of the Pyramids of Egypt." YouTube, October 26, 2018. https://youtu.be/fDiqVB2P5oo.
42. Ibid.
43. Mei, Armando. *36.400 A.C.: Il Segreto degli Dèi*. Casa Editrice Amazon, 2018.
44. Hancock, Graham, and Robert Bauval. *The Message of the Sphinx: A Quest for the Hidden Legacy of Mankind*. New York: Three Rivers Press, 1996.
45. Ibid.
46. "Nile Delta." Wikipedia. https://en.wikipedia.org/wiki/Nile_Delta.
47. Temple, *Egyptian Dawn*, 432.
48. Weisman, *The World Without Us*, 19 (see chap. 1, n. 7).
49. Reymond, Eve A. E. *The Mythical Origin of the Egyptian Temple*. Manchester U.P., 1969, p. 76.
50. Gigal, "Egypt before the Pharaohs."
51. Reymond, *Mythical Origin of the Egyptian Temple*, 83, 41.
52. Ibid., 83.
53. Hancock, Graham, and Santha Faiia. *Heaven's Mirror: Quest for the Lost Civilization*. Three Rivers Press, 1998, p. 105.
54. "Pyramids." Ancient-Wisdom, February 15, 2012. http://www.ancient-wisdom.com/pyramids.htm#alignment.
55. Temple, *Egyptian Dawn*, 33.
56. Ibid., 33, 36.
57. Whiteman, Yvonne. "Guide to the Kolbrin." GrahamHanock.com, October 17, 2015. https://grahamhancock.com/whitemany1/.
58. Ibid.
59. Ibid.
60. "Neanderthal Extinction." Wikipedia. https://en.wikipedia.org/wiki/Neanderthal_extinction.
61. Whiteman, Yvonne. "Was This Eden? Locating the Kolbrin's Gardenplace." GrahamHanock.com, July 29, 2016. https://grahamhancock.com/whitemany4/.

62. Whiteman, "The Kolbrin | The Worldwide Flood."

63. *The Kolbrin*, 27-28, 35.

64. "Abaris the Hyperborean." Wikipedia. https://en.wikipedia.org/wiki/Abaris_the_Hyperborean.

65. Herodotus, *The Histories*, Book 4, Chapters 32-36.

66. *The Kolbrin*, 35.

67. Ibid., 353.

68. Ibid., 111.

69. "Helena Blavatsky." Wikipedia. https://en.wikipedia.org/wiki/Helena_Blavatsky#Tibet.

70. "Helena Petrovna Blavatsky." Theosophy Wiki. https://theosophy.wiki/en/Helena _Petrovna_Blavatsky.

71. Blavatsky, H. P. *The Secret Doctrine*. Vol. 1. Theosophical University Press Online Edition, 57. https://www.theosociety.org/pasadena/sd/sd-hp.htm.

72. Ibid.

73. Reigle, David. "The Book of Dzyan: The Current State of the Evidence," in *Brahmavidyā: The Adyar Library Bulletin*, Supplement, 2013, p. 87-120. http://prajnaquest.fr/blog/ wp-content/uploads/Book-of-Dzyan-The-Current-State-of-the-Evidence.pdf.

74. Ibid.

75. "The Secret Book of Dzyan." BlavatskyTheosophy.com, February 15, 2016. https:// blavatskytheosophy.com/the-secret-book-of-dzyan/.

76. Reigle, "The Book of Dzyan," 90.

77. Atwood with Atwood, *Ancient Solstice*, 28.

78. *Stanzas of Dzyan*. Theosophy Wiki. https://theosophy.wiki/en/Stanzas_of_Dzyan.

79. Waters, Frank. *The Book of the Hopi*. New York: Penguin Books, 1977, p. 14, 16.

80. Hancock, Chap. 6 in *Magicians of the Gods* (see chap. 1, n. 17).

81. Waters, *Book of the Hopi*, 13, 16, 18-20, 115.

82. Ibid., 118.

83. Ibid., 30-31.

84. Brown, Lee. "North American Indian Hopi Prophecies." Talk given at the Continental Indigenous Council, Tanana Valley Fairgrounds, Fairbanks, AK, 1986. https://www. welcomehome.org/prophecy/hopi2.html.

85. Hancock, *Magicians of the Gods*, 390.

86. Reich, David. *Who We Are and How We Got Here*. Oxford University Press, 2018, p. 196. Kindle edition.

87. Ellis, Normandi, trans. *Awakening Osiris: The Egyptian Book of the Dead*. Boston: Phanes Press, 1988.

88. "Yuga." Wikipedia. https://en.wikipedia.org/wiki/Yuga.

89. Hancock, *Fingerprints of the Gods*, location 4373.

90. Ibid., Chap. 30.

91. "Manly P. Hall." Wikiquote. https://en.wikiquote.org/wiki/Manly_P._Hall.

92. Hall, Manly P. *The Secret Teachings of All Ages*. San Francisco: H.S. Crocker company, 1928, p. 35.

93. "Plato." Wikipdia. https://en.wikipedia.org/wiki/Plato.

94. Plato, *Critias*. Translated by Benjamin Jowett, 1817-1893. http://classics.mit.edu/Plato/ critias.html.

95. Plato, *Timaeus*.

96. University of Colorado at Boulder. "Greenland Ice Core Analysis Shows Drastic Climate Change near End of Last Ice Age." ScienceDaily, June 19, 2008. https://www.sciencedaily. com/releases/2008/06/080619142112.htm.

97. "Meltwater Pulse 1B." Wikipedia. https://en.wikipedia.org/wiki/Meltwater_pulse_1B.

98. Plato, *Timaeus*.

99. O'Connell, Tony. "Dating the Atlantis War." Atlantipedia, May 25, 2010. http://atlantipedia. ie/samples/date-of-atlantis/.

100. *Stanzas of Dzyan.*

101. Leonard, R. Cedric. "Ancient Writings: Pre-Platonic Writings Pertinent to Atlantis." Quest for Atlantis, March 17, 2011. https://atlantisquestscience.wordpress.com/culture/ ancient-writings/. Quotes: MacDonnell, Arthur A. *A Practical Sanskrit Dictionary.* London: Oxford University Press, 1974; Ganguli, Kisari Mohan, trans. *The Mahabharata of Krishna-Dwaipayana Vyasa.* Calcutta: Bharata Press (Pratep Chandra Roy), 1883-1896.

102. Blavatsky, *The Secret Doctrine*, 57.

103. "Mahabharata." Wikipedia. https://en.wikipedia.org/wiki/Mahabharata.

104. "Bhishma." Wikipedia. https://en.wikipedia.org/wiki/Bhishma.

105. Ganguli, Kisari Mohan, trans. Book 12, Section CCCXXXVII in *The Mahabharata*. Calcutta: Bharata Press (Pratep Chandra Roy), 1883-1896. https://www.sacred-texts.com/hin/m12/ m12c036.htm.

106. Ibid., Section CCCXXXIX.

107. Ibid., Section CCCXL.

108. Ibid.

109. Swami Harshananda. "Trita." Hindupedia. http://www.hindupedia.com/en/Trita.

110. "Saptarishi." Wikipedia. https://en.wikipedia.org/wiki/Saptarishi.

111. "Gautama Maharishi." Wikipedia. https://en.wikipedia.org/wiki/Gautama_Maharishi.

112. Ganguli, trans., Section CCCXXXIX in *The Mahabharata*.

113. "Bhishma." Wikipedia.

114. Kak, Subash. "The Mahabharata and the Sindhu-Sarasvati Tradition." Baton Rouge: Louisiana State University, 2012. http://www.ece.lsu.edu/kak/MahabharataII.pdf.

115. "Sūta." Wikipedia. https://en.wikipedia.org/wiki/Sūta.

116. Ganguli, trans., Section CCCXL in *The Mahabharata*.

117. "Vyasa." Wikipedia. https://en.wikipedia.org/wiki/Vyasa.

118. "Mahabharata." Wikipedia.

119. Srivastava, trans., *Samba-Purana*, Introduction (see chap. 1, n. 20).

120. "Samba Purana." Wikipedia. https://en.wikipedia.org/wiki/Samba_Purana.

121. "Multan Sun Temple." Wikipedia. https://en.wikipedia.org/wiki/Multan_Sun_Temple.

122. Swami Harshananda. "Saptadvipas." Hindupedia. http://www.hindupedia.com/en/ Saptadvipas.

123. Srivastava, trans., *Samba-Purana*, 79-81.

124. "Sakaldwipiya." Wikipedia. https://en.wikipedia.org/wiki/Sakaldwipiya.

125. "Saka." Wikipedia. https://en.wikipedia.org/wiki/Saka.

126. "Pangaea." Wikipedia. https://en.wikipedia.org/wiki/Pangaea.

127. Swami Harshananda. "Saptadvipas."

128. "Shakya." Wikipedia. https://en.wikipedia.org/wiki/Shakya.

129. Diodorus, *Library of History*.

130. Leonard, R. Cedric. "Writings of the Egyptians: Egyptian Vignettes of the story of Atlantis." Quest for Atlantis, June 15, 2012. https://atlantisquestscience.wordpress.com/culture/ writings-of-the-egyptians/.

131. Hancock, *Magicians of the Gods*, 170.

132. *The Kolbrin*, 351.

133. Ibid., 350-352.

134. "Pico: New Archaeological Evidence Reveals Human Presence before Portuguese Occupation – Azores." Portuguese American Journal, August 28, 2013. https:// portuguese-american-journal.com/pico-new-archeological-evidence-reveals-human-presence-before-portuguese-occupation-azores.

135. Whiteman, Yvonne. "The Kolbrin: On Who Built the Great Sphinx, and Why." GrahamHancock.com, March 10, 2018. https://grahamhancock.com/whitemany6/.

136. *The Kolbrin*, 619.

137. Ibid., 314.

138. Whiteman, "The Kolbrin | The Worldwide Flood."

139. Bitto, Robert. "Mexican Giants." Mexico Unexplained, July 3, 2017. http://mexicounexplained. com/mexican-giants/.

140. "Quinametzin." Wikipedia. https://en.wikipedia.org/wiki/Quinametzin.

141. Gallegos, Fernando S. "Giants of Ancient México." Exploring Traditions, December 19, 2018. https://www.exploringtraditions.com/giants-of-ancient-mexico/.

142. Maestri, Nicoletta. "Aztlán, The Mythical Homeland of the Aztec-Mexica." ThoughtCo, July 3, 2019. https://www.thoughtco.com/aztlan-the-mythical-homeland-169913.

143. Brinton, Daniel G. *American Hero-Myths: A Study in the Native Religions of the Western Continent*. Philadelphia: H. C. Watts & Co., 1882.

144. Waters, *Book of the Hopi*, 17-18, 20.

145. Banyacya, Thomas. "The Hopi Message." The Alpha Institute. http://www.welcomehome. org/rainbow/prophecy/hopi.html.

146. Gurdjieff, G. I. *Meetings with Remarkable Men*, New York: Penguin Compass, 2002, p. 37.

147. *The Kolbrin*, 35

148. Gurdjieff, *Meetings with Remarkable Men*, 36.

149. Ibid., 45.

150. Plato, *Timaeus*.

151. Carlson, "Ice Ages, Atlantis, and the Azores Pyramid," 36:35.

152. Ibid., 38:59-42:50.

153. "What Is Glacial Isostatic Adjustment?" NOAA's National Ocean Service, March 23, 2015. https://oceanservice.noaa.gov/facts/glacial-adjustment.html.

154. Ibid.

155. Kosmographia with Randall Carlson. "Atlantis Mystery - Evidence Revealed Pt3 Vertical Movements of MAR." YouTube, August 5, 2019. https://youtu.be/F1ysskPoyW4.

156. Carlson, "Ice Ages, Atlantis, and the Azores Pyramid," 39:18-42:50.

157. Kosmographia with Carlson, "Atlantis Mystery," 22:27.

158. Ibid.

159. Ibid.

160. Ibid.

161. Kosmographia with Randall Carlson. "Canary Islands Caldera Collapses / Events YDB Coincident." YouTube, September 16, 2019. https://youtu.be/ozsRtWpVj38.

162. Ewing, Maurice. "Exploring the Mid-Atlantic Ridge." *National Geographic Magazine* XCIV (1948), p. 281, quoted by Randall Carlson in "Atlantic Seafloor Recently Exposed? Atlantis Mystery–Evidence Revealed." YouTube, September 3, 2019. https://youtu. be/4b_2YowEr_Q?t=640.

163. Ibid., 12:45.

164. Ibid., 18:00.

165. Petersson, Hans. *The Ocean Floor*. 2nd ed. Yale University Press, 1958. Quoted by Carlson in "Atlantic Seafloor Recently Exposed?," 27:00.

166. Heezen, Bruce C., Maurice Ewing, D. B. Ericson, and C. R. Bentley. "Flat-Topped Atlantis, Cruiser, and Great Meteor Seamounts." *Geographical Society of America Bulletin* 65 (1954), p. 1261. Quoted by Randall Carlson in "Atlantic Seafloor Recently Exposed?," 42:35.

167. "Mysterious Underwater Pyramid Found Near Azores." SurferToday.com, February 12, 2014. https://www.surfertoday.com/environment/9928-mysterious-underwater-pyramid-found-near-azores.

168. Gigal, "Egypt before the Pharaohs."

169. "Golden Age." Wikipedia. https://en.wikipedia.org/wiki/Golden_Age.

170. "Yuga." Wikipedia.

171. "Kali Yuga." Wikipedia. https://en.wikipedia.org/wiki/Kali_Yuga.

172. Waters, *Book of the Hopi*, 12-13, 26.

173. Ibid., 17.

174. Anklesaria, Behramgore Tehmuras, trans. Chap. 1 in *Zand-Akasih*. Bombay, 1956. http://www.avesta.org/mp/grb1.htm.

CHAPTER THREE: THE WISDOM BRINGERS

1. Hancock, *Magicians of the Gods*, 26 (see chap. 1, n. 17).

2. Ibid., 9.

3. Ibid., 185.

4. Ibid.

5. Ibid.

6. *The Kolbrin*, 430, 435 (see chap. 1, n. 21).

7. Budge, E. A. Wallis. *Osiris and the Egyptian Resurrection*. London: Philip Lee Warner, 1911, p. xviii, 1.

8. Ibid., 2.

9. Diodorus, quoted in Budge, *Osiris and the Egyptian Resurrection*, 10-11.

10. *The Kolbrin*, 435.

11. Ibid., 354.

12. Ibid., 434.

13. Budge, *Osiris and the Egyptian Resurrection*, xv.

14. Atwood with Atwood, *Ancient Solstice*, 277, 293, 301, 319, 335-336 (see chap. 1, n. 1).

15. Frawley, *Gods, Sages and Kings*, 226 (see chap. 2, n. 2).

16. Purohit Swami, Shri, trans. *The Bhagavad Gita*. Circa 1935.

17. Frawley, *Gods, Sages and Kings*, 93.

18. Ibid., 166.

19. "Saptarishi." Wikipedia. https://en.wikipedia.org/wiki/Saptarishi.

20. Lord Teignmouth. *The Works of Sir William Jones*. Vol. 13. London: John Stockdale, 1807, p. 367.

21. "Sandhyavandanam." Wikipedia. https://en.wikipedia.org/wiki/Sandhyavandanam.

22. Heyerdahl, Thor. *The Maldive Mystery*. Maryland: Adler & Adler, 1986, p. 287.

23. Hancock, *Magicians of the Gods*, 185-187.

24. Ibid., 186-187.

25. Collins, Andrew. *Gods of Eden*. Rochester: Bear & Company, 2002, p. 295-296.

26. "Enki." Wikipedia. https://en.wikipedia.org/wiki/Enki.

27. Hancock, *Magicians of the Gods*, 165.

28. "Ziusudra." Wikipedia. https://en.wikipedia.org/wiki/Ziusudra.

29. Hancock, *Magicians of the Gods*, 157.

30. Verbrugghe, Gerald P., and John M. Wickersham. *Berossos and Manetho*. University of Michigan Press, 1999, p. 49-50, quoted in Hancock, *Magicians of the Gods*, 164.

31. Hancock, *Magicians of the Gods*, 165.

32. Silberman, Neil Asher, ed. "Ur." In *The Oxford Companion to Archaeology*. 2nd ed. Oxford University Press, 2012. http://www.oxfordreference.com/view/10.1093/acref/9780199735785.001.0001/acref-9780199735785-e-0468.

33. Woolley, Leonard. *Ur Excavations Volume V: The Ziggurat and Its Surroundings*. London: The British Museum, 1939, p. 1.

34. Penprase, Bryan E. *The Power of Stars: How Celestial Observations Have Shaped Civilization*. Springer Science & Business Media, 2010, p. 205-206.

35. Heyerdahl, Thor. *The Tigris Expedition*. London: Flamingo, 1993, p. 141.

36. "Yama." Wikipedia. https://en.wikipedia.org/wiki/Yama.

37. Darmesteter, James, trans. *The Sacred Books of the East*. American Edition. Vol. III. The Zend-Avesta. NY: The Christian Literature Company, 1898, p. 11, 15-16. http://www.avesta.org/vendidad/vd2sbe.htm.

38. "Jamshid." Wikipedia. https://en.wikipedia.org/wiki/Jamshid.

39. Hancock, *Magicians of the Gods*, 379.

40. Darmesteter, *Sacred Books of the East*, 12-14.

41. Davidski. "The Mystery of the Sintashta People." Eurogenes Blog, April 27, 2018. http://eurogenes.blogspot.com/2018/04/the-mystery-of-sintashta-people.html.

42. Sudakov, Dmitry. "Arkaim, Russia's Strongest Anomaly Zone." Pravda.Ru, June 7, 2010. http://www.pravdareport.com/science/113680-arkaim/.

43. Ibid.

44. "Nowruz." Wikipedia. https://en.wikipedia.org/wiki/Nowruz.

45. "Faravahar." Wikipedia. https://en.wikipedia.org/wiki/Faravahar.

46. "Sun Worship." Britannica (see chap. 1, n. 3).

47. Mills, L. H., trans. *The Zend-Avesta*. Oxford University Press, 1887. https://www.sacred-texts.com/zor/sbe31/sbe31096.htm.

48. Waters, *Book of the Hopi*, 21-22, 30-31, 34-35, 113 (see chap. 2, n. 79).

49. "Hopi Mythology." Wikipedia. https://en.wikipedia.org/wiki/Hopi_mythology.

50. Waters, *Book of the Hopi*, 168.

51. Ibid., 67-68.

52. Ouspensky, P. D. *In Search of the Miraculous*. London: Routledge & Kegan Paul, 1950, p. 321.

53. Waters, *Book of the Hopi*, 68.

54. Ibid., Chap. 6.

55. "Casas Grandes." Wikipedia. https://en.wikipedia.org/wiki/Casas_Grandes.

56. Waters, *Book of the Hopi*, 71, 111, 165.

57. Ibid., 6.

58. Hancock, *Magicians of the Gods*, 397.

59. "Ahu Akivi." Wikipedia. https://en.wikipedia.org/wiki/Ahu_Akivi.

60. Grant-Peterkin, James. "Vernal (Spring) Equinox at Ahu Akivi." Easter Island News, September 24, 2012. https://easterislandnews.blogspot.com/2012/09/vernal-spring-equinox-at-ahu-akivi.html.

61. "Ahu Vinapu." Wikipedia. https://en.wikipedia.org/wiki/Ahu_Vinapu.

62. Heyerdahl, Thor. *Easter Island: The Mystery Solved*. London: Souvenir Press, 2014, p. 88, 111, 198.

63. Ibid., 200.

64. Hancock, *Magicians of the Gods*, 399.

65. Hancock and Faiia, *Heaven's Mirror*, 242 (see chap. 2, n. 53).

66. Heyerdahl, Thor. *Aku-Aku: The Secret of Easter Island*. Chicago: Rand McNally & Company, 1958, p. 160.

67. Budge, E. A. Wallis. *An Egyptian Hierogyphic Dictionary*. Vol. 1. London: John Murray, 1920, p. 9. https://www.um.es/cepoat/egipcio/wp-content/uploads/egyptianhierogly.pdf.

68. Seawright, Caroline. "The Ancient Egyptian Concept of the Soul." Tour Egypt. http://www.touregypt.net/featurestories/soul.htm.

69. Kandil, Dr. Hoda Abd allah. "The Function and Symbolism of the Akh in Ancient Egpyt." Faculty of Tourism and Hotel, Minoufiya University. https://platform.almanhal.com/Files/2/14853.

70. Hancock and Bauval, *Message of the Sphinx*, 214 (see chap. 2, n. 44).

71. Hancock and Faiia, *Heaven's Mirror*, 233-234.

72. Gallegos, "Giants of Ancient México" (see chap. 2, n. 141).

73. Hancock, *Fingerprints of the Gods*, 80 (see chap. 2, n. 18).

74. Doutré, Martin. "Ancient Solar Observatories and Surveying Alignments of New Zealand." Ancient Celtic New Zealand, April 5, 2018. http://www.celticnz.co.nz/SolarObservatoriesNZ/SolarObservatoriesPart13.html.

75. Heyerdahl, *Aku-Aku*, 91.

76. Mark, Joshua J. "Osiris." Ancient History Encyclopedia, March 6, 2016. https://www.ancient.eu/osiris/.

77. Cassaro, Richard. "Osiris, The First Messiah: Was Jesus The "Second Coming" Of Egypt's Christ?" RichardCassaro.com, December 28, 2011. https://www.richardcassaro.com/osiris-the-first-messiah-was-jesus-the-second-coming-of-egypts-christ/.

78. "Easter Island." Wikipedia. https://en.wikipedia.org/wiki/Easter_Island.

79. Heyerdahl, *Easter Island: The Mystery Solved*, 165, 196-198.

80. "Kalash People." Wikipedia. https://en.wikipedia.org/wiki/Kalash_people.

81. Heyerdahl, *Easter Island: The Mystery Solved*, 222-224.

82. Hancock, *Magicians of the Gods*, 396.

83. Heyerdahl, *Aku-Aku*, 31.

84. Heyerdahl, Thor. *American Indians in the Pacific*. London: George Allen & Unwin, 1952, p. 735.

85. Heyerdahl, Thor. *Early Man and the Ocean*. Garden City: Doubleday & Company, 1979, p. 94.

86. Heyerdahl, *American Indians in the Pacific*, 737.

87. Ibid.

88. Ibid.

89. Ibid.

90. Ibid.

91. Heyerdahl, *Early Man and the Ocean*, 108.

92. Truman, Dave. "Ancient Alignment in the Andes Hints at a Lost Global High Culture." GrahamHancock.com, January 2, 2016. http://grahamhancock.com/trumand1/.

93. Heyerdahl, Thor. "The Bearded Gods Speak." In *The Quest for America*, edited by Geoffrey Ashe. New York: Praeger, 1971.

94. "San Blas Islands: Kuna Cultures." Tripadvisor, November 17, 2015. https://www.tripadvisor.co.uk/Travel-g298434-c2329/San-Blas-Islands:Panama:Kuna.Cultures.html.

95. Heyerdahl, *American Indians in the Pacific*, 281.

96. Heyerdahl, *Early Man and the Ocean*, 108.

97. Heyerdahl, "The Bearded Gods Speak."

98. Heyerdahl, *American Indians in the Pacific*, 258.

99. "Ancient Temple Found under Lake Titicaca." BBC News, August 23, 2000. http://news.bbc.co.uk/2/hi/americas/892616.stm.

100. Heyerdahl, *American Indians in the Pacific*, 251.

101. Heyerdahl, "The Bearded Gods Speak."

102. Heyerdahl, *American Indians in the Pacific*, 277.

103. Ibid.

104. Ibid., 278.

105. Ibid.

106. Hancock, Chap. 21 in *Fingerprints of the Gods*, 156-163.

107. Maestri, Nicoletta. "Itzamná: The Mayan Supreme Being and Father of the Universe." ThoughtCo, March 14, 2018. https://www.thoughtco.com/itzamna-mayan-god-of-the-niverse-171591.

108. Heyerdahl, *American Indians in the Pacific*, 278.

109. Ibid.

110. Ibid.

111. Ibid., 279.

112. Ibid.

113. Heyerdahl, "The Bearded Gods Speak."

114. Matlock, Gene D. "Was Mexico's God Quetzalcoatl Jesus Christ?" Viewzone Magazine, April 9, 2008. http://www.viewzone.com/gene.word.html.

115. "Mesoamerican Long Count Calendar." Wikipedia. https://en.wikipedia.org/wiki/Mesoamerican_Long_Count_calendar.

116. "Kali Yuga." Wikipedia. https://en.wikipedia.org/wiki/Kali_Yuga.

117. Heyerdahl, "The Bearded Gods Speak."

118. "Itzamna." Wikipedia. https://en.wikipedia.org/wiki/Itzamna.

119. Spence, Lewis. "The Gods of the Maya." *The Open Court* XL, no. 2 (February, 1926), p. 78 (18 in PDF). https://opensiuc.lib.siu.edu/cgi/viewcontent.cgi?article=3863&context=ocj.

120. "Odin." Wikipedia. https://en.wikipedia.org/wiki/Odin.

121. Heyerdahl, *American Indians in the Pacific*, 279.

122. Brinton, *American Hero-Myths* (see chap. 2, n. 143).

123. Heyerdahl, "The Bearded Gods Speak."

124. Heyerdahl, *American Indians in the Pacific*, 276.

125. Ibid., 296.

126. Ibid. See numerous accounts in the chapter "Traces of Caucasian-Like Elements in Pre-Inca Peru."

127. Ibid., 237.

128. Ibid., 297, 308.

129. Ibid., 268.

130. Sturluson, Snorri. "Gylfaginning." In *The Prose Edda*. Translated by Arthur Gilchrist Brodeur, 1916. http://www.sacred-texts.com/neu/pre/pre04.htm.

131. Kvilhaug, Maria. "Pantheism Pt. 2: Ódinn – The Spirit – Hidden Knowledge in Old Norse Myths Pt. 29." YouTube, October 29, 2011. https://youtu.be/plt881LFgnU.

132. Thomas, Wilmer. "Was Odin a Genuine Human Being?" Wilmer-T.net, September 4, 2003. http://www.wilmer-t.net/fornnorden/AncientNordic/HumanOdin.html.

133. Fell, Barry. *Bronze Age America*. Boston: Little Brown and Company, 1982. For a detailed analysis, see the final chapter of the book.

134. "Peterborough Petroglyphs National Historic Site of Canada." Parks Canada Directory of Federal Heritage Designations. https://www.pc.gc.ca/apps/dfhd/page_nhs_eng.aspx?id=487.

135. Kvilhaug, Maria. *The Seed of Yggdrasill: Deciphering the Hidden Messages in Old Norse Myths*. Whyte Tracks, 2016, section 9.2 The Sacred Marriage. Kindle edition.

136. Oates, Shanti. *The Hanged God: Odin Grimnir*. Canada: Anathema Publishing Ltd., 2019, p. 109, 113-114.

137. Rood, Joshua. *Ascending the Steps to Hliðskjálf: The Cult of Óðinn in Early Scandinavian Aristocracy* (Háskóla Íslands, 2017), quoted in Oates, *The Hanged God*, 111.

138. Kvilhaug, *Seed of Yggdrasill*, 4.7 The Verse-Smiths: How the Gods are Known.

139. Heyerdahl, *American Indians in the Pacific*, 274-275.

140. "Odin's Kin." Geni. https://www.geni.com/projects/Odin-s-Kin/12244.

141. Lukyashko, Sergey. "Thor Heyerdahl's Archaeological Expedition to Azov and Prospects for the Development of Archaeology in South-Eastern Europe." In Roggen, Vibeke, ed. *Thor Heyerdahl's Search for Odin*. Novus Press, 2014, p. 228.

142. "Mannus." Wikipedia. https://en.wikipedia.org/wiki/Mannus.

143. Grimm identified Ingvio with Odin (see: Grimm, Jacob. *Teutonic Mythology*. London: George Bell and Sons, 1882, p. 348-349. https://www.norron-mytologi.info/diverse/TeutonicMythology1.pdf); Istro has been identified with Odin (see: "Odin's Kin." Geni. https://www.geni.com/projects/Odin-s-Kin/12244); Irmin is another name for Odin (see: "Irminsul." Wikipedia. https://en.wikipedia.org/wiki/Irminsul).

144. For examples from Betanzos and Cieza de León, see pages 207 and 208 in Bandelier, Adolph F. "Aboriginal Myths and Traditions Concerning the Island of Titicaca, Bolivia." *American Anthropologist* 6, no. 2 (1904): 197-239. https://www.jstor.org/stable/659069.

145. United Nations Development Programme. "The Wuasikamas Movement of the Inga People in Aponte, Columbia." Equator Initiative Case Study Series, 2019, p. 4. https://www.equatorinitiative.org/wp-content/uploads/2019/02/Wuasikamas-Colombia.pdf.

146. "Mannus." Wikipedia.

147. Siikala, Anna-Leena. Jumalat ja Sankarit Chapter, Mytologinen Kokonaisuus section in *Itämerensuomalaisten Mytologia*. Helsinki: Suomalaisen Kirjallisuuden Seura (SKS), Helsinki, 2012. Kindle edition (2013), para. 2. https://kirja.elisa.fi/ekirja/itamerensuomalaisten-mytologia.

148. Siikala, Myyttinen Laulaja section in *Itämerensuomalaisten Mytologia*, para. 3, 4.

149. Castrén, M.A, and Joonas Ahola. *Luentoja Suomalaisesta Mytologiasta*. Helsinki: Finnish Literature Society, 2016, p. 291-293. https://doi.org/10.21435/tl.252.

150. Sarmela, Matti. *Finnish Folklore Atlas*. 4th Partially Revised ed. Translated by Annira Silver. Helsinki: Finnish Literature Society (SKS), 2009, p. 500. https://sarmela.net/_files/200000116-8d4a98e455/folkloreatlas.pdf.

151. Castrén and Ahola, *Luentoja Suomalaisesta Mytologiasta*, 292-294.

152. *The Kolbrin*, 126.

153. Siikala, Aika Ennen Alkua section in *Itämerensuomalaisten Mytologia*, para. 3-5; Ibid., Historialliset tulkinnat section, para. 6.

154. Sarmela, *Finnish Folklore Atlas*, 358.

155. Siikala, Turisas ja Tursas section in *Itämerensuomalaisten Mytologia*, para. 1, 5, 7; Ibid., Kaleva, Alkujättiläinen section, para. 1.

156. Kaitanen, Veijo, Esa Laukkanen, and Kari Uotila, editors. *Muinainen Kalanti ja Sen Naapurit - Talonpojan Maailma Rautakaudelta Keskiajalle*. Helsinki: Suomalaisen Kirjallisuuden Seura (SKS), 2003, p. 237.

157. Siikala, Kaleva, Alkujättiläinen section in *Itämerensuomalaisten Mytologia*, para. 1.

158. Ridderstad, Marianna P. "Arkeoastronomia ja Jätinkirkot. Tähtiuskomuksia ja Megaliitteja - Näkökulmia Arkeoastronomiaan." *Suomen Arkeoastronomisen Seuran Julkaisuja* 1, p. 7-32. *Suomen Arkeoastronominen Seura Ry.*, Helsinki (2017), p. 9, 11. https://www.academia.edu/37047787.

159. Hyppönen, Anna. "Jättiläisten Valtakunta. Jättiläistarinat Osana Suomen Kiinteitä Muinaisjäännöksiä." Master's thesis, University of Oulu, 2016, p. 36, 49. http://jultika.oulu.fi/files/nbnfioulu-201612223336.pdf.

160. Snellman, A. H. *Oulun Kihlakunta: Muinaistieteellisiä ja Historiallisia Lehtiä*. Helsinki: Suomen Muinaismuistoyhdistyksen Aikakauskirja, IX., 1887, p. 69. https://fennougrica.kansalliskirjasto.fi/handle/10024/89978.

161. Haavio, Martti. *Väinämöinen: Suomalaisten Runojen Keskushahmo*. Porvoo: Werner Söderström Osakeyhtiö, 1950, p. 28.

162. Siikala, Kosiomatka ja Ansiotyöt section in *Itämerensuomalaisten Mytologia*, para. 3; Ibid., Väinämöinen, Savon Sankari: Kulttuuriheeros section.

163. Haavio, *Väinämöinen*, 28.

164. Krohn, Kaarle. *Suomalaisten Runojen Uskonto*. Salakirjat, (1915) 2008, p. 324.

165. Haavio, *Väinämöinen*, 20.

166. Siikala, Laulajat ja Loitsijat section in *Itämerensuomalaisten Mytologia*, para. 4.

167. Haavio, *Väinämöinen*, 20.

168. Ibid., 24.
169. Słupecki, Leszek, and Rudolf Simek, ed. "Shamans, Christians, and Things in between: From Finnic–Germanic Contacts to the Conversion of Karelia." In *Conversions: Looking for Ideological Change in the Early Middle Ages*, p. 53-97. *Studia Mediaevalia Septentrionalia* 23. Vienna, Fassbaender (2013), p. 54, 64-65, 75. https://www.academia.edu/4049431.
170."Tietäjä." Wikipedia. https://en.wikipedia.org/wiki/Tietäjä.
171. Sarmela, *Finnish Folklore Atlas*, 33, 39, 41, 309.
172. Słupecki and Simek, ed., "Shamans, Christians, and Things in between," 67.
173. Frog, Anna-Leena Siikala and Eila Stepanova, ed. "Confluence, Continuity and Change in the Evolution of Mythology: The Case of the Finno-Karelian SampoCycle." In *Mythic Discourses: Studies in Uralic Traditions*, 205–254. *Studia Fennica Folkloristica* 20. Finnish Literature Society (SKS), Helsinki (2012), p. 222. https://www.academia.edu/3687105.
174. Stroud, Melissa (Iiddá). "The Origin and Genetic Background of the Sámi." Sami Culture. https://www.laits.utexas.edu/sami/dieda/hist/genetic.htm.
175. Ingman, Max, and Ulf Gyllensten. "A Recent Genetic Link between Sami and the Volga-Ural Region of Russia." *European Journal of Human Genetics* 15 (2007): 115-120. https://doi.org/10.1038/sj.ejhg.5201712.
176. Thomas, Charlie (Kárrál). "Creation Myths and Worldview: Sámi Animism and Christianity." Sami Culture. https://www.laits.utexas.edu/sami/diehtu/siida/religion/creationmyth.htm.
177. Düben, Gustov von. *Om Lappan och Lapparne*. Stockholm: P. A. Norstedt & Söners Förlag, 1873, p. 330. http://urn.fi/URN:NBN:fi-fd2010-00002370.
178. Donner, Otto. *Lappalaisia lauluja*. Helsinki: Suomalaisen Kirjallisuuden Seuran Kirjapaino, 1876, p. 8. https://fennougrica.kansalliskirjasto.fi/handle/10024/85593.
179. Thomas, "Creation Myths and Worldview."
180. Kåven, Elin. "Sami Soga Lávlla – The Sami Anthem." Beneath Northern Lights, February 5, 2019. https://beneathnorthernlights.com/sami-soga-lavlla-the-sami-anthem/.
181. Pulkkinen, Risto. "Saamelaisten Esikristillinen Uskonto." In *Saamentutkimus Tänään*, edited by Irja Seurujärvi-Kari, Petri Halinen, and Risto Pulkkinen. Helsinki: Finnish Literature Society, 2011. https://doi.org/10.21435/tl.234.
182. Sommarström, Bo. "Ethnoastronomical Perspectives on Saami Religion." In *Saami Religion*, edited by Tore Ahlbäck. Åbo/Finland: The Donner Institute for Research in Religious and Cultural History, 1987, p 239. https://www.doria.fi/handle/10024/134157.
183. Gaski, Harald. "When the Thieves Became Masters in the Land of the Shamans." 2004, p. 38. https://septentrio.uit.no/index.php/nordlit/article/download/1906/1772/0.
184. Düben, *Om Lappan och Lapparne*, 331-332.
185. Halinen, Petri. "Arkeologia ja Saamentutkimus." In *Saamentutkimus Tänään*.
186. Kallio, Petri. "Stratigraphy of Indo-European Loanwords in Saami." In *Máttut - Máddagat: The Roots of Saami Ethnicities, Societies and Spaces / Places*, edited by Tiina Äikäs. Oulu: Publications of the Giellagas Institute 12, (2009), p. 39. https://www.academia.edu/1103685.
187. "Assianism." Wikipedia. https://en.wikipedia.org/wiki/Assianism.
188. Ibid.
189."Æsir." Wikipedia. https://en.wikipedia.org/wiki/Æsir.
190."Assianism." Wikipedia.
191. Ibid.
192. Ibid.
193."Udi People." Wikipedia. https://en.wikipedia.org/wiki/Udi_people.
194."Ynglinga Saga." Wikipedia. https://en.wikipedia.org/wiki/Ynglinga_saga.
195."In Search of the Origins of Kalash." Cogniarchae, July 27, 2016. https://cogniarchae.com/2016/07/27/in-search-of-the-origins-of-kalash/.

196. Indo-Iranian Society for Heritage Preservation and Traditional Arts. "Kalash and Ossetian Uatsdin." Facebook, August 9, 2019. https://www.facebook.com/ishpataorg/posts/kalash-and-ossetian-uatsdintwo-people-separated-by-2500-km-of-central-asian-step/2367338363586903/.

197. "Apsat (Mythology)." Wikipedia. https://en.wikipedia.org/wiki/Apsat_(mythology).

198. Thomas, "Was Odin a Genuine Human Being?"

199. "Emperor Wu of Han." Wikipedia. https://en.wikipedia.org/wiki/Emperor_Wu_of_Han.

200. Kvilhaug, *Seed of Yggdrasill*, 2.5: Aesir [Gods] – The First Awareness: Óðinn, Víli and Vé.

201. Frawley, *Gods, Sages and Kings*, 287, 289.

202. "Orion Worship – Part 3 – Nordic Aryans (Ymir,Yama, Gayomart)." Cogniarchae, February 18, 2017. https://cogniarchae.com/2017/02/18/orion-worship-part-3-nordic-aryans-ymiryama-gayomart/.

203. Redalia, Suzanne. "Cracking the Indus Script: A Potential Breakthrough." Swarajya, April 17, 2016. https://swarajyamag.com/culture/how-i-deciphered-the-indus-valley-script.

204. Serith, Ceisiwr. "Proto-Indo-European Deities." Ceisiwr Serith's Homepage, August 25, 2020. http://ceisiwrserith.com/pier/deities.htm.

205. Dundas, Paul. "Jainism." Britannica. https://www.britannica.com/topic/Jainism.

206. "Tirthankara." Wikipedia. https://en.wikipedia.org/wiki/Tirthankara.

207. "Rishabhanatha." Wikipedia. https://en.wikipedia.org/wiki/Rishabhanatha.

208. "Bhagavan Rishabha." Jain Dharma Online. http://www.jaindharmonline.com/tirthan/tir01.htm.

209. Sullivan, Suzanne Marie Redalia. "Are there any similarities between the Nordic and the Hindu gods?" Quora, November 10, 2015. https://www.quora.com/Are-there-any-similarities-between-the-Nordic-and-the-Hindu-gods.

210. "Rishabhanatha." Wikipedia.

211. "Who Is Lord Rishabhnath?" Quora, July 31, 2016. https://www.quora.com/Who-is-Lord-Rishabhnath.

212. "Rishabha (Hinduism)." Wikipedia. https://en.wikipedia.org/wiki/Rishabha_(Hinduism).

213. "Orion Worship – Part 3." Cogniarchae.

214. "Pria, a Proto-Indo-European Goddess." Proto-Indo-European Religion, April 4, 2011. http://piereligion.org/pria.html.

215. Sturluson, Snorri. "Of Odin's Accomplishments." Chap. 1, Part 6 in *Heimskringla: The Chronicle of The Kings of Norway*. London: Samual Lang, 1844. https://www.wisdomlib.org/scandinavia/book/heimskringla/d/doc4937.html.

216. "Shiva." Wikipedia. https://en.wikipedia.org/wiki/Shiva.

217. Redalia, "Cracking the Indus Script."

218. Basavaraddi, Ishwar V. "Yoga: Its Origin, History and Development." Ministry of External Affairs, April 23, 2015. https://www.mea.gov.in/in-focus-article.htm?25096/Yoga+Its+Origin+.

219. Ober, Frederick Albion. Chap. 24 in *Travels in Mexico and Life among the Mexicans*. San Francisco: J. Dewing and Company, 1884. https://en.wikisource.org/wiki/Travels_in_Mexico_and_life_among_the_Mexicans/Chapter_24.

220. "Orion Worship – Part 3." Cogniarchae.

221. Krohn, *Suomalaisten Runojen Uskonto*, 322.

222. Sturluson, Snorri. "Of the People of Asia," Chap. 1, Part 2 in *Heimskringla*. https://www.wisdomlib.org/scandinavia/book/heimskringla/d/doc4933.html.

223. Sturluson, "Gylfaginning."

224. Bitto, Robert. "Vikings in Ancient Mexico? The Story of Votan." Mexico Unexplained, September 12, 2016. http://www.mexicounexplained.com/vikings-ancient-mexico-story-votan/.

225. Landmann, Erhard. *Weltbilderschütterung: Die richtige Entzifferung der Hieroglyphenschriften*. 1986, p. 12.

226. Heyerdahl, *American Indians in the Pacific*, 280.

227. Ibid., 281.

228. "The Marvelous Odyssey of Votan, a Bronze Age Seafarer." Cogniarchae, August 17, 2016. https://cogniarchae.com/2016/08/17/the-marvelous-odyssey-of-votan-a-bronze-age-seafarer/.

229. Thomas, "Was Odin a Genuine Human Being?"

230. "What Is an Ovate?" The Order of Bards, Ovates & Druids. https://www.druidry.org/druid-way/what-druidry/what-druidism/what-ovate. Adapted from *Druid Mysteries* by Philip Carr-Gomm.

231. Maestri, "Itzamná: The Mayan Supreme Being and Father of the Universe."

232. Landmann, *Weltbilderschütterung*, 50.

233. Kashyap, Karthik. "Incas and India: The God Connection." Owlcation, September 9, 2019. https://owlcation.com/humanities/Incas-and-India-The-God-Connection.

234. Drone image by Bogdan.

235. "Carajía." Wikipedia. https://en.wikipedia.org/wiki/Carajia.

236. Englebert, Victor. "Realm of the Cloud People." *Archaeology* 61, no. 1 (2008). https://archive.archaeology.org/0801/abstracts/chachapoya.html.

237. Ibid.

238. Gorgani, Cyrus. "The Irminsul." Real Rune Magick, December 25, 2017. http://realrunemagick.blogspot.com/2017/12/the-irminsul.html.

239. Kvilhaug, *Seed of Yggdrasill*, 2.11 Yggdrasill – The World Tree: The Serpent, the Squirrel and the Eagle.

240. "Djed." Wikipedia. https://en.wikipedia.org/wiki/Djed.

241. "Osiris." Wikipedia. https://en.wikipedia.org/wiki/Osiris.

242. "Æsir." Wikipedia.

243. Frawley, *Gods, Sages and Kings*, 271.

244. Ibid., 268.

245. Gorgani, "The Irminsul."

246. Kvilhaug, *Seed of Yggdrasil*, 3.16 The Mead and the Sun Goddess.

247. Serith, "Proto-Indo-European Deities."

248. Albuquerque, Carlos. "On the Scythian Pantheon." Ichthyoconodon, October 22, 2018. https://ichthyoconodon.wordpress.com/2018/10/22/on-the-scythian-pantheon/.

249. "Tiwaz (Luwian Deity)." Wikipedia. https://en.wikipedia.org/wiki/Tiwaz_(Luwian_deity).

250. "*The Deeds of the Saxons*." Wikipedia. https://en.wikipedia.org/wiki/Deeds_of_the_Saxons.

251. Gorgani, "The Irminsul."

252. Ibid.

253. "Odin's Eyes: Sun and Moon?" We Are Star Stuff, April 26, 2015. https://earthandstarryheaven.com/2015/04/26/odins-eyes-sun-and-moon/.

254. Bansi Pandit. "Lord Shiva." Kashmir Hindu Deities. http://www.koausa.org/Gods/God9.html.

255. Serith, "Proto-Indo-European Deities."

256. Sturluson, Snorri. "Skáldskaparmal." In *The Prose Edda*. Translated by Arthur Gilchrist Brodeur, 1916, XLVIII. https://www.sacred-texts.com/neu/pre/pre05.htm.

257. Sturluson, Snorri. "The Ynglinga Saga – Odin's Lawgiving." In *Heimskringla*. http://www.sacred-texts.com/neu/heim/02ynglga.htm; "Hakon the Good's Saga – Hakon Spreads Christianity," "Saga of Olaf Haraldson – Of the Sacrifices by the People of the Interior of the Throndhjem District," "Saga of Olaf Haraldson – Murder of Olver of Eggja," and "Saga of Olaf Haraldson – Here begins the Story of Asbjorn Selsbane." In *Heimskringla*. https://www.gutenberg.org/files/598/598-h/598-h.htm.

258. Atwood with Atwood, *Ancient Solstice*, 178-181, 187-190.

259. Sturluson, "Skáldskaparmal" in *The Prose Edda*, LXIV.

260. Gray, Martin. "Externsteine." World Pilgrimmage Guide, July 30, 2013. https://sacredsites. com/europe/germany/externsteine.html.

261. Arnbald OR. "The Irminsul and the Externsteine: From Yggdrasil to the Irminsul." The Odinic Rite, August 21, 2009. http://www.odinic-rite.org/main/ the-irminsul-and-the-externsteine-from-yggdrasil-to-the-irminsul/.

262. "Deities of Slavic Religion." Wikipedia. https://en.wikipedia.org/wiki/Deities_of _Slavic_religion.

263. Asov, Alexander Igorevich. *The Book of Kolyada*. 2nd ed. Moscow: FAIR Publishing House, 2010. English excerpts translated for Sura Ondrunar Publishing, 2018.

264. "Svarog." Wikipedia. https://en.wikipedia.org/wiki/Svarog.

265. "Deities of Slavic Religion." Wikipedia.

266. Plato, *Timaeus* (see chap. 2, n. 20).

267. Sturluson, "Gylfaginning."

268. Asov, *The Book of Kolyada*.

269. Ibid.

270. Ibid.

271. Donnelly, Ignatius. "The Deluge Legends of Other Nations." Chap. 4 in *Atlantis: The Antediluvian World*. New York: Harper & Brothers, 1882.

272. Sturluson, "Gylfaginning."

273. Asov, *The Book of Kolyada*.

274. "Slavic Mythology: Svarog | Сварог." A Journey through Slavic Culture, December 20, 2010. https://russianculture.wordpress.com/2010/12/20/slavic-mythology-sv.

275. Asov, *The Book of Kolyada*.

276. "Radegast (God)." Wikipedia. https://en.wikipedia.org/wiki/Radegast_(god).

277. Helmond, and Arnold. "The Rites of the Slavs." Book 1, Section 52 in *The Chronicle of the Slavs*. Translated by Francis Joseph Tschan. Columbia University Press, 1935. https://www. jassa.org/?page_id=10175.

278. "Fuxi." Wikipedia. https://en.wikipedia.org/wiki/Fuxi.

279. Ibid.; *The I Ching or Book of Changes*, Richard Wilhelm 1873-1930, Cary F Baynes, trans, © 1950, 1967 Bollingen Foundation Inc, London: Routledge & Kegan Paul, 1968.

280. *The Kolbrin*, 436.

281. "Fuxi." Wikipedia.

282. "Dongzhi Festival." Wikipedia. https://en.wikipedia.org/wiki/Dongzhi_Festival.

283. "2, 500 Years' History of Winter Solstice in China." TravelChinaGuide.com, August 26, 2019. https://www.travelchinaguide.com/essential/holidays/winter-solstice-history.htm.

284. "Fuxi." Wikipedia.

285. "Three Sovereigns and Five Emperors." Wikipedia. https://en.wikipedia.org/wiki/ Three_Sovereigns_and_Five_Emperors.

286. "Shennong." Wikipedia. https://en.wikipedia.org/wiki/Shennong.

287. "Three Sovereigns and Five Emperors." Wikipedia.

288. Scranton, Laird. *Point of Origin: Gobekli Tepe and the Spiritual Matrix for the World's Cosmologies*. Inner Traditions/Bear & Company, 2015, location 240. Kindle edition.

289. Brinton, *American Hero-Myths*.

290. Budge, *Osiris and the Egyptian Resurrection*, xv.

291. "Uru People." Wikipedia. https://en.wikipedia.org/wiki/Uru_people.

292. Patrón Faustos, Pablo. *Nouvelles Etudes sur les Langues Américaines: Origine du Kechua et de l'Aimará*. Leipzig, 1907, p. 332

293. "Shakya." Wikipedia. https://en.wikipedia.org/wiki/Shakya.

294. "Chimú Culture." Wikipedia. https://en.wikipedia.org/wiki/Chimú_culture.

295. MacCulloch, John Arnott. "Tuatha De Danann and Milesians." In *The Mythology of All Races*. Edited by Louis Herbert Gray and George Foot Moore. Vol. III. Boston: Marshall Jones Company, 1918. https://en.wikisource.org/wiki/The_Mythology_of_All_Races/Celtic_Mythology/Chapter_2.

296. Frawley, *Gods, Sages and Kings*, 259.

297. Whiteman, Yvonne. "The Kolbrin's Origin of the British." GrahamHancock.com, September 30, 2017. https://grahamhancock.com/whitemany5/.

298. Atwood with Atwood, *Ancient Solstice*, 17-20.

299. Ibid., 29.

300. "Kuna People." Wikipedia. https://en.wikipedia.org/wiki/Kuna_people.

301. Heyerdahl, *American Indians in the Pacific*, 281.

302. Hancock, Graham. *America Before*. Great Britain: Coronet, 2019, locations 3707-3728. Kindle edition. Quotes: Reichel-Dolmatoff, G. *Beyond the Milky Way: Hallucinatory Imagery of the Tukano Indians*. UCLA Latin America Center Publications, 1978, p. 1-2.

303. Budge, *Osiris and the Egyptian Resurrection*, 11.

304. Atwood with Atwood, *Ancient Solstice*, 242-245.

305. Heyerdahl, *The Maldive Mystery*, 291-292.

306. Truman, "Ancient Alignment in the Andes."

307. Ibid.

308. Foerster, Brien. *Elongated Skulls of Peru and Bolivia: The Path of Viracocha*. CreateSpace Independent Publishing Platform, 2015.

309. Hancock, *Fingerprints of the Gods*, 49; Hancock, *Magicians of the Gods*, 225.

310. Hancock, *Fingerprints of the Gods*, 49.

311. *The Kolbrin*, 111.

312. Ibid., 353.

313. Brinton, *American Hero-Myths*, 140. Quote edited by Thor Heyerdahl in "The Bearded Gods Speak."

314. *The Kolbrin*, 126, 131.

315. Donnelly, *Atlantis: The Antediluvian World*, locations 1792, 4818. Kindle edition.

316. Ganguli, trans., Book 12, Section CCCXXXVII in *The Mahabharata*, (see chap. 2, n. 105).

317. Ibid., Section CCCXXXVIII. https://www.sacred-texts.com/hin/m12/m12c037.htm.

318. Srivastava, trans., *Samba-Purana*, 82-83 (see chap. 1, n. 20).

319. *The Kolbrin*, 111.

320. Ibid., 57.

321. Ibid., 712.

322. Ibid., 133.

323. Heyerdahl, *American Indians in the Pacific*, 253-254, 237.

324. Ibid., 237.

325. Atwood with Atwood, *Ancient Solstice*, 31.

326. *The Kolbrin*, 315.

327. Sturluson, "The Ynglinga Saga – Of Odin's Feats" in *Heimskringla*. Translated by Samuel Laing.

328. *The Kolbrin*, 315-316.

329. Atwood with Atwood, *Ancient Solstice*, 103.

330. Ibid., 100-105.

331. Hancock, *Magicians of the Gods*, 185.

332. Heyerdahl, *Early Man and the Ocean*, 90.

333. Atwood with Atwood, *Ancient Solstice*, 242-245.

334. Heyerdahl, *Early Man and the Ocean*, 90.

335. "Saptarishi." Wikipedia.

336. Hancock, *Magicians of the Gods*, 165.

337. Ibid., 225.

338. *The Kolbrin*, 239.

339. Heyerdahl, *Early Man and the Ocean*, 186.

340. See my husband Mark's work on out-of-body experiences.

341. Gigal, "Egypt before the Pharaohs," (see chap. 2, n. 22).

CHAPTER FOUR: THE LOST CIVILIZATION OF THE SUN

1. Muscato, Christopher. "What is Western Civilization? - Definition & Overview." Study. com. https://study.com/academy/lesson/what-is-western-civilization-definition-overview.html.

2. "Western Culture." Wikipedia. https://en.wikipedia.org/wiki/Western_culture.

3. Heyerdahl, *Early Man and the Ocean*, 83 (see chap. 3, n. 85).

4. Plato, *Timaeus* (see chap. 2, n. 20).

5. Clynes, Tom. "Exclusive: Laser Scans Reveal Maya 'Megalopolis' Below Guatemalan Jungle." National Geographic, February 1, 2018. https://news.nationalgeographic.com/2018/02/maya-laser-lidar-guatemala-pacunam/.

6. *Stanzas of Dzyan* (see chap. 2, n. 78).

7. Parada, Carlos, and Maicar Förlag. "Hellenes." Greek Mythology Link, 1997. http://www.maicar.com/GML/Hellenes.html.

8. Hancock, *Magicians of the Gods*, 164 (see chap. 1, n. 17).

9. "History of Agriculture." Wikipedia. https://en.wikipedia.org/wiki/History_of_agriculture.

10. Hancock, *Magicians of the Gods*, 7-9.

11. "On Some Connections between Ancient Slavs and India." Cogniarchae, February 4, 2016. https://cogniarchae.com/2016/02/04/on-some-connections-between-ancient-slavs-and-india/.

12. "Urfa Man." Wikipedia. https://en.wikipedia.org/wiki/Urfa_Man.

13. Sidharth, B. G. *The Celestial Key to the Vedas*. Inner Traditions, 1999.

14. Ibid.

15. Gamkrelidze, Thomas V., and V. V. Ivanov. "The Early History of Indo-European Languages." *Scientific American* 262, no. 3 (1990): 110-117. https://www.jstor.org/stable/24996796.

16. Ibid.

17. "Anatolian Hypothesis." Wikipedia. https://en.wikipedia.org/wiki/Anatolian_hypothesis.

18. "Late PIE ground zero now obvious; location of PIE homeland still uncertain, but..." Eurogenes Blog, May 12, 2017. http://eurogenes.blogspot.com/2017/05/late-pie-ground-zero-now-obvious.html.

19. Bouckaert, Remco, Philippe Lemey, Michael Dunn, Simon J. Greenhill, Alexander V. Alekseyenko, Alexei J. Drummond, Russell D. Gray, Marc A. Suchard, Quentin D. Atkinson. "Mapping the Origins and Expansion of the Indo-European Language Family." *Science* 337, no. 6097 (2012): 957-960. https://doi.org/10.1126/science.1219669. Reprinted with permission from AAAS.

20. Gray, Russell D., and Quentin D. Atkinson. "Language-Tree Divergence Times Support the Anatolian Theory of Indo-European Origin." *Nature* 426, (2003): 435–439. https://doi.org/10.1038/nature02029. Reprinted with permission from Springer Nature.

21. Ibid.

22. Gamkrelidze and Ivanov, "The Early History of Indo-European Languages."

23. Ibid.

24. Teryan, Angela. *Ancient Written Sources of European Nations About Their Ancestral Homeland— Armenia and Armenians*. Yerevan: Voskan Yerevantsi, 2017, p. 5.

25. Ibid., 3.

26. Ibid., 16.

27. Haak, Wolfgang, Iosif Lazaridis, Nick Patterson, Nadin Rohland, Swapan Mallick, Bastien Llamas, Guido Brandt, et al. "Massive Migration from the Steppe Was a Source for Indo-European Languages in Europe." *Nature* 522, (2015): 207-211. https://doi.org/10.1038/nature14317.

28. Reich, *Who We Are and How We Got Here*, 145 (see chap. 2, n. 86).

29. Seyfzadeh, Manu, and Robert Schoch. "World's First Known Written Word at Göbekli Tepe on T-Shaped Pillar 18 Means God." *Archaeological Discovery* 7, no. 2 (2019): 31-53. https://doi.org/10.4236/ad.2019.72003.

30. "Megalithic Culture of Talaiotic Menorca." Descobreix Menorca. https://www.descobreixmenorca.com/en/megalithic-menorca/.

31. "Vinča Symbols." Wikipedia. https://en.wikipedia.org/wiki/Vinca_symbols.

32. Boutet, Michel-Gérald. "The Inscriptions of the Danube Civilization Decoded?" Academia.edu, 2018. https://www.academia.edu/37950498; Rankin, Joan. "The Mold Gold Cape." Thoth is the Ibis, July 3, 2012. https://thothistheibis.wordpress.com/2012/07/03/the-mold-gold-cape/.

33. "The Oracular Spherical Stone from Lepenski Vir." Prehistory Knowledge. http://www.prehistory.it/fase2/yugoslavia2.htm.

34. Boutet, "The Inscriptions of the Danube Civilization Decoded?"; Rankin, "The Mold Gold Cape."

35. Boutet, "The Inscriptions of the Danube Civilization Decoded?" 36.

36. Haarmann, Harald (Ed.). *Early Civilization and Literacy in Europe*. New York, 1995. Tab. 32. http://www.prehistory.it/mappadeisegni6i.htm.

37. Boutet, "The Inscriptions of the Danube Civilization Decoded?" 31.

38. "Gareth Alun Owens." Wikipedia. https://en.wikipedia.org/wiki/Gareth_Alun_Owens.

39. "Linear A." Wikipedia. https://en.wikipedia.org/wiki/Linear_A.

40. Lazaridis, Iosif, Alissa Mittnik, Nick Patterson, Swapan Mallick, Nadin Rohland, Saskia Pfrengle, Anja Furtwängler, et al. "Genetic Origins of the Minoans and Mycenaeans." *Nature* 548, (2017): 214–218. https://doi.org/10.1038/nature23310.

41. "Tărtăria tablets. Is Vinca (proto) Linear B script?" Cogniarchae, October 29, 2015. https://cogniarchae.com/2015/10/29/tartaria-tablets-connection-between-vinca-and-proto-linear-b-script/.

42. "The Riddle of the Minoans – Solved?" Cogniarchae, July 11, 2018. https://cogniarchae.com/2018/07/11/the-riddle-of-the-minoans-solved/.

43. Misra, Bibhu Dev. "Indus Valley Cultural Elements in Minoan Crete: Was It Due to Migration?." Ancient Inquiries, March 29, 2017. https://www.bibhudevmisra.com/2017/03/indus-valley-cultural-elements-in.html.

44. Landmann, *Weltbilderschütterung*, 11 (see chap. 3, n. 225).

45. Ibid., 30.

46. Landmann, Erhard. "The Decoding of the So Called Maya-Hieroglyphs and the Language behind Them."

47. Landmann, *Weltbilderschütterung*, 85.

48. "Maya Civilization." Wikipedia. https://en.wikipedia.org/wiki/Maya_civilization#Writing_system.

49. "Old High German." Wikipedia. https://en.wikipedia.org/wiki/Old_High_German.

50. Marsh, Richard Oglesby. *White Indians of Darien*. New York: G.P. Putnam's Sons, 1934, p. 220.

51. Denison, T. S. *A Mexican-Aryan Comparative Vocabulary*. Chicago: T.S. Denison & Co Publishers, 1909, p. 5.

52. Ibid., 13.

53. "Uto-Aztecan Languages." Wikipedia. https://en.wikipedia.org/wiki/Uto-Aztecan_languages.

54. Matlock, Gene D. "Is the Hopi Deity Kokopelli an Ancient Hindu God?" Viewzone. http://www.viewzone.com/kokopeli.html.

55. Waters, *Book of the Hopi* (see chap. 2, n. 79).

56. López, Vicente Fidel. *Les Races Aryennes du Perou*. Paris: A. Franck, 1871.

57. Raina, Neeta. "The Sun Temple of Korikancha, Peru - The Sanskrit & Sri Rama Connection." Vedic Cafe, January 25, 2013. http://vediccafe.blogspot.com/2013/01/the-sun-temple-of-korikancha-peru.html.

58. Raina, Neeta. "Nazca Lines, Peru - The Sanskrit Connection to the Name 'Nazca'." Vedic Cafe, February 14, 2013. http://vediccafe.blogspot.com/2013/02/nazca-lines-peru-sanskrit-connection-to.html.

59. Rajiv Malhotra Official. "Hinduism in Latin America." YouTube, September 23, 2019. https://youtu.be/xyD4Do4WyY0.

60. Patrón, *Nouvelles Etudes sur les Langues Américaines* (see chap. 3, n. 292).

61. "Sumer." Wikipedia. https://en.wikipedia.org/wiki/Sumer.

62. "Proto-Euphratean Language." Wikipedia. https://en.wikipedia.org/wiki/Proto-Euphratean_language.

63. "Indo-European before the Indo-Europeans? - New Evidence from Mesopotamia." University of Copenhagen, 2009. https://rootsofeurope.ku.dk/english/calendar/archive_2009/euphratic/.

64. Whittaker, Gordon. "The Case for Euphratic." *Bulletin of the Georgian National Academy of Sciences* 2, no. 3 (2008): 156-168. http://science.org.ge/old/moambe/2-3/Gordon Whitteker.pdf.

65. Chang, Tsung-tung. "Indo-European Vocabulary in Old Chinese." *Sino-Platonic Papers* 7 (1988), p. 35. http://sino-platonic.org/complete/spp007_old_chinese.pdf.

66. Ibid., 32.

67. Ibid., 36.

68. Ibid., 34.

69. Jixu, Zhou. "The Rise of Agricultural Civilization in China: The Disparity between Archeological Discovery and the Documentary Record and Its Explanation." *Sino-Platonic Papers* 175 (2006), p. 18, 35. http://sino-platonic.org/complete/spp175_chinese_civilization_agriculture.pdf.

70. Ibid.; Jixu, Zhou. "Old Chinese '*tees' and Proto-Indo-European '*deus': Similarity in Religious Ideas and a Common Source in Linguistics." *Sino-Platonic Papers* 167 (2005). http://www.sino-platonic.org/complete/spp167_old_chinese_proto_indo_european.pdf; Jixu, Zhou. "Correspondences of Cultural Words between Old Chinese and Proto-Indo-European." *Sino-Platonic Papers* 125 (2003). (http://www.sino-platonic.org/complete/spp125_chinese_proto_indo_european.pdf; Jixu, Zhou. "Correspondences of the Basic Words between Old Chinese and Proto-Indo-European." *Sino-Platonic Papers* 115 (2002). http://www.sino-platonic.org/complete/spp115_chinese_proto_indo_european.pdf.

71. Jixu, "Old Chinese '*tees' and Proto-Indo-European '*deus,'" 2.

72. Jixu, "The Rise of Agricultural Civilization in China."

73. Klyosov, Anatole A., and Elena A. Mironova. "A DNA Genealogy Solution to the Puzzle of Ancient Look-Alike Ceramics across the World." *Advances in Anthropology* 3, no. 3 (2013): 164-172. http://doi.org/10.4236/aa.2013.33022.

74. "Yin and Yang." Old European Culture, February 5, 2018. http://oldeuropeanculture.blogspot.com/2018/02/yin-and-yang.html.

75. "Taijitu." Wikipedia. https://en.wikipedia.org/wiki/Taijitu.

76. Robinson, Andrew. "Ancient Civilization: Cracking the Indus Script." Nature.com, April 7, 2016. https://doi.org/10.1038/526499a.

77. Redalia, "Cracking the Indus Script" (see chap. 3, n. 203).

78. Redalia, Suzanne. *Indus Script Dictionary*. California: 2013.

79. "Easter Island - Indus Valley Scripts." Ancient-Wisdom. http://www.ancient-wisdom.com/easterislandindusvalley1.htm.

80. JoshuaMessiah, Anonymousfor. "Rongorongo and the Indus Script." Boloji.com, October 27, 2012. https://www.boloji.com/articles/13273/rongorongo-and-the-indus-script.

81. "Boustrophedon." Wikipedia. https://en.wikipedia.org/wiki/Boustrophedon.

82. Heyerdahl, *Easter Island: The Mystery Solved*, 45 (see chap. 3, n. 62).

83. "Easter Island - Indus Valley Scripts." Ancient-Wisdom.

84. Giffhorn, Hans. *Wurde Amerika in der Antike entdeckt?* 2nd ed. München: Verlag C.H. Beck oHG, 2014, p. 173.

85. Redalia, *Indus Script Dictionary*, 526.

86. Ibid., iii.

87. Temple, *Egyptian Dawn*, 422 (see chap. 2, n. 38).

88. "Proto-Sinaitic Script." Wikipedia. https://en.wikipedia.org/wiki/Proto-Sinaitic_script.

89. "Indus Script." Wikipedia. https://en.wikipedia.org/wiki/Indus_Valley_script.

90. Pennick, Nigel. *Magical Alphabets*. S. Weiser, 1992, p. 78.

91. Landmann, *Weltbilderschütterung*, 14.

92. Wadler, Arnold D. *One Language: Source of All Tongues*. Lindisfarne Books, 2006. Originally published by The American Press for Art and Science, 1948.

93. Frawley, *Gods, Sages and Kings*, 57-58 (see chap. 2, n. 2).

94. Ibid., 58.

95. Heyerdahl, *Easter Island: The Mystery Solved*, 213.

96. Heyerdahl, *Early Man and the Ocean*, 6, 10.

97. "Gobustan Rock Art Cultural Landscape." UNESCO World Heritage Centre. https://whc.unesco.org/en/list/1076/.

98. Farajova, Malahat. "Boats in Rock Art of Gobustan." In *Thor Heyerdahl's Search for Odin*, edited by Vibeke Roggen. Novus Press, 2014.

99. Ibid.

100. Heyerdahl, *Easter Island: The Mystery Solved*, 213.

101. Heyerdahl, *Early Man and the Ocean*, 6-7.

102. Ibid., 10-11, 20.

103. Hancock, *Fingerprints of the Gods*, 409 (see chap. 2, n. 18).

104. Ibid.

105. "Possibly World's Oldest Sea Port Found in Egypt." GMA News Online, April 15, 2013. http://www.gmanetwork.com/news/scitech/science/303946/possibly-world-s-oldest-sea-port-found-in-egypt/story/.

106. Hancock, *Fingerprints of the Gods*, 409.

107. Heyerdahl, *The Maldive Mystery*, 63-64 (see chap. 3, n. 22).

108. Frawley, *Gods, Sages and Kings*, 45.

109. Ibid., 45-46.

110. Ibid., 51, 55.

111. Ibid., 53.

112. Ibid.

113. Ibid., 57.

114. Collins, *Gods of Eden*, 214 (see chap. 3, n. 25).

115. Ibid.

116. Heyerdahl, *The Maldive Mystery*, 60.

117. Heyerdahl, *Early Man and the Ocean*, 92.

118. "About Thor Heyerdahl." The Kon-Tiki Museum. https://www.kon-tiki.no/thor-heyerdahl/.

119. Heyerdahl, *Easter Island: The Mystery Solved*, 7.

120. Blair, Betty. "Thor Heyerdahl in Azerbaijan." *Azerbaijan International*, (Spring 1995): 62-63, 76. http://azer.com/aiweb/categories/magazine/31_folder/31_articles/31_thorheyerdahl.html.

121. Heyerdahl, Thor. "Scandinavian Ancestry." *Azerbaijan International*, (Summer 2000): 78-83. https://www.azer.com/aiweb/categories/magazine/82_folder/82_articles/82_heyerdahl.html.

122. "About Thor Heyerdahl." The Kon-Tiki Museum.

123. Ibid.

124. Heyerdahl, "Scandinavian Ancestry."

125. Blair, "Thor Heyerdahl in Azerbaijan."

126. "The Azerbaijan Connection." © 1995 Thor Heyerdahl. *Azerbaijan International*. http://azer.com/aiweb/categories/magazine/31_folder/31_articles/31_thorazerconn.html.

127. Farajova, "Boats in Rock Art of Gobustan," 192.

128. Goshgarli, Goshgar. "Thor Heyerdahl and Azerbaijani Archaeology." In *Thor Heyerdahl's Search for Odin*, 187-88.

129. Foerster, Brien. "Changing Human History: The Amazing Paracas Elongated Skull Results." Hidden Inca Tours. https://hiddenincatours.com/changing-human-history-amazing-paracas-elongated-skull-results/.

130. Olson, Dee. "New DNA Results Released from the Paracas Elongated Skulls." Megalithic Marvels, February 3, 2018. https://megalithicmarvels.com/2018/02/03/new-dna-results-released-from-the-paracas-elongated-skulls/.

131. Foerster, Brien. "DNA Results for the Elongated Skulls of Paracas: Part 4 of 4: European Nobility?" Hidden Inca Tours. https://hiddenincatours.com/dna-results-elongated-skulls-paracas-part-4-4-nobility/.

132. Foerster, "Changing Human History."

133. Foerster, Brien. "Discussion of the Paracas DNA results." Facebook, February 5, 2018. https://www.facebook.com/Shipibospirit/videos/10210935540572279.

134. Olson, "New DNA Results Released."

135. Foerster, "Changing Human History."

136. Ibid.

137. Foerster, Brien. "Latest DNA Results for the Elongated Skulls of Paracas: Part 1 of 4: The Red Haired Baby." Hidden Inca Tours. https://hiddenincatours.com/dna-results-elongated-skulls-paracas-part-1-4-baby/.

138. Foerster, Brien. "Elongated Skulls of Paracas Peru: Paternal Nuclear DNA Testing Results." Hidden Inca Tours. https://hiddenincatours.com/elongated-skulls-of-paracas-peru-paternal-nuclear-dna-testing-results/.

139. Foerster, "Latest DNA Results for the Elongated Skulls."

140. Foerster, Brien. "DNA Results for the Elongated Skulls of Paracas: Part 2 of 4: La Oroya." Hidden Inca Tours. https://hiddenincatours.com/dna-results-elongated-skulls-paracas-part-2-4-la-oroya/.

141. Foerster, Brien. "DNA Results for the Elongated Skulls of Paracas: Part 3 of 4: 'Cleopatra of Paracas.'" Hidden Inca Tours. https://hiddenincatours.com/dna-results-elongated-skulls-paracas-part-3-4-cleopatra-paracas/.

142. Foerster, "Changing Human History."

143. Hay, Maciamo. "Haplogroup U2 (mtDNA)." Eupedia, July 2020. https://www.eupedia.com/europe/Haplogroup_U2_mtDNA.shtml.

144. Genetiker. "Higher-resolution K = 11 analysis of the European admixture in Chinchorro DNA." February 10, 2018. https://genetiker.wordpress.com/2018/02/10/higher-resolution-k-11-analysis-of-the-european-admixture-in-chinchorro-dna/#comment-2659. See comment by Genetiker.

145. Hay, Maciamo. "Haplogroup T (mtDNA)." Eupedia, July 2020. https://www.eupedia.com/europe/Haplogroup_T_mtDNA.shtml.

146. Comment by Genetiker on "Higher-resolution K = 11 analysis."

147. Hay, Maciamo. "Haplogroup H (mtDNA)." Eupedia, July 2020. https://www.eupedia.com/europe/Haplogroup_H_mtDNA.shtml.

148. Comment by Genetiker on "Higher-resolution K = 11 analysis."

149. Hay, "Haplogroup H (mtDNA)."

150. Comment by Genetiker on "Higher-resolution K = 11 analysis."

151. Foerster, "Discussion of the Paracas DNA Results."

152. Allison, Marvin J., Ali A. Hossaini, Nora Castro, Juan Munizaga, and Alejandro Pezzia. "ABO Blood Groups in Peruvian Mummies. I. An Evaluation of Techniques." *American Journal of Physical Anthropology* 44, no. 1 (1976): 55-61. https://doi.org/10.1002/ajpa.1330440108.

153. Foerster, Brien. Facebook, February 3, 2018. https://www.facebook.com/Shipibospirit/videos/10210917559202756.

154. Foerster, "Discussion of the Paracas DNA Results."

155. Ibid.

156. Ibid.

157. "Artificial Cranial Deformation." Wikipedia. https://en.wikipedia.org/wiki/Artificial_cranial_deformation.

158. Trinkaus, Erik. "Artificial Cranial Deformation in the Shanidar 1 and 5 Neandertals." *Current Anthropology* 23, no. 2 (1982). https://doi.org/10.1086/202808.

159. White, Chris. "Head Space: Behind 10,000 Years of Artificial Cranial Modification." Atlas Obscura, May 26, 2015. https://www.atlasobscura.com/articles/head-space-artificial-cranial-deformation. Quotes: Molnár, Mónika, István János, László Szűcs, and László Szathmáry. "Artificially Deformed Crania from the Hun-Germanic Period (5th–6th Century AD) in Northeastern Hungary: Historical and Morphological Analysis." *Neurosurg Focus* 36 (2014).

160. Gigal, "Egypt before the Pharaohs" (see chap. 2, n. 22).

161. Foerster, Brien. "Elongated Skulls of the Ancients; Akhenaten, The Paracas and the Black Sea Connection." YouTube, July 16, 2020, 8:28-8:32. https://youtu.be/3uWGlS9KcNk.

162. "Kon (Inca Mythology)." Wikipedia. https://en.wikipedia.org/wiki/Kon_(Inca_mythology).

163. Heyerdahl, *Easter Island: The Mystery Solved*, 23.

164. Ibid., 248.

165. "File:Kaitae, Nearest Descendant of the Last King of Easter Island, photograph.jpg." Wikimedia Commons. https://commons.wikimedia.org/wiki/File:Kaitae,_Nearest_Descendant_of_the_Last_King_of_Easter_Island,_photograph.jpg.

166. "Rapa Nui People." Wikipedia. https://en.wikipedia.org/wiki/Rapa_Nui_people.

167. Genetiker. "Eske Willerslev is an anti-White Propagandist." February 6, 2015. https://genetiker.wordpress.com/2015/02/06/eske-willerslev-is-an-anti-white-propagandist/.

168. Ibid.

169. Hay, Maciamo. "The Genetic Causes, Ethnic Origins and History of Red Hair." Eupedia. https://www.eupedia.com/genetics/origins_of_red_hair.shtml.

170. Foerster, Brien. "Update from Brien Foerster." YouTube, August 1, 2018. https://youtu.be/o74u336CuT4.

171. Foerster, Brien. Facebook, February 4, 2018. https://www.facebook.com/Shipibospirit/videos/10210920677480711/.

172. Thorsby, Erik. "The Polynesian Gene Pool: An Early Contribution by Amerindians to Easter Island." *Philosophical Transactions of the Royal Society B* 367, no. 1590 (2012): 812–819. https://doi.org/10.1098/rstb.2011.0319.

173. Olalde, Iñigo, Swapan Mallick, Nick Patterson, Nadin Rohland, Vanessa Villalba-Mouco, Marina Silva, Katharina Dulias, et al. "The Genomic History of the Iberian Peninsula over the Past 8000 Years." *Science* 363, no. 6432 (2019): 1230-1234. https://doi.org/10.1126/science.aav4040.

174. Thorsby, "The Polynesian Gene Pool."

175. Giffhorn, Hans. "Celtic Immigrants in Ancient Peru? The merits of Professor Warren Church for the understanding of Chachapoya culture, Eurocentric ideologies and dogmatism at universities and new evidence for a pre-Columbian immigration to South America." Academia.edu. https://www.academia.edu/39508768.

176. Funck, Ronald. "República del Perú." timediver®, March 10, 2014. https://www.timediver. de/Peru_Regionen_San_Martin_Amazonas.html.

177. Giffhorn, "Celtic Immigrants in Ancient Peru?."

178. Genetiker. "More Y-SNP Calls for Chachapoyas." September 2, 2015. https://genetiker. wordpress.com/2015/09/02/more-y-snp-calls-for-chachapoyas/.

179. Allison, Hossaini, Castro, Munizaga, and Pezzia, "ABO Blood Groups in Peruvian Mummies."

180. Ibid.

181. Allison, Marvin J., Ali A. Hossaini, Juan Munizaga, and Rosa Fung. "ABO Blood Groups in Chilean and Peruvian Mummies. II. Results of Agglutination-Inhibition Technique." *American Journal of Physical Anthropology* 49, no. 1 (1978): 139-142. https://doi.org/10.1002/ajpa.1330490121.

182. Jett, Stephen C. "Pre-Columbian Transoceanic Contacts: The Present State of the Evidence." In *Ancient South Americans*, edited by Jesse D. Jennings. W. H. Freeman and Company, 1983, p. 337-393. https://www.researchgate.net/publication/200577481_Pre-Columbian_Transoceanic_Contacts.

183. Foerster, Chap. 5 in *Elongated Skulls of Peru and Bolivia*.

184. "Chinchorro Mummies." Wikipedia. https://en.wikipedia.org/wiki/Chinchorro_mummies.

185. Images of them can be found across the internet. Just a couple of examples appear in this article: https://news.harvard.edu/gazette/story/2015/03/racing-to-save-the-worlds-oldest-mummies/.

186. Genetiker. "Principal Component Analysis Confirms European Admixture in Chinchorro DNA." March 14, 2017. https://genetiker.wordpress.com/2017/03/14/principal-component-analysis-confirms-european-admixture-in-chinchorro-dna/.

187. Genetiker, "Higher-resolution K = 11 analysis."

188. "Haplogroup X (mtDNA)." Wikipedia. https://en.wikipedia.org/wiki/Haplogroup_X_(mtDNA).

189. Brown, Michael D., Seyed H. Hosseini, Antonio Torroni, Hans-Jürgen Bandelt, Jon C. Allen, Theodore G. Schurr, Rosaria Scozzari, et al. "mtDNA Haplogroup X: An Ancient Link between Europe/Western Asia and North America?" *The American Society of Human Genetics* 63, no. 6 (1998): 1852-1861. https://doi.org/10.1086/302155.

190. Ibid.

191. Ibid.

192. "Kennewick Man." Wikipedia. https://en.wikipedia.org/wiki/Kennewick_Man.

193. Derenko, Miroslava V., Tomasz Grzybowski, Boris A. Malyarchuk, Jakub Czarny, Danuta Miścicka-Śliwka, and Ilia A. Zakharov. "The Presence of Mitochondrial Haplogroup X in Altaians from South Siberia." *Am J Hum Genet* 69, no. 1 (2001): 237-241. https://doi.org/10.1086/321266.

194. Raff, Jennifer A., and Deborah A. Bolnick. "Does Mitochondrial Haplogroup X Indicate Ancient Trans-Atlantic Migration to the Americas? A Critical Re-Evaluation." *PaleoAmerica* 1, no. 4 (2015): 297-304. https://doi.org/10.1179/2055556315Z.00000000040.

195. Ibid.

196. Schuenemann, Verena J., Alexander Peltzer, Beatrix Welte, W. Paul van Pelt, Martyna Molak, Chuan-Chao Wang, Anja Furtwängler, et al. "Ancient Egyptian Mummy Genomes Suggest an Increase of Sub-Saharan African Ancestry in Post-Roman Periods." *Nature Communications* 8 (2017). https://doi.org/10.1038/ncomms15694.

197. Ibid.

198. Live Science Staff. "King Tut's Mom and Dad ID'ed." LiveScience, February 16, 2010. https://www.livescience.com/8092-king-tut-mom-dad-id-ed.html.

199. "The Tutankhamun DNA Project." iGENEA. https://www.igenea.com/en/tutankhamun.

200. Pappas, Stephanie. "King Tut Related to Half of European Men? Maybe Not." LiveScience, August 3, 2011. https://www.livescience.com/15388-discovery-channel-tutankhamen-dna.html.

201. "The Tutankhamun DNA Project."

202. Baghdjian, Alice. "Half of European Men Share King Tut's DNA." Reuters, August 2, 2011. https://www.reuters.com/article/oukoe-uk-britain-tutankhamun-dna-idAFTRE7704OR20110801.

203. "Linear Pottery Culture." Wikipedia. https://en.wikipedia.org/wiki/Linear_Pottery_culture.

204. Callaway, Ewen. "First Ancient African Genome Reveals Vast Eurasian Migration." Nature.com, October 8, 2015. https://doi.org/10.1038/nature.2015.18531.

205. Llorente, M. Gallego, E. R. Jones, A. Eriksson, V. Siska, K. W. Arthur, J. W. Arthur, M. C. Curtis, J. T. Stock, M. Coltorti, P. Pieruccini, S. Stretton, F. Brock, T. Higham, Y. Park, M. Hofreiter, D. G. Bradley, J. Bhak, R. Pinhasi, A. Manica. "Ancient Ethiopian Genome Reveals Extensive Eurasian Admixture in Eastern Africa." *Science* 350, no. 6262 (2015): 820-822. https://doi.org/10.1126/science.aad2879.

206. Morelle, Rebecca. "Ancient DNA Reveals 'into Africa' Migration." BBC, October 8, 2015. https://www.bbc.com/news/science-environment-34479905.

207. Hayden, Erika Check. "African Genes Tracked Back." Nature.com, August 27, 2013. https://doi.org/10.1038/500514a.

208. Stockholm University. "The Guanches Originated from North Africa, Shows DNA-Study." Phys.org, October 26, 2017. https://phys.org/news/2017-10-guanches-north-africa-dna-study.html.

209. Llorente, M. Gallego, E. R. Jones, A. Eriksson, V. Siska, K. W. Arthur, J. W. Arthur, M. C. Curtis, J. T. Stock, M. Coltorti, P. Pieruccini, S. Stretton, F. Brock, T. Higham, Y. Park, M. Hofreiter, D. G. Bradley, J. Bhak, R. Pinhasi, A. Manica. "Ancient Ethiopian Genome Reveals Extensive Eurasian Admixture in Eastern Africa." *Science* 350, no. 6262 (2015): 820-822. https://doi.org/10.1126/science.aad2879. Reprinted with permission from AAAS.

210. Hay, Maciamo. "Haplogroup R1a (Y-DNA)." Eupedia, April 2020. https://www.eupedia.com/europe/Haplogroup_R1a_Y-DNA.shtml.

211. Hay, Maciamo. "Haplogroup R1b (Y-DNA)." Eupedia, June 2020. https://www.eupedia.com/europe/Haplogroup_R1b_Y-DNA.shtml.

212. Ibid.

213. Ibid.

214. Ibid.

215. Mathieson, Iain, Songül Alpaslan Roodenberg, Cosimo Posth, Anna Szécsényi-Nagy, Nadin Rohland, Swapan Mallick, Iñigo Olalde, et al. "The Genomic History of Southeastern Europe." *Nature* 555, no. 7695 (2018): 197-203. https://doi.org/10.1038/nature25778.

216. "Haplogroup R1." Wikipedia. https://en.wikipedia.org/wiki/Haplogroup_R1.

217. "Y-DNA Haplogroups in Indigenous Peoples of the Americas." Wikipedia. https://en.wikipedia.org/wiki/Y-DNA_haplogroups_in_indigenous_peoples_of_the_Americas.

218. Oppenheimer, Stephen, Bruce Bradley, and Dennis Stanford. "Solutrean Hypothesis: Genetics, the Mammoth in the Room." *World Archaeology* 46, no. 5 (2014): 752-774. https://doi.org/10.1080/00438243.2014.966273.

219. Malhi, Ripan Singh, Angelica Gonzalez-Oliver, Kari Britt Schroeder, Brian M Kemp, Jonathan A. Greenberg, Solomon Z. Dobrowski, David Glenn Smith, et al. "Distribution of Y Chromosomes among Native North Americans: A Study of Athapaskan Population History." *Am J Phys Anthropol* 137, no. 4 (2008): 412-424. https://doi.org/10.1002/ajpa.20883.

220. St. Fleur, Nicholas. "DNA Clues to an Ancient Canary Islands Voyage." *New York Times*, March 21, 2019. https://www.nytimes.com/2019/03/21/science/canary-islands-indigenous-dna.html.

221. Genetiker. "Phenotype SNPs for Berber Guanches." November 4, 2017. https://genetiker.wordpress.com/2017/11/04/phenotype-snps-for-berber-guanches/.

222. Rodríguez-Varela, Ricardo, Torsten Günther, Maja Krzewińska, Jan Storå, Thomas H. Gillingwater, Malcolm MacCallum, Juan Luis Arsuaga, et al. "Genomic Analyses of Pre-European Conquest Human Remains from the Canary Islands Reveal Close Affinity to Modern North Africans." *Current Biology* 27, no. 21 (2017): 3396-3402. https://doi.org/10.1016/j.cub.2017.09.059.

223. Ibid.

224. Ordóñez, Alejandra C., R. Fregel, A. Trujillo-Mederos, Montserrat Hervella, Concepción de-la-Rúa, and Matilde Arnay-de-la-Rosa. "Genetic Studies on the Prehispanic Population Buried in Punta Azul Cave (El Hierro, Canary Islands)." *Journal of Archaeological Science* 78 (2017): 20-28. https://doi.org/10.1016/j.jas.2016.11.004.

225. Fregel, Rosa, Verónica Gomes, Leonor Gusmão, Ana M González, Vicente M Cabrera, António Amorim, and Jose M Larruga. "Demographic History of Canary Islands Male Gene-Pool: Replacement of Native Lineages by European." *BMC Evolutionary Biology* 9, no. 181 (2009). https://doi.org/10.1186/1471-2148-9-181.

226. Fregel, Rosa, Alejandra C. Ordóñez, Jonathan Santana-Cabrera, Vicente M. Cabrera, Javier Velasco-Vázquez, Verónica Alberto, Marco A. Moreno-Benítez, et al. "Mitogenomes Illuminate the Origin and Migration Patterns of the indigenous People of the Canary Islands." *PLoS ONE* 14, no. 3 (2019). https://doi.org/10.1371/journal.pone.0209125.

227. "Guanche Language." Wikipedia. https://en.wikipedia.org/wiki/Guanche_language.

228. Kennedy, Gordon. *The White Indians of Nivaria*. Mecca, CA: Nivaria Press, 2010, p. 7, 52, 77.

229. Ibid., 52, 53, 83.

230. Ibid., 56.

231. "Hu Gadarn." Wikipedia. https://en.wikipedia.org/wiki/Hu_Gadarn.

232. Doutré, Martin. "The Chinese Pyramids at Xi'an, Shaanxl." Ancient Celtic New Zealand. http://www.celticnz.co.nz/ChinesePyramids/Chinese Pyramids 1.htm.

233. Atwood with Atwood, *Ancient Solstice*, 329-330 (see chap. 1, n. 1).

234. Heath, Robin. *Sun, Moon & Stonehenge*. Blue Stone Press, 1998.

235. "Goseck Henge: (The 'German Stonehenge')." Ancient-Wisdom. http://www.ancient-wisdom.com/germanygoseck.htm.

236. Chapman, John, Bisserka Gaydarska, and Marco Nebbia. "The Origins of Trypillia Megasites." *Frontiers in Digital Humanities* 6, no. 10 (2019). https://doi.org/10.3389/fdigh.2019.00010.

237. "Cucuteni–Trypillia Culture." Wikipedia. https://en.wikipedia.org/wiki/Cucuteni-Trypillia_culture.

238. Tarnovski, Griandr. "Trypilian Temple - Observatory at Nebelivka." Bezvodovka, August 31, 2018. http://www.bezvodovka.com/en/pysmena/nebelivka.html.

239. Ibid.

240. Chirita, Robert. "The Cucuteni Solar Temple - A Potential Interpretation of a Cucuteni Culture Artifact." Academia.edu. https://www.academia.edu/12359153/.

241. Klyosov and Mironova, "A DNA Genealogy Solution."

242. Ibid.

243. Thompson, Lucy. *To the American Indian: Reminiscences of a Yurok Woman*. Eureka, CA: 1916.

244. Lee, Nelson. *Three Years Among the Camanches: The Narrative of Nelson Lee, the Texas Ranger, Containing a Detailed Account of His Captivity Among the Indians, His Singular Escape*. 1859, p. 163. Kindle Edition.

245. Ibid., 164.

246. "Ancestral Puebloans." Wikipedia. https://en.wikipedia.org/wiki/Ancestral_Puebloans.

247. Gannon, Megan. "Ancient Pueblo Used Golden Ratio to Build the Sun Temple." LiveScience, February 13, 2017. https://www.livescience.com/57862-sun-temple-golden-ratio-found.html.

248. De Pastino, Blake. "Mesa Verde's Sun Temple Reveals Geometrical 'Genius,' Physicist Says." Western Digs, April 9, 2017. http://westerndigs.org/mesa-verdes -sun-temple-reveals-geometrical-genius-physicist-says/.

249."Foot (Unit)." Wikipedia. https://en.wikipedia.org/wiki/Foot_(unit).

250. 1874 Hayden Survey. Quotes: Ingersoll, Ernest. New York Tribune, November 3, 1874. http:// www.crowcanyon.org/researchreports/castlerock/text/crpw_oralhistory.asp.

251. "Ancestral Puebloans." Wikipedia.

252. De Pastino, Blake. "Elite 'Dynasty' at Chaco Canyon Got Its Power from One Woman, DNA Shows." Western Digs, March 3, 2017. http://westerndigs.org/ ancient-leaders-at-chaco-canyon-were-members-of-matrilineal-dynasty-dna-shows/.

253. De Pastino, Blake. "Chaco's Elites Were Natives of Chaco Canyon, Not Migrants, Their Remains Show." Western Digs, April 6, 2017. http://westerndigs.org/chacos-elites -were-native-to-the-canyon-not-migrants-their-remains-show/.

254. Vieira, Jim. "The Mark of the Giants | Six Fingers and Toes in the Ancient World | Megalithomania." YouTube, September 15, 2019. https://youtu.be/9vP4-tfFcWc.

255. Donnelly, Deirdre E., and Patrick J. Morrison. "Hereditary Gigantism-the Biblical Giant Goliath and His Brothers." Ulster Med J 83, no. 2 (2014): 86-88. https://www.ncbi.nlm.nih. gov/pmc/articles/PMC4113151/.

256. Kennett, Douglas J., Stephen Plog, Richard J. George, Brendan J. Culleton, Adam S. Watson, Pontus Skoglund, Nadin Rohland, et al. "Archaeogenomic Evidence Reveals Prehistoric Matrilineal Dynasty." Nat Commun 8, no. 14115 (2017). https://doi.org/10.1038/ ncomms14115.

257. "Haplogroup B (mtDNA)." Wikipedia. https://en.wikipedia.org/wiki/Haplogroup_B_(mtDNA).

258. Canada, Rebekah. "The Curious Origin of mtDNA Haplogroup B2 in the Americas." Haplogroup. org. https://haplogroup.org/the-curious-origin-of-mtdna-haplogroup-b2-in-the-americas/.

259. David, Gary A. "The Orion Zone: Ancient Star Cities of the American Southwest." GrahamHancock.com, February 17, 2006. https://grahamhancock.com/davidga1/.

260. Waters, Book of the Hopi, Part Three: The Mystery Plays.

261. "Tellem." Wikipedia. https://en.wikipedia.org/wiki/Tellem.

262. Fell, Barry. Saga America. New York: Times Books, 1980, p. 247.

263. Ibid., xiii.

264. Ibid., 243, 249.

265. "Tellem." Wikipedia.

266. Scranton, Laird. The Cosmological Origins of Myth and Symbol: From the Dogon and Ancient Egypt to India, Tibet, and China. Rochester: Inner Traditions, 2010, locations 140-141. Kindle edition.

267. "Dogon People." Wikipedia. https://en.wikipedia.org/wiki/Dogon_people.

268. Fregel, Rosa, Fernando L. Méndez, Youssef Bokbot, Dimas Martín-Socas, María D. Camalich-Massieu, Jonathan Santana, Jacob Morales, et al. "Ancient Genomes from North Africa Evidence Prehistoric Migrations to the Maghreb from Both the Levant and Europe." bioRxiv (2018). https://doi.org/10.1101/191569.

269. Mathilda. "Eurasian Origins of Berbers and Modern North Africans." Mathilda's Anthropology Blog, May 2, 2008. https://mathildasanthropologyblog.wordpress.com/2008/05/02/ eurasian-origins-of-the-berbers/.

270. "Ancient Libya." Wikipedia. https://en.wikipedia.org/wiki/Ancient_Libya.

271. "Traditional Berber Religion." Wikipedia. https://en.wikipedia.org/wiki/Traditional _Berber_religion.

272. Waters, Book of the Hopi, 23-25.

273. "Southwestern Archaeology." Wikipedia. https://en.wikipedia.org/wiki/Southwestern _archaeology.

274. "Mound Builders." Wikipedia. https://en.wikipedia.org/wiki/Mound_Builders.

275. Hancock, *America Before*, locations 4490-4519 (see chap. 3, n. 302).

276. See the work of Dr. Barry Fell, including his books *Saga America*, *Bronze Age America*, and *America B.C.*

277. Hancock, *America Before*, locations 4633-4702.

278. Panther-Yates, Teresa A. "White People Behaving Badly and Ancient Giants." DNA Consultants, February 6, 2014. https://dnaconsultants.com/white-people -behaving-badly-ancient-giants/.

279. Lepper, Bradley T. "Early Historic American Indian Testimony Concerning the Ancient Earthworks of Eastern North America." *Journal of Ohio Archaeology* 3 (2014): 1-11. https:// ohioarchaeology.org/documents/Lepper_2014-final.pdf.

280. Carlson, Randall. "Archaic America: The Earthworks Mystery (#4/4) Cosmographic Research w/ Randall Carlson 3/14/08." YouTube, February 12, 2019, 9:38. https://youtu. be/uvePXpQdf80.

281. Ibid.

282. Harris, Frederick E. "Exploring Native American Folklore: Little People and Giants." Graduate Student Theses, Dissertations, & Professional Papers, University of Montana, 2006, p. 37-42. https://scholarworks.umt.edu/etd/5813.

283. Carlson, "Archaic America," 5:15, 7:03.

284. "Natchez People." Wikipedia. https://en.wikipedia.org/wiki/Natchez_people.

285. "Natchez." Britannica. https://www.britannica.com/topic/Natchez-people.

286. Patrón, *Nouvelles Etudes sur les Langues Américaines*, 332.

287. "Natchez People." Wikipedia.

288. "Natchez." Britannica.

289. "Natchez People." Wikipedia.

290. "Mound 72." Wikipedia. https://en.wikipedia.org/wiki/Mound_72.

291. "Ancient Egyptian Retainer Sacrifices." Wikipedia. https://en.wikipedia.org/wiki/ Ancient_Egyptian_retainer_sacrifices.

292. "Giants with Double-Rowed Teeth, and Six Fingers." DNA Consultants, October 13, 2012. https:// dnaconsultants.com/giants-with-double-rowed-teeth-flattened-heads-and-six-fingers/.

293. Barrat, John. "Corn Entered Southwest U.S. First along Highland Route, DNA Shows." Smithsonian Insider, February 24, 2015. https://insider.si.edu/2015/02/corn-entered -southwest-u-s-first-along-highland-route-dna-study-shows/.

294. "Mound 72." Wikipedia.

295. De Pastino, Blake. "Victims of Human Sacrifice at Cahokia Were Locals, Not 'Foreign' Captives, Study Finds." Western Digs, December 31, 2015. http://westerndigs.org/ victims-of-human-sacrifice-at-cahokia-were-locals-not-captives-study-finds/.

296. Belknap, Lori. "New Discoveries from Cahokia's 'Beaded Burial'..." Cahokia Mounds, August 22, 2016. https://cahokiamounds.org/new-discoveries-from-cahokias-beaded-burial/.

297. Vieira, Jim, and Hugh Newman, *Giants on Record*, quoted in "The Giants of Cahokia | Secrets of the Ancient American Mound Builders | Megalithomania." YouTube, July 8, 2020. https:// youtu.be/iYpOC07RStA.

298. Hamilton, Ross. "A Tradition of Giants: The Elite Social Hierarchy of American Prehistory." Academia.edu, 2007, p. 30. https://www.academia.edu/4693378.

299. Ibid., 75.

300. Ibid., 67, 90, 91.

301. Hancock, *America Before*, locations 4713-4755.

302. Mills, Lisa A. "Mitochondrial DNA Analysis of the Ohio Hopewell of the Hopewell Mound Group." PhD diss., The Ohio State University, 2003, p. 123. https://etd.ohiolink.edu/!etd. send_file?accession=osu1054605467.

303. Hamilton, Ross. *Star Mounds: Legacy of a Native American Mystery*. North Atlantic Books, 2012.

304."European Megalithic Complexes: (Form and Function)." Ancient-Wisdom. http://www. ancient-wisdom.com/complexes.htm#similarities.

305. Hancock, *America Before*, locations 158-191, 3236-3377, 4045-4077.

306. Ibid. See chapter 15.

307. Boutet, Michel-Gérald. "On the Origins of the Oghamic Writing System." Academia.edu, 2008, p.3. https://www.academia.edu/4134903.

308. Keys, David. "Found: Europe's Oldest Civilisation." Independent, June 11, 2005. https://www. independent.co.uk/news/world/europe/found-europes-oldest-civilisation-5345769. html.

309. Atwood with Atwood, *Ancient Solstice*, 339.

310. Boutet, "The Inscriptions of the Danube Civilization Decoded?," 10.

311. Fell, Barry. *America B.C.* New York: Quadrangle, 1976.

312."Six Mysterious Stone Structures of New England." New England Historical Society, 2020. https:// www.newenglandhistoricalsociety.com/6-mysterious-stone-structures-new-england/.

313."Gavr'inis: (Passage Mound)." Ancient-Wisdom. http://www.ancient-wisdom.com/ francegavrinis.htm.

314. Atwood with Atwood, *Ancient Solstice*, 295.

315. Ibid. 298.

316."Kercado: (Passage Mound)." Ancient-Wisdom. http://www.ancient-wisdom.com/ francekercado.htm.

317. Fell, *America B.C.*

318. Angel, Paul Tudor. "Who Built New England's Megalithic Monuments?" *The Barnes Review* (November, 1997). http://planetvermont.com/pvq/v9n2/megaliths.html.

319. Eccott, David J. "The Ogams of the Sun Temple." Old News. http://www.onter.net/biblio/ eccott.pdf.

320."Ogham." Wikipedia. https://en.wikipedia.org/wiki/Ogham.

321. Boutet, "On the Origins of the Oghamic Writing System."

322. Hale, John P. *History of the Great Kanawha Valley: With Family History and Biographical Sketches*. Brant & Fuller, 1891, p. 40.

323. Wakefield, Jay Stuart. "August 2011 AOM: Michigan Copper in the Mediterranean." GrahamHancock.com, July 29, 2011. https://grahamhancock.com/wakefieldjs1/.

324. Pompeani, David P., Mark B. Abbott, Byron A. Steinman, and Daniel J. Bain. "Lake Sediments Record Prehistoric Lead Pollution Related to Early Copper Production in North America." *Environmental Science & Technology* 47, no. 11 (2013): 5545-5552. https://doi.org/10.1021/ es304499c.

325. Ibid.

326."Passage Mounds: (Form and Function)." Ancient-Wisdom. http://www.ancient-wisdom. com/passagemounds.htm. This page provides an overview of similarities found between the passage mounds of Europe and the Mediterranean, and how this indicates they were built by the same civilization.

327. Fell, *America B.C.*, 5-6.

328. Caesar, Caius Julius. *Caesar's Commentaries*. Translated by W. A. McDevitte and W. S. Bohn. New York: Harper & Brothers, 1869. http://mcadams.posc.mu.edu/txt/ah/Caesar/ CaesarGal03.html.

329. Fell, *Saga America*, 24.

330. Ibid.

331. Doutré, Martin. "Ring O' Brodgar, Orkney Islands: Gateway to the Americas." Ancient Celtic New Zealand. http://www.celticnz.co.nz/Brodgar/Brodgar 1.htm.

332. Heyerdahl, *Aku-Aku*, 357-359 (see chap. 3, n. 66).

333. See color photograph reproductions in *American Indians in the Pacific* by Thor Heyerdahl, XXXV and XXVI.

334. Hancock and Faiia, *Heaven's Mirror*, 13 (see chap. 2, n. 53).

335. Brinton, *American Hero-Myths* (see chap. 2, n. 143).

336. "Toltec." Wikipedia. https://en.wikipedia.org/wiki/Toltec.

337. Brinton, *American Hero-Myths*.

338. Atwood with Atwood, *Ancient Solstice*, 93,186-187, 281-282.

339. "Quinametzin." Wikipedia. https://en.wikipedia.org/wiki/Quinametzin.

340. Cassaro, Richard. "Suppressed by Scholars: Twin Ancient Cultures on Opposite Sides of the Pacific." RichardCassaro.com, May 14, 2012. https://www.richardcassaro.com/suppressed-by-scholars-twin-ancient-cultures-on-opposite-sides-of-the-pacific/.

341. Hancock, *Fingerprints of the Gods*, 115.

342. "Xelhua." Wikipedia. https://en.wikipedia.org/wiki/Xelhua.

343. "Inca Empire." Wikipedia. https://en.wikipedia.org/wiki/Inca_Empire.

344. Hyland, Sabine. *The Quito Manuscript: An Inca History Preserved by Fernando de Montesinos*. New Haven: Peabody Museum, Yale University Publications in Anthropology, 2007, p. 2. https://www.academia.edu/21067469.

345. Genetiker. "More Proof of Whites in Ancient Peru and Chile." April 19, 2016. https://genetiker.wordpress.com/2016/04/19/more-proof-of-whites-in-ancient-peru-and-chile/.

346. Hyland, *The Quito Manuscript*, 2.

347. Foerster, Brien. "The Disappearance of the Children of Viracocha, Part 3: Cuzco: The City Which the Inca Found, Not Founded." GrahamHancock.com, February 7, 2011. https://grahamhancock.com/foersterb4/.

348. Foerster, Brien. "Ollantaytambo: House of the Dawn; an Underestimated Inca Monument." GrahamHancock.com, April 18, 2011. https://grahamhancock.com/foersterb5/.

349. "Amautas." Amautadiaries's Blog. https://amautadiaries.wordpress.com/about/.

350. "Amauta." Encyclopedia.com, February 1, 2020. https://www.encyclopedia.com/humanities/encyclopedias-almanacs-transcripts-and-maps/amauta.

351. "Amauta." Wikipedia. https://en.wikipedia.org/wiki/Amauta.

352. Cassaro, Richard. "Suppressed by Scholars: The Mystery of Twin Cultures on Opposite Sides of the Atlantic." RichardCassaro.com, November 5, 2012. https://www.richardcassaro.com/suppressed-by-scholars-the-mystery-of-twin-cultures-egyptians-incas-on-opposite-sides-of-the-globe/.

353. Marsh, Richard O. "Blond Indians of the Darien Jungle." *Dunstan Times*, June 22, 1925. https://paperspast.natlib.govt.nz/newspapers/DUNST19250622.2.44 .

354. Ibid.

355. Marsh, *White Indians of Darien*.

356. Ibid., 220.

357. "Thule." Wikipedia. https://en.wikipedia.org/wiki/Thule.

358. University of Copenhagen. "Blue-Eyed Humans Have a Single, Common Ancestor." ScienceDaily, January 31, 2008. https://www.sciencedaily.com/releases/2008/01/080130170343.htm.

359. "The Indigenous Guna: Living with Albinism in Panama." Al Jazeera, August 1, 2019. https://www.aljazeera.com/indepth/inpictures/indigenous-guna-living-albinism-panama-190730144647964.html.

360. Jasso, Carlos. "On Panama Islands, Albinos Battle a Bright Foe." Reuters, June 11, 2015. https://www.reuters.com/article/us-panama-albinos-widerimage-idUSKBN0OR1ET20150611.

361. "Cuna Religion." Encyclopedia.com, August 13, 2020. https://www.encyclopedia.com/environment/encyclopedias-almanacs-transcripts-and-maps/cuna-religion.

362. "San Blas Islands: Kuna Cultures." TripAdvisor (see chap. 3, n. 94).

363. "Cuna Religion." Encyclopedia.com.

364. "San Blas Islands: Kuna Cultures." TripAdvisor.

365. Marsh, *White Indians of Darien*, 135, 138.

366. Marsh, "Blond Indians."

367. Marsh, *White Indians of Darien*, 230.

368. Ibid., 60.

369. "San Blas Rebellion." Wikipedia. https://en.wikipedia.org/wiki/San_Blas_Rebellion.

370. "Guna People." Wikipedia. https://en.wikipedia.org/wiki/Guna_people.

371. Giffhorn, Hans. *Keltische Krieger im Antiken Peru*. 2016. DVD.

372. Giffhorn, *Wurde Amerika in der Antike entdeckt?*, 43.

373. Heyerdahl, *American Indians in the Pacific*, 326.

374. De Cieza de Léon, Pedro. Chap. 27 in *The Incas of Pedro de Cieza de Léon*. Translated by Harriet de Onís. Edited, with an Introduction, by Victor Wolfgang von Hagen. Norman: University of Oklahoma Press, 1959.

375. Giffhorn, "Celtic Immigrants in Ancient Peru?," 16-17.

376. Giffhorn, Hans. *Keltische Krieger im Antiken Peru – Zusatzmaterialien*. 2016, p. 26-27. PDF.

377. Ibid., 44.

378. Giffhorn, "Celtic Immigrants in Ancient Peru?," 19-23.

379. Giffhorn, *Wurde Amerika in der Antike entdeckt?*, 147.

380. Ibid., 173.

381. Ibid., 179, 186.

382. Cahill, Mary. "Here Comes the Sun." *Archaeology Ireland* 29, no. 1 (Spring 2015): 32.

383. Wells, S. A. "American Drugs in Egyptian Mummies." Discoveries in Natural History & Exploration. https://faculty.ucr.edu/~legneref/ethnic/mummy.htm.

384. "Marajoara Culture." Wikipedia. https://en.wikipedia.org/wiki/Marajoara_culture.

385. "Religion and Funeral Ritual." Celtiberia Historica. https://celtiberiahistorica.es/en/celtiberia/religion-and-funeral-ritual.

386. Turner, Tej. "Travelblog SA#13: Chachapoyas – Peru." Tej Turner Blog, September 14, 2018. https://tejturner.wordpress.com/2018/09/14/travelblog-sa13-chachapoyas-peru/.

387. "Celtiberians." Wikipedia. https://en.wikipedia.org/wiki/Celtiberians.

388. "The Celtiberians." Celtic Life International, November 17, 2018. https://celticlifeintl.com/the-celtiberians/.

389. Koch, John. "Celtic from the West." Academia.edu, December 2, 2015. https://www.academia.edu/19895000.

390. Giffhorn, *Keltische Krieger im Antiken Peru – Zusatzmaterialien*, 81.

391. Ibid., 77-80.

392. Gayre of Gayre, R. *The Origin of the Zimbabwean Civilisation*. Salisbury: Galaxie Press, 1972, Preface.

393. Clark, Stuart, and Damian Carrington. "Eclipse Brings Claim of Medieval African Observatory." New Scientist, December 4, 2002. https://www.newscientist.com/article/dn3137-eclipse-brings-claim-of-medieval-african-observatory/.

394. Giffhorn, *Keltische Krieger im Antiken Peru*.

395. Heyerdahl, *American Indians in the Pacific*, 372.

396. Heyerdahl, *Easter Island: The Mystery Solved*, 163-173.

397. Heyerdahl, *Aku-Aku*, 75.

398. Ibid., 91, 141.

399. Ibid., 32.

400. Childress, David Hatcher. *The Lost World of Cham: The Transpacific Voyages of the Champe*. SCB Distributors, 2017.

401. "Pukao." Wikipedia. https://en.wikipedia.org/wiki/Pukao.

402. "Sadhu and Swami." Britannica. https://www.britannica.com/topic/sadhu.

403. Srinivasan, Doris. "Unhinging Śiva from the Indus Civilization." *Journal of the Royal Asiatic Society of Great Britain and Ireland*, no. 1 (1984): 77-89. http://www.jstor.org/stable/25211627.

404. Heyerdahl, *Easter Island: The Mystery Solved*, 235.

405. "Lingam." Wikipedia. https://en.wikipedia.org/wiki/Lingam.

406. ET Online. "Steppe Migration to India Was between 3500-4000 Years Ago: David Reich." The Economic Times, October 12, 2019. https://economictimes.indiatimes.com/news/science/steppe-migration-to-india-was-between-3500-4000-years-ago-david-reich/articleshow/71556277.cms?from=mdr.

407. Sharma, Swarkar, Ekta Rai, Prithviraj Sharma, et al. "The Indian Origin of Paternal Haplogroup R1a1* Substantiates the Autochthonous Origin of Brahmins and the Caste System." *Journal of Human Genetics* 54 (2009), p. 47–55. https://doi.org/10.1038/jhg.2008.2.

408. ET Online, "Steppe Migration to India: David Reich."

409. "Dholavira: A Harappan City." UNESCO. https://whc.unesco.org/en/tentativelists/5892/.

410. Iyer, Chandran. "Vastu Shastra at Harappan Site: ASI." DNA, September 20, 2005. https://www.dnaindia.com/technology/report-vastu-shastra-at-harappan-site-asi-2628.

411. Vahia, Mayank, and Srikumar M. Menon. "A Possible Harappan Astronomical Observatory at Dholavira." *Journal of Astronomical History and Heritage* 16, no. 3 (2013). https://arxiv.org/ftp/arxiv/papers/1310/1310.6474.pdf.

412. *A Handbook of Ancient Religions*. Edited by John R. Hinnells. Cambridge University Press, 2007, p. 477.

413. Chopra, Omesh K. *History of Ancient India Revisited*. India: BlueRose Publishers, 2019, p. 40.

414. Heyerdahl, *The Maldive Mystery*, 64-69, 288-291.

415. "Barabar Caves." Wikipedia. https://en.wikipedia.org/wiki/Barabar_Caves.

416. I first saw this hypothesis put forward in this video by Brien Foerster: https://youtu.be/CHl85d42-48.

417. Foerster, Brien. "The Enduring Enigma of Puma Punku in Bolivia." Academia.edu. https://www.academia.edu/5631446.

418. Heyerdahl, *The Maldive Mystery*, 50-51, 66-68, 286-287.

419. Ibid., 65-66.

420. Rao, K. P. "Astronomical Relationship of South Indian Megaliths." In *Viewing the Sky through Past and Present Cultures: Selected Papers from the Oxford VII International Conference on Archaeoastronomy*, edited by Todd W. Bostwick and Bryan Bates. City of Phoenix Parks Recreation and Library, 2006.

421. Fenton, Bruce. "A Global Aboriginal Australian Culture? The Proof at Göbekli Tepe." BruceFenton.info, October 12, 2017. http://brucefenton.info/2017/10/12/a-global-aboriginal-australian-culture-the-proof-at-gobekli-tepe/.

422. Yong, Ed. "Genomes Link Aboriginal Australians to Indians." Nature.com, January 14, 2013. https://doi.org/10.1038/nature.2013.12219.

423. New World Encyclopedia contributors. "Mehrgarh." New World Encyclopedia, September 14, 2018. https://www.newworldencyclopedia.org/entry/Mehrgarh.

424. Whiteman, "Was This Eden?" (see chap. 2, n. 61).

425. Doutré, Martin. Personal communication.

426. Doutré, Martin. "The Ancient Surveying Structures on the Bombay Hills." Ancient Celtic New Zealand. http://www.celticnz.co.nz/AucklandAlignment1.htm.

427. Doutré, Martin. "Megalithic New Zealand." Ancient Celtic New Zealand. http://www.celticnz.co.nz/mnz_pt1.html.

428. Doutré, "The Chinese Pyramids at Xi'an."

429. "European Megalithic Complexes: (Form and Function)." Ancient-Wisdom.

430. Doutré, "Megalithic New Zealand."

431. Ibid.

432. Doutré, "The Chinese Pyramids at Xi'an."

433. Doutré, "Megalithic New Zealand."

434. Monica Matamua in Capper, Raynor. "Listen to the People. Talking with an Extinct Race. Part 1," *eLocal*, 2011. https://www.facebook.com/346003915492277/posts/the-results-dna-to-rock-the-nation-part-2changing-our-nz-history-for-decades-aca/670609243031741/.

435. Doutré, Martin. "Ancient New Zealand Surveyors & Astronomers." Ancient Celtic New Zealand, January 2009. http://www.celticnz.co.nz/SurveyorsNZ/Ancient New Zealand Surveyors.htm.

436. Temple, *Egyptian Dawn*, 409.

437. "Trilithons: (Ancient Constructions)." Ancient-Wisdom, August 28, 2011. http://www.ancient-wisdom.com/trilithons.htm.

438. Atwood with Atwood, *Ancient Solstice*. See chapters on ancient sites.

439. "Ancient Libya." Wikipedia.

440. Temple, *Egyptian Dawn*, 407.

441. Ibid., 410.

442. "African Humid Period." Wikipedia. https://en.wikipedia.org/wiki/African_humid_period.

443. Temple, *Egyptian Dawn*, 391-392.

444. Ibid., 382.

445. Lloyd, Ellen. "Was Megalithic Stone Circle of Mzoura the Tomb of Giant Antaeus?." Ancient Pages, September 5, 2015. http://www.ancientpages.com/2015/09/05/was-megalithic-stone-circle-of-mzoura-the-tomb-of-giant-antaeus/.

446. O'Connell, Tony. "Mzora Stone Circle." Atlantipedia, February 14, 2014. http://atlantipedia.ie/samples/mzora-stone-circle-n/.

447. Temple, *Egyptian Dawn*, 382.

448. "Karahunj." Armeniapedia, April 25, 2013. http://www.armeniapedia.org/wiki/Karahunj.

449. Callaway, "First Ancient African Genome."

450. Temple, *Egyptian Dawn*, 262-263.

451. "Palermo Stone." Wikipedia. https://en.wikipedia.org/wiki/Palermo_Stone.

452. Hsu, Shih-Wei. "The Palermo Stone: The Earliest Royal Inscription from Ancient Egypt." *Altorientalische Forschungen* 37, no. 1 (2010): 68–89, p. 78. https://doi.org/10.1524/aofo.2010.0006.

453. Temple, *Egyptian Dawn*, 262-263.

454. Nesmenser. "The Temehu Tribes of Ancient Libya." Temehu, December 4, 2015. https://www.temehu.com/Temehu.htm.

455. "Ancient Libya." Wikipedia.

456. Ibid.

457. Temple, *Egyptian Dawn*, 424.

458. Ibid.

459. Fregel, Méndez, Bokbot, Martín-Socas, Camalich-Massieu, Santana, Morales, et al. "Ancient Genomes from North Africa."

460. Temple, *Egyptian Dawn*, 419.

461. "Carnac Stones." Wikipedia. https://en.wikipedia.org/wiki/Carnac_stones.

462. Atwood with Atwood, *Ancient Solstice*, 194-196.

463. Whiteman, "Guide to the Kolbrin" (see chap. 2, n. 57).

464. Ibid.

465. *The Kolbrin*, 355.

466. Kennedy, *White Indians of Nivaria*.

467. Ibid., 59.

468. "Atum." Wikipedia. https://en.wikipedia.org/wiki/Atum; Routledge, Katherine. *The Mystery of Easter Island*. London: Hazell, Watson and Viney, 1920, p. 236; "Ātman (Hinduism)." Wikipedia. https://en.wikipedia.org/wiki/Ātman_(Hinduism).

469. *The Kolbrin*, 63, 66, 602.

470."Gautam (Given Name)." Wikipedia. https://en.wikipedia.org/wiki/Gautam_(given_name).

471. "Ātman (Hinduism)." Wikipedia. https://en.wikipedia.org/wiki/Ātman_(Hinduism).

472. Kennedy, *White Indians of Nivaria*, 55.

473. Kennedy, *White Indians of Nivaria*.

474. Heyerdahl, *Early Man and the Ocean*, 67.

475. Misra, Bibhu Dev. "Olmec Yogis with Hindu beliefs: Did They Migrate from Ancient China?." Ancient Inquiries, August 31, 2016. https://www.bibhudevmisra.com/2016/08/olmec-yogis-with-hindu-beliefs-did-they.html.

476. Recino, Adrián, trans. *POPOL VUH: "The Book of the People."* Translated into English by Delia Goetz and Sylvanus Griswold Morley. Los Angeles: Plantin Press, 1954, p. 52.

477. Bender, Chris. "Speakers Discuss Ancient Cultures." Student Media Company, March 31, 2000. https://web.archive.org/web/20010807013907/http://dailycampus.smu.edu/HTMLPages/Spring00/03-31-00/news4_0331.html.

478."La Venta." Wikipedia. https://en.wikipedia.org/wiki/La_Venta.

479."Chinese Pyramids." Wikipedia. https://en.wikipedia.org/wiki/Chinese_pyramids.

480."Xi'an." Wikipedia. https://en.wikipedia.org/wiki/Xi'an.

481. Doutré, "The Chinese Pyramids at Xi'an."

482. Lewis, Ricardo. "Does Chinese Civilization Come from Ancient Egypt?." FP, September 2, 2016. https://foreignpolicy.com/2016/09/02/did-chinese-civilization-come-from-ancient-egypt-archeological-debate-at-heart-of-china-national-identity/.

483."China and Egypt. Cradles of the World." Staatliche Museen zu Berlin. https://www.smb.museum/en/exhibitions/detail/china-and-egypt-cradles-of-the-world.html.

484."Amenmesse." Wikipedia. https://en.wikipedia.org/wiki/Amenmesse.

485."Khasekhemwy." Wikipedia. https://en.wikipedia.org/wiki/Khasekhemwy.

486.Temple, *Egyptian Dawn*, 103-104, 110.

487."A Meeting of Civilisations: The Mystery of China's Celtic Mummies." Independent, August 28, 2006. https://www.independent.co.uk/news/world/asia/a-meeting-of-civilisations-the-mystery-of-chinas-celtic-mummies-5330366.html.

488. Ibid.

489."Golden Hat." Wikipedia. https://en.wikipedia.org/wiki/Golden_hat.

490."A Meeting of Civilisations." Independent.

491. Ibid.

492. Ibid.

493."Tarim Mummies." Wikipedia. https://en.wikipedia.org/wiki/Tarim_mummies.

494."Centum and Satem Languages." Wikipedia. https://en.wikipedia.org/wiki/Centum_and_satem_languages.

495. Adams, Douglas Q. "Tocharian Languages." Britannica. https://www.britannica.com/topic/Tocharian-languages.

496. Gray, Russell D., Quentin D. Atkinson, and Simon J. Greenhill. "Language Evolution and Human History: What a Difference a Date Makes." *Phil. Trans. R. Soc. B* 366, (2011): 1090-1100. https://doi.org/10.1098/rstb.2010.0378. 1092.

497. Li, Chunxiang, Hongjie Li, Yinqiu Cui, Chengzhi Xie, Dawei Cai, Wenying Li, Victor H Mair, et al. "Evidence That a West-East Admixed Population Lived in the Tarim Basin as Early as the Early Bronze Age." *BMC Biology* 8, no. 15 (2010). https://doi.org/10.1186/1741-7007-8-15.

498. Hay, "Haplogroup R1a (Y-DNA)."

499."Afanasievo Culture." Wikipedia. https://en.wikipedia.org/wiki/Afanasievo_culture; Narasimhan, Vagheesh M., Nick Patterson, Priya Moorjani, Nadin Rohland, Rebecca Bernardos, Swapan Mallick, Iosif Lazaridis, et al. "The Formation of Human Populations in South and Central Asia." *Science* 365, no. 6457 (2019). https://doi.org/10.1126/science.aat7487.

500.Adams, "Tocharian Languages."

501."Emperor of Japan." Wikipedia. https://en.wikipedia.org/wiki/Emperor_of_Japan.

502. Heyerdahl, *Early Man and the Ocean*, 84.

503. Kennedy, *White Indians of Nivaria*, 81.

504. Patrón, *Nouvelles Etudes sur les Langues Américaines*, 332.

505. Heyerdahl, *Easter Island: The Mystery Solved*, 217.

506. Heyerdahl, *Aku-Aku*, 30.

507. "Manu." Britannica. https://www.britannica.com/topic/Manu.

508. Heyerdahl, *Aku-Aku*, 75.

509. Ibid., 356-358.

510. Ibid., 358.

511. "Bell Beaker Buddha? (The Samborzec Sage)." Bell Beaker Blogger, June 20, 2017. http://bellbeakerblogger.blogspot.com/2017/06/bell-beaker-buddah-samborzec-sage.html.

512. Budge, E. A. Wallis, trans. "The Chapter of Changing into a Lotus." In *The Book of the Dead: Papyrus of Ani*. Vol. II. New York: G. P. Putnam's Sons, 1913, p. 557.

513. Atwood with Atwood, *Ancient Solstice*, 325.

514. Easwaran, Eknath, trans. *The Upanishads*. 2nd ed. Tomales: Nilgiri Press, 2007, p. 143-144.

515. Reymond, *Mythical Origin of the Egyptian Temple*, 83 (see chap. 2, n. 49).

516. Atwood with Atwood, *Ancient Solstice*, 46-64.

517. Serith, "Proto-Indo-European Deities."

518. Diodorus, *Library of History*, 2.47.1-6 (see chap. 2, n. 19).

519. Scholfield, A. F., trans. *Aelian: On the Characteristics of Animals*. Vol. II. London: William Heinemann, 1959, p. 357, 359. Found at Atsma, Aaron J. "Hyperborea." Theoi Project. http://www.theoi.com/Phylos/Hyperborea.html.

520. Trautz, Nick. "Shambhala in the Kalachakra Tantra." Shambhala Times, October 28, 2018. https://shambhalatimes.org/2018/10/28/shambhala-in-the-kalachakra-tantra/.

521. "Shambhala." Wikipedia. https://en.wikipedia.org/wiki/Shambhala.

522. Trimondi, Victor, and Victoria Trimondi. "The Shadow of the Dalai Lama – Part I – 10. The Aggressive Myth of Shambhala." Translated by Mark Penny. 2003. http://www.trimondi.de/SDLE/Part-1-10.htm.

523. Trautz, "Shambhala in the Kalachakra Tantra."

524. Gurdjieff, *Meetings with Remarkable Men*, 150 (see chap. 2, n. 146).

525. Ibid., 90-91.

526. Ibid., 90.

527. Ibid.

528. Ibid., 156, 158.

529. Ibid., 236-238.

530. Gopalakrishnan, V. S. "The Strange History of Kafiristan." Sulekha, 2010. http://creative.sulekha.com/the-strange-history-of-kafiristan_459575_blog.

531. Gurdjieff, *Meetings with Remarkable Men*, 239, 241.

532. Ouspensky, *In Search of the Miraculous*, 22 (see chap. 3, n. 52).

533. Azize, Joseph. "Solar Mysticism in Gurdjieff and Neoplatonism." *Crossroads* 5, no. 1, (2010): 18-26.

534. Paine, Thomas. "Origin of Free-Masonry." In *Writings of Thomas Paine*. Edited by Moncure Daniels Conway. G.P. Putnam's Sons, 1896.

535. "United States Masonic Founding Fathers." Freemason Information. http://freemasoninformation.com/masonic-education/famous/united-states-masonic-founding-fathers/.

536. Snyder, G. W. "To George Washington from G. W. Snyder, 22 August 1798." Founders Online. https://founders.archives.gov/documents/Washington/06-02-02-0435.

537. "Late Bronze Age Collapse." Wikipedia. https://en.wikipedia.org/wiki/Late_Bronze_Age_collapse.

538. Ibid.

539. Ibid.

540. "Origins of the 'Sea Peoples' – The Sherden, the Shekelesh, the Peleset." Cogniarchae, June 30, 2018. https://cogniarchae.com/2018/06/30/origins-of-the-sea-peoples -the-sherden-the-shekelesh-the-peleset/.

541. "On Fomorians, Pomeranians and Sea People." Cogniarchae, October 27, 2016. https:// cogniarchae.com/2016/10/27/on-fomorians-pomeranians-and-sea-people/.

542. *The Kolbrin*, 447.

543. Bower, Bruce. "Massacre at Sacred Ridge Sparks Debate about Prehistoric Genocide." Archaeology News Network, October 22, 2010. https://archaeologynewsnetwork.blogspot. com.au/2010/10/massacre-at-sacred-ridge-sparks-debate.html.

544. Ibid.

545. "BRIA 18 4 c Climate Change and Violence in the Ancient American Southwest." Constitutional Rights Foundation. https://www.crf-usa.org/bill-of-rights-in-action/ bria-18-4-c-climate-change-and-violence-in-the-ancient-american-southwest.

546. 1874 Hayden Survey. Quotes: Ingersoll, Ernest. *New York Tribune*, November 3, 1874. http:// www.crowcanyon.org/researchreports/castlerock/text/crpw_oralhistory.asp.

547. Human Sacrifice in Aztec Culture." Wikipedia. https://en.wikipedia.org/wiki/ Human_sacrifice_in_Aztec_culture.

548. Heyerdahl, *Early Man and the Ocean*, 123.

549. "Paracas Culture." Wikipedia. https://en.wikipedia.org/wiki/Paracas_culture.

550. Vega, Garcilaso de la. *Royal Commentaries of the Incas and General History of Peru, Volume 1 and Volume 2*. Translated by Harold V. Livermore. University of Texas Press, 1989, chapter I, location 9682. Kindle edition.

551. Ibid.

552. "Chachapoya Culture." Wikipedia. https://en.wikipedia.org/wiki/Chachapoya_culture.

553. Vega, *Royal Commentaries*, chapter XXXVII, locations 4841, 12333, 12351.

554. Heyerdal, *Aku-Aku*, 124.

555. Ibid., 123.

556. Ibid.

557. Ibid., 75.

558. Ibid., 151.

559. Ibid., 74-75.

560. Doutré, Martin. "Bes of Egypt & Taranaich-Thor of Europe in the Ancient South Pacific." Ancient Celtic New Zealand. http://www.celticnz.co.nz/Bes & Thor/Bes&Taranis.htm.

561. Chapman, Paul. "Tribe Wins Justice over 1835 Massacre." The Telegraph, June 16, 2001. https:// www.telegraph.co.uk/news/worldnews/australiaandthepacific/newzealand/1312121/ Tribe-wins-justice-over-1835-massacre.html.

562. Annikal. "The Moriori Genocide." Infogram. https://infogram.com/ the-moriori-genocide-1g143mn34x53pzy.

563. "Ran Min." Wikipedia. https://en.wikipedia.org/wiki/Ran_Min.

564. "Military Campaigns of Julius Caesar." Wikipedia. https://en.wikipedia.org/wiki/ Military_campaigns_of_Julius_Caesar.

565. "Julian (Emperor)." Wikipedia. https://en.wikipedia.org/wiki/Julian_(emperor).

566. "Persecution of Pagans in the Late Roman Empire." Wikipedia. https://en.wikipedia.org/ wiki/Persecution_of_pagans_in_the_late_Roman_Empire.

567. "Edict of Thessalonica." Wikipedia. https://en.wikipedia.org/wiki/Edict_of_Thessalonica.

568. "Persecution of Pagans in the Late Roman Empire." Wikipedia.

569. Kennedy, *White Indians of Nivaria*, 7, 29.

570. "Itzcoatl." Wikipedia. https://en.wikipedia.org/wiki/Itzcoatl.

571. Hancock, *Magicians of the Gods*, 38, 86.

572. Oh-Willeke, Andrew. "The Holocene Climate Events That Shaped Prehistory and Ancient History." Dispatches From Turtle Island, March 2, 2014. http://dispatchesfromturtleisland. blogspot.com/2014/03/the-holocene-climate-events-that-shaped.html.

573. For example, see papers by Joachim Seifert and Frank Lemke: http://www.knowledgeminer. eu/climate/papers.html.

574. Misra, Bibhu Dev. "The Comet Impact in the Indian Ocean That May Have Submerged Dwaraka." Ancient Inquiries, April 18, 2018. https://www.bibhudevmisra.com/2018/04/the-comet-impact-in-indian-ocean-that.html.

575. Thompson, *To the American Indian*.

CHAPTER FIVE: THE CHILDREN OF THE SUN

1. Hancock and Faiia, *Heaven's Mirror*, 318 (see chap. 2, n. 53).

2. Plato, *Critias* (see chap. 2, n. 94).

3. Perry, William James. *The Growth of Civilization*. 2nd ed. London: Methuen & Co. Ltd, 1926, p. 177.

4. Perry, William James. *The Children of the Sun: A Study in the Early History of Civilization*. London: Methuen & Co. Ltd, 1923, p. 64. https://archive.org/details/in.ernet.dli.2015.283090.

5. *The Kolbrin*, 21 (see chap. 1, n. 21).

6. Tomas, Andrew. *Shambhala: Oasis of Light*. London: Sphere, 1977, p. 146.

7. *The Holy Bible*. King James Version (KJV). Genesis 1:26.

8. *Stanzas of Dzyan* (see chap. 2, n. 78).

9. *The Kolbrin*, 22.

10. *Stanzas of Dzyan*.

11. *The Kolbrin*, 48.

12. Grobe, Hannes. "File:Iceage north-intergl glac hg.png." Wikipedia. https://en.wikipedia. org/wiki/File:Iceage_north-intergl_glac_hg.png. Ice coverage: Ehlers, J., and P. L. Gibbard. "The Extent and Chronology of Cenozoic Global Glaciation." *Quaternary International* (June 20 2007): 164-165. Topography: U.S. Department of Commerce, NOAA/NGDC. "2-Minute Gridded Global Relief Data (ETOPO2)." 2006. Map software: Schlitzer, R. Ocean Data View. 2007. http://odv.awi.de.

13. Carlson, Randall. "Pole Shifts, Hapgood, Floods, Impacts & Atlantis -Cosmography101-33.1 with Randall Carlson Dec'08." YouTube, October 30, 2019, 17:45-32:00. https://youtu. be/39nwDNaaupM.

14. Dewhurst, Richard. "February 2014 AOM: The Ancient Giants Who Ruled America." GrahamHancock.com, January 31, 2014. https://grahamhancock.com/dewhurstr1/.

15. See Jim Vieira and Hugh Newman, *Giants on Record*, for the thousands of accounts in America alone.

16. "Yuga." Wikipedia. https://en.wikipedia.org/wiki/Yuga.

17. "Five Suns." Wikipedia. https://en.wikipedia.org/wiki/Five_Suns.

18. Jarrell, Jason, and Sarah Farmer. "The Giant Deception." Road2Ruins.com, January 14, 2016. http:///road2ruins.com/the-giant-deception/.

19. Vieira, Jim, and Hugh Newman. *Giants on Record: America's Hidden History, Secrets in the Mounds and the Smithsonian Files*. Glastonbury: Avalon Rising Publications, 2015, p. xiii in Preface by Ross Hamilton.

20. Dewhurst, "The Ancient Giants Who Ruled America."

21. Ibid.

22. Panther-Yates, "White People Behaving Badly and Ancient Giants" (see chap. 4, n. 278).

23. Cartwright, Mark. "Viracocha." Ancient History Encyclopedia, February 23, 2014. https://www.ancient.eu/Viracocha/.

24. Brodeur, Arthur Gilchrist, trans. *The Prose Edda*. New York: The American-Scandinavian Foundation, 1916. http://www.sacred-texts.com/neu/pre/pre04.htm.

25. Halvorsen, Ingrid. "Norse Gods, Goddesses, Giants, Dwarves & Wights." Runes, Alphabet of Mystery. http://www.sunnyway.com/runes/gods3.html.

26. "Titan (Mythology)." Wikipedia. https://en.wikipedia.org/wiki/Titan_(mythology).

27. "Anunnaki." Wikipedia. https://en.wikipedia.org/wiki/Anunnaki.

28. "Daitya." Hindupedia. http://www.hindupedia.com/en/Daitya.

29. "Asura." Wikipedia. https://en.wikipedia.org/wiki/Asura.

30. "Daitya." Hindupedia.

31. Colavito, Jason. "Akhbār al-Zamān." JasonColavito.com, 2015. http://www.jasoncolavito.com/akhbar-al-zaman.html. Translation by Jason Colavito.

32. Ibid.

33. Ibid.

34. "Dynastic Race Theory." Wikipedia. https://en.wikipedia.org/wiki/Dynastic_race_theory.

35. "Mairu." Wikipedia. https://en.wikipedia.org/wiki/Mairu.

36. "Giants (Welsh Folklore)." Wikipedia. https://en.wikipedia.org/wiki/Giants_(Welsh_folklore).

37. Hamilton, "A Tradition of Giants," 14 (see chap. 4, n. 298).

38. Latham, John. "Soviets and Sun-Gods: The Changing Uses of an 'Alan' Nart Saga." Academia.edu, 2015. https://www.academia.edu/14078753.

39. "Scythians." Wikipedia. https://en.wikipedia.org/wiki/Scythians.

40. Wilford, John Noble. "Mummies, Textiles Offer Evidence of Europeans in Far East." *New York Times*, May 7, 1996. https://www.nytimes.com/1996/05/07/science/mummies-textiles-offer-evidence-of-europeans-in-far-east.html.

41. Hughes, Samuel. "When West Went East." *The Pennsylvania Gazette*, January | February 2011. https://www.upenn.edu/gazette/0111/PennGaz0111_feature2.pdf.

42. "Neolithic Revolution." Wikipedia. https://en.wikipedia.org/wiki/Neolithic_Revolution.

43. McCoy, Daniel. "Giants." Norse Mythology for Smart People. https://norse-mythology.org/gods-and-creatures/giants/.

44. Brinton, *American Hero-Myths* (see chap. 2, n. 143).

45. *The Kolbrin*, 27.

46. Ibid., 788, 790-791, 794.

47. Whiteman, "Was This Eden?" (see chap. 2, n. 61).

48. Ibid.

49. *The Kolbrin*, 28.

50. Whiteman, "Guide to the Kolbrin" (see chap. 2, n. 57).

51. *The Kolbrin*, 57.

52. *The Holy Bible*. New King James Version (NKJV). Thomas Nelson, 1982.

53. "Nephilim." Wikipedia. https://en.wikipedia.org/wiki/Nephilim.

54. "Land of Manu." Wikipedia. https://en.wikipedia.org/wiki/Land_of_Manu.

55. "Rigveda." Wikipedia. https://en.wikipedia.org/wiki/Rigveda.

56. *The Kolbrin*, 34, 57. The names in *The Kolbrin* are Netar, which may either be the same as the Mesopotamian god Namtar or Nergal, and Enkigal, which is likely the Mesopotamian god Enki.

57. "Anunnaki." Wikipedia.

58. Plato, *Critias*.

59. *Stanzas of Dzyan*.

60. *The Kolbrin*, 16, 18.

61. Ibid., 29.

62. Recino, trans., *POPOL VUH*, 8 (see chap. 4, n. 476).

63. Ibid., 49-50.

64. Ibid., 50.

65. *The Kolbrin*, 30.

66. Ibid., 47.

67. Ibid., 84.

68. Castro, Joseph. "Homo Floresiensis: Facts about the 'Hobbit'." LiveScience, March 30, 2016. https://www.livescience.com/29100-homo-floresiensis-hobbit-facts.html.

69. Callaway, Ewen. "Evidence Mounts for Interbreeding Bonanza in Ancient Human Species." Nature.com, February 17, 2016. https://doi.org/10.1038/nature.2016.19394.

70. Reich, *Who We Are and How We Got Here*, 89, 91 (see chap. 2, n. 86).

71. Ibid., 89.

72. Ibid., 99.

73. Ibid., Chap. 4.

74. Ibid., 84.

75. "Evidence." Sirius Disclosure. https://siriusdisclosure.com/evidence/.

76. Andrew, Scottie. "The US Navy Just Confirmed These UFO Videos Are the Real Deal." CNN, September 18, 2019. https://www.cnn.com/2019/09/18/politics/navy-confirms-ufo-videos-trnd/index.html.

77. To The Stars Academy of Arts & Science. "Gimbal: The First Official UAP Footage from the USG for Public Release." YouTube, December 16, 2017. https://youtu.be/tfluLwUTDA0; To The Stars Academy of Arts & Science. "FLIR1: Official UAP Footage from the USG for Public Release." YouTube, December 16, 2017. https://youtu.be/6rWOtrke0HY; To The Stars Academy of Arts & Science. "Go Fast: Official USG Footage of UAP for Public Release." YouTube, March 9, 2018. https://youtu.be/wxVRg7LLaQA.

78. Fish, Tom. "UFO Proof? Pentagon FINALLY Admits Previous Alien Spacecraft Investigations." Express, May 23, 2019. https://www.express.co.uk/news/weird/1131196/ufo-proof-pentagon-alien-spacecraft-investigations.

79. To The Stars Academy of Arts & Science, "Gimbal: The First Official UAP Footage."

80. Conte, Michael. "Pentagon Officially Releases UFO Videos." CNN, April 29, 2020. https://www.cnn.com/2020/04/27/politics/pentagon-ufo-videos/index.html.

81. Atwood, Lara. "Making Contact with Extraterrestrials Through Other Dimensions." Sakro Sawel, August 17, 2013. https://sakrosawel.com/making-contact-with-extraterrestrials-through-other-dimensions/; Atwood, Lara. "Extraterrestrial Contact Experience with Dr Steven Greer." Sakro Sawel, August 21, 2013. https://sakrosawel.com/extraterrestrial-contact-experience-with-dr-steven-greer/.

82. Greer, Steven M. *Hidden Truth: Forbidden Knowledge*. Chap. 39. Kindle edition.

83. *The Kolbrin*, 353.

CHAPTER SIX: JESUS AND THE RELIGION OF THE SUN

1. "Jesus." Wikipedia. https://en.wikipedia.org/wiki/Jesus.

2. *The Holy Bible*. Lexham English Bible (LEB). Logos Bible Software, 2012.

3. Stern, David H., trans. *Complete Jewish Bible* (CJB). Messianic Jewish Publishers, 1998.

4. "Massacre of Verden." Wikipedia. https://en.wikipedia.org/wiki/Massacre_of_Verden.

5. "Jesus in the Talmud." Wikipedia. https://en.wikipedia.org/wiki/Jesus_in_the_Talmud.

6. McGrath, James F. "Notsrim in the Talmud: Mandaeans, Christians, or Both?" Patheos, August 6, 2014. https://www.patheos.com/blogs/religionprof/2014/08/notsrim-in-the-talmud-mandaeans-christians-or-both.html.

7. *The Holy Bible*. New International Version (NIV). Biblica, 2011.

8. *The Kolbrin*, 780 (see chap. 1, n. 21).

9. See the work of scholar Bart D. Ehrman.

10. "Sun God from the First Temple." Old European Culture, September 25, 2017. https://oldeuropeanculture.blogspot.com/2017/09/sun-god-from-first-temple.html.

11. *The Holy Bible.* New International Version (NIV). Biblica, 2011.

12. Ibid.

13. Ibid., 2 Kings 23:4-5, 11.

14. "Sun God from the First Temple." Old European Culture.

15. New World Encyclopedia contributors. "Akhenaten." New World Encyclopedia. https://www.newworldencyclopedia.org/entry/Akhenaten.

16. "Moses and Monotheism." Wikipedia. https://en.wikipedia.org/wiki/Moses_and_Monotheism.

17. Lönnqvist, Kenneth, and Minna Lönnqvist. "Spatial Approach to the Ruins of Khirbet Qumran at the Dead Sea." *XXth ISPRS Congress Technical Commission V* (July 12-23, 2004): 558-563. https://www.isprs.org/proceedings/XXXV/congress/comm5/papers/616.pdf.

18. "Sun God from the First Temple." Old European Culture.

19. "Qumran Calendrical Texts." Wikipedia. https://en.wikipedia.org/wiki/Qumran_calendrical_texts.

20. "Qumran Sundial." Madain Project, April 26, 2019. https://madainproject.com/qumran_sundial.

21. Whiston, William, 1667-1752, trans. *The Wars of the Jews, or The History of the Destruction of Jerusalem*, by Flavius Josephus, 75 AD. https://www.gutenberg.org/files/2850/2850-h/2850-h.htm; https://en.wikiquote.org/wiki/Josephus_on_the_Essenes.

22. "Sun God from the First Temple." Old European Culture.

23. "Bar and Bat Mitzvah." Wikipedia. https://en.wikipedia.org/wiki/Bar_and_bat_mitzvah.

24. "Unknown Years of Jesus." Wikipedia. https://en.wikipedia.org/wiki/Unknown_years_of_Jesus.

25. *The Kolbrin*, 776.

26. "Mandaeans." Wikipedia. https://en.wikipedia.org/wiki/Mandaeans.

27. Dower, E. S. *The Mandaeans of Iraq and Iran.* Leiden: Brill, 1962. http://gnosis.org/library/manda-dower-1937.html.

28. Smith, William Benjamin. "Meaning of the Epithet Nazorean (Nazarene)." *The Monist* 15, no. 1 (1905): 25-45. https://www.jstor.org/stable/pdf/27899560.pdf.

29. McGrath, "Notsrim in the Talmud."

30. Rudolph, Kurt. "Mandaeans ii. The Mandaean Religion." Encyclopædia Iranica, 2012. http://www.iranicaonline.org/articles/mandaeans-2-religion.

31. Dower, *The Mandaeans*.

32. Ibid.

33. Ibid.

34. Rudolph, "The Mandaean Religion."

35. Gündüz, Şinasi. "The Problems of the Nature and Date of Mandaean Sources." *Journal for the Study of the New Testament* 16, no. 53 (1994): 87-97. https://doi.org/10.1177/0142064X9401605305.

36. Dower, *The Mandaeans*.

37. "Edmond Bordeaux Szekely." Wikipedia. https://en.wikipedia.org/wiki/Edmond_Bordeaux_Szekely.

38. "Essenes." Wikipedia. https://en.wikipedia.org/wiki/Essenes.

39. Wolfe, George. *Parallel Teachings in Hinduism and Christianity.* Austin: JOMAR Press, 1995. http://lib.bsu.edu/beneficencepress/exhibitsperformances/wolfe/word/parallelteachings.pdf.

40. Johnsen, Linda. "Gnostic Texts Reveal Jesus in a New Light." Yoga International. https://yogainternational.com/article/view/gnostic-texts-reveal-jesus-in-a-new-light/.

41. Albrile, Ezio. "Zoroaster at Nag-Hammadi." The Circle of Ancient Iranian Studies. https://www.cais-soas.com/CAIS/Religions/iranian/Zarathushtrian/zoroastian_nag_hammadi.htm.

42. See the ancient Gnostic text Pistis Sophia, which recounts the story of the soul and its struggle for salvation from hell. It's similar to the story of the Greek goddess Persephone, who also symbolized the descent of the soul into the underworld, and its salvation from it.

43. Atwood with Atwood, *Ancient Solstice* (see chap. 1, n. 1). We describe many of these similarities in our book.

44. See the ancient Gnostic text Pistis Sophia.

45. "If Jesus Never Called Himself God, How Did He Become One?." NPR, April 7, 2014. https://www.npr.org/2014/04/07/300246095/if-jesus-never-called-himself-god-how-did-he-become-one.

46. *The Kolbrin*, 771.

47. Atwood with Atwood, *Ancient Solstice*, 28-31, 148.

48. Ibid., 150.

CHAPTER SEVEN: SUMMARY OF THE FOUNDING OF THE ANCIENT RELIGION OF THE SUN

1. Martin, Robert D. "Strange Head Shapes: Revisiting Nefertiti, Akhenaten and Tut." Psychology Today, July 30, 2019. https://www.psychologytoday.com/us/blog/how-we-do-it/201907/strange-head-shapes-revisiting-nefertiti-akhenaten-and-tut.

2. New World Encyclopedia contributors. "Hermeticism." New World Encyclopedia, December 22, 2017. https://www.newworldencyclopedia.org/entry/Hermeticism.

CHAPTER EIGHT: WHY DID ANCIENT PEOPLE VENERATE THE SUN?

1. Swami Krishnananda, trans. "Narayana Sukta." In *Daily Invocations*. Rishikesh: The Divine Life Society.

2. Easwaran, trans., *The Upanishads* (see chap. 4, n. 514).

3. Walker, Brian Browne, trans. *The Tao Te Ching of Lao Tzu*. New York: St. Martin's Press, 1995.

4. Hall, *Secret Teachings of All Ages* (see chap. 2, n. 92).

5. Atwood with Atwood, *Ancient Solstice*, 17-18 (see chap. 1, n. 1).

6. Walker, Brian Browne, trans. *Hua Hu Ching: The Unknown Teachings of Lao Tzu*. San Francisco: HarperCollins, 1995.

7. Hall, *Secret Teachings of All Ages*.

8. Atwood with Atwood, *Ancient Solstice*, 18-19.

9. Giles, Lionel, trans. *The Sayings of Lao-Tzŭ*. Edited by L. Cranmer-Byng and Dr. S. A. Kapadia. New York: E. P. Dutton and Company, 1905, p. 19.

10. Easwaran, trans., *The Upanishads*.

11. Atwood with Atwood, *Ancient Solstice*, 31-32.

12. Ibid., 39.

13. Easwaran, trans., *The Upanishads*.

14. Cowell, E. B., trans. *The Maitri or Maitrāyanīya Upanishad*. Calcutta: Asiatic Society of Bengal, 1870.

15. Easwaran, trans., *The Upanishads*.

16. Atwood with Atwood, *Ancient Solstice*, 26-27.

17. Ibid., 125-126.

18. Ibid., 39-40.

19. Ibid., 29.

20. Frawley, *Gods, Sages and Kings*, 168-69 (see chap. 2, n. 2).

21. Budge, E. A. Wallis, trans. *The Book of the Dead: The Papyrus of Ani*. British Museum, 1895, p. liii.

22. "Electric Sun Theory." Electric Universe Theory Project. https://www.electricuniverse.info/electric-sun-theory/.

23. Waters, *Book of the Hopi*, 161 (see chap. 2, n. 79).

24. "Brahma." Wikipedia. https://en.wikipedia.org/wiki/Brahma.

25. "Sun, Thunder, Fire." Old European Culture, June 17, 2017. http://oldeuropeanculture.blogspot.com/2017/06/sun-thunder-fire.html.

26. *The Kolbrin*, 236 (see chap. 1, n. 21).

27. Szekely, Edmond Bordeaux, trans. *The Essene Gospel of Peace: Book One*. International Biogenic Society, 1981, p. 13.

28. Cassaro, Richard. "Pagan 'God Self' Icon Found Worldwide Rewrites History, Reveals Lost Golden Age." RichardCassaro.com, October 15, 2013. https://www.richardcassaro.com/pagan-god-self-icon-found-worldwide-rewrites-history-reveals-lost-golden-age-religion/.

29. Mastin, Luke. "Handedness and the Brain." Right Left Right Wrong?, 2012. https://www.rightleftrightwrong.com/brain.html.

30. My husband Mark's work on self-knowledge.

31. Atwood with Atwood, *Ancient Solstice*, 335.

32. Ibid., 303.

33. Ibid., 279-280, 291.

34. My husband Mark's work on self-knowledge.

35. My husband Mark's work on self-knowledge.

36. "Aker (Deity)." Wikipedia. https://en.wikipedia.org/wiki/Aker_(deity).

37. Paracelsus, quoted in Hall, *Secret Teachings of All Ages*, 40.

CHAPTER NINE: REVIVAL

1. "Stonehenge Summer Solstice: Thousands Gather to Cheer Sunrise." BBC, June 21, 2019. https://www.bbc.com/news/uk-england-wiltshire-48703632.

2. "The One Tree Project." The Order of Bards, Ovates & Druids, August 19, 2015. https://www.druidry.org//events-projects/one-tree-project.

3. "Willkakuti." Wikipedia. https://en.wikipedia.org/wiki/Willkakuti.

4. "'Kitzit' – Laguna Youth Dance Group." Native Pathways, February 24, 2015. http://www.nativepathways-edu.net/kitzit-laguna-youth-dance-group/.

5. Spadaccini, Jim. "Solstice Dancers at Chaco Canyon." Friends of Chaco, June 1, 2015. http://friendsofchaco.org/solstice-dances-at-chaco-canyon.

6. Bakhtavar, Slater. "Millennial Iranians Bring Back Their Persian Roots." Forbes, November 18, 2016. https://www.forbes.com/sites/realspin/2016/11/18/millennial-iranians-bring-back-their-persian-roots.

7. Ravji, Zenobia. "The Religion That the Iranian Mullahs Fear Most." Swarajya, March 29, 2017. https://swarajyamag.com/culture/the-religion-that-the-iranian-mullahs-fear-most.

APPENDIX

1. Heyerdahl, *Easter Island: The Mystery Solved*, 96 (see chap. 3, n. 62).

2. Bitto, Robert. "The Gigantic Atlantean Statues of the Toltecs." Mexico Unexplained, October 24, 2016. http://mexicounexplained.com/gigantic-atlantean-statues-toltecs/.

3. Hill, Jenny. "The Ancient Egyptian Soul." Ancient Egypt Online, 2017. https://ancientegyptonline.co.uk/soul/.

4. "Moai." Wikipedia. https://en.wikipedia.org/wiki/Moai.

5. Childress, *Lost World of Cham* (see chap. 4, n. 400).

6. "Easter Island." Wikipedia. https://en.wikipedia.org/wiki/Easter_Island.

7. Hancock and Faiia, *Heaven's Mirror*, 178 (see chap. 2, n. 53).

8. Cooper, Anderson. "Easter Island's Famous Moai Statues Slowly Fading Away." 60 Minutes, April 21, 2019. https://www.cbsnews.com/news/easter-island-heads-famous-moai-statues-slowly-fading-away-60-minutes-2019-04-21/.

9. Nash, Nathaniel C. "The Mysteries of Easter Island." *New York Times*, July 11, 1993. https://www.nytimes.com/1993/07/11/travel/the-mysteries-of-easter-island.html.

10. "Moai." Wikipedia.

11. Atwood with Atwood, *Ancient Solstice*, 97-102, 139-143, 198 (see chap. 1, n. 1).

12. Heyerdahl, *Easter Island: The Mystery Solved*, 88.

13. Kandil, "The Function and Symbolism of the Akh," 2 (see chap. 3, n. 69).

14. "Tula (Mesoamerican Site)." Wikipedia. https://en.wikipedia.org/wiki/Tula_(Mesoamerican_site).

IMAGE REFERENCES

All Creative Commons works in this book are derivatives which have been processed with cropping, rotation, and/or other image adjustments.

Image credits are listed by page number.

MISC

Chapter Headings: Solar Cross. Symbol re-created by Sura Ondrunar Publishing based on petroglyph at the Three Rivers Petroglyph Site in New Mexico, USA.

PREFACE

4. Left: Varma, Raja Ravi. *Kali,* before 1906. Wikimedia Commons, 2012. https://en.wikipedia.org/wiki/File:Kali_by_Raja_Ravi_Varma.jpg. Public domain.

4. Right: Luidger, photographer. *Statue of Coatlicue,* National Anthropology Museum, Mexico City, 2004. Wikimedia Commons, 2004. https://commons.wikimedia.org/wiki/File:20041229- Coatlicue (Museo Nacional de Antropología) MQ-3.jpg. CC BY-SA 3.0.

CHAPTER ONE: THE ANCIENT RELIGION OF THE SUN

10. Artist unknown. *Anch and Sunwheel.* In *Book of the Dead of Ani*, frame 2, Vignette of sunrise, circa 19th Dynasty (1292 to 1189 BC), British Museum. Wikimedia Commons, 2006. https://commons.wikimedia.org/wiki/File:Totenbuch.jpg. Public domain.

13. Collage top image 1: Egorov, Valery, photographer. *View of West Facade of Chartres Cathedral.* Shutterstock.com. https://www.shutterstock.com/image-photo/view-west-facade-chartres-cathedral-1076537756. Licensed from Shutterstock.com.

13. Collage top image 2: HelloRF Zcool, photographer. *Guangzhou Shushe Sacred Heart Cathedral.* Shutterstock.com. https://www.shutterstock.com/image-photo/guangzhou-shushe-sacred-heart-cathedral-1173463153. Licensed from Shutterstock.com.

13. Collage top image 3: F11photo, photographer. *St. John the Baptist Cathedral in Savannah,* Georgia USA. Shutterstock.com. https://www.shutterstock.com/image-photo/st-john-baptist- cathedral-savannah-georgia-493931884. Licensed from Shutterstock.com.

13. Collage top image 4: Ravi, Joe, photographer. *St. Philomena's Church Is a Catholic Church Built in Honour of St. Philomena in Mysore.* Shutterstock.com. https://www.shutterstock.com/ image-photo/guangzhou-shushe-sacred-heart-cathedral-1173463153. Licensed from Shutterstock.com.

13. Collage bottom image 1: Hendrikse, Boyd, photographer. *Cristo de la Concordia (Christ of Peace) Is a Statue of Jesus Christ Located atop San Pedro Hill, to the East of Cochabamba*, Bolivia. Shutterstock.com. https://www.shutterstock.com/image-photo/cristo-de-la-concordia-christ-peace-192340583. Licensed from Shutterstock.com.

13. Collage bottom image 2: Petrova, Maria, photographer. *Famous Statue of the Christ the Reedemer, Lubango Angola.* Shutterstock.com. https://www.shutterstock.com/image-photo/famous-statue-christ-reedemer-lubango-angola-21157789. Licensed from Shutterstock.com.

13. Collage bottom image 3: Catay, photographer. *Jesus Statue in Beirut 4 February 2018.* Shutterstock.com. https://www.shutterstock.com/image-photo/jesus-statue-beirut-4-february-2018-1041517408. Licensed from Shutterstock.com.

13. Collage bottom image 4: Lashkov, Fedor, photographer. *The Christian Park in Essentuki.* Shutterstock.com. https://www.shutterstock.com/image-photo/christian-park-essentuki-669164776. Licensed from Shutterstock.com.

14. Collage, top left: Bon, Jerome, photographer. *Great Pyramid of Giza,* Egypt, 2008. Wikimedia Commons, 2015. https://commons.wikimedia.org/wiki/File:Great_Pyramid_of_Giza_(2427530661).jpg. CC BY 2.0.

14. Collage, top center: Skubasteve834, photographer. *Monks Mound,* Collinsville, Illinois, 2007. Wikimedia Commons, 2013. https://commons.wikimedia.org/wiki/File:Monks_Mound_in_July.JPG. CC BY-SA-3.0.

14. Collage, top right: Brücke-Osteuropa, photographer. *Pingling,* 2011. Wikimedia Commons, 2011. https://de.wikipedia.org/wiki/Datei:Pingling_1.jpg. Public domain.

14. Collage, second left: Schwen, Daniel, photographer. *Chichen Itza,* Mexico, 2009. Wikimedia Commons, 2009. https://commons.wikimedia.org/wiki/File:Chichen_Itza_3.jpg. CC BY-SA 4.0.

14. Collage, second center: Peaceofangkor, photographer. *Prang (Behind Prasat Thom)* Koh Ker, Cambodia, 2006. Wikimedia Commons, 2006. https://commons.wikimedia.org/wiki/File:0505280017PThompyramid.jpg. Public domain.

14. Collage, second right: Ximenez, Pedro, photographer. *Pyramid Güimar,* Canary Islands, Spain, 1998. Wikimedia Commons, 2009. https://commons.wikimedia.org/wiki/File:Pyramide Güimar.jpg. CC BY-SA 2.0.

14. Collage, third left: Wilson, Captain W. *Marae Mahaiatea on Tahiti Island,* 1799, British Museum. Wikimedia Commons, 2017. https://commons.wikimedia.org/wiki/ File:Oc,G.T.1663,_Mana_Expedition_to_Easter_Island,_British_Museum.jpg. Public domain.

14. Collage, third center: Jagadeesan, Madhuranthakan, photographer. *Sri Kanteshwara Temple Gopuram,* Nanjangud, Karnataka, India, 2007. Wikimedia Commons, 2016. https://commons.wikimedia.org/wiki/File:N-KA-B159_Srikanteshwara_Temple_Gopuram_Nanjangud.jpg. CC BY-SA 4.0.

14. Collage, third right: Duffell, Marjorie V. *The Ziggurat of Nabonidus Restored,* plate 88. In *Ur excavations. Vol. 5, Ziggurat and its surroundings* by Leonard Woolley, publications of the Joint expedition of the British Museum and of the University Museum, University of Pennsylvania, Philadelphia, to Mesopotamia, published for the trustees of the two museums by aid of a grant made by the Carnegie corporation of New York, 1939, p. 255. Internet Archive, 2019. https://archive.org/details/urexcavations5/page/n3. Public domain.

14. Collage Bottom Left: Torbenbrinker, photographer. *Jardim dos Maroicos park,* Pico island, Azores, 2016. Wikimedia Commons, 2016. https://commons.wikimedia.org/wiki/File%3AMadalenaJardim.jpg. CC BY-SA 4.0.

14. Collage Bottom Center Gianf84 at Italian Wikipedia, photographer. *Monte D' Accoddi, Sardinia,* Italy, 2008. Wikimedia Commons, 2009. https://commons.wikimedia.org/wiki/File:Monted%27accoddisardegna.png. CC BY-SA 3.0.

14. Collage Bottom Right Uli sh, photographer. *Mauritius pyramid,* 2014. Wikimedia Commons, 2015. https://commons.wikimedia.org/wiki/File%3AMauritius-Pyramiden-5-4-3.jpg. CC BY-SA 4.0.

15. Collage, top left: Saamiblog: http://saamiblog.blogspot.com, photographer. *Buckle from Oseberg Vikingship Buddha,* found with the Oseberg ship burial circa 800 CE, 2008. Wikimedia Commons, 2009. https://commons.wikimedia.org/wiki/File:Buckle_from_Oseberg_Vikingship_Buddha_3.JPG. CC BY-SA 3.0.

15. Collage, top center: Chirita, Cristian, photographer. *Archeological Artefacts in Sozopol Museum,* Sozopol Museum, Sozopol, Bulgaria, 2011. Wikimedia Commons, 2011. https://commons.wikimedia.org/wiki/File:Sozopol_Archaeological_Museum_IMG_4214.JPG. GNU Free Documentation License, Version 1.2. https://commons.wikimedia.org/wiki/Commons:GNU_Free_Documentation_License,_version_1.2.

15. Collage, top right: Dbachmann, photographer. *Samarra Bowl,* circa 4000 BC, Pergamon Museum, Berlin, 2010. Wikimedia Commons, 2010. https://en.wikipedia.org/wiki/File:Samarra_bowl.jpg. CC BY-SA 4.0.

15. Collage, center left: Haylli, photographer. *Sican Vessel in the Huaca Rajada Site Museum*, Huaca Rajada Site Museum, 2009. Wikimedia Commons, 2009. https://commons.wikimedia.org wiki/File:Sican-Vessel-in-the-Huaca-Rajada-Site-Museum-001.JPG. Public domain.

15. Collage, center: PHGCOM, photographer. *Etruscan Pendant with Swastika Symbols Bolsena Italy 700 BCE to 650 BCE.* Louvre Museum, 2008. Wikimedia Commons, 2010. https://commons.wikimedia.org/wiki/File:Etruscan_pendant_with_swastika_symbols_Bolsena_Italy_700_BCE_to_650_BCE.jpg. CC BY-SA 3.0.

15. Collage, center right: BabelStone, photographer. *Early Anglo-Saxon Cinerary Urn from North Elmham, Norfolk,* circa between 5th and 6th century, British Museum, 2010. Wikimedia Commons, 2010. https://commons.wikimedia.org/wiki/File:British_Museum_cinerary_urn_with_swastika_motifs.jpg. Public domain.

15. Collage, bottom left: Шнапс, photographer. Скоба для стрел (*Bracket for Arrows),* 2009. Wikimedia Commons, 2012. https://commons.wikimedia.org/wiki/File:Скоба_для_стрел. JPG. CC BY-SA 3.0.

15. Collage, bottom center: Tylas at English Wikipedia, photographer. *Zionpictographs*, Zion National Park, 2006. Wikimedia Commons, 2006. https://commons.wikimedia.org/wiki/File:Zionpictographs.jpg. CC BY-SA 3.0.

15. Collage, bottom right: Before My Ken, photographer. *Indus Valley Civilization Seals*, British Museum, 2005. Wikimedia Commons, 2009. https://commons.wikimedia.org/wiki/File:IndusValleySeals_swastikas.JPG. CC BY-SA 3.0.

15. Collage, top left: Pattych at English Wikipedia, photographer. *MocheBeardedMen,* 2008. Wikimedia Commons, 2010. https://en.wikipedia.org/wiki/File:MocheBeardedMen.jpg. CC BY-SA 3.0.

15. Collage, top right: Artist unknown. *Pashupati Seal* from Mohenjo-daro, 2600–1900 BC. Wikimedia Commons, 2010. Public domain.

15. Collage, bottom left: Fortuna, Roberto, and Kira Ursem, photographers. *Gundestrup Cauldron.* Nationalmuseet, Denmark, 2007. Wikimedia Commons, 2016. https://en.wikipedia.org/wiki/File:Gundestrupkedlen-_00054_(cropped).jpg. CC BY-SA 3.0.

15. Collage, bottom right: Ober, Frederick A. *Quetzalcoatl.* In *Travels in Mexico and Life Among the Mexicans,* San Francisco: J. Dewing and Co., 1884, p. 508. Wikimedia Commons, 2017. https://commons.wikimedia.org/wiki/File:TLM_D516_Quetzalcoatl.jpg. Public domain.

16. Zenz, Rainer at German Wikipedia, photographer. *Mount Rushmore,* South Dakota, USA. Wikimedia Commons, 2005. https://commons.wikimedia.org/wiki/File:Mount_Rushmore-2.jpg. Public domain.

17. Terletskaya, Elena, artist. *Seven wonders of the ancient world!!! 3D reconstructions.* Shutterstock. com. https://www.shutterstock.com/image-illustration/seven-wonders-ancient-world-3d-reconstructions-27690895. Licensed from Shutterstoc.com. Image modified by Sura Ondruar Publising.

21. Google Earth. 2018. *Great line.* © Google, Data SIO, NOAA, U.S. Navy, NGA, GEBCO, Image Landsat / Copernicus, Image IBCAO.

CHAPTER TWO: ORIGINS

26. Whitney, William Dwight, and Charles Rockwell Lanman. *Image of Codex Cashmiriensis folio 187a.* In *Atharva-Veda Samhitā,* 1905. Wikimedia Commons, 2015. https://commons.wikimedia.org/wiki/File:Atharva-Veda_samhita_page_471_illustration.png. Public domain.

27. Mystique, Mickey, photographer. *Skeleton at Museum Lepenski Vir*, Serbia, 2018. Wikimedia Commons, 2018. https://commons.wikimedia.org/wiki/File:Lepenski_Vir,_muzej_26.jpg. CC BY-SA 4.0.

28. Simon, Klaus-Peter, photographer. *Göbekli Tepe Settlement hill near Şanlıurfa, Southeast Turkey, Appendix C from the east*, 2012. Wikimedia Commons, 2012. https://commons.wikimedia.org/wiki/File:G%C3%B6bekli2012-14.jpg. CC BY-SA 3.0.

31. Budge, E. A. Wallis. *Depiction of Ra-Horakhty.* In *The Gods of the Egyptians, Vol. 1.* London: Methuen & Co., 1904, p. 331. Wikimedia Commons, 2007. https://commons.wikimedia. org/wiki/File:Ra-Horakhty,_Wallis_Budge.jpg. Public domain.

35. Chernov, Mstyslav, photographer. *Great Sphinx of Giza (foreground) Pyramid of Menkaure (background),* Cairo, Egypt, North Africa, 2009. Wikimedia Commons, 2009. https:// commons.wikimedia.org/wiki/File:Great_Sphinx_of_Giza_(foreground)_Pyramid_of_ Menkaure_(background)._Cairo,_Egypt,_North_Africa.jpg. CC BY-SA 3.0.

38. Hofmann, Florian, photographer. *Pylon of the Horus Temple in Edfu,* 2004. Wikimedia Commons 2004. https://commons.wikimedia.org/wiki/File:Edfu_pylon.jpg. CC BY-SA 3.0

41. Soutekh67, photographer. *Thoth in adoration in front of the Lunar Disc / Oudjat, ceiling of Denérah,* 2014. Wikimedia Commons, 2014. https://commons.wikimedia.org/wiki/ File:Dendera_Deckenrelief_03_(2).JPG. CC BY-SA 4.0.

42. The Culdian Trust. *Cover of The Kolbrin.* The Kolbrin, 1994. © The Culdian Trust.

45. Ogawa, Hiroki, photographer. *Tashilhunpo Monastery,* Shigatse, Tibet, 2014. Wikimedia Commons 2017. https://commons.wikimedia.org/wiki/File:Tashilhunpo_Monastery_ Shigatse_Tibet_China_西藏日喀则扎什伦布寺_-_panoramio_(5).jpg. CC. BY 3.0.

47. Curtis, Edward S, photographer. *Gobuguoy, Walpi girl, half-length portrait, facing front, hair tied in swirls on sides of head, metal bead and bell choker, printed cotton dress, cotton shawl around shoulders,* Arizona Walpi, ca. 1900. https://www.loc.gov/item/93501149/. Public domain.

49. Inspired by Maps, photographer. *Tiwanaku: Spiritual and Political Centre of the Tiwanaku Culture,* Bolivia. Shutterstock.com. https://www.shutterstock.com/image-photo/tiwanaku-spiritual-political-centre-culture-unesco-730144396. Licensed from Shutterstock.com

50. Artist unknown. *Egyptian god Ra in his solar barque.* Wikimedia Commons, 2005. https:// commons.wikimedia.org/wiki/File:Ra_Barque.jpg. Public domain.

53. Nguyen, Marie-Lan, photographer. *Plato, Luni marble, copy of the portrait made by Silanion ca. 370 BC for the Academia in Athens,* 370 BC, Capitoline Museums, 2009. Wikimedia Commons 2009. https://en.wikipedia.org/wiki/File:Plato_Silanion_Musei_Capitolini_ MC1377.jpg. © Marie-Lan Nguyen. CC-BY 2.5.

57. Ramanarayanadatta Astri. *Bishma telling the secret of his death.* In *Mahabharata,* Gorakhpur: Gita Press. University of Toronto Collection, acquired 1965. Wikimedia Commons, 2012. https://commons.wikimedia.org/wiki/File:Bisma_telling_the_secrete_of_his_death.jpg. Public domain.

60. Artist unknown. *Two mythological Character, Narad and Vasudev,* c. 1940s. Wikimedia Commons, 2014. https://commons.wikimedia.org/wiki/File:Narad_-_Vintage_Print.jpg. Public domain.

62. Ramanarayanadatta Astri. *Ugrashravas narrating Mahābhārata before the sages gathered in Naimisha Forest.* In *Mahabharata,* Gorakhpur: Gita Press. University of Toronto Collection, acquired 1965. Wikimedia Commons, 2012. https://commons.wikimedia.org/wiki/ File:Ugrashravas_narrating_Mah%C4%81bh%C4%81rata_before_the_sages_gathered_in_ Naimisha_Forest.jpg. Public domain.

63. Burke, John, photographer. *General view of Temple and Enclosure of Marttand or the Sun, near Bhawan,* 1868, British Museum. Wikimedia Commons, 2007. https://commons.wikimedia. org/wiki/File:Sun_temple_martand_indogreek.jpg. Public domain.

66. Baedeker, Karl. *Drawing of Thoth.* In *Handbook for Traveling, pt.1 Lower Egypt, with the Fayum and the peninsula of Sinai,* Leipsic; London: K. Baedeker, 1885, p. 134. From Travelers in the Middle East Archive (TIMEA), Uniform Resource Identifier: 9937. Wikimedia Commons 2010. https://commons.wikimedia.org/wiki/ File:Thoth._(1885)_-_TIMEA.jpg. CC BY-SA 2.5.

68. Ignati, photographer. *Osiris detail from the grave of Sennedjem,* 2009. Wikimedia Commons, 2009. https://commons.wikimedia.org/wiki/File:Detail_aus_dem_Grab_des_Sennudjem. jpg. Public domain.

70. NOAA. *Atlantic bathymetry.* Wikimedia Commons, 2006. https://commons.wikimedia.org/ wiki/File:Atlantic_bathymetry.jpg. Public domain.

72. Artist unknown. *The Mexica depart from Aztlán*. In *Codex Boturini*, 16th Century. Wikimedia Commons, 2006. https://en.wikipedia.org/wiki/File:Aztlan_codex_boturini.jpg. Public domain.

74. Post of Armenia. Stamp of Armenia, 1997. Wikimedia Commons, 2008. https://commons.wikimedia.org/wiki/File:ArmenianStamps-115.jpg. Public domain.

77. Baviere, Guillaume, photographer. *Island of São Jorge,* Azores, 2010. Wikimedia Commons, 2012. https://en.wikipedia.org/wiki/File:A%C3%A7ores_2010-07-19_(5047589237).jpg. CC BY 2.0.

79. Beauregard, Mike, photographer. *Rebounding beach, Bathurst Inlet,* Nunavut, Canada, 2013. Wikimedia Commons, 2013. https://en.wikipedia.org/wiki/File:Rebounding_beach,_among_other_things_(9404384095).jpg. CC BY 2.0.

81. Pimvantend, artist, map information from NOAA, ETOPO1, GPLATES. *The Azores Triple Junction*, 2011. Wikimedia Commons, 2011. https://en.wikipedia.org/wiki/File:Azorestriple3d.png. CC BY-SA 3.0.

CHAPTER THREE: THE WISDOM BRINGERS

86. Collage, top left: Dr.regosistvan, phtographer. *Oannes*, 2016. Wikimedia Commons, 2016. https://commons.wikimedia.org/wiki/File:Oannes.jpg. CC BY-SA 4.0.

86. Collage, top right: Delange, Audrey and George, photographers. *La Venta Stele 19,* the earliest known representation of the Feathered Serpent in Mesoamerica, 2005. Wikimedia Commons, 2015. https://commons.wikimedia.org/wiki/File:La_Venta_Stele_19_(Delange).jpg. © Audrey and George Delange. Reproduced with permission.

86. Collage, bottom left: Simon, Klaus-Peter, photographer. *Göbekli Tepe*, Şanlıurfa, southeast Turkey, 2012. Wikimedia Commons, 2012. https://commons.wikimedia.org/wiki/File:G%C3%B6bekli2012-18.jpg. CC BY-SA 3.0.

86. Collage, bottom right: Artist unknown, 9th century B.C. *Deity Performing Ritual Purification*, Los Angeles County Museum of Art. Wikimedia Commons, 2013. https://commons.wikimedia.org/wiki/File:Deity_Performing_Ritual_Purification_LACMA_66.4.5_(2_of_3).jpg. Public Domain.

87. Tausch, Olaf, photographer. *Edfu Temple Relief,* Egypt, 2014. Wikimedia Commons, 2014. https://commons.wikimedia.org/wiki/File:Edfu_Tempelrelief_33.jpg. CC BY 3.0.

88. Baedeker, Karl. *Line drawing of Egyptian god Osiris*. In *Handbook for Traveling, pt.1 Lower Egypt, with the Fayum and the peninsula of Sinai*, Leipsic; London: K. Baedeker, 1885, p. 131. From Travelers in the Middle East Archive (TIMEA), Uniform Resource Identifier: 9934. Wikimedia Commons 2010. https://commons.wikimedia.org/wiki/File:Osiris,_prince_of_eternity_(1885)_-_TIMEA.jpg. CC BY-SA 2.5.

92. Ramanarayanadatta Astri. *The fish avatara of Vishnu saves Manu during the great deluge*. In *Mahabharata*, Gorakhpur: Gita Press. University of Toronto Collection, acquired 1965. Wikimedia Commons, 2012. https://commons.wikimedia.org/wiki/File:The_fish_avatara_of_Vishnu_saves_Manu_during_the_great_deluge.jpg. Public domain.

94. Place, Victor and Thomas, Félix. *Winged deity Khorsabad*, 1867. Wikimedia Commons, 2019. https://commons.wikimedia.org/wiki/File:Gegen%C3%BCsberstellung_der_Genien_Nimrud-Khorsabad.jpg. Public domain.

96. Left: Layard, Austen, illustrator. *Plate 6 Fish God (Nimroud)*. In *A second series of the monuments of Nineveh: including bas-reliefs from the Palace of Sennacherib and bronzes from the ruins of Nimroud ; from drawings made on the spot, during a second expedition to Assyria*, London, 1853. Wikimedia Commons, 2018. Henryhttps://commons.wikimedia.org/wiki/File:Plate_6_fish_god_(A_second_series_of_the_monuments_of_Nineveh)_1853_(cropped).jpg. Public domain.

96. Right: Erdenkäufer, Stefan, Photographer. *Panzerreiter*, 2009. Wikimedia Commons, 2009. https://commons.wikimedia.org/wiki/File:Panzerreiter.jpg. Public domain.

97. Bose, Nandlal. *Yama and Savitri*. In *Indian Myth and Legend* by Donald Alexander Mackenzie, London: The Gresham Publishing Company, 1913, p. 52. Wikimedia Commons, 2015. https://commons.wikimedia.org/wiki/File:Yama_and_Savitri_by_Nandlal_Bose_1913.jpg. Public domain.

99. Jvtrplzz. *Arkaim Infographic*, 2012. Wikimedia Commons, 2018. https://commons.wikimedia.org/wiki/File:Arkaim_Infographic.jpg. Public domain.

100. Collage, top left: Ace, Sahand, photographer. *Faravahar Symbol in Persepolis*, Shiraz, Iran, 2012. Wikimedia Commons, 2013. https://commons.wikimedia.org/wiki/File:Farvahar1.JPG. CC BY-SA 3.0.

100. Collage, bottom left: Capillon, photographer. *Mesopotamian sun god Shamash, Assyrian relief*, 865–860 BC, British Museum. Wikimedia Commons, 2008. https://commons.wikimedia.org/wiki/File:Shamash.jpg. Public domain.

100. Collage, bottom right: Sharpe, Samuel. *The winged Sun of Thebes*. In *Egyptian Mythology and Egyptian Christianity*, London: John Russel Smith, 1863, p. 1. Wikimedia Commons, 2006. https://commons.wikimedia.org/wiki/File:Winged_sun_sharpe.png. Public domain.

100. James, George Wharton. *Hopi Snake Dance Ceremony at Oraibi*, Arizona, 1898, University of Southern California, California Historical Society Collection. http://digitallibrary.usc.edu/cdm/ref/collection/p15799coll65/id/16902. Public domain.

102. Kabotie, Fred. *Hopi Tawa mural*, Painted Desert Inn, Petrified Forest National Park, Arizona, National Park Service. Wikimedia Commons, 2012. https://commons.wikimedia.org/wiki/File:Hopi_Tawa_Mural.jpeg. Public domain.

102. Sewell, Ian. *Ahu Akivi*, Easter Island, 2006. Wikimedia Commons, 2006. https://commons.wikimedia.org/wiki/File:Ahu-Akivi-1.JPG. CC BY-SA 3.0.

104. Pouteau, Claire, photographer. *Tiwanaku*, Bolivia, 2003. Wikimedia Commons, 2005. https://commons.wikimedia.org/wiki/File:Tiwanaku1.jpg. CC BY-SA 2.0.

105. Plekhanova, Yulia, photographer. *Glasnevin Cemetery*, Dublin Ireland, 2019. Shutterstock.com. https://www.shutterstock.com/image-photo/glasnevin-cemetery-ireland-august-02-2019-1472088821. Licensed from Shutterstock.com

105. Petrow, Chris, photographer. *Row of Buddhas*. Unsplash.com. https://unsplash.com/photos/j4Wia6JDLm0. Licensed from Unsplash.com.

106. Left: Papiermond, photographer. *Sarcophagi of Karajia*, 2005. Wikimedia Commons, 2006. https://en.wikipedia.org/wiki/File:Karajia1.jpg. CC BY-SA 3.0.

106. Right: Mitzo, photographer. *Sarcophagus*, Kunsthistorisches Museum, Vienna, Austira, 2020. Shutterstock.com. https://www.shutterstock.com/image-photo/vienna-austria-1502-interior-museum-art-1650056077. Licensed from Shutterstock.com.

107. Collage, top left: Gybas DigiPhoto, photographer. *Moai from Ahu Tongariki on Easter Island*. Shutterstock.com. https://www.shutterstock.com/image-photo/moai-ahu-tongariki-on-easter-island-10886431. Licensed from Shutterstock.com.

107. Collage, top center: Ndede, photographer. *Archaeological Work Gobeklitepe Turkey*. Shutterstock.com. https://www.shutterstock.com/image-photo/archaeological-work-gobeklitepe-turkey-1087902086. Licensed from Shutterstock.com.

107. Collage, top right: Kaiser, Jennifer, photographer. *Statue from Gobeklitepe*, Urfa Museum, 2015. Flickr.com, 2015. https://www.flickr.com/photos/kaiserjennifer/20263074231. CC BY 2.0.

107. Collage, bottom left: TheWanderingScot.com, photographer. *Kabul Museum: Kafiristan Statue*, 2009. http://thewanderingscot.com/photos/2009 Stans/Afghanistan/midis/IMG_7902.jpg. © TheWanderingsScot.com. Reproduced with permission.

107. Collage, bottom center: Artist unknown. *Two European Ladies and a Man Are Standing in front of a Statue in Napu, Menado*, before 1937, Tropenmuseum, part of the National Museum of World Cultures, Amsterdam, Netherlands. Wikimedia Commons, 2009. https://commons.wikimedia.org/wiki/File:COLLECTIE_TROPENMUSEUM_Twee_Europese_dames_en_een_man_staan_voor_een_afgodsbeeld_te_Napu_Menado_TMnr_10000852.jpg. CC BY-SA 3.0.

107. Collage, bottom right: Damsea, photographer. *French Polynesia Tahiti Island Carved Stone Tiki Statue on the Marae Arahurahu, South Pacific, Oceania*. Shutterstock.com. https://www. shutterstock.com/image-photo/french-polynesia-tahiti-island-carved-stone-784904116. Licensed from Shutterstock.com.

109. James, Gilbert. *Aged Quetzalcoatl Leaves Mexico on Raft of Serpents*. In *The Myths of Mexico & Peru*, London: G. G. Harrap & Company, 1913, p. 80. https://commons.wikimedia.org/wiki/ File:080-Aged_Quetzalcoatl_Leaves_Mexico_on_Raft_of_Serpents.jpg. Public domain.

111. Cronista Martín de Murúa. *Illustration showing the Inca Pachacútec in the Coricancha*. In *Crónicas de Martín de Murúa*, 17th century. https://en.wikipedia.org/wiki/ File:Pachacuteckoricancha.jpg. Public domain.

113. Rivera, Diego, artist. Kgv88, photographer. *Indian Mexico*, Palacio Nacional, Mexico, 2011. Wikimedia Commons, 2011. https://commons.wikimedia.org/wiki/File:Indian_Mexico_2. JPG CC BY-SA 3.0.

114. Schwen, Daniel, photographer. *El Castillo (pyramid of Kukulcán)* in Chichén Itzá, Mexico, 2009. Wikimedia Commons, 2009. https://commons.wikimedia.org/wiki/File:Chichen_ Itza_3.jpg. CC BY-SA 4.0.

115. Henderson, Keith. *Quetzalcoatl*. In *The Conquest of Mexico*, London: Chatto & Windus, 1922, p.39. https://commons.wikimedia.org/wiki/File:COM_V1_D225_Quetzalcoatl.png

116. Left: Meyrick, S. R., and C. H. Smith. *The Costume of the Original Inhabitants of the British Islands*, 1815. Wikimedia Commons, 2011. https://commons.wikimedia.org/wiki/File:An_ Arch_Druid_in_His_Judicial_Habit.jpg. Public domain.

116. Right: Sammes, Aylett. *A Druid*. In *Britannia Antiqua Illustrata*, 1676. Wikimedia Commons, 2010. https://en.wikipedia.org/wiki/File:ADruid.jpg. Public domain.

117. Pattych at en.wikipedia. *MocheBeardedMen*, 2008. Wikimedia Commons, 2010. https:// commons.wikimedia.org/wiki/File:MocheBeardedMen.jpg. CC BY-SA 3.0.

118. Gehrts, Johannes. *Odhin*. In *Walhall: Germanische Götter- und Heldensagen. Für Alt und Jung am deutschen Herd* by Felix Dahn, Breitkopf und Härtel, 1901. Wikimedia Commons 2008. https://commons.wikimedia.org/wiki/File:Odhin_by_Johannes_Gehrts.jpg. Public domain.

119. Robertson, D. Gordon E., photographer. *Cast of petroglyphs in Learning Centre,* Petroglyphs Provincial Park, Woodview, Ontario, Canada, 2012. Wikimedia Commons, 2012. https:// en.wikipedia.org/wiki/File:Cast_of_boat.jpg. CC BY-SA 3.0.

121. Ekman, Robert. *Väinämöinen's Play*, 1866, Student Union of the University of Helsinki. Wikimedia Commons, 2014. https://commons.wikimedia.org/wiki/ File:V%C3%A4in%C3%A4m%C3%B6isen_soitto1.jpg. Public domain.

127. Collage, top left: Artist unknown. *Adinatha, from a series of Vishnu Avatars, Rishabha, Jaipur*, circa 1860. Wikimedia Commons, 2012. https://en.wikipedia.org/wiki/File:From_a_series_ of_Vishnu_Avataras-_Rishabha.jpg. Public domain.

127. Collage, top right: Artist unknown. *Seal from Mohenjo-daro,* 2600–1900 BC. Wikimedia Commons, 2010. https://en.wikipedia.org/wiki/File:Shiva_Pashupati.jpg. Public domain.

127. Collage, bottom left: Fortuna, Roberto, and Kira Ursem, photographers. *Gundestrup cauldron*, Nationalmuseet, Denmark, 2007. Wikimedia Commons, 2016. https://en.wikipedia.org/ wiki/File:Gundestrupkedlen-_00054_(cropped).jpg. CC BY-SA 3.0.

127. Collage, bottom right: Ober, Frederick A. *Quetzalcoatl*. In *Travels in Mexico and Life Among the Mexicans,* San Francisco: J. Dewing and Co., 1884, p. 508. Wikimedia Commons, 2017. https://commons.wikimedia.org/wiki/File:TLM_D516_Quetzalcoatl.jpg. Public domain.

128. Left: Pogány, Willy, illustrator. *Odin*. In *The Children of Odin: The Book of Northern Myths* by Padaric Colum, 1917. Wikimedia Commons, 2013. https://commons.wikimedia.org/wiki/ File:The_Children_of_Odin_The_Book_of_Northern_Myths_30.jpg. Public domain.

128. Right: Leonard G, photographer. *Terracotta urn of Maya sun god*, De Young Museum, San Francisco, 2007. Wikimedia Commons, 2007. https://en.wikipedia.org/wiki/ File:MayanSunGodEffigyClip.jpg. Public domain.

129. Pogány, Willy, illustrator. *Odin The Wanderer*. In *The Children of Odin: The Book of Northern Myths* by Padaric Colum, 1917. Wikimedia Commons, 2013. https://commons.wikimedia.org/wiki/File:The_Children_of_Odin_The_Book_of_Northern_Myths_37.jpg. Public domain.

129. Left: Klement-Speckner, Marianne. *Irminsul*, 1996. Wikimedia Commons, 2007. https://en.wikipedia.org/wiki/File:Irminsul_als_Weltenbaum.jpg. Public domain.

129. Right: Le Plongeon, Augustus. Illustration in *Sacred Mysteries Among the Mayas and the Quiches*, 1886. Third edition, New York: Macoy Publishing and Masonic Supply Company, 1909, p. 134. Internet Archive, 2017. https://archive.org/details/sacredmysteriesa00lepliala/page/134/mode/2up. Public domain.

131. Drone image by Bogdan.

132. Budge, E. A. Wallis. *Tet with the Head of Osiris*. In *Osiris and the Egyptian Resurrection*, London: P. L. Warner, 1911, p. 52. Internet Archive, 2008. https://archive.org/details/osirisegyptianre00budg/page/52. Public domain.

133. Bjoertvedt, photographer. *Nordens Ark in Sotenäs,* Sweden, 2013. Wikimedia Commons, 2013. https://commons.wikimedia.org/wiki/File:Soten%C3%A4s_Tossene_73-1_Aaby_ID_10161200730001_IMG_8005.JPG. CC BY-SA 3.0.

135. Left: Von Rosen, Georg. *Odin in the guise of a wanderer*, 1886. Wikimedia Commons, 2005. https://commons.wikimedia.org/wiki/File:Georg_von_Rosen_-_Oden_som_vandringsman,_1886_(Odin,_the_Wanderer).jpg. Public domain.

135. Center: Ignati, photographer. *Osiris as ruler of the afterlife, detail from the tomb of Sennedjem,* 2009. Wikimedia Commons, 2011. https://commons.wikimedia.org/wiki/File:Detail_aus_dem_Grab_des_Sennudjem.jpg. Public domain.

135. Right: Muru Photography. *Durga Puja Kolkata*. Shutterstock.com. https://www.shutterstock.com/image-photo/durga-puja-kolkata-677058361 Licensed from Shutterstock.com.

135. Top: Sauber, Wolfgang, photographer. *Picture stone showing a spiral and deer*, Visby (Gotland), Fornsalen Museum, 2007. Wikimedia Commons, 2009. https://commons.wikimedia.org/wiki/File:Fornsalen_-_Bildstein_-_Spirale_und_Hirsche.jpg. CC BY-SA 3.0.

135. Bottom: Kolyan, Artak, photographer. *Armenian tombstone*, Aghout, Sisian, Armenia, 2013. Wikimedia Commons, 2013. https://en.wikipedia.org/wiki/File:Armenian_Tombstone_Aghout_Sisian_Armenia.jpg. CC BY-SA 3.0.

136. Alexander, Mitrofanov, photographer. *Wooden Idol Slavic Culture*. Shutterstock.com. https://www.shutterstock.com/image-photo/wooden-idol-slavic-culture-on-village-722636782. Licensed from Shutterstock.com.

139. Gehrts, Johannes. *Ragnarok*. In *Walhall: Germanische Götter- und Heldensagen. Für Alt und Jung am deutschen Herd* by Felix Dahn, Breitkopf und Härtel, 1901. Wikimedia Commons 2008. https://commons.wikimedia.org/wiki/File:Johannes_gehrts_ragnarok_mindre.JPG. Public domain.

142. Lobachev, Vladimir, photographer. *Ivan Kupala in the Belgorod Region,* 2011. Wikimedia Commons, 2014. https://commons.wikimedia.org/wiki/File:Ivan_Kupala_Day_in_2011_08.JPG. CC BY-SA 3.0.

142. Artist unknown. *Chinese mythological figures Nuwa and Fuxi with an unidentified third party,* Han dynasty, Temple mural. Wikimedia Commons, 2006. https://en.wikipedia.org/wiki/File:NuwaFuxi1.JPG. Public domain.

144. Left: Haha169, photographer. *A leaning tower in the Chinese city of Xi'an*. Wikimedia Commons, 2008. https://commons.wikimedia.org/wiki/File:Xian_Leaning_Tower.JPG. Public domain.

144. Right: Brücke-Osteuropa, photographer. *Pingling,* 2011. Wikimedia Commons, 2011. https://commons.wikimedia.org/wiki/File:Pingling_1.jpg. Public domain.

145. Left: Käyttäjä:Kompak. Derivative by Perhelion. *Ra-Horakhty Based on Nefertari's Tomb,* 2010. Wikimedia Commons, 2016. https://commons.wikimedia.org/wiki/File:Sun_god_Ra.svg. CC BY-SA 3.0.

145. Center: Ellis, Edward S., and Charles F. Horne. *Woden*. In *The Story of the Greatest Nations, from the Dawn of History to the Twentieth Century*, 1900, p. 247. Flickr.com. https://flic.kr/p/oxEEja. Public domain.

145. Right: Mahamuni. *Lord of Gods Vishnu*. In *Shrimad Bhagavata Mahapurana,* Gorakhpur: Gita Press. Wikimedia Commons, 2018. https://commons.wikimedia.org/wiki/File:Lord_of_Gods_Vishnu.jpg. Public domain.

148. Left: Polylerus, photographer. *Model of the reed boat Tigris, boat of Thor Heyerdahl,* 2009. Wikimedia Commons, 2009. https://commons.wikimedia.org/wiki/File:Tigris_Model_Pyramids_of_Guimar.jpg. CC BY-SA 3.0.

148. Right Hajor, photographer. *Tomb KV34 (Thutmose III), 11th hour Amduat*, Valley of the Kings, Luxor, Egypt, 2002. Wikimedia Commons, 2005. https://commons.wikimedia.org/wiki/File:Egypt.KV34.07.jpg. CC BY-SA 3.0.

149. Left: James, Gilbert. *Aged Quetzalcoatl Leaves Mexico on Raft of Serpents*. In *The Myths of Mexico & Peru*, London: G. G. Harrap & Company, 1913, p. 80. https://commons.wikimedia.org/wiki/File:080-Aged_Quetzalcoatl_Leaves_Mexico_on_Raft_of_Serpents.jpg. Public domain.

149. Right: Ramanarayanadatta Astri. *Sheshashayi Vishnu*. In *Mahabharata*, Gorakhpur: Gita Press. University of Toronto Collection, acquired 1965. Wikimedia Commons, 2012. https://commons.wikimedia.org/wiki/File:Sheshashayi_Vishnu.jpg. Public domain.

150. Collage, top left: Bon, Jerome, photographer. *Great Pyramid of Giza*. Wikimedia Commons, 2015. https://commons.wikimedia.org/wiki/File:Great_Pyramid_of_Giza_ (2427530661).jpg. CC BY 2.0.

150. Collage, top center: Skubasteve834, photographer. *Monks Mound,* Collinsville, Illinois, 2007. Wikimedia Commons, 2013. https://commons.wikimedia.org/wiki/File:Monks_Mound_in_July.JPG. CC BY-SA-3.0.

150. Collage, top right: Brücke-Osteuropa, photographer. *Pingling*, 2011. Wikimedia Commons, 2011. https://de.wikipedia.org/wiki/Datei:Pingling_1.jpg. Public domain.

150. Collage, second left: Schwen, Daniel, photographer. *Chichen Itza,* Mexico, 2009. Wikimedia Commons, 2009. https://commons.wikimedia.org/wiki/File:Chichen_Itza_3.jpg. CC BY-SA 4.0.

150. Collage, second center: Peaceofangkor, photographer. *Prang (Behind Prasat Thom),* Koh Ker, Cambodia, 2006. Wikimedia Commons, 2006. https://commons.wikimedia.org/wiki/File:0505280017PThompyramid.jpg. Public domain.

150. Collage, second right: Ximenez, Pedro, photographer. *Pyramid Güimar,* Canary Islands, Spain, 1998. Wikimedia Commons, 2009. https://commons.wikimedia.org/wiki/File:Pyramide Güimar.jpg. CC BY-SA 2.0.

150. Collage, third left: Wilson, Captain W. *Marae Mahaiatea on Tahiti Island,* 1799, British Museum. Wikimedia Commons, 2017. https://commons.wikimedia.org/wiki/File:Oc,G.T.1663,_Mana_Expedition_to_Easter_Island,_British_Museum.jpg. Public domain.

150. Collage, third center: Jagadeesan, Madhuranthakan, photographer. *Sri Kanteshwara Temple Gopuram*, Nanjangud, Karnataka, India, 2007. Wikimedia Commons, 2016. https://commons.wikimedia.org/wiki/ File:N-KA-B159_Srikanteshwara_Temple_Gopuram_Nanjangud.jpg. CC BY-SA 4.0.

150. Collage, third right: Duffell, Marjorie V. *The Ziggurat of Nabonidus Restored*, plate 88, in *Ur excavations. Vol. 5, Ziggurat and its surroundings* by Leonard Woolley, publications of the Joint expedition of the British Museum and of the University Museum, University of Pennsylvania, Philadelphia, to Mesopotamia, published for the trustees of the two museums by aid of a grant made by the Carnegie corporation of New York, 1939, p. 255. Internet Archive, 2019. https://archive.org/details/urexcavations5/page/n3. Public domain.

150. Collage, bottom left: Torbenbrinker, photographer. *Jardim dos Maroicos park, Pico island,* Azores, Portugal, 2016. Wikimedia Commons, 2016. https:// commons.wikimedia.org/wiki/File%3AMadalenaJardim.jpg. CC BY-SA 4.0.

150. Collage bottom center Gianf84 at Italian Wikipedia, photographer. *Monte D' Accoddi,* Sardinia, Italy, 2008. Wikipedia Commons, 2009. https:// commons.wikimedia.org/wiki/File:Monted'accoddisardegna.png. CC BY-SA 3.0.

150. Collage Bottom Right Uli sh, photographer. *Mauritius pyramid,* 2014. Wikimedia Commons, 2015. https://commons.wikimedia.org/wiki/ File%3AMauritius-Pyramiden-5-4-3.jpg. CC BY-SA 4.0.

151. Collage, top left: Heghnaraghpour, photographer. *Zorats Karer,* Armenia, 2014. Wikimedia Commons, 2017. https://commons.wikimedia.org/wiki/File:Karahounch.jpg. CC BY-SA 4.0.

151. Collage, top center: Raymbetz, photographer. *Nabta Playa Calendar Circle,* reconstructed at Aswan Nubia museum, Aswan, Eqypt, 2009. Wikimedia Commons, 2009. https:// commons.wikimedia.org/wiki/File:Calendar_aswan.JPG. CC BY-SA 3.0.

151. Collage, top right: Leandroisola, photographer. *The Calzoene's "Stonehenge,"* Calçoene, Brazil, 2008. Wikimedia Commons, 2008. https://commons.wikimedia.org/wiki/ File:Calçoene, Stonehenge brasileira, Amapá.jpg. CC BY 4.0.

151. Collage, bottom left: Boychou, photographer. *Willong Khullen,* Manipur, India, 2010. Wikimedia Commons, 2010. https://commons.wikimedia.org/ wiki/File:Stone_Erections_ of_Willong_Khullen.jpg. CC BY-SA 3.0.

151. Collage, bottom center: Woods, David, photographer. *A portion of the Orkney neolithic site, the Ring of Brodgar.* Shutterstock.com. https://www.shutterstock.com/image-photo/ portion-orkney-neolithic-site-ring-brodgar-4674436. Licensed from Shutterstock.com.

151. Collage, bottom right: Adwo, photographer. *South Africa's Adam's Calendar Stone Replica – Argentina.* https://www.shutterstock.com/image-photo/south-africas-adams-calendar-stone-replica-630489557. Licensed from Shutterstock.com.

151. Image created for book, based on Truman, Dave. *Ancient Alignment in the Andes Hints at a Lost Global High Culture.* GrahamHancock.com, January 2, 2016. https://grahamhancock. com/truman1. Background © Google Earth, image Landsat / Copernicus, Data SIO, NOAA, U.S. Navy, NGA, GEBCO, Data LDEO-Columbia, NSF, NOAA.

154. Ganguly, Biswarup, photographer. *Vishnu Yajna,* Howrah, 2012. Wikimedia Commons, 2012. https://commons.wikimedia.org/wiki/File:Vishnu_Yajna_-_Howrah_2012-12-16_2078. JPG. CC BY 3.0.

159. Left: Artist unknown. *Egyptian God Sokar-Osiris,* from the Papyrus of Ani, circa 1300 BC, facsimile made by E. A. Wallis Budge, 1890, British Museum. Wikimedia Commons, 2010. https://commons.wikimedia.org/wiki/File:BD_Sokar-Osiris.jpg. Public domain.

159. Right: Artist unknown. *Vishnu Laxmi and Serpent Anant.* Malavli: Ravi Varma Press. Wikimedia Commons, 2012. https://en.wikipedia.org/wiki/File:Vishnu_Laxmi_and_Serpent_Anant. jpg. Public domain.

160. Artist unknown. *Sri Surya Bhagvan, Bazaar Art,* circa 1940s. Wikimedia Commons, 2015. https://commons.wikimedia.org/wiki/File:Shri_Surya_Bhagvan_bazaar_art,_c.1940%27s. jpg. Public domain.

162. Left: Wihelm, Richard. *Meditation, Stage 3: Separation of the spirit-body for independent existence.* In *The Secret of the Golden Flower,* 1930. https://commons.wikimedia.org/wiki/ File:GoldFlwr3.gif. Public domain.

162. Right: Carrington, Hereward, and Sylvan Muldoon. *Example of the astral body or phantom detached from the physical body.* In *The Projection of the Astral Body,* 1929. Wikimedia Commons, 2017. https://commons.wikimedia.org/wiki/File:Astral_Body_from_ Carrington_and_Muldoon.png. Public domain.

163. Ramanarayanadatta Astri. *Yayati ascend to Heaven.* In *Mahabharata,* Gorakhpur: Gita Press. University of Toronto Collection, acquired 1965. Wikimedia Commons, 2012. https:// commons.wikimedia.org/wiki/File:Yayati_ascend_to_Heaven.jpg. Public domain.

CHAPTER FOUR: THE LOST CIVILIZATION OF THE SUN

167. Donnelly, Ignatius. *Map of the Atlantean Empire.* In *Atlantis: The Antediluvian World,* 1882. Wikimedia Commons, 2010. https://commons.wikimedia.org/wiki/File:Atlantis_ map_1882_crop.jpg. Public domain.

169. AntiguoEgipto.org, photographer. *Osireion,* Abidos Egypt, 2004. Wikimedia Commons, 2005. https://commons.wikimedia.org/wiki/File:Osireion.jpg. CC BY-SA 2.5.

171. Sketch by Sura Ondrunar Publishing based on CultureWise, photographer. *Mezin Paleolithic Bird with Swastika*, 2014. https://www.flickr.com/photos/144631630@N07/29755220321/in/ album-72157670845333124/.

172. Left: Sketch by Sura Ondrunar Publishing based on Musi, Vincent J. *Ancient Head with Snake*, 2011. https://www.nationalgeographic.com/content/dam/magazine/rights-exempt/2011/06/gobekli/08-snakes-on-human-head.jpg.

172. Center: Sketch by Sura Ondrunar Publishing.

172. Right: Daderot, photographer. *Pharaoh, 26th Dynasty to Ptolemaic Dynasty, 664-32 BC,* 2011, Nelson-Atkins Museum of Art. Wikimedia Commons, 2011. https://commons.wikimedia.org/wiki/File:Pharaoh_and_two_heads,_two-sided_relief,_Egypt,_Late_Period_to_Ptolemaic_Period,_26th_Dynasty_to_Ptolemaic_Dynasty,_664-32_BCE_-_Nelson-Atkins_Museum_of_Art_-_DSC08138.JPG. Public domain.

173. HP1740-B. *Partial tree of Indo-European languages,* 2009. Wikimedia Commons, 2009. https://commons.wikimedia.org/wiki/File:IndoEuropeanTree.png. Public domain.

174. Jonathan, Joshua. *Indo-European Migrations,* 2015. Based on Anthony, David. *The Horse, The Wheel and Language,* 2007. Wikimedia Commons, 2015. https://commons.wikimedia.org/wiki/File:Indo-European_Migrations._Source_David_Anthony_(2007),_The_Horse,_The_Wheel_and_Language.jpg. CC BY-SA 4.0.

178. Sura Ondrunar Publishing, 2020. Based on Smolenski, Nikola. *Drawing of a clay vessel unearthed near Vinca*, 2003. Wikimedia Commons, 2005. https://en.wikipedia.org/wiki/File:Vinca_vessel.png. © Nikola Smolenski. CC BY-SA 3.0.

179. LBM 1948, photographer. *Clay tablet in Mycenaean Greek*, 2013. Archaeological Museum of Mycenae. Mikines, Argolis, Greece. Wikimedia Commons, 2019. https://commons.wikimedia.org/wiki/File:Micenas,_museo_07.jpg. CC BY-SA 4.0.

180. Morley, Sylvanus Griswold. *Stela 23, Naranjo*. In *An Introduction to the Study of the Maya Hieroglyphs,* 1915. Wikimedia Commons, 2013. https://commons.wikimedia.org/wiki/File:Maya_Hieroglyphs_Fig_84.jpg. Public domain.

184. Chistophe cagé. *Tarim basin with mountains*, 2011. Based on *Map of Asia – 600 CE* by Thomas A Lessman, 2008. Wikimedia Commons, 2011. https://commons.wikimedia.org/wiki/File:Tarim_bassin.png. CC BY-SA 3.0

186. De Hevesy, Guillaume. *Comparing the scripts of the Indus Valley and Easter Island*. In "The Easter Island and the Indus Valley Scripts," *Anthropos*, Sep-Dec 1938 issue, p. 808, 1938. https://www.jstor.org/stable/41104307?seq=1. © Anthropos 1938. Reproduced with permission.

187. Birgirms. *A chart that shows the evolution of Etruscan writing systems*. Wikimedia Commons, 2010. https://commons.wikimedia.org/wiki/File:Etruiska_tafla.png. CC BY-SA 3.0.

189. Left: Ragimov, M, photographer. *Rock paintings in Gobustan State Reserve*, Azerbaijan, 2009. Wikimedia Commons, 2017. https://commons.wikimedia.org/wiki/File:Gobustan_rock_paintings_-_a_boat.jpg. CC BY-SA 4.0.

189. Center: Mariette, Auguste. *Grand Temple, Chambres de la terrasse*, Osiris du sud, Chambre, No. 2. In *Denderah, Vol. IV*, Paris: Librairie A. Franck, 1874, Pl. 64. Public domain.

189. Right: Lidingo. *Petroglyph ship*, Nordic bronze age (1800-550 BC), Tanum, Sweden, 2008. Wikimedia Commons, 2008. https://commons.wikimedia.org/wiki/File:Petroglypgh_Ship_Nordic_Bronze_Age_001.svg CC BY-SA 4.0.

191. ProjectManhattan, photographer. *Lake Titicaca reed boat*, Peru, 2011. Wikimedia Commons, 2013. https://commons.wikimedia.org/wiki/File:Titicaca_reed_boat.jpg. Public domain.

192. Todd, Gary, photographer. *Disha Kaka Boat with Direction Finding Birds, model of Mohenjo-Daro seal*, 3000 BCE, Maritime Heritage Gallery, India National Museum, New Delhi, 2015. Wikimedia Commons, 2019. https://commons.wikimedia.org/wiki/File:Disha_Kaka_Boat_with_Direction_Finding_Birds,_model_of_Mohenjo-Daro_seal,_3000_BCE.jpg. Public domain.

194. Fjørtoft, Bjørn, photographer. *Thor Heyerdahl*, 1955. National Archives of Norway. Wikimedia Commons, 2017. https://commons.wikimedia.org/wiki/File:Thor_Heyerdahl_-_L0061_934Fo30141701190050.jpg. CC BY 4.0.

195. Shyamal, photographer. *Thor Heyerdahl image outside Kon Tiki museum*, Oslo, 2008. Edited by Jacek Halicki. Wikimedia Commons, 2008, 2012. https://commons.wikimedia.org/wiki/File:KonTikiQuote.jpg. CC BY-SA 3.0.

197. Piotrus, photographer. *Model of Thor Heyerdahl's Ra II at Pyramids of Güímar Museum*, Tenerife, 2007. Wikimedia Commons, 2007. https://commons.wikimedia.org/wiki/File:Ra_II_model_at_Guimar_museum.JPG. CC BY-SA 3.0.

198. Valentinapazmunozmarquez, photographer. *Balsa Viracocha II*, 2015. Wikimedia Commons, 2015. https://commons.wikimedia.org/wiki/ File:Balsa_Viracocha_II.jpeg. CC BY-SA 4.0.

200. Tlustochowicz, Marcin, photographer. *Paracas skulls*, Mueseo Regional de Ica, Ica Peru, 2008. Wikimedia Commons, 2010. https://commons.wikimedia.org/wiki/File:ParacasSkullsIcaMuseum.jpg. CC BY 2.0.

202. Left: Ekholm, Oscar, photographer. *Portrait of Tepano*, Easter Island, 1884. Wikimedia Commons, 2018. https://en.wikipedia.org/wiki/File:Tepano_fr%C3%A5n_P%C3%A5sk%C3%B6n,_1-059_glas18x24.tif. Public domain.

202. Center left: Thomson, William J, photographer. *Kaitae, Nearest Descendant of the Last King of Easter Island*, 1886. Wikimedia Commons, 2017. https://commons.wikimedia.org/wiki/File:Kaitae,_Nearest_Descendant_of_the_Last_King_of_Easter_Island,_photograph.jpg. Public domain.

202. Center right: Routledge, Katherine, photographer. *Te Haha, Clan Miru*, 1915. In *The Mystery of Easter Island*, 1919. Wikimedia Commons, 2017. https://commons.wikimedia.org/wiki/File:Te_Haha._Clan_Miru,_The_Mystery_of_Easter_Island,_published_1919.jpg. Public Domain.

202. Right: Unknown artist. Nicolas Pakomio, circa 1940's. *In The Lost Caravel* by Robert Langdon, Sydney: Pacific Publications, 1975.

207. Maulucioni. *Distribution of haplogroup X*, 2010. Wikimedia Commons, 2020. https://en.wikipedia.org/wiki/File:Haplogroup_X_(mtDNA).PNG. CC BY 3.0.

212. Acosta, Carlos. *Los Menceyes de Tenerife in the Court of the Catholic Monarchs*, fresco on wall, 1764, Old Town Hall of San Cristobal de La Laguna, Tenerife. Wikimedia Commons, 2006. https://commons.wikimedia.org/wiki/File:AlonsoFernandezdeLugo2.JPG. Public domain.

214. Left: Raifikiva m, photographer. *Russian: Settlement "Arkaim"*, 2014. Wikimedia Commons, 2015. https://commons.wikimedia.org/wiki/File:Укрепленное поселение Аркаим. Аэрофотоснимок..jpg. CC BY-SA 4.0.

214. Center: Image by Jones, Nicholas E, photographer. *Sunrise at Stonehenge*. Shutterstock.com. https://www.shutterstock.com/image-photo/sunrise-stonehenge-673724080. Licensed from Shutterstock.com.

214. Right: Google Maps. *Goseck Circle*, 2018. Imagery ©2018 Google, Map data ©2018 GeoBasis-DE/BKG (©2009), Google.

215. Lang Antonsen, Kenny Arne and Antonsen, Jimmy John. *Reconstruction of the Trypillian city Maydanets c 4000 B.C*, 2014. Based on information from the book *Looking for Trypillya-Culture Proto-Cities* by Mykhailo Videiko. Wikimedia Commons, 2014. https://en.wikipedia.org/wiki/File:Trypillian_city_(Maydanets).jpg. CC BY-SA 4.0.

216. Lang Antonsen, Kenny Arne. *Cucuteni-Trypillian Temple*. Wikimedia Commons, 2019. https://commons.wikimedia.org/wiki/File:Cucuteni-trypillian_temple.jpg. CC BY-SA 4.0.

217. Left: Daderot, photographer. *Tularosa b/w pitcher with effigy handle, circa 1175 - 1300 AD*, Brooklyn Museum, 2013. Wikimedia Commons, 2014. https://commons.wikimedia.org/wiki/File:Jar,_Anasazi,_southwestern_United_States,_400-800_AD,_ceramic_-_Brooklyn_Museum_-_Brooklyn,_NY_-_DSC08344.JPG. Public domain.

217. Center: CristianChirita, photographer. *Cucuteni Omega Pottery*, Piatra Neamt Museum. Wikimedia Commons, 2009. https://commons.wikimedia.org/wiki/File:CucuteniOmegaPottery.JPG. CC BY-SA 3.0.

217. Right: BabelStone, photographer. *Banshan painted pottery*, 2011. Banshan phase (circa 2700 BC to 2300 BC) of the Yangshao culture, on exhibition at the Museum of the Mausoleum of the Nanyue King, Guangzhou, China. Wikimedia Commons, 2011. https://commons.wikimedia.org/wiki/File:Banshan_painted_pottery_pot_2.jpg. CC BY-SA 3.0.

218. Thompson, Lucy. *Che-na-wah-Weitch-ah-wah*, 1916. Yurok author, Lucy Thompson. Library of Congress Prints and Photographs division. Wikimedia Commons, 2010. https://commons.wikimedia.org/wiki/File:Lucy_Thompson_cph.3c26490.jpg. Public domain.

220. Underawesternsky, photographer. *Panorama of Pueblo Bonito great house in Chaco Canyon National Historic Park*, New Mexico, USA. Shuterstock.com. https://www.shutterstock.com/image-photo/panorama-pueblo-bonito-great-house-chaco-717647170. Licensed from Shutterstock.com.

221. NASA/Ideum. *Chaco Canyon Pueblo Bonito digital reconstruction*. Wikimedia Commons, 2007. https://commons.wikimedia.org/wiki/File:Chaco_Canyon_Pueblo_Bonito_digital_reconstruction.jpg. Public domain.

222. Left: Tobi 87, photographer. *Cliff Palace in Mesa Verde National Park*, Colorado, USA, 2007. Wikimedia Commons, 2008. https://commons.wikimedia.org/wiki/File:Cliff_Palace-Colorado-Mesa_Verde_NP.jpg. CC BY-SA 4.0.

222. Right: Reus, Ferdinand, photographer. *Cliff dwellings in the Bandiagara escarpment*, Mali, 2006. Wikimedia Commons, 2007. https://commons.wikimedia.org/wiki/File:Bandiagara_escarpment_2.jpg. CC BY-SA 2.0.

224. Roe, Herb. *Mississippian cultures*, 2010. Wikimedia Commons, 2010. https://commons.wikimedia.org/wiki/File:Mississippian_cultures_HRoe_2010.jpg. CC BY-SA 3.0.

225. Roe, Herb. *Mississippian culture mound components*, 2011. Wikimedia Commons, 2018. https://en.wikipedia.org/wiki/File:Mississippian_culture_mound_components_HRoe_2011.jpg. CC BY-SA 3.0.

228. QuartierLatin1968, photographer. *The Central Column of Cahokia's Woodhenge,* 2011. Wikimedia Commons, 2013. https://commons.wikimedia.org/wiki/File:Woodhenge_Cahokia_3998.jpg. CC BY-SA 3.0.

229. Collage, top left: Kvaran, Einar E (Carptrash), photographer. *Newark Mounds*, Newark, Ohio, USA, 1980s. Wikimedia Commons, 2017. https://commons.wikimedia.org/wiki/File:Newark_Mounds,_Newark,_Ohio,_USA.jpg. CC BY-SA 4.0.

229. Collage, top center: Saunaluoma, Sanna, photographer. *Fazenda Colorada,* Rio Branco, Acre, Brazil, 2012. Wikimedia Commons, 2012. https://en.wikipedia.org/wiki/File:Fazenda_Colorada.jpg. CC BY-SA 3.0.

229. Collage, top right: Google Maps. 2018. *Goseck Circle*. Imagery ©2018 Google, Map data ©2018 GeoBasis-DE/BKG (©2009), Google.

229. Collage, bottom left: MikPeach, photographer. *Avebury henge and stone circles*, 2009. Wikimedia Commons, 2017. https://commons.wikimedia.org/wiki/File:Wiltshire-Avebury.jpg. CC BY-SA 4.0.

229. Collage, bottom right: 4Kclips, photographer. *Fantastic view over Stonehenge in England,* Brighton, UK, 2019. Shutterstock.com. https://www.shutterstock.com/image-photo/fantastic-view-over-stonehenge-england-brighton-1648235137. Licensed from Shutterstock.com.

230. Left: Webber, Arthur M, photographer. *The Balanced Rock*, North Salem, NY, 2017. Wikimedia Commons, 2018. https://commons.wikimedia.org/wiki/File:AV5I2323_North_Salem_NY_Balancing_Rock.jpg. CC BY-SA 4.0.

230. Right: Klaus Rieder, Helge, photographer. *Carreg Samson*, Neolithic dolmen, southwest Wales, 2018. Wikimedia Commons, 2018. https://commons.wikimedia.org/wiki/File:CarregSamsonH4a.jpg. Public domain.

231. Left: Andriotis, Katharine, photographer. *Wangtown Chamber*, an ancient stone chamber located off Wangtown Road in Kent, Putnam County, New York, USA, 2009. Alamy Stock Photo. https://www.alamy.com/mediacomp/imagedetails.aspx?ref=BARA74. Licensed from Alamy Stock Photo.

231. Right: Kranewitter, Michael, photographer. *Tumulus de Kercado*, 2005. Wikimedia Commons, 2012. https://commons.wikimedia.org/wiki/File:Tumulus_de_Kercado_2005_02.jpg. CC BY-SA 4.0.

235. Sluijs, Peter van der, photographer. *Skeleton near Nazca*, Peru, 2012. Wikimedia Commons, 2012. https://commons.wikimedia.org/wiki/ File:Skull_with_body_of_the_nazca_culture_in_Peru.jpg. CC BY-SA 3.0.

236. Garcia, Alejandro Linares, photographer. *Model of the Cholula Pyramid site at the site museum*, Puebla, Mexico, 2011. Wikimedia Commons, 2011. https://commons.wikimedia.org/wiki/File:ModelCholula2.JPG. CC BY-SA 4.0.

239. S/V Moonrise, *Flag of Guna Yala*, Panama. Wikimedia Commons, 2009. https://en.wikipedia.org/wiki/File:Flag_of_Kuna_Yala.svg. CC BY SA-3.0.

240. St-Amant, Martin, photographer. *Eastern facade of the wall surrounding Kuelap fortress*, 2007. Wikimedia Commons, 2007. https://commons.wikimedia.org/wiki/File:Kuelap_-_Ao%C3%BBt_2007_-_05.jpg. CC BY 3.0.

241. Salvatierra Cuenca, Miguel, artist. *Los Millares*, painting located in the Millares visitor reception center. Used with permission from artist. Photo by Jose Mª Yuste, 2008. Wikimedia Commons, 2008. https://en.wikipedia.org/wiki/File:Los_Millares_recreacion_cuadro.jpg. Photo CC BY-SA 4.0.

241. Left: Calvert, Harley, photographer. *Restored Building Kuelap*, 2007. Wikimedia Commons, 2013. https://commons.wikimedia.org/wiki/File:Kuelap_Restoration.jpg. CC BY-SA 3.0.

241. Right: Madrinan, Maria, photographer. *Celtic Citania, in Santa Tegla mont*, Galicia Spain. Shutterstock.com https://www.shutterstock.com/image-photo/celtic-citania-santa-tegla-mont-galicia-719586133. Licensed from Shutterstock.com.

242. Left: TPYXA_ILLUSTRATION. *Conor Anthony McGregor, Irish professional mixed martial artist and boxer*, 2018. Shutterstock.com. https://www.shutterstock.com/image-illustration/conor-anthony-mcgregor-irish-professional-mixed-1172705026. Licensed from Shuttestock.com.

242. Center: Papiermond, photographer. *Sarcophagi of Karajia*, 2005. Wikimedia Commons, 2006. https://en.wikipedia.org/wiki/File:Karajia1.jpg. CC BY-SA 3.0.

242. Right: Sewell, Ian, photographer. *Ahu Akivi*, Easter Island, 2006. Wikimedia Commons, 2006.https://commons.wikimedia.org/wiki/File:Ahu-Akivi-1.JPG. CC BY-SA 3.0.

244. Left: Hodges, William. *Easter Island man*, 1777. Wikimedia Commons, 2007. https://commons.wikimedia.org/wiki/File:Easter_Island_Man.jpg. Public domain.

244. Right: Lassalle and Melan. *Native Pascuence*. In *Correo de Ultramar*, 1872, París: Lassalle y Melan, 1853-1885, p. 189. Available in Memoria Chilena, Biblioteca Nacional de Chile. http://www.memoriachilena.gob.cl/602/w3-article-70397.html. Public domain.

245. Top left: Hahnewald, Matt, photographer. *MUKTINATH, ANNAPURNA CIRCUIT*, Nepal, 2016. Shutterstock.com. https://www.shutterstock.com/image-photo/muktinath-annapurna-circuit-nepal-april-23-1588730410. Licensed from Shutterstock.com

245. Top right: Du Petit-Thouars, Abel. *Easter Island Native With Topknot and Beard*. In *Voyage autour du monde sur la frégate La Vénus commandée par M. Abel du Petit-Thouars, capitaine de Vaisseau, commandeur de la Légion d'honneur*, Paris: Gide, 1840-1845. Found in *Aku Aku; The Secret Of Easter Island* by Thor Heyerdahl, London: George Allen & Unwin Ltd, 1957, p. 183. Internet Archive. https://archive.org/details/dli.venugopal.701/page/n195/mode/2up. Public domain.

245. Bottom left: https://clevelandart.org/art/1940.53, photographer. *Head of Shiva*, circa 1100, Cambodia, Angkor. Cleveland Museum of Art, Purchase from the J.H. Wade Fund. Wikimedia Commons, 2019. https://commons.wikimedia.org/wiki/File:Clevelandart_1940.53.jpg. Public domain.

245. Bottom right: GTW, photographer. *Ahu Nao-Nao Moais wearing a red hat*, Anakena, Rapa Nui National Park, Easter Island, Chile. Shutterstock.com. https://www.shutterstock.com/image-photo/ahu-naonao-moais-wearing-red-hat-1514915321. Licensed from Shutterstock.com.

247. Collage, top left: Forbes, Alexander Kinloch. *Plan of Temple and Reservoir, Sun Temple, Modhera, Gujarat, India*. In *Râs Mâlâ: Or, Hindoo Annals of the Province of Goozerat, in Western India*, Volume 1, by Alexander Kinloch Forbes, Richardson Bros, 1856, p. 255-256. Wikimedia Commons, 2015. https://en.wikipedia.org/wiki/File:Plan_Modhera_Sun_Temple_Gujarat_India.jpg. Public domain.

247. Collage, top right: Jigar_rayputra, photographer. *Modhera Sun Temple*, Modhera, India, 2018. Wikimedia Commons, 2018. https://commons.wikimedia.org/wiki/File:Stepwell_,Modhera.jpg. CC BY-SA 4.0.

247. Collage, center right: Dhapa Nitaben Harshaddhai, photographer. *Several miniature shrines and niches along the Stepped well in Modhera Sun Temple complex*, Modehera, Gujarat, India, 2019. Shutterstock.com. https://www.shutterstock.com/image-photo/gujarat-india-december-12-2019-several-1579834762. Licensed from Shutterstock.com.

247. Collage, bottom left: Brattarb, photographer. *Tiwanaku*, Bolivia, 2010. Wikimedia Commons, 2010. https://commons.wikimedia.org/wiki/File:3_Tiwanaku.JPG. CC BY-SA 3.0.

247. Collage, bottom right: Brattarb, photographer. *Puma_Punku*, Bolivia, 2010. Wikimedia Commons, 2010. https://commons.wikimedia.org/wiki/File:7_Puma_Punku.jpg. CC BY-SA 3.0.

247. Collage, left: Peppé, Thomas Fraser, photographer. *Vapiya-ka-Kubha cave,* India, 1870. British Library, 2009. http://www.bl.uk/onlinegallery/onlineex/apac/photocoll/g/019pho0000125s1u00058000.html. Public domain.

247. Collage, center: Rehak, Matyas, photographer. *Ancient Inca style door of a house in Ollantaytambo village*, Sacred Valley of Incas, Peru. Shutterstock.com. https://www.shutterstock.com/image-photo/ancient-inca-style-door-house-ollantaytambo-1262553982. Licensed from Shutterstock.com.

247. Collage, right: ckchiu, photographer. *Inca temple doorway*, Machu Picchu, Peru. Shutterstock.com. https://www.shutterstock.com/image-photo/inca-temple-doorway-machu-picchu-peru-63075088. Licensed from Shutterstock.com.

248. Boychou, photographer. *Photograph of stone erected during ancient time at Willong Khullen*, a village in Senapati District, Manipur, India, 2010. Wikimedia Commons, 2010. https://en.wikipedia.org/wiki/File:Stone_Erections_of_Willong_Khullen.jpg. CC BY-SA 3.0.

250. Cherchen Man sketch by Sura Ondrunar Publishing.

251. Artist's impression of Tarim mummy full facial painting, by Sura Ondrunar Publishing.

251. Artist's impression of Tarim mummy full facial painting, by Sura Ondrunar Publishing.

252. en:User:Nomadtales, photographer. *Newgrange Entrance Stone*, 4500-5500 years old, Newgrange tomb, Ireland, 2005. Wikimedia Commons, 2006. https://commons.wikimedia.org/wiki/File:Newgrange_Entrance_Stone.jpg. CC BY-SA 3.0.

252. Robley, Major-General G. *Derivative of a 1910 illustration of Maori chief Hongi Hika*, after the portrait painted in England in 1820. The New Zealand Electronic Text Collection. http://www.nzetc.org/etexts/SmiMaor/SmiMaorP001a.jpg. Wikimedia Commons, 2011. https://commons.wikimedia.org/wiki/File:Hongi_Hika.jpg. CC BY-SA 3.0 NZ.

254. Dalbéra, Jean-Pierre. *A jeweled falcon of Tutankhamun holding the ankh,* Cairo museum, Egypt. Edited by Ra'ike. Wikimedia Commons, 2009. https://commons.wikimedia.org/wiki/File:Tutankhamun_Falcon1_(retouched).jpg. CC BY 2.0.

254. Left: Stolpe, Hjalmar. *Tepano, Easter Islanders in Tahiti*, based on an original photograph by author. In *Über die Tätowirung der Oster-Insulaner (About the Tattooing of the Easter Islanders)*, Berlin: R. Friedlaender, 1899, no. 6, p. 1-13. Wikimedia Commons, 2017. https://commons.wikimedia.org/wiki/File:Tepano,_Oster-Insulaners_auf_Tahiti._Nach_einer_photographischen_Originalaufnahme_des_Verfassers._Fig._4._%C3%9Cber_die_T%C3%A4towirung_der_Oster-Insulaner.jpg. Public domain.

254. Right: MykReeve, photographer. *The golden death mask of the Tutankhamun*, Egyptian Museum, Cairo, 2002. Wikimedia Commons, 2004. https://commons.wikimedia.org/wiki/File:Tutanchamun_Maske.jpg. CC BY-SA 3.0.

256. Weld-Blundell, Mr. H., photographer. *Megalithic Group at Messa in the Cyrenaica*. In *The Hill of the Graces: A Record of Investigation among the Trilithons and Megalithic Sites of Tripoli*, by H. S. Cowper, London: Methuen & Co., 1897, p. 169. Internet Archive, 2009. https://archive.org/details/hillgracesareco01cowpgoog/page/n199/mode/2up. Public domain.

257. Left: De Capell Brooke, Sir Arthur. *L'Uted*. In *Sketches in Spain and Morocco*, London: Henry Colburn and Richard Bentley, 1831, p. 39. Internet Archive, 2009. https://archive.org/details/sketchesinspainm02brok/page/n53/mode/2up. Public domain.

257. Right: MariSha, photographer. *Zorats Karer,* Sisian, Armenia, 2004. Wikimedia Commons, 2008. https://commons.wikimedia.org/wiki/File:Armenian_Qarhunj01.jpg. CC BY-SA 2.0.

258. Artist unknown, *Libyans (Berbers), a Nubian, a Syrian, and an Egyptian,* drawing by an unknown artist after a mural of the tomb of Seti I, copy of drawing by Heinrich Menu von Minutoli, 1820. Wikimedia Commons, 2007. https://commons.wikimedia.org/wiki/File:Races2.jpg. Public domain.

259. Ojj! 600, photographer. *Caucasus mountains,* Svaneti, Georgia, 2005. Wikimedia Commons, 2005. https://commons.wikimedia.org/wiki/File:VittfarneGeorgien_155.jpg. CC BY-SA 3.0.

260. Köppchen, Christian, photographer. *Mencey Pelicar,* sculpture of Mencey Pelicar in the Plaza de la Patrona de Canarias in Candelaria, Tenerife, created by José Abad. Wikimedia Commons, 2013. https://commons.wikimedia.org/wiki/File:Mencey_Pelicar.jpg. CC BY 3.0.

262. Phirosiberia. *The routes of the four Voyages of Christopher Columbus,* 2009. Wikimedia Commons, 2018. https://commons.wikimedia.org/wiki/File:Viajes_de_colon_en.svg. CC BY-SA 3.0.

263. Hajor, photographer. *Olmec head,* La Venta Park, Villahermosa, Tabasco, Mexico, 2001. Wikimedia Commons, 2005. https://commons.wikimedia.org/wiki/File:Mexico.Tab.OlmecHead.01.jpg. CC BY-SA 2.0.

263. Left: Madman2001, photographer. *Olmec mask,* Dumbarton Oaks collection, Washington DC, 2013. Wikimedia Commons, 2013 https://commons.wikimedia.org/wiki/File:Olmec_mask_(Dumbarton_Oaks)_1.JPG. CC BY-SA 3.0.

263. Right: Midloa, photographer. *Peninsula Hotel Chinese Lion,* Kowloon, Hong Kong. 2008. Wikimedia Commons, 2008. https://commons.wikimedia.org/wiki/File:HK_TST_Peninsula_Hotel_Chinese_Lion_01_a.jpg. CC BY-SA 3.0.

264. Brücke-Osteuropa, photographer. *Mausoleum of Han Yang Ling near Xian, model of pyramid,* der Han Yang Ling Museum, Xianyang, China, 2008. Wikimedia Commons, 2010. https://commons.wikimedia.org/wiki/File:Han_Yang_Ling_02.JPG. Public domain.

265. Top: Schengili-Roberts, Keith, photographer. *Amenmesse-Statue Head,* statue Head of the pharaoh Amenmesse, from the 19th dynasty, circa 1203-1200 B.C, Metropolitan Museum, 2007. Wikimedia Commons, 2007. https://en.wikipedia.org/wiki/File:Amenmesse-StatueHead_MetropolitanMuseum.png. CC BY-SA 2.5.

265. Bottom: Bodsworth, Jon, photographer. *Ka statue Rahotep,* Cairo Museum, 2007. Wikimedia Commons, 2008. https://en.wikipedia.org/wiki/File:Rahotep_statue.jpg. © Jon Bodsworth. Reproduced with permission.

266. Martonkurucz, photographer. *Tarim mummy,* 2015. Wikimedia Commons, 2015. https://commons.wikimedia.org/wiki/File:Tarim-mumia-4.jpg. CC BY-SA 4.0.

270. Wikipedia Loves Art participant one_click_beyond, photographer. *Viracocha, Eighth Inca,* oil painting, mid 18th century, Brooklyn Museum, 2009. Wikimedia Commons, 2009. https://commons.wikimedia.org/wiki/File:WLA_brooklynmuseum_18th_century_Viracocha.jpg. CC BY 2.5.

271. Top left: Fewings, Nick, photographer. *Buddha Tooth Relic Temple,* Singapore. Unsplash.com https://unsplash.com/photos/efD1FBZqYuQ. Licensed from Unsplash.com.

271. Top right: Artist unknown. *A Roundel of Brahma,* 19th century, India. Wikimedia Commons, 2012. https://en.wikipedia.org/wiki/File:A_roundel_of_Brahma.jpg. Public domain.

271. Middle left: Ober, Frederick A. *Quetzalcoatl.* In *Travels in Mexico and Life Among the Mexicans,* San Francisco: J. Dewing and Co., 1884, p. 508. Wikimedia Commons, 2017. https://commons.wikimedia.org/wiki/File:TLM_D516_Quetzalcoatl.jpg. Public domain.

271. Middle right: Hildebrand, Gabriel - Historiska Museet, photographer. *Frey statuette found in Rällinge,* 9th century, Historiska Museet, Stockholm, Sweden, 2011. Wikimedia Commons, 2018. https://commons.wikimedia.org/wiki/File:Frej_R%C3%A4llinge.jpg. CC BY 2.5.

271. Bottom: Mystique, Mickey, photographer. *Skeleton at Museum Lepenski Vir,* 2018. Wikimedia Commons, 2018. https://commons.wikimedia.org/wiki/File:Lepenski_Vir,_muzej_26.jpg. CC BY-SA 4.0.

273. Collage, top left: Saamiblog: http://saamiblog.blogspot.com, photographer. *Buckle from Oseberg Vikingship,* found with the Oseberg ship burial circa 800 CE, 2008. Wikimedia Commons, 2009. https://commons.wikimedia.org/wiki/File:Buckle_from_Oseberg_ Vikingship_Buddha_3.JPG. CC BY-SA 3.0.

273. Collage, top center: Chirita, Cristian, photographer. *Archeological Artefacts in Sozopol Museum,* Sozopol Museum, 2011. Wikimedia Commons, 2011. https://commons. wikimedia.org/wiki/File:Sozopol_Archaeological_Museum_IMG_4214.JPG. GNU Free Documentation License, Version 1.2. https://commons.wikimedia.org/wiki/ Commons:GNU_Free_Documentation_License,_version_1.2.

273. Collage, top right: Dbachmann, photographer. *Samarra Bowl,* circa 4,000 BC, Pergamon Museum, Berlin. Wikimedia Commons, 2010. https://en.wikipedia.org/wiki/File:Samarra_ bowl.jpg. CC BY-SA 4.0.

273. Collage, center left: Haylli, photographer. *Sican Vessel in the Huaca Rajada Site Museum*, Huaca Rajada Site Museum, Wikimedia Commons, 2009. https://commons.wikimedia. org/ wiki/File:Sican-Vessel-in-the-Huaca-Rajada-Site-Museum-001.JPG. Public domain.

273. Collage, center: PHGCOM, photographer. *Etruscan Pendant with Swastika Symbols Bolsena Italy 700 BCE to 650 BCE.* Louvre Museum, 2008. Wikimedia Commons, 2010. https:// commons.wikimedia.org/wiki/File:Etruscan_pendant_with_swastika_symbols_Bolsena_ Italy_700_BCE_to_650_BCE.jpg. CC BY-SA 3.0.

273. Collage, center right: BabelStone, photographer. *Early Anglo-Saxon Cinerary Urn from North Elmham, Norfolk,* circa 5th and 6th century, British Museum, 2010. Wikimedia Commons, 2010. https://commons.wikimedia.org/wiki/File:British_Museum_cinerary_urn_with_ swastika_motifs.jpg. Public domain.

273. Collage, bottom left: Шнапс, photographer. Скоба для стрел *(Bracket for Arrows),* 2009. Wikimedia Commons, 2012. https://commons.wikimedia.org/wiki/File:Скоба_ для_стрел. JPG. CC BY-SA 3.0.

273. Collage, bottom center: Tylas at English Wikipedia, photographer. *Zionpictographs*, Zion National Park, 2006. Wikimedia Commons, 2006. https://commons.wikimedia.org/wiki/ File:Zionpictographs.jpg. CC BY-SA 3.0.

273. Collage, bottom right: Before My Ken, photographer. *Indus Valley Civilization Seals,* British Museum, 2005. Wikimedia Commons, 2009. https://commons.wikimedia.org/wiki/ File:IndusValleySeals_swastikas.JPG. CC BY-SA 3.0.

273. Top Left: Wikipedia Loves Art participant va_va_val, photographer. *Buddha head*, stucco, 4th-5th century, Hadda, Afghanistan, 2009. Wikimedia Commons, 2009. https://commons.wikimedia. org/wiki/File:WLA_vanda_Afghanistan_stucco_head_of_the_Buddha.jpg. CC BY-SA 2.5.

273. Top Right: Artist unknown. *Moche mask,* 6th-7th century, Peru. The Michael C. Rockefeller Memorial Collection, Bequest of Nelson A. Rockefeller, 1979. https://www.metmuseum. org/art/collection/search/313442. Public domain.

273. Bottom: Rama, photographer. *Stele of Lady Taperet,* painted wood, 10th-9th century BC (22nd dynasty, Louvre Museum, 2007. Wikimedia Commons, 2007. https://commons. wikimedia.org/wiki/File:Taperet_stele_E52_mp3h9201.jpg. CC BY-SA 3.0 FR.

275. Zenz, Rainer, photographer. *Trundholm Sun Chariot*, 2005. Wikimedia Commons, 2005. https://en.m.wikipedia.org/wiki/File:Trundholm.jpg. Public domain.

276. Kmusser. *Tarim River Basin*, 2008. Digital Chart of the World and GTOPO data, labels based on GEOnet. Wikimedia Commons, 2008. https://commons.wikimedia.org/wiki/ File:Tarimrivermap.png. CC BY-SA 3.0.

278. Millière, Auguste. C. *Thomas Paine*, 1876. After Romney, George. 1734-1802. After Sharp, William. 1792. Wikimedia Commons, 2010. https://commons.wikimedia.org/wiki/ File:Thomas_Paine.jpg. Public domain.

283. Morris, Ann Axtell. *Watercolour reproduction of mural from the Temple of the Warriors at Chichen Itza.* In *Temple of the Warriors at Chichen Itzá, Yucatan,* Morris, E. H., J. Charlot, and A. A. Morris, The Washington Carnegie Institute, 1931, plate 145. University of Illinois Urbana-Champaign. Internet Archive, 2019. https://archive.org/details/templeofwarriors02morr/ page/338/mode/2up. CC BY-NC-SA 4.0

283. Morris, Ann Axtell. *Watercolour reproduction of mural from the Temple of the Warriors at Chichen Itza*. In *Temple of the Warriors at Chichen Itzá, Yucatan*, Morris, E. H., J. Charlot, and A. A. Morris, The Washington Carnegie Institute, 1931, plate 136. University of Illinois Urbana-Champaign. Internet Archive, 2019. https://archive.org/details/templeofwarriors02morr/page/338/mode/2up. CC BY-NC-SA 4.0

284. Artist unknown. *Folio 65r, Codex Mendoza, Aztec codex,* Mid-16th century. Wikimedia Commons, 2006. https://en.wikipedia.org/wiki/File:Codex_Mendoza_folio_65r.jpg. Public domain.

286. Artist unknown. *Moriori people*, late 19th century. Christchurch: Canterbury Museum. Wikimedia Commons, 2012. https://commons.wikimedia.org/wiki/File:Moriori_people.jpg. Public domain.

287. Castaigne, Andre. *Alexander visits the Apis bull at the temple in Memphis*, circa 1898-1899. Wikimedia Commons, 2006. https://commons.wikimedia.org/wiki/File:Alexander_visits_the_Apis_bull_at_the_temple_in_Memphis_by_Andre_Castaigne_(1898-1899).jpg. Public domain.

288. Tataryn. *Roman Empire Trajan 117AD*, 2012. Wikimedia Commons, 2020. https://en.wikipedia.org/wiki/File:Roman_Empire_Trajan_117AD.png. CC BY-SA 3.0.

288. Tuxen, Laurits. *The Taking of Arkona in 1169, King Valdemar and Bishop Absalon,* Late 19th century. The Museum of National History. Wikimedia Commons, 2008. https://commons.wikimedia.org/wiki/File:Bishop_Absalon_topples_the_god_Svantevit_at_Arkona.PNG. Public domain.

289. Nguyen, Marie-Lan, photographer. *Roman coin from 313 AD*. Collection of Carlos de Beistegui, Cabinet des Médailles, France, 2006. Wikimedia Commons, 2007. https://commons.wikimedia.org/wiki/File:Constantine_multiple_CdM_Beistegui_233.jpg. Public domain.

CHAPTER FIVE: THE CHILDREN OF THE SUN

299. Grobe, Dr. Hannes. *Glaciation*. Wikimedia Commons, 2008. https://commons.wikimedia.org/wiki/File:Iceage_north-intergl_glac_hg.png. CC BY 3.0. Ice coverage: Ehlers, J., and P.L. Gibbard. *The extentand chronology of Cenozoic global glaciation*. Quaternary International, 164-165, 6-20,2007. Topography: U.S. Department of Commerce, National Oceanic and Atmospheric Administration, National Geophysical Data Center (NOAA/NGDC), 2-minute Gridded Global Relief Data (ETOPO2) 2006. Map software: Schlitzer, R. 2007. Ocean Data View, http://odv.awi.de.

300. Tampa Tribune. *Giant Indian Skeletons,* 1922. Wikimedia Commons, 2017. https://commons.wikimedia.org/wiki/File:Tampa_giant_skeleton_Hillsboro_Bay_giant.jpg. Public domain.

302. Dr. K, photographer. *Titanomachy at the Gorgon pediment*, at Artemis Temple in Corfu, Greece, 2007. Wikimedia Commons, 2011. https://commons.wikimedia.org/wiki/File:Titanomachy_at_the_Gorgon_pediment_at_Artemis_Temple_in_Corfu.jpg. CC BY-SA 3.0.

303. Daderot, photographer. *Shamash, Sippar*, 870 BC, plaster cast of limestone original, Oriental Institute Museum, University of Chicago, 2014. Wikimedia Commons, 2015. https://commons.wikimedia.org/wiki/File:Shamash,_the_Sun_God,_Sippar,_Early_Iron_Age,_870_BC,_plaster_cast_of_limestone_original_-_Oriental_Institute_Museum,_University_of_Chicago_-_DSC07413.JPG. Public domain.

305. Loubat, Joseph Florimond. *A group of natives in the central highlands of Mexico, capturing and putting to death a giant*. In *Codex Vaticanus 3738 A*, 1900, p. 8v. Universitätsbibliothek Rostock. FAMSI. http://www.famsi.org/research/loubat/Vaticanus%203738/page_08v.jpg. Public domain.

307. MM. *Indus Civilization*. Wikimedia Commons, 2005. https://commons.wikimedia.org/wiki/File:Civilt%C3%A0ValleIndoMappa.png. CC BY-SA 3.0.

310. Bence, Ocskay, photographer. *The eyes of Buddha symbol of buddhism*. Shutterstock.com https://www.shutterstock.com/image-photo/eyes-buddha-symbol-buddhism-506426023. Licensed from Shutterstock.com.

312. Left: Moraes, Cicero et alii, artist. *Second version (2.0) of Archaeological Forensic Facial Reconstruction of the individual LB1 of the species Homo floresiensis*, part of open source exhibition *Facce. I molti volti della storia umana*, 2015. Wikimedia Commons, 2018. https://commons.wikimedia.org/wiki/File:Homo_floresiensis_v_2-0.jpg. CC BY 4.0.

312. Center: The Neanderthal Museum. *Reconstruction of the Homo erectus: Turkana Boy from the site of Nariokotome, Kenya*, exhibited in the Neanderthal Museum in Mettmann, Germany. Wikimedia Commons, 2020. https://commons.wikimedia.org/wiki/File:Homo-erectus_Turkana-Boy_(Ausschnitt)_Fundort_Nariokotome,_Kenia,_Rekonstruktion_im_Neanderthal_Museum.jpg. CC BY-SA 4.0.

312. Right: The Neanderthal Museum. *Reconstruction of Homo sapiens neanderthalensis*, exhibited in the Neanderthal Museum in Mettmann, Germany. Wikimedia Commons, 2020. https://commons.wikimedia.org/wiki/File:Homo_sapiens_neanderthalensis-Mr._N.jpg. CC BY-SA 4.0.

312. Primola, Nicolas, artist. *Digital illustration and render of a Neanderthal man*. Shutterstock.com. https://www.shutterstock.com/image-illustration/digital-illustration-render-neanderthal-man-310746206. Licensed from Shutterstock.com.

313. Left: Laplume, Mark, artist. *Image of Paracas Skulls*. Root Race Research, 2016. https://www.facebook.com/RootRaceResearch/photos/a.250594045060672/1098721666914568. Reproduced with permission.

313. Center: Foerster, Brien. *Paracas Skull*. Hidden Inca Tours, 2018. https://hiddenincatours.com/comparison-elongated-skulls-paracas-peru-egypt-russia-black-sea. Reproduced with permission.

313. Right: Silentlight87, photographer. *Schädel der Chongos*, Regional Museum of Ica, Ica Peru, 2016. Wikimedia Commons, 2016. https://commons.wikimedia.org/wiki/File:Sch%C3%A4del_der_Chongos.jpg. CC BY-SA 4.0.

314. United States Navy. *Gimbal The First Official UAP Footage from the USG for Public Release, 2015*. Gimbal is one of three US military videos of unidentified aerial phenomenon (UAP) that has been through the official declassification review process of the United States government and has been approved for public release. Wikimedia Commons, 2020. https://commons.wikimedia.org/wiki/File:Gimbal_The_First_Official_UAP_Footage_from_the_USG_for_Public_Release.webm. Public domain.

CHAPTER SIX: JESUS AND THE RELIGION OF THE SUN

318. Leutemann, Heinrich. *The destruction of the Irminsul by Charlemagne*. In Nordisch-germanische Götter und Helden by Wägner, Wilhelm, Otto Spamer, Leipzig & Berlin, 1882, p. 159. Wikimedia Commons, 2008. https://commons.wikimedia.org/wiki/File:Zerst%C3%B6rung_der_Irminsaule_durch_Karl_den_Gro%C3%9Fen_by_Heinrich_Leutemann.jpg. Public domain.

319. Angelico, Fra. *Christ the Judge*, 1447, Cappella di San Brizio. Wikimedia Commons, 2011. https://commons.wikimedia.org/wiki/File:Fra_Angelico_-_Christ_the_Judge_-_WGA00679.jpg. Public domain.

319. Unknown author. *End page of the Apocryphon of John and beginning of Gospel of Thomas*, from *The Nag Hammadi Library*, 4th century. Wikimedia Commons, 2011. https://commons.wikimedia.org/wiki/File:Apocryphon_of_John.jpg. Public domain.

322. Jaberian, Morteza, photographer. *Mandeans*, Tasnim News Agency. Wikimedia Commons, 2018. https://en.wikipedia.org/wiki/File:Mandaeans_02.jpg. CC BY 4.0.

CHAPTER EIGHT: WHY DID ANCIENT PEOPLE VENERATE THE SUN?

336. James, Gilbert. *How the Sun Appeared Like the Moon*. In *The Myths of Mexico and Peru*, by Lewis Spence, New York: Thomas Y. Crowell Company Publishers, 1913, p. 330. Wikimedia Commons, 2015. https://commons.wikimedia.org/wiki/File:The_myths_of_Mexico_and_Peru_(1913)_(14783779812).jpg. Public domain.

337. Daniel, Csorfoly, photographer. *Dendera Hathor Temple Complex*, Egypt, 2007. Wikimedia Commons, 2007. https://commons.wikimedia.org/wiki/File:DenderaHathorTempleCom plexQenaEgypt602-2007feb10PhotoByCsorfolyDaniel.JPG. Public domain.

339. Srkris at English Wikipedia, photographer. *Hindu Priest from the Nambudiri Caste Performs a Yajna*, Kerala, India. Wikimedia Commons, 2008. https://commons.wikimedia.org/wiki/File:Yajna1.jpg. Public domain.

341. Van Honthorst, Gerard. *The Adoration of the Shepherds,* 1622. Wallraf–Richartz Museum, Wikimedia Commons, 2011. https://commons.wikimedia.org/wiki/File:Gerard_van_Honthorst_-_Adoration_of_the_Shepherds_-_WGA11657.jpg. Public domain.

343. Cheyne, T.K. and Black, J. Sutherland. *Fig. 12 – Amenhotep IV and his wife worshiping the solar disk*. In *Encyclopaedia Biblica Volume II - E To K*, New York: The Macmillan Company, 1901, p. 1239. Internet Archive, 2015. https://archive.org/details/in.ernet.dli.2015.89084/page/n55/mode/2up. Public domain.

344. Top Left: NASA image by Jeff Schmaltz, MODIS Rapid Response Team, Goddard Space Flight Center. *Cyclone Favio*, 2007. Wikimedia Commons, 2007. https://commons.wikimedia.org/wiki/File:Cyclone_Favio_22_February_2007_0820Z.jpg. Public domain.

344. Top Right: NASA, ESA, and the Hubble Heritage Team (STScl/AURA). *Hubble Space Telescope image showing a group of interacting galaxies,* 2010. Wikimedia Commons, 2011. https://commons.wikimedia.org/wiki/File:UGC_1810_and_UGC_1813_in_Arp_273_(captured_by_the_Hubble_Space_Telescope).jpg. Public domain.

344. Center Right: Wee, Lawrence, photographer. *Unfurling Fern Tip*. Shutterstock.com. https://www.shutterstock.com/image-photo/unfurling-fern-tip-13375597. Licensed from Shutterstock.com.

345. Left: Bjørklid, Finn, photographer. *Runestone*, Gotland, 2005. Wikimedia Commons, 2005. https://commons.wikimedia.org/wiki/File:Gotlandstein.jpg. Public domain.

345. Center: Bkwillwm, photographer. *Minoan Master of Animals jewelry,* from the Aegina Treasure, British Museum, 2010. Wikimedia Commons, 2015. https://commons.wikimedia.org/wiki/File:Minoan_Master_of_Animals_jewellery.jpg. CC BY-SA 4.0.

345. Right: Lee, Ian, photographer. *The Long Man of Wilmington*, Polegate, United Kingdom, 2009. Wikimedia Commons, 2015. https://commons.wikimedia.org/wiki/File:The_Long_Man_of_Wilmington_(4219108070).jpg. CC BY 2.0.

345. Bottom, left: Hjaltland Collection, photographer. *Modern impression on clay of Achaemenid cylinder seal*, 5th. c. BC. Wikimedia Commons, 2014. https://commons.wikimedia.org/wiki/File:Cylinder_Seal,_Achaemenid,_modern_ impression_05.jpg. CC BY-SA 3.0.

345. Bottom, right: National Museum of Iran, photographer. *Chlorite object Jiroft*, Kerman c. 2500 BC, National Museum of Iran, 2017. Wikimedia Commons, 2017. https://commons.wikimedia.org/wiki/File:Chlorite_object_Jiroft,_Kerman_ca._2500_BCE,_Bronze_Age_I,_National_Museum_of_Iran.jpg. CC BY-SA 4.0.

346. Unger, Roland, photographer. *Edfu Temple, first pylon*, Egypt, 2006. Wikimedia Commons, 2012. https://commons.wikimedia.org/wiki/File:EdfuTempleFacade.jpg. CC BY-SA 3.0.

346. Red, Jeremy, photographer. *Philae Temple*. Shutterstock.com. https://www.shutterstock.com/image-photo/philae-temple-isis-trajans-kiosk-sunny-684849580. Licensed from Shutterstock.com.

347. Image by Sura Ondrunar Publishing

347. Mhwater, photographer. *The Gateway of the Sun from the Tiwanaku Civilization in Bolivia*. Wikimedia Commons, 2006. https://commons.wikimedia.org/wiki/File:Zonnepoort_tiwanaku.jpg. Public domain.

347. Lukiyanova Natalia frenta, photographer. *Ancient Mayan pyramid (Kukulcan Temple),* Chichen Itza, Yucatan, Mexico. Licensed from Shutterstock.com. https://www.shutterstock.com/image-photo/ancient-mayan-pyramid-kukulcan-temple-chichen-699889807. Licensed from Shutterstock.com.

348. Hajor, photographer. *Tomb KV34 (Thutmose III) 11.th hour Amduat,* Valley of the Kings, Luxor, Egypt, 2002. Wikimedia Commons, 2005. https://commons.wikimedia.org/wiki/File:Egypt.KV34.07.jpg. CC BY-SA 3.0.

349. Dahl, Jeff. *Aker*, 2008. Wikimedia Commons, 2008. https://commons.wikimedia.org/wiki/File:Aker.svg. CC BY-SA 4.0

CHAPTER NINE: REVIVAL

352. Masalskis, Mantas, photographer. *Hindu-Romuvan ecumenism*. Wikimedia Commons, 2009. https://commons.wikimedia.org/wiki/File:Hindu-Romuvan_ecumenism.png. CC BY 2.0.

352. Asamblea Nacional del Ecuador, photographer. *Ancestral Possession of the President of Bolivia, Evo Morales*, 2010. Wikimedia Commons, 2016. https://commons.wikimedia.org/wiki/File:Asamble%C3%ADsta_participan_en_ la_Posesi%C3%B3n_Ancestral_del_Presidente_de_Bolivia,_Evo_Morales_(4295908812).jpg. CC BY-SA 2.0.

355. Image by Sura Ondrunar Publishing

355. Image by Sura Ondrunar Publishing

APPENDIX

357. Sorensen, Bjarte, photographer. *Ahu Tahai*, a close up of the moai at Ahu Tahai, restored with coral eyes by the American archaeologist William Mullo, Easter Island, 2005. Modified by Zantastik~commonswiki. Wikimedia Commons, 2006. https://en.wikipedia.org/wiki/File:Ahu_Tahai.jpg. CC BY-SA 3.0.

358. Eichmann, Gerd, photographer. *Tula*, archeological site in Mexico, 1980. Wikimedia Commons, 2020. https://commons.wikimedia.org/wiki/File:Tula-04-Tempelpyramide-1980-gje.jpg. CC BY-SA 4.0.

Copyright Acknowledgments

TEXTUAL ACKNOWLEDGMENTS

Copyrighted texts quoted in this book are listed alphabetically by title of work.

"ABO Blood Groups in Chilean and Peruvian Mummies. II. Results of Agglutination-Inhibition Technique." Marvin J. Allison, Ali A. Hossaini, Juan Munizaga, and Rosa Fung. *American Journal of Physical Anthropology* 49, no. 1 (1978): 139-142. © 1978 Wiley-Liss, Inc., A Wiley Company. https://doi.org/10.1002/ajpa.1330490121. Reproduced with permission from Wiley.

"ABO blood groups in Peruvian mummies. I. An evaluation of techniques." M.J. Allison, A.A. Hossaini, N. Castro, J. Munizaga, and A. Pezzia. *American Journal of Physical Anthropology* 44, (1976): 55-61. © 1976 Wiley-Liss, Inc., A Wiley Company. https://doi.org/10.1002/ajpa.1330440108. Reproduced with permission from Wiley.

"About Thor Heyerdahl." © The Kon-Tiki Museum. Kon-Tiki.no, https://www.kon-tiki.no/thor-heyerdahl.

Aelian: On the Characteristics of Animals, Vol. II. A. F. Scholfield, translator. © The President and Fellows of Harvard College. London: William Heinemann, 1959.

"Akhbār al-zamān." © 2015 Jason Colavito, translator. JasonColavito.com, 2015.

Aku-Aku: The Secret of Easter Island. © 1957 Thor Heyerdahl. Chicago: Rand McNally & Company. English edition © 1958 George Allen & Unwin Ltd.

America Before. © 2019 Graham Hancock. Great Britain: Coronet, 2019, Kindle edition.

American Indians in the Pacific. © 1952 Thor Heyerdahl. London: George Allen & Unwin, 1952.

"Ancient Alignment in The Andes Hints at A Lost Global High Culture." © 2016 Dave Truman. The Official Graham Hancock Website, January 2, 2016. http://grahamhancock.com/trumand1.

"Ancient DNA reveals 'into Africa' migration." Rebecca Morelle, quoting Dr. Andrea Manica. BBC, October 8, 2015. https://www.bbc.com/news/science-environment-34479905.

"Ancient Egyptian mummy genomes suggest an increase of Sub-Saharan African ancestry in post-Roman periods." Verena J. Schuenemann, Alexander Peltzer, Beatrix Welte, W. Paul van Pelt, Martyna Molak, Chuan-Chao Wang, Anja Furtwängler, et al. © 2017 Springer Nature. *Nature Communications* 8, (2017). https://doi.org/10.1038/ncomms15694. CC BY 4.0.

"Ancient Ethiopian genome reveals extensive Eurasian admixture in Eastern Africa." M. Gallego Llorente, E. R. Jones, A. Eriksson, V. Siska, K. W. Arthur, J. W. Arthur, M. C. Curtis, J. T. Stock, M. Coltorti, P. Pieruccini, S. Stretton, F. Brock, T. Higham, Y. Park, M. Hofreiter, D. G. Bradley, J. Bhak, R. Pinhasi, A. Manica. © 2015 American Association for the Advancement of Science. *Science* 350, no. 6262, (2015): 820-822. https://doi.org/10.1126/science.aad2879. Reprinted with permission from AAAS.

"Ancient New Zealand Surveyors & Astronomers." © 2009 Martin Doutré. Ancient Celtic New Zealand. http://www.celticnz.co.nz/SurveyorsNZ/Ancient%20New%20Zealand%20Surveyors.htm. Reproduced with permission.

"The Ancient Surveying Structures on the Bombay Hills." © Martin Doutré. Ancient Celtic New Zealand. http://www.celticnz.co.nz/AucklandAlignment1.htm. Reproduced with permission.

"Ancient Writings: Pre-Platonic Writings Pertinent to Atlantis." © 2001, 2011 R. Cedric Leonard. Quest for Atlantis. https://atlantisquestscience.wordpress.com/culture/ancient-writings.

Ancient Written Sources of European Nations About Their Ancestral Homeland—Armenia and Armenians. © 2017 Angela Teryan. Yerevan: Voskan Yerevantsi, 2017.

"Archaic America: the Earthworks Mystery (#4/4) Cosmographic Research w/ Randall Carlson 3/14/08." © 2008 Randall Carlson. YouTube, February 12, 2019. https://youtu.be/uvePXpQdf80.

"Arkaim, Russia's Strongest Anomaly Zone." © 2010 Dmitry Sudakov. Pravda.Ru, June 7, 2010. http://www.pravdareport.com/science/113680-arkaim.

Ascending the Steps to Hlidskjalf: The Cult of Odinn in Early Scandinavian Aristocracy. © 2017 Joshua Rood, Haskoli islands, 2017. Quoted in Oates, The Hanged God.

Awakening Osiris: The Egyptian Book of the Dead. © 1988 Normandi Ellis, translator. Boston, MA: Phanes Press, 1988.

"The Azerbaijan Connection." © 1995 Thor Heyerdahl, Azerbaijan International. *Azerbaijan International*, (1995): 60-61, http://azer.com/aiweb/categories/magazine/31_folder/31_articles/31_thorazerconn.html.

"The Bearded Gods Speak." © 1971 Thor Heyerdahl. In *The Quest for America* edited by Geoffrey Ashe. New York: Praeger Publishers, 1971.

Beyond the Milky Way: Hallucinatory Imagery of the Tukano Indians. Gerado Reichel-Dolmatoff. © 1978 The Regents of the University of California. UCLA Latin America Center Publications, 1978. Quoted in Hancock, America Before.

Blond Indians of the Darien Jungle. Richard O Marsh. © Allied Press Ltd. Dunstan Times, Issue 3275, June 1925, https://paperspast.natlib.govt.nz/newspapers/DUNST19250622.2.44. CC BY-NC-SA 3.0 NZ.

"Boats in Rock Art of Gobustan." © 2014 Novus AS, Malahat Farajova. In *Thor Heyerdahl's Search for Odin*, edited by Vibeke Roggen. Novus Press, 2014.

The Book of Kolyada, 2nd ed. © 2010 Alexander Igorevich Asov. Moscow: FAIR Publishing House. English excerpts translated for Sura Ondrunar Publishing, 2018.

"February 2014 AOM: The Ancient Giants Who Ruled America." © 2014 Richard Dewhurst. The Official Graham Hancock Website, January 31, 2014. https://grahamhancock.com/dewhurstr1.

Fingerprints of the Gods. © 1995 Graham Hancock. Crown/Archetype, 1995, Kindle edition, 2011.

"Genomic Analyses of Pre-European Conquest Human Remains from the Canary Islands Reveal Close Affinity to Modern North Africans." © 2017 Ricardo Rodríguez-Varela, Torsten Günther, Maja Krzewińska, Jan Storå, Thomas H. Gillingwater, Malcolm MacCallum, Juan Luis Arsuaga, et al. *Current Biology* 27, no. 21 (2017): 3396-3402.e5. Published by Elsevier. https://doi.org/10.1016/j.cub.2017.09.059. CC BY-NC-ND 4.0.

"The Giant Deception." © 2016 Jason Jarrell and Sarah Farmer. Road2Ruins.com, January 14, 2016, http:///road2ruins.com/the-giant-deception.

Giants on Record: America's Hidden History, Secrets in the Mounds and the Smithsonian Files. © 2015 Jim Vieira and Hugh Newman, Preface by Ross Hamilton. Glastonbury: Avalon Rising Publications, 2015.

Gods, Sages and Kings. Per the request dated September 12th 2018, reproduced with permission from *Gods, Sages and Kings*, by Dr. David Frawley. Lotus Press, a division of Lotus Brands, Inc., PO Box 325, Twin Lakes, WI 53181, USA, www.lotuspress.com © 1991 All Rights Reserved.

"Goseck Henge: (The 'German Stonehenge')." © Scott Jones, Elaine Jones. Ancient-Wisdom. http://www.ancient-wisdom.com/germanygoseck.htm.

"Greenland Ice Core Analysis Shows Drastic Climate Change near End of Last Ice Age." © 2008 University of Colorado at Boulder. ScienceDaily, June 19, 2008. https://www.sciencedaily.com/releases/2008/06/080619142112.htm.

"Guide to the Kolbrin." © 2015 Yvonne Whiteman. The Official Graham Hancock Website, October 17, 2015. https://grahamhancock.com/whitemany1.

"Half of European men share King Tut's DNA." Alice Baghdjian, quoting Roman Scholz director of the iGENEA Centre. Reuters, August 2, 2011. https://www.reuters.com/article/oukoe-uk-britain-tutankhamun-dna-idAFTRE7704OR20110801.

The Hanged God: Odin Grimnir. © 2019 Shanti Oates. Canada: Anathema Publishing Ltd., 2019.

"Haplogroup H (mtDNA)." Maciamo Hay. © Eupedia. Eupedia, July 2020, https://www.eupedia.com/europe/Haplogroup_H_mtDNA.shtml.

"Haplogroup R1a (Y-DNA)." Maciamo Hay. © Eupedia. Eupedia, April 2020. https://www.eupedia.com/europe/Haplogroup_R1a_Y-DNA.shtml.

"Haplogroup R1b (Y-DNA." Maciamo Hay. © Eupedia. Eupedia, June 2020. https://www.eupedia.com/europe/Haplogroup_R1b_Y-DNA.shtml.

"Haplogroup T (mtDNA." Maciamo Hay. © Eupedia. Eupedia, July 2020. https://www.eupedia.com/europe/Haplogroup_T_mtDNA.shtml.

"Haplogroup U2 (mtDNA." Maciamo Hay. © Eupedia. Eupedia, July 2020. https://www.eupedia.com/europe/Haplogroup_U2_mtDNA.shtml.

"Haplogroup X (mtDNA)." Wikipedia. https://en.wikipedia.org/wiki/Haplogroup_X_(mtDNA). CC-BY-SA 3.0.

"Head Space: Behind 10,000 Years of Artificial Cranial Modification." © 2015 Chris White. Atlas Obscura, May 26, 2015, https://www.atlasobscura.com/articles/head-space-artificial-cranial-deformation. Quotes "Artificially deformed crania from the Hun-Germanic Period (5th–6th century AD) in northeastern Hungary: historical and morphological analysis." Molnár, Mónika, István János, László Szűcs, and László Szathmáry. © AANS, 2014. *Neurosurg Focus* 36, 2014.

Heaven's Mirror: Quest for the Lost Civilization. © 1998 Graham Hancock and Santha Faiia. New York: Three Rivers Press, 1998.

"Higher-resolution K = 11 analysis of the European admixture in Chinchorro DNA" © 2018 Genetiker. Genetiker, February 10, 2018. https://genetiker.wordpress.com/2018/02/10/higher-resolution-k-11-analysis-of-the-european-admixture-in-chinchorro-dna. Reproduced with permission.

The Holy Bible, NEW INTERNATIONAL VERSION®, NIV®. Copyright © 1973, 1978, 1984, 2011 by Biblica, Inc.® Used by permission. All rights reserved worldwide.

"The Hopi Message." © 1992 Thomas Banyacya. The Alpha Institute. http://www.welcomehome.org/rainbow/prophecy/hopi.html.

Hua Hu Ching: The Unknown Teachings of Lao Tzu. © 1992 Brian Browne Walker, translator. San Francisco: HarperCollins, 1995.

"Ice Ages, Atlantis, and the Azores Pyramid." © 2013 Randall Carlson. YouTube, September 30, 2013. https://youtu.be/gQv8DPXwm8Q?t=1670.

The I Ching or Book of Changes. Richard Wilhelm, Cary F Baynes, translator. © 1950, 1967 Bollingen Foundation Inc. London: Routledge & Kegan Paul, 1968.

The Incas of Pedro de Cieza de Léon. Pedro Cieza de Léon, Harriet de Onís, translator, Victor Wolfgang von Hagen, editor. © 1959 University of Oklahoma Press. Norman: University of Oklahoma Press, 1959.

"Indo-European before the Indo-Europeans? - New Evidence from Mesopotamia." © 2009 University of Copenhagen. Roots of Europe, University of Copenhagen, 2009. https://rootsofeurope.ku.dk/english/calendar/archive_2009/euphratic.

"Indo-European Vocabulary in Old Chinese." © 1988 Tsung-tung Chang. *Sino-Platonic Papers* 7 (1988), p. 35. http://sino-platonic.org/complete/spp007_old_chinese.pdf. CC BY-NC-ND 2.5.

In Search of the Miraculous. P.D. Ouspensky. © 1949 Harcourt, Brace & World, Inc. New York: Harcourt, Brace & World, Inc, 1949, London: Routledge & Kegan Paul, 1950.

"The Irminsul." © 2017 Cyrus Gorgani. Real Rune Magick, December 25, 2017. http://realrunemagick.blogspot.com/2017/12/the-irminsul.html. CC BY-NC-ND 4.0.

Itämerensuomalaisten Mytologia. © 2012 Anna-Leena Siikala. Helsinki: Suomalaisen Kirjallisuuden Seura (SKS), Helsinki, 2012. https://kirja.elisa.fi/ekirja/itamerensuomalaisten-mytologia.

"King Tut Related to Half of European Men? Maybe Not." Stephanie Pappas, quoting Roman Scholz director of the iGENEA Centre. LiveScience, August 3, 2011. https://www.livescience.com/15388-discovery-channel-tutankhamen-dna.html.

The Kolbrin. © 1998 The Hope Trust, © 2014 The Culdian Trust. New Zealand: The Culdian Trust, 2014. Reproduced with permission.

"Language-tree divergence times support the Anatolian theory of Indo-European origin." Russell D. Gray and Quentin D. Atkinson. *Nature* 426, (2003): 435–439, © 2003 Springer Nature. https://doi.org/10.1038/nature02029. Reprinted by permission from Springer Nature.

"Lepenski Vir." Wikipedia. https://en.wikipedia.org/wiki/Lepenski_Vir. CC-BY-SA 3.0.

Library of History, Vol 1. Diodorus Siculus, C. H. Oldfather, translator. Harvard University Press, 1933. Reprinted 1989.

"Listen to the People. Talking with an Extinct Race. Part 1." Raynor Capper, quoting Monica Matamua. eLocal, 2011. https://www.facebook.com/346003915492277/posts/the-results-dna-to-rock-the-nation-part-2changing-our-nz-history-for-decades-aca/670609243031741/.

Luentoja Suomalaisesta Mytologiasta, M.A. Castrén. © 2016 Joonas Ahola, translator and editor. Helsinki: Finnish Literature Society, 2016, https://doi.org/10.21435/tl.252. CC BY-NC-ND 4.0.

Magicians of the Gods. © 2015 Graham Hancock. New York: Thomas Dunne Books, St. Martin's Press, 2015, Kindle edition.

The Maldive Mystery. © 1986 Thor Heyerdahl. Bethesda, Maryland: Adler & Adler, 1986.

"Manly P. Hall." Wikiquote. https://en.wikiquote.org/wiki/Manly_P._Hall. CC-BY-SA 3.0.

"Mapping the Origins and Expansion of the Indo-European Language Family." Remco Bouckaert, Philippe Lemey, Michael Dunn, Simon J. Greenhill, Alexander V. Alekseyenko, Alexei J. Drummond, Russell D. Gray, Marc A. Suchard, Quentin D. Atkinson. © 2012 American Association for the Advancement of Science. *Science* 337, no. 6097 (2012): 957-960. https://doi.org/10.1126/science.1219669. Reprinted with permission from AAAS.

"A meeting of Civilisations: The Mystery of China's Celtic Mummies." Independent, August 28, 2006. https://www.independent.co.uk/news/world/asia/a-meeting-of-civilisations-the-mystery-of-chinas-celtic-mummies-5330366.html.

Meetings with Remarkable Men. G. I. Gurdjieff, A. R. Orage, translator. © Editions Janus 1963. Penguin Compass, 2002.

"Megalithic New Zealand." © Martin Doutré. Ancient Celtic New Zealand. http://www.celticnz.co.nz/mnz_pt1.html. Reproduced with permission.

"Mitogenomes illuminate the origin and migration patterns of the indigenous people of the Canary Islands." © 2019 Rosa Fregel, Alejandra C. Ordóñez, Jonathan Santana-Cabrera, Vicente M. Cabrera, Javier Velasco-Vázquez, Verónica Alberto, Marco A. Moreno-Benítez, et al. *PLoS ONE* 14, no. 3 (2019). https://doi.org/10.1371/journal.pone.0209125. CC BY 4.0.

"More Y-SNP calls for Chachapoyas" © 2015 Genetiker. Genetiker, September 2, 2015. https://genetiker.wordpress.com/2015/09/02/more-y-snp-calls-for-chachapoyas. Reproduced with permission.

"mtDNA Haplogroup X: An Ancient Link between Europe/Western Asia and North America?" Michael D. Brown, Seyed H. Hosseini, Antonio Torroni, Hans-Jürgen Bandelt, Jon C. Allen, Theodore G. Schurr, Rosaria Scozzari, Fulvio Cruciani, Douglas C. Wallace. © 1998 The American Society of Human Genetics. *The American Society of Human Genetics* 63, no. 6 (1998): 1852-1861. Published by Elsevier Inc. https://doi.org/10.1086/302155. Reprinted with permission from Elsevier.

The Mythical Origin of the Egyptian Temple. © 1969 Eve A. E. Reymond. Manchester: Manchester U.P., 1969.

"Natchez." The Editors of Encyclopaedia Britannica. © 2019 Encyclopædia Britannica®. https://www.britannica.com/topic/Natchez-people.

"North American Indian Hopi Prophecies." © 1986 Lee Brown. Talk given at the Continental Indigenous Council, Tanana Valley Fairgrounds, Fairbanks, AK, 1986. https://www.welcome-home.org/prophecy/hopi2.html.

"On the Origins of the Oghamic Writing System." © 2008 Michel-Gérald Boutet. Academia.edu, 2008. https://www.academia.edu/4134903.

"Plato." Wikipdia. https://en.wikipedia.org/wiki/Plato. CC-BY-SA 3.0.

Point of Origin: Gobekli Tepe and the Spiritual Matrix for the World's Cosmologies. © 2015 Laird Scranton. Inner Traditions/Bear & Company, 2015, location 240, Kindle edition.

"The Polynesian Gene Pool: An Early Contribution by Amerindians to Easter Island." Erik Thorsby. © 2012 The Royal Society. *Philosophical Transactions of the Royal Society* B 367, no. 1590 (2012): 812–819. https://dx.doi.org/10.1098/rstb.2011.0319.

POPOL VUH: "The Book of the People." © Adrián Recino, translator from Quiché to Spanish. © Delia Goetz and Sylvanus Griswold Morley, translators from Spanish to English. Los Angeles: Plantin Press, 1954.

"Precession of the Equinoxes and Calibration of Astronomical Epochs." © 2011 Burra G. Sidharth. Hyderabad: International Institute for Applicable Mathematics & Information Sciences, B.M. Birla Science Centre, February 3, 2011. https://arxiv.org/pdf/1001.2393.pdf.

"Pre-Columbian Transoceanic Contacts: The Present State of the Evidence." © 1983 Stephen C. Jett. In *Ancient South Americans*, edited by Jesse D. Jennings. W. H. Freeman and Company, 1983. https://www.researchgate.net/publication/200577481_Pre-Columbian_Transoceanic_Contacts.

"Principal Component Analysis Confirms European Admixture in Chinchorro DNA." © 2017 Genetiker. Genetiker, March 14, 2017. https://genetiker.wordpress.com/2017/03/14/principal-component-analysis-confirms-european-admixture-in-chinchorro-dna. Reproduced with permission.

The Prose Edda. Snorri Sturlson, Arthur Gilchrist Brodeur, translator. New York: The American-Scandinavian Foundation, 1916.

"Ring O' Brodgar, Orkney Islands: Gateway To The Americas." © Martin Doutré. Ancient Celtic New Zealand. http://www.celticnz.co.nz/Brodgar/Brodgar%201.htm. Reproduced with permission.

"The Rise of Agricultural Civilization in China: The Disparity between Archeological Discovery and the Documentary Record and Its Explanation." © 2006 Zhou Jixu. *Sino-Platonic Papers* 175 (2006), p. 35. http://sino-platonic.org/complete/spp175_chinese_civilization_agriculture.pdf. CC BY-NC-ND 2.5.

Royal Commentaries of the Incas and General History of Peru, Volume 1 and Volume 2. Garcilaso de la Vega, Harold V. Livermore, translator. © 1966 University of Texas Press. Austin: University of Texas Press, 1989, Kindle edition.

Samba-Purana. © 2013 V. C. Srivastava, translator. Delhi: Parimal Publications, 2013.

The Sayings of Lao-Tzŭ. Lionel Giles, translator, edited by L. Cranmer-Byng and Dr. S. A. Kapadia. New York: E. P. Dutton and Company, 1905.

"Scandinavian Ancestry." © 2000 Thor Heyerdahl, Azerbaijan International. *Azerbaijan International*, (2000): 78-83, https://www.azer.com/aiweb/categories/magazine/82_folder/82_articles/82_heyerdahl.html.

The Secret Teachings of All Ages. © 1928 Manly P. Hall. San Francisco: H.S. Crocker Company.

The Seed of Yggdrasill: Deciphering the Hidden Messages in Old Norse Myths. © 2016 Maria Kvilhaug. Denmark: Whyte Tracks, 2016.

"Shambhala in the Kalachakra Tantra." © 2010 Nick Trautz. Shambhala Times, October 28, 2018. https://shambhalatimes.org/2018/10/28/shambhala-in-the-kalachakra-tantra.

Shambhala: Oasis of Light. © 1977 Andrew Tomas. London: Sphere, 1977.

"Slavic Mythology: Svarog | Сварог." © 2010 A Journey Through Slavic Culture. https://russian-culture.wordpress.com/2010/12/20/slavic-mythology-sv.

Sun, Moon & Stonehenge. © 1998 Robin Heath. Blue Stone Press, 1998.

"Sun Worship." The Editors of Encyclopaedia Britannica. © 2018, 2020 Encyclopædia Britannica®. https://www.britannica.com/topic/sun-worship.

"Svarog." Wikipedia. https://en.wikipedia.org/wiki/Svarog. CC-BY-SA 3.0.

The Tao Te Ching of Lao Tzu. © 1995 Brian Browne Walker, translator. New York: St. Martin's Press, 1995.

"Thor Heyerdahl and Azerbaijani Archaeology." © 2014 Novus AS, Goshgar Goshgarli. In *Thor Heyerdahl's Search for Odin*, edited by Vibeke Roggen. Novus Press, 2014.

"Thor Heyerdahl in Azerbaijan." Betty Blair quoting Thor Heyerdahl. © 1995 Azerbaijan International. *Azerbaijan International*, (1995): 62-63, 76, http://azer.com/aiweb/categories/magazine/31_folder/31_articles/31_thorheyerdahl.html.

"Thor Heyerdahl's archaeological expedition to Azov and prospects for the development of archaeology in south-eastern Europe." © 2014 Novus AS, Sergey Lukyashko. In *Thor Heyerdahl's Search for Odin*, edited by Vibeke Roggen. Novus Press, 2014.

"Three Sovereigns and Five Emperors." Wikipedia. https://en.wikipedia.org/wiki/Three_Sovereigns_and_Five_Emperors. CC-BY-SA 3.0.

The Tigris Expedition. © 1980 Thor Heyerdahl. Garden City, NY: Doubleday & Company, 1982. Reprint London: Flamingo, 1993.

"A Tradition of Giants: The Elite Social Hierarchy of American Prehistory." © 2007 Ross Hamilton. Academia.edu, 2007, https://www.academia.edu/4693378.

"Trypilian Temple - Observatory at Nebelivka." © 2018 Griandr Tarnovski. Bezvodovka, August 31, 2018. http://www.bezvodovka.com/en/pysmena/nebelivka.html.

The Upanishads, 2nd ed. Eknath Easwaran, translator. © 1987, 2007 The Blue Mountain Center of Meditation. Tomales: Nilgiri Press, 2007.

Väinämöinen: Suomalaisten Runojen Keskushahmo. © 1950 Martti Haavio. Porvoo: Werner Söderström Osakeyhtiö, 1950.

"Vikings in Ancient Mexico? The Story of Votan." © 2016 Robert Bitto. Mexico Unexplained, September 12, 2016. http://www.mexicounexplained.com/vikings-ancient-mexico-story-votan/.

The White Indians of Nivaria. © 2010 Gordon Kennedy. Mecca, CA: Nivaria Press, 2010.

Who We Are and How We Got Here. © 2018 David Reich and Eugenie Reich. Oxford: UK: Oxford University Press, 2018, Kindle edition.

"World's First Known Written Word at Göbekli Tepe on T-Shaped Pillar 18 Means God." © 2019 Manu Seyfzadeh and Robert Schoch. *Archaeological Discovery* 7, no. 2 (2019): 31-53. https://doi.org/10.4236/ad.2019.72003. CC BY 4.0.

The World Without Us. © 2007 Alan Weisman. New York: St. Martin's Publishing Group, 2007, Kindle edition, 2012.

"Writings of the Egyptians: Egyptian Vignettes of the story of Atlantis." © 2012 R. Cedric Leonard. Quest for Atlantis. https://atlantisquestscience.wordpress.com/culture/writings-of-the-egyptians.

IMAGE ACKNOWLEDGMENTS

All Creative Commons works in this book are derivatives which have been processed with cropping, rotation, and/or other image adjustments.

Copyrighted images used in this book are listed by page number.

MISC

Chapter Headings: Solar Cross. Symbol re-created by Sura Ondrunar Publishing based on petroglyph at the Three Rivers Petroglyph Site in New Mexico, USA.

PREFACE

4. Right: Luidger, photographer. *Statue of Coatlicue,* National Anthropology Museum, Mexico City, 2004. Wikimedia Commons, 2004. https://commons.wikimedia.org/wiki/ File:20041229- Coatlicue (Museo Nacional de Antropología) MQ-3.jpg. CC BY-SA 3.0.

CHAPTER ONE: THE ANCIENT RELIGION OF THE SUN

13. Collage top image 1: Egorov, Valery, photographer. *View of West Facade of Chartres Cathedral.* Shutterstock.com. https://www.shutterstock.com/image-photo/view-west-facade-chartres-cathedral-1076537756. Licensed from Shutterstock.com.
13. Collage top image 2: HelloRF Zcool, photographer. *Guangzhou Shushe Sacred Heart Cathedral.* Shutterstock.com. https://www.shutterstock.com/image-photo/guangzhou-shushe-sacred-heart-cathedral-1173463153. Licensed from Shutterstock.com.
13. Collage top image 3: F11photo, photographer. *St. John the Baptist Cathedral in Savannah,* Georgia USA. Shutterstock.com. https://www.shutterstock.com/image-photo/st-john-baptist- cathedral-savannah-georgia-493931884. Licensed from Shutterstock.com.
13. Collage top image 4: Ravi, Joe, photographer. *St. Philomena's Church Is a Catholic Church Built in Honour of St. Philomena in Mysore.* Shutterstock.com. https://www.shutterstock. com/ image-photo/guangzhou-shushe-sacred-heart-cathedral-1173463153. Licensed from Shutterstock.com.
13. Collage bottom image 1: Hendrikse, Boyd, photographer. *Cristo de la Concordia (Christ of Peace) Is a Statue of Jesus Christ Located atop San Pedro Hill, to the East of Cochabamba,* Bolivia. Shutterstock.com. https://www.shutterstock.com/image-photo/cristo-de-la-concordia-christ-peace-192340583. Licensed from Shutterstock.com.
13. Collage bottom image 2: Petrova, Maria, photographer. *Famous Statue of the Christ the Reedemer, Lubango Angola.* Shutterstock.com. https://www.shutterstock.com/ image-photo/famous-statue-christ-reedemer-lubango-angola-21157789. Licensed from Shutterstock.com.
13. Collage bottom image 3: Catay, photographer. *Jesus Statue in Beirut 4 February 2018.* Shutterstock.com. https://www.shutterstock.com/image-photo/jesus-statue-beirut-4-february-2018-1041517408. Licensed from Shutterstock.com.
13. Collage bottom image 4: Lashkov, Fedor, photographer. *The Christian Park in Essentuki.* Shutterstock.com. https://www.shutterstock.com/image-photo/christian-park-essentuki-669164776. Licensed from Shutterstock.com.
14. Collage, top left: Bon, Jerome, photographer. *Great Pyramid of Giza,* Egypt, 2008. Wikimedia Commons, 2015. https://commons.wikimedia.org/wiki/File:Great_Pyramid_of_Giza_ (2427530661).jpg. CC BY 2.0.

14. Collage, top center: Skubasteve834, photographer. *Monks Mound,* Collinsville, Illinois, 2007. Wikimedia Commons, 2013. https://commons.wikimedia.org/wiki/File:Monks_Mound_in_July.JPG. CC BY-SA-3.0.

14. Collage, second left: Schwen, Daniel, photographer. *Chichen Itza,* Mexico, 2009. Wikimedia Commons, 2009. https://commons.wikimedia.org/wiki/File:Chichen_Itza_3.jpg. CC BY-SA 4.0.

14. Collage, second right: Ximenez, Pedro, photographer. *Pyramid Güimar,* Canary Islands, Spain, 1998. Wikimedia Commons, 2009. https://commons.wikimedia.org/wiki/File:Pyramide Güimar.jpg. CC BY-SA 2.0.

14. Collage, third center: Jagadeesan, Madhuranthakan, photographer. *Sri Kanteshwara Temple Gopuram,* Nanjangud, Karnataka, India, 2007. Wikimedia Commons, 2016. https://commons.wikimedia.org/wiki/File:N-KA-B159_Srikanteshwara_Temple_Gopuram_Nanjangud.jpg. CC BY-SA 4.0.

14. Collage Bottom Left: Torbenbrinker, photographer. *Jardim dos Maroicos park*, Pico island, Azores, 2016. Wikimedia Commons, 2016. https://commons.wikimedia.org/wiki/File%3AMadalenaJardim.jpg. CC BY-SA 4.0.

14. Collage Bottom Center Gianf84 at Italian Wikipedia, photographer. *Monte D' Accoddi, Sardinia*, Italy, 2008. Wikimedia Commons, 2009. https://commons.wikimedia.org/wiki/File:Monted%27accoddisardegna.png. CC BY-SA 3.0.

14. Collage Bottom Right Uli sh, photographer. *Mauritius pyramid*, 2014. Wikimedia Commons, 2015. https://commons.wikimedia.org/wiki/File%3AMauritius-Pyramiden-5-4-3.jpg. CC BY-SA 4.0.

15. Collage, top left: Saamiblog: http://saamiblog.blogspot.com, photographer. *Buckle from Oseberg Vikingship Buddha,* found with the Oseberg ship burial circa 800 CE, 2008. Wikimedia Commons, 2009. https://commons.wikimedia.org/wiki/File:Buckle_from_Oseberg_Vikingship_Buddha_3.JPG. CC BY-SA 3.0.

15. Collage, top center: Chirita, Cristian, photographer. *Archeological Artefacts in Sozopol Museum,* Sozopol Museum, Sozopol, Bulgaria, 2011. Wikimedia Commons, 2011. https://commons.wikimedia.org/wiki/File:Sozopol_Archaeological_Museum_IMG_4214.JPG. GNU Free Documentation License, Version 1.2. https://commons.wikimedia.org/wiki/Commons:GNU_Free_Documentation_License,_version_1.2.

15. Collage, top right: Dbachmann, photographer. *Samarra Bowl,* circa 4000 BC, Pergamon Museum, Berlin, 2010. Wikimedia Commons, 2010. https://en.wikipedia.org/wiki/File:Samarra_bowl.jpg. CC BY-SA 4.0.

15. Collage, center: PHGCOM, photographer. *Etruscan Pendant with Swastika Symbols Bolsena Italy 700 BCE to 650 BCE.* Louvre Museum, 2008. Wikimedia Commons, 2010. https://commons.wikimedia.org/wiki/File:Etruscan_pendant_with_swastika_symbols_Bolsena_Italy_700_BCE_to_650_BCE.jpg. CC BY-SA 3.0.

15. Collage, bottom left: Шнапс, photographer. Скоба для стрел (*Bracket for Arrows)*, 2009. Wikimedia Commons, 2012. https://commons.wikimedia.org/wiki/File:Скоба_для_стрел.JPG. CC BY-SA 3.0.

15. Collage, bottom center: Tylas at English Wikipedia, photographer. *Zionpictographs*, Zion National Park, 2006. Wikimedia Commons, 2006. https://commons.wikimedia.org/wiki/File:Zionpictographs.jpg. CC BY-SA 3.0.

15. Collage, bottom right: Before My Ken, photographer. *Indus Valley Civilization Seals*, British Museum, 2005. Wikimedia Commons, 2009. https://commons.wikimedia.org/wiki/File:IndusValleySeals_swastikas.JPG. CC BY-SA 3.0.

15. Collage, top left: Pattych at English Wikipedia, photographer. *MocheBeardedMen,* 2008. Wikimedia Commons, 2010. https://en.wikipedia.org/wiki/File:MocheBeardedMen.jpg. CC BY-SA 3.0.

15. Collage, bottom left: Fortuna, Roberto, and Kira Ursem, photographers. *Gundestrup Cauldron.* Nationalmuseet, Denmark, 2007. Wikimedia Commons, 2016. https://en.wikipedia.org/wiki/File:Gundestrupkedlen-_00054_(cropped).jpg. CC BY-SA 3.0.

17. Terletskaya, Elena, artist. *Seven wonders of the ancient world!!! 3D reconstructions*. Shutterstock. com. https://www.shutterstock.com/image-illustration/seven-wonders-ancient-world-3d-reconstructions-27690895. Licensed from Shutterstoc.com. Image modified by Sura Ondruar Publising.

21. Google Earth. 2018. *Great line*. © Google, Data SIO, NOAA, U.S. Navy, NGA, GEBCO, Image Landsat / Copernicus, Image IBCAO.

CHAPTER TWO: ORIGINS

27. Mystique, Mickey, photographer. *Skeleton at Museum Lepenski Vir*, Serbia, 2018. Wikimedia Commons, 2018. https://commons.wikimedia.org/wiki/File:Lepenski_Vir,_muzej_26.jpg. CC BY-SA 4.0.

28. Simon, Klaus-Peter, photographer. *Göbekli Tepe Settlement hill near Şanlıurfa, Southeast Turkey, Appendix C from the east*, 2012. Wikimedia Commons, 2012. https://commons. wikimedia.org/wiki/File:G%C3%B6bekli2012-14.jpg. CC BY-SA 3.0.

35. Chernov, Mstyslav, photographer. *Great Sphinx of Giza (foreground) Pyramid of Menkaure (background)*, Cairo, Egypt, North Africa, 2009. Wikimedia Commons, 2009. https:// commons.wikimedia.org/wiki/File:Great_Sphinx_of_Giza_(foreground)_Pyramid_of_ Menkaure_(background)._Cairo,_Egypt,_North_Africa.jpg. CC BY-SA 3.0.

38. Hofmann, Florian, photographer. *Pylon of the Horus Temple in Edfu*, 2004. Wikimedia Commons 2004. https://commons.wikimedia.org/wiki/File:Edfu_pylon.jpg. CC BY-SA 3.0

41. Soutekh67, photographer. *Thoth in adoration in front of the Lunar Disc / Oudjat, ceiling of Denérah*, 2014. Wikimedia Commons, 2014. https://commons.wikimedia.org/wiki/ File:Dendera_Deckenrelief_03_(2).JPG. CC BY-SA 4.0.

42. The Culdian Trust. *Cover of The Kolbrin*. The Kolbrin, 1994. © The Culdian Trust.

45. Ogawa, Hiroki, photographer. *Tashilhunpo Monastery*, Shigatse, Tibet, 2014. Wikimedia Commons 2017. https://commons.wikimedia.org/wiki/File:Tashilhunpo_Monastery_ Shigatse_Tibet_China_西藏 日喀则扎什伦布寺_-_panoramio_(5).jpg. CC. BY 3.0.

49. Inspired by Maps, photographer. *Tiwanaku: Spiritual and Political Centre of the Tiwanaku Culture*, Bolivia. Shutterstock.com. https://www.shutterstock.com/image-photo/tiwanaku-spiritual-political-centre-culture-unesco-730144396. Licensed from Shutterstock.com

53. Nguyen, Marie-Lan, photographer. *Plato, Luni marble, copy of the portrait made by Silanion ca. 370 BC for the Academia in Athens*, 370 BC, Capitoline Museums, 2009. Wikimedia Commons 2009. https://en.wikipedia.org/wiki/File:Plato_Silanion_Musei_Capitolini_ MC1377.jpg. © Marie-Lan Nguyen. CC-BY 2.5.

66. Baedeker, Karl. *Drawing of Thoth*. In *Handbook for Traveling, pt.1 Lower Egypt, with the Fayum and the peninsula of Sinai*, Leipsic; London: K. Baedeker, 1885, p. 134. From Travelers in the Middle East Archive (TIMEA), Uniform Resource Identifier: 9937. Wikimedia Commons 2010. https://commons.wikimedia.org/wiki/ File:Thoth._(1885)_-_TIMEA.jpg. CC BY-SA 2.5.

77. Baviere, Guillaume, photographer. *Island of São Jorge*, Azores, 2010. Wikimedia Commons, 2012. https://en.wikipedia.org/wiki/File:A%C3%A7ores_2010-07-19_(5047589237).jpg. CC BY 2.0.

79. Beauregard, Mike, photographer. *Rebounding beach, Bathurst Inlet*, Nunavut, Canada, 2013. Wikimedia Commons, 2013. https://en.wikipedia.org/wiki/File:Rebounding_beach,_ among_other_things_(9404384095).jpg. CC BY 2.0.

81. Pimvantend, artist, map information from NOAA, ETOPO1, GPLATES. *The Azores Triple Junction*, 2011. Wikimedia Commons, 2011. https://en.wikipedia.org/wiki/File:Azorestriple3d.png. CC BY-SA 3.0.

CHAPTER THREE: THE WISDOM BRINGERS

86. Collage, top left: Dr.regosistvan, phtographer. *Oannes*, 2016. Wikimedia Commons, 2016. https://commons.wikimedia.org/wiki/File:Oannes.jpg. CC BY-SA 4.0.

86. Collage, top right: Delange, Audrey and George, photographers. *La Venta Stele 19,* the earliest known representation of the Feathered Serpent in Mesoamerica, 2005. Wikimedia Commons, 2015. https://commons.wikimedia.org/wiki/File:La_Venta_Stele_19_(Delange). jpg. © Audrey and George Delange. Reproduced with permission.

86. Collage, bottom left: Simon, Klaus-Peter, photographer. *Göbekli Tepe,* Şanlıurfa, southeast Turkey, 2012. Wikimedia Commons, 2012. https://commons.wikimedia.org/wiki/File:G%C3%B6bekli2012-18.jpg. CC BY-SA 3.0.

87. Tausch, Olaf, photographer. *Edfu Temple Relief,* Egypt, 2014. Wikimedia Commons, 2014. https://commons.wikimedia.org/wiki/File:Edfu_Tempelrelief_33.jpg. CC BY 3.0.

88. Baedeker, Karl. *Line drawing of Egyptian god Osiris.* In *Handbook for Traveling, pt.1 Lower Egypt, with the Fayum and the peninsula of Sinai,* Leipsic; London: K. Baedeker, 1885, p. 131. From Travelers in the Middle East Archive (TIMEA), Uniform Resource Identifier: 9934. Wikimedia Commons 2010. https://commons.wikimedia.org/wiki/File:Osiris,_prince_of_eternity_(1885)_-_TIMEA.jpg. CC BY-SA 2.5.

100. Collage, top left: Ace, Sahand, photographer. *Faravahar Symbol in Persepolis,* Shiraz, Iran, 2012. Wikimedia Commons, 2013. https://commons.wikimedia.org/wiki/File:Farvahar1. JPG. CC BY-SA 3.0.

102. Sewell, Ian. *Ahu Akivi,* Easter Island, 2006. Wikimedia Commons, 2006. https://commons. wikimedia.org/wiki/File:Ahu-Akivi-1.JPG. CC BY-SA 3.0.

104. Pouteau, Claire, photographer. *Tiwanaku,* Bolivia, 2003. Wikimedia Commons, 2005. https://commons.wikimedia.org/wiki/File:Tiwanaku1.jpg. CC BY-SA 2.0.

105. Plekhanova, Yulia, photographer. *Glasnevin Cemetery,* Dublin Ireland, 2019. Shutterstock. com. https://www.shutterstock.com/image-photo/glasnevin-cemetery-ireland-august-02-2019-1472088821. Licensed from Shutterstock.com

105. Petrow, Chris, photographer. *Row of Buddhas.* Unsplash.com. https://unsplash.com/photos/j4Wia6JDLm0. Licensed from Unsplash.com.

106. Left: Papiermond, photographer. *Sarcophagi of Karajia,* 2005. Wikimedia Commons, 2006. https://en.wikipedia.org/wiki/File:Karajia1.jpg. CC BY-SA 3.0.

106. Right: Mitzo, photographer. *Sarcophagus,* Kunsthistorisches Museum, Vienna, Austira, 2020. Shutterstock.com. https://www.shutterstock.com/image-photo/vienna-austria-1502-interior-museum-art-1650056077. Licensed from Shutterstock.com.

107. Collage, top left: Gybas DigiPhoto, photographer. *Moai from Ahu Tongariki on Easter Island.* Shutterstock.com. https://www.shutterstock.com/image-photo/moai-ahu-tongariki-on-easter-island-10886431. Licensed from Shutterstock.com.

107. Collage, top center: Ndede, photographer. *Archaeological Work Gobeklitepe Turkey.* Shutterstock.com. https://www.shutterstock.com/image-photo/archaeological-work-gobeklitepe-turkey-1087902086. Licensed from Shutterstock.com.

107. Collage, top right: Kaiser, Jennifer, photographer. *Statue from Gobeklitepe,* Urfa Museum, 2015. Flickr.com, 2015. https://www.flickr.com/photos/kaiserjennifer/20263074231. CC BY 2.0.

107. Collage, bottom left: TheWanderingScot.com, photographer. *Kabul Museum: Kafiristan Statue,* 2009. http://thewanderingscot.com/photos/2009 Stans/Afghanistan/midis/IMG_7902.jpg. © TheWanderingsScot.com. Reproduced with permission.

107. Collage, bottom center: Artist unknown. *Two European Ladies and a Man Are Standing in front of a Statue in Napu, Menado,* before 1937, Tropenmuseum, part of the National Museum of World Cultures, Amsterdam, Netherlands. Wikimedia Commons, 2009. https://commons. wikimedia.org/wiki/File:COLLECTIE_TROPENMUSEUM_Twee_Europese_dames_en_een_man_staan_voor_een_afgodsbeeld_te_Napu_Menado_TMnr_10000852.jpg. CC BY-SA 3.0.

107. Collage, bottom right: Damsea, photographer. *French Polynesia Tahiti Island Carved Stone Tiki Statue on the Marae Arahurahu, South Pacific, Oceania.* Shutterstock.com. https://www. shutterstock.com/image-photo/french-polynesia-tahiti-island-carved-stone-784904116. Licensed from Shutterstock.com.

113. Rivera, Diego, artist. Kgv88, photographer. *Indian Mexico*, Palacio Nacional, Mexico, 2011. Wikimedia Commons, 2011. https://commons.wikimedia.org/wiki/File:Indian_Mexico_2.JPG CC BY-SA 3.0.

114. Schwen, Daniel, photographer. *El Castillo (pyramid of Kukulcán)* in Chichén Itzá, Mexico, 2009. Wikimedia Commons, 2009. https://commons.wikimedia.org/wiki/File:Chichen_Itza_3.jpg. CC BY-SA 4.0.

115. Henderson, Keith. *Quetzalcoatl*. In *The Conquest of Mexico*, London: Chatto & Windus, 1922, p.39. https://commons.wikimedia.org/wiki/File:COM_V1_D225_Quetzalcoatl.png

117. Pattych at en.wikipedia. *MocheBeardedMen*, 2008. Wikimedia Commons, 2010. https://commons.wikimedia.org/wiki/File:MocheBeardedMen.jpg. CC BY-SA 3.0.

119. Robertson, D. Gordon E., photographer. *Cast of petroglyphs in Learning Centre*, Petroglyphs Provincial Park, Woodview, Ontario, Canada, 2012. Wikimedia Commons, 2012. https://en.wikipedia.org/wiki/File:Cast_of_boat.jpg. CC BY-SA 3.0.

127. Collage, bottom left: Fortuna, Roberto, and Kira Ursem, photographers. *Gundestrup cauldron*, Nationalmuseet, Denmark, 2007. Wikimedia Commons, 2016. https://en.wikipedia.org/wiki/File:Gundestrupkedlen-_00054_(cropped).jpg. CC BY-SA 3.0.

133. Bjoertvedt, photographer. *Nordens Ark in Sotenäs*, Sweden, 2013. Wikimedia Commons, 2013. https://commons.wikimedia.org/wiki/File:Soten%C3%A4s_Tossene_73-1_Aaby_ID_10161200730001_IMG_8005.JPG. CC BY-SA 3.0.

135. Right: Muru Photography. *Durga Puja Kolkata*. Shutterstock.com. https://www.shutterstock.com/image-photo/durga-puja-kolkata-677058361 Licensed from Shutterstock.com.

135. Top: Sauber, Wolfgang, photographer. *Picture stone showing a spiral and deer*, Visby (Gotland), Fornsalen Museum, 2007. Wikimedia Commons, 2009. https://commons.wikimedia.org/wiki/File:Fornsalen_-_Bildstein_-_Spirale_und_Hirsche.jpg. CC BY-SA 3.0.

135. Bottom: Kolyan, Artak, photographer. *Armenian tombstone*, Aghout, Sisian, Armenia, 2013. Wikimedia Commons, 2013. https://en.wikipedia.org/wiki/File:Armenian_Tombstone_Aghout_Sisian_Armenia.jpg. CC BY-SA 3.0.

136. Alexander, Mitrofanov, photographer. *Wooden Idol Slavic Culture*. Shutterstock.com. https://www.shutterstock.com/image-photo/wooden-idol-slavic-culture-on-village-722636782. Licensed from Shutterstock.com.

142. Lobachev, Vladimir, photographer. *Ivan Kupala in the Belgorod Region*, 2011. Wikimedia Commons, 2014. https://commons.wikimedia.org/wiki/File:Ivan_Kupala_Day_in_2011_08.JPG. CC BY-SA 3.0.

145. Left: Käyttäjä:Kompak. Derivative by Perhelion. *Ra-Horakhty Based on Nefertari's Tomb*, 2010. Wikimedia Commons, 2016. https://commons.wikimedia.org/wiki/File:Sun_god_Ra.svg. CC BY-SA 3.0.

148. Left: Polylerus, photographer. *Model of the reed boat Tigris, boat of Thor Heyerdahl*, 2009. Wikimedia Commons, 2009. https://commons.wikimedia.org/wiki/File:Tigris_Model_Pyramids_of_Guimar.jpg. CC BY-SA 3.0.

148. Right Hajor, photographer. *Tomb KV34 (Thutmose III), 11th hour Amduat*, Valley of the Kings, Luxor, Egypt, 2002. Wikimedia Commons, 2005. https://commons.wikimedia.org/wiki/File:Egypt.KV34.07.jpg. CC BY-SA 3.0.

150. Collage, top left: Bon, Jerome, photographer. *Great Pyramid of Giza*. Wikimedia Commons, 2015. https://commons.wikimedia.org/wiki/File:Great_Pyramid_of_Giza_(2427530661).jpg. CC BY 2.0.

150. Collage, top center: Skubasteve834, photographer. *Monks Mound*, Collinsville, Illinois, 2007. Wikimedia Commons, 2013. https://commons.wikimedia.org/wiki/File:Monks_Mound_in_July.JPG. CC BY-SA-3.0.

150. Collage, second left: Schwen, Daniel, photographer. *Chichen Itza*, Mexico, 2009. Wikimedia Commons, 2009. https://commons.wikimedia.org/wiki/File:Chichen_Itza_3.jpg. CC BY-SA 4.0.

150. Collage, second right: Ximenez, Pedro, photographer. *Pyramid Güimar,* Canary Islands, Spain, 1998. Wikimedia Commons, 2009. https://commons.wikimedia.org/wiki/File:Pyramide Güimar.jpg. CC BY-SA 2.0.

150. Collage, third center: Jagadeesan, Madhuranthakan, photographer. *Sri Kanteshwara Temple Gopuram*, Nanjangud, Karnataka, India, 2007. Wikimedia Commons, 2016. https://commons.wikimedia.org/wiki/ File:N-KA-B159_Srikanteshwara_Temple_Gopuram_Nanjangud.jpg. CC BY-SA 4.0.

150. Collage, bottom left: Torbenbrinker, photographer. *Jardim dos Maroicos park, Pico island,* Azores, Portugal, 2016. Wikimedia Commons, 2016. https:// commons.wikimedia.org/wiki/File%3AMadalenaJardim.jpg. CC BY-SA 4.0.

150. Collage bottom center Gianf84 at Italian Wikipedia, photographer. *Monte D' Accoddi,* Sardinia, Italy, 2008. Wikipedia Commons, 2009. https:// commons.wikimedia.org/wiki/File:Monted'accoddisardegna.png. CC BY-SA 3.0.

150. Collage Bottom Right Uli sh, photographer. *Mauritius pyramid,* 2014. Wikimedia Commons, 2015. https://commons.wikimedia.org/wiki/ File%3AMauritius-Pyramiden-5-4-3.jpg. CC BY-SA 4.0.

151. Collage, top left: Heghnaraghpour, photographer. *Zorats Karer*, Armenia, 2014. Wikimedia Commons, 2017. https://commons.wikimedia.org/wiki/File:Karahounch.jpg. CC BY-SA 4.0.

151. Collage, top center: Raymbetz, photographer. *Nabta Playa Calendar Circle,* reconstructed at Aswan Nubia museum, Aswan, Eqypt, 2009. Wikimedia Commons, 2009. https://commons.wikimedia.org/wiki/File:Calendar_aswan.JPG. CC BY-SA 3.0.

151. Collage, top right: Leandroisola, photographer. *The Calzoene's "Stonehenge,"* Calçoene, Brazil, 2008. Wikimedia Commons, 2008. https://commons.wikimedia.org/wiki/File:Calçoene, Stonehenge brasileira, Amapá.jpg. CC BY 4.0.

151. Collage, bottom left: Boychou, photographer. *Willong Khullen*, Manipur, India, 2010. Wikimedia Commons, 2010. https://commons.wikimedia.org/ wiki/File:Stone_Erections_of_Willong_Khullen.jpg. CC BY-SA 3.0.

151. Collage, bottom center: Woods, David, photographer. *A portion of the Orkney neolithic site, the Ring of Brodgar*. Shutterstock.com. https://www.shutterstock.com/image-photo/portion-orkney-neolithic-site-ring-brodgar-4674436. Licensed from Shutterstock.com.

151. Collage, bottom right: Adwo, photographer. *South Africa's Adam's Calendar Stone Replica – Argentina*. https://www.shutterstock.com/image-photo/south-africas-adams-calendar-stone-replica-630489557. Licensed from Shutterstock.com.

151. Image created for book, based on Truman, Dave. *Ancient Alignment in the Andes Hints at a Lost Global High Culture*. GrahamHancock.com, January 2, 2016. https://grahamhancock.com/trumand1. Background © Google Earth, image Landsat / Copernicus, Data SIO, NOAA, U.S. Navy, NGA, GEBCO, Data LDEO-Columbia, NSF, NOAA.

154. Ganguly, Biswarup, photographer. *Vishnu Yajna,* Howrah, 2012. Wikimedia Commons, 2012. https://commons.wikimedia.org/wiki/File:Vishnu_Yajna_-_Howrah_2012-12-16_2078.JPG. CC BY 3.0.

CHAPTER FOUR: THE LOST CIVILIZATION OF THE SUN

169. AntiguoEgipto.org, photographer. *Osireion,* Abidos Egypt, 2004. Wikimedia Commons, 2005. https://commons.wikimedia.org/wiki/File:Osireion.jpg. CC BY-SA 2.5.

171. Sketch by Sura Ondrunar Publishing based on CultureWise, photographer. *Mezin Paleolithic Bird with Swastika*, 2014. https://www.flickr.com/photos/144631630@N07/29755220321/in/ album-72157670845333124/.

172. Left: Sketch by Sura Ondrunar Publishing based on Musi, Vincent J. *Ancient Head with Snake*, 2011. https://www.nationalgeographic.com/content/dam/magazine/rights-exempt/2011/06/gobekli/08-snakes-on-human-head.jpg.

172. Center: Sketch by Sura Ondrunar Publishing.

174. Jonathan, Joshua. *Indo-European Migrations*, 2015. Based on Anthony, David. *The Horse, The Wheel and Language*, 2007. Wikimedia Commons, 2015. https://commons.wikimedia.org/wiki/File:Indo-European_Migrations._Source_David_Anthony_(2007),_The_Horse,_The_Wheel_and_Language.jpg. CC BY-SA 4.0.

178. Sura Ondrunar Publishing, 2020. Based on Smolenski, Nikola. *Drawing of a clay vessel unearthed near Vinca*, 2003. Wikimedia Commons, 2005. https://en.wikipedia.org/wiki/File:Vinca_vessel.png. © Nikola Smolenski. CC BY-SA 3.0.

179. LBM 1948, photographer. *Clay tablet in Mycenaean Greek*, 2013. Archaeological Museum of Mycenae. Mikines, Argolis, Greece. Wikimedia Commons, 2019. https://commons.wikimedia.org/wiki/File:Micenas,_museo_07.jpg. CC BY-SA 4.0.

184. Chistophe cagé. *Tarim basin with mountains*, 2011. Based on *Map of Asia – 600 CE* by Thomas A Lessman, 2008. Wikimedia Commons, 2011. https://commons.wikimedia.org/wiki/File:Tarim_bassin.png. CC BY-SA 3.0

186. De Hevesy, Guillaume. *Comparing the scripts of the Indus Valley and Easter Island*. In "The Easter Island and the Indus Valley Scripts," *Anthropos*, Sep-Dec 1938 issue, p. 808, 1938. https://www.jstor.org/stable/41104307?seq=1. © Anthropos 1938. Reproduced with permission.

187. Birgirms. *A chart that shows the evolution of Etruscan writing systems*. Wikimedia Commons, 2010. https://commons.wikimedia.org/wiki/File:Etruiska_tafla.png. CC BY-SA 3.0.

189. Left: Ragimov, M, photographer. *Rock paintings in Gobustan State Reserve*, Azerbaijan, 2009. Wikimedia Commons, 2017. https://commons.wikimedia.org/wiki/File:Gobustan_rock_paintings_-_a_boat.jpg. CC BY-SA 4.0.

189. Right: Lidingo. *Petroglyph ship*, Nordic bronze age (1800-550 BC), Tanum, Sweden, 2008. Wikimedia Commons, 2008. https://commons.wikimedia.org/wiki/File:Petroglypgh_Ship_Nordic_Bronze_Age_001.svg CC BY-SA 4.0.

194. Fjørtoft, Bjørn, photographer. *Thor Heyerdahl*, 1955. National Archives of Norway. Wikimedia Commons, 2017. https://commons.wikimedia.org/wiki/File:Thor_Heyerdahl_-_L0061_934Fo30141701190050.jpg. CC BY 4.0.

195. Shyamal, photographer. *Thor Heyerdahl image outside Kon Tiki museum*, Oslo, 2008. Edited by Jacek Halicki. Wikimedia Commons, 2008, 2012. https://commons.wikimedia.org/wiki/File:KonTikiQuote.jpg. CC BY-SA 3.0.

197. Piotrus, photographer. *Model of Thor Heyerdahl's Ra II at Pyramids of Güímar Museum*, Tenerife, 2007. Wikimedia Commons, 2007. https://commons.wikimedia.org/wiki/File:Ra_II_model_at_Guimar_museum.JPG. CC BY-SA 3.0.

198. Valentinapazmunozmarquez, photographer. *Balsa Viracocha II*, 2015. Wikimedia Commons, 2015. https://commons.wikimedia.org/wiki/File:Balsa_Viracocha_II.jpeg. CC BY-SA 4.0.

200. Tlustochowicz, Marcin, photographer. *Paracas skulls*, Mueseo Regional de Ica, Ica Peru, 2008. Wikimedia Commons, 2010. https://commons.wikimedia.org/wiki/File:ParacasSkullsIcaMuseum.jpg. CC BY 2.0.

202. Right: Unknown artist. Nicolas Pakomio, circa 1940's. *In The Lost Caravel* by Robert Langdon, Sydney: Pacific Publications, 1975.

207. Maulucioni. *Distribution of haplogroup X*, 2010. Wikimedia Commons, 2020. https://en.wikipedia.org/wiki/File:Haplogroup_X_(mtDNA).PNG. CC BY 3.0.

214. Left: Raifikiva m, photographer. *Russian: Settlement "Arkaim"*, 2014. Wikimedia Commons, 2015. https://commons.wikimedia.org/wiki/File:Укрепленное поселение Аркаим. Аэрофотоснимок..jpg . CC BY-SA 4.0.

214. Center: Image by Jones, Nicholas E, photographer. *Sunrise at Stonehenge*. Shutterstock.com. https://www.shutterstock.com/image-photo/sunrise-stonehenge-673724080. Licensed from Shutterstock.com.

214. Right: Google Maps. *Goseck Circle*, 2018. Imagery ©2018 Google, Map data ©2018 GeoBasis-DE/BKG (©2009), Google.

215. Lang Antonsen, Kenny Arne and Antonsen, Jimmy John. *Reconstruction of the Trypillian city Maydanets c 4000 B.C*, 2014. Based on information from the book *Looking for Trypillya-Culture Proto-Cities* by Mykhailo Videiko. Wikimedia Commons, 2014. https://en.wikipedia.org/wiki/File:Trypillian_city_(Maydanets).jpg. CC BY-SA 4.0.

216. Lang Antonsen, Kenny Arne. *Cucuteni-Trypillian Temple*. Wikimedia Commons, 2019. https://commons.wikimedia.org/wiki/File:Cucuteni-trypillian_temple.jpg. CC BY-SA 4.0.

217. Center: CristianChirita, photographer. *Cucuteni Omega Pottery,* Piatra Neamt Museum. Wikimedia Commons, 2009. https://commons.wikimedia.org/wiki/File:CucuteniOmegaPottery.JPG. CC BY-SA 3.0.

217. Right: BabelStone, photographer. *Banshan painted pottery*, 2011. Banshan phase (circa 2700 BC to 2300 BC) of the Yangshao culture, on exhibition at the Museum of the Mausoleum of the Nanyue King, Guangzhou, China. Wikimedia Commons, 2011. https://commons.wikimedia.org/wiki/File:Banshan_painted_pottery_pot_2.jpg. CC BY-SA 3.0.

220. Underawesternsky, photographer. *Panorama of Pueblo Bonito great house in Chaco Canyon National Historic Park*, New Mexico, USA. Shuterstock.com. https://www.shutterstock.com/image-photo/panorama-pueblo-bonito-great-house-chaco-717647170. Licensed from Shutterstock.com.

222. Left: Tobi 87, photographer. *Cliff Palace in Mesa Verde National Park*, Colorado, USA, 2007. Wikimedia Commons, 2008. https://commons.wikimedia.org/wiki/File:Cliff_Palace-Colorado-Mesa_Verde_NP.jpg. CC BY-SA 4.0.

222. Right: Reus, Ferdinand, photographer. *Cliff dwellings in the Bandiagara escarpment*, Mali, 2006. Wikimedia Commons, 2007. https://commons.wikimedia.org/wiki/File:Bandiagara_escarpment_2.jpg. CC BY-SA 2.0.

224. Roe, Herb. *Mississippian cultures*, 2010. Wikimedia Commons, 2010. https://commons.wikimedia.org/wiki/File:Mississippian_cultures_HRoe_2010.jpg. CC BY-SA 3.0.

225. Roe, Herb. *Mississippian culture mound components*, 2011. Wikimedia Commons, 2018. https://en.wikipedia.org/wiki/File:Mississippian_culture_mound_components_HRoe_2011.jpg. CC BY-SA 3.0.

228. QuartierLatin1968, photographer. *The Central Column of Cahokia's Woodhenge,* 2011. Wikimedia Commons, 2013. https://commons.wikimedia.org/wiki/File:Woodhenge_Cahokia_3998.jpg. CC BY-SA 3.0.

229. Collage, top left: Kvaran, Einar E (Carptrash), photographer. *Newark Mounds*, Newark, Ohio, USA, 1980s. Wikimedia Commons, 2017. https://commons.wikimedia.org/wiki/File:Newark_Mounds,_Newark,_Ohio,_USA.jpg. CC BY-SA 4.0.

229. Collage, top center: Saunaluoma, Sanna, photographer. *Fazenda Colorada,* Rio Branco, Acre, Brazil, 2012. Wikimedia Commons, 2012. https://en.wikipedia.org/wiki/File:Fazenda_Colorada.jpg. CC BY-SA 3.0.

229. Collage, top right: Google Maps. 2018. *Goseck Circle*. Imagery ©2018 Google, Map data ©2018 GeoBasis-DE/BKG (©2009), Google.

229. Collage, bottom left: MikPeach, photographer. *Avebury henge and stone circles*, 2009. Wikimedia Commons, 2017. https://commons.wikimedia.org/wiki/File:Wiltshire-Avebury.jpg. CC BY-SA 4.0.

229. Collage, bottom right: 4Kclips, photographer. *Fantastic view over Stonehenge in England,* Brighton, UK, 2019. Shutterstock.com. https://www.shutterstock.com/image-photo/fantastic-view-over-stonehenge-england-brighton-1648235137. Licensed from Shutterstock.com.

230. Left: Webber, Arthur M, photographer. *The Balanced Rock*, North Salem, NY, 2017. Wikimedia Commons, 2018. https://commons.wikimedia.org/wiki/File:AV5I2323_North_Salem_NY_Balancing_Rock.jpg. CC BY-SA 4.0.

231. Left: Andriotis, Katharine, photographer. *Wangtown Chamber*, an ancient stone chamber located off Wangtown Road in Kent, Putnam County, New York, USA, 2009. Alamy Stock Photo. https://www.alamy.com/mediacomp/imagedetails.aspx?ref=BARA74. Licensed from Alamy Stock Photo.

231. Right: Kranewitter, Michael, photographer. *Tumulus de Kercado*, 2005. Wikimedia Commons, 2012. https://commons.wikimedia.org/wiki/File:Tumulus_de_Kercado_2005_02.jpg. CC BY-SA 4.0.

235. Sluijs, Peter van der, photographer. *Skeleton near Nazca*, Peru, 2012. Wikimedia Commons, 2012. https://commons.wikimedia.org/wiki/ File:Skull_with_body_of_the_nazca_culture_in_Peru.jpg. CC BY-SA 3.0.

236. Garcia, Alejandro Linares, photographer. *Model of the Cholula Pyramid site at the site museum*, Puebla, Mexico, 2011. Wikimedia Commons, 2011. https://commons.wikimedia.org/wiki/File:ModelCholula2.JPG. CC BY-SA 4.0.

239. S/V Moonrise, *Flag of Guna Yala,* Panama. Wikimedia Commons, 2009. https://en.wikipedia.org/wiki/File:Flag_of_Kuna_Yala.svg. CC BY SA-3.0.

240. St-Amant, Martin, photographer. *Eastern facade of the wall surrounding Kuelap fortress*, 2007. Wikimedia Commons, 2007. https://commons.wikimedia.org/wiki/File:Kuelap_-_Ao%C3%BBt_2007_-_05.jpg. CC BY 3.0.

241. Salvatierra Cuenca, Miguel, artist. *Los Millares*, painting located in the Millares visitor reception center. Used with permission from artist. Photo by Jose Mª Yuste, 2008. Wikimedia Commons, 2008. https://en.wikipedia.org/wiki/File:Los_Millares_recreacion_cuadro.jpg. Photo CC BY-SA 4.0.

241. Left: Calvert, Harley, photographer. *Restored Building Kuelap*, 2007. Wikimedia Commons, 2013. https://commons.wikimedia.org/wiki/File:Kuelap_Restoration.jpg. CC BY-SA 3.0.

241. Right: Madrinan, Maria, photographer. *Celtic Citania, in Santa Tegla mont*, Galicia Spain. Shutterstock.com https://www.shutterstock.com/image-photo/celtic-citania-santa-tegla-mont-galicia-719586133. Licensed from Shutterstock.com.

242. Left: TPYXA_ILLUSTRATION. *Conor Anthony McGregor, Irish professional mixed martial artist and boxer*, 2018. Shutterstock.com. https://www.shutterstock.com/image-illustration/conor-anthony-mcgregor-irish-professional-mixed-1172705026. Licensed from Shuttestock.com.

242. Center: Papiermond, photographer. *Sarcophagi of Karajia*, 2005. Wikimedia Commons, 2006. https://en.wikipedia.org/wiki/File:Karajia1.jpg. CC BY-SA 3.0.

242. Right: Sewell, Ian, photographer. *Ahu Akivi*, Easter Island, 2006. Wikimedia Commons, 2006.https://commons.wikimedia.org/wiki/File:Ahu-Akivi-1.JPG. CC BY-SA 3.0.

245. Top left: Hahnewald, Matt, photographer. *MUKTINATH, ANNAPURNA CIRCUIT*, Nepal, 2016. Shutterstock.com. https://www.shutterstock.com/image-photo/muktinath-annapurna-circuit-nepal-april-23-1588730410. Licensed from Shutterstock.com

245. Bottom right: GTW, photographer. *Ahu Nao-Nao Moais wearing a red hat*, Anakena, Rapa Nui National Park, Easter Island, Chile. Shutterstock.com. https://www.shutterstock.com/image-photo/ahu-naonao-moais-wearing-red-hat-1514915321. Licensed from Shutterstock.com.

247. Collage, top right: Jigar_rayputra, photographer. *Modhera Sun Temple*, Modhera, India, 2018. Wikimedia Commons, 2018. https://commons.wikimedia.org/wiki/File:Stepwell_,Modhera.jpg. CC BY-SA 4.0.

247. Collage, center right: Dhapa Nitaben Harshaddhai, photographer. *Several miniature shrines and niches along the Stepped well in Modhera Sun Temple complex*, Modehera, Gujarat, India, 2019. Shutterstock.com. https://www.shutterstock.com/image-photo/gujarat-india-december-12-2019-several-1579834762. Licensed from Shutterstock.com.

247. Collage, bottom left: Brattarb, photographer. *Tiwanaku*, Bolivia, 2010. Wikimedia Commons, 2010. https://commons.wikimedia.org/wiki/File:3_Tiwanaku.JPG. CC BY-SA 3.0.

247. Collage, bottom right: Brattarb, photographer. *Puma_Punku*, Bolivia, 2010. Wikimedia Commons, 2010. https://commons.wikimedia.org/wiki/File:7_Puma_Punku.jpg. CC BY-SA 3.0.

247. Collage, center: Rehak, Matyas, photographer. *Ancient Inca style door of a house in Ollantaytambo village*, Sacred Valley of Incas, Peru. Shutterstock.com. https://www.shutterstock.com/image-photo/ancient-inca-style-door-house-ollantaytambo-1262553982. Licensed from Shutterstock.com.

247. Collage, right: ckchiu, photographer. *Inca temple doorway*, Machu Picchu, Peru. Shutterstock. com. https://www.shutterstock.com/image-photo/inca-temple-doorway-machu-picchu-peru-63075088. Licensed from Shutterstock.com.

248. Boychou, photographer. *Photograph of stone erected during ancient time at Willong Khullen*, a village in Senapati District, Manipur, India, 2010. Wikimedia Commons, 2010. https://en.wikipedia.org/wiki/File:Stone_Erections_of_Willong_Khullen.jpg. CC BY-SA 3.0.

250. Cherchen Man sketch by Sura Ondrunar Publishing.

251. Artist's impression of Tarim mummy full facial painting, by Sura Ondrunar Publishing.

251. Artist's impression of Tarim mummy full facial painting, by Sura Ondrunar Publishing.

252. en:User:Nomadtales, photographer. *Newgrange Entrance Stone*, 4500-5500 years old, Newgrange tomb, Ireland, 2005. Wikimedia Commons, 2006. https://commons.wikimedia.org/wiki/File:Newgrange_Entrance_Stone.jpg. CC BY-SA 3.0.

252. Robley, Major-General G. *Derivative of a 1910 illustration of Maori chief Hongi Hika*, after the portrait painted in England in 1820. The New Zealand Electronic Text Collection. http://www.nzetc.org/etexts/SmiMaor/SmiMaorP001a.jpg. Wikimedia Commons, 2011. https://commons.wikimedia.org/wiki/File:Hongi_Hika.jpg. CC BY-SA 3.0 NZ.

254. Dalbéra, Jean-Pierre. *A jeweled falcon of Tutankhamun holding the ankh,* Cairo museum, Egypt. Edited by Ra'ike. Wikimedia Commons, 2009. https://commons.wikimedia.org/wiki/File:Tutankhamun_Falcon1_(retouched).jpg. CC BY 2.0.

254. Right: MykReeve, photographer. *The golden death mask of the Tutankhamun*, Egyptian Museum, Cairo, 2002. Wikimedia Commons, 2004. https://commons.wikimedia.org/wiki/File:Tutanchamun_Maske.jpg. CC BY-SA 3.0.

257. Right: MariSha, photographer. *Zorats Karer,* Sisian, Armenia, 2004. Wikimedia Commons, 2008. https://commons.wikimedia.org/wiki/File:Armenian_Qarhunj01.jpg. CC BY-SA 2.0.

259. Ojj! 600, photographer. *Caucasus mountains*, Svaneti, Georgia, 2005. Wikimedia Commons, 2005. https://commons.wikimedia.org/wiki/File:VittfarneGeorgien_155.jpg. CC BY-SA 3.0.

260. Köppchen, Christian, photographer. *Mencey Pelicar*, sculpture of Mencey Pelicar in the Plaza de la Patrona de Canarias in Candelaria, Tenerife, created by José Abad. Wikimedia Commons, 2013. https://commons.wikimedia.org/wiki/File:Mencey_Pelicar.jpg. CC BY 3.0.

262. Phirosiberia. *The routes of the four Voyages of Christopher Columbus,* 2009. Wikimedia Commons, 2018. https://commons.wikimedia.org/wiki/File:Viajes_de_colon_en.svg. CC BY-SA 3.0.

263. Hajor, photographer. *Olmec head,* La Venta Park, Villahermosa, Tabasco, Mexico, 2001. Wikimedia Commons, 2005. https://commons.wikimedia.org/wiki/File:Mexico.Tab.OlmecHead.01.jpg. CC BY-SA 2.0.

263. Left: Madman2001, photographer. *Olmec mask*, Dumbarton Oaks collection, Washington DC, 2013. Wikimedia Commons, 2013 https://commons.wikimedia.org/wiki/File:Olmec_mask_(Dumbarton_Oaks)_1.JPG. CC BY-SA 3.0.

263. Right: Midloa, photographer. *Peninsula Hotel Chinese Lion*, Kowloon, Hong Kong. 2008. Wikimedia Commons, 2008. https://commons.wikimedia.org/wiki/File:HK_TST_Peninsula_Hotel_Chinese_Lion_01_a.jpg. CC BY-SA 3.0.

265. Top: Schengili-Roberts, Keith, photographer. *Amenmesse-Statue Head,* statue Head of the pharaoh Amenmesse, from the 19th dynasty, circa 1203-1200 B.C, Metropolitan Museum, 2007. Wikimedia Commons, 2007. https://en.wikipedia.org/wiki/File:Amenmesse-StatueHead_MetropolitanMuseum.png. CC BY-SA 2.5.

265. Bottom: Bodsworth, Jon, photographer. *Ka statue Rahotep*, Cairo Museum, 2007. Wikimedia Commons, 2008. https://en.wikipedia.org/wiki/File:Rahotep_statue.jpg. © Jon Bodsworth. Reproduced with permission.

266. Martonkurucz, photographer. *Tarim mummy,* 2015. Wikimedia Commons, 2015. https://commons.wikimedia.org/wiki/File:Tarim-mumia-4.jpg. CC BY-SA 4.0.

270. Wikipedia Loves Art participant one_click_beyond, photographer. *Viracocha, Eighth Inca*, oil painting, mid 18th century, Brooklyn Museum, 2009. Wikimedia Commons, 2009. https://commons.wikimedia.org/wiki/File:WLA_brooklynmuseum_18th_century_Viracocha.jpg. CC BY 2.5.

271. Top left: Fewings, Nick, photographer. *Buddha Tooth Relic Temple*, Singapore. Unsplash.com https://unsplash.com/photos/efD1FBZqYuQ. Licensed from Unsplash.com.

271. Middle right: Hildebrand, Gabriel - Historiska Museet, photographer. *Frey statuette found in Rällinge*, 9th century, Historiska Museet, Stockholm, Sweden, 2011 . Wikimedia Commons, 2018. https://commons.wikimedia.org/wiki/File:Frej_R%C3%A4llinge.jpg. CC BY 2.5.

271. Bottom: Mystique, Mickey, photographer. *Skeleton at Museum Lepenski Vir,* 2018. Wikimedia Commons, 2018. https://commons.wikimedia.org/wiki/File:Lepenski_Vir,_muzej_26.jpg. CC BY-SA 4.0.

273. Collage, top left: Saamiblog: http://saamiblog.blogspot.com, photographer. *Buckle from Oseberg Vikingship,* found with the Oseberg ship burial circa 800 CE, 2008. Wikimedia Commons, 2009. https://commons.wikimedia.org/wiki/File:Buckle_from_Oseberg_Vikingship_Buddha_3.JPG. CC BY-SA 3.0.

273. Collage, top center: Chirita, Cristian, photographer. *Archeological Artefacts in Sozopol Museum,* Sozopol Museum, 2011. Wikimedia Commons, 2011. https://commons.wikimedia.org/wiki/File:Sozopol_Archaeological_Museum_IMG_4214.JPG. GNU Free Documentation License, Version 1.2. https://commons.wikimedia.org/wiki/Commons:GNU_Free_Documentation_License,_version_1.2.

273. Collage, top right: Dbachmann, photographer. *Samarra Bowl,* circa 4,000 BC, Pergamon Museum, Berlin. Wikimedia Commons, 2010. https://en.wikipedia.org/wiki/File:Samarra_bowl.jpg. CC BY-SA 4.0.

273. Collage, center: PHGCOM, photographer. *Etruscan Pendant with Swastika Symbols Bolsena Italy 700 BCE to 650 BCE*. Louvre Museum, 2008. Wikimedia Commons, 2010. https://commons.wikimedia.org/wiki/File:Etruscan_pendant_with_swastika_symbols_Bolsena_Italy_700_BCE_to_650_BCE.jpg. CC BY-SA 3.0.

273. Collage, bottom left: Шнапс, photographer. Скоба для стрел (*Bracket for Arrows),* 2009. Wikimedia Commons, 2012. https://commons.wikimedia.org/wiki/File:Скоба_для_стрел.JPG. CC BY-SA 3.0.

273. Collage, bottom center: Tylas at English Wikipedia, photographer. *Zionpictographs*, Zion National Park, 2006. Wikimedia Commons, 2006. https://commons.wikimedia.org/wiki/File:Zionpictographs.jpg. CC BY-SA 3.0.

273. Collage, bottom right: Before My Ken, photographer. *Indus Valley Civilization Seals,* British Museum, 2005. Wikimedia Commons, 2009. https://commons.wikimedia.org/wiki/File:IndusValleySeals_swastikas.JPG. CC BY-SA 3.0.

273. Top Left: Wikipedia Loves Art participant va_va_val, photographer. *Buddha head*, stucco, 4th-5th century, Hadda, Afghanistan, 2009. Wikimedia Commons, 2009. https://commons.wikimedia.org/wiki/File:WLA_vanda_Afghanistan_stucco_head_of_the_Buddha.jpg. CC BY-SA 2.5.

273. Bottom: Rama, photographer. *Stele of Lady Taperet*, painted wood, 10th-9th century BC (22nd dynasty, Louvre Museum, 2007. Wikimedia Commons, 2007. https://commons.wikimedia.org/wiki/File:Taperet_stele_E52_mp3h9201.jpg. CC BY-SA 3.0 FR.

276. Kmusser. *Tarim River Basin*, 2008. Digital Chart of the World and GTOPO data, labels based on GEOnet. Wikimedia Commons, 2008. https://commons.wikimedia.org/wiki/File:Tarimrivermap.png. CC BY-SA 3.0.

283. Morris, Ann Axtell. *Watercolour reproduction of mural from the Temple of the Warriors at Chichen Itza*. In *Temple of the Warriors at Chichen Itzá, Yucatan*, Morris, E. H., J. Charlot, and A. A. Morris, The Washington Carnegie Institute, 1931, plate 145. University of Illinois Urbana-Champaign. Internet Archive, 2019. https://archive.org/details/templeofwarriors02morr/page/338/mode/2up. CC BY-NC-SA 4.0

283. Morris, Ann Axtell. *Watercolour reproduction of mural from the Temple of the Warriors at Chichen Itza*. In *Temple of the Warriors at Chichen Itzá, Yucatan*, Morris, E. H., J. Charlot, and A. A. Morris, The Washington Carnegie Institute, 1931, plate 136. University of Illinois Urbana-Champaign. Internet Archive, 2019. https://archive.org/details/templeofwarriors02morr/page/338/mode/2up. CC BY-NC-SA 4.0.

288. Tataryn. *Roman Empire Trajan 117AD*, 2012. Wikimedia Commons, 2020. https://en.wikipedia.org/wiki/File:Roman_Empire_Trajan_117AD.png. CC BY-SA 3.0.

CHAPTER FIVE: THE CHILDREN OF THE SUN

299. Grobe, Dr. Hannes. *Glaciation*. Wikimedia Commons, 2008. https://commons.wikimedia.org/wiki/File:Iceage_north-intergl_glac_hg.png. CC BY 3.0. Ice coverage: Ehlers, J., and P.L. Gibbard. *The extentand chronology of Cenozoic global glaciation*. Quaternary International, 164-165, 6-20,2007. Topography: U.S. Department of Commerce, National Oceanic and Atmospheric Administration, National Geophysical Data Center (NOAA/NGDC), 2-minute Gridded Global Relief Data (ETOPO2) 2006. Map software: Schlitzer, R. 2007. Ocean Data View, http://odv.awi.de.

302. Dr. K, photographer. *Titanomachy at the Gorgon pediment*, at Artemis Temple in Corfu, Greece, 2007. Wikimedia Commons, 2011. https://commons.wikimedia.org/wiki/File:Titanomachy_at_the_Gorgon_pediment_at_Artemis_Temple_in_Corfu.jpg. CC BY-SA 3.0.

307. MM. *Indus Civilization*. Wikimedia Commons, 2005. https://commons.wikimedia.org/wiki/File:Civilt%C3%A0ValleIndoMappa.png. CC BY-SA 3.0.

310. Bence, Ocskay, photographer. *The eyes of Buddha symbol of buddhism*. Shutterstock.com https://www.shutterstock.com/image-photo/eyes-buddha-symbol-buddhism-506426023. Licensed from Shutterstock.com.

312. Left: Moraes, Cicero et alii, artist. *Second version (2.0) of Archaeological Forensic Facial Reconstruction of the individual LB1 of the species Homo floresiensis*, part of open source exhibition *Facce. I molti volti della storia umana*, 2015. Wikimedia Commons, 2018. https://commons.wikimedia.org/wiki/File:Homo_floresiensis_v_2-0.jpg. CC BY 4.0.

312. Center: The Neanderthal Museum. *Reconstruction of the Homo erectus: Turkana Boy from the site of Nariokotome, Kenya*, exhibited in the Neanderthal Museum in Mettmann, Germany. Wikimedia Commons, 2020. https://commons.wikimedia.org/wiki/File:Homo-erectus_Turkana-Boy_(Ausschnitt)_Fundort_Nariokotome,_Kenia,_Rekonstruktion_im_Neanderthal_Museum.jpg. CC BY-SA 4.0.

312. Right: The Neanderthal Museum. *Reconstruction of Homo sapiens neanderthalensis*, exhibited in the Neanderthal Museum in Mettmann, Germany. Wikimedia Commons, 2020. https://commons.wikimedia.org/wiki/File:Homo_sapiens_neanderthalensis-Mr._N.jpg. CC BY-SA 4.0.

312. Primola, Nicolas, artist. *Digital illustration and render of a Neanderthal man*. Shutterstock.com. https://www.shutterstock.com/image-illustration/digital-illustration-render-neanderthal-man-310746206. Licensed from Shutterstock.com.

313. Left: Laplume, Mark, artist. *Image of Paracas Skulls*. Root Race Research, 2016. https://www.facebook.com/RootRaceResearch/photos/a.250594045060672/1098721666914568. Reproduced with permission.

313. Center: Foerster, Brien. *Paracas Skull*. Hidden Inca Tours, 2018. https://hiddenincatours.com/comparison-elongated-skulls-paracas-peru-egypt-russia-black-sea. Reproduced with permission.

313. Right: Silentlight87, photographer. *Schädel der Chongos*, Regional Museum of Ica, Ica Peru, 2016. Wikimedia Commons, 2016. https://commons.wikimedia.org/wiki/File:Sch%C3%A4del_der_Chongos.jpg. CC BY-SA 4.0.

CHAPTER SIX: JESUS AND THE RELIGION OF THE SUN

322. Jaberian, Morteza, photographer. *Mandeans*, Tasnim News Agency. Wikimedia Commons, 2018. https://en.wikipedia.org/wiki/File:Mandaeans_02.jpg. CC BY 4.0.

CHAPTER EIGHT: WHY DID ANCIENT PEOPLE VENERATE THE SUN?

344. Center Right: Wee, Lawrence, photographer. *Unfurling Fern Tip*. Shutterstock.com. https://www.shutterstock.com/image-photo/unfurling-fern-tip-13375597. Licensed from Shutterstock.com.

345. Center: Bkwillwm, photographer. *Minoan Master of Animals jewelry,* from the Aegina Treasure, British Museum, 2010. Wikimedia Commons, 2015. https://commons.wikimedia.org/wiki/File:Minoan_Master_of_Animals_jewellery.jpg. CC BY-SA 4.0.

345. Right: Lee, Ian, photographer. *The Long Man of Wilmington*, Polegate, United Kingdom, 2009. Wikimedia Commons, 2015. https://commons.wikimedia.org/wiki/File:The_Long_Man_of_Wilmington_(4219108070).jpg. CC BY 2.0.

345. Bottom, left: Hjaltland Collection, photographer. *Modern impression on clay of Achaemenid cylinder seal*, 5th. c. BC. Wikimedia Commons, 2014. https://commons.wikimedia.org/wiki/File:Cylinder_Seal,_Achaemenid,_modern_ impression_05.jpg. CC BY-SA 3.0.

345. Bottom, right: National Museum of Iran, photographer. *Chlorite object Jiroft*, Kerman c. 2500 BC, National Museum of Iran, 2017. Wikimedia Commons, 2017. https://commons.wikimedia.org/wiki/File:Chlorite_object_Jiroft,_Kerman_ca._2500_BCE,_Bronze_Age_I,_National_Museum_of_Iran.jpg. CC BY-SA 4.0.

346. Unger, Roland, photographer. *Edfu Temple, first pylon*, Egypt, 2006. Wikimedia Commons, 2012. https://commons.wikimedia.org/wiki/File:EdfuTempleFacade.jpg. CC BY-SA 3.0.

346. Red, Jeremy, photographer. *Philae Temple*. Shutterstock.com. https://www.shutterstock.com/image-photo/philae-temple-isis-trajans-kiosk-sunny-684849580. Licensed from Shutterstock.com.

347. Image by Sura Ondrunar Publishing

347. Lukiyanova Natalia frenta, photographer. *Ancient Mayan pyramid (Kukulcan Temple),* Chichen Itza, Yucatan, Mexico. Licensed from Shutterstock.com. https://www.shutterstock.com/image-photo/ancient-mayan-pyramid-kukulcan-temple-chichen-699889807. Licensed from Shutterstock.com.

348. Hajor, photographer. *Tomb KV34 (Thutmose III) 11.th hour Amduat,* Valley of the Kings, Luxor, Egypt, 2002. Wikimedia Commons, 2005. https://commons.wikimedia.org/wiki/File:Egypt.KV34.07.jpg. CC BY-SA 3.0.

349. Dahl, Jeff. *Aker*, 2008. Wikimedia Commons, 2008. https://commons.wikimedia.org/wiki/File:Aker.svg. CC BY-SA 4.0

CHAPTER NINE: REVIVAL

352. Masalskis, Mantas, photographer. *Hindu-Romuvan ecumenism*. Wikimedia Commons, 2009. https://commons.wikimedia.org/wiki/File:Hindu-Romuvan_ecumenism.png. CC BY 2.0.

352. Asamblea Nacional del Ecuador, photographer. *Ancestral Possession of the President of Bolivia, Evo Morales*, 2010. Wikimedia Commons, 2016. https://commons.wikimedia.org/wiki/File:Asamble%C3%ADsta_participan_en_ la_Posesi%C3%B3n_Ancestral_del_Presidente_de_Bolivia,_Evo_Morales_(4295908812).jpg. CC BY-SA 2.0.

355. Image by Sura Ondrunar Publishing

355. Image by Sura Ondrunar Publishing

APPENDIX

357. Sorensen, Bjarte, photographer. *Ahu Tahai*, a close up of the moai at Ahu Tahai, restored with coral eyes by the American archaeologist William Mullo, Easter Island, 2005. Modified by Zantastik~commonswiki. Wikimedia Commons, 2006. https://en.wikipedia.org/wiki/File:Ahu_Tahai.jpg. CC BY-SA 3.0.

358. Eichmann, Gerd, photographer. *Tula*, archeological site in Mexico, 1980. Wikimedia Commons, 2020. https://commons.wikimedia.org/wiki/File:Tula-04-Tempelpyramide-1980-gje.jpg. CC BY-SA 4.0.

SŪRA ONDRÚNAR

PUBLISHING

suraondrunar.org

For More Information Visit

SAKROSAWEL.COM